SHOSTAKOVICH

A Life Remembered

Shostakovich

A Life Remembered

ELIZABETH WILSON

PRINCETON UNIVERSITY PRESS
PRINCETON, NEW JERSEY

First published in the United States of America by
Princeton University Press
41 William Street, Princeton, New Jersey 08540

Published in Great Britain
by Faber and Faber Limited
3 Queen Square London WC1N 3AU

Photoset by Wilmaset Ltd, Wirral
Printed in England by Clays Ltd, St Ives plc

Elizabeth Wilson is hereby identified as author
of this work in accordance with Section 77 of the Copyright,
Designs and Patents Act 1988

ISBN 0–691–02971–7

Library of Congress Cataloging-in-Publication Data
A CIP catalog record for this book
is available from the Library of Congress

2 4 6 8 10 9 7 5 3

To the memory of my father

Contents

List of Illustrations

Preface

By the time he died (9 August 1975), Dmitri Dmitriyevich Shostakovich was universally acclaimed as one of the great composers of the
twentieth century. Yet no biography written in Russia or outside it
since his death has done justice to him. More often than not they failed
because speculation and ideological tendentiousness played a greater
role in them than objective assessment. Perhaps it is still too early for a
definitive biography of Dmitri Shostakovich to be written – many
archives are closed, and we may not have reached the right distance
from his life and times to enjoy a true perspective on them. Whatever
the truth, now is the time, while some key witnesses are still alive, to
try and tap living memory with a view to capturing the atmosphere of
the epoch in which the composer lived and worked.

In the West, there was a drastic re-evaluation of the composer's
personality after the publication of *Testimony: The Memoirs of Shostakovich as Related to and Edited by Solomon Volkov* in 1979. Hitherto, the
official Soviet point of view had represented Shostakovich as an
obedient socialist-realist and model Soviet citizen; he emerges from
Volkov's book as a passionate anti-communist and embittered, life-
weary individual. (The image of a composer forced to lead a double
life, one official and ideologically correct, and the other clandestine,
reserved for his real feelings, had a distinctly dramatic allure; in recent
years at least one play [David Pownall's *Masterclass*] and one film
[Tony Palmer's *Testimony*], both loosely based on events in Shostakovich's life, have been devoted to this theme.) However, extreme
representations of whatever kind cannot help to facilitate our understanding of Shostakovich's enormous range and depth of vision. A
balanced reappraisal is required to discover where the truth lies.

Shostakovich: A Life Remembered is therefore an attempt to present the
biography of Dmitri Shostakovich within the social context of his time,
using the perception of his contemporaries as a means to make this

possible. It does not aim to deal with his musical output in any depth, or to foist new political interpretations on his life or music.

The idea of using reminiscence material as the basis of a book on Shostakovich originated from a commission I had from Faber & Faber in 1988 to edit and collate a book for their 'Composers Remembered' series. As I started collecting material and studying the printed Soviet sources, I realized that there was no Shostakovich biography available to the English-speaking reader which had made use of these sources. Very soon I had collected enough material for a book that was outside the scope of the original commission. At that point I decided to extend the book into a kind of full-length 'documentary' biography.

My initial objective was to collect as much fresh 'first-hand' material as possible. I therefore talked to dozens of people in Moscow and Leningrad, and also to many Russian musicians living in the West. The majority were extremely generous in their response to my request for reminiscence material.

The collaboration of the participants took two forms: some agreed to be interviewed, while others preferred to contribute a written article. In the first instance I transcribed and translated the interview, edited it in rough form, and then, whenever possible, showed it to the interviewee for comment. In some cases this edited transcript was accepted. In others I was asked to introduce changes and corrections, and in one case my informant was prompted to write an article of recollections to replace the interview. Because the space is limited, interviews and articles have been cut and utilized selectively. Indeed, in certain instances I have had to reject material specifically collected for the book.

Additionally, I conducted several 'off-the-record' interviews; often these private conversations gave me a deep insight into the background and context of my subject.

I conducted my research in the Soviet Union from 1988 to early 1990, in a time of excitement and confusion there as the country as I had known it over the past twenty-five years fast disintegrated. As Gorbachov's policy of 'glasnost' took root, Russians became ready to speak openly and without fear about their past. This worked largely in my favour. Naturally, I had on occasion to discount the sometimes dubious benefits of hindsight on a person's memory, and there were instances when reminiscences were coloured by the personal issues at stake. Some Russians also continued to speak in allusions and metaphors, a habit acquired in harsher times, where the 'sub-text' was often more important than the surface meaning. In some measure my experience of Russia had prepared me to deal with this.

Of the many people I approached, very few refused to contribute to the book. In general, those who chose not to participate were close friends of Shostakovich, who did not wish to share their intimate memories with the outside world. Naturally, I respect this point of view. Such refusals came from Galina Ustvolskaya, Kurt Sanderling, Boris Tishchenko and Dmitri Frederiks. The latter, having written an article for me, then had second thoughts about publishing his memoirs. Others who did not wish to contribute to this book for a variety of reasons include Alexander Solzhenitsyn, Boris Tchaikovsky, Leonid Trauberg and Dmitri Tsyganov.

Shostakovich was extremely cautious in his dealings with the outside world, conditioned as he was by an in-built mistrust of people, whether as petty gossips or potential informers. Naturally suspicion of his fellow men was exacerbated by the conditions of life in a police state. Hence he rarely revealed himself fully, even with those he trusted and liked, and his extreme sensibility towards others defined his attitudes and behaviour in every particular instance. Therefore I have attempted to describe the nature of the relationship and the degree of trust that each contributor enjoyed with Shostakovich, as a guide to the reader in his or her own assessment of the material. To be fair, many contributors themselves have been the first to point out if their connection with Shostakovich was only tenuous. On the other hand, the quality of a contribution is not exclusively governed by the closeness of the informant's relationship with the composer. After all, the gift of observation and sensitive perception is by no means the exclusive right of close friends.

Not unnaturally, much of the testimony comes from musicians – composers, performers, pupils and musicologists – all of whom had some professional connection with Shostakovich. But the testimony from such non-musicians as Zoya Dmitriyevna Shostakovich, Tatyana Glivenko, Flora Litvinova, Natalya Vovsi-Mikhoels and others is of the greatest value in shedding light into the private world of Shostakovich.

In the case of Shostakovich's closest family (his widow Irina Antonovna, his son Maxim Dmitriyevich and daughter Galina Dmitriyevna), I myself felt that it would be ridiculous to ask any of them for a short memoir when each could write a book on the subject.

Maxim Shostakovich has stated his intention of writing his memoirs, whose appearance must be eagerly awaited. Irina Shostakovich has confirmed that she is resolute in her intention not to write any. In this she has no doubt been influenced by Dmitri Dmitriyevich's avowed dislike and suspicion of memoirs. On the other hand, I greatly appreciate the encouragement all three gave me in this venture.

In order to attempt a comprehensive coverage of the life, I realized that it was necessary to provide more documentary material to back up the testimony I had gathered directly from my various informants. Hence I studied the available published sources. Apart from several Soviet books devoted to Shostakovich and his music, I discovered a lot of valuable material in Soviet (and now Russian) journals and news-papers, most of which had never previously been translated into English or quoted in Western publications on Shostakovich. All the information on my various sources is given at the end of the book in an annotated list.

I was influenced by various factors in my choice of extracts for the book. In general, I preferred to use first-hand material where possible. But when some aspect of Shostakovich's life was not covered, and this applies more particularly to the early period of his life (obviously fewer witnesses from these times are alive today), I made use of published sources. At other times the choice was influenced by the quality of the material, which speaks for itself.

It was my conscious decision also to include extracts by individuals who have been hostile towards Shostakovich, provided that their attitude was representative of a particular point of view. Hence Nicholas Nabokov's malicious description of Shostakovich at the 1949 New York Peace Congress is included as a typical instance of a 'first-wave' Russian emigré's hatred of Soviet Bolshevism, its exponents and victims.

In addition to material by others about my subject, I have included extracts from Shostakovich's own letters. On the other hand, as far as possible I have avoided using his published statements, because it is well known that Shostakovich rarely wrote the articles published under his name; certainly this is true after 1936.

Shostakovich developed a vivid epistolary style reminiscent of his music; it shows the marked literary influence of Zoshchenko. His language bristles with an understated sardonic humour, rhythmic repetitions, and a parodying use of Soviet officialese.

Shostakovich was withdrawn in his early years, but his youthful letters reveal quite a lot about his state of mind and personal feelings. Later in life the composer jealously guarded his personal privacy and came to express himself with increasing restraint in his letters and speech. Furthermore, because of the necessity for self-imposed censorship, he developed a coded linguistic style, only alluding to risky subjects in cryptic references. For the most part, Shostakovich's correspondents were themselves expert in recognizing innuendo; thus they would not have turned a hair reading statements that meant the exact opposite of what was written.

Although I attempted to base the book on documentary evidence, I found that there were still many gaps left to fill. Hence my own contributions as editor cum narrator serve several purposes: to remind the reader of the historical and political context, to give the chronology of events in Shostakovich's life and the sequence and background of his compositions, and to introduce the reader to the contributor.

In establishing the guiding rules as to what material to include in the book, I was anxious to make the biography read as a continuous story. I had to avoid too much repetition. I wished to balance many points of view, and not to eliminate contradictions. Wherever possible, I have tried to verify facts and to make sure that contributions from witnesses do not contain misdatings or other obvious factual errors. Obviously, I have discarded evidence that I found to be unreliable.

I have tried as far as possible to use the words of my informants exactly as written or spoken. Inevitably their views are individual and their personal reactions differ – sometimes even factual accounts of events are contradictory. But I leave the reader to form his or her opinion of where the truth lies in such instances. I have tried not to interfere unduly or to fall into the trap of adapting testimony for the sake of convenience.

For the most part the translations from Russian to English have been undertaken by myself. However, I have had some valuable help from Mr Grigori Gerenstein in transcribing and translating some of the interviews. Inevitably I have gone over the translations in the course of editing. My aim has been to try to capture the diverse linguistic styles of the contributors, and not to impose uniformity on the language.

I have divided the book into chapters dealing with the various stages of Shostakovich's life. The subheads within each chapter relate either to a more confined period in the composer's activity, or to some pertinent theme related either directly to his life or to the social and political background of it.

Although this book is largely about Shostakovich, it is populated by a *dramatis personae* of secondary characters. Each person who recounts something of another unfailingly leaves something of himself or herself in the telling of the story. I do not regard these interludes as digressions, rather they serve an important function in re-creating the psychological outlook and atmosphere of the times. To aid the reader in his way around this gallery of minor portraits, I have included biographical notes at the end of the book that give relevant information about both the contributors and a large number of the participants of the story. Hopefully this will serve not only to identify them, but to minimize the confusion over difficult Russian names.

As far as possible I have checked the veracity of everything in the book. Due to a variety of circumstances, I did not apply to work in the Moscow or Leningrad/St Petersburg archives. True, not all the Soviet archives were open at the time I was researching, and the restrictions that then applied to foreigners meant that material was usually only made available if it had already appeared in publications by Soviet scholars. Regrettably, this has meant that I have often had to rely on secondary sources to check information. I can only apologize to my readers for any errors I have unwittingly left in the text.

Needless to say, it is impossible to be comprehensive in covering the life and work of a man of Shostakovich's stature. Many important themes relating to his music and the influences behind it, the literary stimulus and so on are barely touched on. But I hope that this book will not only give a fresh outlook on the composer's life, but raise questions which must perforce remain unanswered. I have tried not to include contentious claims without believing in their possible veracity, for example, the dating of the Tenth Symphony and the lampoon *Rayok*. Future scholars will have an opportunity to confirm or dismiss such claims when the archives are opened and all manuscripts can be examined and scientifically dated. I would be happy if this book provokes argument that leads to the discovery of the truth.

I believe that, despite contradictions and differences of opinion, the overall picture of Dmitri Shostakovich built up from this mosaic of many pieces is a consistent one. Certainly, to my mind, he emerges as a person of great humanity, integrity and dignity. Furthermore, in his understanding and acceptance of the moral responsibilities that come as part and parcel of the gift of genius, Shostakovich shows himself to have been a truly great artist. Hence his binding commitment to fight evil and to lend support to those in distress. In the final analysis, I believe that any human weaknesses he displayed are far outweighed by the steadfast courage he found in order to live by his convictions.

ELIZABETH WILSON
Giaveno, Italy, 1994

Acknowledgements

This book owes its existence to the help of many people. To start with, it would never have come into being without the co-operation of the many contributors, who either agreed to be interviewed or to write articles specially for this publication. I thank them not only for being so generous with their time and knowledge, but in many cases for giving me hospitality. I have been touched by the continuing interest that several of them have expressed in the project. The contributors are all named and acknowledged in the appendix of sources.

I have made every effort to contact all publishers concerned to gain the necessary permission to quote from various books, journals and magazines. In some instances I received no response. However, I wish to thank the following publishers and individuals for granting permission to quote from the following books and journals:

The Britten-Pears Library for use of extracts from *Moscow Christmas* by Peter Pears

Faber & Faber, for use of extracts from *Dialogues and a Diary* by Igor Stravinsky and Robert Craft

Harcourt Brace Jovanovich and Hodder & Stoughton, for use of extracts from *Galina: A Russian Story* by Galina Vishnevskaya

Kompozitor (Moscow), for use of extracts from *D. D. Shostakovich: Articles and Materials* (ed. G. M. Shneyerson); *Music, Contacts and Destinies* by Grigori Fried; *Alexander Vasiliyevich Gauk: Memoirs, Selected Articles and Reminiscences* edited by L. Gauk, R. Glezer and Y. Milstein; *Discourses on Conducting* by Boris Khaikin

Kompozitor (St Petersburg) and DSCH publishing house, for use of extracts from *Letters to a Friend: Dmitri Shostakovich to Isaak Glikman*

Little, Brown & Co., for use of extracts from *Old Friends and New Music* by Nicholas Nabokov

Krzysztof Meyer for use of his obituary article published in *Rych Muzyczny*

Boris Lossky, for use of his article 'New Facts about Shostakovich', published in *Russkaya Mysl'*

Dmitri Frederiks for use of Shostakovich's 'Letters to Mother', published in *Neva*.

I wish to acknowledge a debt of deepest gratitude to Irina Antonovna Shostakovich, the composer's widow, who has encouraged me and given me assistance in so many ways. I thank her in particular for providing photographs from the family archive collection. I also thank the composer's son, Maxim Dmitriyevich Shostakovich, and daughter, Galina Dmitriyevna Shostakovich, for their help and support. Galina Dmitriyevna kindly effected my introduction to her aunt, Zoya Dmitriyevna Shostakovich, and her cousin, Dmitri Vsevolodovich Frederiks.

My thanks to Manashyr Yakubov, the curator of the Shostakovich family archive for much stimulating discussion and for generously providing me with material.

I wish to thank the staff of the Glinka Museum, Moscow, for making photographs available, and Mariya Yurevna Konniskaya for providing me with the cover photograph.

In St Petersburg (or Leningrad as it was then), I had the good fortune to be assisted by Lyudmila Kovnatskaya, who introduced me to many people and new sources, and actively collaborated in collecting material from various contributors. I warmly thank her and various of her students who were involved on this project.

I also wish to express my gratitude to Laurel Fay, who has simultaneously been engaged in writing a biography of Shostakovich for Dent's Master Musicians series. Apart from allowing me to indulge in stimulating discussions, arguments and speculation with her, she kept me up to date with new publications when I was housebound in Italy.

I owe my thanks to those who provided material or granted me interviews, but whose contributions I have been unable to include due to lack of space. They include V. Uspensky, Moisei Weinberg, Nadezhda Yureneva, Vitali Buyanovsky and Alan George. I also gained much insight from speaking privately to many individuals who preferred not to give interviews to be quoted in the book. I also completely respect the privacy of that small category of people who refused to co-operate in my project.

I am most grateful to the many people who gave me hospitality while on research trips to Moscow and Leningrad: principally to Sir Roderic and Lady Braithwaite, Nina Zarkhi and her family, Alexander Knaifel and Tatyana Melentyeva, and also to Natalya Gutman, Mariya Konniskaya and Zoya Tomashevskaya.

I owe a great debt of gratitude to Grigori Gerenstein for providing invaluable help in transcribing and translating some of the interviews.

Amongst many others I need to thank for various acts of assistance, kindness and support are Dmitri and Tatyana Alexeev, Rosamunde Bartlett, Michael Bird, Felicity Cave, Jim Devlin, Alexander and Natasha Ivashkin, Sofiya Khentova, Gerard MacBurney, Alan Mercer, Irina Semyonova, Dmitri Smirnov, Rosamunde Strode, Vladimir Tonkha, Emanuel Utwiller, Eliso Virsoladze, Ann Wilson, Catherine Wilson and Jagna Wright.

My thanks to my editors at Faber & Faber. Patrick Carnegie entrusted me with the initial idea, Helen Sprott encouraged me through the years of research, and Andrew Clements backed the idea of expanding the length and scope of the original commission. Throughout this time Jane Feaver has been consistently helpful and patient.

My thanks to Malcolm Ward, who accomplished the onerous task of copy-editing with great tact and understanding. He was both supportive and severe, while maintaining his good humour and bolstering mine throughout the editing period.

I wish warmly to thank my mother for her constant interest in my work. She has read and re-read the entire manuscript at its various stages, always offering useful comment and criticism as well as encouragement. At home, Francesco Candido has given me support of every kind, and our daughter Fanny has offered welcome distraction. I am also grateful to Nadia Giacone and Francesca Gatto for their help.

I would never have undertaken this book if I had not been a student at the Moscow Conservatoire during 1964–71. I owe an enormous debt of gratitude to Mstislav Rostropovich, not only for teaching me then, but for stimulating my interest in all things Russian, and for providing me with the opportunity to be present (as a fly on the wall) in the company of Dmitri and Irina Shostakovich on some unforgettable occasions. And not least I should thank him for introducing me to and encouraging my passion for Shostakovich's music.

EW

Acronyms

ASM	Association of Contemporary Music (Sometimes referred to as LASM, i.e. the Leningrad Association)
CHEKA	Extraordinary Commission for Struggle with Counter-Revolution and Sabotage
FEKS	Factory of the Eccentric Actor
GABT	State Academic Bolshoi Theatre (Moscow)
GATOB	State Academic Theatre of Ballet and Opera (Formerly known as the Mariinsky Theatre in St Petersburg/Petrograd, then later as the Kirov Theatre in Leningrad)
GITIS	State Institute of Theatre and Art
GPU (OGPU)	State Administration for the Struggle Against Espionage and Counter-Revolution
KGB	Committee for State Security
KOMSOMOL	Communist Youth Movement
LEF	Front for Left Art
MALEGOT	Leningrad 'Maly' State Opera Theatre
MKHAT	Moscow Arts Theatre
MUZGIZ	State Music Publishers
NARKOMPROS	People's Commissariat of Enlightenment (Education)
NEP	New Economic Policy
NKVD	People's Commissariat of Internal Affairs
OBERIU	Association for Real Art
OBKOM	Regional Committee of the Communist Party
PROKOLL	Production Collective of Student Composers' Conservatoire
PROLETKULT	Proletarian Cultural and Educational Organization
PROMET	Industrial Metals

Rabfak	Workers' Faculties
RAPM	Russian Association of Proletarian Musicians
RAPP	Russian Association of Proletarian Writers
TRAM	Working Youth Theatre

CHAPTER ONE

Childhood and Youth

A start in life and music

The Russia where Dmitri Dmitriyevich Shostakovich was born in 1906 was in the process of enormous social upheaval. Discontent and unrest throughout the country had led to instability and bloodshed, and a premonition of approaching catastrophe prevailed. Widespread outbreaks of violence culminated in the St Petersburg Palace Square massacre on 9 January 1905 (more commonly referred to at the time as 'Bloody Sunday'). This tragic slaughter of an unarmed crowd of peaceful demonstrators by Imperial troops was the first in a chain of events which came to be termed the 1905 Revolution. It marked a psychological turning point in the country's attitude to the monarchy. In the eyes of the people Tsar Nicholas II lost his credibility, and he was forced to grant fundamental civic liberties and to concede the creation of an elected parliament, the Duma. The intransigence of the monarchy seemed to be outweighed merely by the ineffectiveness of the Duma. Nicholas's regime was generally detested, and no one doubted its days were numbered.

The general mood of ferment and anticipation of impending change was reflected in Russia's artistic circles, notably in the literary scene. The Symbolists looked to the future with foreboding and gloom, and foresaw the death of the country's culture, while the many new movements that had come into being searched for new forms and a new and vigorous language to express them. The most dynamic of these groups were the Futurists, who advocated total cultural anarchy.

In the world of music, this search for a new means of expression was evident in Alexander Skryabin's 'decadent' harmonies and mystic philosophy. Rebels of a different kind, Igor Stravinsky and Sergei Prokofiev broke their ties with the academic schools which had fostered them and dazzled the world with the vitality of their new musical idiom. And in the years preceding the 1917 Revolution, such composers as Nikolai Roslavets and Arthur Lourié had started using elements of dodecaphony, and even graphic notation, in their music, which reflected such diverse influences as Skryabin's late 'Promethean' style, the esoteric and refined sonorities of Claude Debussy, and Pablo Picasso's visual experiments.

The traditional rivalry that existed between the more 'Western' Moscow Conservatoire and the 'Russophile' St Petersburg Conservatoire (personified by 'The Mighty Handful') from the second half of the nineteenth century continued (and continues!). Nikolai Rimsky-Korsakov was regarded as being musically conservative, but he was liberal in his politics. Indeed, he was dismissed from his position as director of the St Petersburg Conservatoire for his outspoken condemnation of the 1905 Uprising.

The St Petersburg Conservatoire could boast of having produced the two greatest Russian composers of the early twentieth century – Stravinsky and Prokofiev. Shostakovich later graduated from the same Conservatoire and thus felt himself rooted in the Russian tradition. He was to be hailed as the Soviet Union's first 'home-grown' composer.

The first written testimony of the future composer is given by his aunt, NADEZHDA (NADEJDA) GALLI-SHOHAT:

The child was born at five o'clock on the afternoon of the 12th of September 1906[1] – a fine healthy boy.

The day of his christening was a busy one in the Shostakovich household. His father, Dmitri, had come home early from work loaded down with packages of delicacies for the celebration. The whole house was in a busy turmoil. A room had to be prepared for the baptism and the dining room arranged for the tea. The baby slept peacefully in his crib, oblivious of the excitement and gaiety that surrounded him. His three-year-old sister, Marusia, ran about under everyone's feet, eager to participate and to miss nothing. At three o'clock the priest and his attendant arrived, the font was placed in the middle of Dmitri's study, and the family gathered for the ceremony.

'What name do you want to give to your boy?' the priest asked the parents. 'We want to call him Jaroslav,' they replied. The priest raised his eyes in astonishment. 'That is a very unusual name,' he said. 'You wouldn't know what nickname to give him, and his friends in school wouldn't know what to call him. No, no, that name will not do.'

The family looked at each other, smiling a little, not understanding the priest's objection to the chosen name.

'Why don't you call him Dmitri?' continued the priest; 'it is a good Russian name and his father's name too.'

'But,' said Sonya, 'Jaroslav Dmitrievich sounds much better than Dmitri Dmitriyevich.'

---

1 This date is according to the old-style calendar. The new-style date is 25 September.

But the priest waved aside her objections. 'Dmitri is a good name,' he said; 'we'll call him Dmitri.'

So the matter was settled.[2]

Family background

Shostakovich's forebears hailed from Siberia. His mother's father, Vasili Kokaoulin (1850–1911), a Siberian by origin, made his way from humble beginnings to the position of manager at the Lena Gold-mines at Bodaibo in Eastern Siberia, where he was respected for his liberal attitudes and enlightened concern for the miners. He wished to give education rather than riches to his six children. Sofiya Kokaoulina (1878–1955), the composer's mother, commended herself as an exemplary student at her exclusive Irkutsk school and as a special honour she was chosen to dance for the Crown Prince (later Tsar) Nicholas. She went on to study piano at the St Petersburg Conservatoire.

Her younger sister, Nadezhda, studied physics at the Bestuzhev Courses for Women in St Petersburg (as did Nina Varzar, the composer's wife, in later years). Three of Vasili's children became actively involved in revolutionary politics, which was not unusual as the Romanov monarchy was detested in intellectual circles for its narrow-minded and repressive policies. Indeed, in reaction to the 1905 Uprising, Nadezhda joined the Social Democrat Bolshevik Party. The youngest Kokaoulin sister, Lyubov', married the socialist revolutionary Vyacheslav Yanovitsky while he was under arrest in the Kresti Prison, Petrograd, in 1907. Nadezhda later lost faith in Bolshevism and emigrated to the United States in 1923.

Shostakovich's paternal grandfather, Boleslav Shostakovich (1845–1919) was of Polish extraction, but born and brought up in Siberia. Following family tradition, he became involved in revolutionary politics and joined the Zemlya i Volya group[3] while still a student. In 1864 he organized the escape from prison of Jaroslav Dombrovsky, who had been arrested for his participation in the Polish Uprising. Two years later Boleslav himself was arrested in connection with the investigation into Alexander II's assassination. Despite his probable innocence, Boleslav was sentenced to exile in Siberia, first to Tomsk, then Narym. In 1869, while in exile, he married Varvara Shaposhnikova, whose

2 Victor Seroff in collaboration with Nadejda Galli-Shohat, *Dmitri Shostakovich: The Life and Background of a Soviet Composer*, pp. 37–8.
3 Land and Will, a radical group active in the early 1860s that was influenced by the ideas of Nikolai Chernyshevsky. It maintained close links with the Polish revolutionary movement. After the arrest of its most active members in the autumn of 1863, the organization ceased to exist, although its project to release the revolutionary Dombrovsky was carried out by a splinter group, of which Boleslav Shostakovich was a member.

family were on friendly terms with Nikolai Chernyshevsky, the radical publicist and critic. Hence, even if his family was not 'working class', the composer could boast an impeccable revolutionary ancestry to satisfy the requirements of Soviet class ideology.

The composer's father, Dmitri Boleslavovich (1875–1922) attended St Petersburg University, graduating in 1899. In 1902, he found employment as senior keeper at the Palace of Weights and Measures, which had recently been founded by the famous chemist Dmitri Mendeleyev, discoverer of the periodic table. The following year he married Sofiya Kokaoulina,[4] and their first daughter, Mariya, was born on 12 November. After Mendeleyev's death in 1910, the Palace of Weights and Measures went into a period of decline, and D. B. Shostakovich left his job there. From 1910 to 1916 he held the post of Manager of the Rennenkampf Estates at Irinovka. During the First World War he also worked as commercial manager at Promet, the munitions industry. The family by now enjoyed a comfortable standard of living, even having two cars at their disposal.

Zoya Dmitriyevna Shostakovich, the composer's younger sister, was born on 8 August 1908 in Vyborg, then part of Finland, where the Shostakovich family was on holiday. She studied ballet and music in her youth, but later graduated in veterinary science. In her early years she was the much-loved (and perhaps little understood) eccentric of the family. Boris Lossky, the art historian, remembers that while a schoolgirl she was an enthusiastic supporter of the Bolsheviks, to the annoyance of the rest of the family. Whereas Dmitri Dmitriyevich always remained on very close terms with his elder sister Mariya, his ties with Zoya weakened in adult life, but he was reportedly proud to have a sister who 'could cure elephants'. (Zoya was apparently on occasion called in by the Moscow Zoo to treat these exotic animals.[5]) Zoya died in Moscow in February 1990.

The young Dmitri in these and other reminiscences is often referred to by the diminutive Mitya. Similarly, his mother Sofiya Vasilyevna is referred to as Sonya, and his elder sister Mariya as Marusya or Musya.

ZOYA DMITRIYEVNA SHOSTAKOVICH recalls the Shostakovich family life:

We came from a good family. Father was trained as a biologist and worked as an engineer. Both Mama and Papa were Siberians. Father's family came from Tomsk. His father had been arrested, then exiled to Narym as a revolutionary. Father was not allowed to serve in the army because he was the child of a revolutionary. It was one of the few advantages for children of political prisoners that they could not be

---

4 On 12 February 1903.
5 Lydia Zhukova, *Epilogues: First Book*, p. 30.

called up. Mama's family came from Bodaibo, in Eastern Siberia, where her father, Vasili Kokaoulin, was general manager of a gold-mine. Although he was not the owner, he was a person of great local importance. So Mama was brought up in deepest Siberia. She studied piano and graduated from the Institute for Noblewomen in Irkutsk, and then came to St Petersburg to continue her studies at the Conservatoire. Then she got married and the children came, and that was that as far as her career went. We never knew our grandparents, they all died early.[6]

As soon as we reached our ninth birthdays, Mother started each of us at the piano. Two days after she began lessons with Mitya, she announced, 'We have an outstandingly gifted boy on our hands.' He was able to grasp things like musical notation instantly, and in a few days' time he was playing four-hand music with Mother.

Otherwise he was a normal boy, although somewhat reserved and introspective. He liked nature. He enjoyed going for strolls, but he was always listening to something. If we went mushrooming, it was me who found them and Mitya who picked them. He could stand right on top of a mushroom and not notice it. He was somewhat absent-minded. Yet he was a wonderfully kind and cheerful child. He was full of mischief and good spirits in the first years of his life, and indeed he remained so until they started beating the fun out of him.

Up to 1917 we spent a lot of time outside Petrograd living in a large *dacha* at Irinovka, but after the Revolution we stayed in town and never went anywhere. The *dacha* didn't belong to us, but to a family friend, Adolf Rennenkampf. Father worked for him as general manager of his estates. Rennenkampf took us children under his wing. This *dacha* was on his estate, and it was an enormous and eccentric house. Apparently, when it was built they got the measurements muddled, and substituted metres for centimetres, so the rooms were huge and out of proportion. For instance, a room of fifty square metres had only one small window! It was certainly a strange house.

In Petrograd we lived in quite a large flat on Nikolayevskaya Street. Although we weren't very rich, we lived a comfortable life; we even had servants before the Revolution. Of course, things were a bit easier then, certainly for my parents. When the shortages started in the years

6 Zoya's maternal grandfather died in 1911, predeceased by his wife in 1905. Her paternal grandmother was survived by her paternal grandfather, who died in 1919. However, as they lived in distant Siberia, it is unlikely that they met their grandchildren.

following the Revolution, we children nevertheless always got fed something, and didn't go hungry like the adults.

The first school that Mitya went to was called the Shidlovskaya. It was a co-educational school with high standards attended by children of the intelligentsia, who came from the most varied backgrounds. Mitya's schoolmates included Leon Trotsky's son, Alexander Kerensky's two sons, Boris Kustodiev's children, and the Princess Tarakanova. However, my sister and I went to a different school nearer to home. Mitya was diligent and got good marks in all subjects, although he had problems with maths.

After the Revolution everything was hard to come by, and there were no exercise books to be had. We had to write on any old thing, newspaper or whatever. We also couldn't get manuscript paper, and I remember drawing staves on blank paper for Mitya. When Papa was alive he brought home a contraption which allowed you to draw five lines on paper at once with ink. Papa was very fond of all kinds of gadgets.

The Shidlovskaya School was not far from the Finland Bridge. When the Revolution started and Lenin arrived at the Finland Station, a whole group of boys rushed off there. Mitya came back home in raptures, saying he had seen Lenin. Well, he was only a young boy of ten. I remember Father coming home after the February Revolution and shouting, 'Children, Freedom!'

Our parents were not church-goers, and I do not remember talk of politics in the house. They lived a hard life, but in great harmony and friendship. The atmosphere in our house was very free and liberal. As Mama was incredibly hospitable, it was always full of people, and there was much laughter and entertainment. People kept coming and coming to the house. Mama accepted everybody. Our rooms were on the ground floor, and Mama gave all kinds of people shelter for the night, Chernosotintsy[7] and communists included. Amongst the latter was our Uncle Maxim. Some Jews came for the night too. Mama told us, 'There's going to be a pogrom tomorrow.' She said, 'The Kingdom of the Jews is coming to an end,' and then, 'Come and I'll hide you.' Mama's nature was generous and compassionate.

When Mitya entered the Conservatoire, everything changed. He

7 'Chernosotintsy' were the 'Black Hundreds', the name of a reactionary, anti-semitic group.

was only just thirteen, while his friends were all adults in their twenties and thirties. Although he still enjoyed playing some childish games with us, like *lapta*,[8] he started befriending these solid chaps like Valerian Bogdanov-Berezovsky, who was about twenty;[9] and he had one friend who was approaching forty. Mitya was tied to them through their mutual interests in life and their studies together. This age difference meant that he didn't experience the usual difficulties of the complex teenage years, but his childhood came to an end when he entered the Conservatoire and circumstances dictated that his friends were all 'respectable' adults.

Mitya simultaneously continued his studies at school. The Shidlovskaya School was closed after the Revolution and he started attending our school, the Stoyunina Gymnasium. But as he couldn't attend regularly, the director, Boris Afanasyev, said as a malicious joke, 'I can do without these geniuses. He has to be at school every day.' Although the Conservatoire did have some school classes, they didn't teach maths or science, so Mitya went to another school where he was able to combine school studies with those at the Conservatoire. He was allowed to sit his exams 'externum', thereby gaining a certificate of graduation. This, despite being thrown out by the director of the Gymnasium. It wasn't easy for Mitya, but then in those days one studied 'approximately'.

When he was young, Mitya's health was fragile. He got tuberculosis of the lymphatic system and had a swelling on his neck. Everyone feared for his life. He was operated on by Professor Grekov, a friend of the family, and then he was sent to the Crimea. Fortunately, tuberculosis of the lymphatic system is less dangerous than of the lung and everything turned out all right for him. This happened when he was a student. He went to sit his exams with his neck still in bandages. He carried the scars of the operation for a long time.

Mitya practised hard in those days; he was a very good pianist. He spent most of his time composing, playing and improvising. Sometimes he played for our home entertainments, for the dancing. Mama kept an open house and organized an incredible number of 'balls', as we called these informal parties. We invited up to thirty people. There was nothing much to feed the guests on, but we would dance until six

8 *Lapta* is a game similar to rounders or softball.
9 In fact Bogdanov-Berezovsky was only three years older than DDS.

in the morning. Mama usually invited a professional pianist who came for the fee of two pounds of bread and was willing to play right through the night for it. Alexander Glazunov was amongst our guests, and there were all kinds of other important people. Life was quite fantastic in those days. Mitya enjoyed himself with the rest of us, and didn't miss out on the dancing either. We certainly knew how to have fun.

Father died early and Mother had a very difficult time with three children to look after. My sister Mariya went to work straight away and Mitya also had to take a job playing in the cinema. He had to improvise and compose for the films. It was a terrible hardship for him and a mark of sorrow on our conscience. Knowing how Mitya suffered, Mama tried to release him from this drudgery, but we had to eat and drink, so Mitya had to keep at it. Sometimes he would fall asleep at the cinema, but sometimes he managed to use the time for himself. I remember that, when he had composed his Piano Trio, Mitya and his friends the violinist Venyamin Sher and the cellist Grigori Pekker rehearsed it in the cinema as the accompaniment to the film. That's how they learnt it. The cinemas usually tolerated him, but often there were scandals, and the people whistled and booed. I myself was actually rather glad that Mitya had this work as it meant that I got free tickets. He was only released from this torture when he got a job as pianist in Meyerhold's Theatre in Moscow.

The Trio in question was dedicated to Tatyana Glivenko. I think she was the only true love of my brother. She got to know him at the age of seventeen in the Crimea. Her father was a philologist. Although she didn't graduate from university, she was a very well-educated, well-read and altogether knowledgeable person. One couldn't call her a beauty, but she was very interesting and had a certain charm which she has preserved to this day.

Mitya graduated from the Conservatoire as a pianist, and then as a composer. He completed his studies very early. Everybody assumed he would win the pianists' medal,[10] but as I remember he was wiped out. My sister Marusya was given a medal and a diploma, and she was a much less good pianist than he was.

In the 1920s I also studied at the Conservatoire. We went to Mitya's

---

10 The medal in question was awarded during the graduation exams. Both DDS and his sister Mariya graduated as pianists from the Conservatoire in spring 1924.

concerts, where his compositions were played. First there were the Circle of Friends of Chamber Music, where Mitya performed some of his preludes and other piano pieces. My sister also played there. It was a professional organization and had its own posters and programmes.

Mitya's graduation piece in composition was his famous First Symphony. Glazunov sat and listened and listened to it; he left the hall saying, 'I don't understand anything. Of course the work shows great talent, but I don't understand it.' Glazunov was a man of the old regime, and he drank an awful lot. Mama even helped him get hold of liquor. There was a woman, Lenochka Gavrilova, who looked after him and whom he eventually married. He was a fat and paunchy man and I had the impression he was a rather abnormal character.

Mitya had a natural facility and wrote very fast, but in addition he was incredibly hard working. He wrote out his music in full score straight away. He would then take his scores to lessons without having even played them through. I always found it amazing that he never needed to try things out on the piano. He just sat down, wrote out whatever he heard in his head and then played it through complete on the piano.

He never demanded or appeared to need silence in order to compose. He had his own room, and there was also the room with the two pianos in it, so he wasn't hindered while working. My sister and mother were out at work most of the time. We had a lot of room in the apartment, not like in Soviet flats nowadays.

Mitya was also a great letter-writer. He wrote lots of letters in general, including many to Mother. His handwriting was appalling but it was surprisingly easy to decipher his scribbles. When Mama died, Mitya was abroad, in Vienna. He got back for the funeral and the first thing he did was to burn all his letters to her. I remember him coming into the room, a bundle of nerves, and going directly to the chest where Mama kept the letters. He took them out and burnt them all in the stove.[11,12]

11 Actually, some of the correspondence has survived, and many of the early letters of DDS to his mother are in private family archives. A few have been published in Soviet journals.
12 Recorded interview with EW.

Discovery of musical talent

Shostakovich gives this brief account of his early musical education:

Until I started to play the piano I had no desire to learn, although I did show a certain interest in music. When our neighbours played quartets I would put my ear to the wall and listen.

Seeing this, my mother insisted that I begin piano lessons. I put up stubborn resistance. In the spring of 1915 I went to the theatre for the first time to see Rimsky-Korsakov's *The Tale of Tsar Saltan*. I liked the opera, but it still did not overcome my reluctance to learn music. 'The root of knowledge is too hard to grasp – it's not worth the trouble to learn to play,' I thought to myself, but mother insisted all the same, and in the summer of 1915 began to give me piano lessons . . . Things then went ahead very fast. It turned out that I had perfect pitch and a good memory. I learnt music very quickly, I memorized without repetitious learning – the notes just stayed in my memory by themselves. I could also sight-read well. . . . Soon after I made my first attempts at composition.[13]

NADEZHDA GALLI-SHOHAT describes this visit to the opera (which she dates, almost certainly mistakenly, back to 1911). She also reports on Mitya's early improvisations on the piano:

They sat breathless through the performance, and the next day little Mitya surprised the family with his unusual memory and ear. He recited and sang correctly most of the opera. Sonya did not conclude from this, however, that her son was a musical genius or a child prodigy; she kept to her decision that he would take up his music in due time, as Marusia had done, and that meanwhile he would play and grow up as any child does.[14]

The summer of 1916,[15] when the family went back to Irinovka [the estate outside Petrograd], Mitya had his first lessons on the piano with his mother. She was surprised how easily he learned and memorized his little pieces. Nadejda remembers very well the first time Mitya improvised for her. He sat down at the piano one evening and, with an

13 D. D. Shostakovich, 'Autobiography', p. 24.
14 Seroff in collaboration with Galli-Shohat, *Shostakovich*, p. 59.
15 This date should be given as 1915.

absorbed expression on his handsome little face, started to make up a story.

'Here is a snow-covered village far away –' a run and the beginning of a little tune accompanied his words – 'moonlight is shining on the empty road – here is a little house lit by a candle –' Mitya played his tune and then, looking slyly over the top of the piano, he suddenly flicked a note high in the treble – 'Somebody peeks in the window.'

But these improvisations were rare; music was not yet all-absorbing, and the children spent most of the time with their playmates. Mitya grew very fond of Jurgensen, the handyman around the estate. Whenever things didn't go as Mitya liked them at home, he would declare, pouting: 'Well then, I'll go and live with Jurgensen.' One day, when he had misbehaved and Sonya had scolded him, he again threatened to leave. 'All right,' said Sonya, 'get dressed. I'll take you myself to Jurgensen.' Muttering to himself, Mitya dressed very quickly and Sonya took him firmly by the hand and they started out across the field for Jurgensen's house. At first Mitya swaggered along bravely. Then gradually Sonya felt his pace slacken and lag; then his hand began slowly to slip out of hers, finger by finger. Suddenly he burst into tears, turned, and ran back home as fast as he could.[16]

According to his sister Mariya, one of the things that put the young Mitya off learning the piano was the sight of notated music. Nevertheless, under his mother's guidance he made excellent progress, and soon was transferred to the school (or courses) run by Ignati Glyasser. Initially he was taught by Glyasser's wife, but in 1916 he was transferred to Glyasser himself.

The composer describes his first attempts at composition:

In his class I played Haydn and Mozart Sonatas, and the following year Bach's Preludes and Fugues. Glyasser was very sceptical about my attempts to compose and did not encourage me to continue. Nevertheless I persisted, and composed a lot at the time.[17]

School years

Shostakovich gave this brief account of his schooling:

In 1915 I was enrolled at Mariya Shidlovskaya's Private Commercial School, where I remained until the middle of 1918. Then I attended

16 Seroff in collaboration with Galli-Shohat, *Shostakovich*, pp. 64–5.
17 D. D. Shostakovich, 'Autobiography', p. 24.

Gymnasium No. 13 [the former Stoyunina Gymnasium] for a year, and completed my secondary education at the School of Labour No. 108.[18,19]

While he was at the Shidlovskaya School, Shostakovich met BORIS NIKO-LAYEVICH LOSSKY, who was also a pupil there. Thereafter they both went to the same schools. Lossky was a year older than Shostakovich and his grandmother ran the Stoyunina Gymnasium. Here are Lossky's memories of those years:

I first encountered Mitya Shostakovich in the beginning of 1916 in the Recreation Hall of the Shidlovskaya Gymnasium during one of the breaks between classes. The nine-year-old boy, with fragile, sharp features, looked somewhat like a small sparrow. He sat at the window looking blank-faced through his spectacles while his schoolmates played and amused themselves. Probably his introspection was due to his being under the spell of his inner hearing. At the time he seemed out of place and helpless amongst the other children, and I felt a desire to protect him in some way.

Soon after that I was astonished to see this same boy in the Hall of the Stoyunina Gymnasium. This was at one of the annual class concerts, and that evening it was the turn of the Third Class to play. Musya (Mariya) Shostakovich was amongst the performers, and it transpired that she was the elder sister of this interesting boy. Later, in January 1918, I was to hear one of the first compositions of Musya's brother in this same hall. The occasion was a memorial service commemorating those who had been massacred at the demonstration against the dissolution of the Constituent Assembly, and also Fyodor Kokoshkin and Shingaryov, who had been bestially slaughtered. The service at my grandmother's Gymnasium was attended by teachers and pupils alike. Musya had brought her brother Mitya along, and he played his recent composition, 'Funeral March in Memory of Victims of the Revolution'. It was most probably inspired by the events of the last few days.

Mitya's first school was the Shidlovskaya Gymnasium, which we

18 D. D. Shostakovich, 'Description of Life', written in June 1926 for his curriculum vitae.

19 There remains some confusion as to the new names of private schools after the enforced nationalization of all educational institutions after 1917. The institutions were usually given a number, and the names and numbers of different sources do not coincide with one another.

both started to attend in autumn 1915. It was officially entitled 'The Commercial School', but despite the name the Gymnasium had no connection with trade or commerce. The pupils were chiefly drawn from the ranks of the 'out-lived' liberal intelligentsia who were unsympathetic to the 'official' bureaucracy of the day. Instead of the standard school uniforms of peaked caps and leather belts with metal buckles, we wore blue and white striped 'sailor' tops and sand-coloured overalls. I remember the names of all of Mitya's classmates. They included George Pozner, who recently died in Paris after achieving fame as an Egyptologist. Then there were two cousins, with a claim to certain notoriety, Shura Rozenfeld and one of the Bronstein boys – in other words the sons of the Bolshevik leaders Lev Borisovich Kamenev and Lev Davydovich Trotsky. Mitya was not on friendly terms with either of these boys, and particularly not with the latter. During the spring of 1918, during Trotsky's rise to power, Mitya never so much as hinted at any kind of sympathy with the 'existing regime', and I can vouch that this was the case until 1922. Gleb, Alexander Kerensky's younger son studied in the class below Mitya. But, most important, there was Irina Kustodieva, who was able to initiate a friendship between the boy composer and her father, the artist Boris Kustodiev. Kustodiev was tied to a wheel-chair through illness; but despite the disparity in ages they had a touching and tender relationship. Kirill, Irina's elder brother, studied in the class above mine; he, like his father, was to become a well-known painter. He teased us smaller boys in those years and was a real hooligan. Also in his class was the elder Kerensky son, Oleg, and the elder Pozner boy, Vova, who became a poet, and after emigrating to France won renown as a French communist writer. In the years of the old Tsarist regime he expressed his revolutionary sympathies through his inspired rendering of the Marseillaise, which was only tolerated then as France was our ally in the War. All this gives you the atmosphere of the Shidlovskaya School's predominantly 'intellectual' make-up. After the nationalization of all private schools in summer 1918, the Shidlovskaya Gymnasium became in all probability, the 'Soviet School of Labour No. 108'.

In the autumn of 1917 my parents, on the advice of Mitya's mother, decided to send me to study the piano at the Glyasser Courses, which Mitya had already been attending for two years. I clearly remember him playing Beethoven's C minor Sonata (no. 5) at the examination concert in April 1918. I can still hear the music sounding in my head as he played it. Through his reflective and introspective performance he showed a remarkable quality of concentration.

I also remember attending a concert with Glyasser and his class in the Hall of the Nobleman's Assembly (today the Large Hall of the Leningrad Philharmonic) on Mikhailovsky Square. We sat on the right side of the hall behind the pillars on a velvet-upholstered bench which was reserved for Ignati Albertovich Glyasser and his pupils. Beethoven's 8th and 9th Symphonies were played by the Philharmonic Orchestra under the inspired direction of Serge Koussevitsky. Mitya and his classmate, Lyonya Diderichs, sat on either side of Glyasser, avidly following the score laid out on his knees. Then, during the interval, they went up to the stage to examine all the instruments of the orchestra, hazarding guesses as to their names.

I think that, sadly for Glyasser, plans were already afoot for both Mitya and Musya to leave his courses and to transfer to the Conservatoire class of Alexandra Rozanova, their mother's former teacher. This occurred at the very end of the year (1918). Sofiya Vasilyevna felt forced to take this decision because of Glyasser's irritable temper (which I had also experienced on many occasions) and his impatient demands. Many of his pupils used to arrive home in tears after lessons. After this the Shostakoviches did not maintain their relationship with Glyasser. Incidentally this is in contradiction with the dates given in Shostakovich's own 'autobiography', written in 1926, where he states that 'in February 1917 I got bored with studying with Glyasser . . . From 1917–1919 I studied with A. Rozanova'. The group photograph of Glyasser with his pupils was taken a month after the aforesaid concert in April 1918. I also remember a lesson of music theory given by Glyasser in November of that year, which we all attended; hence the transfer to Rozanova could only have taken place at the very end of 1918.

In the spring of 1917 I transferred to the Gymnasium run by my grandmother, M. N. Stoyunina, on Kabinetskaya Street, and from 1919 Mitya also attended this school. After the Revolution, it was renamed 'Soviet School No. 10'.

I don't remember that much about Mitya's presence at the Stoyunina Gymnasium, no doubt because from autumn 1919 he started his Conservatoire studies of piano, theory and composition. In the autumn of 1920, my grandmother, then in her seventy-fourth year, handed over the running of the Gymnasium to Boris Afanasyev, the physics and chemistry teacher at the school since 1915; but she remained the life and soul of the place until we were expelled from the USSR in 1922.

According to Soviet sources, it was this Afanasyev who summoned Mitya's father, Dmitri Boleslavovich, and announced that it was going to be impossible for Mitya to combine studies in two institutions simultaneously. Shostakovich's Soviet biographer, Sofiya Khentova, also states that Mitya had to continue his general education in the 'School No. 8' on Kuznechny Lane. This statement leaves me bewildered, as I remember events in a different light.

The question of Mitya combining study in two schools simultaneously was indeed raised in the early spring of 1921. I believe that this resulted from the solicitous intervention of my grandmother, who was always sensitive to the needs of each pupil's individual gifts. It was decided to let the fourteen-year-old Mitya sit a sort of premature 'graduation' exam, a hypothetical test that would at least give him a certificate of his studies at secondary school. But, alas, Mitya did not even have time to prepare for these specially devised tests, and because of the categorical and insistent protests of our very severe maths teacher, he was awarded no such certificate. Under such circumstances, there could have been no question of his enrolling in any other institution of secondary education. So I can state with assurance that, from spring 1921, Mitya was able to devote himself exclusively to his musical studies, without the annoying disruption of ordinary school subjects.

Mitya possessed an amazingly lively mind and a refined literary perception. He had an unusually wide knowledge and love of Russian prose and poetry. With his innate humour and large vocabulary, he was very inventive with words.

I remember how we used to amuse ourselves by inventing an absurd imagined dynasty. Many of the names derived from Gogol's story 'The Overcoat', or from Ivan Turgenev or Alexander Ostrovsky: Akaki, Moki, Sossi, Khozdozaty, Guli Ivlich, Sysoi Psoich, Pstoy Stakhich, and so on.

Once I met Mitya in front of his home on Nikolayevskaya Street. He invited me up, and we spent a pleasurable hour together before his mother's return. First of all he started to recount to me the subject of an Alexander Kuprin story that had obviously made a great impression on him. It concerned a Japanese spy who was able to pass himself off as a Russian despite his oriental looks. 'A sheep's mug, but a human soul,' was Mitya's witty comment. Then he sat at the piano and sang in a somewhat hoarse voice Khivrya's aria from Mussorgsky's *Sorochinsky Fair*, gaily accentuating the refrain 'The Devil take you'.

This was in sharp contrast to his performance of Beethoven's 'Appassionata' Sonata, which he gave at my grandmother's Gymnasium that same winter. It was remarkable for its overall grasp of the work, rather than any depth of inner passion.

I heard Mitya again as a performer of his own works when he was a guest in our house. That was in 1921. He played a suite of either preludes or variations. Grandmother, who had been brought up on Glinka and regarded Tchaikovsky as an unredeeming modernist, remarked after each piece, 'Interesting . . .' No doubt she meant well, but she didn't sound all that convinced.[20]

The artist, Boris Kustodiev left several fine portraits of the young Shostakovich children. He developed a touching friendship with the young composer. Here his daughter, IRINA KUSTODIEVA describes their first meeting:

Mitya Shostakovich, a small boy with a shock of hair, gave Papa a list of works that he had learnt, and sat down at the piano. The success of the occasion exceeded all expectations, and he won Papa over with his playing. That day was the beginning of a deep and tender friendship between our family and that of Shostakovich . . .

Even in those years of hunger and devastation, our parents tried as far as possible to give us young every chance of enjoyable entertainment. They held dances and parties, and family celebrations. Mama used to bake cakes, concocted from black rusks and cranberries. Our guests, naturally, included Marusya and Mitya Shostakovich, and also my brother's friends, the Dobuzhinskys. We would dress up, dance and play charades. Papa helped us to think up funny charades; he would chuckle, pretend to be an oracle, and then foretell our fortunes, each more ridiculous than the last. He also played forfeits with us. It was such fun, and we were all truly happy.[21]

The actress, N. L. Komarovskaya describes her impressions of this relationship:

20 Boris Lossky, 'New Facts about Shostakovich', p. 9.
21 Irina Kustodieva, 'Dear Memories', in V. A. Kapralov (ed.), *Boris Mikhailovich Kustodiev*, pp. 324–5.

They would put at the piano a small pale youth with a disobedient lick of hair on his forehead. He sat down and started to improvise. 'Mitya,' Irina would shout, 'don't invent anything – just play us a foxtrot!' Mitya was, of course, Dmitri Shostakovich . . . He submitted to the general chorus of dissatisfied voices, but in the music of his foxtrot all kinds of unexpected rhythms and intonations suddenly broke through. Kustodiev wheeled his chair closer to the piano and, bending forward to the pianist, whispered: 'Just take no notice of them, Mitya, play your own thing.'[22]

A political schooling

In the space of less than twenty years, Shostakovich's native city of St Petersburg was to change its name twice: firstly, it was russified into Petrograd as a patriotic gesture when the country went to war with Germany in 1914; and secondly, after Lenin's death in 1924, the city assumed the name of Leningrad.

If the events of World War I seemed far removed from Petrograd, the city became the main stage for Russia's revolutions. The first 'bloodless' revolution of 1917, the one that finally toppled the Romanov monarchy, broke out on 18 February (5 March, new-style calendar). A provisional government was formed, which came to be headed by Alexander Kerensky, giving the Russians a taste of democracy. The Bolshevik leader Vladimir Lenin, operating from a hidden base in the Finnish Gulf, organized the military coup in Petrograd on 25 October (7 November, new-style calendar) by which the Bolsheviks seized power. However, the Bolsheviks remained in a minority in the elected body, the Constituent Assembly. On 5 January 1918, Lenin gave orders to dissolve it with the use of force. This action served as a sure sign to other political parties that no compromise could be reached with the Bolsheviks. Opposition to the new Soviet (Workers and Peasants') government rapidly gained ground. The ensuing Civil War (1918–21) brought terrible suffering and hardships to Russia's people, and saw the birth of organized terror.

NADEJDA GALLI-SHOHAT gives a vivid description of the atmosphere of revolutionary Petrograd:

The precarious balance of a 'bloodless Revolution' could not be kept for long. The victims of violence on both sides grew steadily in number, and soon funerals for those who had died for the Revolution in its first days were being held throughout Russia. A gigantic funeral

---

22 N. L. Komarovskaya, 'My Meetings with B. M. Kustodiev', in *ibid.*, p. 388.

procession filled the streets and avenues of Petrograd on the way to the Marsovo Field, where the bodies were to be put into one common grave. A great sea of people moved solemnly up the Nevsky Prospect – soldiers, sailors, workmen, students and the new 'free citizens' of the capital; on their shoulders rocked the coffins covered with brilliant red banners. The procession moved slowly between the packed lines of spectators to the strains of the revolutionary funeral song 'You Fell Victims in the Fatal Struggle'. Platforms had been erected at the street corners, and here the procession stopped while men made speeches in the name of freedom, revolution and the dead. Clinging to trees and lamp-posts, leaning from windows and balconies, perched on roofs and on fences, men and women watched the impressive parade; they lifted their children to their shoulders so that they, too, might see. They had been gathering since early morning, and many of them had stood shivering in the cold dawn wind of that grey March day, awaiting the procession.

The Shostakovich family was there in the crowd and the children had climbed to the top of an iron fence surrounding an old church-yard. The sad air of the funeral song filled their hearts with a strange pain and pride.

When the tired family returned home that evening, Mitya went to the piano and played quietly for a long time; he might have been thinking of a tragic incident he had witnessed a few days before and which had left a deep impression on him – the brutal killing of a small boy by a policeman. Then he played to them the piece he had just composed, his 'Funeral March for the Victims of the Revolution'. This and his 'Hymn to Liberty'[23] were the two things he was always asked to play when anyone came to the house.[24]

The young Shostakovich's 'revolutionary' sympathies were given excessive prominence in all Soviet biographical literature (with a certain amount of encouragement from the composer himself). Nowadays there are doubts about the matter, and about some of the 'legendary' events of the composer's childhood.

It is alleged, for instance, that the young Shostakovich was present at the Finland Station when Lenin arrived in Petrograd in April 1917, and that this

23 These two pieces are usually dated to spring 1917, although some sources state that 'Hymn to Liberty' was composed a year or even two years earlier.
24 Seroff in collaboration with Galli-Shohat, *Shostakovich*, pp. 72–3.

incident had a formative influence on the young composer. Without actually denying it, the Shostakovich of Solomon Volkov's book *Testimony* disclaims any specific memory of being there.

On the other hand, Zoya Shostakovich claims that her brother did witness Lenin's arrival, whereas Shostakovich's daughter Galina and son-in-law Evgeny Chukovsky[25] had no memory of the composer ever giving them an account of this event. It is worth pointing out that many who knew Shostakovich really well recall his love of mystification and invention just for the sake of a good story.

Chukovsky, however, recalled that the composer occasionally talked of other incidents from this period. For instance, in the years immediately after the Revolution lists of the names of 'Enemies of the People' who had been 'liquidated' were pinned up on the street pillars which normally served as theatre billboards in Petrograd. The names were given in alphabetical order. The scale of this calculated slaughter was horrifying. The pillar with the 'A's' list on it usually only had room for the 'B's' as well.

Certainly, the turbulent events of 1917 must have left their mark on an impressionable ten-year-old. Most probably, if the young Mitya did indeed witness the arrival of Lenin, he would have been taken to the Finland Station by his Bolshevik uncle, Maxim Lavrentyevich Kostrykin.[26] Kostrykin had suffered arrest and exile for his part in the 1905 Uprising. He subsequently escaped from Siberia, and returned to St Petersburg to finish his studies using the pseudonym of Sokovnitsky. On occasion, he was given refuge in the Shostakovich family flat in the years preceding the Revolution. The Kostrykin family lived in Moscow, and during his student years Shostakovich often visited them there. Like so many old Bolsheviks, Maxim Kostrykin was arrested in 1937 and perished.

Boris Lossky claims that these childhood incidents of 'formative ideological influence' are more often than not mere legend:

The story of Shostakovich's walk along Nevsky Prospect in the first days of the events of February 1917 has been given much credence. Allegedly, while the Police were attempting to disperse the demonstration of workers, a little boy was slashed by a sabre in front of the young Shostakovich's very eyes. According to Volkov's account in *Testimony*, 'He rushed home to tell them all about it.' I should point out that Mitya was only ten years old at the time, I was eleven, and that it was inconceivable that my parents, or his, would have allowed us on

25 Private conversation with EW, Moscow, March 1989.
26 It is often stated that the composer's son was named in honour of this uncle. Maxim Shostakovich, in a private interview with EW (Turin, December 1991), denied that this was so.

to the streets unchaperoned. And all the more unlikely during those particular days, when schools were closed and life disrupted because of the shooting in the streets. I ask myself if, in reality, the boy's death that impressed Mitya actually refers to another incident witnessed slightly earlier by his elder sister Musya (Mariya). She was a pupil at the Stoyunina Gymnasium. One day, as the pupils were dispersing after lessons were over, they watched a demonstration of workers emerging on to the streets from the nearby Bogdanov tobacco factory. One of its youngest participants, still only a lad, was slashed to death by a policeman's sabre in front of them.

I regard with even greater scepticism the second episode which is supposed to be of such important formative influence on the development of Shostakovich's revolutionary ideology: Mitya's alleged presence at Lenin's famous speech delivered from the armoured train on arrival at the Finland Station on 3 April 1917.[27] The arrival was in the evening, which precludes the idea that a group of boys ran along to the station after school. Evidently Shostakovich did not dare refute the authenticity of this story in the predominantly candid memoirs 'Testimony'. From this I permit myself to conclude that if the first of these episodes is to a large extent a 'stylized' account, then the second is sheer invention by the guardians of this Soviet composer's 'ideological purity'.[28]

The Conservatoire years

The thirteen-year-old student

The cinema director LEO (LYOLKA, LYOLIK) ARNSHTAM's close friendship with Shostakovich started in their student years and continued till the composer's death. Arnshtam studied piano at the Petrograd/Leningrad Conservatoire. Lydia Zhukova described him at the age of sixteen as a virtuoso pianist who dazzled with his incredible tempi 'the speed of light', and his powerful chord technique: 'He hammered away flamboyantly, but he did not live the music.'[29]

'Mariya Nikolayevna, they've brought the cabbages.' I heard someone whisper conspiratorially behind my back.

27 Or 16 April according to the new-style calendar. This date fell during the period of the Easter holidays, so it is unlikely that schools would have been open.
28 Lossky, 'New Facts', p. 9.
29 Zhukova, *Epilogues*, p. 24.

Lost in the sensuous sonorities of a Chopin nocturne, I didn't take my hands off the keyboard straight away, but when I turned my head I saw the 'Classic of Russian Music', Alexander Glazunov, bending over Mariya Barinova, my piano teacher. She sat by the piano, her legs crossed in their frayed felt boots. Even when dressed in these tattered boots and several layers of warm woollies, Mariya Nikolayevna somehow succeeded in preserving an artistic elegance. Her eyes lit up at this interesting piece of information. Within seconds she shot out of the class, with Glazunov lumbering heavily after her. Her head reappeared for an instant round the door. Recalling her duty as a teacher, she hurriedly instructed me, 'Repeat that passage one hundred times.'

So they had brought the cabbages! Of course the cabbage was pickled, maybe sprinkled with the odd cranberry, and preserved in small barrels. It was intended as a supplement to the food ration, and maybe not just for the teachers and world famous musicians, but also for us humble students. After all, the Petrograd Commune was, despite its limited resources, concerned about us as well, the musicians of the future. It was the winter of 1919, the second hard winter after the Great October Revolution.

The Conservatoire smelled of sour cabbage soup. In the canteen we were fed on this cabbage soup or a watered down porridge – and this thanks to the charity of the Petrograd Commune. Towards one o'clock, a hungry queue started to form, consisting of our revered teachers and students ranging in age from thirteen to thirty.

A student of thirteen, you ask? This may seem incredible, but the old Conservatoire of the pre-revolutionary and transitional years was in no way similar to what it has become today. There were no preparatory music schools, and people were accepted on one of the three courses (lower, middle, and upper) according to their level of achievement and regardless of age. So it happened that you might find a 'mature' student approaching thirty on the lower course, and some gifted adolescent on the upper course.

The Conservatoire of my youth smelled of cabbage, but despite everything it breathed inspiration!

From the unheated, icy classrooms music sung out as always. The cold piano keyboard singed your fingers. In the concert hall the angel on the ceiling strummed a lyre covered in a tracery of hoar-frost. Before sitting at the piano, we would warm our hands on a contraption invented by some ingenious student: smooth little tin boxes filled with a couple of pieces of smouldering charcoal.[30]

Bach, Mozart, Beethoven, Tchaikovsky and Mussorgsky looked down on us in aloof contempt from the Conservatoire walls, as if urging us to ignore the pangs of hunger.

Music triumphed. And not just the music that we played on our instruments, but the music of revolution!

Submerged under snowdrifts, the city of Petrograd lived an intense artistic life. In the Hall of the former Nobleman's Assembly, a newly-created symphony orchestra played the cycle of Beethoven Symphonies. At the last concert, where the Ninth Symphony was performed, the hall was packed. The audience consisted not only of seasoned music-lovers, but sailors from the Baltic Fleet. A detachment of sailors went straight on to the front lines from the concert hall. It was hellishly cold! The conductor wore his traditional tails, but underneath his 'bourgeois' attire, one could discern several formless layers of thermal underwear. It would seem that the icy brass mouthpieces of the trumpets and trombones were about to freeze directly on to the players' lips. Schiller's words came out of the singers' mouths together with clouds of steam. And steam swirled in thick gusts over the heads of the chorus. . . .

'The streets are our brushes, the squares are our palettes,' declaimed Mayakovsky in his 'Instruction to the Armies of Art' . . . He goes on to insist, 'Drag the pianos out on the streets.'

This last demand, unusual even by the standards of those times, was fulfilled literally. Grand or upright pianos, requisitioned from the homes of the bourgeois, were heaped on to jolting old lorries which had long seen their day. Each lorry was allocated, apart from its chauffeur, a pianist, a singer and, less commonly, a violinist or cellist. These 'artists' were often students from the Conservatoire. The musical lorries would trundle over to the Red Army quarters and the workers' suburbs; sometimes they drove right into the factories on the Vyborg Side, or stopped at the drill grounds where the Red Guard workers' brigades were instructed in the science of vanquishing its enemies. The musical department (Muzo) of the Commissariat for Enlightenment required that serious repertoire, mostly selected from

---

30 Lydia Zhukova recalled 'once running home after a concert. It was frosty and a biting wind blew from the Neva – we shared one glove between four hands, and we took turns to stuff our numbed fingers into it, as we sprinted along, laughing' (*ibid.*, p. 30).

the classics, be played. Usually the audience was well-disposed to 'the artists', sometimes even sharing its meagre rations and donating them a stale crust of bread.

. . . I attempt to convey the flavour of those unrepeatable times when Dmitri Shostakovich started his career. He enrolled at the Conservatoire in 1919. In that hungry, but nevertheless happy year, he was thirteen years old. This thin and apparently fragile adolescent was exceptionally animated and always in rapid motion.

His sharp profile, crowned by a jaunty lick of hair, would flash past me at different corners of the Conservatoire. His outward appearance and behaviour did not lead one to suspect the artist in him. People spoke of him as a gifted pianist, and his amazing ear and phenomenal musical memory were already a legend within the Conservatoire. When he played at auditions and exams, one was struck by his musical maturity and a particular enhanced rhythmic sense in his performance. But this heightened rhythmic pace was inherent to his spirit and the intensity with which he perceived the outside world. This rhythmic sense lay at the very core of Shostakovich's world, and it was forged by the rhythm and pace of the Revolution.

Like the rest of us, he waited his turn for the cabbage soup in the Conservatoire queue. And he too, before touching the icy keyboard, had to warm his hands, frozen to the point of numbness.

And he too would not have missed a single rehearsal of the Beethoven cycle, and would have crept in and hidden like the rest of us students behind the columns of the hall.

But don't pity him, he needs no pity or sympathy! Like all of our generation whose conscious awakening in life coincided with the Revolution, he did not notice deprivation. Neither did he know the constraints of routine or the fetters of everyday life.[31]

After the Revolution and the onset of civil war, life in Soviet Russia became increasingly difficult for one and all. Material conditions only eased slightly when Lenin introduced the New Economic Policy (NEP) in 1921, which effectively authorized a free market policy. Consumer goods became available and peasants were allowed to grow and sell their own produce, thereby putting an end to the worst food and fuel shortages. This concession to the realities of a bankrupt economy was interpreted by many communists (and

31 Leo Arnshtam, 'Immortality', in G. Shneyerson (ed.), *D. D. Shostakovich: Articles and Materials*, pp. 105–9.

indeed ordinary people) as a sell-out. As prices were uncontrolled and inflated, many families continued to experience great hardship.

But in the preceding years, not only were food and firewood hard to come by, but other 'essentials' like clothes, books and manuscript paper. Some institutions closed down in 1918 and 1919 because of the general chaos and lack of supplies and fuel. It says much of its Director, Glazunov, that the Petrograd Conservatoire kept its doors open in those hard times; he did so through constant badgering of the new political administrators for essential funds, and, incidentally, at great cost to his own health. He also spared no effort in helping needy students. Glazunov personally interceded on behalf of the young Shostakovich during his years at the Conservatoire, thereby gaining him ration cards and funds for study. In 1921 he appealed to Maxim Gorky prior to his departure for Italy so as to procure the so-called 'academic' ration which Gorky helped to administer.

Glazunov also petitioned the Commissar for Enlightenment, A. V. Lunacharsky:

> We have at the Petrograd Conservatoire a most gifted pupil studying piano and theory of composition. He will undoubtedly be a composer in the future. His name is Dmitri Shostakovich. He is making outstanding progress, but unfortunately his sickly organism is much affected, weakened as it is by malnutrition. I humbly ask you not to refuse my request on his behalf to provide the means of feeding this most talented boy and building up his strength.[32]

Fortunately Lunacharsky took a personal interest in the fate of talented artists, on the assumption that they would bring credit to the young Soviet regime.

The composer VALERIAN BOGDANOV-BEREZOVSKY became Shostakovich's closest friend during his early years at the Petrograd/Leningrad Conservatoire. This friendship was gradually replaced by others, notably with the Muscovite group of composers and slightly later with Ivan Ivanovich Sollertinsky. This perhaps can be explained by Bogdanov-Berezovsky's tendency towards seriousness and pomposity born of a somewhat mediocre talent:

We met in the class of Maximilian Oseyevich Steinberg during the first-year courses in the winter of 1919/20, when the Conservatoire building was completely unheated. Our classes were continuously interrupted because of the cold, and everyone sat in their coats and galoshes; gloves or mitts were only removed so as to write in the harmony of a choral on the blackboard, or to play some modulation on an icy keyboard. The first-year class was initially very large, but quite

32 Dated 16 August 1921. This was the first of several appeals that Glazunov addressed to Lunacharsky.

quickly its numbers melted away; but the youngest of all its members, a calm, polite, even-tempered and modest boy in glasses obstinately attended all the lessons, and was streets ahead of the others in his progress.

What struck one then about Shostakovich? His quick and thorough assimilation of everything that concerned music, from the laws of polyphony, the principles of harmony, techniques of modulation and specifics of musical texture. We usually practised sight-reading of four-hand transcriptions of symphonic and chamber works in the late autumn and the spring when the temperature in the classrooms was tolerable for music-making.

Shostakovich undoubtedly outstripped everyone else in this art, as well as in aural dictation. One could already compare his hearing in its refinement and precision to a perfect acoustical mechanism (which he later was to develop still further), and his musical memory created the impression of an apparatus which made a photographic record of everything he heard.

Once while waiting for a lesson to begin, we met in the corridor and sat down together by the window and started talking. We both got so carried away that after lessons were over we continued our conversation outside on the street. This marked the start of a close and intimate friendship of many years standing. I frequently visited the Shostakovich family. We attended symphonic concerts together at the Philharmonia, and chamber music concerts at the Circle of Friends of Chamber Music, and went to the opera and ballet at the so-called GATOB.[33]

Almost every day we made music together, showed each other what we had written, and played through virtually the whole four-hand piano literature – everything that we could lay hands on. We went for walks about town, often making long 'diversions on foot' from the Conservatoire to Nikolayevskaya Street (now renamed Marat Street) where Shostakovich lived.

Thinking back to those distant hard but happy times, I see in my mind's eye the cosy apartment No. 7 on the top floor of 9 Nikolayevskaya Street. The head of the family was Dmitri Boleslavovich, a welcoming, open-hearted and energetic figure. I also retain a vivid

33 State Academic Theatre of Opera and Ballet, previously known as the Mariinsky Theatre.

memory of Sofiya Vasilyevna, who undoubtedly dominated family life and initiated the musical development of her son. After the untimely death of her husband, this courageous woman had to take a job, yet she still managed to maintain an exemplary household and take endless pains to secure her children's education. Her firm guiding influence played an important part in Mitya's upbringing.

Mitya's sisters were of sharply contrasted character. Mariya, the elder, a pianist and student in Professor Alexandra Rozanova's class at the Conservatoire, was very vivacious, but gentle and amenable. The younger sister, Zoya, was then an angular schoolgirl with a mischievous character; she was somewhat of an eccentric. I remember how, despite the protests of the family, she insisted on hanging all the pictures in her small room to the left of the entrance hall at strange angles.

The hospitable and cheerful atmosphere in the Shostakovich household attracted a wide circle of friends. The parents' friends, such as the Grekovs, the Kustodievs, Klavdia Lukashevich, mixed with those of the children. This circle was always on the increase. Originally it consisted mainly of the Conservatoire contemporaries of the elder children, but soon people were irresistably drawn to this house, which became a magnet for the city's intelligentsia. As the young composer rapidly started to acquire fame, he could count among his new friends such luminaries as Ivan Sollertinsky, Nikolai Malko, Alexander Gauk, Leonid Nikolayev, Leo Arnshtam, Grigori Kozintsev, Leonid Trauberg, Sergei Yutkevich, Mikhail Zoshchenko, Evgeny Zamyatin, Nikolai Radlov, and Marshal Mikhail Tukhachevsky.

However, despite the family's intense social life and the constant stream of visitors, a regime of work was strictly and systematically observed, first and foremost by Dmitri Dmitriyevich, who was always totally absorbed in some creative idea, if not several at once. He was meticulous in observing a sequence and order of work, and assiduously conscientious in its execution. To be the 'architect' of one's life, to plan and construct on an enormous scale, and to carry out one's aims systematically – all this was striking in one so young. Shostakovich was not only determined to succeed, but possessed the most remarkable powers of endurance. This attribute, already evident in his youth, later helped him to live through many bitter experiences.

Another outstanding feature of the young Shostakovich was his early independence of thought and behaviour. Not that he disregarded advice from friends and relatives, but he himself took all the fundamental decisions (after careful consideration) in his fledgling life. But once he had decided on something, his resolve was unflinching.

In the beginning of 1923 Shostakovich fell ill with tuberculosis of the bronchial and lymph glands, and he underwent an operation. But his illness did not affect his studies. He appeared at the spring exam session with a bandaged neck, and (now I can make these facts public!) he even slipped information to several of his comrades. The session lasted from morning till evening, and after it was over he couldn't resist going with me to see *Sleeping Beauty*. This was the period of his enormous enthusiasm for Tchaikovsky's scores. We sat up in the Gods looking through binoculars at the dancers far below, and shared our delight over the orchestration of the epilogue of this fairy tale, particularly enjoying the ogre's dance, in which the theme is broken up and scattered amongst various instruments at wide intervals of the register.[34]

Hard times at home

The Shostakovich family shared in the general deprivation and hunger of the population at large. Despite the issue of ration cards, food was very scarce – the children only received four spoons of sugar a month. Dmitri Boleslavovich was fortunate in finding employment with the Central Co-operative Guild, as well as holding a position on the directive management of the Petrograd Factories of Mass Production. But his salary was not enough to buy bread for the family at the inflated prices of the day. Sofiya Vasilyevna boosted the family income by giving piano lessons for payment in bread.

When Dmitri Boleslavovich died suddenly in February 1922, it was nothing short of a disaster for the family. Sofiya Vasilyevna, like most women of her generation, had never before had to go out to work. She found employment as a shop-cashier, but was soon dismissed. She managed to find other work (including a clerical job at the Palace of Weights and Measures) but suffered dismissal again in January 1925. In any case, she only earned a pittance, so the elder children went out to work to help make ends meet.

Thus from November 1923, Dmitri started 'service' on and off in the cinema, illustrating silent films at the piano. He resented the time away from his studies and composition, missing evening concerts, and most of all the dishonesty of some of his employers. In desperation, he took the manager of

34 Valerian Bogdanov-Berezovsky, 'Adolescence and Youth', in G. M. Shneyerson (ed.), *D. D. Shostakovich: Articles and Materials*, pp. 27–9.

the 'Picadilly' cinema to court for non-payment and won the case. Shostakovich described the family's desperate financial plight in a letter to Lev Oborin,
his close friend in their student years, dated 3 October 1925:

> Life is really bad with me. Especially in the material sense. My debts equal
> 244 roubles. From Tuesday I shall start the drudgery of a job at the
> 'Splendid Palace'. I will earn 100 roubles 50 kopecks. If I work there for two
> months then I will have earned 200 roubles. If I use them to pay my debts,
> I'll still be 44 roubles in the red. And one has to eat . . . ? and [one needs]
> manuscript paper? One just spins around like a squirrel on a wheel. It
> would be a good thing if all my creditors just dropped dead. But there's
> very little hope of that. They are a tenacious lot. I've come to a slight halt
> with my composing.

After his father's death, the young Dmitri regarded it as a sacred duty to
give his mother every support, financial and moral. As it was, Sofiya
Vasilyevna's most persistent worry was the children's health. Dmitri in
particular was a fragile boy whose physique had been undermined by
constant cold and hunger. His godmother, Klavdia Lukashevich gave this
account of his pitiful physical condition:

> From lack of nutrition – he almost never has any milk, eggs, meat, sugar,
> and only very rarely butter – our dear young boy is very pale and
> emaciated. He shows signs of nervous disorder, and, what is more terrible,
> he has severe anaemia. The hard Petersburg autumn is approaching, and
> he has no strong footwear, no galoshes and no warm clothes. It is terrible to
> think what future awaits him. Despite their love and best intentions,
> neither his parents nor close friends are in a position to give him the bare
> essentials for his survival and the development of his talent. He gets a
> school ration, the so-called 'talented' ration, but lately it has been so
> miserable that it cannot possibly save him from hunger . . . he is issued
> with two spoons of sugar and half a pound of pork every fortnight. Besides
> his exceptional musical gifts, I can testify that Mitya Shostakovich, whom I
> have known since birth, has a timid and noble character and an elevated,
> pure and childish heart. He loves reading and all that is beautiful, and he is
> exceptionally modest. In the field that is dear to him, music, he does not
> miss a single concert of serious music; he follows the music with a score,
> and always welcomes every good performance with special delight. His
> brain is working without tire and to excess.[35]

Illness heaped further burdens on the family. Sofiya Vasilyevna's family
had a history of tuberculosis – two of her siblings had died of it. A swelling on

35 Letter to Anatoly Lunacharsky, 16 August 1921 (N. S. Zelov, 'Scholarships of the
Commissariat of Enlightenment', pp. 101–2).

Mitya's neck was diagnosed as tuberculosis of the lymphatic system; he underwent an operation in spring 1923. The family, already in debt, sold one of their pianos to raise money for his and his elder sister's convalescence in the Crimea.

The Shostakovich family seemed to be incessantly in debt, struggling to survive cold and hunger. Nevertheless, in the best Russian liberal intellectual traditions, education always took priority, and there was never any question that the children should cease their studies.

Through the intercession of friends and colleagues, sufficient material support was found for Dmitri in the form of various study scholarships. However, from 1923 onwards the increasing political pressures in educational institutions inevitably influenced the attitudes of the Conservatoire authorities towards Shostakovich. There was talk of dismissal and Shostakovich's personal stipends were under threat. The composer M. F. Gnessin described how:

> the assistant director of the Conservatoire decided to deprive Shostakovich of his stipend, saying, 'The name of this student means nothing to me.'
>
> 'If this name means nothing to you,' replied the outraged Glazunov, 'then what are you doing here with us? This is no place for you – Shostakovich is one of the best hopes for our art.'[36]

According to Galli-Shohat, in the early spring of 1924 a group of students tried to oust Shostakovich and have his 'personal' stipend suspended:

> Glazunov, since it was a gift in his own name, prevented this . . . Mitya did not belong to any party, nor did Sonya [Sofiya Vasilyevna, his mother]; and Sonya had lost her job partly on account of it. It was clear that Mitya's position in the conservatory during this winter was only tolerated[37]

On the other hand, however, certain of his politically motivated fellow students were no doubt envious of the 'special' treatment accorded to the young star.

In September of 1924 things went from bad to worse, as Shostakovich wrote to his friend Lev Oborin:

> By the way our piano was taken away. Muzpred refuses to continue the free loan of pianos. However much we remonstrated, there was nothing to be done. They've taken it away. We're left with our time-honoured piano, which, after many years of use, emits a sound like an old pot. Maybe I'll grow rich all of a sudden and can put two new pianos in my flat. At the moment, such hope of sudden riches is very dim.[38]

36 Mikhail Gnessin, *My Thoughts and Reminiscences about Rimsky-Korsakov*, p. 252.
37 Seroff in collaboration with Galli-Shohat, *Shostakovich*, p. 121.
38 Letter dated 27 September 1924 (G. M. Kozlova [ed.], *Letters to Lev Oborin*, p. 85).

Nevertheless, the young Shostakovich possessed a remarkably resilient spirit. However difficult the circumstances, he got the most he could out of life, enjoying the company of his friends and teachers, eagerly absorbing impressions of the concerts and ballets that he attended as frequently as possible. He was a disciplined student, but, more than that, he was keenly aware that his life's work was music. As he explained to Boleslav Yavorsky, the composer and music theorist:

> I passionately love music. I have dedicated myself completely to music, or it would be more correct to say that I will dedicate myself completely to music. There are no other joys in life apart from music. For me, all of life is music.[39]

Here is BORIS LOSSKY on these difficult times, and particularly on the death of Shostakovich's father:

Mitya's parents, and particularly his mother, belonged to the liberal traditions of the Russian intelligentsia. But at the same time the family was of a fairly conservative nature. They observed at least the most common of the Church customs, as was evident at the time of the death of Mitya's father in February 1922. Dmitri Boleslavovich had caught a cold on a trip to the provinces in quest of food for the family. His cold developed into pneumonia with fatal consequences.[40] These trips were made on provision trains which certain categories of workers had the right to use so as to acquire food products against barter of goods in the villages. In reality the trains were only open goods wagons which hardly merited the name of *teplushka* (heated goods van).

I attended the funeral services for Dmitri Boleslavovich and also the subsequent burial service with my elder brother, Vladimir and Shura Shalnikov. The latter had to help the grave diggers take the measurements from the dead man. Expense was not spared at the funeral service, which was held at home. The priest Vertogradsky officiated. He was a family friend, the father of one of the girls who attended the Glyasser Courses. The service was accompanied by the singing of two or three nuns from the Novodevichy Convent. Sofiya Vasilyevna demonstrated her hardy spirit and powers of endurance, remaining on her knees for far longer than the requirements of the service. In response to somebody's verbose expressions of condolence, I remem-

39 Letter dated 16 April 1925 (D. D. Shostakovich, Letters to Boleslav Yavorsky).
40 According to Galli-Shohat's account in Seroff's book, D. B. Shostakovich died of a heart ailment, and not of pneumonia (Seroff with Galli-Shohat, *Shostakovich*, p. 85).

ber her saying, 'Now I feel like a stone.' I happened to overhear a snatch of her conversation with the priest who advised her to hold another service (this time in a church) for her dead husband prior to the burial. I remember his words to her, 'Well, you could hold just the one service, but somehow it would be a bit lonesome for his soul.'

These words evidently did not go unheeded, since, the next day, a choir of five or six monks met the funeral procession with singing as it approached the gates of the Alexander Nevsky Monastery. Then a full service for the dead was held in one of the baroque side chapels. I remember the children collapsing on to the face and hands of their dead father just before the coffin lid was closed and nailed down. The burial followed at the Lazarevsky Cemetery (later to be renamed 'The Necropolis of the Eighteenth Century'). At the graveside a speech was given by the wife of the surgeon Ivan Grekov. The Grekovs were family friends, and Dr Grekov had attended Dmitri Boleslavovich in his last illness. Madame Grekov had literary pretensions, and although her intentions were of the best, her speech was somewhat out of place, addressing the gathering in a burst of flowery rhetoric as 'the thinning ranks of the intelligentsia'.

Lossky describes his last meeting with the Shostakovich family:

My brother and I were invited to a party at their home shortly before our family was expelled from the USSR in November 1922. My brother had on several other occasions attended these lively 'balls', as these homely festivities were called. Because of the restricted space in the apartment, the guests were seated in two separate rooms. The adults sat in the dining room, presided over by the prodigious figure of Glazunov with a carafe of vodka placed in front of him. The young people were in the sitting room, and we too were served with the 'Russian nectar'. With the advent of NEP[41] vodka, after a long absence, had reappeared on our tables.

As for such newcomers to the drink as Mitya and myself, one could have compared us to the proverbial siskin, 'who drank one glass, then another, and lost his head altogether'. Therefore I have a somewhat blurred memory as to how Mitya persuaded the foregathered that he was absolutely sober. This didn't thwart our high spirits, and we reached an agreement to enter into a sort of stylized 'united brother-

41 The acronym for the New Economic Policy.

hood'. We had to pass each other three times in various outlandish poses, in imitation of Egyptian and Assyrian reliefs, then we grasped each other and soon tumbled on to the floor, rolling over and over on the carpet until we landed under the piano. I then noticed that Mitya's face was as white as a sheet, without a fleck of colour on it; it was soon apparent that he had fainted. The anxious Sofiya Vasilyevna came to the rescue, and in answer to my no doubt incoherent explanations and reassurances that everything was all right, she fixed me with a glare that was far from her customary welcoming expression. After this, my brother and I, heeding the voice of reason, forsook the gathering. That was the last friendly contact I had with Mitya Shostakovich.[42]

NADEJDA GALLI-SHOHAT describes perhaps the same occasion – Mitya's sixteenth birthday party, which Glazunov attended:

Glazunov's weakness for alcohol was well known to everyone, and although there was no wine to be had, Sonya managed to find some vodka for him. Mitya proudly played host and, while keeping his guest's glass filled, he added to his own. Glazunov first proposed a toast to Mitya, and one of the guests immediately followed this with one to the composer of *Scheherazade* – raising her glass and indicating Glazunov. The fact that *Scheherazade* was written by Rimsky-Korsakov did not bother Glazunov in the least, for the toast merely meant to him a chance to have his glass refilled.

Mitya, partly from embarrassment at this mistake and partly from an exaggerated courtesy to Glazunov, was all this time keeping up with his famous guest glass for glass. It soon became evident that the host was not feeling very well; he was rather green in the face and his mother took him hastily into the music room.

There he lay throughout the rest of the party with cold compresses on his head. He had for the first time 'looked upon the wine when it was red'.[43]

Musical studies

Little survives of the young Shostakovich's pre-Conservatoire compositions. His Opus 1, the Scherzo in F sharp minor, his first orchestral piece, was

42 Compiled from Boris Lossky's 'New Facts' (p. 9), and from his unpublished 'Reactions of a Schoolmate of Mitya Shostakovich to Sofiya Khentova's "Shostakovich's Young Years"'.
43 Seroff in collaboration with Galli-Shohat, *Shostakovich*, pp. 93–4.

written in the autumn of 1919 and dedicated to Maximilian Steinberg his composition teacher. Much of what he composed next was for his own instrument, the piano: Eight Preludes Op. 2, Five Preludes, the Suite for Two Pianos Op. 6, and notably his Three Fantastic Dances Op. 5. In 1923 he wrote three works which can be regarded as preparation for his single most important student work, the First Symphony: the one-movement Piano Trio (or Poème), Three Cello Pieces and his second orchestral Scherzo. The Trio was at least heartily approved of by Steinberg.

Steinberg happened to be Rimsky-Korsakov's son-in-law; not surprisingly he indoctrinated his students in the canons of the Korsakov School, giving them a thorough but arid training. Students were first subjected to a rigid course on Form and Analysis before being allowed to move on to a slightly less inflexible two-year 'academic' course of 'free composition'.

Although Glazunov was a follower of Rimsky-Korsakov, he recognized the need to introduce changes in the Conservatoire curriculum. In 1923 he invited the composer Vladimir Shcherbachov on to the staff. Under his radical influence, and that of the composer Boris Asafiev, the composition and theoretical courses were reformed.

The composer and musicologist YURI TYULIN taught at the Petrograd/ Leningrad Conservatoire during Shostakovich's student years. He was a follower of Shcherbachov, and hence a 'reformer':

When after a long absence I returned to Petrograd in the spring of 1921, the composer Vladimir Shcherbachov told me of a small circle of composers which met every Monday to make music together.[44] He spoke with great warmth about the younger members of the circle, who formed its nucleus, and in particular about the youngest and most talented of them all, Mitya Shostakovich. In those years there was no course of practical composition at the Conservatoire, and the formative part of young people's musical education derived from friendly discussion and debate. The circle had a small membership, mostly consisting of young people. Apart from Shcherbachov, its frequenters included his pupils Khristofor Kushnarov and Pyotr Ryazanov, the composers Vladimir Deshevov, Boris Asafiev, and the conductor Nikolai Malko. Once or twice we were visited by a small group of friendly Muscovites, amongst whom I clearly remember Vissarion Shebalin and Lev Oborin. When I joined in 1921, the circle had already been in existence for three or four years, and was so well

44 This circle met at the apartment of Anna Fogt; hence it is usually referred to as 'the Fogt Circle'. Shostakovich also attended another circle made up of Conservatoire students.

known that Rachmaninov himself once sent some scores as presents. There was no defined programme or study schedule. Each of us talked uninhibitedly of his current work, and we all were delighted to share in each other's creative projects. Apart from new composition, which in fact wasn't shown that often, we also enjoyed making music and listening to familiar repertoire. We were much interested in contemporary foreign music, and we got to know scores by Stravinsky, Hindemith, Křenek, Schoenberg and the composers of Le Six. Our reactions to it differed from whole-hearted acceptance to censure.

The participation of Shcherbachov, one of the most fascinating and erudite musicians that I have ever encountered, much enhanced these discussions. But our attention was focused on the circle's youngest member, the fourteen-year-old Mitya Shostakovich. We watched him grow as a composer and as a pianist before our very eyes. We were particularly delighted by the sure mastery of his striking and individual *Fantastic Dances*. From the beginning it was clear to everyone that this was a composer with an enormous gift and his own particular destiny.

Glazunov followed his extraordinary progress with close attention, which is not to say that he necessarily understood or approved of Mitya Shostakovich's innovations. After all, he was a representative of a completely different musical culture, and new fashions were alien to him. One has only to remember his outraged reactions earlier in the century to the work of Stravinsky and Prokofiev. All the more remarkable that Glazunov, who had no patience with Prokofiev, and who did not understand Shostakovich's early style, supported his talent during his Conservatoire years. Furthermore, he retained faith in Shostakovich the artist till the end of his days, and in addition nurtured a special respect for his person. And indeed, Mitya Shostakovich was a youth quite unlike any other.

Not only did he possess an incredible memory and perfect ear, but he was a superb sight-reader. It may be true that these are inherent qualities of every child prodigy, but Mitya, unlike so many, went on to fulfil this early promise. But it was his powerful intellect that provided the basis for the growth of his talent. He possessed amazing powers of musical observation and, while he remembered everything he heard, he knew how to use his memory selectively. Apart from his official academic studies, he avidly absorbed all the music he came across in concerts or through reading scores. This is what enabled him to master the art of orchestration so early, of which his First Symphony was living proof.

As befitting his youth, Mitya Shostakovich had a lively spirit. But his serious attitude to his work was unique and extraordinary. He was exacting in his professionalism and discipline, and possessed an unusual capacity for hard work. His ability to concentrate was an example to us all, and had a beneficial influence on his elder as well as his younger colleagues. Despite the pressure of combining his Conservatoire studies with his general education, he always managed to do all that was required of him. In this he showed a maturity far beyond his years.

One must remember that at that time the Conservatoire teaching of compositional technique was still very backward. Only in 1925 were radical reforms introduced. Harmony was studied according to rigid and restrictive rules, and strict-style Counterpoint was taught on the basis of the outmoded methods of Fuchsian combinations. The second-year free-style composition course was as inhibiting as the harmony course. One could not talk of anything approaching a modern technique. Even during the years of my youth (1912–17), young composers rebelled against the scholastic dogma, Prokofiev being the most notable example. Those who accepted it in blind faith could only go on to become teachers and musicologists. But for a true composer, it was well-nigh impossible to write music while restricted by these rigid rules and teaching methods.

During this time of crisis, when the split between the teaching of a scholastic dogma and real compositional practice was at its most extreme, Mitya Shostakovich felt as free as a fish in water. He absorbed only what was useful to him, both within his study course and outside it. I maintain that it was through his stubborn insistence that he gained a high degree of professional mastery without compromising his artistic principles. By following his own path he achieved creative freedom.[45]

Study with Nikolayev

In view of his extreme youth, it was natural that the student Shostakovich should seek guides and mentors amongst his Conservatoire teachers. Both his composition teacher, Maximilian Steinberg, and piano teacher, Leonid Niko-

45 Yuri Tyulin, 'The Youthful Years of D. D. Shostakovich', in L. Danilevich (ed.), *Dmitri Shostakovich*, pp. 36–8.

layev, exhibited a touching paternal interest in their protégé, taking trouble on his behalf that went far beyond a teacher's usual obligations. The young composer also attended counterpoint classes with Nikolai Sokolov, violin lessons with Victor Walter and conducting classes with Nikolai Malko.

Shostakovich nurtured a particular respect for his piano teacher Leonid Nikolayev. Bogdanov-Berezovsky described him as 'a musician and performer with a composer's conception and wide intellectual and cultural horizons. He educated his students not just as pianists but first and foremost as thinking musicians.'[46] Nikolayev's school embraced wide stylistic variety; he had that rare gift of knowing how to encourage every pianist to develop his own individuality. When Shostakovich considered leaving Leningrad for Moscow, it was Nikolayev rather than Steinberg whom he did not wish to abandon. Thus he wrote to Oborin: 'You say that in Moscow I will work with real musicians – Myaskovsky and Igumnov.[47] Of course Myaskovsky is 100,000 times better than 'Oatsovich',[48] but I don't agree with you about Igumnov. Nikolayev is a much finer musician than Igumnov.'[49]

A remarkable event at the Conservatoire in 1921 was the graduation of two star Nikolayev pupils, Mariya Yudina and Vladimir Sofrinitsky. They both presented the Liszt Sonata at their diploma concert, and Shostakovich remembered this as one of the strongest impressions of his student years. Shostakovich also profited from his contacts with Yudina:

[Yudina and I] would sometimes play four-hand music together. The thing was our Professor was very often late. He would schedule the class, say, for eleven o'clock, and then only arrive at three, or even four. Most of the students dispersed – times were hard, and people had enough cares and worries. But Mariya Yudina and I were the most persistent of his pupils; we would get some music out of the library and sight-read it while waiting for Nikolayev's arrival. . . . I would show her my works and she was very encouraging to me! And she in turn acquainted me with works by Hindemith, Bartók and Křenek.

Yudina advised me to play the 'Hammerklavier'. 'Why do you keep playing the Moonlight and Appassionata?' she once reproached me. 'Why don't you tackle the Hammerklavier?' Nikolayev gave his approval and before taking it to him I played it several times to her.[50]

46 V. M. Bogdanov-Berezovsky, *The Roads of Art*, p. 60.
47 The pianist, Konstantin Igumnov (1873–1948).
48 A nickname for M. O. Steinberg, a play of words on his patronymic.
49 Letter dated 17 March 1924. (Kozlova, *Letters to Lev Oborin*, p. 241).
50 A. Kuznetsov (ed.), 'D. D. Shostakovich: Reminiscences of Friends and Relatives', *M. V. Yudina: Articles, Reminiscences and Materials*, pp. 39–40.

A student's point of view

The conductor, GAVRIIL YUDIN was born in Vitebsk. At the instigation of his cousin, the remarkable pianist Mariya Yudina, he came to study composition and conducting at the Leningrad Conservatoire in 1921:

Already at that time the recognized leader of the younger generation of composers was Shostakovich. I remember for instance the exams in aural harmony, as it was then called. We all clustered around the door of Glazunov's study when Shostakovich went in to take the exam. Most of us could cope with the task of playing a modulation into some distant key at a more or less sedate moderato speed. But then Shostakovich's turn came. After a short pause while he was being told what to play, the silence from behind the closed doors was suddenly broken by a cascade of chords played at prestissimo speed. This tempo was so fantastic that we were left suspended in disbelief and awe. Shostakovich then ran out of Glazunov's study and here started the real fireworks. After the decorous atmosphere of the examination room, he relaxed and displayed his ferocious wit and lively spirit. We witnessed all kind of pranks, jokes and improvised parodies which tumbled out of him in rich abundance.

I often played four-hand piano music with Shostakovich. We installed ourselves in classroom no. 30, the 'Rimsky-Korsakov', now used by Steinberg, where there was an excellent instrument. There was also another covered piano which nobody could touch – it was the piano Rimsky-Korsakov himself had played during lessons. Some-times Steinberg himself appeared unexpectedly and grumbled in dissatisfied tones that we would destroy the poor piano if we continued to pound on it so long and so energetically. At that Mitya would pronounce the hallowed words, 'Well, so that's it then, let's be off to lead a life of luxury! We'll down a couple of beers and treat ourselves to a portion of sausage each.'[51]

Dissatisfaction

Shostakovich soon started to resent the limitations of the Leningrad Conservatoire's formal teaching methods. He found Steinberg's dogmatic approach sterile and inhibiting, although later in life he was to credit Steinberg for professional thoroughness as a teacher. At the same time he kept his distance from Shcherbachov and the 'reformers', although he developed an important, if somewhat uneasy relationship with Boris Asafiev.

51 Gavriil Yudin, *Beyond the Frontiers of Past Years*, p. 39.

In the spring of 1924, the Conservatoire Council refused to take Shostako-vich on the post-graduate piano course because of 'his youth and immaturity'. Nikolayev, in protest against Shostakovich's suspension, continued to give his pupil private piano lessons without charging a fee. Shostakovich's mother was mortified at once more being forced to accept charity: 'And how should I feel now that I have landed a pupil on you and am in no position to pay you a single penny . . . Mityusha and I live in the hope that one day we may be able to repay our immense debt to you.'[52]

It was at this point that Shostakovich seriously considered a transfer to the Moscow Conservatoire. In Moscow there were many musicians sympathetic to him, notably a group of young composers calling themselves 'The Six', Lev Oborin, Vissarion Shebalin, Mikhail Starokadomsky, Yuri Nikolsky, Misha Cherimukhin and Mikhail Kvadri, most of whom he had met in September 1923 on his way home from the Crimea. Oborin and Kvadri were particularly insistent that Shostakovich should transfer his studies to Moscow.

In the spring of 1924 Shostakovich went to Moscow, and on 3 April he filed his application to enter the Conservatoire there. The following day he wrote to his mother assuring her that with Kvadri's help he had fulfilled all the formalities and had also succeeded in fixing the material side of things, as he had promised her before his departure. On 8 April he was able to report to her:

> Yesterday a sort of exam was arranged at the Conservatoire by Professors Myaskovsky, Vasilenko, Konyus and the assistant director Bryusov. I played my cello pieces and my piano trio. I played the cello pieces myself, and the Trio with the Violinist Vlasov and the cellist Klevensky. They played disgustingly . . . but the result was completely unexpected. I would never have imagined it. They decided to regard the Trio as my sonata form piece, and immediately I was accepted on the free composition course . . . Konyus, an official old chappie, asked Myaskovsky, 'Will you take him in your class?' Myaskovsky replied, 'Without question.' Konyus: 'You accept him in the class of Form?' (That is what I have been studying this year with Oatsovich.) Myaskovsky: 'Why Form, when he already is a complete master of form. I'll take him immediately on the free composition course. What he has just played can be considered his test piece for sonata form.' . . . I listened to this dialogue and was bursting with joy. Mishka [Kvadri] was in transports of delight. In Leningrad they would never have accepted the Trio as my sonata form test piece. What stupid formalists.[53]

But reluctantly Shostakovich had to abandon the idea of Moscow, princi-pally because of his mother's (no doubt justified) worry over his poor health.

52 Letter dated 12 March 1924 (Sofiya Khentova, *Shostakovich: Life and Work*, vol. I, p. 124).
53 D. D. Shostakovich, 'Letters to Mother', pp. 169–70.

Back in Leningrad, Shostakovich got down to work at his graduation piece, his Symphony. Although conceived in 1923, he wrote most of it between December 1924 and February 1925, with intermittent interruptions while he earned money working in the cinema.

By the spring of 1925, Shostakovich was again pressing to leave 'Peter' and move to Moscow. By now he had met the brilliant music theorist and composer, Boleslav Yavorsky, and already in February 1925 he told his friend Tatyana Glivenko that if he moved to Moscow he would do so on account of Yavorsky. He wrote to Oborin: 'What attracts me to Moscow is Yavorsky, and not the Moscow State Conservatoire with its distinguished composers [Alexander] Gedike and Myaskovsky. After all they're old and I'll not get anything new out of them . . . In fact since I met Yavorsky my whole musical perception has changed.'[54]

In the meantime, Shostakovich had met a powerful patron, MARSHAL MIKHAIL TUKHACHEVSKY, who promised to help with any material problems involved in the move:

In Moscow there lives a very famous person. He occupies a high position, has his own car, but like so many famous people he has a weakness. He adores music and himself plays the violin a little. Kvadri introduced me to this person, whose name is Tukhachevsky. I played for him and he asked if I wanted to come to Moscow. I answered, 'I want, but . . .' 'Well, what?' 'How can I arrange things here?' 'It's enough for you only to want it, and it won't be difficult to arrange for such a person as you.'[55]

Again it was Sofiya Vasilyevna that held Dmitri back. He wrote to Yavorsky that the matter was not merely:

a question of material support; my mother says she will on no account allow me to go to Moscow, if she can't be certain that I will be looked after and provided for. I understand her. It will be hard for her to think that in Moscow I will not drink milk and eat porridge regularly, and do all that is essential to conquer the tuberculosis bacillus that sits in me.[56]

Indeed Shostakovich was divided between the desire to acquire his freedom and leave home, and a sense of duty towards his family, especially his widowed mother, however much he resented her control.

So it was that Shostakovich graduated from the Leningrad Conservatoire, and on 21 April 1926 he was unanimously accepted on the Post-graduate Composition Course. Steinberg wrote in his Dean's Report:

54 Letter dated 17 April 1925 (Kozlova, *Letters to Lev Oborin*, p. 247).
55 Letter to Boleslav Yavorsky, 16 April 1925 (D. D. Shostakovich, Letters to Boleslav Yavorsky).
56 Letter dated 16 April 1925 (*ibid.*).

Shostakovich had commended himself for his remarkable conscientious-ness and effort in his academic work. At the same time Shostakovich is undoubtedly the most talented of the young composers of Leningrad . . .

Now a fully fledged professional, Shostakovich was quick to show his independence as a composer, although formally he remained under the wing of the Conservatoire until 1929.

CHAPTER TWO

The Young Composer Established

Achieving independence

MIKHAIL SEMYONOVICH DRUSKIN, the Leningrad pianist and musicologist was very close to Shostakovich during the years he lived in Leningrad. They were introduced by their mutual friend Ivan Sollertinsky in the late 1920s. In the following extract Druskin writes of how the young composer was perceived by his contemporaries in the 1920s:

His exterior was deceptive: fragile and nervously agile, Shostakovich preserved his youthful charm for many years. From his adolescent years, he was very observant, and showed curiosity for all sides of life. He had a keen eye for the ridiculous, often noticing the absurd where others paid no attention. He was gifted with an abundant sense of humour. Gogol and Chekhov remained his favourite authors throughout life. He loved satirical literature, Saltykov-Shchedrin, and Zoshchenko amongst Soviet writers. Humour and high spirits, which in Shostakovich sometimes acquired a youthful daring, are a sure sign of vitality and zest for life.

This was one aspect of his complex make-up. There was another deeply arcane side to his nature. In his adolescence, he experienced hardship: he lost his father early, suffered deprivation and ill health, and had to take mundane jobs to help support the family. These sufferings were reflected in his First Symphony, with its dramatic collisions. But simultaneously, it seemed to forebode more distress and suffering in the future, both personal and general; it was this that gave rise to his predilection for the tragic in art. It was Shostakovich's vocation to realize the concept of tragedy, for this was how he perceived the world. One can draw an analogy in this with Dostoevsky's work; in particular, the last act of *Katerina Izmailova* was written under the influence of Dostoevsky's *From the House of the Dead*.

The polarities in Shostakovich's psychological make-up also found their expression in his music. These sharp contrasts stare you in the face in works which were created side by side in chronology. For example, the 'neighbouring couples', the Fifth and Sixth Symphonies, the Eighth and Ninth, the comic opera *The Nose* and the tragic opera *Katerina Izmailova* [*Lady Macbeth of Mtsensk District*], then the same *Katerina Izmailova* and the First Piano Concerto, where parody is evident throughout. Then this last work was followed by the more traditional Cello Sonata.

These ambivalences became evident by the age of twenty, by which time Shostakovich as an individual and an artist had been formed. It goes without saying that the successive decades brought their changes and corrections; some features of his character weakened and dimmed, while others were strengthened, especially during the 1960s, when his health went into a steep decline. Can one point to analogies in his music?

While noting these polarities, one must not forget that there existed a multitude of psychological nuances between their extremes. Already in his youth, Shostakovich was unpredictable and given to sudden vacillations of mood; at one moment, jolly and easy, the next pensive; then suddenly he would switch off altogether. And as the years went by these changes intensified. And does not this mass of varying moods also exist in his music, with its exclusively wide range of genre, often in diametric opposition, and the unexpected twists in the unfolding of its drama?

Without doubt his individual destiny was not easy, to live with exposed nerves and to react acutely to everything surrounding him. But he also had remarkable self-possession, and however difficult the circumstances, he was always able to contain himself and did not give in to his whimsical moods; for his deep sense of responsibility towards life and art was an organic constituent of his make-up, and he totally accepted the moral principles behind these concepts.

It seems to me that in Shostakovich's nature one can discover a quality that is genetically traceable to the best features of the old-world St Petersburg intellectual; but these characteristics have been touched by the spirit of his 'Soviet' surroundings, with their peculiar demands, human contacts and civic duties.[1]

1 During my interview with him in January 1990, Druskin elaborated on this idea: the features of a St Petersburg 'official' (he used this word rather than 'intellectual') were punctuality ('Neither DD or I would ever have arrived late like you did today!') formality

He was disciplined and restrained. Although this restraint cost him great moral effort, it became the mainstay of his stoic spirit. He was sociable and absolutely lacking in arrogance; he was well-disposed towards people and at the same time aloof, (only in his own music could he be completely open and sincere); he had natural good manners, but simultaneously kept his distance from the vast majority of people whom he met (he was secretive because he was vulnerable). At the same time, despite his enormous workload – or you might say his obsession with work – he never refused any requests for help of a personal or professional kind. (His favourite phrase was, 'Not a day without writing a line'.) He was like this both in his youth and in his mature years.

. . . And life seethed around the young Shostakovich, sucking him into its vortex. Anyone who did not experience those years together with Shostakovich must find it difficult to imagine the intensity of this whirlpool, which threw up an explosion of creative energy and provided the strongest impulse to increased artistic endeavour and innovation.

The fresh wind of the Revolution revitalized the whole pattern of life, thrown up as it was on the open spaces of the streets and squares. Youth, driven by the force of its tempestuous gusts, avidly reached out for all that was new and futuristic; often their ideas were idealized and illusory, and did not relate to reality. For only a few creators of spiritual values knew how to listen to the true voice of history, the 'Noise of Time', to use Alexander Blok's expression. One way or another the times held sway over people, and left their imprint on them, the impressionable Shostakovich included. His future as an artist was conditioned and formed by those years. Shostakovich had many diverse and significant sides to him, comparable to the multifarious levels of artistic and cultural life of the time.

. . . Shostakovich did not develop good relations with his Conservatoire teachers, the adherents of Rimsky-Korsakov, including his composition teacher Steinberg. But Shostakovich did not belong to the other camp which opposed these 'scholastic' circles, headed by 'the disturbers of the peace', Boris Asafiev and Vladimir Shcherbachov,

---

(answering like a good schoolboy'), a terror of officials (which produced in Shostakovich a total incapacity to say 'no'), and a deep mistrust of everybody (which on occasion included his closest family). The last two features were exacerbated by the conditions of Soviet life.

each of whom had his circle of pupils and associates and his own sphere of influence. Shostakovich did not take an active part either in the Circle of New Music or the LASM (Leningrad Association of Contemporary Music), and what is more, he evaded their leaders. On the other hand, he willingly made music with his contemporaries, and often met with his fellow-composers, especially the Muscovites Vissarion Shebalin and Lev Oborin. (With the first he preserved close ties, especially during the 1930s and 1940s. With the latter his friendship later weakened.)

So, from his first creative efforts, Shostakovich, already crowned with success, occupied an independent position and defined his own terms in art without submitting to the aesthetic of the recognized authorities. He also did not succumb to passing fashion or temporary enthusiasms for new music, but accepted them with discrimination.

As far as I know (and in those years, as concert pianists, we were on close terms), Shostakovich had no interest in avant-garde trends in art (after all, Malevich, Tatlin and Filonov were all working in Leningrad) or in the theatre. The premieres of productions by the talented director Terentyev and the young Kozintsev and Trauberg, the directors of FEKS, 'The Factory of the Eccentric Actor' caused much stir in Leningrad. In Moscow there was the analogous studio of Nikolai Foregger. As for Meyerhold, Shostakovich, while holding him in the greatest respect, remained sceptical about some of his productions.

Shostakovich was also not touched by the polemics in the literary world, under the volatile leadership of LEF, which centred around Mayakovsky. Shostakovich met Mayakovsky when he wrote the music for *The Bedbug*, but he failed to establish a personal contact with him. I think that he was indifferent to the poetry of Pasternak and Khlebnikov. He was not affected by the furious arguments about 'constructivism' and 'urbanism' which were supposed to reflect the spirit and requirements of the age – for instance, Tatlin's model for the Tower of the Third International, Rodchenko's work, Lyubov' Popova's theatrical constructions, and so on. Whereas in music Alexander Mosolov acquired fame in the West during the 1920s as a constructivist. All this speaks not so much of his narrow cultural horizons as the fact that from the beginning of his career Shostakovich swept aside all that was alien to his individuality as a composer, and did not seek to examine it more closely.

In his youth Shostakovich aspired to Rachmaninov's double role of

virtuoso pianist and composer (incidentally, he didn't like Rachmaninov's music). He started to perform in public from 1923, and soon his
concert activity had grown extensively. Apart from his own works, he
only played music from the standard classical and romantic repertoire.
One exception was Prokofiev's First Concerto, which he performed
towards the end of the 1920s when his concert career was in decline.
Soon he was only to perform his own works.

. . . It was his independent position that served to underline
Shostakovich's basically traditional musical outlook, notwithstanding
some daring innovation in his composition of this period. . . . With his
Aphorisms, the opening of the Second Symphony, and likewise the
thirteen-voice fugue in the same work, the kaleidoscopically shifting
episodes in the Third Symphony, where, according to the composer's
concept, not one idea was to be repeated, and the amazingly daring
Percussion Entr'acte in *The Nose* – all these were symptoms which
meant that, had he wanted to, he could have become the leader of the
musical avant-garde. However, his 'sorties' into different expressive
spheres were not the result of external pressure but of his conscious
recognition that he should break away from the limitations of the
petrified traditionalism that was imposed on him during his Conservatoire years. He searched for a more dynamic, complete expression of
the national tradition within the context of modern-day actuality,
resonant as it was with the dramatic events of a turbulent history, and
a threatening sense of catastrophe.[2]

The First Symphony

Shostakovich conceived the idea of the First Symphony in July 1923. Probably
his early Scherzo Op. 7 was initially intended as its third movement. The
young composer noted, not without satisfaction, that he had provoked
Steinberg's displeasure with this piece: 'What is this obsession with the
Grotesque? The [Piano] Trio already was in part Grotesque. Then the cello
pieces are Grotesque and finally this Scherzo is also Grotesque!'[3] Steinberg's
comments did not have much effect. The young composer went on to ridicule
the traditional tenets of his teacher: 'The inviolable foundations of The Mighty
Handful, the sacred traditions of Nikolai Andreevich [Rimsky-Korsakov] and

2 Mikhail Druskin, 'Shostakovich in the 1920s', in *idem*, *Sketches, Articles, Notes*, pp. 45–
59.
3 Letter dated 26 February 1924 (D. D. Shostakovich, Letters to Tatyana Glivenko).

other such pompous phrases. Unfortunately, I can no longer indulge him with my music.'[4]

In the autumn of 1924 the Conservatoire set a symphony as the composers' graduation test piece. This prompted Shostakovich to get down to work in earnest. He knew what he wanted; hence, when he wrote to his friend Lev Oborin in early December saying that the first two movements were completed, he declared that 'it would be more fitting to call this work 'Symphony-Grotesque'.[5] Shostakovich worked in fits and starts, with various interruptions ranging from cinema hack work to composing a completely different piece: in December 1924 he completed a Prelude 'and the beginning of a Fugue' for string octet.[6]

The composer was developing a pattern of work that was generally to hold true throughout his life. He wrote with great intensity and enormous speed; hence composition was both exciting and exhausting. In his letters to friends of that period Shostakovich writes of great contrasts: on the one hand of the thrills of inspiration and the happiness of creating music, and on the other of the gloom and doom of everyday life. Before completing the Symphony, he wrote to Lev Oborin:

> I am in a terrible mood. I cannot find a room in Moscow, I cannot find work, Volodya[7] is dying, darkness surrounds me, and to cap it all my neck has started to swell up. The horrid town of Moscow doesn't want to nurture me in its cradle. Its teeming masses make a horrible impression on me – its low houses, the crowds on the streets – but nevertheless I yearn to go there with all my soul. So there. Sometimes I just want to shout. To cry out in terror. Doubts and problems, all this darkness suffocate me. From sheer misery I've started to compose the Finale of the Symphony. It's turning out pretty gloomy – almost like Myaskovsky, who takes the cake when it comes to gloominess.[8]

The Finale was completed shortly on 26 April 1925, and by early July Shostakovich had put the finishing touches to the orchestration of his symphony.

Shostakovich showed the score to Moscow's musical luminaries, Myaskovsky, Zhilyaev and Yavorsky. They were warmly appreciative and talked of immediate performances. In the event it was Yavorsky, in collaboration with Shostakovich's teacher Maximilian Steinberg, who arranged for the score to be

4 *Ibid.*
5 Letter dated 4 December 1924 (G. M. Kozlova, *Letters to Lev Oborin*, p. 244).
6 Letter from 'St Leninsburg' dated 14 December 1924 (*ibid.*, p. 245).
7 A reference to Shostakovich's friend Volodya Kuvcharov.
8 Letter dated 17 April 1925 (Kozlova, *Letters to Lev Oborin*, p. 247).

shown to Nikolai Malko, the chief conductor of the Leningrad Philharmonic. Malko was duly impressed, and undertook to perform it.

For the next few months, Shostakovich was kept busy writing out the orchestral parts. His moods swung from excitement to despair in anticipation of hearing his music in the 'real' sound of the orchestra. Despite his fears that the orchestration might not be effective, he displayed remarkable confidence in his own music. When Malko and Steinberg declared the Finale unplayable at such a fast tempo, Shostakovich decided to find out for himself. Having written out the relevant parts, he took them to the clarinettist and trumpeter in the cinema orchestra, who had no difficulty in playing them. Shostakovich, vindicated, was able to convince Malko and Steinberg that his speeds should not be altered. The young composer obviously quite enjoyed proving his teachers wrong. This episode confirmed his opinion that practicalities should be learnt from performers and not from academics.[9]

The First Symphony was premiered on 12 May 1926 by the Leningrad Philharmonic under Malko in a programme entirely made up of new music. (Iosif Shillinger's *March on the East* and Julia Weisberg's symphonic cantata *The Twelve* were the other works.) Shostakovich celebrated this date for the rest of his life as his 'second birth'. He dedicated his work to his friend Misha Kvadri, the moving spirit behind the Moscow group of composers called 'The Six'. As an afterword, it should be mentioned that Kvadri was arrested and shot in 1929, the first of Shostakovich's friends to perish in the years of Stalinist repression.

Malko first met Shostakovich in Leningrad, probably in 1923, when he heard the boy composer play his *Scherzo for Orchestra*.[10] Malko judged it to be 'the scholastic work of a talented pupil'.

Malko held the position of chief conductor of the Leningrad Philharmonic from 1925 to 1928. Steinberg was responsible for Malko's appointment as professor of conducting at the Leningrad Conservatoire during this period. Shostakovich attended these classes during the academic year of 1925/26.

Shostakovich's attitude to Malko was one of grudging respect for his musicianship, and a certain intolerance of his pomposity. He wrote to his friend Oborin: 'I believe Malko to be a rather ungifted person. But professionally, he knows his stuff.'[11] As for Malko's conducting classes, he complained to Oborin:

> I am incensed by his verbosity. He chatters away and wastes our time. If he is asked a question, he gives the most lengthy answers which leave you dumbfounded. I prefer practice to theory. But his lessons are all social chit-

9 Letter dated 12 November 1925 (D. D. Shostakovich, Letters to Tatyana Glivenko).
10 This was his Opus 1 (1919), also known as 'The Officer's Scherzo'.
11 Letter dated 6 October 1925 (Kozlova, *Letters to Lev Oborin*, p. 257).

chat, such as: 'Nikisch, in one of his letters to me . . .', or 'When I was a guest at Mahler's summer house . . .' This is only of possible interest to Malko's future biographer.[12]

Here is the other side of the story, NIKOLAI MALKO on Shostakovich:

One day Steinberg asked me to listen to a symphony by one of his students – and thus it was that I again came into contact with Dmitri Shostakovich. He had changed greatly by that time. He was no longer a child, although he was still frail, shy, and silent.

Since all the classrooms were filled, we went into the big concert hall, and there, in that quiet and empty auditorium, Mitya Shostakovich played his symphony for me.

I was amazed both by the symphony and by his playing. . . . It was in no sense a 'pupil's work', for nothing of the boy-composer of the 'Scherzo' was now evident. An entirely different composer seemed to be before me, and it was extremely noticable that this symphony did not have the 'academic stamp' that usually characterizes the beginning composer. . . . It was immediately clear that this First Symphony by Shostakovich was the vibrant, individual, and striking work of a composer with an original approach. The style of the symphony was unusual; the orchestration sometimes suggested chamber music in its sound and its instrumental economy. . . .

Shostakovich played his symphony on the piano remarkably, producing the effect of a full score in spite of his small, non-pianistic hands. But characteristically, as do most composers, he played with great attention to the notes and without much expression. No single counterpoint or technical passage seemed to hinder him; no intricate harmony upset his attention. Everything was fluent, clear and accurate, although his tempi were constantly too fast. By his own estimation the symphony should last twenty-five minutes. Toscanini used to play it in twenty-six minutes forty-five seconds. Other conductors need from thirty-two to thirty-three minutes. However, if the symphony were played in the tempi indicated it would be physically impossible in many sections and would actually take less than twenty minutes.

. . . After I had heard Mitya Shostakovich's symphony, I decided immediately to perform it. There was a certain amount of displeasure on the part of some members of the Conservatory who thought that

12 Letter dated 26 September 1925 (*ibid.*, p. 249).

Shostakovich should wait another year, but I did not pay much attention to this.

In passing I should like to mention that when I performed this symphony in other cities, and when I showed it to Bruno Walter, I met with real opposition from a group of prominent musicians who grumbled that I was pushing Shostakovich too energetically. (Time, as always, has shown who was right.)

Our concert was scheduled for sometime in the spring. Meantime I had many opportunities to listen to the symphony played by Mitya himself. Each rendition was a real pleasure, and this alone speaks much for the symphony.

At last the exact date for the concert was fixed, 12 May. . . .

The presence of the composer during the rehearsal of a new composition has great significance. Much depends upon how much the composer hears and how he listens. By 'hear' I mean just that . . . Shostakovich immediately showed what we call attentiveness to listening. He did not reveal his nervous state and did not fidget,[13] but listened with full concentration and answered sensibly when questions were asked. . . . I remember clearly that he never stopped the rehearsal nor interfered with it, nor did he interrupt the work of the conductor during the rehearsal. This might be explained by his shyness and his youthful good behaviour, but I do not think so. Mitya, for all his shyness and reserve, was quite self-assured and never, prior to the performance of his symphony or as a regular student of the Conservatory, had exhibited any tendency toward compliance. The fact is that he knew exactly what he wanted when he wrote his score. The first sounds that issued from the orchestra confirmed the correctness of his imagination, and he had no reason to make any fuss.

An orchestra is like a responsive barometer, . . . and always takes young composers with a grain of salt. When we rehearsed the First Symphony of Shostakovich, this attitude was scarcely noticeable: there were almost no mistakes in the parts, the composer himself having carefully checked the orchestral material. Technically everything was playable, and the orchestra musicians could not overlook

---

13 Steinberg, DDS's teacher, had a different story, as shown by this extract from his diary: 'Mitya's symphony sounds very good. Mitya himself is in a state of such indescribable excitement from hearing the sound of his own music that I only restrained him with difficulty from gesticulating and displaying his agitation' (Sofiya Khentova, *Shostakovich: Life and Work*, vol. I, p. 141).

the quality of the music itself. The usual mistrust disappeared fairly quickly. An elderly cellist did grumble when he had to play a solo (without a mute) while accompanied by other strings (celli), also without mutes.

At the concert, the symphony had a pronounced success. The second movement, the Scherzo was encored. The audience was thrilled, and there was a certain festive mood in the hall. This kind of response is a difficult thing to describe in words, but it is positive in character and, in this instance, there was no mistake about it. Such a feeling is usually apparent when something really outstanding and exceptional is performed. It is not a casual success warmed by casual conditions, but a genuine, spontaneous recognition. And so it was on this occasion.[14]

Shostakovich's mother, SOFIYA VASILYEVNA, left a moving description of the premiere of her son's symphony in this extract from her letter to Klavdia Lukashevich, her son's godmother. She also copied this letter and sent it to her sister Nadejda Galli-Shohat:

At last came 10 May, the day of the first orchestral rehearsal. (The symphony has been postponed from the 8th to the 12th May because *Salome* was being performed at the Mariinsky Theatre, and many of the brass players needed in our symphony were occupied there.)

While at work, I was unable to think about anything else, and only awaited the telephone call. At last I heard Mitya's happy voice. 'Everything sounds good – everything is all right.' Mitya was given his first ovation by the musicians and those present in the hall. I managed to get away from work to attend the next rehearsal on the 11th. I heard all the musical authorities heap praise on Mitya. Glazunov told me that he was particularly struck by Mitya's mastery of orchestration – something that is usually acquired only after years of experience and study. But it shone through brightly in this first large-scale orchestral work. Again much praise and compliments – another ovation – and Mitya's happy little face.

At last the day of the concert dawned. Our anxieties started from early morning. Mitya hadn't slept all night, and could neither eat nor drink anything. At half past eight we arrived at the Philharmonic. By nine o'clock the hall was completely packed. I cannot describe my emotions on seeing the conductor, Nikolai Malko, about to pick up his

14 Nikolai Malko, *A Certain Art*, pp. 160–7.

baton. I can only say that even the greatest happiness is very hard to bear! Everything went off brilliantly – the magnificent orchestra, and the superb execution! But the greatest success went to Mitya. The audience were very attentive, and the Scherzo was encored. It was over, and Mitya was called out again and again. When our young composer came out on stage, seemingly still only a boy, the audience expressed its joy and enthusiasm in a long and tumultuous ovation.

After the concert we celebrated at home with the luminaries of the musical world in attendance (Steinberg, Malko and Nikolayev). Glazunov couldn't come, as, still weak after his illness, he couldn't walk up the five flights of stairs. When Mitya arrived with Malko, Nikolayev and Steinberg played Glazunov's *Fanfare* on the piano and gave him three cheers. . . . The guests stayed until five o'clock in the morning.[15]

MAXIMILIAN STEINBERG wrote of this occasion in his diary:

A most memorable concert. The enormous success of Mitya's Symphony. The Scherzo was encored. After the concert we supped at the Shostakovich's until 2 a.m., predominantly in the society of youth. We returned home with Malko and his wife by foot as far as the Sadovaya [street]. A white night, but cold (2°C).[16]

The First Symphony was given its first public performance in Moscow at the packed-out Grand Hall of the Conservatoire. Shostakovich's young friends attended in force; many of them did not however possess a ticket. Pavel Lamm's daughter OLGA writes of this exciting occasion:

The ticket controllers had to fight off the students who were pushing their way through. They succeeded in grabbing hold of Misha Kvadri, who, waving the score in his hand, demanded loudly that he should be let into the hall, because they 'are going to perform my symphony, the author himself has dedicated it to me'. While Kvadri gesticulated and expounded, the others, with Shebalin at their head quickly slipped into the hall.[17]

At NIKOLAI MALKO's instigation, Shostakovich was invited to play two concerts in Kharkov in July 1926. At the first, on 12 July, he was soloist in

15 Compiled from Victor Seroff in collaboration with Nadejda Galli-Shohat, *Dmitri Shostakovich: The Life and Background of a Soviet Composer*, pp. 138–9, and Khentova, *Shostakovich*, vol. I, p. 141.
16 Khentova, *Shostakovich*, vol. I, p. 142.
17 Olga Lamm, 'Vissarion Yaklovlevich Shebalin', in A. Shebalina, *In Memory of Y. Y. Shebalin: Reminiscences, Materials*, p. 213.

Tchaikovsky's First Piano Concerto, conducted by Malko. On 17 July he played a solo recital. In another symphonic programme Malko conducted his First Symphony. MALKO also wrote about these Kharkov performances:

The rehearsals for the symphony were getting along nicely. The orchestra liked the composition, and the presence of the young composer intrigued the musicians, particularly since the nineteen-year-old Shostakovich still looked rather like a child.

In the role of 'composer' he again behaved very modestly and tactfully. He did not come to the platform, did not interfere, and in no way made a show of himself. It was not on his part a lack of interest in the performance but quite the contrary. Since everything had been previously discussed with the conductor, he was simply displaying good professional upbringing.

The symphony was a pronounced success. As I had expected, the presence of the boy-composer thrilled the public and resulted in the announcement of his forthcoming piano recital.

So Mitya had to practise.

Our kind host arranged for him to work on a fine Steinway located in a club. Here he was allowed to play as long as he desired. I must admit that Shostakovich actually practised very little. Instead, we discovered a billiard table in the club and he started practising on that 'instrument'. Neither of us had ever played before, so our initial attempts were rather poor. Finally, after long fiddling around, I succeeded in getting two balls into a pocket. Mitya got one in. I was called to the telephone and when I returned he said, 'While you were away I went on playing and I got another ball.'

'Splendid,' I congratulated him, and we continued our game.

The program for his recital was in two parts: his trio for piano, violin, and cello,[18] then his own piano works and some Liszt. Mitya, as I have already mentioned, did not trouble himself with much practising. My own orchestral rehearsals were also not too time-consuming. Thus we had sufficient leisure for trips to the country, visiting and café sessions. He was interested in absolutely everything and possessed a critical mind plus a good sense of humor. When he was given to playing pranks, these were not always childish. There was something in his make-up, stemming from his unsettled and nervous nature, that

18 The Trio was performed with local musicians, the violinist I. Dobrzhints and the cellist A. Kassan.

seemed to interweave his dignity and his bright and observant mind with a petty and silly vanity, a mischievousness, and a bent for tomfoolery.

. . . At last came the night of his recital. I started in due time to prepare Mitya for his appearance. He was dressed in a white shirt, white trousers and white shoes, but alas! the shoes proved to be far from white. What to do? I mixed some tooth powder into a paste and daubed his shoes. Satisfactory. Something was wrong with his belt. I happened to have a suitable one, but for him we had to fasten it with safety pins. Everything else was in order. (In passing I might mention that in the course of the week I had become accustomed to looking after his clothes and linen – and to picking up his socks and everything else from the most unexpected places.)

We took a coach to the hall. On the way Mitya started talking about the mating instincts of animals and insects. He became so engrossed that I had to stop him, saying, 'We have only half an hour left. The club is next door; go practise a bit.'

In twenty-five minutes I went after him. 'How do you feel?'
'OK.'
'Did you play?'
'Yes, some Liszt.'
'And your own works?'
'I rehearsed the Trio before.'
'But the other pieces?'
'No.'
'Are they ready?'
'I hope so. I did not play them.'
'What? Not at all?'
'No.'
'Not a single time during the whole week?'
'No.'
'But why not? You are starting your recital in one minute.'
'Yes, but they are *my* works. I do not need to repeat them. And I have rehearsed the Trio.'

With these parting words, Shostakovich went on to the stage. He performed quietly, without any trace of nervousness, and with self-assurance, precisely, without any special enthusiasm; I should say even with a little reserve.

The audience was not very large, but it was warmly appreciative.

Shostakovich made about three hundred rubles, so he went to the Caucasus, where he spent several weeks.[19] This was a very important thing for his health. He was indeed a happy boy. And I, probably even more so because everything had succeeded so well.[20]

The young SHOSTAKOVICH did not share Malko's opinion that the Kharkov performance of the First Symphony was a success. The following extract is from a letter to his mother dated 6 July 1926:

[At the rehearsal] I listened and was in despair: instead of three trumpets there were only two, instead of three timpani, only two, and instead of a grand piano a revolting, rattling old upright. All this I found most upsetting. Then the solo violinist is useless. At the second rehearsal, despite all Malko's efforts, nothing much was achieved, or rather nothing at all. Malko himself said that he was satisfied, so I didn't pursue the matter. The third rehearsal took place yesterday evening. It went better than the second, and the musicians gave me an ovation. At last it came to the concert. Malko came out. (The concert took place outside in the Gardens. The acoustic was garden-like, with the strings sounding terribly thin, while the upright piano was inaudible; on the other hand the timpani drowned everything else.) Malko stood at the conductor's desk, and somewhere close at hand some dogs started to bark loudly. They went on barking for an awfully long time, and the longer they went on the louder they got. The public was beside itself with laughter. Malko stood there motionless on stage. At last the dogs stopped barking. Malko started. The trumpet (there were three players at the concert) immediately bungled his first phrase. He was followed by the bassoon playing piles of wrong notes (we stumbled on an exceptionally awful bassoon player here). After about ten bars, the dogs started barking again. And throughout the first movement the dogs often added their solo. The orchestra barely got through the first movement. Then the second movement started. In the first two bars, however much Malko had gone over them at rehearsals, the celli and double basses made a terrible hashup. Then the clarinet started playing slower than the strings . . . Here I was rather surprised by the following: Malko, after a lot of effort, managed to steady the tempo; but he did so at the expense of the dynamics.

19 Shostakovich went to Anapa in the Caucasus on 19 July, where he met up with Tatyana Glivenko (see p. 84).
20 Malko, *A Certain Art*, pp. 173–6.

Instead of playing *piano*, the violins played *forte*, and Malko somehow didn't bother to call them to order. Then it was the turn of the bassoon solo. No words can describe it. The bassoonist caused me dire distress. And do you remember the wonderful bassoon solo at the [Leningrad] Philharmonic? Then they dragged the middle section, and a certain amount of confusion ensued. I almost burst into tears at that point. Instead of good strong chords on the piano, all one could hear were some pitiful, watered-down and out-of-tune plinks; the timbre didn't resemble that of a piano, rather a cymbalum or a toy harpsichord. I sat there thinking, 'What rubbish.' They finished the second movement. Applause broke out, they clapped for a while and some voices cried out 'encore'. Malko bowed, and they started playing again. I should say straight away that the third and fourth movements went considerably better. The cellist played his solo very well. They rushed the coda, and the percussion made such a racket that you couldn't hear anything else. It was over at last. The applause started, and the composer was called. I didn't want to take a bow, but Malko started clapping in my direction (I was sitting in the front row). It was awkward not to go. So I took a bow, and then another one, and then clambered on to the stage and bowed again. Outwardly it was successful, but of course the audience didn't understand anything, and only clapped from inertia. But there was no booing. Afterwards I went backstage to see Malko. He was satisfied and basked in glory. The musicians came backstage and there was a lot of hand-shaking. The rituals were observed.

When we got home, Malko said, 'It's a good thing that the Symphony was played.' A good thing or not, it wasn't all right. It's all right that I am going to be paid the author's rights, and also that on 12 July I'll play the Tchaikovsky Concerto with orchestra. It means that I'll be earning money. But there's nothing good in the fact that the local orchestra has spattered dirt all over my symphony.[21]

The professional pianist

The success of the First Symphony catapulted Shostakovich overnight to international fame. In May 1927, Bruno Walter performed the work in Berlin, and before long it was taken up by Arturo Toscanini and Otto Klemperer,

21 D. D. Shostakovich, 'Letters to Mother', p. 173.

amongst others. Such diverse figures as Darius Milhaud and Alban Berg were impressed by it.[22]

In the meantime, in April 1926 Shostakovich was accepted on the post-graduate composition course at the Leningrad Conservatoire, and continued his piano studies. At the preceding graduate diploma exam it was obligatory to play a classical work. His friend LYDIA ZHUKOVA was amazed at Mitya's nonchalant attitude towards this exam:

> Two weeks beforehand he still didn't know what he would play. Eventu-
> ally he chose Beethoven's 'Hammerklavier' Sonata. He said that it was
> inconceivably difficult, and that some of the ninths and tenths were
> unperformable. The evening before the exam I dropped by around nine
> o'clock at his house on Marat Street. He played for me. He was a wonderful
> pianist, with strong hands and his own precise and somewhat dry manner
> of playing. But I felt quite sick at heart. This was only a sketchy
> performance. How could he be ready in time? But at the exam next day he
> played with authority and maturity, displaying a symphonic grasp of the
> whole grandiose work. Already then he thought in massive symphonic
> boulder-like sections. . . . Then with his sister, Marusya he played his Suite
> for Two Pianos, one of his earliest works, which was still boyish, prickly
> and rumpled in style.[23]

After completing the First Symphony and the Octet Op. 11 (both in July 1925), Shostakovich underwent something of a creative block and for the best part of a year he stopped composing. At some point during 1926 he reached a point of despair and burnt many of his manuscripts, including sketches for an opera based on Pushkin's poem 'The Gypsies'. When he returned to composition he wrote two works for piano: the Piano Sonata Op. 12 (in November 1926) and the Ten Aphorisms for Piano Op. 13 (February–April 1927). At the same time he started thinking seriously about a career as a concert pianist.

This was a difficult period for Shostakovich when he felt alienated not only from his Conservatoire teachers, but from musical life. He looked more and

---

22 Darius Milhaud wrote in his book *Notes sans musique*: 'Despite its rather conventional form and construction [the Symphony] betrayed genuine gifts and even had certain qualities of greatness, if it is to be remembered that its composer, Shostakovich was only eighteen at the time . . .'
Alban Berg wrote to Shostakovich after hearing a performance of the symphony in Vienna on 28 November 1928: 'It was a great joy for me to get to know your symphony. I find it quite marvellous, especially the first movement' (Khentova, *Shostakovich*, vol. I, p. 152). In Solomon Volkov's *Testimony* it is alleged that Shostakovich complained that this letter never reached him, since it was sent to Asafiev, who didn't pass it on.
23 Lydia Zhukova, *Epilogues: First Book*, p. 27.

more to the brilliant Moscow music theorist Boleslav Yavorsky as his mentor. It was Yavorsky who suggested the title of 'Aphorisms' to Shostakovich, who dedicated this set of piano pieces to him. The Aphorisms were obviously intended to be subversive. For instance, Shostakovich talked about writing a waltz, combining it with another piece and calling it 'Dance of Shit', a play of words produced by changing one letter in the usual title of 'Dance of Death'.[24]

It was also through Yavorsky's initiative that Shostakovich was chosen (very much at the eleventh hour) to be one of the Soviet team to take part in the Chopin Competition in Warsaw in late January 1927. Shostakovich does not seem the obvious choice to represent Nikolayev's School, if one bears in mind that there were some outstanding Chopinists amongst his students, notably Vladimir Sofronitsky. Nevertheless, Nikolayev approved his candidature and worked intensively with him in the weeks prior to the competition.

Despite his own and others' expectations, he was not awarded one of the prizes. SHOSTAKOVICH's own disappointment is reflected in his detailed letters to his mother. The jury was exclusively Polish, as were seventeen of the thirty-one contestants. On 1 February 1927 he wrote to his mother from Warsaw:

> I played the programme well, and had a great success. Eight people were selected for the final round with orchestra. . . . Everybody said that there were two candidates for first prize, Oborin and myself. And, what's more, they wrote in the press that the Soviet pianists were by far the best, and that if they were to award the four prizes, then all of them should go to us. But the jury decided, 'with grief in their hearts', to give only the first prize to a Russian, so it was awarded to Lyova [Oborin]. The decision regarding the other prizes bewildered the audience. I only got a diploma. Malishevsky, who read out the order of prizes, even forgot to mention my name. In the audience cries of 'Shostakovich, Shostakovich' were heard. . . . Malishevsky then read out my name, and the audience gave me a great ovation – rather demonstratively at that. But don't you be upset. There is an impresario here who wants to talk about some concert tours. I'm off to Berlin next week, and I'm playing a concert on Saturday.[25]

Shostakovich was not a man to relish failure, and gradually he relinquished his ambitions of becoming a concert pianist. He continued to enjoy performing – partly for the opportunities it provided for travel and adventure. Surprisingly his repertoire was not adventurous, although he played Prokofiev's First Piano Concerto and participated in a performance of Stravinsky's Les Noces

24 Tatyana Glivenko in interview with EW. The play of words is achieved by turning 'Tanets Smert'i' ('Dance of Death') into 'Tanets Smerd'i' ('Dance of Shit').
25 D. D. Shostakovich, 'Letters to Mother', p. 175.

where Mariya Yudina was one of the other piano soloists. In the last three years of the decade Shostakovich once more turned to intensive composition and turned out a staggering volume of work in a remarkable variety of genres and styles. But soon he was to give up performing all music except his own.

The Leningrad pianist NATHAN PERELMAN was an exact contemporary of the composer. He recalls Shostakovich as a Chopinist:

Early in 1927 it was decided to send Shostakovich to participate in the Chopin competition in Warsaw. It seemed a very strange and unexpected choice. I heard Shostakovich's performance at the Philharmonic Hall in Leningrad just prior to his departure for Warsaw. His Chopin playing didn't resemble anything I have heard before or since. It reminded me of his performances of his own music, very direct and without much plasticity, and very laconic in expression. It was an altogether idiosyncratic manner of playing. Shostakovich left for the competition together with Lev Oborin, Grigori Ginzburg and Yuri Bryushkov. As you know Oborin won the competition and Ginzburg was also awarded some prize, but Shostakovich was only given a diploma. After that he went to Berlin for a few days and while he was there he bought his first hat. I remember his first appearance wearing a hat when he returned to Leningrad.

While he was preparing for the competition he was no longer officially studying with Nikolayev, but he would go to his home and play for him there. Nikolayev was an extraordinary personality, a man of great erudition and a wonderful musician. He was also a musicologist and composer, in fact the old-fashioned type of Russian intellectual who had an enormous range of interests and grasp on things. He was an outstanding teacher.

Few people now remember Shostakovich's amazing and idiosyncratic pianism. He expressed his individuality in his approach to performance. He never allowed himself the slightest hint of 'Chopinesque' sentiment, and this in its own way had much charm. He had a wonderful technique, with fantastic octaves. He played Tchaikovsky's First Piano Concerto excellently, with brilliant octave passages. There was nothing left to chance in his playing, it was all very closely and precisely heard in his head. If he chose to use little pedal, it wasn't because he did not know how to use it, but because he heard the music this way. It didn't at all coincide with our notions and expectations of piano playing. In our youthful years we were very sensitive, aiming for beauty of expression, using a range of soft and delicate dynamics and nuances. I participated at the next Chopin competition in 1932, and, together with others of my generation, I was reproached for playing too softly.

Shostakovich emphasized the linear aspect of music and was very precise in all the details of performance. He used little rubato in his playing, and it lacked extreme dynamic contrasts. It was an 'anti-sentimental' approach to playing which showed incredible clarity of thought. You could say that his playing was very modern; at the time we accepted it and took it to our hearts. But it made less impression in Warsaw, where Oborin's more decorative, charming and 'worldly' approach, albeit somewhat militaristic, was the order of the day. However, Shostakovich seemed to foresee that by the end of the twentieth century, his style of playing would predominate, and in this his pianism was truly contemporary.

Shostakovich played his own works marvellously. I heard him perform his own First Piano Sonata in the foyer of the Leningrad Philharmonic Hall.[26] It was interesting that during the 1920s and 1930s he continued working at the piano and giving concerts, but increasingly he performed his own music. Later in the 1930s he played some concerts with the cellist Arnold Ferkelman. I remember with great pleasure how sensitively Dmitri Dmitriyevich performed in this duo.[27]

PERELMAN, like Shostakovich, played in the cinema, providing sound for the silent movies. Here he remembers these experiences:

Shostakovich, or Mitya as he was to us in those years, played a lot in the cinemas during the 1920s, illustrating the silent movies. However there was nothing exceptional in this, we all played at various cinemas to earn money. Mitya played in the Piccadilly cinema on Nevsky Prospect which today is now called the Aurora. Another well-known composer used to play at another cinema on the Nevsky called the Coliseum. I played at a cinema on Liteiny Prospect. After its closure, it became the home for TRAM,[28] the theatre where Shostakovich worked for a couple of years.

26 The first performance took place on 12 December 1926. On that occasion Shostakovich's teacher Leonid Nikolayev commented wryly, 'Is this a piano sonata? No, it is a sonata for metronome to the accompaniment of the piano' (Khentova, *Shostakovich*, vol. I, p. 213.
27 Nathan Perelman: recorded interview with EW.
28 Leningrad Workers' Youth Theatre.

I believe that Dmitri Dmitriyevich used to improvise while playing for the films in much the same style as he wrote music in the 1920s – very 'progressively'. The audiences now and then protested. Once there was such a terrible scandal that the director of the cinema decided to dismiss Mitya and to deprive him of the payment he was already due. As this was the only means we had of making a living of any kind it was no laughing matter. I remember that an article appeared in the magazine *Rabochii i Teatr* in his defence, saying what a talented young man he was, how well he improvised, and so the affair ended happily and he was reinstated. I heard some of his improvisations, but wasn't present during these scandalous episodes. We all knew about them through the cinema grapevine.

I also had my share of scandals. I arranged a mirror at the piano which reflected the screen, and this allowed me to read a book simultaneously, without having to glue my eyes continuously on the film. It meant that I often played music that didn't fit the action. As they were dying on the screen, I was dancing on the piano, and while they were dancing on the screen, I was playing tragic funeral music. The director came to reprimand me: 'How much longer are you going to mock the viewers?' I also learnt a lot of repertoire while playing at the cinema, like the Chopin concertos, a Metner sonata, and so on. I think that many people went to the cinema to hear Shostakovich, certainly those who were in the know. Of course the crowd preferred the more sentimental music played by popular composers of the day.[29]

For Shostakovich, the scandals sometimes had an element of fun in them:

I have now given myself over to serving in the cinema. Yesterday an event occurred not without a certain interest. They were showing a picture called *Marsh and Water Birds of Sweden*. I started to illustrate it. I got worked up into a passion and depicted such birds that the sky itself grew hot. Suddenly in the hall there was a loud volley of applause and some penetrating whistles. Usually applause in the hall is a sign of protest and not of delight. I thought to myself, 'I suppose the picture is a load of rubbish and that the public is protesting.' Then everything grew quiet. After a while, another burst of applause. Then the picture finished. A certain lady, Scheffer, came up to me and declared, 'The

29 Nathan Perelman: recorded interview with EW.

public say you must escape from such "Musik".' Then the head of the theatre went up to Vladimirov [the conductor] and started to speak to him. I asked Vladimirov what he had said. Vladimirov laughed and said, 'The public complained to the boss during the show, saying, "Your pianist is undoubtedly drunk".' But Vladimirov defended me and told the boss, 'The illustration is first-rate and your public doesn't understand a thing.' Afterwards the musicians of the orchestra came up to me and shook my hand. I was left with a feeling of real satisfaction that I had managed to exasperate the cinema goers. It was only a pity that none of my friends were in the cinema yesterday.[30]

Shostakovich worked at the cinema on and off for three years, from 1923 to 1926. Apart from the Picadilly he played at the Bright Reel and the Splendid Palace cinemas. The musicians at these cinemas often had difficulty in getting their wages, and Shostakovich actually went so far as to sue his employer, Akim Volynsky:

. . . for non payment of two weeks' wages to us musicians for our work at the 'Bright Reel' cinema. It's all rather unpleasant. I never thought that I would ever have to take somebody to court, let alone Volynsky, whom I previously used to respect. But now I see that he is only a rogue and exploiter.[31]

The Second Symphony

In February 1927 Shostakovich was commissioned by the agit prop department of the State Publishing House to write a symphonic work in honour of the tenth anniversary of the October Revolution. The resulting Opus 14 was finished in August, and first performed by Malko and the Leningrad Philharmonic on 5 and 6 November.

In 'To October' Shostakovich set verses by the poet Alexander Bezymensky which he heartily disliked, calling them 'quite disgusting'.[32] The work called for special effects, such as factory whistles tuned to a particular pitch. Many people found the music bewildering and difficult; not least the musicians. Malko noted that in rehearsal Shostakovich was very demanding on the orchestral musicians, who 'curse him for the uncomfortable writing (pizzicato)'. Two days later he stated, 'Shostakovich suggested changing the

---

30 Letter dated 28 October 1925 (*ibid.*, p. 252).
31 Letter dated 16 February 1925 (Kozlova, *Letters to Lev Oborin*, p. 247).
32 Interview with Tatyana Glivenko.

pizzicato to spiccato. It works better. He keeps saying either, 'I have capitulated ignominiously' or, 'One day they will learn to play pizzicato.'[33]

Maximilian Steinberg remarked on the symphony's 'utter emancipation from vertical line', while wondering 'can this really be "New Art"? Or is it only the daring of a naughty boy?'[34] Shostakovich himself remained satisfied, pleased to be called out on stage four times.[35]

During this period Shostakovich's relationship with Malko underwent ups and downs; in particular he took great offence that Malko, having suggested that his new symphony should be entered in a competition organized by the Leningrad Philharmonic, did not see that it was awarded first prize.[36]

However, Malko continued to remain an important figure in Shostakovich's life at this period, both musically and socially. It was in Malko's house that Shostakovich met Sollertinsky, and there, as a consequence of a bet, he transcribed and orchestrated in forty minutes flat Victor Youman's 'Tea for Two' (known in Russia as 'Tahiti Trot'). At Malko's request he also made transcriptions of two Domenico Scarlatti pieces for wind orchestra. Together with 'Tahiti Trot', they were first performed in Moscow on 25 November 1928 as a complement to the Suite from the newly-finished opera *The Nose*.

Here are NIKOLAI MALKO's reminiscences of 'To October':

After his graduation from the Conservatory, Shostakovich's attitude toward the academic status of the school was very critical. This was quite natural. Moreover, neither could he sympathize with VAPM[37] and its limited ideas of simplification. Thus his interests and leanings became very understandable. With such attendant circumstances, Shostakovich was commissioned to compose a cantata for the Tenth Anniversary of the Soviet Regime – 7 November 1927 – set to the words of Bezymensky's poem 'To October'. Although the acceptance of the European calendar had changed the date of the Revolution from 25 October 1917 to 7 November, the terminology 'October Revolution' has continued to exist.

One must admit that Bezymensky's words were bad. Shostakovich did not like them and simply laughed at them. His musical setting did

33 From Malko's Philharmonic Diary, 2 and 4 November 1927, archive of the Leningrad Institute of Theatre, Music and Cinema.
34 Khentova, *Shostakovich*, vol. I, p. 213.
35 Letter to Lev Shulgin, director of the Leningrad Philharmonic, 7 November 1927.
36 Shostakovich shared second prize with a presumed protégé of Boris Asafiev, who, like Malko, was on the jury. (Later it transpired that the presumed protégé was actually a composer from Argentina! [Malko, *A Certain Art*, p. 206.])
37 The All-Union Association of Proletarian Musicians. Usually referred to as RAPM.

not quite take them seriously, and it showed no enthusiasm whatsoever.

Shostakovich quite often, and willingly, would play this cantata on the piano. It has a long developed introduction, several independent episodes, and a final chorus. Some of the chorus phrases were to be recited rather than sung. In one of the episodes, Shostakovich tried to express the personal impression he had experienced when he had seen a boy killed in Letny Prospect. The boy's crime had been stealing an apple. This episode, described in music, brings forth some intricate atonal fugato, partly in a very high register. Why the memory of that poor boy was expressed in precisely this way remains forever a mystery to me. . . . Shostakovich later named this cantata his Symphony Number Two.[38]

Friendship with Ivan Sollertinsky

Shostakovich's first close friends from his Conservatoire years were Valerian Bogdanov-Berezovsky and Leo Arnshtam. The Arnshtams' house was a lively centre for the Conservatoire youth. Lydia Zhukova, one of the bright sparks of that circle, recalled that the young composer was nicknamed 'Shtozhtakovich' (roughly meaning 'What's-the-matter-ovich'), and that his best friend was Volodya Kuvcharov, who had a 'mystical' resemblance to Shostakovich. Kuvcharov's main talent was to be a sympathetic listener, and he appeared to be Shostakovich's shadow rather than equal partner. He fell ill and died in 1925, 'as if fading into oblivion'.

It was sometime during 1927 that Shostakovich got to know Ivan Ivanovich Sollertinsky. By profession a specialist in the Spanish and Romance languages, Sollertinsky was a man of amazingly diverse gifts and interests. Endowed with a phenomenal memory, he was a brilliant linguist, an expert on philosophy, art history and theatre. But it was in the sphere of music that he came to have most public recognition and influence. He founded the Gustav Mahler and Anton Bruckner circles, and was responsible for having the music of these composers first performed in the Soviet Union. Later he assumed the position of artistic adviser to the Leningrad Philharmonic. His pre-concert talks at the Philharmonic were often considered more inspiring than the music that followed. He became vital to Shostakovich as a loyal and ardent supporter of his work, and in particular of his stage works.

38 Malko, *A Certain Act*, p. 204–5. The work was published in 1927 with the title 'To October: A Symphonic Dedication with Final Chorus on Words by Bezymensky for Large Orchestra and Mixed Chorus'.

SHOSTAKOVICH wrote of a first meeting with this paragon during the exams on Marxism/Leninism which he sat when applying for the post-graduate course in 1926:

I was extremely nervous before the exam. We were called up in alphabetical order. After a while Sollertinsky was called in to answer for the examining commission. Soon he came out of the room. I summoned up my courage and asked him: 'Tell me, please, was it a difficult exam?' He answered: 'No, not in the least difficult.' 'And what did they ask you?' 'Oh, the easiest questions imaginable: about the origin of materialist philosophy in Ancient Greece, Sophocles' poetry as an expression of realistic tendencies, the English philosophers of the seventeenth century, and something else.' I need hardly say that Sollertinsky's account caused me no uncertain anguish.[39]

Shostakovich's sister, ZOYA recalled her brother coming home to announce:

'I have met a wonderful new friend.' This, of course, was Ivan Ivanich Sollertinsky. They had an insane friendship. Sollertinsky came to see us every day in the morning and stayed until the evening. They spent the whole day together, laughing and chuckling. Sollertinsky was an incredible witty person, but he had a horrible squeaky voice. His tongue was poisonous, and it was no fun to be the butt of his wit. On the days they didn't meet, Mitya and Ivan Ivanich wrote to each other.

Zoshchenko also came to see us. Mitya loved him. He visited us frequently after he was denounced in 1946, when he was very unhappy. He was by nature quite a despondent character, you couldn't expect any fun from him. Even before the Decree of 1946 he was pretty gloomy; he only knew how to be jolly in his stories.

Then later on we used to see a lot of Isaak Glikman. But the really close friendship of Mitya's was with Sollertinsky. Sollertinsky's son told me how during the evacuation from Leningrad most of the family's things got left behind, but all of Mitya's letters got taken as part of his father's most treasured belongings.[40]

IRINA DERZAYEVA, Sollertinsky's first wife, described the two young men's early encounters:

39 Lyudmila Mikheeva, *In Memory of I. I. Sollertinsky: Reminiscences, Material and Research*, p. 92.
40 Zoya Shostakovich: recorded interview with EW.

We lived in those days in a large communal flat on Pushkin Street. Sollertinsky, like Shostakovich, was absolutely oblivious of his every-day surroundings and to any form of comfort. Usually they retired by themselves and indulged in non-stop conversation. Shostakovich would make music. They demanded an unlimited supply of the strongest, bitter tea. When they didn't manage to meet, Shostakovich would usually ring up. They called each other with comic reverence by name and patronymic – Van Vanich, and Dmi Dmitrich – while using the 'thou' form of address. They were simply in love, and didn't conceal their delight in each other. Sollertinsky never tired of repeat-ing: 'Shostakovich is a genius.'[41]

LYDIA ZHUKOVA describes how their youthful circle perceived Sollertinsky:

As a university professor, he seemed to us to belong to another generation, although actually the age difference between us was insignificant. He would appear unexpectedly and noisily in our 'Arnshtam' circle with news and gossip. He would spread his shaggy greatcoat on the floor and recite Petrarch Sonnets, or sing right through a Mahler symphony in his funny falsetto, recalling every voice note for note with complete precision. Our jaws dropped open, we revered him like a god. But this great and erudite original remained on an equal footing with us; he would fall about with laughter or get involved in some quarrel; would swear – sometimes not at all elegantly either – and behave boisterously; and then suddenly he would disappear. . . .

Sollertinsky was no mean drinker. We, great purists that we were, shunned drink and made do with cranberry juice. Once we all went in a gang to the beach near Stroretsk. The bathing wasn't much in that shallow puddle, as you had to wade out half a kilometre, and even then you only got your heels wet. Two figures – that of Sollertinsky and our slim Mitya – could be seen striding through the water, staggering from side to side, until they became shadows in the distance. We saw them swigging down brandy from the same bottle. Sollertinsky, it is said, taught Shostakovich to drink. But Mitya never learnt . . . he was just a boy wishing to appear like an adult. When Kolya Chukovsky and Lyonya Mess discoursed on ladies' legs, Mitya surveyed the beauties on the beach and with a sense of importance held forth knowingly . . .

41 Khentova, *Shostakovich*, vol. I, p. 217.

Today Sollertinsky's name is venerated. Much of what he wrote with such temperament and genius has retained its freshness. But alas, many of his brilliant, erudite articles display a vulgar sociological vein, a reminder of those 'Marxist' times.[42]

And lastly the reminscences of NIKOLAI MALKO:

Involuntarily I was instrumental in bringing into his life another very important influence, aside from that of his mother. This influence gradually spread into the innermost corners of his spiritual interests and, as time went by, it did not diminish but instead strengthened, continuing for many years. The influence I speak of came from Ivan Ivanovich Sollertinsky, whom I introduced to Mitya. They became fast friends, and eventually one could not seem to do without the other.

When Shostakovich and Sollertinsky were together, they were always fooling. Jokes ran riot and each tried to outdo the other in making witty remarks. It was a veritable competition. Each had a sharply developed sense of humor; both where bright and observant; they knew a great deal; and their tongues were itching to say something funny or sarcastic, no matter whom it might concern. They were each quite indiscriminate when it came to being humorous, and if they were too young to be bitter they could still come mercilessly close to being malicious.

. . . Each of these young men had a profound knowledge of music. They accepted it as though it were a live thing, a living body. They experienced it emotionally, with a deep admiration and love. They would esteem and praise something, or they might hate, despise and ridicule a composition. Once they hit upon a sad and monotonous melody from the symphony of a contemporary composer. They started singing it in a humorous fashion. The caricature was so apropos and so genuinely funny that it stuck permanently.

Both knew Russian literature well and often cited witty quotations. Shostakovich loved and admired Gogol, and when quoting him he would speak the words with a special deep sense of enjoyment as he brought out the inner meaning of each word.

. . . Mitya was vibrantly interested in all music, not just in his own compositions. This statement may seem odd, but there do exist composers who are completely disinterested in anyone else's music.

42 Zhukova, *Epilogues*, pp. 35-7.

. . . But the young Shostakovich was interested in everybody, and he listened attentively, thoughtfully, and critically to everything. He often played for me whatever I might ask. I remember his performance at my home of Tchaikovsky's *The Nutcracker Suite*. At that time I was sharing an apartment with a family of ballet people. The two daughters were dancers, and the mother had been a member of the ballet corps. While listening to Mitya's playing, I opened, by chance, the door into the corridor, and there they all were, sitting and listening in rapture to his playing. The old lady was experiencing again the entire ballet. Her daughter told us later how the mother, with tears in her eyes, had recognized every note, and how from time to time she would say, 'Here comes the Mouse King,' or, 'Here the Nutcracker turns into the Prince,' or, 'Here comes the cannon.'

Mitya was interested not only in music and literature, but in everything. He had a passion for roller coasters (in Russia they were called 'American Mountains') which were put up in the 'People's House.'

. . . However, Sollertinsky knew much more than Shostakovich. He was stronger in criticism and less reserved. His outlook in music, strange as this statement may sound, was much wider than that of Shostakovich. Rumor had it that Shostakovich had given Sollertinsky a few music lessons. I do not know what it was that he taught him, but I am sure that Sollertinsky learned more in those few sessions than someone else would have learned in two or three full courses.

Sollertinsky knew the symphonies of Gustav Mahler and Bruckner very thoroughly. It was certainly his influence that made Shostakovich interested in Mahler. . . . Let me say that from his own personal standpoint this influence was quite natural. The angularity of Mahler, his sharpness, the peculiarity of his humor, and his tendency towards grandiose forms with stretched-out expositions – all of this, as well as his musical grimaces, found a vivid response in Shostakovich both in himself and as a person and as a musician, in fact, perhaps more as a person than as a musician.[43]

Social upheaval and cultural revolution

The political and social climate in the USSR changed radically after Lenin's death in January 1924, marked by the gradual but irresistible rise to power of

43 Malko, *A Certain Art*, pp. 187–97.

Joseph Stalin. Until the late 1920s opposition groups within the Communist Party still enjoyed an official existence, but Stalin, in his role as General Secretary, developed a cunning and lethal strategy of manipulating and eliminating his rivals. By 1927 he had stripped his arch-enemy Leon Trotsky of all power and had him sent into exile. Lev Kamenev and Grigori Zinoviev, the principal leaders of the 'right' opposition, were suppressed somewhat differently; forced to recant and submit to the role of obedient puppets, the road was open to their eventual destruction in the political show trials of 1936/7.

The principal problem that faced the Party in the mid-1920s was that of regenerating the country's bankrupt economy. The free market policies of the NEP had been successful up to a point, but they were much resented because the NEP's 'capitalist' values flew in the face of all that the Party was meant to stand for. The term 'Nepmen' was coined as a pejorative not only for the entrepreneurs who were able to exploit the free market, but for all those who indulged in such 'bourgeois' pastimes as dancing, American jazz, living it up in restaurants, and so on. This aspect of the NEP was heavily satirized in the literature, films and plays of the period, of which Mayakovsky's play *The Bedbug* and Shostakovich's ballet *The Golden Age* are striking examples.

In order to resolve the social problems that had been thrown up by the NEP, the Party got embroiled in an urgent debate over how to create socialism in a worker's state and how rapid a pace could be set for the industrialization of the country. At the 15th Party Congress in 1927, a decision was taken to collectivize the land, which was implemented from 1929. The following year, 1928, saw the introduction of the First Five Year Plan, with its ambitious programme of industrial growth. The social consequences of these measures cannot be overstated. The doors were opened for a new ruling class of workers who gained education and privilege by joining the Party. These future Party plutocrats were to oust the 'bourgeois specialists', the products of the old-time professional classes and intelligentsia.

When it proved impossible to meet the quotas set by the Party for the enforced pace of industrialization and collectivization, scapegoats were required. Accusations of sabotage, wrecking, hoarding and espionage were bandied about with frightening results. In 1928, at the notorious 'Shakhti' trial, fifty-three mining engineers (or 'bourgeois' specialists) stood accused of wrecking equipment. This was the first of a series of public trials which convulsed Soviet society between 1928 and 1931. These sweeping purges were set in motion by Stalin as a means to reinforce his political power and to execute his often unpopular policies. The climate of suspicion and distrust that characterized the Stalinist era came into being.

On the other hand, the challenges of meeting and 'overfulfilling' quotas for the Five Year Plans stimulated a pioneering spirit and a certain pride in the country's progressive achievements. It was an era of heroic deeds and daring feats, which culminated in the much-publicized exploit of Alexei Stakhanov, a Donbass miner who in 1935 allegedly exceeded the 'norm' of production for a single shift by nearly fifteen times.

This 'Revolution from above' was based on the principle of class warfare, which threatened not only the intelligentsia but the richer peasants (the kulaks) and the professional and managerial classes. From 1928 the educational institutions were subject to attack from militant groups, and in addition a virulent anti-religious campaign was unleashed. In the countryside the 'de-kulakization' campaign saw wide-scale arrests and deportations. The beleaguered intelligentsia seemingly had two choices open to them – to conform, or to lie low. Only a few outspoken voices dared challenge the authorities. The writer Evgeny Zamyatin, who had worked on the libretto of Shostakovich's The Nose, (1927–8), had the courage to tackle Stalin directly, declaring his view that to be deprived of the freedom of expression was equivalent to 'the death penalty'. While other writers such as Daniil Kharms and Osip Mandelstam suffered arrest, Zamyatin was allowed to emigrate in 1931.

Shostakovich inevitably found himself involved with topical political themes, particularly in the theatre and cinema. His ballet Bolt (1930–1) takes sabotage in industry as its subject, and The Limpid Stream (1934–5) is concerned with collectivization. The vaudeville show Declared Dead,[44] for which Shostakovich wrote the music in 1931, is populated by such archetypal caricatures as 'Mr Beat-the-Bourgeois' and crafty priests and depraved dancing girls. Most of the films that Shostakovich wrote music to had historical-revolutionary subjects. But of all the works of this period it was the music for the film Counterplan (1932) that brought Shostakovich enormous popular success. The film describes the spontaneous creation of a workers' plan (or 'counterplan') to boost production and increase their factory's norm. The 'Song of the Counterplan'[45] became Shostakovich's greatest hit, and was sung all over the country. It was later re-used in the composer's own scores, and even adapted to become the United Nations Hymn in 1942.

Such was the background to the cultural revolution which gripped the country from 1928 to 1931. The multifarious society that had been a positive feature of the 1920s gradually disintegrated; from 1928 onwards it was totally stamped out by the militant groups acting in the name of the proletariat. In 1932, the Party, intolerant of all independent associations, including the militants', decided to assume control in cultural matters. It did so by creating 'unions' (initially of writers, soon followed by unions of artists, composers,

44 More commonly known as 'Hypothetically [or Conditionally] Killed' (see p. 101).
45 Often (incorrectly) translated as 'Song of the Meeting' or 'Song of the Passer-by'.

cinematographers, and so on) which became servants of its policy. Conformity (or uniformity) was imposed in all walks of life, from the sphere of economics to that of culture.

The prevailing winds of left art

The early and mid-1920s had been characterized by a proliferation of independent associations and groups in the world of literature and arts. The most experimental of them embraced elements of revolutionary ideology and were referred to in Russia as leftist. They included LEF, which was associated with Mayakovsky, FEKS, the cinema laboratory of Kozintsev and Trauberg, and OBERIU,[46] to which the absurdists Kharms and Alexander Vvedensky belonged. Others were overtly political, claiming the right to represent the proletariat's views. In the minority were those who merely wished to defend professional artistic standards.

In music the most important of the proletarian groups was RAPM, the Russian Association of Proletarian Musicians, the counterpart of RAPP, the writers' association. RAPM was founded in 1925, and by the late 1920s it was very powerful. (Like all other independent organizations, it was dissolved in 1932 to make way for the Union of Composers, which lay under exclusive Party control.) RAPM's platform proclaimed that music should have a social message and be accessible to the wide masses, whether it be the mass song or Beethoven's Ninth Symphony. Tchaikovsky was seen as decadent (even Lunacharsky criticized his music as too 'salonish and perfumed'), whereas most modern experiment was labelled 'formalist'.

RAPP and RAPM's policies are often confused with those of PROLET-KULT,[47] which, under the leadership of Alexander Bogdanov, advocated an anarchic ideology towards the arts. RAPM advocated a simplification that debased professional standards, while Proletkult believed in training workers to become artists, in sweeping aside all inherited bourgeois values and destroying habitual context. The climax of Proletkult's activity was the mounting of an enormous public spectacle in the squares and streets of Petrograd: 'The Mystery of Emancipated Labour' was held on May Day 1920, involving thousands of participants. Although Proletkult was disbanded by Lenin in 1920, its spirit lived on in the work of Russia's most progressive artists (e.g. in Sergei Eisenstein's Proletkult theatrical experiment *The Wise Man* [1924] and in the work of FEKS and OBERIU, and elements of it are also present in Shostakovich's opera *The Nose*).

Shostakovich consciously evaded all these groups, preferring to remain an

46 Association for Real Art.
47 Proletarian Cultural and Educational Organization.

outsider. True he had occasional dealings with the ASM (Association of Contemporary Music), an organization which in the mid-1920s promoted a wide range of composers from the constructivist Mosolov to the more academic Asafiev. The fact that Shostakovich wrote music celebrating revolutionary events (notably the Piano Sonata and the Second and Third Symphonies) was probably prompted as much by a desire to be seen as artistically 'progressive' as to prove himself politically in tune with the ideals of the Revolution. However, these works did not gain him support from RAPM or its break-away organizations, such as PROKOLL.[48] They criticized his Second Symphony and regarded *The Nose* as not merely experimental but 'formalist' and 'decadent'.

After 1928, radical groups such as RAPP and RAPM increasingly took it upon themselves to act as spokesmen for the Party as well as 'the proletariat' during this period of cultural revolution. These vigilant groups also took every opportunity to harass and humiliate intellectuals, and they wreaked havoc within the institutions of higher education. Officially Shostakovich only finished his post-graduate course at the Leningrad Conservatoire in autumn 1929; his Conservatoire report is full of statements to the effect that he wishes to create music for the people, although emphasizing that accessibility did not mean debasing standards. Earlier that year the Conservatoire had been 'purged' of 'unwelcome elements', a notable victim of which was Mariya Yudina, who was dismissed from her professorship for her espousal of religion. In the spring of 1929 Shostakovich himself was dismissed from a teaching position he had held for a few months at the Choreographic Technical College.

No musician could afford to ignore the implications of RAPM's militancy. The need to protect himself from their attacks was a guiding factor in Shostakovich's decision to accept a position at TRAM in 1929, and also influenced his choice of themes in the Third Symphony and the ballet scores.

The musicologist DANIIL ZHITOMIRSKY, an exact contemporary of Shostakovich, made his early career in the circles of RAPM and PROKOLL. In 1929 he wrote a polemic article in the journal *Proletarsky Muzikant* condemning Shostakovich's opera *The Nose*, noting that Shostakovich 'had strayed from the main road of Soviet Art'.

After the dissolution of RAPM in 1932, Zhitomirsky, like many of his colleagues, changed his radical ideological position. While he became increasingly sympathetic to Shostakovich, he could never be counted amongst the circle of the composer's friends.

I first saw Shostakovich close to in the winter of 1927, when I met him in the cramped room of Nikolai Sergeyevich Zhilyaev, one of my

48 Production Collective of Student Composers.

teachers at the Conservatoire. I was labouring over an exercise in 'strict style' counterpoint. Somewhere from the opposite end of this enormous communal flat the signal of 'four short buzzes' sounded and Nikolai Sergeyevich shuffled off in his slippers to the main entrance to open the door. It was his guest from Leningrad. He seemed only a boy, although the expression of his eyes through the thick black-framed glasses was adult. He was very sparing with words. Soon, at Zhilyaev's request, he sat down at the piano to show us his newly-finished Piano Sonata. At that time I already knew his First Symphony, with its vivid theatricality, humour, its refined lyricism; the music, whose features obviously converged on those of Stravinsky and Prokofiev, was markedly individual and accessible. The Piano Sonata was completely different, and I hardly understood it. But this hearing created a strong impression on me. The composer was unusually severe, very concentrated, and played with faultless clarity. As an artist he had great authority, and he seemed to hold one in a hypnotic grip with his seriousness and conviction. He was not simply playing, he seemed to be casting spells and imposing his will upon us.

His Second Symphony ('October' from 1927) was not only hardly comprehensible to me, but I actively disliked it. Why was this? I belonged to a student circle which aimed to create a new 'revolution-ary' music. Our ideal was music that, while completely professional and serious, would be accessible to the People. The musical language of Shostakovich's Second Symphony seemed to be artificially com-plex, and the composer made no concessions to the tastes and the habits of the 'proletarian listener'. Now I dislike the Symphony for other reasons. In itself the aim which motivated the composer (or had been instilled in him by official propaganda) to glorify the October Revolution was a false aim. It was a child of our illusions of the 1920s.

Only a very few people would have been able to guess where this 'Path of October' would lead us, attended as it was at the time by hymns and fanfares. In addition the picture of revolution depicted in the symphony was extremely schematic; it did not originate out of contact with real life, but out of the Marxist textbooks of the time.

In the 'left' art of that period, energy and dynamism, 'revolutionary' innovation were taken to be the antithesis of the real human indi-vidual, where, it seemed, there was too much of the unpredictable, the introspective, too much posturing or 'Hamletizing'. In this idio-syncratic form we underwent the dehumanization of art; this process left us twenty-five years later completely bankrupt in the avant-garde of world culture.[49]

Experiment on stage and screen

Shostakovich conceived the idea of his opera *The Nose* (Op. 15) in 1927. The overall composition took three and a half months spread over a period of eighteen months. Part of it was written in Meyerhold's flat in Moscow while Shostakovich was working at Meyerhold's Theatre in January 1928.

The composer's sister Zoya recalled that:

> Mitya had great difficulty finishing the third act of *The Nose*. It simply wouldn't come. But then I remember him coming into our living room one morning and telling us that he had heard the whole of the third act in a dream; he there and then sat down and wrote it all out.[50]

This was not the first occasion when Shostakovich experienced the phenomenon of 'hearing' an entire piece of music. The composer mentioned writing an 'ultra-modern' cello piece 'not in my style' (one of the Op. 9 cello pieces dating from 1924). He recounted how late at night he heard the whole piece in all its polyphonic complexity as if it were being dictated to him note by note. His own role in all this was merely that 'of copyist'.[51]

The score of *The Nose* was completed by the summer of 1928. In July of that year the opera was accepted for production by the Leningrad Maly Theatre (MALEGOT), in whose chief conductor, Samuel Samosud, Shostakovich found a champion. The Bolshoi Theatre also expressed interest in staging the work, and Meyerhold in directing the production there. However this latter project came to nothing.

A concert performance was put on to vet the new work in June 1929, against Shostakovich's wishes. In a letter to the director, Nikolai Smolich, Shostakovich reiterated the principles that lay behind his stage work, akin to those which he adopted when writing music to Kozintsev and Trauberg's films:

> *The Nose* loses all meaning if it is seen just as a musical composition. For the music springs only from the action. . . . It is clear to me that a concert performance of *The Nose* will destroy it. . . . And offering *The Nose* at 10 per cent of its potential, instead of 100 per cent will provoke a terrible song and dance.[52]

49 Daniil Zhitomirsky, 'Dmitri Shostakovich: Reminiscences and Reflections', unpublished article.
50 Zoya Shostakovich in interview with EW.
51 Tatyana Glivenko in interview with EW.
52 Gavriil Yudin, 'Letters to Smolich', p. 90.

As Shostakovich predicted, the concert performance only caused bewilderment. The inaccessibility of the music became a subject of heated controversy. The most ferocious attacks came from RAPM; Shostakovich was forced to defend his work strongly, backed by Samosud, Nikolayev, Asafiev and, principally, Sollertinsky. The accusation of 'Formalism' was first directed at Shostakovich in connection with this opera.

Malko stated that Samosud had an inordinate number of rehearsals in the year preceding the stage premiere on 18 January 1930: 150 piano rehearsals, 50 orchestral rehearsals, and innumerable stage rehearsals. This may well be an exaggeration, but undoubtedly the new music was difficult for the performers.

Malko spoke of the opera's 'tremendous success'. However, in all there were sixteen performances, and the reviews were mostly unfavourable. A certain Gvozdev wrote that 'it cannot be considered a Soviet opera; rather an example of decadent Western traditions, of an outlived genre in the process of extinction.'[53] Shostakovich bitterly remarked to Smolich:

> [The reviews] will make me suffer a week, and I will have to bear the malicious delight of my friends at the flop of *The Nose* for the next two months. Then I'll calm down and work; I'd like most of all to write something on [Nikolai] Oleinnikov's story, 'The Carp'.[54]

In the meantime Shostakovich had written his first film score, and embarked on a career as occasional cinema composer. This was to be a useful fall-back when times were hard. At the end of December 1928 the film directors Kozintsev and Trauberg invited him to write a score for the silent film *New Babylon*. The film called for the accompaniment of a large orchestra, but the complexities of the score proved too much for the cinema orchestras and the film had only a few showings with the music until it was revived in the 1980s. Shostakovich was able to re-use some of the score for the music to Mayakovsky's play *The Bedbug*, which he wrote more or less simultaneously.

GRIGORI KOZINTSEV and Trauberg worked as members of FEKS, the Factory of the Eccentric Actor. The ideas of FEKS were embodied in their first films. The two directors worked as a team until the beginning of World War II.

Shostakovich not only wrote the music for their film *New Babylon*, but he continued his association with the Kozintsev/Trauberg team when sound was introduced into the cinema. Many of their films achieved lasting popularity, not least *The Maxim Trilogy* (1934–8). Later, when the directors went their

---

53 Review in *Krasnaya Gazeta*, no. 17, 20 January 1930.
54 Letter dated 2 January 1930 (Yudin, 'Letters to Smolich', p. 91). Nikolai Oleinnikov, a founder member of the OBERIU group, was a well-known children's writer. This was the period of Shostakovich's short-lived fascination with the dadaist Leningrad Oberiu writers.

separate ways, Shostakovich continued to work with Kozintsev, writing music for his stage productions and notably for his Shakespearean films *Hamlet* (1964) and *King Lear* (1970):

The film makers of the 1920s were all young men. I was probably the very youngest of all; at the time of shooting *The Adventures of Octyabrina* I was only nineteen years old. I became used to this idea, as the next generation of film directors were all older than I was. And then suddenly there appeared to work with us a man who was still younger than me.

Happily for us, rumours reached us about a young composer who had just composed an opera on the subject of Gogol's *The Nose*. This was the best recommendation we could have.

I soon saw a rehearsal of *The Nose* at the Maly Opera Theatre. Vladimir Dmitriev's sets spun and reeled to the sounds of rollicking gallops and dashing polkas; Gogol's phantasmagoria was transformed into sound and colour. The particular imagery of Russian art that was linked to urban folklore – the signs of taverns, shops and picture booths, cheap dance orchestras – all burst into the kingdom of *Aida* and *Il Trovatore*. Gogol's grotesque raged around us; what were we to understand as farce, what as prophecy? The incredible orchestral combinations, texts seemingly unthinkable to sing ('And what makes your hands stink?' sung Major Kovalyov) . . . the unhabitual rhythms (the mad *accelerando* when the Nose is being beaten up at the police station and the chorus shrieks: 'Take that, take that, and that!'; the incorporating of the apparently anti-poetic, anti-musical, vulgar, but what was in reality the intonation and parody of real life – all this was an assault on conventionality. . . .

When in 1928[55] Shostakovich came at our invitation to the cinema studios to compose music for the silent film *New Babylon*, his face was almost that of a child. He was dressed unusually for an artist in a white silk scarf, a soft grey hat, and he carried a large leather briefcase. He spoke with a slight stutter, using ordinary phrases. Often, to his own delight, he would recall from memory whole chunks of Chekhov or Gogol: isn't it well put, how wonderful!

After viewing the film, which was still not edited to final cut, he agreed to write the score. Our ideas coincided. In those years film

55 Shostakovich signed his contract to write the film music on 28 December 1928, and wrote the score in January and February 1929.

music was used to strengthen the emotions of reality, or, to use the current terminology, to illustrate the frame. We immediately came to an agreement with the composer that the music would be linked to the inner meaning and not to the external action, that it should develop by cutting across events, and as the antithesis of the mood of a specific scene. Our general principle was not to illustrate, and not to complement or coincide on this point. In the score the tragic themes intrude on to vulgar can-cans, the German cavalry galloped into Paris to the accompaniment of Offenbach's *La Belle Hélène* (transformed suddenly out of the 'Marseillaise'); the themes interwove with great complexity, changing the mood from the farcical to the pathetic.

There was much that was unusual for those times. Even the repertoire committee of those days evokes particular memories. The viewing hall was situated in the basement of the Sovietsky Kino[56] building, which was under repair. There were puddles on the concrete floor. Several varicoloured chairs were placed at random on the floor. The composer, balancing on boards, had to make his way across the water to sit down at the piano and try it out. His face expressed complete bewilderment. One experiences all kinds of viewing sessions: happy ones, sad ones. Film directors are constantly irritated by bad lighting, mediocre copy, the rasping quality of the sound, but, my God, on this occasion the screen was ghastly, the piano out of tune, the hall filthy. And yet how wonderful that session seemed when Shostakovich himself played the first music he had composed for cinema.

. . . But alas, the path from the viewing halls of Sovkino to the orchestras of the cinemas was a thorny one. The score was met with hostility. It was much easier to continue the old way of life.

'And not only does this young man understand nothing about the cinema,' the conductor at the Piccadilly cinema raged, 'but he is very arrogant. I made certain suggestions to help him – I proposed orchestrating his music, but he refused!'

A few days later the offending sounds were silenced. The orchestra returned to its robust and hardened performances of 'The East – the River – Boating'. The music was only performed for a few showings of the film.[57]

56 Soviet cinema.
57 Grigori Kozintsev, *The Complete Works*, vol. I, pp. 156–7; vol. IV, pp. 253–4.

Theatre music

As the young Dmitri began to earn money from commissions and concert performances, the Shostakovich family gradually emerged from its years of poverty. Undoubtedly, financial as well as artistic considerations motivated Shostakovich to accept the job of music director at Meyerhold's Theatre in Moscow from January 1928. In fact it allowed him to give up the 'drudgery' of playing at the cinemas.

Shostakovich had first met the brilliant theatre director Vsevolod Meyerhold in Leningrad in 1927. After a subsequent hearing of the First Symphony, Meyerhold declared that he was greatly impressed by the young composer's talent. It is Malko who takes the credit for suggesting that Shostakovich be employed at Meyerhold's Theatre; but no doubt Leo Arnshtam, Shostakovich's predecessor in the job, also promoted his friend. In all Shostakovich only remained at Meyerhold's Theatre for two months (January and February). During this time he lived in Meyerhold's flat as a member of his family.

At the end of the year Meyerhold commissioned Shostakovich to write the music for Mayakovsky's play *The Bedbug*, which was staged in January 1929. Although it was the first of many plays Shostakovich wrote music for, he never again worked with Meyerhold, much to their mutual regret.

The painter NIKOLAI SOKOLOV was a member of Kukryniksy, a collective group of artists who achieved fame for their theatre designs, illustrations, and in particular for their political and satirical cartoons which appeared in the magazine *Krokodil*. Here are his memories of Shostakovich at Meyerhold's Theatre:

I first got acquainted with Dmitri Dmitriyevich Shostakovich in 1928. In fact it wasn't so much an acquaintance as a working contact with him at Meyerhold's Theatre during the time when our collective, Kukryniksy, mounted the staging of the first part of Mayakovsky's play *The Bedbug*. I was then twenty-five years old and Shostakovich was several years younger than me. 'Mitenka', as V. E. Meyerhold fondly called him, was writing the music to the play. His appearance was that of a boy – very thin and scrawny, pale, with a thick head of hair; he created the impression of being very modest and shy. His light-coloured myopic eyes looked out in bewilderment through his spectacles at all that surrounded him. His gait was nervous and rapid, as were the constant movements of his hands.

He also spoke very quickly, but quietly, and he didn't open his mouth often. He came down from Leningrad for the rehearsals, bringing with him the music composed for the scenes of the March and the Intermezzo. The music was sharp, angular and unusual, but it was easy to remember, and Meyerhold himself commented, 'That'll blow away the cobwebs in our brains!'

At the rehearsals we several times observed Meyerhold, Mayakovsky and Shostakovich sitting together.

Once we met Shostakovich looking distraught and upset. It turned out that somewhere in the Theatre he had lost the music of the March that he had just brought with him. The theatre workers, including Meyerhold himself, were all urgently set the task of finding the vanished March. On seeing how upset his darling Mitya was, Vsevolod Emilievich said to him gently, embracing him around the shoulders, 'Don't you worry, my dear, your March will be found. And if the worst comes to the worst, we'll manage without it.'

The music was found shortly and the happy composer was soon walking around the theatre smiling.[58]

Shostakovich worked at TRAM from 1929 to 1931. His position there shielded him from ideological attack at a time when the proletarian associations such as RAPM were at the height of their power. Shostakovich's Conservatoire progress report of October 1929 shows that he was aware of the ideological issues at stake. He declared that he was about to start work on a 'Soviet' opera and in connection with this was working at TRAM, where 'real workers' art is being forged', and that he wished to imbibe the principles of 'Tramism'. In the same document he moots the conviction that music was one of the arts most accessible to the 'masses'. While wishing to write accessible music, he also considered it a duty to wage war on the 'musical pornography' which was being heaped on the mass listeners in the name of accessibility.

Run by the talented director Mikhail Sokolovsky, TRAM was an attempt at theatre run on collective principles, loosely based on the Brechtian aesthetic, which relied heavily on agitprop and placard art. The political bias of its authors was 'leftist'. Shostakovich wrote music for three plays (none of which he actually liked!) during his time there, Alexander Bezymensky's *The Shot*, A. N. L'vov and N. F. Gorbenko's *Virgin Soil*, and Adrian Piotrovsky's *Rule Britannia*.

PAVEL MARANCHIK, one of the founders of TRAM, recalled the polemic discussions that took place at the TRAM commune in Nekrasov Street, Leningrad:

Dmitri Dmitriyevich used to come to our meetings often . . . I remember one occasion when some representatives of RAPM came to

58 Nikolai Sokolov, *Sketches from Memory*, pp. 52–3.

see us. A fierce argument arose over the various ways in which Soviet musical culture should be developed. Shostakovich proved that in itself the term 'proletarian composer' was absolutely meaningless, that an enormous amount of work lies ahead in the assimilation of our cultural heritage, and that many proletarian composers write noisy declarations and very mediocre music. He supported his passionate speech with an example:

'There is a song from Civil War times called "Over the Seas, Over the Valleys" written by a proletarian composer, and an old lullaby "Sleep, My Lovely Child" . . . It would appear that these two songs have nothing in common, but I will prove to you that they are as alike as two peas in a pod.'

Shostakovich then proposed that these two songs should be sung simultaneously. The right side of the hall was to sing 'Over the Seas, Over the Valleys', while the left side sung the lullaby. Shostakovich conducted, and the hall sung these two songs, which sounded identical.[59]

The Georgian composer ANDRÉ BALANCHIVADZE met Shostakovich in Leningrad when he came to take his entrance exam at the Conservatoire in 1927. The two composers became close friends and Shostakovich enjoyed visiting Balanchivadze at his Tbilisi home in Georgia, where in 1932 he wrote part of the second act of *Lady Macbeth of Mtsensk*. Balanchivadze was one of the few people to come to the defence of *Lady Macbeth* when the opera was criticized in 1936:

As I remember, in the late 1920s Shostakovich started working at the Leningrad TRAM. At that time the young workers' theatre defended its position and artistic principles from the attacks of 'proletarian' critics. I followed Shostakovich's example, and so as to avoid being hounded from all sides by the Georgian branch of APM,[60] I started to work at the equivalent TRAM theatre in Tbilisi as musical director. In that period I often met and corresponded with Shostakovich.

Once, in answer to my question about the essence of musical ideology, Shostakovich wrote to me:

'Ideology in my view can be demonstrated in this manner. Let us take literature. In two different works we have the description of one and the same subject. For instance, Gogol's description of the River

59 Pavel Maranchik, *The Birth of Komsomol Theatre*, pp. 225–6.
60 Association of Proletarian Musicians.

Dnieper ('Wondrous Is the Dnieper'), and then the description of the same River Dnieper in the Afinogenov play *Construction on the Dnieper*. Here we are dealing with two authors' completely different attitudes to the same subject.

'It is the attitude of the author that gives rise to the ideology. And the same in music. Let us suppose that the two composers Ivanov and Petrov each decide to write a composition on the theme of 'The Factory'. Ivanov goes to the factory and sees the machines, the stock, the activity and motion, the clatter and grinding, chugging and churning of the machinery. Ivanov comes home and conscientiously attempts to depict all these noises and movements using the greatest professionalism. Petrov also goes to the factory and hears the same noises, clatter and grinding, but notwithstanding also notices something else. For instance, he notices the pathos of socialist labour, the enthusiasm and dynamic energy of the creative force of the working class, its tragedy in relation to its failures and its joys at the success in the overfulfilling of the Plan. Petrov comes home, and, with the same professionalism as Ivanov, depicts the noises of the factory, but additionally that important thing that has excited him, which Ivanov was not able or did not want to notice. Here we now have two compositions on the theme of 'The Factory'. Which of them is closest to us? Clearly, Petrov's. In this way it is the attitude of the composer to a particular subject which he wishes to illustrate that defines his ideology.'[61]

Shostakovich was invited by the director Nikolai Akimov to write music for his controversial production of *Hamlet* at the Moscow Vakhtangov Theatre. He started work on the music in December 1931. The play's première was on 19 May 1932, just a week after his marriage to Nina Varzar. The violinist YURI YELAGIN led the Vakhtangov Theatre orchestra for several years, where he got to know many of the best Soviet composers:

Soon after I started work in the theatre, the rehearsals for *Hamlet* started. The plan for the production of *Hamlet* was conceived by the artist and director, Nikolai Pavlovich Akimov, who co-produced and created the sets for *Treachery in Love*. His plan was eccentric to the highest degree, but Akimov presented it so entertainingly at the

61 André Balanchivadze, 'Contemporaries Write on D. D. Shostakovich', in L. V. Danilevich (ed.), *Dmitri Shostakovich*, pp. 96–7.

meeting of the artistic council that it was difficult to raise any objections to it.

'Nobody in this turbulent age of ours is interested in the philosophical ponderings of the Danish Prince,' said Akimov. 'The contemporary theatre-goer doesn't wish to languish from boredom during the abstruse, time-worn monologues. The adventurous element of the tragedy holds much greater interest; duels, sword-fights, bloody and deceitful intrigues, brilliant court feasts, the young prince Fortinbras returning victorious to his native country. And Ophelia will not be the usual pale, weak-minded girl, but a seductive beauty, dissolute in her behaviour, and of dubious moral standards. Our Hamlet will be a hearty young rake and a good fencer. We will have hunts and spectacular battle scenes. Horses will charge across the stage ridden by knights in shining armour. The audience will gasp at the sight of the royal banquet. We will fill our *Hamlet* with music – music that is sharp-edged, brilliant and witty, and full of innovation. And we will invite Shostakovich to compose it.'

. . . I remember first seeing Shostakovich at the rehearsals of *Hamlet* in 1932. He was still a very young man, of about twenty-five or twenty-six. He behaved with extreme modesty, and made no comments at the rehearsals, but also seldom handed out praise.

One evening a dinner was arranged in his honour at the home of one of the actors. It was here that I met him personally for the first time. He drank a lot at the table, but instead of getting drunk he became more reserved, silent and polite. The only visible sign was that his usually very pale face grew still paler. Our girls paid court to him incessantly, but he gave them scant attention. Towards the end of the evening, one of the actresses started singing gypsy romances to guitar accompaniment. Shostakovich sat down next to her and listened in rapt attention. She sang marvellously. When everybody started to leave, he thanked her and kissed her hand. He himself never touched the piano throughout the evening, however much we urged him.

The music he wrote for *Hamlet* was exceptional in its originality and innovation. It was much closer to Shakespeare's *Hamlet* than anything else in Akimov's production. Of course there were moments of great eccentricity in the music which were in the style of the production; for instance, at the ball, under a biting, spicy jazz accompaniment, the drunken Ophelia (played by our most beautiful actress, Valentina Vagrina) sang a jolly song with a frivolous text in the style of German chansonnières from the beginning of the century. It was interesting how, in the famous scene with the flute, Shostakovich angrily mocked both the Soviet authorities and a group of proletarian composers who at that time were at the height of their power and caused much harm to Russian music and musicians. In this scene, Hamlet held the flute to the lower part of his torso, and the piccolo in the orchestra, accompanied by double bass and a drum, piercingly and out of tune played the famous Soviet song 'They Wanted to Beat Us, to Beat Us' written by the composer Alexander Davidenko, the leader of the proletarian musicians. The song had been written on the occasion of the victory of Soviet troops over the Chinese in 1929.[62]

First love

Shostakovich met Tatyana Glivenko in 1923, when he was sixteen, while recuperating from tuberculosis at the Crimean sanatorium of Koreiz near Gaspra. Mariya Shostakovich, who accompanied her brother on this trip, wrote home to her mother: '(Mitya) has grown, got a suntan, is cheerful and has fallen in love. This is now clear to me. The girl in question is a bit strange, a flirt, and I don't like her; but then it is hard to please your sister in such matters.'[63]

Evidently Sofiya Vasilyevna was sufficiently alarmed to write a cautionary letter to her son. His reply is an interesting document, showing him to be in tune with the fashionable spirit of free love that had been strongly instilled in Russian youth of the day:

You write that I should be careful, and not get entangled. In reply I want to submit a little philosophy. Pure animal love . . . is so vile that one doesn't need to begin to speak about it. I don't think that was what you had in mind. In such an instance, a man is no different from an animal. But now, suppose that a wife ceases to love her husband and gives herself to another, and that they start living together openly, despite the censorious opinions of society. There is nothing wrong with that. On the contrary, it's even a good thing, as Love is truly free. The oath sworn before the altar is one of the worst features of religion. Love cannot last for long. Of course the best thing one could imagine would be the complete annulment of the institution of marriage, with all its fetters and responsibilities, but that is of course a utopian wish. If there is no marriage then there can be no family, and that would be a terrible thing. But there can be no question but that

62 Yuri Yelagin, *The Taming of the Arts*, pp. 38–40, translated from the Russian by EW.
63 D. D. Shostakovich, 'Letters to Mother', p. 168.

–82–

Love is free. And, Mamochka, let me warn you, that if I at some point fall in love I do not intend to bind myself by marrying. But if I do marry, and if my wife loves another, then I won't say a word; if she wants a divorce, I'll give it to her, and take the blame on myself. . . . But at the same time I know that there exists the sacred vocation of parenthood. So, when you start to ponder the subject, your head bursts. But in any case, Love is free![64]

On return to Leningrad Shostakovich set about writing his first Piano Trio (or Poème) which he dedicated to Tatyana.[65] Their ensuing relationship was not an easy one, due to the pressures of separation, Shostakovich's inability to commit himself and the innuendoes of family disapproval. However, it continued over several years and was of real importance in both their lives. In 1929 Glivenko met and married Alexander Berlin, a professor of chemistry, while in the meantime Shostakovich had met Nina Varzar, his future wife, in the summer of 1927. His relationship with Nina likewise had its ups and downs, both before their marriage in May 1932 and afterwards. Here are TATYANA GLIVENKO's memories of their relationship:

My family comes from Moscow. My father was a philologist by profession, whereas both my husband and son were professors of chemistry. I was the only one in the family not to complete a university course, and, so to speak, never had a 'profession'.

I met Shostakovich in the summer of 1923 at Gaspra in the Crimea. We were exact contemporaries; we shared the same birth date, only his birthday was on 25 September New Style, and mine 25 September Old Style; in other words I was two weeks younger than him. Mitya had been sent to recuperate; he had been seriously ill with inflammation of the lymph glands (a form of tuberculosis), and had swellings on his neck. Times were very hard then. Alexander Glazunov, the director of the Petrograd Conservatoire, arranged a grant for him to be sent to a sanatorium on the grounds of his poor health. My father, a great lover of social work, held a position in the state organization responsible for sanatoriums and 'rest-houses'. He was the representative of the 'House of Scientists', which had its sanatorium at Koreiz. He decided that my sister and I should go there that summer for a holiday. It was at this sanatorium that I got to know Mitya, although

64 Letter dated 3 August 1923 (ibid., p. 168).
65 Shostakovich was fond of dedications. The first girl (apart from his sister) to whom he dedicated a piece of music was the unsuspecting ten-year-old Natalya Kubé'. Numbers 6–8 of the Op. 2 Preludes for Piano (written in 1919) bear the initials N.K. The dedicatee only discovered about this honour after Shostakovich's death.

unfortunately this only happened towards the end of his stay. Later Mitya wrote to me saying what a pity that we had lost so much time there before we met.

We fell in love then. It was a love that endured throughout our lives; here I believe that I am not only speaking for myself. For both of us it was the experience of first love. It turned into a complicated story, as we lived in different cities. We kept the relationship alive through corresponding regularly. Mitya was a complex person, and his family's situation was extremely difficult. After his father's death in 1922, they suffered great deprivations. True, it was a time of hardship for us all, the country was in a state of ruin and devastation and there was widespread hunger. His mother, Sofiya Vasilyevna was left with three children to fend for. Marusya, the eldest was only seventeen, a student at the Conservatoire, and she had to go out to work. Mitya was fifteen and very sickly. Zoya was only a young girl, and, before long she too went out to work. Later, when she married and came to live in Moscow, we became the greatest of friends. There was only two months' difference in the age of our eldest sons.

Mitya and I met only occasionally, usually when he was visiting Moscow. We spent a summer together at Anapa in the Caucasus when we were nineteen. In those days it was accepted that you didn't have to marry; people were not aiming at marriage as they seem to today. We were in no hurry to tie ourselves down. When Mitya wrote to invite me to join him I replied that he should find me a room there, and then I would come down and live and work there independently. He was terribly offended and said, 'Why this way, why can't we live together?' In the end we spent most of that summer together, and I intended to go and live with him in Leningrad.

In general Mitya found it very difficult to commit himself, as his moods kept fluctuating. All this when we lived in different cities contributed to the instability of our relationship. I never knew what was going on in Leningrad. Perhaps he had another girlfriend there? In the end it was I who didn't wait for him and married someone else. But even then Mitya continued to come down to Moscow to see me and on many occasions tried to persuade me to leave my husband and to come and live with him in Leningrad. Only when I became pregnant with my first child did he accept that the relationship was over.

I was twenty-two when I married in February 1929. My husband took a very firm stand and said, 'Either you marry me or I'll stop coming to your house.' Then Mitya came to Moscow and rang me. I went to see him in the hotel and told him that I was going to marry. He thought I was having him on. His face just darkened. The very next day we were celebrating the wedding at my parents' house. In those days there were no ceremonies or other formalities. We had a modest sort of celebration at home with just a few friends present to drink a toast to our good health. My niece and her nanny lived with our family in the apartment. They were also very fond of Mitya. Suddenly, during this party, the nanny came up to me and whispered in my ear, 'Tatyana, go to the phone, it's Mitya for you.' I picked up the phone.

'It's me – Shostakovich . . .'

'Yes, I'm listening . . .'

No more was said, and that was that. He returned to Leningrad. According to Zoya, when he walked into his flat his first words were, 'Tanya's got married.' Thereafter my name wasn't mentioned for some time in their house, but later on he got to know my husband and they became friends.

However, a year later Mitya wrote to me, asking me to come to see him and saying that he would like me to live with him. We started corresponding again. I agreed to go up to Leningrad. I said I'd consider his proposal on return to Moscow and would write to him from there with my final answer. It's very hard to explain, on the one hand he had asked me to come to stay with him, on the other he was curiously non-committal. When I came up to Leningrad, his sister Marusya burst into tears, saying, 'Thank you for coming, stay with Mitya and with us now.'

For two months Mitya and I corresponded, and I wrote telling him that yes, I was about to take the decision to leave my husband and to be with him. Then Mitya would answer, 'But you probably love your husband more . . .' And so it continued until he informed me one day that he had got married himself – in secret. Of course there wasn't an ounce of truth in it, it was all invention on his part. (He wrote saying, 'Of course, she's a real fool, but I've committed myself.') He was trying to call my bluff, and to provoke me to leave by giving me a fright.

Maybe this is conceit on my part, but his marriage to Nina Varzar in 1932 was connected with the birth of my first child. Mitya's sister Marusya came to see me while on a visit to Zoya, who had recently married and moved to Moscow. She told Zoya, 'Now it's really all over, Tanya is pregnant.' Her intention had been to persuade me to leave and come and live with Mitya. My son was born on 3 May. Zoya, who was shortly expecting her first child, came to see me and my new baby and then left for Leningrad to have her baby at home. Only two weeks later Mitya and Nina got married. Zoya wrote to tell me that they had gone ahead with the marriage, and in secret! Although Mitya was by then a man of twenty-five, his mother had also tried to dissuade him from this marriage.

However, Sofiya Vasilyevna was a strange and complicated woman. You would think that she would have been delighted that her son had found happiness, as she was always complaining how miserable he was. But no, Mitya was forced to act in secret. His relationship with Nina had been going on and off for some time prior to this; they had decided to marry, then he withdrew, then he wrote asking me to come and live with him, so it was a complicated affair. In the middle of May 1932, Mitya was going to Moscow to attend the première of Akimov's strange production of *Hamlet* at the Vakhtangov Theatre for which he'd written the music. The Shostakoviches lived very near the station. Mitya announced to the family that he was taking the night train to Moscow, but that he would go to the station on his own as it was within walking distance of their house. 'There's no need to accompany me.' No sooner was he out of the door than Sofiya Vasilyevna rushed out and followed in order to see what was going on. According to Zoya, when she came back home, she sat down and cried. Zoya asked what the matter was and her mother replied, 'I saw the silhouette of Nina Vasilyevna in the window of the compartment.' Then the two of them sobbed all night long, although Zoya now says she can't think why she joined in, there was nothing to cry about. After all Nina was an interesting, highly educated woman and a hundred times more intelligent than I was.

Mitya's mother was largely responsible for preventing the development of our relationship. It's true that she felt Mitya couldn't take on the responsibility of marriage as he had no regular source of income. There's no doubt that she did much to dissuade him from being with me. However, Sofiya Vasilyevna felt she could afford to love me once I was married to somebody else and wasn't going to take Mitya away from her. A mother's jealousy can be a terrible thing, particularly once a woman is widowed.

Sofiya Vasilyevna was very ambitious for her son. Sometimes I blame her for pushing Mitya, despite his fragile health. He was the centre of her world, and she paid far more attention to him than to his sisters, who were physically much stronger than him. I don't think this did him much good. She followed every step in his education and professional career very closely, and was always delighted and thrilled by his every success. But this close identification with his professional life also created a lot of pressure on him. As it was, Mitya worked incredibly hard.

I remember for instance one occasion when I visited them in Leningrad. Mitya had pressed me very hard to come up, so I came. He was writing some piece and he wanted to finish it. He asked me to sit beside him while he wrote because it gave him a sense of security and pleasure if I just sat there quietly beside him. Then his mother came into the room and said, 'Go out and leave Mitya to finish his work.' But Mitya said, 'No, I want Tanya to stay here, it helps me.' This was only a detail, but typical of Sofiya Vasilyevna's over-solicitous and interfering attitude to her beloved son.

Once, many years later, Mitya said to me when I was visiting him in his hotel in Moscow, 'Why are you friendly with my mother? She is responsible for everything.' Indeed, after I married my husband, I became a good friend of Sofiya Vasilyevna's. In the 1930s I always saw her during her visits to Moscow, when she came to intercede for her son-in-law, Marusya's husband Vsevolod Frederiks, who had been arrested. I even accompanied her when she visited those unpleasant institutions like the GPU.[66] By this time Marusya had actually already divorced Frederiks, and I must say it was Sofiya Vasilyevna who made the most effort on his behalf.

I feel it was a real pity that Mitya and I didn't marry. At the age of seventeen we had a wonderful love and we let it go. It may sound conceited, but I do think that Mitya would have been happier with me. He didn't really have much happiness in life. He always wanted children. Nina created a family for him and he was terribly attached to his children. However, she lived much of the time with another man, and this cannot have been good for his self-esteem, however much he loved her. But Shostakovich would never have left her, he was a man of principle. He used to say, 'Shostakovich will never abandon his children,' and it was he more than Nina who created a sense of family.

66 State Administration for the Struggle Against Espionage and Counter-Revolution.

After her early death in 1954, he married again, first very briefly (Zoya called the woman in question a charlatan) and then to Irina Anton-ovna, who was a devoted wife. It was her fate to look after him in the years of his sickness.[67]

Tatyana Glivenko's claim that Shostakovich's mother was often over-solicitous and interfering in her relationship to her son is reinforced by NIKOLAI MALKO:

After the performance of his First Symphony, Shostakovich assumed a definite position in the musical sphere of Leningrad. Gradually his name became known outside of Leningrad. This obliged him to 'grow up', and he did, but he still had much childishness within him. It originated in part from his position in the family. He was the centre of life and the idol. His mother was so devoted that she constantly petted and spoiled him. She worked for him when he should have been working for himself, and often, thinking only of him, she even did his worrying for him. . . . He was automatically freed from any household worry, and it made him impractical to a degree. He always bore the imprint of his mother's influence.

. . . The guardianship of his mother never relaxed. Sofiya Vasily-evna would telephone almost every day to tell me her worries and to ask for advice or help concerning Mitya.

The telephone would ring. It would be she, worried. 'Mitya wants to marry.'

'Well. What then? Let him.'

'How can you say that? He's still a child.'

The next day the telephone would ring again. 'It is not so bad.'

'What?' I ask.

'Mitya's getting married.'

'Why?'

'I looked through his diary and found a note, "Find a room." I know him. He will never start looking. He does not even know how to start.'

Usually, after such a telephone call, my wife and I would ask Mitya to come over to the house; but I definitely do not remember that we had to discuss any of these matters with him or to comfort him in any such problems. It was not in his nature to mope, after the fashion of the old-time, romantic Russian student. In spite of all the hardship and deprivation he went through, Mitya remained spiritually strong

67 Tatyana Glivenko: recorded interview with EW.

and self-assured. He showed no signs of strain. This was partly due to his mother's devoted care, and partly to the environment of Soviet times in which there was no room for slobbering or whimpering. But chiefly it was simply not his nature to whine. He had a positive attitude, and he was spiritually strong and self-reliant.[68]

The ballets

In 1929, the Leningrad Theatre Commission, in an attempt to help the creation of a modern and significant 'Soviet' ballet, announced a competition for a ballet libretto. The cinema director Alexander Ivanovsky won it with *Dynamiada* (later renamed *The Golden Age*), the story of the triumph of a Soviet football team over its bourgeois-fascist rivals. Shostakovich was invited to write the score for it, which he completed by the end of February 1930. The ballet went into rehearsal at the Leningrad Kirov Theatre with a strong team of dancers (including the young Galina Ulanova in the role of the 'Western Komsomolka'). Due to the many problems that arose in its production, the première was postponed more than once, eventually taking place on 26 October 1930.

Initially Shostakovich had doubts about the libretto and claimed that he did 'everything possible to fight away' from it. In a letter to Zakhar Lyubimsky, the director of Leningrad's State theatres, Shostakovich talks of an anti-religious ballet libretto called *Morals* for which he expresses his preference over that of *Dynamiada*.[69] However, Smolich, the director of *The Nose*, and Sollertinsky encouraged Shostakovich to tackle *Dynamiada*; the composer himself was attracted by the sporting element in its subject. His declared aim was that the music should play a primary role by creating 'real symphonic tension and dramatic development'.

The Golden Age met with what Shostakovich defined as a 'frosty success' and was soon eased out of the repertoire. Afterwards he wrote to Smolich:

> I am more than ever convinced that in every piece of music theatre the music must play the main, and not the supporting role. . . . But this didn't happen in *The Golden Age*. The staging functioned on its own, the music on its own. . . . I cannot defend my ballet convincingly, since, in regard to the artistic content, I know I have written an anti-artistic work. And I hold you, Lyubimsky, Sollertinsky and others responsible. I can answer for the music of *The Golden Age*; I believe it to be exceptionally successful. But in future I shall write only on subjects that truly kindle my imagination.[70]

68 Malko, *A Certain Art*, pp. 187, 191–2.
69 Letter dated 1 July 1929 (V. Kisilev, 'Letters from the 1930s', p. 85).
70 Letter dated 30 October 1930 (Yudin, 'Letters to Smolich', pp. 91, 92).

As if trouble with one ballet was not enough, Shostakovich immediately took on another![71] He was soon aware that he was again dealing with a defective subject. He informed Sollertinsky:

> Comrade Smirnov has read me the libretto for a ballet, *The New Machine*. Its theme is extremely relevant. There once was a machine. Then it broke down (problem of material decay). Then it was mended (problem of amortization), and at the same time they bought a new one. Then everybody dances around the new machine. Apotheosis. This all takes up three acts.[72]

This facetious version was in essence the libretto of *Bolt*, a topical story of industrial sabotage, reflecting the preoccupations of the industrialization campaign and the First Five Year Plan. *Bolt* was premièred on 8 April 1931, met with a cool reception from a bewildered public and provoked a negative reaction in the press. The journal *Rabochii i Teatr* wrote that '*Bolt* was a flop and should serve as a last warning to its composer.'

Shostakovich was decidedly unlucky in this genre. His third ballet, *The Limpid Stream*, commissioned by Fyodor Lopukhov for a new ballet troupe at MALEGOT (Leningrad Maly Theatre) was premièred on 4 June 1935. Once more Shostakovich was landed with a simplistic libretto (about life on a collective farm), for which he decided to adjust his musical language. In the event the ballet's music was considered by some its single redeeming feature, whereas others disparaged its banality. However, *The Limpid Stream* enjoyed great public success and ran until it was subjected to a vicious attack in the newspaper *Pravda* with the article 'Ballet Falsehood' (6 February 1936). Following hard on the heels of the notorious article 'Muddle Instead of Music', it sealed Shostakovich's disgrace.

The conductor Alexander Gauk studied at the St Petersburg Conservatoire and made his name as a ballet conductor at the Leningrad State Theatre of Opera and Ballet (formerly the Mariinsky Theatre and later re-named the Kirov Theatre). His contact with Shostakovich dates from the late 1920s, when he gave the premières of the ballets *The Golden Age* and *Bolt*. From 1930 he briefly held the position of director of the Leningrad Philharmonic. With this orchestra he gave the first performance of the Third 'Mayday' Symphony on 21 January 1930.

The comments on Gauk attributed to Shostakovich are far from flattering.[73] Allegedly, Gauk was responsible for the loss of the manuscript of the Fourth

---

71 He received the commission to write the music for *Bolt* in February 1930, while in Moscow.
72 Undated letter February 1930 (Lyudmila Mikheeva, 'The Story of a Friendship', Part 1, p. 29).
73 Solomon Volkov, *Testimony: The Memoirs of Dmitri Shostakovich*, p. 28.

Symphony, which was kept in a suitcase that disappeared during the Second World War. According to that source, the manuscripts of the Fifth and Sixth Symphonies were lost at the same time.

Here is ALEXANDER GAUK on the production of the two ballets:

I was working at the time as chief conductor at the Kirov Theatre.[74] One day I was approached by the director, Emmanuil Kaplan, with the proposal to start work on a new ballet. He said that the designer was to be the artist Vladimir Dmitriev, whom I already knew.

'What is the subject of this ballet, and who's the composer?' I asked. He replied, 'It's called *The Golden Age*, and Shostakovich is writing the music.'

I was delighted, and at the same time a bit intimidated. It would undoubtedly be very interesting to work on Shostakovich's music, which promised to be full of innovation and surprises, and would display the wonderful orchestra of the Mariinsky Theatre in all its glory. But on the other hand, I feared that the ballet company would create problems. . . .

Kaplan had just completed his studies at the Conservatoire as a singer, and also had studied stage direction. He was a fanatical admirer of Meyerhold. But he had no experience, and *The Golden Age* was his first production. . . . The choreographic side was consigned to the care of Fyodor Lopuhkov, L. Leontev and M. Petrov. It turned out that Kaplan did not have the necessary authority to deal with the ballet company or the choreographers.[75] Soon, arguments started which sometimes brought our work to a halt. In certain newspaper bulletins, hints were dropped that the music of the ballet was not up to standard. Naturally, this aroused the fury of Shostakovich. . . .

In the end, Lopukhov took over the choreography, leaving Kaplan as the producer.

Unfortunately, the ballet was not successful. This was natural in so far as success was defined by the ballet buffs, who were addicted to tradition and unable to accept this unusual music. And yet the music was the best part of the whole production. Dmitri Dmitriyevich later

---

74 Formerly the Mariinsky Theatre.
75 Shostakovich evidently also did not trust Kaplan. In a letter to Smolich dated 3 February 1930, he wrote 'two days ago, in the office of the Director of Leningrad Theatres, and again in the evening at a meeting of the artistic council, I spoke very strongly against Kaplan's outline of the production' (Yudin, 'Letters to Smolich', p. 91).

made a concert suite from the ballet, which I conducted with the Leningrad Philharmonic.

While learning the orchestral part, there was a certain section that never came off in rehearsal. It was written for strings, with the first violins in an extremely high *tessitura*. I once suggested to Shostakovich that he should double this line in certain places with piccolo, as this might cover the intonation problems. But Dmitri Dmitriyevich immediately refused. I now realize that this would have ruined the sound effect he wanted to achieve. . . .[76]

Dmitri Dmitriyevich amazed us with his extraordinary professionalism and punctiliousness. He was never late in providing a new piece for the ballet or in orchestrating it. He was very restrained in his bearing. He never argued; what he had to say or demonstrate was always of interest, and we all tried to fulfil his every demand. He already had tremendous authority. I remember that before the first orchestral rehearsal I was extremely nervous, as the music was very difficult . . . I admit that I was worried that I would not hear the wrong notes. But on the contrary, it all worked out well. The musicians found that their parts were very comfortably written. The logic of the composition was so clear that the slightest fault of intonation was immediately obvious. I felt that I had never before heard so well. That is an inherent feature of Shostakovich's music.

Shortly before writing *The Golden Age*, Dmitri Dmitriyevich had made a transcription of 'Tahiti Trot'.[77] At my request Dmitri Dmitriyevich included this piece as an entr'acte before the third act of the ballet. The audience always applauded it vigorously and demanded its encore. There was much superb music in *The Golden Age*, and it is a real shame that everyone (including the composer) has swept it aside into the dust of oblivion. Today much of it would sound contemporary and relevant.

The Golden Age stayed in the repertoire for the whole season. Soon, at Lopukhov's request, Shostakovich wrote his new ballet *Bolt*.

By this time the orchestra and ballet company had come to love Shostakovich's music. The reviews of this second ballet all remarked on the success of the musical side; but the music, unfortunately, was not enough to guarantee the ballet's success. The primitive subject,

76 As Gauk points out, this was an effect that Shostakovich used frequently in the future (i.e. in the Fifth Symphony).
77 As Youman's 'Tea for Two' was known (see p. 62).

lack of classical dance, and the very theme of the ballet (a factory, workers' dances, sabotage in the factory, and so on) did not appeal to the ballet buffs. *Bolt* was a flop, and was taken off after the second performance. There was nothing we could do, despite our distress.

The music of *Bolt* is permeated with Russian intonations. When Shostakovich was accused of cosmopolitanism, I always tried to point to the forgotten score of *Bolt*, but nobody knew the music. There are some wonderful musical characterizations there worthy of Chekhov's short stories. Dmitri Dmitriyevich allowed me to make up a suite from the ballet score, which I then performed frequently. It enjoyed an overwhelming success, and we always had to encore some of the numbers from it.[78]

The ballerina TATYANA VECHESLAVA, who danced in the premiere of *Bolt*, confirms the difficulties that Shostakovich's new music created for the ballet company:

I first heard Shostakovich's name when I was twenty years old. His opera *The Nose* appeared on the stage. Soon after that the première of his ballet *Bolt* was given. P. Gusev and I danced the roles of the young Komsomols.[79] in this ballet. We found it difficult to assimilate the music of the ballet; it was full of complex harmony which sometimes acquired grotesque overtones. We had never met with such music before in ballet, and it soon opened up new horizons which were not by any means immediately evident to everyone. To be honest, at the time we did not understand how significant it was that this musical genius and contemporary of ours was making a new contribution to ballet. Much of his music just seemed incomprehensible to us. We had to 'grow' in order to learn to appreciate it. . . .

Although I had no further occasion to dance to Dmitri Dmitriyevich's music, I was fortunate to enjoy the friendship of his family, particularly of his mother, Sofiya Vasilyevna, and his sister Mariya Dmitriyevna. I remember how warmly I was received by them. After the premiere of *Bolt*, several of us dancers went to celebrate at their home. Sofiya Vasilyevna very touchingly kept insisting, 'Tanyusha, please, I beg you, dance with Mitya.'

But 'Mitya' for a long time stubbornly refused, although he eventu-

78 Alexander Gauk, 'Creative Contacts', in L. Gauk, R. Glezer and Y. Milstein (eds), *Alexander Vasiliyevich Gauk: Memoirs, Selected Articles, Reminiscences of His Contemporaries*, pp. 127, 128.
79 A member of the Communist Youth Organization.

ally gave in. We danced a foxtrot. And to his embarrassment he kept treading on my feet! Yes, he was unable to keep time! And this threw him into even greater confusion.

What a remarkable man he was, so modest and shy![80]

Lady Macbeth of the Mtsensk District

Despite a period of intense creativity, by 1930 Shostakovich had produced no major work (apart from his First Symphony) which could claim a permanent place in the concert repertoire. His overriding urge now was to dedicate himself to an opera on a serious or tragic subject; he had no intention of lumbering himself with a 'topical' libretto and a mediocre production as he had done in the ballets. In an article entitled 'Declaration of a Composer's Responsibility' he wrote that it was intolerable for a composer to have to subjugate his personality to a producer's superficial tastes or a theatre's inflexible methods, where 'music is employed as a series of clichés – a 'jolly' dance for the hero, a 'foxtrot' to portray decadence, and 'brisk' music for the optimistic finale'.[81]

Shostakovich's first opera *The Nose* (1930) had provoked much polemical discussion as to the ideological validity of avant-garde experiment. To placate his critics he made frequent statements that he was now engaged in a search for a 'Soviet' theme for his next opera. In the event, he turned to a nineteenth-century Russian writer, Nikolai Leskov, for his subject. Leskov's story 'Lady Macbeth of the Mtsensk District' was suggested to Shostakovich by Boris Asafiev, the original dedicatee of the work. Initially Shostakovich himself undertook the writing of the libretto, but later he sought the aid of the writer Alexander Preis to consolidate his work. The composer started to work out his ideas in October 1930, and then worked intensively on the opera in the autumn of 1931. He informed Sollertinsky, his confidant in all his creative projects, that he had completed the first act on 30 October in the Black Sea resort of Batumi, and 'in the intervals between bathing and partaking of food, I'm orchestrating it'.[82] He combined work on the opera with other commissions for cinema and theatre music. *Lady Macbeth* was finally completed in December 1932, and Shostakovich dedicated it to his new bride, Nina Varzar.

In March 1933 the Leningrad Maly Theatre (MALEGOT) approved the decision to stage *Lady Macbeth*, with the same team that had worked on *The Nose*. (Director – Smolich; designer – Dmitriev; conductor – Samosud.) The opera opened in Leningrad on 22 January 1934, and two days later the

80 Tatyana Vecheslava, *About All That Is Dear*, pp. 169, 170.
81 *Rabochii i Teatr*, no. 31, 1931, p. 6.
82 Mikheeva, 'The Story of a Friendship', Part 1, p. 31.

Moscow premiere took place at the Nemirovich-Danchenko Theatre, under the title of *Katerina Izmailova*. It was directed by Vladimir Nemirovich-Danchenko, the co-founder with Konstantin Stanislavsky of the Moscow Arts Theatre. (It is a reflection of the times that the Moscow performances were announced as part of the production campaign for the 17th Party Congress to keep on a par with the 'production quota' of the Donbass coal-miners.)

The opera was given a triumphant reception in both cities. Shostakovich professed himself satisfied with both productions, although in private he expressed a preference for MALEGOT's. He confided to the director Smolich: 'Overall, I have to say that your production of *Lady Macbeth* reaches the audience. It sustains the tension and interest throughout, and evokes sympathy for Katerina.'[83]

Naturally, the opera stimulated much discussion. The conductor Alexander Gauk recalled that it provoked an enormous number of arguments for and against:

> Many people were put off by some of the naturalistic scenes and situations. It seems to me that this defect originated from the desire to give utmost expression to the subject, and better to convey the sordid character and the depraved atmosphere in which the action takes place.[84]

A more critical point of view was expressed by Daniil Zhitomirsky, who pointed out with hindsight that the opera:

> was not free from the propaganda tendencies of the 1920s. Both composer and librettist considered it necessary to portray the image of the 'dark ages' of Old Russia. They removed from Leskov's story all the poetic pages which illustrated the deluded beginnings of Katerina Izmailova's love – the illusion of her first womanly passion which led to such a tragic end. They introduced primitive satire into the opera. The caricature of the priest in the end of the fourth scene, the whole of the seventh scene at the police station remind me of the so-called 'Blue Blouses',[85] who presented collective propaganda in clubs and factories, and in which I participated in my student years to earn some money. Yet it is in the final scene of *Lady Macbeth* that Shostakovich revealed with incredible force the expression of human sorrow and the despair of the lost soul.[86]

83 Letter dated 18 February 1934 (Yudin, 'Letters to Smolich', p. 92).
84 Gauk, 'Creative Contacts', in Gauk, Glezer and Milstein, *Alexander Gauk*, pp. 127, 128.
85 A reference to the educational form of agitprop, also known as the 'speaking newspapers'. Items of news, culture and art were explained (often with an element of theatre) through direct contact with the masses. The audience were usually factory workers or peasants. The 'blue blouses' referred to the dress of the instructors.
86 Zhitomirsky, 'Shostakovich', unpublished article.

Shostakovich felt it necessary to justify his sympathy with a heroine who was driven through passion to brutal murder. He explained that 'Leskov was unable to interpret correctly the events taking place in his story. My role as a Soviet composer consists in retaining the power of Leskov's narrative while using a critical approach to explain these events from our Soviet point of view.'[87] In effect Shostakovich maintained that Katerina was a victim of the sordid circumstances of her narrow-minded, provincial, petty merchant background. Conveniently, these happenings belonged to the bad old days of Tsarist Russia.

Overall, *Lady Macbeth* was an unprecedented success and secured Shostakovich's reputation as a composer of dramatic genius both at home and abroad. Within a year from its première, MALEGOT had given fifty performances, and outside the Soviet Union the opera reached stage production in the USA (Cleveland and the Metropolitan Opera House in New York), Argentina, Czechoslovakia and Sweden, all before the end of 1935. Not that the opera lacked its critics. Igor Stravinsky, who was present at a performance in Cleveland, dismissed the work as 'lamentably provincial; the music plays a miserable role as illustrator in a very embarrassing realistic style'.[88]

But the opera's fortunes were dramatically reversed with the publication of 'Muddle Instead of Music' in January 1936, when it was effectively dealt a sudden death-blow.

Here are memories of the writing and production of *Lady Macbeth*, the first from GALINA SEREBRYAKOVA. A writer and expert on Karl Marx, she was on friendly terms with the Shostakovich family during the 1920s. Arrested in 1937, she languished in the Gulag camps until the years of the Nikita Khrushchev 'thaw'. Reputedly, her experiences in the camps did not shake her Marxist convictions. After her rehabilitation, Shostakovich renewed his contacts with her:

[Shostakovich] was thirsting to recreate the theme of love in a new way, a love that knew no boundaries, that was willing to perpetrate crimes inspired by the devil himself, as in Goethe's *Faust*. *Lady Macbeth of Mtsensk* attracted him because of the fierce intensity and the fascination of Katerina's magnetism . . .

In the murky room he was writing this new work on a large desk. He would play bits of it through on the piano. I was entertained to tea by two beautiful light-haired girls, Shostakovich's sisters, and his charmingly simple and affectionate mother. The young composer admitted

87 Introduction to a libretto of *Katerina Izmailova* (State Music Publishers, Moscow, 1934), p. 11.
88 From a letter to Ernst Ansermet dated 4 April 1935 (*Selected Correspondence*, vol. I, [Faber & Faber, London, 1982], p. 224).

to me that he was about to get married. He was unable to hide his agitation, and, gulping down his words, he told me about his fiancée, trying to remain cool and objective about her, an impossible feat for those in love![89]

The singer NADEZHDA WELTER played the part of Sonetka in the original MALEGOT production of *Lady Macbeth*. Here she describes the first rehearsals of the opera.

Long before rumours had reached us about this new opera, we became accustomed to seeing in the theatre a slim young man in glasses, who was very shy, modest and unusually refined. He came to all the preliminary rehearsals with singers, and also all the stage and orchestral rehearsals of whatever opera was currently being produced. He usually arrived with Samosud, and, sitting somewhere in the corner, he listened and observed very attentively. In this way he got to know the company, which had been reformed after *The Nose* had been taken off the MALEGOT repertoire.

He spoke very little. One only occasionally caught a glimpse of his feelings through a hardly perceptible smile or a flash from the depths of his eyes.

The company, and particularly the singers, were intrigued to know what this daring experimenter had brought to us now. And Samosud, who was totally enthralled by Shostakovich's exceptional talents, was engrossed in studying the score of the new opera. The lights burned in his study long past midnight; he and the composer were discussing the new opera.

At long last our meeting with Shostakovich was fixed. It was not to be the usual play through of a new opera for the company, as the decision had already been made to produce it. Neither was it our first acquaintance with Dmitri Dmitriyevich – we had already known each other for several years.

The meeting took place in a relaxed atmosphere, which Samosud knew so well how to create. Here for the first time we saw that Shostakovich's restraint was only a superficial skin, and that a passionate spring of energy and dynamic creative force was bubbling underneath it.

At this memorable meeting, Sollertinsky explained to us with

89 Galina Serebryakova, 'About Myself and Others', pp. 309, 310.

characteristic passion and brilliance how Shostakovich was not only revealing the cruelties of an old world, but how this world had crippled and disfigured the life of this woman. Samosud sang various phrases for us with enthusiasm, and at his bidding Shostakovich played various episodes from the opera with great sincerity and extraordinary expression.

The music captivated and disturbed us. My heart literally stopped beating as I was gripped by a passionate desire to take on the part of Katerina. The next day I went to see Samosud. When I entered his study I was overcome with confusion on seeing Sollertinsky there sitting in an armchair. All the same I asked Samosud if he would ask Shostakovich to add some phrasing and articulation to Katerina's part as, in his time Bizet had done with the part of Carmen. I assured him that the dramatic intensity of the part and the whole character of Katerina's image was best-suited to a mezzo-soprano.

Samosud laughed heartily and said, 'Surely you are not so spell-bound by this opera that you are prepared to risk losing your voice altogether? The problem has nothing to do with phrasing, but with the tessitura.' And Sollertinsky, nervously pacing up and down the study, came to a halt opposite me and shrieked, 'The thought should not even cross your mind that the slightest change can be made in this brilliant music.'

Samosud supported him wholeheartedly and suggested that I take on the role of Sonetka. But I didn't want to hear of it, still cherishing my dream to sing Katerina.

Then something unexpected occurred. Having learnt the part of Katerina, trying it out at home, I gradually became convinced that Samosud was right: the tessitura of the part was hard even for a soprano. Then, watching A. Sokolova rehearsing the role of Katerina, I was struck by the simplicity of her theatrical interpretation and the accuracy of her feeling for the part. In her vocal and dramatic gifts she corresponded to both Smolich's and Samosud's prerequisites. As a performer she was young and inexperienced, having previously only sung the role of Micaëla [in Bizet's Carmen], but I understood why the composer should have chosen her in particular. Her naivety and ingenuousness in combination with the tragic pathos of the music created an amazing contrast. The purer her Katerina, the more terrible the tragedy. Sometimes one was overcome with a feeling of cold fear and horror at Shostakovich's brilliant manner of offsetting the eternal themes, good and evil, the striving for freedom and the struggle with brutality.

Both our piano and orchestral rehearsals always took place in Shostakovich's presence, and the reigning atmosphere of agitation intensified with each new-found detail of the staging. We were all gripped by a special feeling; before our very eyes a new and exceptional work of art was coming to life.

At the first orchestral rehearsal, Shostakovich was trembling from anxiety. He was so thoroughly engrossed by the production that only when Samosud stopped the orchestra and put some question to him, 'Well Mitya, how goes it?', 'Dmitri Dmitriyevich, how does it sound?' did he return to reality.

While Samosud was running down from the stage on the ramp which covered the orchestral pit to say something to the conductor, Shostakovich and Sollertinsky were already standing beside the conductor's desk. Ivan Ivanich, who was also present at all the rehearsals, usually sat next to Shostakovich and responded animatedly to every little success and failure. Helping first the singers and then the orchestral musicians with his advice, he could not keep still; he was forever jumping up and running to either the conductor or the producer.

Shostakovich's intense concentration during rehearsals was manifested in the sudden lighting up of his eyes and the involuntary movements of his hand, with which he mechanically stroked his temples, his ears or his lips each time the orchestra paused. It would appear that he had stopped breathing, but when he covered his eyes with his hand and nervously rubbed his temple with his thumb and middle finger, we soon recognized this as a sign that he was about to voice some comment. Shostakovich would explain something, and the experienced musicians would perform his demands without a murmur, while Sollertinsky nodded his head approvingly. Sometimes friendly laughter burst out in the orchestra: Sollertinsky had cracked another brilliant joke.

Overtaken by the general atmosphere of enthusiasm, I gradually became immersed in my work on the role of Sonetka. However, I didn't succeed in keeping it up for long. Once I arrived for a rehearsal at the theatre early and saw Shostakovich on his own by the window. He hurriedly greeted me and continued writing in his notebook. I nevertheless took my courage in my hands and asked, 'Am I in your way?'

'No, not at all, not at all.'

'Dmitri Dmitriyevich, I am finding it very hard to feel the essence of Sonetka's character. I don't only want to see her as vulgar and coarse.'

Shostakovich put the pencil to his lips and thought for a second, and then, as if thinking aloud, he said, 'It is difficult to speak of a definite image because that is only born during the process of work. Each role is a part of an actor's soul. In my conception of her, Sonetka is not so much vulgar as reckless and unbridled. Her actions are guided not by cruelty but by the bitterness caused by the injustices and continual humiliations she has suffered. But she has preserved up to a point her youthful passion and feminine spirit.'[90]

Shostakovich spoke so simply and vividly that I saw my Sonetka at once. In the last scene, it is not so much cruelty but the daring of a degraded street urchin that dictates her image. Uncontrolled and hasty in her whims, she cruelly torments Katerina out of envy for her genuine passion; she laughs at the joys of love, which she herself has never experienced.[91]

Variety – the spice of life

As was to become a life-long pattern, Shostakovich combined 'serious' composition with commissions for film and theatre music. One of the first Soviet composers to compose for cinema soundtracks, Shostakovich wrote music to no less than fifteen films and seven theatre productions in between 1930 and 1940. The opportunity to work with Soviet directors of great distinction, whose ideas had been formulated during the experimental era of the 1920s, contributed much to Shostakovich's outlook. Thus Arnshtam, Yutkevich, Trauberg and Kozintsev, Mikhail Tsekhanovsky and Friedrich Ermler were all influential figures in his development.

Not only did Shostakovich enjoy testing out his own professional skills, but

---

90 Shostakovich wrote to Smolich on 28 February 1934: 'There are a couple of shortcomings, which are a shame in view of the overall high quality of the production. The first concerns the scene after Zinovy Borisovich's murder. Each time Sergei starts humping the corpse away, the audience bursts out laughing. The second defect lies in Sonetka. All the performers (Welter, Golovina and Leliva) make Sonetka into a female vampire, a hoity-toity courtesan, or a worldly coquette. . . . As far as I remember, you persuaded them against such an interpretation, but they have all reverted terribly since your departure. Sonetka, as I see her, should be a simple, flirtatious girl, without any demoniacal side to her.' (Yudin, 'Letters to Smolich', p. 92.)

91 Nadezhda Welter, *About Opera and Myself*, pp. 78–83; also from her reminiscences in O. L. Dansker (ed.), *S. A. Samosud: Articles, Reminiscences, Letters*, p. 84.

he was able to appreciate the professionalism of others in every kind of musical genre; he definitely had no time for musical snobs. In 1930 he made the acquaintance of Leonid Utyosov and his 'Tea Jazz' orchestra in Odessa, the term being derived from *Teatralny Djazz* or 'Theatre Jazz'. Utyosov had a checkered career, working his way from being a violinist, acrobat, restaurant crooner and actor to become the most famous and popular Soviet 'jazz' musician. His jazz orchestra played a mixed bag of music, much of which it would be fairer to describe as popular light music than jazz. Shostakovich informed Sollertinsky of his impressions: '. . . I'm not enraptured by "Tea Jazz", although they play well . . . But undoubtedly Utyosov is the greatest living artist in the USSR that I have come across. He reminds me of Meyerhold.'[92]

In 1931, Utyosov, together with Isaac Dunayevsky, the writer of popular songs and marches, decided to create a vaudeville entertainment 'Declared Dead'[93] at the Leningrad Music-Hall. Shostakovich agreed to write the music for the show, which dealt with the topical subject of a civilian air alert. These practice drills were common in those times of orchestrated hysteria in the face of possible enemy air or chemical attack. During the alert, should any disobedient citizen be found 'above ground', he would have been 'declared dead' and whisked away to a sanitary point in a militia van. The vaudeville follows the adventures of a 'dead' hero, involving his visits to some strange versions of purgatory and paradise, which were a good excuse for some topical anti-religious propaganda. Undoubtedly the main purpose of the plot was to allow Utyosov a lion's share of the limelight in his double role as singer and actor. However, the fun was too outrageous and the vaudeville was soon closed after a hostile reception from RAPM activists.

Despite this setback, Shostakovich later returned to jazz, wishing to raise its level from light music played in cafés and music-hall to music with a professional status. In 1934 he agreed to form part of a jazz commission to organize a competition in Leningrad. This prompted him in turn to write his First Jazz Suite which reveals Shostakovich's brilliance and wit in orchestration, although the music hardly corresponds to the accepted understanding

92 Mikheeva, 'Story of a Friendship', Part 1, p. 30.
93 Usually known as 'Hypothetically Killed', 'Conditionally Killed' or 'Allegedly Murdered'. Shostakovich's music to this vaudeville show had been preserved only in sketches and a few piano arrangements. In 1991, the English composer Gerard McBurney reconstructed much of the music on the basis of these sketches, finding in it a wealth of material which the composer re-used in his 'serious' compositions of those years. I am grateful to Gerard McBurney, and in particular to Laurel Fay, for information about the content of the piece. Both Fay and I felt that all the translations of the title, including the striking 'Hypothetically Killed' are misleading. Hence the decision to offer yet another translation of the title.

of jazz. Rather the composer utilizes a light music idiom he had already used extensively in his film and theatre music. This Suite was followed four years later by his Second Jazz Suite in three movements written at the request of the newly-formed State Orchestra for Jazz and its conductor Victor Knushevitsky. This latter work should not be confused with a 'Suite for Variety Stage Orchestra'[94] which was compiled from the most catchy numbers of Shostakovich's film music. One suspects that this latter work, which is rooted in the world of Johann Strauss, was prepared not only with dance bands in mind, but with the Red Army Orchestras as well, which provided popular concert entertainment throughout the country. The Second Jazz Suite manuscript has been lost, and is yet to be resurrected.

Since 1930 Shostakovich had virtually stopped performing in public, but riding high on the crest of the wave on completing *Lady Macbeth*, he felt the need to return to the concert platform. With this in mind, he immediately embarked on the composition of his Piano Preludes Op. 34 in December 1932. In the spring of 1933 he followed this with his First Piano Concerto Op. 35, which had a prominent solo trumpet part written with the Leningrad Philharmonic trumpeter Alexander Schmidt in mind (although later he gave preference to the expressive playing of Leonid Yuriev, the Moscow Philharmonic's trumpeter). Both the attractive and varied Preludes and the exuberant, high-spirited Piano Concerto, with its wealth of in-joke quotations and parody, won immediate popularity. Shostakovich played the premières of both pieces in Leningrad, and before long was performing them widely across the country.[95]

For Shostakovich, concertizing was a way of escaping from the pressures of life, and provided a welcome opportunity to travel. He was even given the rare chance to go abroad in his capacity as a performer, when, in April and May 1935, he formed part of a Soviet delegation of artists sent to Turkey.

Shostakovich was anxious to follow up the success of *Lady Macbeth* with another opera and considered many projects during the mid-1930s, ranging from an operatic farce to a full-blown Wagnerian trilogy of operas on the theme of women. The press published reports that the composer had joined forces with Mikhail Sholokhov to create an opera from his novel *Virgin Soil Upturned*, while Shostakovich himself approached the writer Alexei Tolstoy for a subject, and asked Alexander Preis to start writing a libretto on a compilation of works by Chekhov and Saltykov-Shchedrin. In 1933 he actually

---

94 I am grateful to Laurel Fay for pointing this out to me. Cf. her review of D. Hulme's *Dmitri Shostakovich: A Catalogue, Bibliography and Discography*, 2nd edition (Clarendon Press, Oxford, 1991).
95 Shostakovich gave the first performance of the complete cycle of Preludes in Moscow on 24 May 1933, having played groups of them earlier in Leningrad. The First Piano Concerto was premièred in Leningrad on 15 October 1933.

embarked on work for a 'Cinema opera' based on Pushkin's poem 'The Priest and his Servant Balda' with the director and animator Mikhail Tsekhanovsky. Shostakovich, much taken by this new form, completed the music ahead of the animation. However, the project met with a blow when Lenfilm annulled its contract with Tsekhanovsky. Shostakovich valued his own work sufficiently to create a Concert Suite on 'The Priest and His Servant Balda', which was performed in Leningrad in the spring of 1935. What existed of the animation footage was largely destroyed during the Second World War.

The symphony's pure instrumental form next claimed Shostakovich's attention. Conceived in the autumn of 1935, the Fourth Symphony had all the makings of an epic drama realized in the orchestral medium.

Cello Sonata Op. 40

This work was written during August and September 1934, at a time of emotional turmoil, when Shostakovich was involved in an affair with the translator Elena Konstantinovskaya. He wrote to her from Polenevo where he was holidaying:

> I cannot compose anything, but, as I am incapable of being idle, I have started writing a fugue every day. I've already composed three. They are turning out very badly, and that makes me miserable. In general it is much pleasanter to work feverishly without a let-up than to sit around doing nothing, 'resting'.[96]

In August Shostakovich and his wife decided on a temporary separation, and in a state of despondency he turned to the composition of his Cello Sonata. It was completed by 19 September and received its first performance in Leningrad on 25 December 1934.

The work was dedicated to the cellist Victor Kubatsky. Shostakovich had originally met him when, as a member of the Stradivarius Quartet, he participated in the first performance of the Octet Op. 11 in 1925. During the 1930s Shostakovich maintained close ties with Kubatsky, who actively promoted his music. Kubatsky, a member of the Bolshoi Theatre Orchestra, also conducted this orchestra in concert repertoire.

Shostakovich subsequently performed his Cello Sonata with other famous cellists, including A. Livshits, A. Ferkelman, Daniil Shafran and notably Mstislav Rostropovich, with whom he recorded it.

ARNOLD FERKELMAN lived in Leningrad during the 1930s. After becoming

---

96 Letter dated 26 July 1934 (Sofiya Khentova, 'Dmitri Shostakovich: We Live in a Time of Stormy Passions and Actions', p. 13).

a prize winner in the First All-Union Competition for performing musicians, he played in concerts all over the USSR. He met Shostakovich in the early 1930s, and they made music together for their own pleasure. In 1939 they gave two concerts together in Moscow and Leningrad. The programme consisted of three sonatas, by Grieg, Rachmaninov and Shostakovich. Here are his memories of the Cello Sonata and of Shostakovich:

I heard the first performance of the Cello Sonata in Leningrad, played by Victor Kubatsky with Dmitri Dmitriyevich at the piano. Kubatsky played at the Bolshoi Theatre in Moscow, he conducted and he taught at the Conservatoire. He had a great talent as a musical organizer, but his technical skill as a cellist was limited. Undoubtedly the sonata has received many better performances since then, and of course is now a part of every cellist's repertoire.

I have to say that when the sonata was first performed, it got a hostile reception. People didn't understand it and were somewhat disappointed, and I regret to say that I was amongst them. It wasn't the sort of new music we were used to. Later I played the sonata very often, not only with Shostakovich but with many other pianists, and then I understood the great value and beauty of the work.

Over the years I used to make music with Dmitri Dmitriyevich for fun. Then, in 1939, we decided to go on a concert tour. In the event we only performed together twice, once in Moscow, once in Leningrad. When it came to deciding on the programme, it was Shostakovich who selected from a list of sonatas I put forward. I remember suggesting Brahms and Chopin, but he very much wanted to play the Rachmaninov sonata, as he was very fond of it.

During our rehearsals, Dmitri Dmitriyevich made very few remarks; apparently he accepted my interpretation of his sonata. In general he was very modest, and it was very easy to play with him. He had no sense of ambition or pride, and he wasn't offended if one made a suggestion. Most of his comments in regard to his sonata related to the tempi. Dmitri Dmitriyevich was a brilliant pianist and had an incredible technique, but in those years he didn't practise very much. He must have been a natural pianist, and of course he had a sound technical grounding as a Nikolayev pupil. He knew all the music from memory, not just his own sonata. When we started rehearsing, he gave the impression he had been practising day and night. He had no difficulties with the virtuoso passages in the Rachmaninov sonata and the Finale of his own sonata. In fact he liked playing quickly and loudly, and he took incredibly fast tempi. I never succeeded in getting any other pianist to take such tempi. His playing was on the dry side, but on the other hand he played very loudly, no doubt because of his great force of temperament.

In life Shostakovich was very nervous. His moods would swing very suddenly from one extreme to another. We would be sitting and having a conversation, or rehearsing, and it was as if something in him suddenly switched off. He would go quiet and limp, then, just as suddenly, he would switch on again and become lively and active. These contrasts of moods could also happen when he was playing, although not during a concert, when he pulled himself together and was very concentrated.

When the war started I was evacuated to Tashkent and then came to live in Moscow in 1943. Shostakovich also came to Moscow at that time and we saw quite a lot of each other. During that period we got together to play cards – usually poker – with his pupil, the composer Yuri Levitin. Sometimes Tikhon Khrennikov joined our party. Dmitri Dmitriyevich was quite a poker fiend. Those were hard and hungry years, and food was rationed, but we were able to get coffee with our ration cards, and my wife used to bake pancakes out of the used grounds. They were much appreciated by Dmitri Dmitriyevich. Although it was a difficult time, life went on and we met and enjoyed ourselves.[97]

Personal happiness

The following two descriptions are of Shostakovich's physical appearance in the early and mid-1930s. The first is by ISAAK GLIKMAN:

I was enthralled not only by his talent, but by his outward appearance. I was captivated by the refinement of his face, its individuality, its noble aspect, with his wonderful grey eyes flashing from behind his spectacles, with their wise expression, penetrating, thoughtful or splintering with laughter.

In many early descriptions, Shostakovich is depicted as physically weak, frail, and even puny, but these are extremely misleading statements. In my view, Shostakovich was of decent height, slender, yet supple and strong. His clothes always suited him, and he looked

97 Arnold Ferkelman: recorded interview with EW.

irresistable in tails or a dinner jacket. His head was crowned with wonderful dark copper-coloured hair, which was carefully combed, or else fell in poetic disorder with that dashing unruly lick of hair falling forward onto his forehead. When he smiled, his excellent teeth were visible. In the 1930s, Dmitri Dmitriyevich looked much younger than his years.[98]

This is reinforced by the film director MIKHAIL TSEKHANOVSKY, who worked with Shostakovich on the animation film/opera based on Pushkin's 'The Tale of the Priest and His Servant Balda':

Shostakovich is twenty-seven or twenty-eight years old. He is at the age when a person can live for four or five years without any external changes in appearance. He is very handsome . . . It would appear that such handsome people are always talented or even 'brilliant'! . . . When Shostakovich played today, I looked down at the crown of his head with its reddish hair. He brushed aside a strand that fell on to his temples, but his curly hair obstinately kept covering his forehead, almost reaching his eyebrows. This feature, a kind of uncontrollable disorder on the head, the oval of his pale face, the form of his lips, the round receding chin and his intelligent eyes, which seem clouded as if in some kind of fog – all this recalls the inspired images of the heads of Beethoven and Mozart.[99]

The first half of the 1930s was not only a period of intense creative activity, but also of important events in Shostakovich's personal life. After putting off the wedding more than once, he finally married Nina Varzar in May 1932 and settled down to relative domestic security.

Nina Varzar was the youngest of three sisters from a well-known Leningrad family. She was a physicist by profession and had a wide knowledge of music and culture. Evidently her buoyant spirits and sharp practical intelligence made her an excellent foil to Shostakovich's sensitive and neurotic nature. Their marriage was explicitly based on the recognition of each partner's freedom. It survived some shaky moments and rough patches, including a temporary separation caused by Shostakovich's open affair with the translator Elena Konstantinovskaya. Additionally, relations between Dmitri's mother and the Varzar family were far from easy. Sofiya Vasilyevna perceived the Varzars as pushy and ambitious, and felt that they had forced her son into marriage. Divorce proceedings were initiated in the spring of 1935, but they were ultimately withdrawn, evidently as a result of pressure applied by Nina's

98 Isaak Glikman, *Letters to a Friend*, p. 6.
99 From his unpublished diary (Khentova, *Shostakovich*, vol. I, p. 308).

parents. In later years, Nina herself spoke of the couple's divorce and immediate remarriage when they realized that they were indispensable to each other. Their daughter Galina was born in May 1936, and their son Maxim two years later in May 1938. The birth of their children stabilized the marriage and brought the Shostakovich family happiness.

On the eve of his thirtieth birthday, Shostakovich had, so it would seem, all a man could wish for: happiness, imminent parenthood, fame, success and an enviable list of compositional achievements. However, any sense of security or peace of mind were rudely shattered for Shostakovich in January 1936. While he was on tour in Arkhangel'sk with Victor Kubatsky and the Bolshoi Theatre Orchestra, the defamatory article 'Muddle Instead of Music' appeared as a *Pravda* editorial. This vicious attack on Shostakovich had consequences that were felt by all who were involved in Soviet musical life.

CHAPTER THREE

Criticism and the Response to Criticism

'Muddle Instead of Music'

Within two years of its premiere, *Lady Macbeth* had achieved such popularity that the Bolshoi Theatre decided to stage a new production of the opera. It opened in Moscow on 28 December 1935 under Alexander Melik-Pashayev's baton. Simultaneously MALEGOT toured both *Lady Macbeth* and Ivan Dzerzhinsky's *Quiet Flows the Don* in Moscow.[1]

Shostakovich came to Moscow for these performances, and also played his First Piano Concerto in concert on 11 January 1936. Two days earlier he had written to Sollertinsky:

> I am extremely tired, but not from banquets in my honour or that of MALEGOT . . . I am tired from the anxieties and success surrounding *Quiet Flows the Don*. . . . Here, in *Evening Moscow*, there was a review of *Quiet Flows the Don*,[2] where the critic E. Kann pointed to the influence of Tchaikovsky, Blaramberg, Serov and Shostakovich. It also stated *en passant* that the worst aspect of the opera was the music. There is a certain truth in what *Evening Moscow* says.[3]

On 26 January 1936 Shostakovich returned to Moscow for twenty-four hours, before proceeding to Arkhangel'sk for a concert tour. That evening, he was ordered to attend a performance of *Lady Macbeth* in the new Bolshoi Theatre production. Shostakovich described the occasion to Sollertinsky:

> Comrade Stalin, and Comrades Molotov, Mikoyan and Zhdanov were all present.[4] The show went very well. At the end I was called out (by the audience) and took a bow. I only regret that I did not do so after the third

1 The tour lasted from late December 1935 through the first part of January 1936.
2 5 January 1936.
3 Letter dated 9 January 1936 (Lyudmila Mikheeva, 'The Story of a Friendship', Part 2, p. 78).
4 The date for Stalin's visit to *Lady Macbeth* is usually given – incorrectly (by Sofiya Khentova, amongst others) – as 26 December 1935, when he is alleged to have attended the MALEGOT production in Moscow. Had this indeed been the case, an explanation is needed of why the Party organs took over a month to voice his displeasure.

act. Feeling sick at heart, I collected my brief-case and went to the station. . . . I am in bad spirits. As you can guess, I kept thinking about what happened to your namesake, and what didn't happen to me.[5]

This cryptic last sentence is a reference to Ivan Ivanovich Dzerzhinsky, whose name and patronymic were identical to Sollertinsky's. While writing his opera *Quiet Flows the Don*, Dzerzhinsky, a composer of limited talents, had received generous assistance from Shostakovich, who had orchestrated large chunks of the opera on his behalf. Sollertinsky had all along ridiculed Dzerzhinsky's helplessness, and didn't disguise his opinion in an article which had recently appeared in *Sovietskaya Muzyka*.

Nevertheless, *Quiet Flows the Don* enjoyed considerable success in Moscow, and Stalin had attended a performance. During the interval Dzerzhinsky had been called to the State Box, and held conversation with the Great Leader. In contrast, the government delegation had demonstratively left before the end of *Lady Macbeth* (evidently after the third act).

Shostakovich was right to have gloomy presentiments about the significance of Stalin's walk-out from his opera. With the publication on 28 January 1936 of the article 'Muddle Instead of Music' in *Pravda*, Shostakovich's fortunes suffered a dramatic reversal. The crass criticism of *Lady Macbeth* was shortly followed by another *Pravda* article, 'Ballet Falsehood', a crude attack on Shostakovich's ballet *The Limpid Stream*. Since *Pravda* was the Party's mouthpiece, these articles were overtly political. Rumour had it that Stalin himself had written the editorial, but it is more probable that its author was David Zaslavsky, a high-ranking party official and journalist who was at home in the corridors of power. Shostakovich must have felt incredibly isolated and bitter as colleagues, friends and admirers distanced themselves and looked on with fascinated horror to see how the 29-year-old composer would extricate himself from this sudden public disgrace. Those friends who faithfully stuck by him at this time became all the more valued because of it.

The Leningrad literary critic Isaak Glikman enjoyed a lifelong friendship with Shostakovich. The two men met in 1931 through their mutual friend Sollertinsky. By 1934 Shostakovich had invited Glikman to act as his secretary in dealing with his correspondence.

Shostakovich evidently enjoyed Glikman's sense of humour, and found his company entertaining. Additionally, he much valued Glikman's literary judgement. Indeed, in the 1950s he entrusted to Glikman the task of making the necessary changes to the libretto of *Lady Macbeth*.

The opinion has been voiced that Glikman's enthusiastic admiration for Shostakovich may have made him less than objective in his perception of the

---

5 Letter written from Arkhangel'sk, dated 28 January 1936 (Mikheeva, 'The Story of a Friendship', Part 2, p. 79).

composer, but in the times, such a capacity for loyalty and devotion was a rare and much appreciated gift. The trust this evoked in Shostakovich is evident in his letters to ISAAK GLIKMAN, which were written over a period of more than thirty years:

During the 1930s it was Shostakovich's lot to undergo extremely hard experiences, and I was filled with admiration for his bearing. It somehow reminded me of the . . . heroes of his symphonies and chamber works, their propensity for mournful contemplation in conjunction with an indestructible force of spirit. My views were confirmed by much of what Dmitri Dmitriyevich expressed in his letters of this period. . . .

The opera *Lady Macbeth of Mtsensk* brought Shostakovich fantastic and incomparable fame which has no analogy in living memory. Its productions both in the Soviet Union and abroad generated immense praise and delight. And when the triumph reached its apogee, all of a sudden the catastrophic article 'Muddle Instead of Music', published in *Pravda* in late January 1936, struck Shostakovich down from those dizzy heights whither he had been borne on the crest of the opera's success.

The publication of the article found Shostakovich in Arkhangel'sk on a concert tour. At this critical moment in his life, the 29-year-old Shostakovich sent me an extraordinary telegram asking me to send him all newspaper reports and articles relating to his work. It was a sign of wisdom more characteristic of an experienced psychologist. After all Dmitri Dmitriyevich had never shown any interest in reviews when his works were being praised, so why this sudden need for press cuttings? I found it most disconcerting, but carried out his request: evidently he was suddenly overcome by curiosity to discover what well-known musicians would now write about *Lady Macbeth*.[6]

Alas, he was not deceived in his sombre expectations. Many of the opera's former admirers criticized the work in various publications. Dmitri Dmitriyevich read these cuttings which came flooding in daily, and he reacted to them with his habitual restraint and self-control. As I visited Shostakovich nearly every day, we read them together; we

6 Elena Konstantinovskaya remembered how Shostakovich visited her after her release from prison early in 1936, and showed her an album filled with derogatory press cuttings in the wake of 'Muddle Instead of Music'. His comment to her was, 'You see how fortunate it is that you didn't marry me' (Sofiya Khentova, 'Dmitri Shostakovich: We Live in a Time of Stormy Passions and Actions', p. 13).

reacted differently, I with disgust and irritation and sometimes indignation, whereas Dmitri Dmitriyevich remained silent and made no comments.

Although his noble spirit was deeply wounded, he retained his dignity and composure to a remarkable degree. He did not seek support or sympathy from anybody. Some false friends harped on about 'the sunset' of the composer of *Lady Macbeth*, while sadly shaking their heads. Although self-opinion and complacency were completely foreign to Dmitri Dmitriyevich, he continued to believe unhesitatingly in his own creative powers. And I must add that these powers were unquenchable and measureless. The Fourth Symphony was close to completion, and through a magic crystal ball the outlines of the Fifth were already discernable!

It was during this very period of time that Dmitri Dmitriyevich one day announced to me: 'Even if they chop my hands off, I will still continue to compose music – albeit I have to hold the pen in my teeth.' This was said in a calm, business-like fashion, with no sense of drama or affectation. I was totally shaken. Goose-flesh crawled up my spine, and words forsook me. For a moment I felt as if I had crossed into some malignant phantasmagoria from Dante. Dmitri Dmitriyevich had not intended to shock me with this admission; he looked me in the eyes intently and calmly, then immediately changed the subject. That morning we had been standing opposite one another while talking, and the sun came streaming through the window of his study, lighting up his youthful figure. Shostakovich . . . was graced with an attractive physique, and emanated a resolute and fearless confidence.

Dmitri Dmitriyevich had no intention of attending the discussion of the *Pravda* article, which lasted for many days at the Leningrad Union of Composers; this was looked on by certain high-up persons as a sign of arrogance. The harrowing discussion was unsparing and hard-hitting. It transpired that there were many who lost no time in practising their rhetorical skills, and were all too happy to trample the disgraced opera in the mud.

Dmitri Dmitriyevich went to Moscow at this time and asked me to write to him describing in detail the progress of the discussions. He requested that I recount everything in a formal style, as if writing an official report and without any personal emotion. I complied with his wishes. Many years later Dmitri Dmitriyevich expressed his regret that these letters, which bore the irrefutable stamp of those times, had been lost for ever; although, to be honest, this regret was mainly rhetorical, as he never preserved any letters. But amazing as it may seem, his phenomenal memory, undimmed by the passage of time, allowed him to recall their content many years later.[7]

The test of friendship

After the criticisms of *Lady Macbeth* and *The Limpid Stream*, countless public debates were called where further criticism in line with Party directives was heaped on Shostakovich. Fear effectively tested people's loyalty to Shostakovich. Many friends and colleagues deserted him at this crucial time, and even those who came to his defence did not always do so as unswervingly as might be expected. Shostakovich's friends were under particular pressure to recant. Early in February, the Leningrad Composers' Union, at the instigation of one of its senior secretaries, V. Iochelson, convoked meetings specifically to discuss the *Lady Macbeth* issue. At the first day's gathering, Mikhail Druskin and Ivan Sollertinsky sat outside the main circle of the hall near the door, trying to hide their disgust at the alacrity with which certain colleagues poured dirt over Shostakovich. On the third day Sollertinsky was forced to 'unbend' slightly when he took the stand; he admitted that *Lady Macbeth* did have certain faults, and he promised to 'review' his opinion.[8] For his support of Shostakovich Sollertinsky was dubbed 'the troubadour of Formalism'.

According to Isaak Glikman, Shostakovich had told Sollertinsky that he should vote for 'any resolutions' if the pressure on him became too great. He no doubt realized that Sollertinsky would be victimized for his enthusiastic support of his music, and in particular of *Lady Macbeth*.[9]

The Leningrad Composers' Union took an 'unanimous' vote in support of *Pravda*'s editorial article.

Sollertinsky, governed by fear, conceded his principles on this issue. However, there was one abstention, that of the composer Vladimir Shcherbachov, who, although not a great admirer of *Lady Macbeth*, could not bring himself to condemn a fellow-composer.

Whereas he was sympathetic to Sollertinsky's dilemma, Shostakovich never forgave Boris Asafiev's treachery. Asafiev, to whom Shostakovich had considered dedicating the opera at one point, was quick to admit his error of judgement, and declared that Ivan Dzerzhinsky's opera *Quiet Flows the Don* reflected all the requirements of perfect 'Soviet' art.[10]

7 Isaak Glikman, *Letters to a Friend*, pp. 8–10.
8 From a private interview with Mikhail Druskin, Leningrad, January 1990.
9 Glikman, *Letters to a Friend*, pp. 321–2.
10 Boris Asafiev, *Selected Works*, vol. 5, p. 67.

Shostakovich did not attend the discussion at either the Leningrad or Moscow Composers' Union. Thus, in contrast to 1948, he was not forced to recant publicly.

Amongst the few people from whom he received unequivocal support were the composers Shebalin and Balanchivadze. To the latter Shostakovich wrote:

> One must have the courage not only to kill one's work, but to defend them. As it would be futile and impossible to do the latter, I am taking no steps in this direction. In any case, I am doing much hard thinking about all that has happened. Honesty is what is important. Will I have enough in store to last for long, I wonder? But if you ever learn that I have 'disassociated' myself from *Lady Macbeth*, you will know that I have done so 100 per cent. I doubt that this will happen soon, however. I am a ponderous thinker and am very honest in all that concerns composition.[11]

Vissarion (Ronya) Shebalin met Shostakovich in 1924 through Lev Oborin. At the time he was a student of Nikolai Myaskovsky's at the Moscow Conservatoire, and a member of the group of young Moscow composers, 'The Six'. The two young composers became steadfast friends. Here are ALISA MAXIMOVNA SHEBALINA's (Vissarion's wife) reminiscences of their friendship:

Shostakovich and Shebalin had a lifelong friendship. From the 1920s on, Mitya always used to stay with us in Moscow, and similarly Shebalin stayed with the Shostakoviches during his visits to Leningrad.

I well remember Mitya's visits to our home in Moshkov Pereulok. On one occasion Mitya went to the bathroom to wash his hands. Suddenly he rushed out of the door in a fright. 'What have you got in there?' he exclaimed. Our good maid used to buy us fresh fish from a nearby fish shop in Pokrovka Street. She would then put them in the bathtub until she was ready to cook them. On that day she had bought a couple of carp which were enjoying a swim in the tub. We told Mitya, 'Oh, that's our aquarium.'

Mitya and Vissarion then got down to some work on music, as usual. In the meantime, as evening approached, I told our maid to get the supper ready, so she extracted the carp from the bath, cleaned them, fried them and served them. Mitya relished the dish: 'How delicious! What wonderful fish! Where did you get them?'

I said, 'That was fresh carp.'

11 R. Tsurtsumiya (ed.), *André Melitonovich Balanchivadze: Collection of Articles and Material*, pp. 15–16.

'And where ever did you get hold of them?'

'But Mitya, you saw them in the bath, they gave you a fright!'

'Well, well, what wheeler-dealers you are.'

Both Mitya and Sollertinsky were such frequent guests that they became part of our household. Our maid once greeted me when I came home by announcing in her inimitable language that 'Your Leninsky-gradskyie have arrived.'[12]

Shostakovich was a great football fan, and often came down to Moscow specially for a match. He would send Ronya a telegram the day before to ask him to reserve tickets. On the other hand, his wife Nina (or Nita as she was called) was a boxing fan.

After the appearance of the articles in *Pravda* in 1936 attacking *Lady Macbeth of Mtsensk* and *The Limpid Stream*, Shostakovich was bitterly persecuted. In Leningrad he was supported by his friend Sollertinsky, and in Moscow by Shebalin. A 'dispute' or 'discussion' was organized in Moscow at the House of Writers (the so-called Herzen House), where a large number of Moscow composers gathered. All the old RAPM activists were there, their teeth bared, ready for a killing. Shostakovich was criticized, purged, disciplined and scolded by one and all on every count. Each person who spoke felt it his duty to express sentiments similar to those printed in the *Pravda* articles. Only Shebalin maintained silence throughout the meeting. But then he too was asked to speak; it was hardly a request but a demand; he refused all the same. A short while elapsed and again it was 'suggested' that he should take the stand. Vissarion then got up, but, remaining where he was without going up to the podium, he announced in a loud and clear voice for all to hear: 'I consider that Shostakovich is the greatest genius amongst composers of this epoch.' And with this statement he sat down.

After this Shebalin was also persecuted; his music was no longer performed or printed and he was deprived of all material means of earning a living. For a certain time we lived in great poverty, and it wasn't until the war started that things started changing for the better.[13]

12 An ingenious play on words: 'Your Lenin-y Town-y folk have arrived,' or 'Lenin-burghers'.
13 Alisa Shebalina: recorded interview with EW.

The Fourth Symphony

Shostakovich's recipe for preserving his sanity in the face of unfair and crass criticism was to press on with his composition. He completed the score of his grandiose Fourth Symphony in April 1936 and waited impatiently for its performance. But at one of the final rehearsals the composer decided – with great reluctance – to withdraw the work. It would appear that he was pressurized by the Leningrad party organs and the director of the Philharmonic to take this eleventh-hour decision.

However, there remains some controversy in the varying accounts of the rehearsals of the Fourth Symphony, and the reasons behind the decision to cancel its performance. Many people have laid the blame at Fritz Stiedri's feet, accusing him of being unco-operative, even hostile towards the new music. M. S. Shak, a violinist of the Leningrad Philharmonic, describes the rehearsal process:

> Our acquaintance with the score started with a string sectional, rather than a play through with the whole orchestra. In the hall sat a thin young man who in our eyes still had not got much authority as a symphonist. Even in later years, when he had reached a position of world fame, he preferred not to interfere with the orchestra's work. But in the tangibly tense atmosphere of those times he sat there timidly and quietly. Bent low over the score, Fritz Stiedri pointed at it with his finger. Checking the text, he impatiently demanded its author: 'Is it correct? Is this how it should go?' The orchestra would stop and a quick answer would follow: 'Correct, correct.'[14]

The conductor Alexander Gauk, on the other hand, gives the impression of professional ineptitude on Stiedri's part:

> They were rehearsing the first movement. It was a shambles. Stiedri obviously did not understand the music, and the orchestra played messily. It was quite depressing. This was a terrible period for Dmitri Dmitriyevich, when he was being demolished by all and sundry.[15]

According to Flora Litvinova, years later, after the Fourth Symphony had eventually been performed, Shostakovich stated that Stiedri had not prepared for the rehearsals, that he and the musicians were at sea and could not cope with the complexities of the score. He himself said to Stiedri that he needed to re-work the Symphony before it could be performed, ostensibly to save the

---

14 Sofiya Khentova, *Shostakovich: Life and Work*, vol. I, p. 439.
15 Alexander Gauk, 'Creative Contacts', in L. Gauk, R. Glezer and Y. Milstein (eds), *Alexander Vasiliyevich Gauk: Memoirs, Selected Articles, Reminiscences of His Contemporaries*, p. 223.

face of the conductor and musicians.[16] Isaak Glikman firmly refutes these accounts, defending Stiedri. Another violinist of the Leningrad Philharmonic, Mark Reznikov, recalled that Stiedri, who admired and promoted Shostakovich's music, had rehearsed the Fourth Symphony very thoroughly and achieved the necessary level for performance.[17]

Ultimately, whether or not the final decision to withdraw the Symphony was imposed on him or taken independently, Shostakovich must have realized that for all concerned it was better to be 'safe than sorry'.

Isaak Glikman gives a vivid account of events surrounding the Fourth Symphony:

At the end of May 1936 the world-famous conductor Otto Klemperer came to Leningrad to give two concerts. Klemperer was a great admirer of Shostakovich's First Symphony, and also one of its first performers. The chief purpose of this visit was to acquaint himself with Dmitri Dmitriyevich's newly-composed Fourth Symphony. On 29 May I went to the Grand Hall of the Philharmonic to hear Klemperer rehearsing Beethoven's Third and Fifth Symphonies. A handsome man, enormously tall and powerfully built, appeared on the stage with a very severe and dictatorial expression. The orchestral musicians greeted him with an ovation. They knew this wonderful musician from his frequent concert appearances in the 1920s.

Here I should point out in parenthesis that the orchestral musicians of that time behaved in a very independent fashion and were very choosy about conductors. They made it known if they were dissatisfied with the level of performance. But not only that: the veterans amongst the orchestral soloists, such as the cello section leader, Ilya Brik (a one-time artistic director of the Philharmonic), or the first-rate bassoon player Alexander Vasilyev, and several others, often did not bother to disguise their critical or sceptical attitude to certain new scores by contemporary Moscow or Leningrad composers. It is essential to bear this circumstance in mind when talking about the atmosphere that prevailed during the preparation of Shostakovich's symphonies. Otto Klemperer's rehearsals were brilliantly conducted, and there was no room for tedious routine or mishaps.

The evening of that self-same spring day I told Dmitri Dmitriyevich

---

16 Flora Litvinova, article commissioned for this book.
17 Mark Reznikov, *Reminiscences of an Old Musician*, p. 70.

about my visit to the Philharmonic. Shostakovich informed me that tomorrow at midday he was to show the famous visitor his Fourth Symphony, and asked me if I would come along too.

Dmitri Dmitriyevich said that it would be a hard task for him to play this enormous and complex symphony, and to show it at its best. He had great hopes for this work, for which he nurtured a great love, all the more so as it was still fresh off the stands. Later on, Shostakovich was to speak very differently about it, either completely disparagingly or with passionate approbation. But this lay ahead.

That evening he conferred with his wife, Nina Vasilyevna, and myself as to how we should entertain Klemperer after he had played through the Symphony. While we were discussing the menu for dinner, the door bell rang. Completely unexpectedly there in the hall stood Otto Klemperer in all his glory, with Ivan Sollertinsky. They told us how they had slipped away from the Maly Opera Theatre, where they had gone to see *The Marriage of Figaro* conducted by Fritz Stiedri. Stiedri himself had insisted that Klemperer and Ivan Ivanovich come to the show, but after the first act Klemperer had a better idea: to sneak away and go and find Shostakovich, rather than wait for the appointed hour the following day.

Dmitri Dmitriyevich did not like unexpected guests, regarding them with barely disguised hostility. But he was touched by the sudden appearance of Klemperer, who had come to Leningrad from the other end of the world to meet him with all possible haste.

The celebrated and impatient guest was received courteously and without any fuss and bother. He turned out to be a man of immense culture, a wonderful raconteur and conversationalist. By the way, Klemperer told me that in his large repertoire he had a favourite 'Shostakovich' programme, with which he had toured all over North and South America, consisting of the First Symphony, the Piano Concerto, the Suites from *The Golden Age* and *Bolt*. The audience always received it favourably . . . 'et toujours avec un succès formidable'. (I still recall his exact words.) The conversation was largely held in French for the benefit of Dmitri Dmitriyevich's wife, Nina Vasilyevna.

It was after midnight before we dispersed. Early that very morning Dmitri Dmitriyevich rang me up to inform me of the happy news that very late that night he had become a father, with the birth of his first child Galina.[18] Without further ado I rushed to congratulate the happy parents with a bottle of champagne tucked under my arm. By twelve o'clock Klemperer, Stiedri, Sollertinsky, Gauk, Oborin and E. Nellius, the secretary of the Philharmonic Board, had arrived for the official appointment. On hearing the glad tidings, they all immediately dashed out to buy champagne. It was then decided to send a letter of congratulations to Nina Vasilyevna in hospital. For some reason Klemperer took it upon himself to write it in French and we all added something to his note.

Dmitri Dmitriyevich, after a sleepless and anxious night, was not himself, but he, more than anybody else I knew, was capable of pulling himself together. He played the Symphony through with great elan. The score lay on the desk, and the conductors Klemperer, Gauk and Stiedri were all huddled over it. I remember that Klemperer occupied the most favourable position, using his powerful build to advantage.

The Symphony made an enormous impression. (Sollertinsky and myself had heard it previously.) Klemperer and Stiedri were fired with genuine enthusiasm, and they both scheduled the work for performance in the autumn of 1936, Klemperer in South America, the latter in Leningrad in his capacity as chief conductor of the Leningrad Philharmonic. But things turned out differently.

Afterwards, at dinner, Klemperer spoke with passion, saying that the heavens themselves had granted him a marvellous gift, the chance of conducting the Fourth Symphony. Delighted as he would be to conduct it, he nevertheless had one humble request to make of the composer: to reduce the number of flutes, as by no means would it be possible everywhere to find six first-rate flautists while on tour. However Dmitri Dmitriyevich was adamant. Smiling he answered, 'What is written with the pen cannot be scratched out with an axe.' Sollertinsky translated this proverb, not without some effort on his part, into German, French, Spanish and English, all languages which Klemperer knew.

That evening, in an overflowing Grand Hall of the Philharmonic, Klemperer conducted Beethoven with colossal success. Dmitri Dmitriyevich, who was totally exhausted and drained after the agitation of the last twenty-four hours, did not attend the concert.

18 Galina Shostakovich was born on 30 May.

Sollertinsky and myself were there, and at the end went backstage to give Klemperer our warmest congratulations. He declared firmly that today the congratulations did not belong to him, but to Shostakovich, the composer of the Fourth Symphony.

Rehearsals for the Fourth Symphony began in the autumn of the same year (1936). Fritz Stiedri was a great conductor and musician. He had escaped from Fascist Germany, settled in Leningrad and was now chief conductor of the Philharmonic. Shostakovich had a high opinion of him. Their first working contact had been a joyful occasion, when, in the autumn of 1933, for the opening concert of the Philharmonic Season they gave the première of Dmitri Dmitriyevich's First Piano Concerto, which the composer played exquisitely.

Dmitri Dmitriyevich invited me to the rehearsals of the Fourth Symphony, of which there were an impressive number. It goes without saying that Stiedri learnt the score of this massive-scale work, using all the resources of his masterful talent. I don't know how Dmitri Dmitriyevich felt, but I sensed an atmosphere of tension and caution in the hall. The trouble was that rumours were circulating in musical circles that Shostakovich, in defiance of criticism, had written a work of devilish complexity that was chock-a-block full of Formalism.

And one fine day a secretary of the Union of Composers, V. E. Iochelson, and another official from Smolny,[19] appeared at a rehearsal; Dmitri Dmitriyevich was requested to report with them to I. M. Renzin, the director of the Philharmonic. They climbed up the inner spiral staircase to Renzin's office, and I remained in the Hall. About 15 or so minutes later Dmitri Dmitriyevich came to fetch me and we set off on foot to his flat at 14 Kirovsky Prospect.

I was confused and upset by the long silence of my dejected companion, but finally he told me, in an even, expressionless voice, that the Symphony would not be performed, that at the express recommendation of Renzin it had been cancelled, but that he had not wished to invoke his administrative authority and therefore had requested that the composer himself should take the decision for cancelling the performance.

Many years have since gone by, and a legend has grown up around the Fourth Symphony, which unfortunately has firmly established

19 Smolny: the headquarters of the Leningrad party administration.

itself in all that has been written about Dmitri Dmitriyevich. Essentially the rumour is that Shostakovich, being convinced that Stiedri could not cope with the Symphony, decided to cancel its performance. It would be hard to invent anything more absurd and unfair.

In 1956 Shostakovich wrote about the faults of the Fourth Symphony. In his words, it suffered from 'folies de grandeur'. But only five years later, on the 30 December 1961, its première took place in the Grand Hall of the Moscow Conservatoire under the baton of Kirill Kondrashin. I sat next to Dmitri Dmitriyevich during the concert, and when the devastating music of the introduction resounded around the Hall, it seemed to me that I could hear his heart knocking audibly in agitation. He was in the grip of an unconquerable anxiety which only subsided at the start of the superb coda.

After the colossal success of the concert, we went to his home. Under the fresh impression of what he had just heard, Dmitri Dmitriyevich told me, 'It seems to me that in many respects my Fourth Symphony stands much higher than my most recent ones.' A remarkable admission! Given that this statement contained an element of exaggeration, it was nevertheless provoked by his impulse to defend a composition which had suffered unjust oblivion in the last twenty-five years. During this long period, the composer himself had regarded this work with a cold and detached eye; but when it actually came to life in sound, he identified totally with the overwhelming musical force of this lost child.[20]

Terror on the doorstep

Following Sergei Kirov's murder in December 1934, a new wave of repression broke out in the country. An atmosphere of hostility and grim suspicion came into being, and, with no little encouragement from the authorities, it became second nature for people to regard anybody near to them as a possible informer or saboteur. The year of 1936 is remembered now as the first of the great purges and 'show trials', where Stalin's political enemies were forced into abject confessions and humiliation prior to their liquidation. It is estimated that over seven million people were arrested between 1936 and 1939. Stalin imposed the Terror so as to transform all institutions – the Party, heavy industry and the armed forces – into obedient tools. It affected people from all walks of life.

20 Glikman, *Letters to a Friend*, pp. 10–13.

The publication of 'Muddle Instead of Music' had found Shostakovich in Arkhangel'sk on a concert tour with the cellist and conductor Victor Kubatsky. Before returning to Leningrad, the composer passed through Moscow, where he consulted with the chairman of the Arts Committee, P. Kerzhentsev, and with Marshal Tukhachevsky as to how to react to party criticism. Kerzhentsev advised Shostakovich that his best tactic would be to 'admit his errors', while Tukhachevsky wrote a letter on Shostakovich's behalf to Stalin.[21]

Tukhachevsky may have seemed a powerful patron at the time, but he was arrested only a year later and shot in the summer of 1937 as an enemy of the people. Shortly afterwards, another of Shostakovich's close friends, the musicologist Nikolai Zhilyaev, was arrested because of his association with Tukhachevsky.

Shostakovich's position was now precarious to a degree, and remained so until the successful performance of the Fifth Symphony in November 1937. The Terror was at its height, and he must have felt increasingly hemmed in and helpless as colleagues, friends and relatives were arrested and disappeared without trace. These included his brother-in-law, the distinguished physicist Vsevolod Frederiks, his mother-in-law, the astronomer Sofiya Varzar (released just before the Second World War), his uncle, the Bolshevik Maxim Kostrikin; the poet Boris Kornilov, author of the text of 'Song of the Counterplan', Adrian Piotrovsky, the author of the play *Rule Britannia* and librettist of *The Limpid Stream*, and the Marxist writer Galina Serebryakova. His friend, the famous theatre director Vsevolod Meyerhold, was arrested in the summer of 1939, and perished in prison six months later. It is known that Shostakovich, at the request of Meyerhold's wife Zinaida Raikh (shortly herself to be brutally murdered) wrote a letter interceding for Meyerhold. His own sister Mariya was exiled to Frunze in 1937. And his former mistress Elena Konstantinovskaya was arrested in 1936, but exceptionally, she was released the following year. It is instructive to remember that this catalogue of disasters formed the background to the composition and première of the Fifth Symphony.

Friendship with Nikolai Zhilyaev

The composer GRIGORI FRIED here describes a meeting with Shostakovich at Zhilyaev's home shortly before his arrest:

I first got to know Shostakovich in 1937. Most Fridays I used to visit my teacher Nikolai Sergeyevich Zhilyaev at home. He was a composer, musicologist and an incredible personality. He had been a pupil of Tanyeev, and in those years was an excellent pianist. He was on friendly terms with Skryabin, Prokofiev and Myaskovsky amongst

21 *Ibid.*, p. 317.

others. Zhilyaev had a unique erudition and knew many languages. At the age of twenty he learnt Norwegian, and then set off to visit Grieg in Bergen. Grieg had always been his idol, and he stayed in his home for two weeks.

He counted amongst his friends Marshal Mikhail Tukhachevsky, who had in the past been his pupil. Shostakovich wrote: 'I met the wonderful musician Nikolai Sergeyevich Zhilyaev at Tukhachevsky's home. I consider him to be one of my teachers. Tukhachevsky had an enormous respect for Zhilyaev, but this did not stop them from quarrelling ferociously. The three of us often met together; usually I played them something new, and they would both listen very attentively, and then make their comments; their views were often diametrically opposed.'[22]

Once Zhilyaev came up to me in the Conservatoire, and said, while placing his massive hand on my shoulder and, as was his wont, exerting great downward pressure, 'Come along and see me today, it'll be worth your while.' That evening I arrived at the familiar communal flat at 15 Chistiye Prudy. Zhilyaev occupied a small room there which seemed all the more cramped because of the profusion of books and music. It also housed a grand piano, a simple wooden table and an iron bedstead on which we usually sat. On the wall hung a large portrait of Tukhachevsky.

'Mitya Shostakovich is about to come along,' Zhilyaev said. I was surprised and naturally delighted. Soon, at the appointed hour, Shostakovich arrived, absolute punctuality being one of his distinguishing features. He was on his way back from a journey in the south, and later that evening was to return to Leningrad. His thin body was always in motion; later in life his quick, angular movements were to acquire an exaggerated character. He was then thirty years old. He had brought his new Pushkin Romances and the first two movements of the still-unfinished Fifth Symphony to show Nikolai Sergeyevich. The manuscript of the score was written in Shostakovich's characteristic nervous hand, which was a testimony to the speed at which he worked. (Subsequently, I myself witnessed this amazing speed of composition, when he was composing the Preludes and Fugues for Piano at the House of Creativity at Ruza.) I did not understand the Pushkin

22 N. I. Koritsky, S. M. Mel'nik-Tukhachevsky and B. N. Chistov (eds), *Marshal Tukhachevsky: Memoirs of His Friends and Comrades in Arms*, p. 159.

Romances at all well, but the Symphony produced an enormous impression on me. Zhilyaev patted Shostakovich on the head with paternal tenderness, repeating almost inaudibly, 'Mitya, Mitya . . .'

When Dmitri Dmitriyevich left for the station, I asked Nikolai Sergeyevich about his impressions. He answered, "The Romances have still retained something of his "hooliganism". But the Symphony is quite wonderful. Mitya is a genius, a genius . . .' he repeated in a near-whisper.[23]

The consequences of friendship with Marshal Tukhachevsky
The composer VENYAMIN BASNER was never officially a composition student of Shostakovich's. However, he regarded him as his Teacher with a capital T, and received constant encouragement from him. Shostakovich will have appreciated Basner's warm and generous personality as well as his affectionate devotion. The two men went on to develop a close and lasting friendship. Here he gives an account of Shostakovich's near-arrest:

It is difficult to imagine with what fear and trembling we lived through the Stalinist reign of terror. Dmitri Dmitriyevich was in some ways broken by this terror. The events of 1936 and, in particular, the 1948 Decree took a heavy toll on him. One should therefore discount the articles and statements that Dmitri Dmitriyevich 'signed'; we knew that they were meaningless acts to him, but served him as a public shield. His many courageous actions were taken in private.

But Shostakovich did also show great courage, particularly during 1936. He would never have cancelled the performance of the Fourth Symphony if it had not been for the heavy-handed hints that were dropped by 'the bosses'. He had no choice in the matter. After all it wasn't only Dmitri Dmitriyevich that was threatened; it was insinuated that all the performers would live to regret the day if the performance of the symphony went ahead.

Dmitri Dmitriyevich suffered tremendously after the attacks on him in early 1936. He decided the best thing to do was to go away on his own. He had some concerts arranged in Odessa, Rostov-on-Don and the Caucasus; the purpose of the tour was largely to distract himself and to avoid seeing people.

An episode of great significance occurred the next year. I know that

23 Grigori Fried, *Music, Contacts and Destinies*, pp. 48, 49.

he never confided this incident to anybody, not even to his great friend Isaak Davydovich Glikman.

One day in the spring of 1937 he received an order to appear in such and such a room at a certain hour at the 'Big House', the headquarters of the NKVD.[24] Can you imagine how he suffered during the hours preceding this interview? He assumed that it was all over for him, yet he didn't know for sure why he had been summoned. He assumed that it was to do with the derogatory articles in *Pravda* criticizing *Lady Macbeth* and his ballet *The Limpid Stream*. He arrived at the appointed hour. An investigator called Zanchevsky received him, asked him politely to sit down and then opened the conversation. Zanchevsky started with ordinary everyday topics: 'What are you working at now? How are your professional affairs?' After a while he went on, 'Are you acquainted with Marshal Tukhachevsky?'

'Yes I know him,' Dmitri Dmitriyevich replied.

'Tell me how and when did you make his acquaintance?'

Dmitri Dmitriyevich told the investigator that Tukhachevsky was a great music lover and had been to many of his concerts. Once he came up to him to offer his congratulations and they had started talking. Tukhachevsky played the violin, and he had invited Shostakovich to his house and they had made music together. (Indeed Tukhachevsky also used to make violins as a hobby.)

'And who else was present at these meetings?' the investigator continued.

'Only members of the family circle.'

'Any politicians there, by chance?'

'No, no politicians.'

'And what did you talk about?'

'About music.'

'And politics?'

'No, there was never any talk of politics in my presence.'

'Now, I think you should try and shake your memory. It cannot be that you were at his home and that you did not talk about politics. For instance, the plot to assassinate Comrade Stalin? What did you hear about that?'

At this point Dmitri Dmitriyevich realized that his end was nigh. The investigation into Tukhachevsky had only just started, and as yet

24 NKVD: the acronyme for the People's Commissariat of Internal Affairs, or, in other words, the security organ, later renamed the KGB.

it was not public knowledge that the Marshal was in disgrace. Dmitri Dmitriyevich fell silent. The only thing he kept repeating was, 'No, there was never any such talk in my presence'; he refused to answer any more questions. Then the investigator said, 'All right, today is Saturday, and you can go now. But I only give you until Monday. By that day you will without fail remember everything. You must recall every detail of the discussion regarding the plot against Stalin of which you were a witness.'

Dmitri Dmitriyevich told me that it was impossible to imagine how terrible he felt over that weekend. He had his family to protect; his daughter Galya was only a small baby. He had to try and disguise his agitated state from all those around him, although he obviously told his wife Nina the whole story. He hurriedly destroyed many of his papers and put things in order. Then, on Monday, having prepared the bare necessities to take with him, he summoned up his courage and returned to the 'Big House'. Naturally, he assumed that this time he himself would be arrested.

As a matter of procedure, he had to announce his name to the soldier on duty before being granted admittance. The soldier looked at the list, but couldn't find his name. He asked Shostakovich, 'What is your business? Whom have you come to see?'

'Zanchevsky.'

Then came the surprise. The soldier said, 'You can go home. Zanchevsky isn't coming in today, so there is nobody to receive you.'

It turned out that over the weekend Zanchevsky himself had been arrested and imprisoned, and thereby Shostakovich was miraculously saved.

I think Dmitri Dmitriyevich only ever told this story to me, and that was many years after the event. This fact contributes to the various reasons why I am forced to believe that the memoirs attributed to Shostakovich in Solomon Volkov's *Testimony* are in fact a falsified account, as this story does not appear there. The book is full of stories that we all had heard many times from Dmitri Dmitriyevich's own lips. I personally don't believe that Dmitri Dmitriyevich himself told Volkov all these things, but that he heard them repeated by those in Shostakovich's inner circle. Surely Dmitri Dmitriyevich would have included this story if he was writing his candid memoirs.[25]

25 Venyamin Basner: recorded interview with EW.

The Fifth and Sixth Symphonies

It took Shostakovich a year to gather up his strength and start his Fifth Symphony (April 1937); once under way, work proceeded quickly and the score was finished by 20 July.

The triumphant reception of the Fifth Symphony at its première on 21 November 1937[26] was seen as a public vindication of the humiliating and unfair criticism Shostakovich had suffered. One of the audience, a certain A. N. Glumov, remembered how:

> many of the listeners started to rise automatically from their seats during the finale, one after the other. The music had a sort of electrical force. A thunderous ovation shook the columns of the white Philharmonic Hall, and Evgeny Mravinsky lifted the score high above his head, so as to show that it was not he, the conductor, or the orchestra who deserved this storm of applause, these shouts of 'bravo'; the success belonged to the creator of this work.[27]

Another musician, Yuri Yelagin, who attended a performance in Leningrad a month later,[28] recalled a similar audience reaction:

> As soon as the last chord of the finale had died away, the hall shuddered from applause and the audience got to its feet. It stood clapping for an incredibly long time, and the intensity of the applause never let up. Shostakovich came out to take a bow countless times: ten, twenty, maybe forty times. He walked to the centre of the stage, returned to the door at the side, and without so much as stopping had to come back immediately to take another bow.[29]

The authorities were, on the whole, willing to accept the Symphony as Shostakovich's offering to the shrine of socialist-realism. As such, the Fifth Symphony was immediately widely performed, and the composer's pardon appeared to be secured. Incidentally, the Symphony's subtitle, 'a Soviet artist's creative reply to just criticism', was coined by a journalist, and it was first used for the Moscow première in January 1938. Shostakovich never officially accepted it, although at the time he probably allowed it to remain in programmes as a seemingly expedient afterthought, which could be interpreted as an admission of his errors and gesture of repentance.

26 The Symphony formed part of a programme of new Soviet music, which also included Aram Khachaturian's Piano Concerto.
27 Khentova, *Shostakovich*, vol. I, p. 454.
28 Yelagin attended a performance on 21 December, not the world première as he states.
29 Yuri Yelagin, *The Taming of the Arts*, p. 221.

Shostakovich must have known that he was on a tightrope when it came to the critics' interpretation of his new work. The conductor Boris Khaikin recalled a conversation with the composer in late 1937:

Shostakovich told me: 'I finished the Fifth Symphony in the major and fortissimo. . . . It would be interesting to know what would have been said if I finished it pianissimo and in the minor?' Only later did I understand the full significance of these words, when I heard the Fourth Symphony, which does finish in the minor and pianissimo. But in 1937 nobody knew the Fourth Symphony.[30]

Between the Fourth and Fifth Symphonies, Shostakovich wrote only one serious and highly personal work, the Four Pushkin Romances Op. 46, which remained unperformed until 1940. For the rest, Shostakovich's output during this period was chiefly limited to music for the cinema. Apart from providing a useful source of income, film music gave Shostakovich an opportunity to prove his identification with Soviet themes of actual relevance.

But the great importance of the Pushkin Romances is evident in the way that the composer uses quotations from the first song, 'Rebirth', in the Finale of his Fifth Symphony. The four notes which set the first three words of that poem[31] form the kernel of the initial march theme, while a whole later section makes reference to the lilting accompaniment to the poem's final quatrain, 'Thus delusions fall off/ My tormented soul/ And it reveals to me visions/ Of my former pure days.'[32] Although self-quotation was to become an increasingly familiar feature of Shostakovich's work, its use in this symphony was totally arcane – insomuch as the Pushkin Romances were unpublished and unperformed at the time of the Fifth Symphony's performance. Perhaps the composer hoped that in the event of the Symphony's failure to rehabilitate his position, his private signals would be deciphered sometime in the future.

As it was, the success of the Fifth Symphony may have served to re-establish Shostakovich's public standing. But Shostakovich played safe and kept making public announcements that he was working on a grandiose symphony dedicated to Lenin.[33] His Sixth Symphony, completed in October

30 Boris Khaikin, *Discourses on Conducting*, p. 89.
31 'A barbarian painter with his somnolent brush/ Blackens the genius' painting,/ Slapping over it senselessly/ His own lawless picture.'
32 David Rabinovich (in *Dmitri Shostakovich, Composer*) was the first to recognize the significance of the quotation from the last quatrain of 'Rebirth'. Whereas it was Gerard McBurney in his most perceptive Radio 3 talk (January 1993) who first pointed out that the derivation of the opening march theme is a setting of the words 'Khudozhnik Varvar' (A Barbarian Painter).
33 In *Sovietskoye Iskusstvo*, of 20 November 1938, Shostakovich states that his Sixth Symphony will be devoted to Lenin's memory, which will consist of 'no less than four movements'. Here he stated his intention of using texts by Vladimir Mayakovsky, the

1939, was anything but such a work. And if audiences were expecting something along the lines of the Fifth, they were in for a surprise. This three-movement symphony did not follow the traditional symphonic layout: the long and static first movement, written in a spirit of introspection, gives way to demonic energy in the Scherzo, and an almost flippant hilarity in the Finale.

In reality Shostakovich was getting on with what he wanted. Increasingly, he was drawn to chamber music. The first in his magnificent cycle of quartets was composed in July 1938, a work of transparent purity and innocence. This was followed by the Piano Quintet (completed in September 1940), which achieved immediate popular success.

Shostakovich was an awkward figure for the authorities to pin down. In his music and life he remained a non-conformist, although outwardly his music corresponded to the precepts of Soviet 'socialist-realism'. As a prominent public figure, he had to justify his every creative step verbally and in print. Thus his candidature and election as a deputy to the Leningrad City Council in March 1939 were necessitated by the need to appear involved in 'community' work. This was undoubtedly a factor in his decision to accept a professorship at the Leningrad Conservatoire in the spring of 1937, and to increase his involvement in the administrative affairs of the Leningrad Branch of the Union of Composers.

ISAAK GLIKMAN recalls the successful premières of the Fifth and Sixth Symphonies:

Unlike the Fourth Symphony, the Fifth Symphony enjoyed a happy fate. The première took place on 21 November 1937 under Mravinsky's direction. This memorable occasion marked the beginning of a specta-cular career for the conductor, his ascent to the heights of Olympus.

Of course Dmitri Dmitriyevich did have enemies and maligners – and what genius does not have them? But I can vouch that the whole of musical Leningrad was intensely proud of the young Shostakovich, and displayed a passionate love and touching and tender affection for him. The entire audience demonstrated its enthusiastic delight. I was shaken by the fact that during the third movement, the Largo, very many people were in tears, both men and women.

Present at the concert was a famous philologist, Vladimir Fyodoro-vich Shishmarev, a fine musician and remarkable man. He was no lover of pompous epithets; he told me that he had only once before

Kazakh poet Dzhambul Dzhabayev, and the Dagestan poet Suleiman Stalsky. Subse-quent reports in Soviet newspapers (i.e. *Leningradskaya Pravda*, 28 August 1939, 1 and 20 January 1940; *Moskovskii Bolshevik*, 14 November 1940, etc.) state that the Seventh Symphony will be dedicated to Lenin's memory.

experienced such excitement at a concert, and seen such a triumph for a composer. That was at the première of Tchaikovsky's Sixth Symphony, conducted by the composer shortly before his death. This comparison from the lips of Shishmarev, well-known for his objectivity, utterly delighted me. Of course I was convinced that, unlike his great forebear, Shostakovich had many years of life ahead of him.

At one of the following [Leningrad] performances of the Fifth Symphony, something unprecedented happened. As soon as the last notes of the finale had died away, a group of Party Activists for Culture, Science and the Arts mounted the stage and proposed that a greetings telegram should be sent from the whole audience to Shostakovich, who was in Moscow for the première. I was not a witness to this event as I had gone to Moscow with Dmitri Dmitriyevich, but Ivan Sollertinsky told me the details of this incident, while recalling the analogous telegrams sent by the Moscow Arts Theatre Company to Chekhov in the Crimea.

The Moscow première was conducted by Alexander Gauk, and was received with the same thrilled excitement as in Leningrad. Looking around the Conservatoire Hall before the concert started, I recognized many of the capital's most famous personalities, whose photos were to be seen in the newspapers and magazines of those days. They were also in the thrall of the general enthusiasm.[34]

I should comment that Shostakovich was not affected by the success that hit him with the force of a hurricane. It did not turn his head or knock him off balance. He comported himself with a certain severity, and did not lose his habitual restraint and dignity. However, his face was more frequently lit up with smiles. In those days of heady success, Dmitri Dmitriyevich told me philosophically that in the musical world, just as in all other matters, success was relative and deceptive. In differing circumstances one should not fall victim either to gratification or to despair. We remembered how, during the rehearsals of the Fifth Symphony, certain people had doubts about the work; there was nothing extraordinary in their trepidation.

34 The violinist David Oistrakh wrote of the first Moscow performance: 'When [Gauk] put down the baton the hall broke out into thunderous applause. Everybody rose to their feet and rushed forward towards the stage, their ecstatic shouts blending into a single roar. I remember perfectly how Vladimir Ivanovich Nemirovich-Danchenko stood up, an imposingly majestic, white-haired figure, and approached the stage applauding' (V. A. Yusefovich, *David Oistrakh*, p. 312, quoted in Khentova, *Shostakovich*, vol. I, p. 460).

Only after the première did I tell Dmitri Dmitriyevich how some of the orchestral musicians warned me that the Symphony would definitely be torn to shreds by the critics, especially the first movement, which they considered to be clumsy and angular and too abstruse. This was said without a trace of malice on their part, but rather with regret. All my attempts to convince them otherwise were in vain. With hindsight I was able to laugh at these musicians' gloomy predictions. But when Dmitri Dmitriyevich heard what I told him, he was saddened and said that he didn't find anything funny here. And he was right.

And what is one to say about the orchestral musicians, if the professional critics could not make sense of the Fifth Symphony? For instance, the Largo, a jewel of inspired and pathetic lyricism, was variously misinterpreted. Once Dmitri Dmitriyevich thrust a magazine in front of me, pointing at a certain page. There I read that the Largo was permeated with 'an atmosphere of dejection and of the morgue'. Dmitri Dmitriyevich kept his silence about this famous critic's 'discovery', but his expression could not disguise his bewilderment. He read all kinds of absurdities about himself, all kinds of abuse, without ever entering into argument with his opponents. As the ancient Roman moralist Cato the Younger remarked, 'He who knows how to retain his silence when unjustly maligned is equal to the gods.' In this way Dmitri Dmitriyevich was god-like. Truly his silence was eloquent and often brought his noisy critics to a halt. . . .

The Sixth Symphony was finished in the summer of 1939 and scheduled for the opening of the 1939 autumn season of the Leningrad Philharmonic. It was impatiently awaited.

Long before the premiere Dmitri Dmitriyevich showed the Symphony to Ivan Sollertinsky and me. He played the Finale through twice, and, against his custom, praised it himself: 'It's the first time I ever wrote such a successful Finale. I think even the most fastidious critics won't have anything to pick at.' He said nothing about the first and second movements. But we spoke enthusiastically of the majestic beauty of the first movement, the Largo, the brilliance of the Scherzo and the overwhelming and intoxicating Finale. I immediately fell in love with it, and, with little regard for the composer's self-effacing modesty, I enthusiastically expounded, 'If Mozart and Rossini had lived in the twentieth century, and had collaborated in writing the finale of a symphony, it would have turned out like this. . . .'

The première of the Sixth Symphony took place on 5 November 1939 under Mravinsky's baton, and it enjoyed an enormous success. The Finale was encored – a rare occurrence at a première of a symphonic work – but the enthralling atmosphere that pervaded the hall at the premiere of the Fifth Symphony was lacking. That particular concert had been a unique event, even unrepeatable, you might say, had not Shostakovich gone on to write the Seventh, Eighth and Fourteenth Symphonies, which all had a similar force of inspired revelation.

For very grave reasons, Dmitri Dmitriyevich was unable to attend the Moscow première of the Sixth Symphony. He asked me to go in his stead to attend the rehearsals and the concert and to write to him with my impressions. I did so, remaining in Moscow for quite a protracted stay. I would write the letters in the evening and send them to Leningrad with somebody travelling by the night train, so that Dmitri Dmitriyevich already had them in his hands next morning.

Naturally, I hid from the composer the inevitable musicians' talk. With rare exceptions, it drove me to despair. Some musicians held that the conceited young composer, having dared to break with the tradition of the symphonic cycle, had produced a formless piece in three movements. Others maliciously implied that Shostakovich had locked himself away in an ivory tower, and no longer knew what was going on around him; the result was that the opening Largo was so dull and inert as to bring on a stupefied torpor. And a third group just laughed goodheartedly, saying that the Finale was nothing more than a depiction of a football match with its successes and reversals of fortune. This vulgar and trivialized opinion has unfortunately persisted and gained widespread credence.

However, all these discussions were swept aside at the première of this brilliant work, when it was played at the Grand Hall of the Conservatoire. But, strangely, when I returned to Leningrad, I could not rid myself of the memory of these conversations for a long time.

After the Sixth Symphony, which aroused so much censure, Shostakovich wrote his Piano Quintet in the spring of 1940; it was received with great acclaim by public and critics alike, and opinion was unanimous. Each performance by the wonderful Glazunov and Beethoven String Quartets with the composer at the piano were hailed as great events in the musical life of Leningrad and Moscow.[35]

---

35 D. Y. Mogilevsky, the cellist of the Glazunov Quartet, recalled their interpretation of the Piano Quintet with DDS: 'We, the string players, wanted to "sing", to play with more emotion. Shostakovich accentuated the constructive, motor elements and

According to his original plan, Shostakovich informed me that he intended to write a second string quartet. Why did he change his plan? Dmitri Dmitriyevich explained to me that it was governed not so much by artistic reasons as by practical ones. 'Do you know why I added the piano part to this quartet? So that I could have the chance to perform myself and thereby travel on concert tours. Now the 'Glazunovs' and the 'Beethovens' won't be able to do without me – and I'll get a chance to see the world.'

We both burst out laughing.

'Are you joking?' I asked.

Dmitri Dmitriyevich answered, 'Not in the slightest! You are an inveterate stay-at-home, while at heart I'm an inveterate traveller!' But from the expression on his face it was impossible to tell if he was joking or not. We had this conversation in the summer of the year preceding the war.[36]

The bureaucrats' interpretation of the Fifth Symphony

In the years preceding the Second World War, the composer MIKHAIL CHULAKI was director of the Leningrad Philharmonic. Chulaki moved in official circles, and as such in 1948 joined the persecutors of Shostakovich, criticizing him for Formalism. He was however respected as a competent composer and a good teacher. Undoubtedly, he was much more cultivated than the average party functionary or union official. In these reminiscences Chulaki recalls how Soviet bureaucrats assessed the Fifth Symphony:

In spring 1937 Shostakovich feverishly worked at his Fifth Symphony, which was to be an answer to the party criticism contained in the *Pravda* articles, 'Muddle Instead of Music' and 'Ballet Falsehood'. Everybody in the music world eagerly awaited the appearance of the new symphony, knowing the pressure, the critical circumstances, under which Shostakovich was writing it.

And at last the symphony was completed and performed by the Leningrad Philharmonic Orchestra, under the baton of Evgeny Mravinsky.

---

achieved his effect through clarity and the flow of the music. The emotional restraint of his playing led to a certain contradiction with the nature of strings. He demanded the minimum use of vibrato. The fast tempi excluded in themselves any possibility of emotional exaggeration and an "open" cantelena' (Khentova, *Shostakovich*, vol. I, p. 504).

36 Glikman, *Letters to a Friend*, pp. 13–15, 19–21.

It is difficult to convey the enthusiasm with which the Fifth Symphony was hailed by the general public. Mingled with genuine appreciation of this outstanding musical composition was a feeling of enormous relief that Shostakovich's new work possessed all the qualities essential to his being rehabilitated as a composer at this tense time. It was simple in language, was full of extended melodies, and what was particularly important, it finished with victorious fanfares whose 'outspoken' nature could not be called into doubt. In other words, it was accessible to professional listeners without making concessions to the pretensions of the general public – that same general public which so bombastically referred to itself as 'the People' (or took it upon itself to speak in the name of 'the People'). It was a real joy to observe how the 'general public' was indeed delighted at the appearance of a new work. It understood that at this moment the fate of a young talented composer was at stake, and it had come to love this composer not just as a musician, but as a man of crystal purity.

But there was another category of persons who had a particular allegiance to art – the bureaucratic stratum. They formulated the judgements of the authorities through writing official reports in which they tried to divine what the 'bosses'' opinions on the matter might be. And for God's sake, should you get it wrong, it could cost you your position. Their anxiety to be 'more Catholic than the Pope himself' was motivated by the wish to insure their own safety. They therefore assessed compositions by the quantity of dissonances and their deviations from the standard 'norms' of folk and classical music. (The 'norms' were established, and were therefore safe.) It was even possible in certain instances that some of the ruling comrades, not being specialists, might not have insisted on such categorical limitations had it not been for the 'authoritative' judgements of these 'artistic' bureaucrats, who were responsible for formulating the rulers' judgement and defining their taste. All this led to the appearance of such pseudo-musicological articles as 'Muddle Instead of Music' and 'Ballet Falsehood', and, what was worse, such official decrees as 'About the Film "The Great Life" ', or 'On Muradeli's Opera *The Great Friendship*'. These were to determine the development of Soviet art and literature for many years to come.

This bureaucratic stratum also attempted to interfere with the fate of Shostakovich's Fifth Symphony. As I have already said, the first performance had a tremendous, unparalleled success. The public ('the

People') filled the hall of the Leningrad Philharmonic to bursting, and at the end demonstrated its enthusiasm for over half an hour. Eventually, the conductor, Mravinsky, lifted the score in both hands and waved it in the air. This provoked an even greater ovation.

Nevertheless, this generally accepted gesture provoked extreme displeasure in official circles, since it was seen as an explicit comment in regard to the criticism expressed on the pages of the Party press.[37] Surely, the composer could not have 'restructured'[38] his outlook and created a 100 per cent Soviet symphony in such a short space of time? And what is more, no official opinion on the symphony had yet been formulated. So what did this mean – a demonstration?[39]

Immediately two high-up officials from the committee responsible for the arts, V. N. Surin and B. M. Yarustovsky,[40] were sent to Leningrad. They were present at one of the next performances of the symphony. Their brief was to find out how it was that the concert

37 'The chairman of the Leningrad branch of the Union of Composers, I. Dunayevsky, wrote to the governing commission of that institution, warning against the dangers of excessive success, in a letter written in dreadful 'bureaucratese' dated 29 January 1938: 'The beating of drums and blowing of trumpets that heralds the composer [Shostakovich] and his new work drowns the healthy – or at least justified – sentiments of doubt and negative criticism, which even the most talented work must provoke. . . . The brilliant mastery of the Fifth Symphony . . . does not preclude the fact it does not by any means display all the healthy symptoms for the development of Soviet Symphonic Music' (TsGALI Archive, F. 2048, op. 1, ed Khr. 160).

38 The Russian word used ('perestroilsya') of course refers to the concept of Stalinist 'Perestroika'. When Mikhail Gorbachev more recently coined the expression, he gave it different connotations. In this instance, the implication is of repentance for errors, and the wish to be 'restructured' with Party guidance.

39 Alexander Gauk, who gave the first Moscow performance of the Symphony, also attended the première in Leningrad. He returned to Moscow immediately to conduct a rehearsal next morning: '. . . Shatilov, the director of the Musical Department of the Repertoire Committee was in attendance. I heard him recounting to another official his version of the Symphony's Leningrad premiere. He belittled its enormous success, saying that it had been a put-up job arranged by Shostakovich's Moscow friends, who had gone up to Leningrad for this very purpose. At this point I interrupted and said that I too had been at the concert, and that six or seven-odd people from Moscow could hardly have been capable of inciting the 2,500-odd Leningraders present' (Gauk, 'Creative Contacts', in Gauk, Glezer and Milstein, *Alexander Gauk*, p. 129).

40 Surin and Yarustovsky, in their capacity as Party officials, acquired some notoriety for the harm they brought to Soviet music. Their hounding of Shostakovich was repaid by the composer when he wrote *Rayok*. In the pseudo-preface, he distorts their names to Srulin and Yavustovsky, both of which thereby assume lavatory connotations. Another story about the latter used to delight Shostakovich. Yarustovsky, the author of a tendentious biography of Stravinsky, met his subject when he returned to Russia in 1962. Stravinsky refused to shake his hand, but proffered his walking stick instead.

organizers had managed to inspire such a loud and demonstrative success. Yarustovsky in particular was most assiduous. After the concert, standing next to Surin in the choir stalls, having just personally witnessed Shostakovich's unheard-of triumph, he made a constant stream of snide remarks, shouting to make himself heard over the noise in the hall: 'Just look, all the concert-goers have been hand-picked one by one. These are not normal concert-goers. The Symphony's success has been most scandalously fabricated,' and so on in this manner. In vain did I, as director of the Philharmonic, try to convince the rabid official that the public attending the concert had bought tickets at the box office in the normal manner. Yarustovsky, supported by the silent Surin, remained implacable. Having made a negative assessment of this matter, the representatives of 'the centre' made off to Moscow.

For some time, echoes of the 'symphonic scandal' stirred up by the two officials continued to reach Leningrad. I had to write explanations, fill in questionnaires and prove the absence of a criminal. Then these passions died down. And in the meantime the symphony continued its life, and was widely performed, invariably exciting a lively and enthusiastic response from its audiences.

But what was to be done about the 'official opinion', which would at some point in time have to be formulated by the big-wigs so that it could filter downwards?

At last the Leningrad District Party Committee showed interest in the Symphony. Evidently the bosses had decided that for a start it was necessary to define their relation to this 'answer by Shostakovich to the criticism of his work by the Central Organs' (i.e. *Pravda*).[41] A special performance of the Symphony for the Leningrad Party Active should be arranged. In my capacity of director of the Leningrad Philharmonic, I was called up by the local committee responsible for the arts to see a certain Rabinovich, a very decisive, butch lady. I can reproduce the following dialogue exactly, as it is imprinted on my memory word for word. It took place in Rabinovich's study at Smolny.

'They tell me, Comrade Chulaki, that Shostakovich has written a good symphony.'

I affirmed that this was so.

'It must be shown to the Party Active.'

41 A reference to the subtitle ascribed to the Fifth Symphony.

I expressed my willingness to organize a performance.

'You will put together a concert programme and present it to us for approval.'

I went away to fulfill this task, and within twenty-four hours I reappeared in Rabinovich's study with the following proposal:

GLINKA
Overture and Arias from *Ruslan and Lyudmila*
TCHAIKOVSKY
Fantastic Overture *Francesca da Rimini*

Interval

SHOSTAKOVICH
Symphony No. Five

Rabinovich did not like it.

'What's all this, symphonies and more symphonies? No, Comrade Chulaki, this won't do. We need something for the People (?!). And besides, what's this 'Franchyoska'?' she asked looking at the proposal.

I tried to explain to her the nature of a Fantastic Overture, and added that it didn't last too long.

'Now then, Comrade Chulaki, you must play both symphonies in one part of the concert, both the 'Franchyoska' and the Shostakovich, and in the second part, you will play something for the People, for instance, a performance by the Red Army Ensemble . . .'

I interrupted her flow by explaining that the Ensemble was on tour in Paris. Her confusion was only momentary. '. . . or the Piatnitsky Choir.'

In a state of furious disbelief, I started to argue the principle on which I had constructed the programme. But soon I had to take recourse to a more devious form of argument; instead of proving the anti-artistic nature of mixing diverse genres, I started to give the practical reasons, which someone of Rabinovich's mentality was better able to grasp.

'You understand,' I insisted, 'that Shostakovich's symphony consists of four movements, each lasting about fifteen to eighteen minutes. 'Franchyoska' (I retained her pronunciation so as not to confuse her) 'is nearly the same length, just a little longer. Therefore the listener may get confused as to where one work ends and another begins.' (It turned out I was predicting the future as if through 'a crystal ball'.)

I could see that my argument was getting me nowhere. 'You see, one and a half hours of symphonic music without any interval is very tiring. The People won't stand for it.'

'Our People can put up with anything!' Rabinovich interrupted.

In the end I was forced to agree that the second half of the concert would be given over wholly to the Moisseyev Ensemble of Folk Dance. In this instance it seemed to me preferable to have dances than songs.

After confirming her approval of the whole programme, Rabinovich proceeded to the details. First of all she wanted to know which orchestra the Moisseyev troupe would dance to. I explained that they used their own special orchestra.

'And how many people are in their orchestra?' asked Rabinovich

'Forty-five', I answered.

'And in yours?'

'One hundred and five,' I answered, without guessing what she was driving at.

'No, Comrade Chulaki, this won't do, they will dance to your orchestra.' Rabinovich was adamant in her desire to secure the maximum quality of this concert she was organizing.

I had the answer this time: 'When our orchestra is in place on the stage they occupy all the space, and there will be no room left for the dancers.'

'Well, put your orchestra in the pit!'

Due to the absence of a 'pit' (!) in the Philharmonic's concert hall, the Ensemble of Folk Dance were eventually allowed to keep their own orchestra.

And so this memorable concert for the Leningrad Party Active took place with the programme dictated by the authorities.[42] As a postscript I should note that, after the extremely long first half, only about a quarter of the hall overcame their exhaustion and stayed on for the second half, the part designed 'for the People'.

Soon after these events, the official lady, Rabinovich, called the director of the Leningrad Union of Composers, Isaak Osipovich Dunayevsky to see her in the District Committee office. She asked him

---

42 It was after this concert that the Party formulated the Soviet definition of the Fifth Symphony as an 'optimistic tragedy' (Khentova, *Shostakovich*, vol. I, p. 455).

if he had known Comrade Chulaki for a long time. Having received an affirmative reply, she then put it to him directly: 'And don't you think that this Chulaki is a saboteur?' In those times the fashionable accusation of sabotage could lead to the most tragic consequences.

Many years later, as fate would have it, Shostakovich and I were being treated in the same clinic in Granovsky Street. We recalled that mammoth concert put together for 'the People' by the official lady, Rabinovich. Shostakovich told me how he had been walking up and down in a state of agitation in the so-called 'blue' foyer outside the hall. There you could hear everything perfectly. *Francesca da Rimini* was coming to an end, and his hour of agony was approaching. Just as the clapping started, after the end of the so-called 'Franchyoska', the writer X, the nicest and kindest of men, and one of the country's most well-loved and read writers, came running into the foyer.[43] Throwing himself on Shostakovich's neck with tears of gratitude in his eyes, he exclaimed, 'Mitya, I always knew that you were able to write beautiful and melodic music!' Shostakovich was so touched by this show of friendship and loyalty that, as he told me laughingly, 'I didn't have the heart to tell him that it was Tchaikovsky.'[44]

Authentic interpretation

Mravinsky, more than any other musician, is identified as the authentic interpreter of Shostakovich's symphonic music. Even when, in the early 1960s, relations between the two musicians deteriorated with Mravinsky's refusal to perform the Thirteenth Symphony, Shostakovich continued to acknowledge Mravinsky's supremacy in the interpretation of his music.

Here EVGENY MRAVINSKY writes of the preparation of the Fifth Symphony, thereby giving an insight into his own and the composer's working methods:

I had my first genuine contact with Shostakovich and his music in 1937, when I started working on his Fifth Symphony. Of course, I knew his work already, and I was also acquainted with him personally. After all we had both been students at the Leningrad Conservatoire in the 1920s. But although I was three years older than Dmitri Dmitriyevich, circumstances were such that I only succeeded in entering the Conservatoire in 1924, when he was already on the fifth-year course. Therefore we had hardly any social contact at that time.

43 This story refers to Mikhail Zoshchenko.
44 Mikhail Chulaki, 'Today I Will Talk about Shostakovich', pp. 190–2.

In the following years I would meet Dmitri Dmitriyevich at concerts and at the theatre, and I observed him at the rehearsals of his ballets *The Golden Age* and *Bolt* at the Kirov Theatre, where he was then working. But there was no close rapport between us, although we shared many friends in common, including Ivan Sollertinsky.

And then in 1937 I, a young conductor with no 'name', was given the task of preparing the newly-finished Fifth Symphony by Shostakovich for a concert dedicated to the 'Decade of Soviet Music'. Until this day I cannot understand how I dared to accept this proposal unhesitatingly, without giving it much thought. If it was put to me now, I would think it over for a long time, undergo many doubts, and finally perhaps refuse to undertake it.

For what was at stake was not only my own reputation, but, much more important, the future of a new and as yet unknown work by a composer whose *Lady Macbeth of Mtsensk* had recently been subjected to cruel attacks, and who had been forced to withdraw his Fourth Symphony from performance.

But I can be excused by reason of my youth and my ignorance of the ensuing difficulties and the responsibility which fell to my part. Besides which, I very much relied on the composer's help.

However, my first meeting with Shostakovich shattered my hopes. However many questions I put to him, I didn't succeed in eliciting anything from him. In the future I encountered this reticence in regard to his other compositions. This made his every meagre comment all the more valuable. In truth, the character of our perception of music differed greatly. I do not like to search for subjective, literary and concrete images in music which is not by nature programmatic, whereas Shostakovich very often explained his intentions with very specific images and associations. But one way or another, any remark on his own compositions that you can wrest from a composer is always of enormous value to a performer.

Initially I could get no information about the tempo indications in the Fifth Symphony. I then had recourse to cunning. During our work together I sat at the piano and deliberately took incorrect tempi. Dmitri Dmitriyevich got angry and stopped me, and showed me the required tempo. Soon he caught on to my tactic and started to give me some hints himself.

The tempi were soon fixed with metronome markings and transferred into the score. They were reproduced in the printed edition. But now, when I check them with recordings of performances, I realize that in many cases the metronome indications in the Fifth Symphony have proved to be incorrect, and the long life of this symphony has in itself brought about essential changes to the tempi that we marked down at that time.

(Incidentally, I suspect that it is precisely these incorrect tempi markings in the score that prevented Toscanini from realizing his intention to perform the Fifth Symphony. Evidently he could not accept the indicated tempi, but at the same time considered them to be authoritative, and did not dare deviate from them.)

Eventually our work on the Symphony reached a successful con-clusion. On 21 November 1937 the first performance took place in the Hall of the Leningrad Philharmonic. The work was received with enormous enthusiasm by the public. And the greatest reward for me were the lines written by the composer and printed a few months later after my winning the All-Union Competition for Conductors. Recal-ling our work on the Symphony, Shostakovich wrote that to start with he was frightened by the conductor's working method: 'It seemed to me that he was delving into too much detail, that he paid too much attention to the particular, and it seemed that this would spoil the overall plan, the general conception. Mravinsky subjected me to a real interrogation on every bar, on my every idea, demanding an answer to any doubts that had arisen in him. But by the fifth day of our collaboration, I understood that his method was undoubtedly correct. A conductor should not just sing like a nightingale.'

Always retaining a friendly manner, and with the same close rapport, but with no fewer difficulties, we worked together on all the following symphonies up to and including the Twelfth. . . .

Every time I start learning a new Shostakovich score with the orchestra, I am amazed by the detail with which he can hear the sound of his own music in his head. Everything has been heard in advance, lived through, thought out and calculated.

Over the many years of our collaboration, I only once ever made a suggestion to retouch a detail of orchestration. In the Eighth Sym-phony, where the daring of the orchestration matches the innovation of the music, there was one place in the second movement where the doubling of the woodwind by trumpet was called for, and similarly in the third movement by the horns. These changes were accepted by the composer, although not immediately, and have been incorporated into the printed edition of the score. But I have to repeat that this was exceptional. One could say that Shostakovich had perfect orchestral hearing. He heard everything in the orchestra as a unity and at the same time each instrument separately, both in his head and in the real sounding.

I remember a specific occasion. We were rehearsing the Eighth Symphony. In the first movement, not long before the general climax, there is an episode in which the cor anglais has to go up quite high into the second octave. The cor anglais is doubled by the oboes and the cellos and is almost indistinguishable in the general sound of the orchestra. Taking this into consideration, the player decided to put his part down an octave, so as to save his lip for the important long solo which comes straight after the climax. It was almost impossible to hear the cor anglais amidst the overpowering noise of the orchestra and to expose the player's little trick. But suddenly, from behind me in the stalls, Shostakovich's voice rang out, 'Why is the cor anglais playing an octave down?' We were all stunned. The orchestra stopped playing, and after a second of complete silence applause broke out.[45]

Shostakovich – the complete professional

In 1939 Shostakovich turned his attention to re-orchestrating Mussorgsky's opera *Boris Godunov*. He was no doubt inspired by the centenary celebration of the composer's birth that year, when there was ample opportunity to hear much of Mussorgsky's music. On completion of the score, Shostakovich gave his only manuscript to Samosud at the Bolshoi Theatre, which had announced its intention of staging a new version. Samosud hesitated about committing himself to Shostakovich's version, but he also didn't return the manuscript to Shostakovich, thereby holding up the composer's negotiations with the Leningrad Kirov Theatre. Ultimately, Shostakovich had to wait twenty years to hear his orchestration of *Boris Godunov*, which was eventually staged at the Kirov in 1959.

In 1958 Shostakovich was commissioned to re-orchestrate and edit Mussorgsky's other masterpiece, *Khovanshchina*, for a film version. A few years previously he had already orchestrated a few scenes from this opera at the request of the conductor, Boris Haikin. In 1962 Shostakovich turned again to Mussorgsky, making an orchestral version of 'The Songs and Dances of Death'.

45 Evgeny Mravinsky, 'Thirty Years of Shostakovich's Music', in L. V. Danilevich, *Dmitri Shostakovich*, pp. 111, 112–14.

Shostakovich believed that a composer should be able to use his skills in any sphere. Apart from the music he wrote for film and theatre, he demonstrated his eclectic tastes by writing two Jazz Suites and making numerous orchestral transcriptions of other composers' works. Whether dealing with a popular American song, as in 'Tahiti Trot' (1927), or pre-classical music, as in the 'Two Pieces by Scarlatti' (1928), or in a miniature by Johann Strauss, Shostakovich left his unmistakable imprint on the orchestral colouring of all his transcriptions, injecting zest and sparkle into the original scores. The orchestration of J. Strauss's 'Pleasure Train Polka' from *Vergnugungzug* was commissioned for a production of *The Gypsy Baron* at the Leningrad Maly Theatre (MALEGOT) in 1940.

Although BORIS KHAIKIN was best known as an opera conductor, he frequently performed Shostakovich's symphonic music. He himself disclaimed any close friendship with the composer, but he obviously enjoyed his trust as a man and musician of integrity:

I myself never conducted a Shostakovich opera, but on two occasions I had a working contact with him in the theatre.

The first of these was in 1940, when we put on *The Gypsy Baron* at MALEGOT. The production promised to be most interesting; it aimed at widening the musical potential of operetta by using a large first-rate orchestra and a mixed choir. Wonderful costumes were to be created by the best designers. In the third act, the director, A. Feona, had decided to add a choreographed number, a polka, to be performed by the talented caricature actress G. Isayeva. I went to the library of the Leningrad Philharmonic to choose a Strauss polka. The librarian said, 'Take your pick, we have about two hundred of them.' Leaving aside the most famous and popular, I found a very attractive polka, and the librarian had a copy made. Soon a very charming dance had been choreographed by B. Fenster.

Then the time came to try out the polka with orchestra. I went again to the Philharmonic Library to collect the orchestral parts, but it transpired that there weren't any, they only had the piano score, two pages of it including the obligatory 'da capo'. What were we to do? I phoned Shostakovich and told him of my problem. He immediately came to the rescue. I showed him the polka, and incidentally pointed out to him an augmented seventh which I considered to be a misprint, as the edition seemed a very dubious one. Shostakovich said nothing, took the piano score away, and in parting said, 'I'll be back tomorrow.'

The next day he appeared with the score completed. I glanced at it and what I saw was a composition by Shostakovich. He had not changed a single note of Strauss's. He had left the dubious chord as it was, and did not consider it to be a misprint. And I too soon stopped regarding the chord as something out of place, but rather saw that it added a special charm. And Shostakovich's orchestration, as always, was so distinctive that the brilliant Johann Strauss paled beside him.

. . . Even in such a trifle as this Strauss 'polka', whose orchestration will have only occupied a couple of hours of Shostakovich's time, it was simply amazing how everything just came to life. The orchestral musicians broke into smiles playing it; and these were the same musicians who had played in the premieres of *The Nose* and *Lady Macbeth*.

. . .

In 1951/52 I conducted *Khovanshchina* in a production at the Leningrad Kirov Theatre. . . . The opera was put on in Rimsky-Korsakov's version. At the time there was no other in existence, but there were some additional scenes added to the first and second acts which had been taken from Mussorgsky's sketches restored by Pavel Lamm. These had also been staged at the Bolshoi Theatre but no orchestral score existed there. . . . I decided for old times' sake to ask Shostakovich to help out; this was before he started work on his own edition of *Khovanshchina*. It was my luck that Dmitri Dmitriyevich happened to be in Leningrad. Again he reacted with great interest and promptly came to see me. I had all the new scenes copied and ready for him. He looked at them with great attention and said, 'Yes, here it will stay like that,' pointing at the semi-breves and minims in the accompaniment. Evidently he wanted to warn me that he wasn't going to add any figuration or fantastical decoration in the score. Not that I had expected it. In addition we decided to include in the first act that scene of utmost brilliance, the destruction of the scribe's booth, which had not been part of the Bolshoi Theatre's production. I anticipated with immense pleasure the performance of this episode in Shostakovich's orchestration. A few days later Shostakovich came to see me with the score completed. As far as I remember now the musical text remained untouched and was orchestrated as only Shostakovich knew how. If in *The Gypsy Baron* Johann Strauss paled beside him, here it was Rimsky-Korsakov who suffered the comparison.

I do not know if it was this occasion which provided the stimulus for Dmitri Dmitriyevich to take on the new edition and orchestration of

Khovanshchina as a whole. Perhaps he had conceived the idea even earlier, or again perhaps it arose later.[46]

A holiday interlude

Shostakovich talked of himself as an 'inveterate traveller'. He certainly enjoyed performing concerts as an excuse for travel, and also did much of his composing away from home. Before the War he and Nina made regular trips to the Crimea, usually in the spring. And as Shostakovich disliked heat, he preferred to spend the summer months in the cooler climes of North Russia. ALISA SHEBALINA recalls one of the spring trips to the Crimea:

In May 1941, shortly before the start of the War, I took my fourteen-year-old son Nikolai to the Crimea to recuperate after a bout of pneumonia. We were allocated a place in the sanatorium that was attached to the House of Scientists in Gaspra. We arrived there to discover Mitya and Nina staying in the next door room.[47] It was a very cold May that year, and Mitya sat in his room freezing, while Nina went off trekking in the mountains with two artists who were paying court to her; apparently she also found them attractive.[48] Mitya was bored and lonely, and often came to see me in my room. If it wasn't raining, he would sometimes go down to the volleyball pitch and climb up on the referee's platform to umpire matches between teams made up of holiday-makers. This was one of his occupations. One day he came to my room, saying how cold it was and how we must find a way to keep warm. 'You know, Ronya once treated me to a wonderful vodka at your dacha in Nikolina Gora made from juniper berries. Do you know that I've just seen some juniper bushes in the park near the sports ground? Let's go and collect some berries and marinate them in vodka – we need some *vodichka* to warm ourselves up.'

Indeed, our rooms had no heating in them as they were only intended for summer accommodation. We went down to the park and found the bushes with the most enormous berries hanging on them, as large as cherries. We collected several handfuls and came back to Mitya's room. There was an empty water carafe on the piano; he

46 Khaikin, *Discourses on Conducting*, pp. 90, 91, 92.
47 The Shostakoviches stayed in Gaspra from 28 April to 20 May.
48 Unlike her husband, whose interest in sport was that of a spectator, Nina Shostakovich was an excellent sportswoman. She was a good skier and enjoyed mountaineering.

sprinkled a couple of fistfuls of berries into it and said, 'I'm off to buy the vodka.' He went to the nearby village and soon he was back with his acquisition, which he poured over the berries.

'Do you think it'll be ready soon? How long does it need to stand? I'm dying to try it,' he kept asking me persistently.

I said that it wouldn't need that long, seeing that he had used so many berries. We waited a while, and then he decided to taste the brew. He poured some into a large tea glass. I said, 'You go ahead and taste it.' Mitya took a gulp, and the next moment I saw him clutch his throat, while his eyes stood out on stalks. 'What's wrong with you?' 'Try it and you'll see.' I only ventured a sniff, but that was enough to make me reel. It was pure turps. For some reason those berries were resinated and incredibly powerful. Mitya put the carafe back on the piano and said, 'Never mind, I'll invite those artist friends of Nina's for a drink. That'll teach them!'

A few days later we left Gaspra together. The Shostakoviches were given a car, so Mitya and Nina gave us a lift to the station at Simferopol, thirty-odd kilometres away. We had hardly started the journey when one of the tyres went flat. The driver, who was a local, changed the wheel and we drove off. We travelled a certain distance and then another of the tyres went flat. This time there was no spare. Our driver turned around and asked us, 'Have you got a five kopeck coin?' Mitya produced one and the driver promptly used it to block the puncture, then pumped air into the tyre, and off we drove. Shortly afterwards another tyre went flat, and the same operation was repeated with another five kopeck coin. I don't remember how many coins we had, three or four, but we barely managed to reach Simferopol, as the tyres kept puncturing. Just as we were arriving at the main square in front of the station, we had yet another puncture. Mitya had run out of coins, and there was no time to spare, the train was due to depart in a few minutes. The driver drove on with the flat tyre, the wheel clattering and rattling across the cobblestones. We arrived on the platform just as the final bell rang. We just managed to get ourselves and our baggage on the train as it pulled out of the station. Mitya was in a state of terrible nervous anxiety – it was unbearable to witness his agitation. I suffered terribly on his behalf. Nina sat in the compartment calmly, apparently indifferent to the situation, while Mitya paced up and down the train corridor for a long time, pale as a sheet and unable to calm down.

He and Nina were travelling in 'international' (first) class, whereas Nikolai and I were in ordinary second class. In the evening Mitya came down to invite us to join them in their compartment. As we were sitting and talking, Miron Polyakin, the wonderful violinist, suddenly walked into the compartment. He was on his way back to Moscow after a concert tour. He produced a large box of chocolates which he offered all round. Then Polyakin and Mitya started playing cards. I didn't join in as I personally have always hated cards and the attendant quarrels and noise. That evening Mitya was on a winning streak; now it was Polyakin's turn to get nervous. He was in such a terrible state that after a while I turned to Mitya and said, 'Don't torture him any more, stop playing.' So the party broke up for the evening, and we all went off to our various compartments.

In the morning we arrived in Moscow. I looked out of the window to see if anyone had come to meet us, and what did I see? Mitya was rushing up and down the platform like a wounded animal, his face as white as a sheet. I realized that something had happened. I told Nikolai to wait and rushed out on to the platform. I asked Mitya what the matter was. 'Polyakin is dead.' It turned out that he had been sleeping in the compartment next to Mitya's. When the train reached Moscow that morning, Polyakin appeared to be still asleep. The person sharing the compartment called the attendant. They then discovered that he was dead.

The worst lay ahead. Mitya was hauled off to the Militia Point at the station. The carriage attendant had testified that the deceased had been sitting in Mitya's compartment all through the previous evening, and therefore Mitya had been the last person to see him. The implications were frightening. They kept Shostakovich there for one and a half hours interrogating him. I decided to go and help. When necessary I am quite good at making a point. I decided that assertive tactics were called for. 'Are you out of your mind? Do you realize to whom you are talking? This is the People's Artist, our most famous composer, Shostakovich. If you need any details about him I can give them to you. He is resident in Leningrad at such and such an address; just now he is coming to stay at our home in Moscow.'

I eventually succeeded in getting them to release Mitya. He was unbelievably upset, firstly because of the shock of Polyakin's death, and secondly because he had been suspected of playing some part in it. We went back to our flat, and Mitya stayed on with us for a few days. He had been anxious to hurry back to Moscow for a football match, so I said to Vissarion, 'Take Mitya along, he needs to unwind,' and they went off together to the match. Such was the end of that awful day.[49]

49 Alisa Shebalina: recorded interview with EW.

CHAPTER FOUR

The War Years – A Respite

The Seventh Symphony

Hitler's troops invaded the Soviet Union on 22 June 1941. Two years previously the Soviet–Nazi pact had been signed, and Stalin had thereby lulled the country into a false sense of security. The Soviet Union found itself unprepared for war, and the German armies made spectacular advances into Soviet territory. By the end of August they had encircled Leningrad; the ensuing siege lasted for seventeen months.

The outbreak of war found Shostakovich examining the graduation composition students at the Leningrad Conservatoire. His immediate preoccupation was to be of use to his country, but his poor eyesight prevented him from enlisting in any kind of active service or home guard. Nevertheless, he did his stint as an auxiliary of the Fire Brigade, and a photograph that shows him standing on the Conservatoire roof and holding a fire hose appeared in all the national newspapers. In early July, before turning to serious composition, he made arrangements of songs for the concert brigades to perform at the Front. He was then able to settle down to write his Seventh Symphony. The massive first movement was written in less than six weeks, the next two movements in under three weeks.

Shostakovich was evacuated from Leningrad with his family on 1 October; he took with him three completed movements of the Seventh Symphony. Aram Khachaturian described how 'Shostakovich played the Seventh Symphony through to me at my flat on Miusskaya Street, straight after getting off the plane from besieged Leningrad. Shostakovich was very agitated and said, "Forgive me, will you, if this reminds you of Ravel's *Bolero*." '[1] Two months earlier Isaak Glikman noted an almost identical reaction from the composer after playing through the first movement: 'Idle critics will no doubt reproach me for imitating Ravel's *Bolero*. Well, let them, for this is how I hear the war.'[2]

The Shostakovich family spent the next two weeks in Moscow before being

---

1 Sofiya Khentova, 'Shostakovich and Khachaturian: They Were Drawn Together by 1948', p. 10.
2 Isaak Glikman, *Letters to a Friend: Dmitri Shostakovich to Isaak Glikman*, p. 22.

allocated places on a train heading for Sverdlovsk. But they decided to stop in Kuibyshev rather than continue what turned out to be a nightmarish journey further east.

The Seventh Symphony was completed on 27 December 1941 in Kuibyshev, and first triumphantly performed there by the Bolshoi Theatre Orchestra under Samuel Samosud on 5 March 1942. By the end of the month, Samosud gave the first performances in Moscow. Performances in other Soviet cities soon followed, and the score was sent abroad. Henry Wood performed the Seventh Symphony in London on 22 June, and and a month later Toscanini gave the American premiere in New York.

The performance of the symphony in besieged Leningrad on 13 August by the Radio Orchestra under Karl Eliasberg was an event of the greatest significance. The Leningrad Philharmonic had been evacuated to Novosibirsk, and the Radio Orchestra was the only remaining ensemble in the city. A hungry and miserably cold winter under siege had reduced it to a mere fourteen players. Eliasberg summoned up all his energy to organize reinforcements; retired musicians were ferreted out, and soldiers with musical training were released from the army units defending Leningrad. Eliasberg himself, weak from hunger, fainted one day on the long walk home in the transportless city. To help restore his strength, the authorities provided the conductor with a bicycle, living quarters in the vicinity of the Philharmonic hall, a telephone and food supplies. Likewise, the orchestral musicians were issued with extra rations.

The creation of an enormous orchestra in these conditions seemed hardly credible. Their performance of the Seventh Symphony was a feat that fired the imagination of the outside world. The playwright Alexander Kron summed up the Leningraders' reaction to the music: 'People who no longer knew how to shed tears of sorrow and misery now cried from sheer joy.'[3] Never before had music acquired such heroic force or become such an effective symbol of patriotism. Shostakovich's fame was at its zenith.

The journey to evacuation

On 16 October 1941 Shostakovich and his family left Moscow on the long journey to safety along with a large group of other composers, artists and writers. Karen Khachaturian, the young composer, who had come to see off his uncle Aram Khachaturian, was a witness to the chaotic scenes of departure:

3 Alexander Kron, 'The Seventh, Leningrad Symphony', *Komsomolskaya Pravda*, 9 August 1967.

I suddenly caught sight of Dmitri Dmitriyevich on the platform. He looked completely bereft. He was holding a sewing machine in one hand and a children's potty in the other, while his wife Nina Vasilyevna stood beside the children and a mountain of stuff. I helped them load their things on to the train. Later, when I made my way home from the station, I was struck by the number of howling dogs roaming the snowy streets, having been abandoned by their owners.[4]

Amongst Shostakovich's fellow-passengers was Nikolai Sokolov, the artist from the collective 'Kukrysniki'. Sokolov, like Shostakovich, chose to stay in Kuibyshev, the seat of government in evacuation. Various institutions like the Bolshoi Theatre and the editorial offices of *Pravda* and *Krokodil* were now based there, as well as the diplomatic corps. NIKOLAI SOKOLOV describes the train journey and the first days in Kuibyshev:

We arrived at ten o'clock in the morning at Kazan Station. It was chock-a-block with evacuees, and the square in front of it was also black with people. Inside the station writers, painters, musicians and artists from the Bolshoi and Vakhtangov Theatres were huddled beside their belongings, trying to make themselves comfortable. The loudspeakers continuously blared announcements. At last we were informed that the train was ready to board. People put on their rucksacks, picked up their bundles and suitcases, and made for the platform, which was enveloped in terrible darkness. Underfoot the snow was wet and squelchy. Everybody pushed and shoved at each other with their belongings. We had a single ticket for a whole group of artists, which got torn in half in the crush. We had been designated carriage no. 7; a queue had formed outside it. Somebody stood guarding the door, blocking the entrance, shouting, 'This carriage is only for the Bolshoi Theatre.' I recognized the tall silhouette loudly arguing with this man as Dmitri Kabalevsky: 'Allow Shostakovich and his children to pass!'

At last Shostakovich was allowed through, and we pressed in behind his children, slowly squeezing our way into the bowels of the carriage. The whole carriage was bursting with people and their possessions. On my back I carried a rucksack with its emergency minimum: one change of underwear, a shirt, socks, a candle, some bread and tins of food. I also had a little sketch album and a pencil. In my coat pocket I closely guarded a slim album of V. Serov's

4 Recorded interview with EW.

illustrations to Krylov's Fables. I never parted company from it, even during the air alerts.

After forty minutes the train set off. It travelled very slowly. Near Ryazan it picked up speed; the town was being bombed by the Fascists. Some of us were on our feet throughout the night. As morning dawned we started to scrutinize each other in the light. Some people gave up their seats to those who had been standing. In other words, people started to soften and show kindness.

Members of the Bolshoi, ballerinas, composers and artists, were travelling in this carriage. Amongst the other composers travelling were Aram Khachaturian, Tikhon Khrennikov, Dmitri Kabalevsky and Vissarion Shebalin. Some of the lady 'artistes' were crying. Others were sighing over the possessions they had left behind.

It took seven days and nights to reach Kuibyshev. The train kept stopping, and would stand still for long stretches of time, often for hours on end. Trains filled with military units were travelling to Moscow. Lines of fuel trucks stretched along the tracks. On the station platforms, tanks and ammunition stood under tarpaulins. Whole factories were being evacuated from Moscow together with their machinery stock; the workers and their families all travelled in the goods wagons.

A wet snow, almost rain, was falling. By morning it had frozen. People got out of the train and wandered by the carriages. They looked to each other for reassurance. It was difficult to get any sleep, there was nowhere to rest. The women lay down at night, the men by day – and in rota at that.

I saw Shostakovich getting out at the stations to fetch boiling water; he washed his crockery with snow at the side of the carriage. He was travelling in an old worn suit, and his legs got soaked through. He desperately looked for his things and got very upset at not finding them. It turned out that his two suitcases with all his personal possessions and the children's things had been left behind at the station in Moscow. I gave him some new socks.

'Thank you! How noble of you,' he said.

Somebody else gave him a shirt, and so on. He took these things very shyly and thanked everybody in a state of great agitation.

The further we got from Moscow, the more difficult it became to decide where to stop off. Sverdlovsk? Novosibirsk? Tashkent? Alma-Alta? Kazan? Kuibyshev?

We noisily argued as to which was the best destination.

I observed people telling Shostakovich what to do; some persuaded him to go to Kuibyshev, others to Tashkent, and a third group suggested some other destination.

'Dmitri Dmitriyevich, why take the children to Kuibyshev? Everybody is going there. There will be problems with food supplies, and the accommodation situation will be worse still. Why not continue to Tashkent? Things will be better there, and the children will be happier. It's not for nothing that people say, "Tashkent has bread in abundance!" '

'Yes . . . yes . . .' Shostakovich replied uncertainly.

'No! Why drag the children on another eight days' journey to Tashkent, when tomorrow he'll already be in Kuibyshev itself?' protested another adviser, a composer.

'But in Tashkent he won't go hungry; but what awaits him in Kuibyshev?' the first persisted.

'What d'you mean? Khrapchenko's in Kuibyshev, and he'll fix everything! Right? After all, he is the chairman of the Committee for Arts! It's his duty!'

'Possibly, possibly,' Dmitri Dmitriyevich muttered finally.

'And nothetheless, in your place I would go to Tashkent.'

'But, Dmitri Dmitriyevich, how about . . .'

But poor Shostakovich had long stopped listening to the 'how about' suggestions, and picked his way back through packages and bundles to his children.

Nevertheless Shostakovich decided on Kuibyshev. When we arrived his family and I were given space on a classroom floor in one of the town schools. It was already full of artists from the Bolshoi Theatre who had arrived previously, and they were now joined by the new arrivals. The numbers kept swelling. Each classroom housed eighteen people with their goods and chattels. At the entrance one was confronted by thirty-six pairs of galoshes, which bore evidence of the profuse autumn mud from the market square just outside the school!

We slept on the floor, without any mattress, on whatever could be adapted for the purpose, all squeezed one against the other. In the morning we all crowded down the long corridor to the washrooms. Sturdy men whistling excerpts from operatic arias – People's Artists, soloists, musicians – all kept coming out of the door which had pinned to it a notice, 'Boys'. You never knew whom you might meet here!

Shostakovich and I were given access to the Bolshoi Theatre commissariat, where we were issued a daily ration of butter, sweets, bread and salami.

I remember that on the day of our arrival I met Shostakovich in the corridor carrying the rations he had just received. With quick steps he hurried off to the classroom, a bright smile lighting up his face.

In a week's time the Shostakoviches were given a room to themselves, furnished and with beds. Dmitri Dmitriyevich was also provided with a grand piano.

Once I dropped in on him, and we started chatting about life.

'You know, Nikolai Alexandrovich,' Shostakovich addressed me, nervously drumming on the table with his beautiful fingers, 'when I got into that dark carriage with the children in Moscow I felt that I was in paradise! But by the seventh day of the journey I felt that I was in hell. When we were settled in the classroom of the school, and what's more given a carpet and surrounded by suitcases, I again felt myself to be in paradise; but after three days I was fed up; in these circumstances you can't get undressed, being surrounded by a mass of strangers. I again perceived this as hell. And then we were allocated this room to ourselves, with decent conditions. . . . And what do you think? Shortly, I felt that I must have a piano. I was given a piano. Everything seemed just fine, and I thought to myself again, "This is paradise." But now I notice how inconvenient it is to work in a single room; the children are rowdy and disturb me. Yet they have every right to be noisy, they are only children, but unfortunately I can't work.'

Soon I attended a house-warming party; the Shostakoviches had been given a separate three-roomed flat, which even had its own bathroom.[5]

Knowing that I was living in a miserable room, Mitya (as he asked me to call him) suggested that I move into their flat, but I refused, thanking him for his concern.

Once I asked Mitya what stopped him from completing his Seventh Symphony. He replied: 'You know, as soon as I got on that train, something snapped inside me . . . I can't compose just now, knowing how many people are losing their lives.'

But as soon as the news came through that the Fascists had been

5 The Shostakoviches moved to 2a Vilonovskaya Street on 11 March 1942. Before that they were living in a two-room flat at 140 Frunze Street.

smashed outside Moscow, he sat down to compose in a burst of energy and excitement. He finished the Symphony in something less than two weeks.

I wanted to do a drawing of Shostakovich but did not wish to disturb him while composing. I was against his posing specially for me, although he suggested it himself.

In the evenings, Shostakovich liked playing cards with the pianist Lev Oborin and others. He got so caught up in the game that he was oblivious to everything else. This was perfect for me, and I made several sketches in black wash and pencil, and I also made a series of caricatures. Mitya, by the way, liked caricatures and was never offended by them.[6]

Evacuation in Kuibyshev

The following two articles by Flora Litvinova and her sister-in-law Tatyana Litvinova describe Shostakovich's life in evacuation in Kuibyshev.

The Shostakovich family soon settled down to a life of apparent normality, their home becoming a focal meeting point for the intelligentsia. As soon as the most basic working conditions were available, Shostakovich got back to composing. During the year and a half he was based in the city, the composer finished the Seventh Symphony, wrote forty-five minutes of music for his unfinished opera *The Gamblers* (based on Gogol's play), composed the 'Six Romances on Verses by English Poets' Op. 62 (later the title was corrected to 'British Poets') and in February 1943 started his Second Piano Sonata Op. 61 (dedicated to the memory of his teacher, Leonid Nikolayev).

Flora Litvinova describes her youth in the 1930s as being infected with Shostakovich's music, notably with that of 'The Song of the Counterplan', and later *Lady Macbeth (Katerina Izmailova)*, which she attended many times as a schoolgirl. She met her future husband Mikhail (Misha) Litvinov and his sister Tatyana (Tanya) at the first Moscow performance of Shostakovich's Fifth Symphony. Flora and Misha were married in May 1939, and their son Pavel (Pavlik) was born the following summer.

Misha and Tanya were born in London, children of the Bolshevik and political refugee Maxim Maximovich Litvinov and the English writer Ivy Low. The Litvinovs soon returned to the newly formed Soviet Union, where Maxim became Commissar for Foreign Affairs, a position he held until May 1939, when he was dismissed in disgrace and replaced by Vyacheslav Molotov. When war with Germany broke out, Maxim Litvinov was called back into

6 Nikolai Sokolov, 'Sketches from Memory', pp. 54–7.

government service, and in November 1941 he was appointed Soviet ambassador in Washington.

Flora and Misha, both university students, dug trenches outside Smolensk
in the summer of 1941. Then Misha was called up and sent on a course at the
Aviation Academy in Sverdlovsk. In October 1941 Maxim Litvinov arranged
for the evacuation of Flora, Pavlik and Tanya to Kuibyshev. Shortly after their
arrival Tanya met and married the sculptor Ilya Lvovich Slonim.

It was in Kuibyshev that the Shostakovich family befriended the Litvinovs,
and they saw each other regularly during this period. Flora was adopted by
Nina Shostakovich as a youthful protégé and accepted into the family on equal
terms. She was treated by Dmitri Shostakovich with fatherly concern. Here
FLORA LITVINOVA describes the Shostakovich family during three months of
evacuation in Kuibyshev:

One day the painter Pyotr Villiams's wife Anusya, an amusing petite
actress, informed us that Shostakovich had arrived in town from
besieged Leningrad with his wife and two small children. She added
that the Shostakoviches had arrived virtually without any luggage.
Dmitri Dmitriyevich had been promised that his mother and sister
would be flown out on the next plane; but they hadn't come. In the
meanwhile, the family was living in the Grand Hotel, formerly a
merchants' hotel, which now housed the elite of the evacuees. Their
children lacked essential clothing. So I got out the suitcase specially
prepared by my mother with clothing and footwear for my son 'to
grow into'. Timidly, I suggested that Anusya should pass this on to
the Shostakoviches.

The next day Dmitri Dmitriyevich's wife, Nina Vasilyevna, came to
see us. I took to her immediately, with her high clear forehead, light
brown eyes and bright even features. She was of medium height and
well-proportioned in build. Without wasting words, she thanked me
for my help. I was only too happy to have been able to do something
for Shostakovich's children.

'You know, we're going to be neighbours. We've been given the flat
below yours on the first floor,' she told me. And indeed, in a few days'
time a grand piano was brought to the building, then four very spartan
iron bedsteads, several Viennese chairs, a desk and a dining table, and
a crudely built cupboard. And once, when looking out of our
bathroom window, which overlooked the courtyard, my heartbeat
quickened as I saw Dmitri Dmitriyevich walking across it, holding by
the hand a five-year-old girl with plaits and an even younger boy in a

black fur coat. Nina Vasilyevna came to our door to ask to borrow a hammer. I offered to feed them.

'Thank you, but we lunched for the last time at the Grand Hotel. However, maybe something for the children, as they ate very poorly.'

The next day Nina and I managed to buy some bowls, saucepans, cut crystal glasses and mugs in the department store. Soon such things were to disappear from the shops, and the department store became the distributing point for rationed goods and things sold to special order. Before long I was on Christian-name terms with Nina, but we used the formal 'you', and never changed to 'thou', even when we became very close friends. During the move, Nina introduced me to Dmitri Dmitriyevich. He also hastened to thank me in his refined St Petersburg manner.

They were given a two-room flat. They put the piano and desk in one room, and they all slept in the other one. I immediately became attached to Nina, sensing her sympathetic attitude towards me. My feelings for her were akin to the adulation one might develop for an elder school friend. Although it existed at a subconscious level, it undoubtedly sprung from my awareness that she was Shostakovich's chosen one.

We often went out for walks with Galya and Maxim and my young son Pavlik in the public gardens that flanked the banks of the Volga. If Nina was busy I would take the children on my own.

My life was radically changed by the Shostakoviches' arrival. I knew that Dmitri Dmitriyevich was finishing his Seventh Symphony. At that time I jotted down some notes: 'Today (2 December) I heard the piano and some obviously Shostakovich-like sounds. I got terribly excited. I stood next to the radiator so that I could hear better, but soon this music stopped, and then I heard Galya and Maxim singing "Three soldiers in a tank, three jolly friends". What a travesty – Shostakovich's children singing *that*.'

Not long afterwards Nina invited me to a party one evening. I was all of a flurry. Pavlik obviously sensed my agitation as he stubbornly refused to go to sleep. Although I sang to him and told him stories, he only quietened down very late. I nearly wept hearing the cheerful voices and sounds of the piano from the flat below. At last Pavlik was asleep, and I rushed downstairs. The party was in full swing. Some friends had brought some sausages, and there was vodka and an improvised vinaigrette salad. People were chattering away noisily.

Dmitri Dmitriyevich was sitting at the piano with the round-faced Lev Oborin, whom I had previously only seen on the concert platform. He was a wonderful musician and pianist. When I walked in they were playing a song from some operetta called *Pupsik* – 'Being called Pupsik has never riled,/ That was my name when I was a child.' An atmosphere of gaiety reigned – people sang along, they drank and laughed. I felt embarrassed and overwhelmed by it all – that *those* fingers in this house should be playing such trash! Oborin approached me and we were introduced. We sat down at the table and he poured me some vodka, which I drank for the first time. I found it unpleasant to taste, but immediately a feeling of warmth spread inside me, and I got tipsy. I felt light-headed and gay, and my anxious fears evaporated, together with my sense of timid adulation. I realized that I was a pleasing young woman. Dmitri Dmitriyevich continued to play some funny songs, laughing and jesting. There in the small corridor people were dancing. I particularly remember Shostakovich singing some romance in a deliberate parody with an unnaturally low voice which he accompanied with heart-tugging chords: 'The chrysanthemums have faded in the garden, but love still blossoms in my sick heart.' He also sung 'A Pair of Bays'[7] with Oborin at the piano. Sometimes they stopped to drink and chat, eat something and have a coffee. (At that time you could still get coffee beans in Kuibyshev, despite the fact that by then all other produce had disappeared from the shops. Food was obtained through special passes and rationing cards.)

Every now and then I ran upstairs to check on Pavlik, but he slept through it all soundly. One time, as I came downstairs, I heard some infectiously jolly piano, obviously by Shostakovich. 'It's the Gallop from *The Bedbug*[8] – it turned out an excellent piece,' Dmitri Dmitriyevich said, and repeated the phrase over and over. I observed with delight a Shostakovich new to me: not the tense, inhibited, nervous St Petersburg type, but a witty, gay and jocular young man (he was then thirty-six years old). He twirled Nina round in some sort of 'pas', then the ballerina Muda Petrova, a lovely girl whom the Shostakoviches were very fond of.

It was on that occasion that I realized that not only was Shostakovich the great composer, the satirist and tragedian, the creator of the Fifth

7 These were romances sung by his father.
8 Shostakovich enjoyed the rhyming phrase, while pronouncing these words with an added 'soft' sign: 'Gallyop iz Klyopa'.

Symphony and *Lady Macbeth*, but at heart he was carefree, gay, kind and homely – not at all the frightening figure I had imagined!

'And, d'you know, today I finally finished my Seventh,' Dmitri Dmitriyevich suddenly announced quietly. That evening was altogether extraordinary and incredible, and I felt how lucky I was to be an accomplice to something so wonderful. In my diary entry for 28 December I wrote: 'How happy I am! I spent the whole evening at the Shostakoviches. Dmitri Dmitriyevich has finished his Seventh, and we will hear it soon. What a marvellous, merry evening it was.'

Soon afterwards Dmitri Dmitriyevich finished the piano score of the Seventh Symphony and invited the conductor Samosud and various friends to hear it. Nina asked me along as well. I was so excited that I cannot remember who was present on that occasion, except for Lev Orborin, the harpist Vera Dulova[9] and the Villiams couple. So much has already been said about the Symphony; I can only add that I was overwhelmed by the impression made on me by the famous theme in the first movement. Initially just playful, primitive, if unserious, it is gradually transformed into something terrifying, acquiring a force capable of obliterating everything in its path. Mechanical and relentless, it possesses a seemingly unlimited and inexorable strength.

When Dmitri Dmitriyevich finished playing, everybody rushed up to him. He was exhausted and highly agitated. Everybody spoke at once, about this theme, Fascism, the war and victory. Someone immediately dubbed the theme 'rat-like'. Samosud declared that the Symphony was destined to have a great success, and that it would be performed all the world over. I went to put Pavlik to bed, and then, very late, I looked in on the Shostakoviches when they were alone. We drank tea, and the talk again revolved naturally around the Symphony. Dmitri Dmitriyevich said pensively, 'Of course – Fascism. But music, real music, can never be literally tied to a theme. National

9 Vera Dulova remembered another occasion when Shostakovich played through the Symphony at their home in the presence of her husband Baturin, Lev Oborin and the conductor Melik-Pashayev, who, it was hoped, would perform the Symphony: 'There were five of us gathered. Shostakovich started playing, and Oborin, following the score, filled in some of the upper voices. During the performance the telephone rang. Samosud, who lived in the flat underneath us, had heard the music and asked if he could join us. The Symphony made a shattering impression on him, and he immediately took the score away, announcing that he would start rehearsals the next day. Our chief conductor was firm and resolute. Shostakovich said that Samosud would guarantee him lots of rehearsals' (Sofiya Khentova, *Shostakovich: Life and Work*, vol. II, p. 51.

Socialism is not the only form of Fascism; this music is about all forms of terror, slavery, the bondage of the spirit.' Later on, when Dmitri Dmitriyevich got used to me and started to trust me, he told me straight out that the Seventh Symphony, and for that matter the Fifth as well, were not just about Fascism, but about our system, or any form of totalitarian regime.

By February 1942 the rehearsals of the Symphony were in full swing. Samosud worked intensively with the orchestra, aware of the immense responsibility invested in him as its first performer. Everybody realized that a performance of the Symphony in the middle of the war would be an event of political significance. Its creator was refuting the axiom that 'When cannons fire, the Muses remain silent.' Nina took me to one of the last rehearsals. We sat in the choir-stalls. They were rehearsing the third movement, the Largo, with its palpable lyrical purity in the marvellous duet between flute and bassoon. Here were absent those tempestuous emotions which Shostakovich so disliked both in real life and in art. Samosud stopped the orchestra twice, and they repeated some sections. Dmitri Dmitriyevich made a remark to the flautist. Then they played right through the movement without stopping. After the rehearsal was over, the musicians noisily put their instruments away, wiping the sweat off their brows, while a flock of ballerinas in tricot came running out of a rehearsal room and fluttered through the hall.

On 5 March 1942, the day of the first performance, I dropped in at the Shostakoviches' flat to get my ticket from Nina. Dmitri Dmitriyevich was in a state of feverish agitation and tension. He ran from one room to the other, mumbling a greeting in passing. He looked pale and was clenching his fists. I glanced at Nina. She seemed very calm and collected. When she saw me out of the door, she divulged: 'He's always like this on the day of a first performance. He gets terribly wrought up. He is frightened it'll be a flop.' Later I observed, and Dmitri Dmitriyevich himself acknowledged, that before a première of his work, he felt physically ill to the point of nausea.

There was an enormous gathering in the theatre where the concert was held. All sorts of famous people were there, as well as high-ranking officials and the diplomatic corps. I was there with my sister-in-law Tanya and her husband Slonim. Nina and Dmitri Dmitriyevich came up to me. 'You know,' Shostakovich said, 'I signed programmes for each of the orchestral musicians. I think that maybe each one of them will try a little harder, and the performance will benefit as a result.' Needless to say, the Symphony had a phenomenal success.

There were always a lot of people at the Shostakovich house – friends, acquaintances, and strangers who just dropped by casually. Basically our life centred round the Information Bureau in anticipation of news bulletins. In one sense we lived without a daily routine, yet our everyday lives were very difficult. People wandered around, calling on each other with and without good cause; they came if they were acquaintances, or merely the acquaintances of acquaintances.

Of those who were closest to Dmitri Dmitriyevich I remember Lev Oborin and the Villiams couple, the harpist Vera Dulova and her husband, the baritone Alexander Baturin, who had given the first performance of the Pushkin Romances.[10] At various times Ilya Ehrenburg and his wife would appear, then the cinema director Trauberg, the young conductor Kirill Kondrashin, and some attractive young girls. A certain Soso[11] attached himself to the family; he worked in provisions and used to hand out supplements to the Shostakoviches. It was more than likely that he was performing other functions as well. Suspecting that he worked as an informer, Nina somehow managed to get rid of him.

Their life in evacuation was very different from their former life in Leningrad, where they had a large flat and servants. Here they lived in very cramped style. In the kitchen there was a small stove which they heated only at lunchtime. In the mornings Dmitri Dmitriyevich ran across the courtyard with two kettles to fetch boiling water from a large urn. I myself rarely went out for this purpose, but once, going into the boiler room, I saw Dmitri Dmitriyevich standing next to a ballerina. She simpered, 'You know, Dmitri Dmitriyevich, I saw in the

10 At a concert on 8 December 1940 at the Moscow Polytechnic museum, where Shostakovich also performed his new Piano Quintet with the Beethoven Quartet. Then, in Kuibyshev, on 4 November, 1942, Baturin gave the first performance of Three Romances on Texts by Burns (from the Six Romances Op. 62. written during 1942).
11 In a letter to Isaak Glikman dated 4 January 1942, DDS writes: 'My friend Soso Begiashvili considers that the fourth movement [of the Seventh Symphony] doesn't manifest enough optimism . . . My friend Soso Begiashvili is a marvellous person, but he can't boast of much intelligence, so one should regard his comments critically.' When DDS referred to someone as 'a marvellous person' in a letter, the recipient knew that this meant the opposite, and in fact this coded information was a warning to steer clear of him. Soso Begiashvili had studied music at the Leningrad Conservatoire, but in the pre-war period made his career in administration (Glikman, Letters to a Friend, p. 35).

papers that they are putting forward candidates for the Stalin Prize. But in our ballet world there is no one worthy of it, I would say . . .' Shostakovich was a member of the Prize Selection Committee. He mumbled a reply, and when we went out into the courtyard, he said with a wry grimace 'I, of course, should have replied, "What do you mean, no one worthy of the Prize? And you? Your incomparable performance of Dulcinea in *Don Quixote*?" ' For Shostakovich nothing was more hateful than vulgar banality.

I grew steadily closer to Nina. She told me about her background and her parents, her father Vasili Vasiliyevich Varzar, an old-world St Petersburg engineer, and her mother, Sofiya Mikhailovna, an astronomer. Nina had graduated from the Bestuzhev Courses, the first institution of women's higher education in Russia. Nina liked to talk of her childhood. She was one of three sisters, all of them interesting and talented girls, and well-known throughout St Petersburg. Nina had studied at a music school and played the piano well. Once when I was with her, she sat down at the piano and I saw that she was indeed a good pianist. 'But now I don't play at all, Mitya does not tolerate amateurs.' She had also studied in ballet school, but by the time she was sixteen her figure had become robust and lost its gracefulness. So she gave up the ballet school and, as she had a bent for the sciences, enrolled as a student of physics and maths at Leningrad University. In those years the Leningrad School of Physics was at its zenith, and her co-students were Lev Landau, Georgi Gamov, Abraam Alikhanov and Artyom Alikhanyan, all of whom were to become world-class physicists. She told me proudly that even in such company she had proved to be one of the best students. After graduating from university she worked with success in a physics laboratory.

It was at that time that she met Shostakovich, and before long they married. 'No sooner would I arrive at the laboratory and get started on an experiment than Mitya would ring up and ask when I would get home. He didn't like me being away from home, and he still doesn't. Even when he goes out himself, he likes to know that we're all at home, so that he returns to find his wife and children waiting for him.' She also told me how they had quarrelled and got divorced, officially at that. However, they soon realized that they couldn't live without one another, and they got married again. This time she changed her name to Shostakovich, and soon, in 1936, she gave birth to Galya, and two years later to Maxim. Nina was very ready to talk, but she never overstepped those bounds of friendship to recount sordid gossip, their private quarrels or flirtations; nor did she feel the need to prove herself right. She was a very strong, self-confident woman, and I don't believe that she ever required such a relationship with a friend. As we lived at such close quarters, we saw each other daily, and their family life was open for me to see; Nina was its stay and support.

Dmitri Dmitriyevich by nature was completely incapable of saying 'No' to anybody. He did indeed help a lot of people, but he also fell victim to many unscrupulous and brazen types. He himself used to say, 'When somebody starts pestering me, I have only one thought in mind – get rid of him as quickly as possible, and to achieve that I am prepared to sign anything!' That autumn a well-known playwright, who also dabbled in operatic librettos, made his appearance at their house. He importuned Shostakovich to write the music to his new operetta libretto: 'With my text, the relevance of its themes, and your music, Dmitri Dmitriyevich, our total success is assured – the operetta will be put on all round the Soviet Union.' Dmitri Dmitriyevich politely kept the libretto saying, 'I will read it and better acquaint myself with it.' But he had no intention of writing an operetta. The writer kept coming to the house to exercise his powers of persuasion. At last Nina said to Dmitri Dmitriyevich when he was off to Moscow for a few days, 'Mitya, don't worry, I'll deal with him.' Nina laughingly showed me the note that Shostakovich had left, listing chores for her to do in his absence; it included, 'Tell the librettist to f— off.' Nina got rid of him, even if she didn't have to use those very words. He didn't come to the house again, although he left his masterpiece behind. In fact it came in very useful since there was a shortage of toilet paper at that time.

The affronted author, and others who were similarly insulted by Nina, did not like her. When Shostakovich turned down somebody's request it was attributed to her influence, and it was said that she controlled his affairs. Sometimes Nina had to fend people off in no uncertain terms; then her face became impenetrable, and I was amazed at the cruelty of her words and her unswerving will. I think that in this Nina was only fulfilling Dmitri Dmitriyevich's wishes, as he himself was incapable of such behaviour. To those close to the family Nina was welcoming and showed her concern without gushing words or excess of sentiment. This is how she behaved towards our family.

And I myself was in love with the whole Shostakovich family. My attitude to Shostakovich was imbued by my perception of his genius. I was full of delighted admiration for Nina, her exceptional and independent mind, her decisive yet calm character, and I was much influenced by her. Without my husband and my university friends, I felt unsure of myself, as if I had lost my bearings.

Dmitri Dmitriyevich got used to me and was welcoming towards me, although we spoke little, and then more or less casually. He worked incessantly, and additionally he was busy with business matters and had to attend many official meetings. Probably the first time that he paid much attention to me was when, on a certain occasion, Mahler was mentioned in the conversation. I told him that my father-in-law Maxim Litvinov had brought us the record of *The Song of the Earth* at Misha's request. Mahler's music was not performed in the Soviet Union then, as it was dubbed as 'formalist'. Moscow musicians came specially to our home to listen to this recording. Suddenly Dmitri Dmitriyevich asked me, 'How many movements does it have?'

'Five. But you knew that anyway,' I replied, offended that he was checking on me. 'I have the record here, you can listen to it if you like.'

'You've brought your records? I'll take a look at what you've got,' he said, and we went upstairs to our flat. Dmitri Dmitriyevich selected Mozart's *Jupiter* Symphony from my records and put it on the wind-up gramophone. We listened to it sitting on Pavlik's small mattress.

From that time on he was much more attentive towards me, and became a sort of mentor to me. I was the youngest of their friends. He did not like me to be flirtatious. Once, seeing me sitting too close to a man on the sofa (which also served as a bed), Dmitri Dmitriyevich called me over: 'Flora, what kind of behaviour is that? He will have every reason to believe that you are provoking him. Surely, that's not what you have in mind?' But I was young, slightly tipsy, and I had no idea what I wanted or didn't want.

Dmitri Dmitriyevich also tried to encourage me to study and to better myself. Soon after we had listened to the *Jupiter* Symphony, I told him that it was one of Misha's and my favourite pieces. 'Yes, yes, it is an amazing symphony – it has that absolute crystal clarity, whereby you hear the most complex polyphony, and all the themes weaving in and out in the last movement.' And he started to recall it minutely, using many technical terms.

I listened, but did not understand much of what he was saying. 'Dmitri Dmitriyevich, you know, I never studied music theory, so I simply listen because I like it. Sometimes I do try to follow the music with attention, but I lose the thread, and then I just go into a dream . . .'

'My goodness, Flora, you're just lazy and have no curiosity. You know all this can and should be studied and understood. Get hold of a textbook and study. Although it requires effort, it is an attainable objective for you. You can have no idea how much I got from Professor Steinberg at the Conservatoire. He was very severe, and made great demands on me. We analyzed all the classics of musical literature. Many students didn't like his classes, saying that he was dry and pedantic, and that he analyzed the harmony to death. But I myself liked to analyze works thoroughly even before I went to the Conservatoire, to find out how things are written. It in no way hinders one's pleasure in listening; on the contrary, it enhances it. Now they listen to recorded music at Conservatoire classes, and that too is very important, as a way of getting to know the interpretation of great conductors and soloists. But nevertheless it cannot be compared to playing through these same symphonies on the piano, and studying scores with one's eyes. Music made with your own hands, and heard in your own head and heart is incomparably the best.'

I should add that once Dmitri Dmitriyevich said that no single performance of his works sounded as perfectly as it did in his own head.

Shostakovich adored Gogol and Chekhov; he knew these authors incredibly well. He read unbelievably fast. Once, seeing him quickly leafing through page after page of a book he held in his hands, I asked him, 'Are you just glancing through it?'

'No, Flora. You see I am used to reading scores, and I therefore also read very fast.'

He obviously possessed that rare gift of being able to read a whole page in a glance.

Chekhov he not only admired as a writer, but as a personality. 'His father was a chandler, but Chekhov educated himself by reading, by hard work, and a constant struggle with himself.' And he also said: 'And after all, he didn't like women, he saw straight through them, and hated all that was vulgar in them.' He recalled the stories 'The Wife', 'Ariadne' and 'The Grasshopper'. He had no good words for

Olga Knipper-Chekhov, although he spoke about this later, when her correspondence with Chekhov had been published:

'Can you imagine what Chekhov's reaction would have been had he known that his wife would expose him in front of honest people? She should be ashamed of herself, publishing all the intimate details of their life together. Chekhov was right in nicknaming her the Aktrissu-lya.[12] What these actresses won't do to please the public! And the public doesn't want to be fed on bread alone, they want to know whether the goings on in famous people's bedrooms are the same as in everybody else's, or whether they get up to something more inventive . . .'

But in the long run it was Gogol whom Dmitri Dmitriyevich loved better than all other Russian writers. In my opinion it is Gogol who is closest to Shostakovich by nature of his talent and his personality. His penetrating insight, his qualities of sarcasm, anger and the grotesque were combined with an infinite and aching compassion for people. On my rough bookshelf were the few books I had brought with me: six volumes of Pushkin, *War and Peace*, some Tyutchev poems, Pasternak's translations, Burns's poems translated by Marshak, Gogol's stories and two volumes of Chekhov.

Dmitri Dmitriyevich borrowed them all. Once, while reading Gogol's 'The Portrait' out loud, he said, 'When I was writing my opera *The Nose*, I kept thinking that I must write something on 'The Portrait', on the theme of the artist who sells himself.'

I then said that I had never heard *The Nose*.

'In that case, let's go,' he said, and we went downstairs, and Dmitri Dmitriyevich sat at the piano and sang long extracts from his opera.

I well remember the police officer's aria, and Kovalyov's conversation with the Nose set against the background of the Liturgy. Nina and the children also listened and laughed in delight.

'So you see what kind of music I produced, it turned out really funny? It's great stuff, don't you think?' Dmitri Dmitriyevich, usually busy, immersed in work and full of cares, was now calm and happy.

And this happened so rarely. It's true that he got merry on a glass of vodka, but then he would usually soon go and sleep it off. But now we enjoyed a long, calm and wonderful evening. (My diary entry for that

---

12 A disparaging diminutive for an actress.

January day reads: 'Today Dmitri Dmitriyevich played *The Nose* for us. How lucky I am! What good fortune!')

Shostakovich's amazing memory is much talked about. He knew all of classical music by heart, and much contemporary music as well. It was enough for him to look at a score or to listen to a work once for him to remember it. One day the conversation touched on his pupil, X. I had somehow heard an aria from X.'s opera before the war, and I mentioned that I felt this piece was 'pseudo-pathétique'. Dmitri Dmitriyevich ran to the piano and instantly reproduced the aria, singing, 'Oh, mother!' His musical memory was a delight to us all, but on the other hand it didn't surprise me, because it seemed like a natural extension of his genius. But I was flabbergasted by the way he knew and remembered literature.

Once I was lamenting the fact that I didn't bring Gogol's *Dead Souls* with me; Dmitri Dmitriyevich immediately starting quoting long extracts from it, about the carriage, the speculation as to whether the wheel would arrive in Moscow. Laughing, he recited the piece about Chichikov dressing for the evening party:

' "He ordered that the washing utensils be brought up to him, and for an excessively long time he scrubbed both his cheeks with soap, inflating them from inside his mouth with his tongue; then taking the towel from the shoulders of the inn servant, he dried his fleshy face on all sides, starting from behind his ears, snorting first a couple of times in the servant's face." Can you imagine this scene? Here I would use a bassoon, trumpet and drum. Then when he puts on his shirt-front, "having plucked two hairs from his nose", I'd use the piccolo – "and naturally found himself wearing a dress-coat the colour of whortle-berries shot with shiny lights." '

Then, when Gogol goes on to describe the Governor's party, Dmitri Dmitriyevich gave each personage a musical characterisation.

In general one might say that sounds of any kind played an important role in Dmitri Dmitriyevich's musical memory. An example of this is the story of how he was travelling by train with a companion. They were drinking vodka, and outside their compartment they noticed a legless war invalid on a wooden platform with wheels, singing some smutty limerick. The man rolled up to them and Dmitri Dmitriyevich poured him out a glass of vodka. They clinked glasses: 'And do you know, because there was a different amount of vodka in each glass, our clinking produced a triad.'

Towards the spring of 1942, Dmitri Dmitriyevich's mother, Sofiya Vasilyevna arrived in Kuibyshev from Leningrad, together with his sister Mariya Dmitriyevna and her son Mitya.[13] Shostakovich had been terribly worried and nervous about their fate. While getting ready to go and meet them, he kept repeating, 'How will they be, I wonder what state they'll be in?' They arrived extremely emaciated after living through several months of the siege.

'You know, once we ate a cat,' Mariya Dmitriyevna told us. 'Of course, I didn't tell Mother or little Mitya.'

Dmitri Dmitriyevich was churned up by their stories of the cold and the hunger, the deaths of their friends and near and dear ones. He nervously drummed his fingers against the table. Soon Nina's parents also arrived, and the nanny who had looked after her and then looked after Galya and Maxim; she was to stay with the family until her death.[14]

Sofiya Vasilyevna was very sociable and had many friends and acquaintances. Outwardly Dmitri Dmitriyevich was very like his mother. They were drawn together by a great friendship and love. But one was aware of the undercurrents in the relationship between Nina and Sofiya Vasilyevna. The latter always spoke well of Nina, but she did so in such a way as to make her praise sound like a reproach. And despite the fact that Dmitri Dmitriyevich was always a respectful and loving son, their relationship was complex.

In spring 1942 the Shostakoviches moved to a larger flat. There was now space to work and for the children. We saw less of each other. Dmitri Dmitriyevich went away to Moscow and other towns, and Nina often went with him. In the autumn of 1942 I first heard from Nina that they had decided to move to Moscow. They loved Leningrad, the city where they had spent their childhood, youth and first years of family life. But so many of their friends had perished, some in the war, while others had been arrested. It had been a difficult decision for them, but

13 Dmitri (Mitya) Frederiks.
14 In a letter to Vissarion Shebalin from Moscow dated 1 April 1942, Shostakovich wrote: 'A few hours before I left for Moscow, my mother, my sister Marusya, and my nephew Mitya arrived. They were followed just after my departure by my parents-in-law. My father-in-law looks awful. Mama looks pretty bad too. The others are in a passable state. Now I have the task of feeding them and restoring them to health.' (Alexei Nikolayev, 'Letters to Shebalin', p. 81.)

By early June the family of ten expanded to thirteen with the arrival in Kuibyshev of Nina's sister with her husband and child.

they realized that they would find it easier to live and work in Moscow.

To begin with the Shostakoviches stayed at the 'Moscow' Hotel, where they had a two-room suite with a grand piano in it. When I managed to make a short visit to Moscow in 1943, I went to see them there. Dmitri Dmitriyevich was working. We went for a meal in the restaurant, where we were fed quite decently. Dmitri Dmitriyevich was very silent, gloomy and preoccupied by something. After lunch, he said to me, 'Why have you put on such bright lipstick? It doesn't suit you at all.'

In the spring of 1943 my father-in-law Maxim Litvinov was called back from Washington to Moscow. Molotov had been to the USA on a visit a few months earlier, and the mutual antagonism of the two men had deepened. Maxim Maximovich understood that he was now to be retired. He was allotted a large flat for all the family in the large, grey, inhospitable block overlooking the Moscow River, the 'House on the Embankment'.[15] We arrived there from Kuibyshev in the autumn of 1943.

In the spring the Shostakoviches had been allocated their first Moscow home, a dark apartment on Kirov Street that looked out on the courtyard. But they were delighted with it, as it meant that at last they could establish a normal family life in their own home. I remember the house-warming party. They had moved in a grand piano, a table, some boxes. There were no plates or cutlery. Everybody was very tired but happy. Some tins of food were opened and a bottle of vodka. We drank out of mugs or cut-crystal glasses, and ate directly out of the tins, breaking the bread in our hands. The Shostakoviches stayed in that flat until 1947.[16],[17]

Tatyana (Tanya) Litvinova and her husband Ilya Slonim shared their Kuibyshev apartment with their sister-in-law Flora. But they tended to keep their lives apart from hers, and established very different relationships than hers with their neighbours, the Shostakoviches. Tanya and Ilya enjoyed a kind of 'man-to-man' contact with Dmitri Dmitriyevich and were not close to the

15 This house became famous as the subject and title of Yuri Trifonov's story (later staged as a play at the TAGANKA Theatre).
16 Shostakovich arrived in Moscow on 3 March 1943. Later that month he settled into flat no. 48 at 21 Kirov Street. He was soon joined by his family.
17 Flora Litvinova, article commissioned for this book.

1 Zoya, Mitya and Mariya at Irinovka, 1911

2 Sofiya Vasilyevna, 1878–1955

3 Dmitri Boleslavovich Shostakovich,
1875–1922

4   Ignati Glyasser's class, 1918. Boris Lossky kneeling bottom left, Glyasser
seated middle with Mariya at right of him

5   DDS, 1925

6   Alexander Glazunov, Director of
    the Petrograd and Leningrad
    Conservatoires

7   Boleslav Yavorsky, late 1920s

8   DDS with Ivan Sollertinsky and Nina Varzar, 1932

9   After the première of *Bolt*, 1931. DDS middle front holding Tatyana
Vecheslava; bottom right, smoking, Ivan Sollertinsky; next to each other, top
right, Mariya Shostakovich and Galina Ulanova; top left, seated, third along,
Mikhail Zoskoker

10   DDS playing the Piano Quintet with Glazunov Quartet, who gave the
Leningrad première in December 1940

11   *Left*, Portrait by Nikolai Sokolov of DDS playing cards, Kuibishev, 1941

12   Ilya Slonim's bust of DDS sculpted in late 1941/early 1942, Kuibishev

13   At a football match, 1940s

14   Aram Khachaturian and his wife with DDS looking at the score to the
Eighth Symphony, 1943

15 DDS at Ivanovo with Galya and Nina, early 1940s

16 DDS, 1943

17   *Left*, Flora Litvinova.   18   DDS with students, late 1940s. Karen
Khachaturian far left

19   DDS with Maxim and Galya, late 1940s

rest of the family. Here TATYANA LITVINOVA describes their life as Shostako-vich's neighbours:

The Shostakovich family had been allotted an apartment in the same building where we had settled a month or so prior to their arrival. To accommodate us, the apartments had been vacated by the local functionaries who had lived there.

We introduced ourselves right away, and more or less the next day my husband began to sculpt a bust of Shostakovich – it had been his dream for years to make one.

Shostakovich was just completing his Seventh Symphony and was at the zenith of his fame. At the same time he was very distraught. At the Leningrad airfield they had promised to put his mother Sofiya Vasilyevna on the next plane out, but they hadn't. Now he was obsessed with the idea of chartering a plane to go and fetch her. After a month or so he succeeded in prevailing upon the authorities to bring her to Kuibyshev. When she arrived she was amazed to see so many dogs roaming the streets freely. In Leningrad all the dogs had been eaten.

The thing that struck one most about Shostakovich was his nervous-ness, which went together with a Leningrader's reserve and a eunuch's youthfulness. Nobody who saw him taking his bows on the platform after his music had been performed could forget his crooked figure, his grimace of misery and the fingers that never stopped drumming on his cheek. It was torture just to watch him! He minced his steps and bowed like a circus pony. There was something robot-like in his movements.[18]

The next thing that impressed one was his perfect mind, just like his perfect pitch, and his amazing knowledge of Russian literature from Pushkin and Lermontov to Babel and Zoshchenko. Once, during a sitting, he noticed that I was reading Dostoevsky's *A Raw Youth*. He began to recite the book from memory, paragraph by paragraph. His favourite place was the following dialogue:

'Prince Dolgoruky?'

'No, simply Dolgoruky.'

At that time he was writing his opera, *The Gamblers*. His aim was not

18 Ilya Slonim wrote of Shostakovich's extreme outward discomfort while acknowledg-ing the audience's enthusiastic ovations at the première of the Seventh Symphony: 'The severe young man mounted the stage as if going to the scaffold' ('Shostakovich as a Model for a Portrait', p. 94).

to omit a single word from Gogol's play. He regretted the absence of a female part. We jokingly suggested that he should write a part for 'Adelaida Ivanovna' (as the gamblers referred to the pack of marked cards). He was also very fond of Chekhov and wanted to write music to 'Gusev', which he considered the most musical prose in all Russian literature. He could also recite from memory whole pages of Zoshchenko. I remember him telling us many years later of his futile attempts to drag some writers holidaying near Leningrad to Zoshchenko's pauper's funeral.

My husband and I were in love with Shostakovich. Between his daily sittings we talked only about him. We decided that he was the 'closest approximation to genius' that we had ever encountered.

He came for his sittings at eleven o'clock in the morning. He was always very punctual and always warned us in advance if he couldn't make it. He always concluded the sessions with the same formula: 'It's thirteen hundred hours. Don't you think . . .?' That meant it was time to drink some beer.

We also met apart from the sittings. Whenever either of us got hold of some vodka or pure spirit we signalled to the others by tapping on the central heating pipes. Shostakovich didn't need much to get drunk. After his second glass he would start looking for an unoccupied bed. Once I saw him very drunk. He was trying to repair with a hammer an alarm clock on top of the piano.

His humour was deadpan and cruel. He excelled in parodying the bureaucratic lingo. Despite all that, to us more expansive Muscovites he appeared somewhat dry, and to begin with we did not have a sense of real friendship. So the following incident was all the more surprising to us.

After the third or fourth sitting, my husband said to Shostakovich, 'I think I'll be seeing you for the last time tomorrow. I've been summoned to the recruiting office.' My husband was thirty-five, the same age as Shostakovich. He wasn't fit for front-line service and he hadn't been trained. But during the first months of the war he had served in the army; his unit was based in Oryol. When the Germans had taken the town, his unit was dispersed, and my husband managed to escape through the surrounding German lines and found his way to Kuibyshev.

Dmitri Dmitriyevich didn't seem to react to my husband's announcement in any way. But an hour later he came back and asked,

'Ilya Lvovich, do you need any money?' We were touched. But what followed was totally unexpected. It turned out that, directly upon leaving us, Shostakovich had gone to the State Committee for the Arts. There he announced that the sculptor Slonim was working on his bust, and it was therefore desirable that he should be exempted from army service. The Shostakovich of the moment was a Big Noise. To appreciate what he had done, one must realize how squeamishly humble he was, how he detested any contact with the powers that be. My husband was accordingly exempted and enlisted in the so-called 'golden heritage of the creative intelligentsia'.

Shostakovich's bust is Slonim's best work. However the then chairman of the Committee for the Arts wasn't pleased with it. 'What we need is an optimistic Shostakovich.' Shostakovich was fond of repeating this phrase.[19]

ILYA SLONIM gave the following description of Shostakovich's behaviour during these sittings in Kuibyshev:

For the first five minutes he sat bolt upright, then he would practise five-finger exercises on his cheek, then he hung his head between his knees and covered his whole head with his hands. We tried to distract him and put music on the wind-up gramophone, which helped things along greatly . . . He couldn't stand generalized conversation. When he spoke of music, he would rush to the piano to illustrate his point, just as, when talking about books, he would quote whole passages verbatim. I remember him playing nearly all of Boris Godunov when the conversation touched on Mussorgsky, and nearly all of Petrushka when we talked of Stravinsky.[20]

ISAAK GLIKMAN confirms Tanya Litvinova's impressions of Shostakovich's diffidence over asking for anything for himself. While visiting the composer in Kuibyshev in April 1942, he noted that Shostakovich insisted on walking rather than ask the authorities to provide him with transport:

Of course, had Shostakovich put in a request to the local powers that be, undoubtedly he would have been given a car, but he would agonize before ever making even the most trivial request . . . Thus when I left Kuibyshev, we set off on foot at night for the station, even

---

19 Tatyana Litvinova, article commissioned for this book. 'Shostakovich in Kuibyshev'.
20 Slonim, 'Model for a Portrait', p. 94.

though I was carrying a heavy rucksack (all the heavier for the provisions that Nina Vasilyevna had given me, knowing that food products were essential to survival in hungry Tashkent).[21]

Similarly, I remember how worried Dmitri Dmitriyevich was before setting off to see the administrator of the affairs of the Soviet of People's Commissars, to ask permission for me to feed with him and his family in the restaurant of the National Hotel in Kuibyshev. I was deeply touched when he returned, clutching in his hands the treasured pass; his face shone with delight . . . But until the moment he actually held the pass in his hands, he doubted whether his request would be granted. Even after the historic performances of the Seventh Symphony, Shostakovich was completely unaware of the power of his authority and reputation. Although he often interceded on behalf of others, he never asked for anything for himself. It was so much against his nature that he was actually incapable of doing so.[22]

The Gamblers

David Rabinovich, Shostakovich's biographer, wrote that Shostakovich started work on *The Gamblers* the day after he finished the Seventh Symphony. However, the composer's own references to this work point to its mostly being written in May and June 1942. In his correspondence with Vissarion Shebalin, Shostakovich first mentions *The Gamblers* on 10 June. By November he was complaining:

> I am still composing the unrealistic opera *The Gamblers*. I call it unrealistic for reasons of its unreality: I've composed thirty minutes of music already, and this is only about one-seventh of the whole work. It's too long. Nevertheless it is not without pleasure and satisfaction that I work on it.[23]

Soon after Shostakovich abandoned the work. After the war he gave the manuscript to his pupil and friend Galina Ustvolskaya. In 1974 he asked her to return it; significantly an excerpt from *The Gamblers* is quoted in the composer's swan song, the Viola Sonata.

The opera director Boris Pokrovsky recalled that at this time Shostakovich contacted the Bolshoi Theatre in Moscow to ask for precise timings of the best-known Russian operas (*Ruslan and Lyudmilla, The Queen of Spades*, and so on.) It

21 Shostakovich's choice to stay in Kuibyshev proved to be a wise one, because, as the seat of government, it was better supplied than the other large centres of evacuation.
22 Glikman, *Letters to a Friend*, p. 27.
23 Letter dated 11 November 1942 (Nikolayev, 'Letters to Shebalin', p. 82).

is Pokrovsky's opinion that Shostakovich should have ignored the question of length and have gone on to finish this potential masterpiece.[24]

In September 1941 ISAAK GLIKMAN was evacuated with the Leningrad Conservatoire to Tashkent. The first performance of the Seventh Symphony from Kuibyshev was transmitted on the National Radio. On hearing this broadcast, Pavel Serebryakov, the director of the Leningrad Conservatoire, supported by the enthusiastic Glikman, decided that the symphony must be performed in Tashkent by the Conservatoire Orchestra.[25] At the express wish of Shostakovich, Glikman was entrusted the mission of going to Kuibyshev to collect the score. The journey by train took ten days, and Glikman arrived in Kuibyshev on 15 April 1942. He stayed in the composer's home until the middle of May:

During my stay in Kuibyshev, Dmitri Dmitriyevich more than once played through much of Verdi's *Otello*; I remember his performance of Iago's 'Credo' monologue, Desdemona's 'Willow Song' and 'Prayer', and Otello's final scene. Back in the 1930s, Dmitri Dmitriyevich had told me that *Otello* was one of his favourite operas and he had an enduring love for this work. While listening to these fragments I wondered if Dmitri Dmitriyevich didn't have some plan to write something on a Shakespearean theme. He had indeed conceived the idea of a new opera, but its subject was not Shakespearean; he was going to set to music Gogol's play, *The Gamblers*.

'Yes, after a gap of fourteen years I have decided to return to Gogol. But *The Gamblers* will not be like *The Nose*; it will be composed on a completely different basis. In *The Nose* I allowed myself to treat Gogol's text very freely, but I wish to reproduce the complete Gogol text of *The Gamblers*, setting every word, in the same way as Dargomyzhsky did in *The Stone Guest*. So Gogol himself will be the librettist. It's probably a bad thing that there are no female roles here; it seems they exist in every opera written so far. On the other hand, what an extraordinary comedy Gogol wrote. You remember of course that it includes a comedy within a comedy, the latter belonging to the hero of the story, Stepan Ivanovich Uteshitelny. What an original idea!'

I rejoined, 'Don't you think that this new work of yours could become the third in a wonderful operatic trilogy based on the theme of cards: Tchaikovsky's *Queen of Spades*, Prokofiev's *The Gambler*, and your new opera; after all this theme retains its perpetual interest.'

24 Recorded interview with EW.
25 It was performed there in June 1942.

'Well, in my youth I enjoyed playing cards and always lost. So maybe I can put my limited experience to use in your dreamt-up trilogy!'

I was surprised and delighted as the concept of *The Gamblers* meant a return to opera, to which it had appeared that Dmitri Dmitriyevich had finally bidden farewell after the miserable affair of *Lady Macbeth*. In addition, it was a return to his beloved Gogol, notwithstanding the unhappy fate that had befallen *The Nose*. And thirdly, it proved his desire to write a comedy after the tragic and epic Seventh Symphony. Ahead lay the creation of his most tragic work – the Eighth Symphony. *The Gamblers* would thereby fulfil the function of a comic interlude as in the satirical dramas of the Greek tragedists.

It is common knowledge what fate overtook this opera. Dmitri Dmitriyevich was afraid that without drastic cutting, Gogol's one-act play would grow out of hand and be unsuitable for operatic treatment. He therefore ceased to work on it after composing forty minutes of first-rate music, bubbling over with brilliant wit and humour.[26]

The Eighth and Ninth Symphonies

If the Seventh Symphony was hailed as the ultimate example of Patriotic Art, Shostakovich's following two symphonies aroused very different reactions. Shostakovich is reputed to have considered the Eighth Symphony his Requiem, and its tragic canvas is arguably one of his greatest compositional achievements. It was written incredibly quickly between 2 July and 9 September 1943 at Ivanovo. It was first performed by the dedicatee, Evgeny Mravinsky (whose profound understanding of the music inspired Shostakovich's dedication), in Moscow on 4 November of that year. By this time, the tide of the war was changing, and the Soviets had started to repulse the Germans. 'Optimistic' celebration rather than 'pessimistic' tragedy was the order of the day. Hence the official reception of the Eighth Symphony was subdued, if not positively icy.

More surprisingly, few musicians at the time appreciated the significance of this great music. Sollertinsky, on the eve of his death, introduced Mravinsky's performance of the Symphony in Novosibirsk on 6 February 1944. He stated that Shostakovich, the tragic poet of music, had an artist's right to tragedy as 'the fruit of maturity, courage and moral freedom'. Shostakovich himself was fully aware that the Eighth Symphony was not to be accorded the triumphant

26 Glikman, *Letters to a Friend*, pp. 28, 29.

reception of the Seventh. In a letter dated 8 December 1943, he wrote to Isaak Glikman:

> A discussion of my Symphony was to be held at the Union of Soviet Composers but it was postponed because of my illness. Soon this discussion will take place, and I don't doubt that many valuable critical observations will be made then, which will inspire me to future creativity, and which will make me review all my previous works, and accordingly, instead of one step backwards, I will make one step forwards.[27]

By now, Shostakovich, along with many of the intelligentsia, realized that victory over the Germans would give Stalin opportunities to abuse his immense power and newly acquired international prestige. In particular he feared a return to the pre-war policies of lawlessness and terror. In his New Year greeting to Glikman, written on 31 December 1943, Shostakovich uses an unmistakable irony:

> 1944 is around the corner. A year of happiness, joy, and victory. This year will bring us much joy. The freedom-loving Peoples will at long last throw off the yoke of Hitlerism, and peace will reign throughout the world under the sunny rays of Stalin's Constitution. I am convinced of this, and therefore experience the greatest joy. Now we are apart; how I miss you; would that together we could rejoice at the victories of the Red Army led by its Great Commander, comrade Stalin.[28]

Shostakovich's fears were justified. At a Composers' Plenum at the end of March 1944, the Eighth Symphony was subjected to heated discussion and criticism. Its unequivocal supporters were few: the musicologists D. Rabinovich and L. Maazel, and the composer Gavriil Popov. Even Prokofiev criticized the work for its undue length and lack of 'a clear, melodic line'. Mravinsky was effectively the only performer of the Eighth Symphony; after the Leningrad première (in the liberated city) in December 1944, the work was to all effects and purposes withdrawn from concert repertoire.

While the Eighth Symphony can be seen as a complement to and continuation of the epic Seventh, the Ninth Symphony, written after victory in 1945, was an about-turn typical of Shostakovich's paradoxical nature. It caused consternation in official circles for failing to be a grandiose hymn extolling Soviet victory over the Germans. Its light-hearted parodying tone was obviously open to misinterpretation.

At the time DANIIL ZHITOMIRSKY wrote 'positive' (if somewhat cautious) critical reviews of these two symphonies. Here he describes the background to their creation:

27 Glikman, *Letters to a Friend*, p. 61.
28 *Ibid.*, p. 62.

In the high-ranking Party officials' attitude towards Shostakovich two motivating and conflicting factors were prevalent. The first was irritation provoked, on the one hand, by the composer's courage and unpredictable behaviour, and, on the other, by their inability to control his work sufficiently. For his work had a formulative and 'pernicious' influence in the circles he moved in. The second factor was Shostakovich's usefulness as a symbol of international prestige for his country, as a convenient mouthpiece to show his country in a favourable light, thereby disguising as far as possible what was really going on in our society. In the same way, Shostakovich had his uses for internal propaganda: 'You see how we value our most distinguished artists, our intelligentsia.' These two factors determined the incredible fate of the composer and the frenetic swings in attitudes towards him in the official evaluation of his status. First he was seen as a high-flying and powerful artist, then he fell from grace. This was also organized by the big Party bosses with the active help of subservient officials, a pack of small-minded and jealous cowards devoid of conscience and honour.

At the Moscow première of the Eighth Symphony in 1943, I was not only a listener but one of its reviewers. From the concert hall I went straight to the editorial office of *Komsomolskaya Pravda*. My article was read meticulously and cautiously corrected; all mention of my fresh impressions was ironed out. At the same time the chief editor made some phone calls to high-up places to obtain special authorization for its publication; this in the end never materialized. Here are some lines from my diary entries of the time:

'The clock showed midnight, then one o'clock, two o'clock. Still there was no answer. But I realized from the editor's expression that some serious trouble was brewing – some 'bigwig' had been outraged. After two o'clock in the morning I left for home. There was no transport and the curfew was on. Despite having to keep an anxious look-out for patrols I had time for reflection. All this seems strange and inexplicable. But no, in essence there's nothing strange here. At the Front the tide has turned and we now can expect victory. The newspapers blare forth fanfares, our evening skies are lit up by ever-more extravagant displays of fireworks. But the Eighth Symphony described something completely different. Good God, who should dare hint that Shostakovich does not share the general delight in our victory over Hitler? His symphony does not reflect this triumphal, fanfare-like actuality, but its converse side. It has something of the retrospective in it, and also of the prophetic . . . such integrity in the face of monstrous evil, sorrow and anger. The Scherzo gave me goose-flesh. The Passacaglia portrays a soul in distress, seeking and questioning with imploring looks. The Finale achieves the greatest spiritual heights, an enlightened resignation. Should some vigilant observer notice something awry, and whisper in the necessary quarters: "Take care, this music is not what you think it is at all, you will answer for this and pay due retribution." '

The next morning my review was not to be found in the paper. Soon after the Eighth Symphony was relegated to the list of works 'not recommended' for performance.

In August 1945 I lived in the composers' 'House of Creativity' at Ivanovo I saw Shostakovich daily. In the small front garden of his shabby dwelling, several friends had concocted a sort of table for him, a board nailed down on top of poles driven into the ground. Every morning Dmitri Dmitriyevich worked here on his Ninth Symphony. Again I quote some lines from my diary:

'For a few days nobody has been around at dinner. Dmitri Dmitriyevich and Nina Vasilyevna have left for Moscow. I met them at Ivanovo station. On the way back here, Dmitri Dmitriyevich first told me about the "uranium" bomb, of the inconceivable, terrible catastrophe of Hiroshima. Nina Vasilyevna explained with great authority about the significance of the splitting of the atom. Dmitri Dmitriyevich was gloomy and taciturn, yet at the same time he could not disguise his inner agitation. He spoke in short quick phrases; the husky, pinched tone of his voice, his absent gaze and pallid complexion all transmitted his distress. We then walked in silence to his little dacha. I thought in bewilderment about Hiroshima, of the complexities of this moment in time (even though the war had ended for us), and wondered what the near future had in store. I started to give voice to my despondency, but Dmitri Dmitriyevich, his eyes fixed on some point overhead, quickly cut short my lamentations: "Our job is to rejoice!" '

I have remembered this reply all my life. It conveyed a certain fatalism, but also a spark of protest. Shostakovich had developed a fatalistic attitude towards what was 'demanded' of him, which often had an oppressing effect on him. But actually, in his work on the Ninth Symphony he could no longer subjugate himself to this oppression. As far back as the spring of 1944 Shostakovich had said to a certain

Moscow musicologist, 'Yes, I am thinking of my next symphony, the Ninth. I would like to employ not only full orchestra but a choir and soloists, if I can find a suitable text; in any case I don't want to be accused of drawing presumptuous analogies.'[29]

According to G. Orlov, 'In the winter of 1944/45 it was common knowledge that Shostakovich had started work on his Ninth Symphony. Certain musicians had the opportunity to listen to the first pages of the new score – a triumphal heroic major which surged with energy. Very soon, literally a few days later, the exposition of the first movement was completed, and, after another week, the development. Then suddenly the composer interrupted his work. He gave no explanation, and in general avoided any mention of this subject. Subsequently, over a year later, he recounted that, after this first version, he had started on another which he also was unable to complete.'[30] In the meantime in the summer of 1945 the papers carried a TASS bulletin reporting that Shostakovich's new symphony 'devoted to the Celebration of our Great Victory' would soon be performed.

But in fact in August of that year, at his crude country table at Ivanovo, Shostakovich was creating something entirely different, indeed totally contrary to what these reports suggested. Instead of a lavish glorification, a modest chamber score emerged. In one of the more favourable reviews of the time it was called a 'Symphony-Scherzo'. I remember how clearly I sensed the novelty of this symphony, its inherent relevance and manifold implications, which were by no means immediately obvious. Superficially there was much that was playful and carefree in the music, even at times a sort of festive swagger; but this then was transformed into something tragic and grotesque. It showed up the senseless vacuity and triteness of that everyday 'rejoicing' which so gratified our authorities.[31]

29 David Rabinovich, *Dmitri Shostakovich, Composer*, p. 96. Shostakovich was obviously referring to Beethoven's Ninth Symphony.
30 Georgi Orlov, *Shostakovich's Symphonies*, p. 221.
31 Daniil Zhitomirsky, 'Dmitri Shostakovich: Reminiscences and Reflections', unpublished article.

The Soviet national anthem

Shostakovich met Aram Khachaturian in 1934, while travelling by train to Baku. The composer described this meeting in a letter to Elena Konstantinovskaya dated 15 June 1934:

> In Moscow the Armenian composer Khachaturian got on the train in the same carriage as me. He turned out to be an excellent travelling companion. We dined together in the restaurant car; I have to say that I liked Khachaturian considerably more than the dinner. In fact, I remained hungry after the meal! Khachaturian brought some wonderful salami and wouldn't leave me in peace until I had eaten it.[32]

The two men were to develop a lifelong friendship based on deep mutal trust.

In July 1943 both composers took part in a national competition for a new national anthem. Previously the Internationale had served this purpose. The competition took place at the Bolshoi Theatre amidst much pomp and ceremony. The final judge was no less a person than Stalin, whom Shostakovich was to meet for the first time. In the event Alexander Alexandrov's 'Bolshevik Party Anthem' was chosen, with a new text by Sergei Mikhailkov and G. El-Registan, which became obsolete after 1956 because of its fawning references to Stalin. Here ARAM KHACHATURIAN gives his account of the competition:

It was during the war that the decision was made to create a new national anthem of the USSR. A special competition to choose the new words and music was announced. First writers and poets, then composers were asked to submit their entries. Stalin entrusted the running of the competition to Voroshilov, Shcherbakov and Khrapchenko. Voroshilov himself used to sing and enjoyed listening to the Bolshevik Party Anthem, which was always performed by the Red Banner Ensemble of the Red Army.

Around 500 anthems were submitted to the competition. Many composers put forward several versions. The auditions took place at the Beethoven Hall of the Bolshoi Theatre. To begin with, anthems of other countries (the 'Marseillaise', 'God Save the King' and the 'Internationale') were played in Stalin's presence. Khrapchenko, chairman of the Committee for Arts at that time, came out and announced, 'Khachaturian and Shostakovich backstage please.' We

32 Sofiya Khentova, 'Dmitri Shostakovich: We Live in a Time of Stormy Passions and Actions', p. 12.

went to the green room. Standing in semi-profile at the door was Stalin's chief of staff, General Vlasik. I summoned up courage and entered first. I saw Stalin standing alone on the right; on the left were all the members of the Politburo. I stood nearest to the door with Shostakovich and Khrapchenko next to me. Stalin outlined the characteristics of a national anthem and defined how to make it 'Soviet'.

The auditions began. The following rule was established: the stage curtains were drawn back, the choir sang the anthem alone, then Melik-Pashayev conducted the orchestral version, and lastly a joint performance by choir and orchestra was given.

Voroshilov suggested that Shostakovich and I wrote an anthem together. For two days we didn't get anywhere with it. We composed separately, then corrected together. By the third day, something started taking shape. We used the words of the poet Mikhail Golodny. But then there was a small hitch: who should orchestrate it? Shostakovich said, 'Let's break a match. Whoever gets the head will do it.' The 'head' fell to me, so I did the orchestration.[33] My own anthem, our joint effort, and those of Alexandrov, Shostakovich and Iona Tuskiya were judged on the same day. Each was played in its three forms: a capella choir, the orchestral version and then the version with choir and orchestra.

We were called again to see Stalin. He asked Melik-Pashayev, 'Do you like their joint anthem?'

He answered, 'I prefer the anthems that they wrote separately to the one they wrote together.'

Stalin rejoined, 'And I like their joint effort better than their separate anthems.'

Many of the anthems (including Alexandrov's) had been orchestrated by Victor Knushevitsky. Shostakovich praised Knushevitsky for his excellent orchestrations. Molotov asked, 'And was your joint anthem also orchestrated by Knushevitsky?'

Shostakovich answered, 'A composer should be able to orchestrate himself,' and then repeated this phrase convulsively.

The question arose about an alteration in the refrain of our anthem. It meant having to rewrite all the music.

33 In the description of this episode in Solomon Volkov's *Testimony: The Memoirs of Dmitri Shostakovich*, p. 201, it was Shostakovich who had to do the orchestration.

Stalin asked, 'Will three months be enough time for you?'
Shostakovich answered, 'Five days will do.'[34]

Soon after that Stalin left for Tehran to meet Roosevelt and
Churchill. On his return he decided in favour of Alexandrov's entry,
the previous Bolshevik Party Anthem.[35]

The Ensemble of Song and Dance of the NKVD Dzerzhinsky Club

This curious offshoot of the NKVD[36] came into being during the war years
under the patronage of Lavrenti Beriya. The Ensemble was made up from
mobilized artists, released from military duty so as to provide entertainment
for the troops at the various front lines, in the cities and also at official Kremlin
receptions. The Ensemble boasted a symphony orchestra, a folk orchestra, a
jazz orchestra, a choir and a dance company. Split up into smaller units, it
travelled all over the country. In reality, the Ensemble constituted a collection
of the country's artistic elite. Shostakovich wrote the music for some of the
theatrical concert entertainments, known as patriotic stage spectacles. The
first of his scores for the Ensemble was a suite entitled 'Native Leningrad' Op.
63 (1942), followed by 'The Great Russian River' Op. 66 (1944) and lastly
'Victorious Spring' Op. 72 (1945).

The theatre director YURI PETROVICH LYUBIMOV started his career as an
actor, and by the time he met Shostakovich he was well-known for his work in
the theatre and cinema. Lyubimov later went on to found the famous
TAGANKA Theatre in Moscow in 1963:

I first met Shostakovich at a dismal institution called 'The Ensemble of
Song and Dance of the NKVD' which was presided over by Beriya. I
was a soldier then and was ordered to join the Ensemble. Shostakovich had been asked to collaborate. Too scared to refuse, he wrote
songs like 'Burn, Burn, Burn' (otherwise known as 'The Torches').[37]
The song described the torches used during the night-time blackouts,
which were necessitated so that the enemy should not see us. The
song became incredibly popular and everybody hummed it. As our

---

34 According to the version in *Testimony*, Shostakovich said that five hours would have
been sufficient time to make the corrections, p. 204.
35 Khentova, 'Shostakovich and Khachaturian', p. 11.
36 Acronym for the People's Commissariat for Internal Affairs. Lavrenti Beriya was the
much-feared head of the NKVD from 1939–53.
37 'The Torches', also known as 'Song of the Lantern', from *Victorious Spring* Op. 72
(1945).

boss used to say, 'We need a song to set the People singing. Both words and tune should easily sink into their ears.'

Once our boss, a secret police officer, expressed a wish for a dance depicting football. Suddenly Shostakovich piped up, 'May I compose the music for "Football",[38] if you have nothing against it?' I don't know why he was so keen on writing football music. He was a funny man; I believe he was a football fan. . . .

I remember how he came begging for jam. There were tremendous food shortages, and he had his family and two children to feed. He hung around for several days with his empty can as he didn't have the nerve to ask for anything himself. I witnessed the scene. The librarian of the Ensemble, Karen Khachaturian,[39] his pupil, put in a good word for the composer with his boss, who then ordered half a can of jam to be issued to Shostakovich. We took Shostakovich's can and went to see the storeman. He kindly gave Shostakovich more than half a can.

The Ensemble ceased to exist after the war, before 1948. It was a remarkable organization. Apart from Shostakovich, among its members were Asaf Messerer, the actor Ruben Simonov, the director Sergei Yutkevich and Kasyan Galizovsky who had produced Stravinsky's *Rite of Spring* at the Bolshoi in the late 1920s and had been duly berated for his ideological oversight. Tarkhanov was in charge of the artistes. The playwright Robert Erdman wrote the scripts. I did the compèring. We gave concerts at the Front, in Leningrad during the siege, and during the destruction of our volunteer divisions near Moscow. We were caught up in all that. We also took part in concerts to entertain the Kremlin dignitaries, including one given at a Moscow Underground station. Shostakovich didn't go to the Front with us, he just wrote the music for the songs.

For all his withrawal from 'real life', Shostakovich knew it as well as Zoshchenko did. Everybody had to face 'real life' during the war years. Even Prokofiev had to sell foreign clothes in the Alma-Alta market in order to buy food. He was reputedly quite good at it. I think that Stalin's Terror had an especially painful effect on Shostakovich, more than on the rest of us. Prokofiev was less affected by it; his European upbringing protected him.

38 'Football' is the second piece from *The Great Russian River* Op. 66 (1944).
39 Karen Khachaturian had a job in the commissioning department of the Ensemble and worked as a pianist.

After 1948 Shostakovich was dismissed from teaching posts in two conservatoires, in Moscow and in Leningrad. His pupils were forced to repent of having studied under a formalist. Undoubtedly, despite his wit and irony, Shostakovich was deeply hurt. He realized it was in the nature of the time for children to denounce their parents, let alone pupils their teacher; but all the same he was hurt.

People close to him told me that he used to carry a briefcase with a change of underwear and a toothbrush in constant expectation of arrest. Many people did that. It is also recounted how he waited for his arrest at night out on the landing by the lift, so that at least his family wouldn't be disturbed if they came to get him. Many people went into hiding and survived, but Shostakovich never got over the trauma of those days.

For all his nervousness and defencelessness, Shostakovich was a caustic man. His table talk was full of sarcasm. He liked his drink and, when in his cups, revealed his wit and irony. His mind was similar to Zoshchenko's. It's not for nothing that he counted Zoshchenko, Sollertinsky and Erdman amongst his friends. His letters were written with 'English humour', but in the style of 'a Soviet communal apartment'.

Later on his nervousness assumed the character of panic, a kind of conditioned reflex. He used to say: 'I'd sign anything even if they hand it to me upside down. All I want is to be left alone.' I think he was only pretending he didn't care. He knew what it implied when he signed such letters and deep down he suffered. Perhaps he was afraid for his family, especially for his son whom he dearly loved. He was always ready to admit his 'mistakes' ('Yes, yes, yes, I've been wrong. Of course, I'll write an operetta which the People will easily understand.'), but I think that this was done cynically and in cold blood. Akhmatova took the same line when talking to foreigners. Zoshchenko, however, tried to justify himself: 'On the one hand . . . but on the other . . .' and he was punished for it. Because he sought rational explanations, he was not allowed to exist as an artist. On the other hand, Akhmatova was able to keep going after a fashion.

Shostakovich, however, was a man with exposed nerves and a keen perception. The fact that he was more vulnerable and receptive than other people was no doubt an important feature of his genius.[40]

40 Yuri Lyubimov: recorded interview with EW.

Teacher and Master

In the autumn of 1942 Vissarion Shebalin was called to Moscow from evacuation in Sverdlovsk and offered the position of director of the Conservatoire. His widow recalled that:

> he accepted it much against his will, as he was uncertain that he was ready to assume this important responsibility. He had to start his directorship during the difficult war years. One of his first new appointments was made in 1943 when he invited Shostakovich to join the teaching staff of the composition faculty.[41]

Shostakovich accepted this professorship and held both composition classes and orchestration classes. He was now able to bring his family from Kuibyshev to settle in Moscow. When the war was over, Shostakovich decided against returning to Leningrad, and while retaining close contacts with his native city, he made Moscow his home for the rest of his life. But he returned to his teaching position at the Leningrad Conservatoire in 1947, keeping a small class of post-graduate composition students.

KAREN KHACHATURIAN first met Shostakovich before the war at the home of his uncle Aram Khachaturian. From 1943 he studied composition with Shostakovich and Shebalin at the Moscow Conservatoire:

After the war was over, I became a full-time composition student of Dmitri Dmitriyevich's at the Moscow Conservatoire. He was a wonderful teacher, because he recognized and respected the individuality of each student. Everything he said was very much to the point, and his attention to detail was always of great relevance in the context of the whole. However, most of his comments concerned matters of form and instrumental texture.

As a rule, the class started with each of us playing some of our own music, which Shostakovich then analysed very thoroughly. He required that we showed him a large span of composition – either a whole movement or at least the whole exposition – even if all the details were not filled in. Shebalin, on the other hand, preferred to work on small sections, maybe only a theme. Then the class went on to play music in four-hand piano arrangements. Shostakovich himself played with each of us; he was of course an outstanding reader. We performed the classics, Haydn, Schubert, Brahms, and also learned a lot of new music this way. Thirdly, he would ask us to bring a piece of

41 Recorded interview with EW.

unfamiliar music to the lesson, so that we students could share our discoveries. To give an example, I might choose a piece like Hindemith's *Nobilissima Visions*. This work would also be played and analysed in detail. I remember Dmitri Dmitriyevich getting hold of a copy of Stravinsky's *Symphony of Psalms*, and he himself made a four-hand version for piano of this wonderful score, thereby allowing us to get to know it really well.

We students would also ask him to play his own compositions for us. Thus, we were the first to get to know such marvellous works as the First Violin Concerto, long before its public performance, and his unfinished opera *The Gamblers*. Naturally we attended every concert where Shostakovich's music was performed, and we travelled to Leningrad specially to attend the premières of his works.

Dmitri Dmitriyevich was the soul of kindness to his students. We attended parties at his home to celebrate birthdays and the New Year. On these occasions we were welcomed as part of his extended family. Shostakovich's favourite New Year toast reflected his philosophical irony: 'Let's drink to this – that things don't get any better!' After all, it was constantly being drummed into us that things would improve in our society; whereas we knew perfectly well that in reality things only ever got worse![42]

Mstislav (Slava) Rostropovich studied cello and piano from an early age with his father Leopold. At the beginning of the War, the Rostropovich family was evacuated to Orienburg, where Leopold Rostropovich died. As for Shostakovich in 1922, the loss of his father was a tremendous blow for the sixteen-year-old boy. In Rostropovich's own words, 'When my father died I became a man; therefore I see the period I spent in Orienburg as the epicentre of my life.'[43] And, like Shostakovich before him, he took on responsibility for his family, left without any means of support. In Orienburg Rostropovich started his composition studies with Mikhail Chulaki.

When the family returned to Moscow in 1943, MSTISLAV ROSTROPOVICH entered the Moscow Conservatoire as a student of cello and composition and attended Shostakovich's orchestration classes. Shostakovich was always more than just a teacher to him and actively supported him in his career as a cellist:

I got to know Shostakovich in the autumn of 1943 when I enrolled at the Moscow Conservatoire. My composition teacher was the director

42 Karen Khachaturian: recorded interview with EW.
43 Recorded interview with EW.

of the Conservatoire, Vissarion Shebalin. I naturally very much wanted to study with Shostakovich, but I did not want to transfer completely from my own professor, Shebalin. So I asked Dmitri Dmitriyevich to accept me in his orchestration class. At that time Shostakovich was tremendously popular, in the wake of the success of the Seventh Symphony and his recent arrival in Moscow. So his class was literally overflowing with students.

My professor of cello, Semyon Kozolupov (incidentally also my uncle), talked to Shostakovich on my behalf. He said, 'My nephew is a talented cellist and composer. He would very much like to study with you. I realize that your class is full to bursting, but perhaps you could spare the time to meet him and listen to him?'

Shostakovich gave me an appointment to come to see him at the Conservatoire. His classes were held in classroom 35 on the fourth storey of the main building of the Conservatoire. I arrived at the appointed hour with my piano concerto, written while we lived in evacuation in Orienburg. I was extremely shy, because the concerto showed the obvious influence of Rachmaninov and Skryabin. In a state of great confusion, and furiously blushing, I handed the score to Shostakovich. Then I played the concerto through on the piano, while Dmitri Dmitriyevich leafed through the pages of the score. Then he showered me with a mass of compliments, which I of course did not for a moment take seriously. An absolute mass of compliments, he almost choked on them, such was his delight! Then finally he said, 'Of course I would consider it a great honour, so to speak, to take you on in my class, a great honour.'

From that moment I started attending his classes on Thursdays. These classes were preceded by some terrible hours, as I had to stay up virtually the whole night writing out the scores. I never had enough time to prepare for the lessons, and Shostakovich was merciless in his demands, always setting me an enormous amount of work. I had to orchestrate all of Chopin's Piano Studies and Preludes, for instance, Schumann's *Carnival*, and so on.

On Thursdays I also had my cello lessons with Professor Kozolupov. I would be the first to arrive at nine o'clock in the morning so as to get my lesson over with as soon as possible. Then I went up to Dmitri Dmitriyevich's class, my cello in tow. Often I was the first to arrive there too. If there were no other students in the class, Dmitri Dmitriyevich would make me take out my cello and play something for him. For instance, he might check with me if a certain passage lay comfortably on the instrument.

Then the other students began to arrive, and the class was brimful of people. We would then play through scores on the piano in four hands. We played through many of Stravinsky's scores on the piano, and also a lot of Mahler, whom Dmitri Dmitriyevich adored. I never ceased to be amazed by Dmitri Dmitriyevich's memory and his capacity for total recall when it came to details of scoring and orchestration. He might look at one of our scores and say: 'You know, it wouldn't be a bad idea to add trumpets, and to give them an accent on this note. You remember for instance that in such and such a symphony at such and such a place Beethoven used this device.' Or for instance he would tell us that the alto flute lacked a lower G, but Tchaikovsky had once used it in his Second Symphony. Of course all of us in the class felt overwhelmed by Shostakovich's erudition. But with his incredible sensitivity, he took pains never to offend anyone.

On one occasion, however, I experienced his real displeasure. The night before that particular Thursday class I had been at a student party. After it was over I stayed up all night doing my set task in orchestration. I probably only finished at five minutes to nine. And then I dashed off with my cello to the Conservatoire for my lesson with Kozolupov. From there I went on to Shostakovich. I opened the score I had prepared for him, and, together with him, I started to look slowly and attentively at what I had done. I immediately blushed red as a lobster because I was ashamed of what I had produced. Then Dmitri Dmitriyevich started questioning me: 'Well, here, do you see, is this an oboe playing? This melody here, have you given it to the oboe?'

I replied sheepishly, 'I understand that it doesn't work, but yes, in this instance I've given it to the oboe.'

And then Dmitri Dmitriyevich lost his temper with me. It was the only occasion that I remember him ever being angry with me. He said: 'You see, Slava, you are a person of genius, of complete genius, and with such a talent in life, with such a talent . . .'

Here I thought to myself, 'What is he babbling on about?'

Then he said, 'You understand that for the next lesson you're to do it again, orchestrate this score again, and you're to make sure that it doesn't bear the slightest resemblance to what you have brought for me today.'

Contrary to what is written in Solomon Volkov's *Testimony*, Dmitri

Dmitriyevich worshipped Stravinsky, and considered the *Symphony of Psalms* to be one of the most brilliant works in existence.

I have to say that I consider that Volkov's book is not a balanced account. It is like a series of anecdotes; or rather, as basically everything that is stated there is true, one might say a series of 'interesting little stories'. Shostakovich was a man who, for the sake of a good story, could go so far as to invent a tale. For instance, to this day I don't give much credence to some of his stories. Two of them he used to tell me regularly, maybe twice a year. One was about how, when a young boy, he met the chess-player Alekhine at the cinema. There was nobody around, and Dmitri Dmitriyevich, who didn't recognize Alekhine approached him and asked him for a game. I don't believe this story, particularly as I then had occasion to recount it to Boris Spassky. Spassky said that Shostakovich would have had to be very young indeed as Alekhine left Russia in 1919 or 1920.

The second story Dmitri Dmitriyevich was fond of telling went as follows:

'I was an eye-witness, you know, an eye-witness to this event. After the siege of Leningrad I saw a funeral procession in the streets . . . The coffin was being loaded onto an open lorry. Just imagine, an open coffin on the back of the lorry, which is bumping and shaking, together with a band of musicians playing Chopin's *Funeral March*. All of a sudden the corpse gets up from his coffin, and all the relatives and friends fall into a faint. Can you imagine, it wasn't a corpse they were going to bury, but somebody who was in a state of lethargic sleep. Only the musicians kept their wits about them, and seeing that the man was all right they stopped halfway through a bar of the *Funeral March* and started playing the "Internationale". Yes, I saw this with my very own eyes . . .'

Shostakovich claimed he had witnessed this happening – and he told me this story many times.

Before I joined Dmitri Dmitriyevich's orchestration class, he had never heard me play the cello. I think that the first time Shostakovich heard me play in concert was when I participated in the All-Union competition of instruments in 1945. Before that I had won the Conservatoire competition for the best performance of a Soviet work, when I played the Myaskovsky Cello Concerto, a work I dearly love to this day. But I don't believe that he heard me then.

But at the All-Union competition Shostakovich was the chairman of the jury. There was a great conflict as to who should win, a conflict behind closed doors, of course. It was largely to do with my personal biography, as I considered myself my father's pupil. But my uncle, Semyon Kozolupov, had all his life dreamed of teaching me. He used to put pressure on my mother, his wife's sister. But my father wanted to teach me himself. Kozolupov let it be known through his wife that he considered that my father didn't know how to teach, and that Slavka would be much better off with him, and only with him. On account of this a great family scandal erupted. Of course he was accused of tempting me away by virtue of the fact that he occupied the position of professor at the Moscow Conservatoire, where he had effectively barred the way against my father. So we were in a dire situation. If it wasn't for a letter that my father wrote and left under his pillow when he knew that he was dying, I would never have agreed to study with Kozolupov. But one of the points that my father made in this letter was that I should complete my education with Kozolupov. This gives you the background to our strained relationship.

So it was that when I participated in the All-Union Competition, Kozolupov wanted the first prize to be awarded to another of his pupils, Luzanov. He didn't mince his words, and once told my mother outright, 'Slavka is very young and has lots of time ahead. But this is Luzanov's last chance of playing in a competition. Slavka will have plenty of time to achieve lots of things in life. And I consider it early to give him a first prize.' When he used these arguments at the competition, Shostakovich intervened. He apparently said to the jury, 'You know, not only do I consider that Rostropovich should be given the first prize, but I consider that, as he has set such a gap in the standard, we should not award a second prize. All the others are way behind Rostropovich.' And that is how the final decisions worked out. I was given first prize, and in the piano competition the first prize was shared by Svyatoslav Richter and Victor Merzhanov. No second prizes were awarded. Luzanov was given third prize for cello. In the violinists' category, neither first nor second prize were awarded and the third prize was given to Julian Sitkovetsky. This was the competition which opened all doors for me.[44]

Shostakovich had a profound effect on Soviet musical life because he was so approachable, and was always willing to listen and give advice to composers

44 Mstislav Rostropovich: recorded interview with EW.

and performers. Both Moisei Weinberg and Venyamin Basner were regarded by many to be Shostakovich pupils, although officially neither of them ever studied with him. Many other composers, such as MIKHAIL MEYEROVICH, enjoyed the occasional contacts with Shostakovich. Here Meyerovich recounts how he benefited from the master's wisdom and tactful advice:

I learned a lot from Shostakovich. Being in his company meant always learning something. He radiated a kind of charm I can't describe. He was exaggeratedly polite, and made an effort never to hurt people's feelings. He was always the first to greet you. His conversation was very mundane, even intentionally so. He was not like a great thinker pronouncing on every subject. But in that mundane conversation, there was always something new from which you could learn. We once played through Mahler's Fourth Symphony on the piano in a four-hand arrangement. Suddenly Dmitri Dmitriyevich stopped and said, 'What a marvellous passage this is.' He showed me why it was wonderful, and we played it over again. Without him I might never have noticed that passage.

It is said that Isaac Babel, the great writer, once met Shostakovich when he was a youth. Babel didn't know who Shostakovich was, but he had an intuitive understanding of people. Apparently he wrote that he had just met a young man who had a hypnotic effect on people. I also experienced this quality in Shostakovich as a positive influence. Once I came to see him. I was depressed for some reason, everything had been going wrong for me. I left him a different person. I suddenly saw what I should do to improve my affairs. Shostakovich had this effect on many people. His presence was calming; it was enough to boost your self-confidence.

Shostakovich never scolded his pupils in class, although he sometimes made fun of them. He had pupils of all kinds, including ones that were ignorant or without talent. He treated them with a gentle irony, but he never said a harsh word to them. Somehow he was able to affect them in such a way that even the most hopeless of them began to soar a little. They didn't fly high, but they produced music to the best of their ability.

All Shostakovich's pupils imitated him, even in his mannerisms. You could tell a Shostakovich pupil a mile off; they all wore glasses, both those who needed them and those who didn't. They imitated his jerky movements and stuttering manner of speech. They all seemed to look like him. I didn't see Shostakovich regularly. I didn't like the flock of satellites who surrounded him. They were sycophants who picked up his cigarette butts, so to speak, pretending to be his dearest friends and asking him for favours. He had a lot of enemies, private and official, so he was profoundly affected by any token of friendship, even if disingenuous.

Once, during a concert at the Hall of Columns, I witnessed behaviour untypical of Shostakovich. The music was very vulgar with clashing cymbals. In a pause I heard hysterical laughter behind me. I turned round to see Shostakovich accompanied by his pupils Georgi Sviridov and Kara Karayev in paroxysms of laughter. In the interval I asked Sviridov, 'What's going on?' He told me that, after having had a few drinks, they became somewhat boisterous, and that an usher had tried to chase them out of the Hall. Here I must mention the fact that Shostakovich never wore his medals in public, while his two pupils were wearing their Stalin prize-winner's badges. When the usher got close enough to see Sviridov's medal, he started apologizing for having threatened to throw them out, and said, 'I didn't mean you, I meant that one,' pointing at Shostakovich. It wasn't typical of Shostakovich to play the fool in public, but the usher's reaction shows how self-effacing Shostakovich was.

Shostakovich was our whole life and our school. Even composers of totally different styles, like Edison Denisov, had a lot of support and encouragement from him. In general, Shostakovich showered praise on every composition that was shown to him. In order to learn from him, one had to be able to see through this praise. I too used to show Shostakovich my newly-finished works. Once I composed a Gypsy Rhapsody. I couldn't cope with one passage to my satisfaction, and, impatient to finish the piece, I made a fair copy and took it to Shostakovich. I played it to him. He praised it to the skies. Then he said, 'I have one unimportant criticism.' With amazing delicacy, he shoved my nose right into the very place that I knew wasn't good enough. He said that the variations were too formal, and suggested that I give my fantasy free play there. He sketched a few chords as a possible idea. I went back home and re-wrote the whole thing. I now saw my way to improving it. You couldn't learn from him if you expected wrath and upbraiding; you had to listen carefully to his self-effacing remarks.

In 1948, when the 'historical' Zhdanov Decree was published, he was working on his Violin Concerto. When the concerto was finished he played it on the piano for me and some other composers. I asked him: 'At which point were you exactly in the score when the Decree was published?' He showed me the exact spot. The violin played semiquavers before and after it. There was no change evident in the music. [45],[46]

Ivanovo

In 1939, the Organizational Committee of the Union of Composers was set up with Rheingold Glière as chairman, Isaac Dunayevsky vice-chairman, and Aram Khachaturian first deputy chairman. Under the Committee's jurisdiction the Composers' Retreats, known as 'Houses of Rest and Creativity', were authorized in 1943. The first such Retreat was set up near the town of Ivanovo, housed in what had been a nobleman's country estate in pre-revolutionary times. The composers and their families were each given a room in the main building, fed in the communal dining room and additionally provided with working 'studios' on the grounds. For wartime, the conditions were unique – composers enjoyed on the one hand the benefits of a kind of health farm, on the other an ideal haven to work in, plus the stimulus of the company of colleagues.

Shostakovich spent the first of several summers at the Ivanovo Retreat in 1943, where during August he wrote most of his Eighth Symphony. In the following two summers he achieved some of his best composition there: the Second Piano Trio, the Second String Quartet and the Ninth Symphony.

Later in life ARAM KHACHATURIAN remembered Ivanovo with nostalgia:

The musicians lived there, enjoying great freedom, without any limitations as to how long they stayed, coming and going as they pleased. Huts were rented and barns repaired for us to work in. I worked in a little log cabin, and Shostakovich in a poultry barn. And how we worked! The history of music has yet to evaluate what was achieved at Ivanovo. Many Soviet classics were produced there in a stimulating, heady atmosphere conducive to creative invention. As we worked, we played our compositions for each other, sought advice and exchanged opinions. It is a remarkable fact, but while we were at Ivanovo our work seemed to progress without any hitches. Were we

45 Isaak Glikman recalls Shostakovich telling him: 'In the evenings, after the convocations with their disgraceful, dismal debates, I returned home and wrote the third movement of the Violin Concerto. I finished it and it turned out well' (Glikman, *Letters to a Friend*, p. 78).
46 Mikhail Meyerovich: recorded interview with EW.

influenced by nature and our surroundings? Or was it the feeling of victory round the corner? Or simply that we were getting properly fed? The war drew us together in an atmosphere of unity.[47]

MSTISLAV ROSTROPOVICH spent a winter vacation at Ivanovo in company with the Shostakovich family:

I got to know the whole Shostakovich family very closely after winning the All-Union competition. In the winter of 1945/46, as a result of my first prize, I was given the opportunity to go to the Ivanovo 'House of Creativity and Rest'. A very interesting group of people gathered there at the time, including Shostakovich, Prokofiev and Khachaturian. Shostakovich's young son Maxim used to run up and down the corridors shouting and screaming, and I think that Prokofiev was longing to box his ears. He used to slink out of his room and hiss, 'Can't you be a bit quieter?' I played charades with Maxim, which made us very happy. We went skiing. And on one occasion I got soaked through to the skin. It was there that Dmitri Dmitriyevich subsidized my first concert dress, a dinner jacket which we bought in a second-hand commission shop in the town of Ivanovo. He gave me a thousand roubles towards this purchase. The Ivanovo Retreat lay outside the town, and we were taken into town by horse-drawn sleigh. After we had acquired the dinner jacket, Dmitri Dmitriyevich decided we must celebrate and we went to the booths in a small market where Dmitri Dmitriyevich selected some 'moonshine' liquor to wash down our purchase. The bottle had a piece of paper stuck down its neck serving as a stopper. On our return we went downstairs to the dining room where there was always some pickled cabbage available. Dmitri Dmitriyevich opened the bottle of moonshine. I was only eighteen at the time, and not too experienced. We immediately threw back a glass of the stuff. I have to say that in all my life I have never tasted anything so terrible. I nearly fainted. And Dmitri Dmitriyevich's face went into complete convulsions. He said, 'You understand, Slava, the woman, the woman who sold us this bottle, but she had a face with such a noble aspect! That's why I bought it from her, she had such a noble face. And to think she could sell us such a thing. How dishonourable!'[48]

47 Khentova, 'Shostakovich and Khachaturian', p. 11.
48 Mstislav Rostropovich: recorded interview with EW.

The musicologist ALEXEI IKONNIKOV only had a passing acquaintance with Shostakovich. However, he kept a diary record of his meetings with him at the Ivanovo Retreat. These form the basis of an article of reminiscences which give a valuable account of Shostakovich's routine.

Dmitri Dmitriyevich arrived at Ivanovo on 27 February 1946 with his wife Nina Vasilyevna and his children Galina (Galisha as they called her) and Maxim to get away from the hurly-burly of Moscow life in mid-winter. This happened only after 'a lot of pressure from Nina Vasilyevna', Dmitri Dmitriyevich told me subsequently. . . .

During this visit Dmitri Dmitriyevich was not working – at least not at his desk. . . . From my conversations with Nina Vasilyevna, Dmitri Dmitriyevich's wife, and from some of his own remarks, I understood that usually he did not compose during the winter. He liked best to compose in spring, summer and the early autumn. A new composition was conceived and carried in his mind in full detail from beginning to end. Only then was it committed to paper. The writing process was therefore very quick, and as a rule he made no corrections in his manuscripts; they were then only modifications in the details of the score. While Dmitri Dmitriyevich willingly listened to the advice of his friends, he never changed his music. . . .

Everyone is curious about the actual composition process, particularly when talking of a composer of Shostakovich's stature. One can only assume that this process of inner composition rarely ceased in Shostakovich's case. When he was alone, he immediately appeared to be completely disconnected from his surroundings; his look became unseeing and neutralized. He appeared to be a man of great inner tension, with his continually moving, 'speaking' hands, which were never at rest. Either they were squeezing his knees, or nervously brushing his forehead; at the same time his pose was natural and relaxed, almost floppy, but his hands continued to live their own life, especially the fingers, which were continually fidgeting and picking at something. Observing Dmitri Dmitriyevich at such moments, it seemed that he was absorbed in extremely concentrated thought, and one would never dream of disturbing his 'rest', as he called this state. If anybody did disturb him, then it was usually Maxim. Dmitri Dmitriyevich would then 'switch off' from his thoughts and open himself up to contact, never showing that he had been disturbed. In his dealings with people he displayed tact and refinement, whether it was a famous, important personage, or a waitress or some other member of the house staff.

Dmitri Dmitriyevich followed a regular routine: he got up quite early, around eight o'clock. Before breakfast he would sometimes stay in his room or else come to the dining room – he was always the first to appear. And around eleven he would set off with the children cross-country skiing. Usually Slava Rostropovich went with them, as a more experienced skier, and the initiator of these excursions. Sometimes I also joined them; Dmitri Dmitriyevich never objected to my presence, although I felt uncertain about imposing myself on the family outing.

I should say that Dmitri Dmitriyevich hardly knew how to ski. This was partly due to his bad eyesight (his myopia was minus nine or ten diopters), and to the fact that he couldn't bear the glare from the snow; he therefore wore dark glasses. On his head he wore a tall Rumanian sheepskin hat.

Although he was insecure on his legs, he tried to copy Rostropo-vich, who was very agile on skis. The biggest hurdle for him was a rather tricky steep hill which led from the path to the stream, which never froze over due to the springs in it. (The women from the village came here to do their washing.) Although the stream was not deep, it was a potential danger as one accelerated on the run downhill; the slope finished some twenty metres before the water. Dmitri Dmitriye-vich persisted in skiing down this hill so as to overcome this hurdle. He nearly always fell, and usually very clumsily: his skis would shoot out in different directions and his hat would fly off his head. It was very funny to watch. Slava Rostropovich and I tried our best not to laugh, but the village boys did not deprive themselves of this pleasure and would taunt the unfortunate skier. This of course embarrassed Shostakovich, but he stoically put up with their jibes and made his way up the hill again for another attempt.

On the other hand, when Maxim skied down the hill (usually much more skilfully than his father), Dmitri Dmitriyevich could not hide his agitation. He would cry out, 'Maxim, throw yourself down, fall down!' fearing that the boy would not be able to stop before reaching the stream, even though he was still a long way from the water.

The trouble was, Dmitri Dmitriyevich told us, that as he skied down the hill . . . he was possessed by a 'mortal fear'. . . . When I asked him why he continued his attempts despite this 'mortal fear', Dmitri Dmitriyevich replied, 'As an example, you see, an example, so that

Maxim does not experience fear.' During the family's stay at Ivanovo, Dmitri Dmitriyevich didn't miss a day of skiing outings with Maxim. . . .

Usually the later afternoon pastime was a walk, and after dinner the evenings were spent playing charades. The prime motivators of the game were Maxim and Galya (in particular the former), who long before the appointed hour of entertainment besieged Slava Rostropovich with the question, 'What shall we do at charades tonight?'[49]

The 1944 chamber compositions

On 11 February 1944, Ivan Sollertinsky died suddenly in Novosibirsk at the age of 41. Shostakovich had spent much of November and December 1943 with him in Moscow; Sollertinsky had come to Moscow for the première of the Eighth Symphony, a work to which he lent his full support. Shostakovich was devastated by the news of his death, and he dedicated his Piano Trio Op. 67 to the memory of his dearest friend. The work, however, was conceived when Sollertinsky was still alive. Shostakovich had informed Isaak Glikman in his habitual laconic style in a letter dated 8 December 1943: 'I am now writing a trio for violin, cello and piano.'[50] The last three movements were written in Ivanovo, where Shostakovich spent his second summer. The Trio was completed on 13 August. Almost immediately he embarked on his Second String Quartet Op. 68, which he finished in under a month on 20 September. It was dedicated to Vissarion Shebalin in honour of twenty years of their friendship. Writing to Shebalin on 6 September, Shostakovich confessed:

> I worry about the lightning speed with which I compose. Undoubtedly this is bad. One shouldn't compose as quickly as I do. Composition is a serious process, and in the words of a ballerina friend of mine, 'You can't keep going at a gallop.' I compose with diabolical speed and can't stop myself. . . . It is exhausting, rather unpleasant, and at the end of the day you lack any confidence in the result. But I can't rid myself of the bad habit.[51]

The composer MIKHAIL MEYEROVICH describes his dismay at the apparent ease and speed with which Shostakovich composed these two works:

I met Shostakovich after I graduated from the Moscow Conservatoire in 1944. He was chairman of the Examination Committee, and he

---

49 Alexei Ikonnikov, 'Some Strokes of a Portrait of Shostakovich', pp. 145–7.
50 Glikman, *Letters to a Friend*, p. 61.
51 Nikolayev, 'Letters to Shebalin', p. 83.

supported me warmly. So I graduated with good results and became a member of the Union of Composers. As such I was entitled to a spell at the Ivanovo House of Creativity. Ivanovo was very popular during the war as it had its own farm, and the food was good and plentiful. I spent a month there during August and September 1944.

When I arrived I saw Shostakovich, who was still a comparatively young man. Shostakovich was not too fond of the other composers of his own age, and he spent most of his time with me and my friend, his former pupil Yuri Levitin; we were the youngest composers there. He used to search us out and suggest we play some four-hand piano music. We took walks together. I had long been an admirer of Shostakovich and I quickly fell under his spell. I discovered him to be a very lively man who was always in motion and could not spend a minute without some occupation. Now he played billiards, now he played football. He insisted we join him in a game of football; he played with passion, throwing himself wholeheartedly into the game. Once I inadvertently knocked his glasses off his nose. I was embarrassed, but he said, 'That's all right. That's what the game is about.'

It was a mystery to me how he managed to compose so much music at the same time. He had just finished his famous Piano Trio and was working on his Second String Quartet. I wondered when he did the actual composing. The Trio took him a month. The Quartet was written in under four weeks before my very eyes. But nobody saw him at the desk or at the piano. I was intrigued and began to observe him closely. He would play football and fool around with friends; then he would suddenly disappear. After forty minutes or so he would turn up again. 'How are you doing? Let me kick the ball.' Then we would have dinner and drink some wine and take a walk, and he would be the life and soul of the party. Every now and then he would disappear for a while and then join us again. Towards the end of my stay, he disappeared altogether. We didn't see him for a week. Then he turned up, unshaven and looking exhausted. He said to me and Levitin, 'Let's go to an empty cottage with a piano in it.'

He played us the Second Quartet. He had only just completed it, as the score had that very day's date on it. He played somewhat haltingly, as if sight-reading. My friend, who knew Shostakovich better than I did, surprised me. He was not famous for his tact, and on that occasion he suddenly piped up, 'Dmitri Dmitriyevich, I have a criticism to make!' That took my breath away. Every note written by

Shostakovich was sacred to me, and he has a criticism to make! I was amazed.

'You know, these chords here,' my friend went on, 'are not really necessary.'

Shostakovich replied politely, but slightly on the defensive: 'What do you mean, not necessary?'

'I mean that you could very well do without them.'

'Well, I could very well do without the whole thing.'

The chords in question were very beautiful, and I especially liked them.

'If I were you,' my friend said, 'I'd scrap those chords.'

Shostakovich said, 'Yes, yes, I'll think it over.'

Later I realized that he had agreed out of politeness. When I heard how the same musician, having listened to a Shostakovich symphony, said to the composer, 'Dmitri Dmitriyevich, you know that place where a solo violin plays? In my opinion it would sound much better if the whole violin section played there.'

Shostakovich answered, 'Don't worry, that passage will flash past so quickly, nobody will notice anything.'[52]

52 Mikhail Meyerovich: recorded interview with EW.

CHAPTER FIVE

The Final Years of Stalinism

'Zhdanovshchina': the post-war hounding of the intelligentsia

In 1946 the Shostakovich family inaugurated a tradition of spending the summer months in the village of Komarovo outside Leningrad. Until 1950 they rented a State-owned dacha in the village, and thereafter they occupied the second floor of a two-storey dacha owned by V. V. Varzar, the composer's father-in-law.

Komarovo provided Shostakovich with a peaceful haven in which to compose. It was there that he completed his great five-movement Third String Quartet on 2 August 1946, which he had conceived in the early months of that year. Written on an almost symphonic scale, it follows the five-movement plan typical of Shostakovich's greatest and most serious compositions. The Quartet was premièred by its dedicatees, the Beethoven Quartet, in Moscow on 16 December. But soon, like so many of the composer's works of that period, it was withdrawn from public performance.

Shostakovich's time was now increasingly being swallowed up by official duties. In February 1947 he was nominated chairman of the Leningrad Composers' Organization, elected a deputy for Leningrad to the Supreme Council of the RSFSR and reappointed professor at the Leningrad Conservatoire. He also continued his teaching duties in Moscow. The family finally decided against moving back to Leningrad, although Shostakovich's mother and elder sister continued to reside there, and in February 1947 they settled in a new flat in Moscow on Mozhaiskoye Highway (later renamed Kutuzovsky Prospect).

In May and June 1947, Shostakovich spent some time in Prague, where he participated in several concerts of his own music, which included a performance of the Second Piano Trio with David Oistrakh and the Czech cellist Milos Sadlo. Oistrakh and Shostakovich had first met and played together in Turkey in 1935. On their return to Moscow, they continued to make music frequently together, playing through all the Mozart and Beethoven sonatas, amongst other things. Inspired by Oistrakh's artistry, the composer set to work on his First Violin Concerto; he had two movements completed by early December 1947. While he was working on the Finale,[1] the Central Committee of the Party published on 10 February 1948 the Decree 'On the Opera *The Great Friendship'*. The Decree made Vano Muradeli, the composer of the opera in question, into a scapegoat for all the most prominent Soviet composers, whom the Party condemned for so-called 'formalist tendencies'.

Despite the devastating implications of the Decree, it hardly came as a surprise. After the euphoria of victory, the politics of the cold war provided a pretext for internal repression. Ferocious campaigns were unleashed in the arts and sciences. Andrei Zhdanov, to whom Stalin had delegated responsibility for culture, had dealt with literature in 1946 with the Decree attacking Akhmatova and Zoshchenko for 'bourgeois degeneracy'.[2] The two writers were immediately expelled from the Writers' Union, and effectively deprived of all means of livelihood. This was followed by purges in the cinema and theatre, with music lagging a little behind in the Party's schedule of priorities.

But the ensuing persecution of scientists and doctors was, if anything, even more menacing and boorish. Whereas the purges of the late 1930s seemed to hit indiscriminately at people from all walks of life, the post-war terror was principally directed at the intelligentsia, and aimed at imposing an Orwellian ideological uniformity in every discipline. This relentless repression of the arts and sciences only came to an end with Stalin's death.

The Union of Composers reacted to the 10 February Decree by calling their first 'All-Union' Congress in April 1948, where an unprecedented spectacle of treachery occurred. Shostakovich was forced to repent publicly; he pronounced himself willing to write for the People, and follow Party directives.

In his initial despair, Shostakovich had even contemplated suicide, but with characteristic determination he decided that work must continue. As a consequence of the Decree, he was dismissed from his teaching posts and deprived of all sources of income. In these years he divided his compositional work into three distinct categories: serious music for 'the desk drawer', which had no chance of public performance; occasional music, such as *The Song of the Forests*, to be seen as evidence of his rehabilitation as a socialist composer; lastly, commissions for film music (the films in question were usually no more than propaganda vehicles for Stalin), which provided money to feed his family.

1 The concerto was completed on 24 March 1948.
2 The Decree was published in the Leningrad journals *Zvezda* and *Leningrad*, which themselves came under attack for publishing works by these authors.

Survival in a hostile environment

Here FLORA LITVINOVA writes about the tensions of everyday life as repression mounted in the post-war years.

In 1947, the Shostakoviches moved to a new home on the Mozhaiskoye Highway. They were given two adjoining flats, which had two separate entrances, although inside there was access from one flat to the other. In one were the children's quarters, and in the other, which was longer and narrower, were a large study with two grand pianos and the bedroom.

The Shostakovich children did their studies at home. Nina thought that they would gain nothing by going to school, and teachers came to the home to give them lessons in arithmetic, Russian, French, history and, of course, music. They went out for walks either with their nanny or with Nina. They were only allowed to play in the courtyard on their own for very short periods. Our Pavlik, who had acquired his freedom relatively early, travelled independently on public transport, and went to 'normal' school. Nina was horrified by our 'liberal' education. Pavlik would take the trolleybus on his own to come and play with her children.

Once, when I was approaching the Shostakovich's building, I saw Galya and Maxim recklessly darting in and out of the traffic on the Mozhaiskoye Highway. I promised that I wouldn't tell Nina, if they gave their word to stop running across the road. They were afraid of their mother and obeyed her.

Needless to say, Dmitri Dmitriyevich was very upset by the Zhdanov Decree on the writers Zoshchenko and Akhmatova which was published in 1946. He then became convinced that there would be no changes in cultural politics as had been hoped. He told us that he had met Zoshchenko on the street after the publication of the Decree. Zoshchenko complained that he was starving. Shostakovich gave him material support, without of course ever broadcasting this fact.

Once, later in the 1950s, I read out Akhmatova's poem 'Music', dedicated to Dmitri Dmitriyevich. I was delighted by it.

'It's very flattering, very flattering,' said Dmitri Dmitriyevich.

I interrupted, 'And what feeling and love she has for music.'

'No, no, what feeling and love she has for poetry,' he quipped.

It was soon after the war that Dmitri Dmitriyevich first talked to us about an incredibly gifted musician, the wonderful cellist and composer Rostropovich. 'He has a God-given talent. I want to help him to enter the Union of Composers, as he needs a flat. And as I have long been intending to take you out, let's all go together to the Aragvi Restaurant – I'll introduce you to him.'

I was thrilled by this proposal. I had never been to a proper restaurant before, let alone in such company!

Dmitri Dmitriyevich came to fetch me at the Biology Faculty at University. We walked to the Aragvi, where we met Slava. He turned out to be very slim and youthful, with a distinctive forelock and a fresh-coloured complexion. We were seated in a separate alcove and fed incredibly well and abundantly. The two men talked at length about the programmes of Rostropovich's forthcoming concert tour to Italy[3] (it was to be his first abroad, I believe). I remember them berating one of the musical bureaucrats, speaking sarcastically of his complete lack of culture.

'It's as if they deliberately appoint somebody to be in charge of music who knows absolutely nothing about it.'

'And I suppose they put a musician in charge of the visual arts?' I chipped in.

'No, no, more likely a carpenter or a chemist.'

We continued the tradition of spending New Year's Eve together. On December 1947 the Shostakoviches were living at the 'House of Creativity' at Ruza. They were in a despondent mood. Ideological attacks were now proceeding from all quarters. In *Pravda*, an article appeared on 'The Anti-Party Group of Theatre Critics', which stated that 'the critics have abandoned their responsibility before the People, and are the advocates of a rootless cosmopolitanism, so despicable to Soviet Man.' (A 'rootless cosmopolitan' was synonymous with the word 'Jew'.) The hostile nature of the 'cosmopolitans' was now revealed; the pseudonyms they hid behind were being exposed.

Before the New Year, we were hit by very hard frosts. Misha was unwell, but Nina insisted that we came to join them at Ruza.

---

3 Rostropovich went on a concert tour of Italy in 1950. The previous year he went to Finland as part of a delegation of artists. This had been his first trip to a 'capitalist' country.

Alikhanyan came to fetch us in his car. As we got into the car, Pavlik banged the door on his finger. The journey took a long time, and on arrival we found the Shostakoviches lodged in a cold, dark and uncomfortable house in the Ruza grounds.

Most of the musicians living there chose to see the New Year in together in the communal dining room. But Nina and Dmitri Dmitriyevich didn't wish to be with so many people, and our supper was brought to us separately at their house. The food provided was very tasty, and there was drink as well, but we were unable to throw off our gloomy mood. Everything seemed dreary, listless and uncosy that evening. Pavlik's hand had swollen up, and he developed a temperature. The woman who came to serve us some course or other remarked reproachfully, 'If we had such food and drink, we'd know how to have fun.' Indeed, these were still hungry times, and she no doubt thought it wicked that we weren't making merry when we had so much food. But a sense of foreboding hung in the air, as if trouble was only round the corner. And indeed it soon burst upon us.

My diary of 11 February 1948 says: 'How terrible. Poor Dmitri Dmitriyevich! How many times can they smash him? How much must a man bear? Why is he continually prevented from working, composing the music generated by his genius? What will happen to him? And once again it is all phrased in that same terrible style: "The enemies of Russian music, Shostakovich, Prokofiev, Shebalin, adherents of decadent, formalist music . . . are bringing about the extermination of true music." '

Soon the Plenum of the Union of Composers was opened. Nina decided to safeguard Dmitri Dmitriyevich by taking him off to the 'Uzkoye' Sanitorium for Academicians outside Moscow. She rang me to ask if I would go to visit them there. I arrived to find them in a state of great alarm, although they hoped that Dmitri Dmitriyevich would not be discovered and made to repent and castigate himself publicly. We walked in the silent forest. Dmitri Dmitriyevich and Nina gossiped about their academician neighbours at the Sanatorium. I went home, feeling somewhat relieved.

But a few days later I learnt that Shostakovich had appeared and spoken at the Plenum; his refuge had been ferreted out. Friends and advisers had warned that the Plenum would not close until he made an appearance. So he made the speech, reading out what had been written for him.

For the Shostakoviches, the following two years were very difficult. Dmitri Dmitriyevich wrote music for the film *The Young Guard*, and he wrote the insignificant oratorio *The Song of the Forests*. He travelled at Stalin's behest to the United States for the Cultural Peace Congress. He lived in a state of constant tension and fatigue.

So in the summer of 1950 Nina decided that they should take a holiday in the Crimea. It was decided they would drive there, 'inaugurating' the newly opened Moscow–Simferopol highway. She invited me to join them. We travelled in a carefree mood in two cars, the Shostakoviches' and Alikhanyan's. We took our time and stopped overnight en route at a hotel. On arrival, we stayed at the Writers' House in Yalta.

Before the war, the Shostakoviches used to go to the Crimea twice a year, once in spring and once in the autumn. They spent their summers outside Leningrad. It was my first trip to the Crimea, and I was enchanted by the sea, the mountains, the warm climate and beautiful landscapes. We drove all round the Crimea, climbed Ai-Petri, and I swam in the sea with the children. But I sensed that Dmitri Dmitriyevich felt oppressed away from home and without work. Living in the midst of many people, eating in company at high table was not to his taste. He remained untouched by the beauties of the scenery, and he cursed the expedition that we made to Alupka by sea, as the boat rolled with the slight swell.

When I shared these observations with Nina, she said, 'Yes, but you see it is absolutely essential that he gets some rest. Although he is bored, he is resting.' We returned to Moscow by train, to the visible relief of Shostakovich. In the meantime, events in the academic world, particularly in the fields of genetics and biology, continued to give cause for alarm. The 'Lysenko' session at the Academy of Sciences was followed by the 'Pavlov' session.[4] These campaigns reached their apogee on 13 January 1953 with press publication of 'the arrests of the groups of saboteur-doctors'. A ferocious form of anti-semitism was now openly espoused. The population at large was seized by panic,

4 At the 'historic' session of LAAS (the Lenin All-Union Academy of Agricultural Sciences) in August 1948, the biologist Trofim Lysenko imposed his views on genetics as dogma, causing untold damage to Soviet science. As early as 1945 Lysenko had been actively promoting his pet theory (the denial of intraspecific struggle), thereby coming into open conflict with the scientific community, and even with Zhdanov. But he won Stalin's support when he presented this theory as 'class biology', stating that acquired characteristics can be inherited, enabling the creation of new species and the transfor-

believing the rumours that had been deliberately put around that dentists were filling their patients' teeth with terrible infections, and that doctors were spreading the plague. Each day, when we arrived at work, we discovered who had been arrested the previous day.

It must have been my innate frivolity which prevented me at the time from grasping that these events could have a direct effect on our family. On the other hand, my mother-in-law, Ivy Litvinova, saw things for what they were. She bought four little suitcases for each of her grandchildren, and filled them with clothing and footwear. 'If we are arrested or deported,' she said, 'the children will be taken to an orphanage, and this will provide them with essential clothing to begin with. And you, Flora, must take this money to Nina Shostakovich. Ask her to help the children as far as possible.'

Feeling somewhat embarrassed, I went to see Nina and said, 'My mother-in-law has this notion that the children might be sent to an orphanage if something happens to us.' I expected Nina to reassure me that nothing of the sort could happen, but instead she took the money, put it on the table, and then sadly but seriously declared, 'I will of course do everything in my power. You understand, Flora, that if it were only a question of your children, I would simply take them in. After all Mitya and my children know them already. But with Tanya's children that makes four, and I fear it's simply unrealistic for us. I have no reason to doubt Mitya's kindness and goodwill; but you yourself know his enhanced sense of responsibility, and his nervous disposition. I am afraid that it would be beyond his strength.'

It was only then that, for the first time, I was overcome by alarm and fear for my children. Dmitri Dmitriyevich walked into the room, and Nina recounted our conversation.

'Cosmopolitans, Jews, so they are responsible, and we are slaves. Anti-semitism is a struggle against reason and culture. In reality, it is an admission that we are stupider, worse, and less well brought-up than the Jews,' he said.

---

mation of old ones. The idea that nature's development can be planned was no doubt appealing to the dictator.

Lysenko's position was reinforced in 1949 when the session of the Academy of Medical Science made Pavlov's theory of conditioned reflexes obligatory.

Litvinova recalls how in the autumn of 1947 Professor Dmitri Sabinin gave a brilliant speech attacking Lysenko at an open university discussion. As Sabinin was wildly applauded by the students, Lysenko's face went black with anger.

On my way home, it seemed to me that all those sitting in the bus were either of hostile disposition, or themselves unfortunate.[5]

The Violin Concerto

VENYAMIN BASNER gives an account of how he participated at the first hearing of Shostakovich's First Violin Concerto:

In the middle of March 1948, Shostakovich came up to Leningrad, soon after the publication of the Zhdanov Decree. It was the last occasion he taught before being dismissed from the Leningrad Conservatoire, although Shostakovich himself only discovered about his dismissal during his next trip to Leningrad.

I attended his class, and played some new work on the violin. Afterwards, Dmitri Dmitriyevich invited several of us to accompany him: Isaak Davydovich Glikman, Galya Ustvolskaya, Mitya Tolstoy and myself. He then played to us for the very first time his newly-finished violin concerto. Because of the political circumstances, the concerto was to wait until 1955 for its official première. Shostakovich played the work through once; then we asked him to play it again, as we were all bowled over by this shattering music.

It was then that Dmitri Dmitriyevich asked if I wouldn't mind trying something out on the violin: 'Venya, please give it a go, as I have my doubts about some of the violin writing. I want to know whether it is feasible to perform.'

Shaking like a leaf, I got my violin out. The very idea, that I should be the first violinist to attempt to play this difficult music, and, what's more, to sight-read it in the presence of the composer! Dmitri Dmitriyevich asked me if the B flat octaves were possible in the Scherzo, and checked some of the other double stops and passage work. I told him that I saw no reason why the music couldn't be performed as it was. To begin with I was extremely nervous, but as we continued, I relaxed and gained some courage, inspired by the intimate and charged atmosphere of this occasion.

I was of course present at the first performance of the First Violin Concerto, given by David Oistrakh in Leningrad in 1955. I attended all the rehearsals. The Concerto is a relentlessly hard, intense piece for the soloist. The difficult Scherzo is followed by the Passacaglia, then

5 Flora Litvinova, article commissioned for this book.

comes immediately the enormous cadenza which leads without a break into the Finale. The violinist is not given the chance to pause and take breath. I remember that even Oistrakh, a god for all violinists, asked Shostakovich to show mercy. 'Dmitri Dmitriyevich, please consider letting the orchestra take over the first eight bars in the Finale so as to give me a break, then at least I can wipe the sweat off my brow.'

Immediately Dmitri Dmitriyevich said, 'Of course, of course, why didn't I think of it?' By the next day he had made the necessary correction by giving the first statement of the theme in the Finale to the orchestra. The violin soloist comes in with the passage work afterwards. Dmitri Dmitriyevich was able to make this small but significant alteration without in any way changing the form and structure of the music.

In such cases of detail, Shostakovich was never obstinate, and he liked to take into consideration any valid objection from a performer. On the other hand, he always refused to make any correction that would affect the overall shape or structure of a work. If he didn't like something, his motto was 'I'll correct it in my next composition'. He certainly never cut a single bar out of any of his symphonies.[6]

The 1948 campaign against formalism in music

The 10 February Decree 'On the Opera *The Great Friendship*' had been preceded by a convocation of the 'Activists of Soviet Music' at the Central Committee in mid-January, where the question of formalism in music was discussed under Zhdanov's chairmanship. The initial furore centred on Vano Muradeli's opera *The Great Friendship*, which had allegedly been infiltrated by 'formalist and decadent' influences. Muradeli, a Georgian composer, who prided himself on his socialist realist style, had taken nationalist themes for the subject of his opera, thereby inadvertently stirring up a hornet's nest. His error had been to show the peoples of the north Caucasus (the Georgians, Osetians and Lezgins) as enemies of the Russians during the period of civil war (1918–20). Stalin, an Osetian, had a different version of history: the Osetians and Georgians were brothers of the great Russian people, and together they had won the civil war. Muradeli had further sinned by writing a dance in the style of a 'Lezginka', rather than quoting an authentic Lezgin folk dance. Shostakovich was to write into his lampoon *Rayok* an absurd parody of the Lezginka rumpus.

6 Venyamin Basner: recorded interview with EW.

To defend himself from Zhdanov's accusations that his music lacked melody and was 'a muddled collection of shrieking sound combinations',[7] Muradeli cast around wildly for somebody to blame. He criticized his Conservatoire teachers and the big names in Soviet music. But he stressed in particular the pernicious influence of Shostakovich, naming *Lady Macbeth* as the main source of evil. Zhdanov pointedly kept referring to the 'still valid' criticisms levelled at Shostakovich in the 1936 article 'Muddle Instead of Music'. The Eighth Symphony (in company with Prokofiev's Sixth) was also singled out for its 'unhealthy individualism' and pessimism.

The minutes of these meetings make depressing reading. Vissarion Shebalin's was the only voice of sanity; instead of criticizing his colleagues, he asked that funds be made available to repair the leaking Conservatoire roof.

The publication of the 'historic' Decree[8] unleashed a ferocious campaign against the most prominent Soviet composers; its main targets were Shostakovich, Prokofiev, Shebalin and Khachaturian. Muradeli seemed like an accidental intruder in this company, and in retrospect his inclusion in the gang of 'formalists' became something of a joke. Incidentally, Dmitri Kabalevsky, having discovered in advance that his name was to be included in this list, succeeded at the last minute in having it removed, and substituting that of Gavriil Popov instead.

The composer, YURI ABRAMOVICH LEVITIN studied with Shostakovich at the Leningrad Conservatoire from 1938. He quickly became a close friend of Shostakovich's, with whom he shared an interest in football and other sports. Levitin's strong allegiances with the hierarchy of the Union of Composers and the Party did not hinder this friendship, which continued throughout Shostakovich's lifetime. Here he writes about 'The Year 1948':

In January 1948, I was living together with my wife and son in the Composers' Union 'House of Creativity' at Ruza. Shostakovich was also staying there with his family. It was a wonderful winter. Dmitri Dmitriyevich was working, but he spent a lot of time out of doors. I was also working to the best of my ability, and I too didn't neglect my leisure activities. In a word, we were in excellent spirits, and various amusing incidents occurred.

But suddenly some alarming rumours started to loom out of the dark. It would appear that a meeting of the Central Committee was being prepared to deal with matters musical. Everyone understood

7 The Convocation of Activists for Soviet Music by the Central Committee of the Communist Party, Moscow, 1948.
8 The Decree of 10 February 1948 was always referred to in Soviet sources as the 'historic' Decree.

perfectly well what this implied, not least because of the recent Decrees published in the magazines *Zvezda* and *Leningrad*, where the names of Akhmatova and Zoshchenko had been trampled in the mud.

And indeed, soon afterwards the notorious January meeting was convoked by Zhdanov. As a group of young composers we were not called to attend. It was the academician Boris Asafiev who played a perfidious role in preparing the initial measures for the Central Committee's Decree that followed. Although he himself did not take an active part in the ensuing persecutions, he lent his protection to his willing and trusty assistants. The chief targets were, of course, Shostakovich and Prokofiev, although others were not forgotten either. Reading the stenographic report of the meeting, one is first and foremost struck by the tone of the speeches. After all, these were musicians speaking about their colleagues. They proved to be intractable, abusive, coarse and malicious in expressing themselves.

Here are some of the sentiments expressed for instance about Shostakovich's symphonies:

ZAKHAROV: 'I consider that from the point of view of the People, the Eighth Symphony can be in no way called a musical composition; it is a "composition" which has absolutely no connection with the art of music.'

KHRENNIKOV: 'Remember what was written about the Seventh Symphony, that it is a work of super-genius, and that Beethoven is a puppy beside Shostakovich.'

NESTYEV: 'Shostakovich's Eighth Symphony made an enormous impression on me – something similar to suffering a nervous shock or a profound physical injury.' (Fortunately, as we know, he was soon enough cured of this injury.)

And at last Zhdanov himself, who spoke of a 'series of works', but evidently with Shostakovich primarily in mind: 'Without mincing words, I have to say that a whole series of works by contemporary composers are infiltrated and overloaded to such a degree by naturalistic sounds that one is reminded – forgive the inelegant expression – of a piercing road drill, or a musical gas-chamber.'[9]

With the latter, he was referring to a 'dushegubka', a special vehicle

---

9 These lines, spoken by Zhdanov at the 1948 Central Committee Convocation of Activists for Soviet Music, are quoted more or less verbatim in Shostakovich's lampoon, *Rayok*.

supplied with gas used by the Fascists to kill their victims. Therefore Zhdanov's accusation was tantamount to an uncouth jeer.

Poor Muradeli found himself like a plucked chicken amongst those implicated by this meeting and the 'historic' Decree. After all, neither he nor his music had any connection with so-called 'formalism'. But Stalin, having seen his opera *The Great Friendship* at the Bolshoi Theatre, considered that Muradeli had misinterpreted the role of the Chechen-Ingush people, and from there everything started rolling. So the 'historic' Decree of the Central Committee was trumpeted abroad. It was followed by 'purging' sessions in all the creative organizations, and first and foremost in the Union of Composers. Much of interest went on at these meetings. At the time, many were accused of pronouncing or writing favourably on certain composers because they enjoyed a personal contact with the given composer. They were accused of not expressing their true convictions. I will never forget how one musicologist, who was chastised for writing a book about Shostakovich which was born of a personal relationship with the composer, publicly beat his breast, and, looking round the hall, his eyes fixed on me: 'Well, Yuri Abramovich, you at least can confirm that I haven't even been inside Shostakovich's house,' he cried out.

And I answered unhesitatingly: 'Yes, I can testify to that with a clean conscience. You never so much as set foot inside his house.'

There was ample opportunity for observation at these meetings. People's behaviour differed greatly. Vladimir Zakharov, Marian Koval' (both former 'RAPM men') and their ilk, having now reached a position of power, gave voice to their aggression and demanded unremitting repentance. There were many comic occurrences, but much tragedy as well.

Nina Vasilyevna, Dmitri Dmitriyevich's first wife, together with his close friend, the cinema director Leo Oskarovich Arnshtam, and myself went by car to the Sanatorium outside Moscow, where Dmitri Dmitriyevich stayed for some days. He was in a terrible state. We calmed him down as best we could. I reminded him how he had succeeded in overcoming all the difficulties which had been created by the article 'Muddle Instead of Music' in 1936, and how he had composed so many marvellous works afterwards. But, quite honestly, our persuasions were of little effect. Nina Vasilyevna went for a walk in the garden with Dmitri Dmitriyevich, while Leo Arnshtam and I sat on a bench and waited, our hearts saddened. After a while Nina

Vasilyevna returned in tears and said that it would probably be best to take Dmitri Dmitriyevich home.

'You cannot imagine our position. Mitya is on the verge of suicide.'

We have often heard talk of the incredible force of Shostakovich's spirit, of his great willpower. This was indeed so, but who knows what it cost him, this man who put kindness and justice above all else, and who was himself so unjustly insulted and humiliated. Fortunately, Dmitri Dmitriyevich was able to overcome these blows of fortune on this occasion as well, and before long he rebounded on his feet.

Once, some time afterwards, Dmitri Dmitriyevich said with habitual irony, 'I have decided to start working again, so as not to lose my qualifications as a composer. I am going to write a prelude and a fugue every day. I shall take into consideration the experience of Johann Sebastian Bach.'

And what do you think? In a few months' time, Dmitri Dmitriyevich showed the finished result of his labour, the brilliant Twenty-Four Preludes and Fugues for Piano solo at the Union of Composers, a work that has gone on to achieve world fame. The audition was an interesting and salutary experience. I have to say at once that the Preludes and Fugues aroused no enthusiasm from the Union officials. Zakharov and others like him severely criticized Dmitri Dmitriyevich's work. The only person who expressed sentiments worthy of the music was the outstanding pianist Mariya Venyaminovna Yudina. She said something along these lines: 'Comrades, what has got into you, are you out of your minds? Surely you understand what we are dealing with? This music will soon be performed as frequently as Bach's Preludes and Fugues are today. We should bow down to the very ground in front of Dmitri Dmitriyevich!'

As Yudina was considered to be not completely normal, nobody paid any attention to her words, which were the only normal words pronounced on that occasion.

I am afraid that maybe you have got the idea that perhaps I expressed myself unworthily on that occasion. No, of course not. Nevertheless, although I and the composer Grigori Fried both praised the work up to a point, our speeches certainly couldn't bear comparison with Yudina's.

This nevertheless didn't stop the authorities at the Union of Composers from calling the two of us up to the Party Bureau, where, as Party members, we were questioned and admonished for our 'incorrect' behaviour. After a dressing down, Fried was 'given a warning' and I was given a strange reprimand, whereby 'my attention was directed to my mistakes'.

But to return to 1948. After the Decree, these dubious revelries continued for a considerable length of time, with the Zakharovs and Kovals assuming prominent positions. This continued until, a year later, Dmitri Dmitriyevich received an unexpected telephone call. Immediately after the Decree, the State Committee responsible for Repertoire (Glavrepertkom) drew up a blacklist of compositions defined as 'formalist'; the performance and distribution of all the listed works were forbidden. I hardly need say that the works of Shostakovich and Prokofiev occupied a prominent position on this list. But it affected a wide circle of composers, and, amongst others, my name was also included.

At the end of February or the beginning of March of 1949, I was visiting the Shostakoviches during the daytime. Dmitri Dmitriyevich wasn't feeling very well. I sat talking to him and Nina Vasilyevna. The telephone rang, and Dmitri Dmitriyevich picked up the receiver. A second later he said helplessly: 'Stalin is about to come on the line . . .'[10]

Nina Vasilyevna, a woman of determination and energy, immediately jumped up and went to the next room and picked up the other receiver. I froze in position on the sofa. For the next moments, naturally all I heard were Dmitri Dmitriyevich's answers, but from them I could clearly deduce the nature of the talk. Stalin was evidently enquiring after Shostakovich's health. Dmitri Dmitriyevich answered disconsolately: 'Thank you, everything is fine. I am only suffering somewhat from stomach-ache.'

Stalin asked if he needed a doctor or any medicine.

'No, thank you, I don't need anything. I have everything I need.'

Then there was a long pause while Stalin spoke. It transpired that he was asking Shostakovich to travel to the USA for the Congress of Peace and Culture.

---

10 This conversation is also described in Solomon Volkov's *Testimony*. All the accounts differ very slightly one from the other, although in substance they are the same. According to certain sources, Leo Arnshtam was also present on this occasion.

' . . . Of course I will go, if it is really necessary, but I am in a fairly difficult position. Over there, almost all my symphonies are played, whereas over here they are forbidden. How am I to behave in this situation?'

And then, as has been recounted many times since, Stalin said with his strong Georgian accent, 'How do you mean forbidden? Forbidden by whom?'

'By the State Commission for Repertoire (Glavrepertkom),' answered Dmitri Dmitriyevich.

Stalin assured Shostakovich that this was a mistake, which would be corrected; none of Dmitri Dmitriyevich's works had been forbidden; they could be freely performed. Afterwards we spent a long time discussing all of this; for some reason we didn't really believe that the ban would be lifted. Nevertheless, in a few days' time, all the composers whose names appeared on the 'blacklist' received the following document, and I quote it verbatim:

'Copied Extract from the Order No. 17 of the Chief Direction in Control of Representations and Repertoire of the Commission in Charge of the Arts under the Auspices of the Council of Ministers of the USSR. Moscow, 14 February 1948.

'To forbid the performance and to remove from the repertoire the following works by Soviet composers, which have been planned in programmes of concert organizations . . .'

Here followed a list of all the works by those composers to whom this document was addressed. Evidently the works of mine on that list had been selected at random. There were three of them: Festive Overture, Piano Concerto, and Quintet for Mixed Ensemble.

The document was signed: 'Head of the Chief Command in Control of Representations and Repertoire, M. Dobrynin.'

This document lay underneath another which had been stapled on top of it. That read:

'The Council of Ministers of the USSR. Order No. 3197 of 16 March 1949. Moscow, The Kremlin.

'1. To recognize as illegal the Order No. 17, dated 14 February 1948, of the State Repertoire Committee in charge of the Arts attached to the Council of Ministers of the USSR which forbids the performance of a series of works of Soviet composers, and demands that they are removed from all programmed repertoire, and to rescind this Order.

'2. To reprimand Glavrepertkom for publishing an illegal order.

'Signed: Chairman of the Council of Ministers of the USSR, J. Stalin.'

That was the document. This probably is the only occasion of which I am aware when an institution rather than an individual person received an official reprimand!

And so, ever so slightly, the bird had its feathers singed. But ever so slightly. Strange as it may seem today, I have to say that there was no shortage of those wishing to participate in the pogroms. Not to mention those who didn't miss an opportunity to use the tribune at any audition, discussion, plenum or congress of the Composers' Union to hurl abuse at their colleagues; they were also more than ready to appear in print with their accusations. It is impossible to forget that disgraceful squib on Shostakovich printed in several editions of the magazine *Sovietskaya Muzyka* which was written by its then chief editor, M. Koval'.[11] Many angry and malicious articles were published in various newspapers, signed by composers and musicologists.

In conclusion, I will recount one amusing episode. In 1948 an article was printed in the newspaper *Kultura I Zhisn* written by M. I. Chulaki. It constituted a ferocious attack on the Leningrad Philharmonic and its conductor E. A. Mravinsky, who, instead of performing worthy compositions, went on promoting 'formalist' creations by such composers as Shostakovich, Bunin, and LeviTAN. (This misprint of my name allowed my poor mother to say, when questioned, that they were no doubt referring to some other composer.) Since the Leningrad Philharmonic had only ever performed two works of mine, *Requiem in Memory of Fallen Heroes*[12] and the oratorio *Fatherland*, it was obvious that Chulaki was delivering a 'well-aimed' blow specifically at these works.

Eighteen years later, with these events well behind us, I thought to myself: 'And maybe I should resurrect the *Requiem in Memory of Fallen Heroes* and see if a performance might be sanctioned?'

11 Koval' wrote a long article, 'The Creative Path of Shostakovich', which appeared in three consecutive issues of *Sovietskaya Muzyka* immediately after the publication of the 'historic' Decree in February 1948. He found evidence of 'decadence' and 'cacophony' in almost all of the composer's works, dubbing them 'formalist vermin'. According to Abraam Gozenpud, Shostakovich only reacted to this disgraceful calumny with the laconic comment, 'Surely he is ashamed of himself.'

12 At the time Shostakovich defended this work in print.

Soon after I played the *Requiem* at the Secretariat of the Union of Composers. After listening to the work, the first to pronounce on it was M. I. Chulaki. He declared, 'I simply cannot understand how it should come to be that such a good composition should lie on the shelf unperformed all these years.'[13]

Loyalty and treachery

The consequences of the Decree on Formalism in Music

The series of Decrees issued by the Central Committee were part of Stalin's scheme (whose realization was initially entrusted to Zhdanov) to implement a rigorous ideological uniformity in all cultural and scientific institutions. Anything that did not conform to the Party guidelines had no right to exist. The effects of the Decree on Formalism in Music cannot be underestimated; they were profound, far-reaching and influenced the perceptions of Soviet composers and musicians for several decades. In the short term, the consequences of the Decree were appalling; many people lost their jobs and financial security. People from all walks of life, including students and school children were encouraged to report on their colleagues and teachers. Meetings were called where the victims of the Decree were publicly humiliated.

Vissarion Shebalin's widow, ALISA MAXIMOVNA, recounted how her husband was driven out of his job as director of the Conservatoire:

I shall never forget his departure from the Conservatoire. A meeting was called at the Grand Hall where Shebalin was given a 'working over'. He was made to sit on stage while he was maligned and vilified on all sides. I went up to the balcony and observed him through a pair of binoculars; I was frightened that his health would not bear the strain of all this abuse. I must say I felt tremendous pride at the dignity with which he behaved that day. After everyone had spoken, Shebalin gave a short and dignified speech. The hall was packed full, mainly with teachers, students and the Conservatoire staff. When he finished speaking the whole hall burst into thunderous applause – this was nothing less than a spontaneous show of support for Shebalin. In other words it was the administrators and officials who suffered a defeat that day.[14]

MSTISLAV ROSTROPOVICH remembers the devastating effect of the Zhdanov Decree on professional musicians and Conservatoire students.

13 Yuri Levitin, 'The Year 1948', unpublished article.
14 Alisa Shebalina: recorded interview with EW.

After the infamous Decree of 1948 Shostakovich was dismissed from the Conservatoire. I was transferred to Nikolai Rakov's orchestration class. Although he was a very nice and knowledgeable man, whom I greatly liked, he wasn't Shostakovich. I attended his classes for a while, but soon I couldn't bear it any more. I decided to leave, and I never graduated as a composer from the Conservatoire.

It was an unhappy time in many ways, as the Decree was a very divisive issue among the students and teachers of the Conservatoire. The students generally were grouped in various categories. The first, and, I regret to say, rather numerous category, was of those students who realized that this was an opportunity to make a career for themselves. An article was published in *Pravda* about the reaction of students to the Decree on 'Formalism in Music'. It reported that a certain student of composition, Kirill Molchanov, had told our correspondent: 'I now feel myself completely liberated. I walk on the streets and sing, my heart pours out melody!' When I met Molchanov in the Conservatoire (we were fellow students), I looked at him: 'So,' I said, 'you are singing, then, but do you have a voice?'

He looked a bit abashed. But his whole subsequent career at the Bolshoi Theatre showed him up in the light of such behaviour. This first group was fairly numerous. There was also a second, smaller group of decent people with consciences who tried to get on with their everyday lives.

I remember how we students were called to a meeting at the Conservatoire. A certain Klavdia Uspenskaya, who taught music history, spoke with rabid frenzy against the 'formalists'. Other speeches were made in a similar vein by those who were, in essence, our teachers. Many students were forced into line by these teachers. Nonetheless, they were deserters.

In general Shostakovich was left almost totally exposed in his surroundings. There was only a tightly-knit group of people who were close to him, and, as genuine friends, they were well aware of the force and genius of Shostakovich the composer. For instance, such people as Yuri Levitin, Metak Weinberg and Lev Lebedinsky, notwithstanding their Party affiliation, retained a good relationship with Dmitri Dmitriyevich. In Leningrad there was also a cluster of faithful friends, including such distinguished people as the great composer Galina Ustvolskaya, who had been a pupil of Dmitri Dmitriyevich. She certainly regarded Shostakovich very highly, and indeed there was a very 'tender' relationship between them. Dmitri Dmitriyevich was also tied by a very close friendship to Isaak Davydovich Glikman. Such were the people whose silent, unvoiced understanding lent support to Shostakovich. Although we maintained silence, we were perfectly aware of what he suffered in this situation. Naturally my own loyalty to Shostakovich knew no bounds, and Dmitri Dmitriyevich was undoubtedly aware of this.

For me the Decree served the function of a biological experiment. I believe that only a great force of talent could help one resist such a cruel stroke of fortune. The director of the Moscow Conservatoire, Vissarion Shebalin, a close friend of Dmitri Dmitriyevich, was one of those who bore himself with great dignity. He was a profoundly honest and pure man. Shebalin suffered tremendously from the Decree, you might simply say that it killed him. He was without doubt a great composer. Had he lived in a different country than Russia, he would have been a prominent national composer. But he was obscured by the shadows of Shostakovich and Prokofiev, and in a sense, Stravinsky, who also belongs to our Russian culture; he did not possess the same creative potential as these composers.

Shebalin was so profoundly affected by this injustice that it ended with him suffering a very bad stroke. His right hand ceased to function, and he temporarily lost his speech. He learnt to write with his left hand. I (amongst others) supported him, and used to go and see him. One of his very last works, an excellent cello sonata, was dedicated to me, and I performed it during his lifetime.

Nikolai Yakovlevich Myaskovsky also underwent serious sufferings, but not to the same extent as Shebalin; because his talent was greater, he possessed greater resistance. So in this biological sense, he weathered the Decree better. I remember the celebrations when his Second Cello Sonata was awarded the Stalin Prize. I was at Richter's place at the Arbat, and on learning the news I immediately ran off to see Nikolai Yakovlevich. He was a humorous man, a sort of real Russian intellectual, who in some ways resembled Turgenev. Neither Prokofiev or Shostakovich were in the same way representative of this kind of post-Turgenev intelligentsia. On that evening, there was a gathering of guests who had come to celebrate with him, and he got slightly tipsy. He was so happy about the award that he took a copy of the Cello Sonata and inscribed it to me there and then: 'To dear Slava Rostropovich, the wonderful performer of this music which is not quite worthy of him.' This was his Turgenev-like reticence.

Aram Khachaturian suffered from the Decree to roughly the same extent as Myaskovsky, but for different reasons. He felt deprived of his social status. For him it was very important that he could ring up Comrade Alexei Kosygin, and that he was on friendly terms with the chairman of the Council of Ministers. In this way he set himself up on a pedestal. He was a wonderful man, but he didn't realize that his music alone was enough to raise him to these heights. For instance, he would tell me, 'Slava, I rang the chairman of the Armenian Council of Ministers, we had a little chat . . .' So Khachaturian suffered from the loss of position, and from the fact that he, a great national composer, had been trampled in the mud, after having been raised to such heights of glory. How could this happen to him . . .? I have to say that Shostakovich often told me that he considered that Khachaturian was the most decent and honourable of all the composers whom he knew. Unlike Dmitri Kabalevsky, who was far from being a decent person.

Shostakovich was, of course, aware that Kabalevsky was a time-server. Dmitri Dmitriyevich used to laugh, telling me how he had once been invited to Kabalevsky's home when Kabalevsky's mother was still alive. She challenged him: 'Tell me Mitya, how do you manage to arrange for so many performances of your music? How do you do it? Please teach *my* Mitya.'

At the next level of reaction to the 1948 Decree came Shostakovich and Prokofiev. Their suffering was experienced first and foremost as a blow to their finances. I have often recounted that famous occasion when Prokofiev told me, 'Slava, I have no money left to buy our breakfast. We have nothing to eat.'

Shostakovich also experienced tremendous hardship; I don't know which of them suffered more profoundly. Although there was a certain childish naivety in the way Prokofiev lived through this ordeal. He was offended to the very core of his being. Shostakovich saw things on a tragic level. For him it was a calamity that the people for whom he had written his works with his very blood, to whom he had exposed his very soul, did not understand him. He was very conscious of this. Therefore, each person who remained near to him and still openly demonstrated admiration and affection towards him was as precious as a diamond.

In the years after the Decree, Shostakovich's works were, practically speaking, no longer publicly performed. For this reason I despised

Oistrakh, because the brilliant Violin Concerto written for him in 1948 was allowed to lie around waiting for its first performance. Whereas Richter fought to be able to perform Prokofiev's Ninth Piano Sonata, which was dedicated to him. I was a witness to Richter's refusal to play, cancelling his concerts until he was granted permission to perform the Ninth Sonata. Unlike Oistrakh, who calmly held back the Violin Concerto for several years before he played it. To my mind this was shameful and cowardly.[15]

A master's integrity defended

The composer, Isaak Schwartz was born into a highly cultivated Leningrad family. Schwartz's father was a professor of history and archaeology at Leningrad University, and a friend of Sollertinsky's

Schwartz describes his childhood as being infused by an awareness of Shostakovich's unique personality. His father had a great admiration for the young composer, and when *Lady Macbeth* was unjustly criticized, he took it as a personal misfortune. Schwartz's father was arrested in 1936 and died the following year in prison.

As a son of an 'enemy of the People', ISAAK SCHWARTZ's experiences are typical of many of his generation, and as such evoked a sympathetic and helpful response from Shostakovich.

During the late 1920s, when the country was undergoing a 'total and all-sweeping' subjugation to ideology, Father made a joking observation at a university gathering. He stated that he was doubtful if there was much future in combining archaeology and Marxism. This joke cost him dearly; he was dismissed from the university, and he had to find other employment as a cashier in the house management office. In December 1936, at the very start of the Ezhovshchina,[16] he was arrested and thrown into prison.

A repercussion of Father's arrest was the exile of my mother, my sister and me from Leningrad to Frunze, Kirghizia, in the summer of 1937. Mother was a school teacher of literature, but she was forbidden to teach in exile; she had to learn a new profession, that of economist. It was there that, as a fourteen-year-old I started my working life as a musician, having my first composition lessons from Vladimir Ferré.

15 Mstislav Rostropovich: recorded interview with EW.
16 Ezhovshchina, 'The Era of Ezhov' is a reference to the worst period of the Stalinist purges.

We were surrounded by many wonderful people. But how great was our suprise to discover that Shostakovich's sister, Mariya Dmitriyevna was amongst those exiled here. I saw her constantly at concerts, in which I often participated. Mariya Dmitriyevna took me under her wing.

Thanks to her, Dmitri Dmitriyevich later received me in his Leningrad home, in 1945 in his flat on Kirovsky Prospect. He gave me a heart-felt welcome. 'In the foreseeable future,' Dmitri Dmitriyevich said, 'I will only be in Leningrad rarely, and then on short visits, so I cannot teach you. You badly need regular teaching on a weekly basis.' He recommended that I enroll in Boris Arapov's class, and promised to talk to him in advance. Shostakovich also sent me to Benedict Schnittke for some most useful harmony lessons prior to the Conservatoire entrance exam. In other words, all the teachers that taught me the rudiments of my profession were recommended to me by Shostakovich.

Dmitri Dmitriyevich followed my development. Sometimes he would complain that I didn't compose enough. Life was difficult for me then as I had to work to support my family and small child and was unable to devote myself to composition. Then in 1946 I was suddenly released from paying the Conservatoire fees for my education; for two years I didn't pay a penny. I couldn't understand how this had happened; however, after a while I stopped questioning the situation. It was certainly a great help to me in life.

Years later, at the première of my ballet, *On the Eve*, at the Maly Opera, Pavel Serebryakov, the director of the Conservatoire congratulated me and exclaimed, 'You see it wasn't for nothing that Shostakovich paid for your education!' I was stunned. Only then did Serebryakov remember that Dmitri Dmitriyevich had pleaded that his charity be kept a strict secret.

. . .

I was fortunate in having wonderful teachers at the Conservatoire. Additionally, there were three musicians who played a tremendously important role in my life; they were my Teachers with a capital T: Shostakovich, Nikolai Rabinovich and Mikhail Druskin. At a time of enormous hardship, these were the great individuals whose independent minds personified for us younger people the concept of progressive enlightenment in our culture.

I used to attend Shostakovich's classes. His principles, both moral and pedagogical were of the greatest importance to me. His judgements on music were never biased; he urged us to learn from the great masters. I always remember his formula, 'Know less works, but know them inside out.'

I was sincerely glad when others mistook me for a Shostakovich pupil, although I have to admit that the consequences were sometimes strange, if not positively frightening.

At the end of the 1940s, during the anti-formalist campaign, I was labelled an 'out-and-out formalist'. (I still have the Conservatoire newspaper which printed this statement.) The accusation pointed to Shostakovich's influence in my music. Imitation, said Anatole France, is an indeterminate form of admiration. Shostakovich was my idol, and it was only natural that this was reflected in my music. I wrote symphonic music in those years, and it seemed to me that the essence of what I wrote was indeed born under Shostakovich's influence. I didn't just listen to his symphonies, I studied them untiringly.

Shostakovich's dismissal from the Leningrad Conservatoire was accompanied by a terrifying and relentless hounding of the composer. This was a true drama for those who loved him and were aware of his stature and great personality.

The secretary of the Party Organization of the Composers' Faculty, A. Ostrovsky invited me to come to his office one day. He suggested, or to be more accurate, ordered me to make a public statement denouncing Shostakovich as a bad teacher. He tried hard to convince me; in his opinion, as a 'formalist' I had nothing to lose. Psychologically this was a very difficult situation for me; I was a marked man, in so far as my father was an 'enemy of the People', and my mother remained exiled. I lived in constant fear for my own family. Nevertheless, I answered Ostrovsky ingenuously, saying that I didn't understand what he was getting at, that, on the contrary, Shostakovich was an excellent teacher. It was unthinkable for me to betray him. I decided that, rather than stoop so low, I would prefer to be thrown out of the Conservatoire.

Later Shostakovich came up to me and gave me a ticking off: 'I am most displeased by your behaviour. You had no right to act like that. You have a family, a wife, small children. You should think about them, and not about me. If I am criticized, then let them criticize me – that's my affair.' But I saw in his eyes such a penetrating look of sympathy and affection for me, and such compassion! I think that it was something Shostakovich never forgot, after all his response was completely spontaneous and heart-felt.[17]

Eradicating Formalism in the Conservatoire

The musicologist MARINA DMITRIYEVNA SABININA describes the restrictive atmosphere of the Moscow Conservatoire after the publication of the Zhdanov Decree. She herself suffered personal tragedy during this period, when her father, the distinguished biologist Dmitri Sabinin, committed suicide in 1952, following the hounding of scientists in the wake of the 'Lysenko' and 'Pavlov' campaigns:

The chief professors amongst the formalists had already been dismissed, including Shostakovich and Shebalin, the director of the Conservatoire (who was replaced by the choir-master, Alexander V. Sveshnikov). Already, the Conservatoire staff and students had been called to a meeting which had been fully attended. On that occasion the orators had liberally strewn their speeches with quotations from the Central Committee's 10 February Decree, castigating the adherents of the 'Anti-People Movement', while eagerly avowing renewed allegiance to 'realism'. Only a hint of discord undermined the reigning atmosphere of officious solemnity when some anonymous written messages were presented to the Presidium, and when from the upper balcony some disorderly voices shouted down angry and mocking interpolations. Naturally, the messages were not read out.

But now a meeting was convoked for us students of the Compositional and Musicological Faculty. Its purpose was to rid us of any further contamination by the plague of 'formalism', and to indoctrinate us the more forcefully with the Party's guiding ideas.

The meeting was held in classroom no. 21, where our course lectures on Party history usually took place. Normally, these lectures were packed out; but today there were relatively few of us, as only our faculty, the smallest in the Conservatoire, were being called to order. However, the atmosphere was emphatically official, like that of a mass demonstration: a long table was placed on the platform, and seated behind it were the Presidium members. One after the other, severe-faced, they went up to the tribune to speak. At the beginning it was incredibly dull, and we sat there rigidly, listening quietly and attent-

17 Isaak Schwartz, 'Reminiscences of Shostakovich', article commissioned for this book.

ively. Klavdia Uspenskaya, a teacher famous for her semi-literacy, a one-time Komsomol-activist of the 'Rabfak',[18] and a member of RAPM of the 1920s was spouting some phrases full of high-flown slogans; the solid and pedantic Y. V. Keldysh was grinding out the standard phrases about the wisdom of the Decree in his colourless, whining voice. I now only have a hazy memory as to who else spoke and when. But I do remember Kiril Molchanov's performance that evening. He had already surpassed himself in a wonderfully effective interview which had recently appeared in the national press. He had stated that, 'Finally I feel free and happy, my spirit sings from joy.'

The critical moment was reached during the speech of the newly-appointed secretary of the Party Bureau of the Conservatoire, Semyonov. He was a man with a rough-hewn, simple face and a manner of speech notable for its lack of culture and education. He succeeded in awakening the auditorium from its apathy when he declared belligerently that, had it not been for the Decree which had now restored order, our music would have disintegrated into a state of shameful anarchy: 'So any old Shostakovich or any old Prokofiev could have written whatever he felt like.'

At this point the hall erupted. Hermann Galynin, one of Shostakovich's brightest and most talented pupils, a lad of spontaneous and ungovernable temper who worshipped his teacher, attempted to jump up from his seat. His wife N. Shumskaya and myself, who were sitting on either side of him, clung on to him and tried to hold him down.

'What are you up to?'

'Let me go, I'm going to kill the bastard.'

As is my wont when dealing with slightly unbalanced people, I asked him brusquely how he intended to carry out his threat: 'What will you kill him with?'

'A chair!' Hermann shrieked furiously, trying to grab a chair from the row in front.

Fortunately all the chairs were firmly welded together, and nothing came of the intended 'murder'; but he continued to shout and struggle in our arms. And behind us, Lolya Kaluzhsky, who had sufferred concussion at the Front, normally an introverted and silent type, was

18 In the 1920s, Workers' Faculties (Rabfak) were established for the education of the proletariat, on the premise that education was no longer the sole right of the intelligentsia.

clawing the back of my chair, shouting hysterically, 'Out, Out!' and shaking in nervous paroxysm.

The rest of the happenings are now jumbled indiscriminately in my memory: pandemonium, shambolic stamping and banging, riotous mass hysteria. The members of the Presidium were completely unable to make themselves heard over the noise of the hall. I returned home worn out and hoarse. I too had evidently been shouting at the top of my voice, and indeed had done such damage to my vocal chords that I could only talk in a whisper for the next three days.

One can only suppose that this meeting convinced the authorities that dangerous and seditious currents were rampant among the students of our faculty, and we were in need of serious 're-education'. The graduation exams were postponed until the autumn, so that there would be time to correct our 'errors' and adjust our written thesis in line with the theories postulated by the Decree.

Things were more difficult for the composition students, particularly for Shostakovich's ex-pupils. For their graduation they had to prepare new 'realistic opuses', preferably cantatas or symphonic works with programmes. Therefore it was decided to keep them back for a year or two, after they were transferred from their 'formalist' teachers (now dismissed) to professors who had survived the campaign of devastation. Naturally, it was hardest of all for the really talented, such as Galynin and Boris Tchaikovsky. The latter's interesting one-act opera *The Star* was censured and mangled beyond recognition; apart from the fact that it showed the unmistakable influence of Shostakovich, its libretto was based on a story by the disgraced writer, Emanuel Kazakevich. Moreover, the work ended tragically, which at the time was evaluated as 'pessimism'. Galynin rehabilitated himself with his *Epic Poem* (1950) where he successfully utilized folklore. This work was awarded the Stalin prize. But the trauma that he had experienced in 1948 decisively accelerated his inherent psychiatric disorders, and by the beginning of the 1950s he had developed schizophrenia.

It was easier for the less gifted to adapt. Thus a student from my year, who had been studying with Shebalin, hurriedly took down from the wall over his bunk in the hostel the photographs of his former idols, Shostakovich and Prokofiev. He then assured us that he had always respected and loved the Russian classics of the nineteenth century, rather than these formalists and modernists.

But the repercussions of that notorious February meeting stayed with us for a long time, and were still in the air one June evening the following year. We made music throughout the night to our hearts' content, and we played through Shostakovich's *Songs from Jewish Poetry* and his Third String Quartet. Then suddenly we decided to salute those 'heroes' who had instructed us at the meeting. In the early hours of the morning, we rang Uspenskaya and Keldysh, and huskily croaked obscenities down the telephone, until our 'heroes' stopped answering the calls. No doubt a stupid, senseless piece of daring or hooliganism? Yet I think it arose from a profound need for emotional release, a necessity to get rid of our pent-up anger and to protest against those insults so injustly heaped on our idols.[19]

The following is another of Sabinina's short stories about the Zhdanov Decree period:

On a winter evening of 1949/50, I was sitting alone on a bench in the cloakroom foyer of the Small Hall of the Conservatoire, where I had a rendezvous with a friend. Shostakovich appeared, glanced around, obviously on the lookout for somebody whom he couldn't spot. On seeing me he came up and greeted me. 'Are you waiting for somebody? So am I. So, shall we wait together?'

It was amazing, considering the circumstances, to see Dmitri Dmitriyevich as jolly and as mischievous as he was that evening. After all we were within the walls of that very Conservatoire which had just dismissed the disgraced composer from its staff. A solemn procession trailed passed us towards the cloakroom – a meeting of the Academic Council had just finished and the professors and teachers were dispersing. And here Dmitri Dmitriyevich started to imitate their smug, obsequious and fawning behaviour, their pompous manners of speech. Miming certain of the professors, he played out whole scenes, displaying a brilliant gift for comedy in his simultaneous impersonations of several characters. It is said that in his youth he adored such theatrical scenarios; but right here and now, one would have hardly thought he was in the mood for such pranks.

Some of the more notorious musicologists processed before us. Dmitri Dmitriyevich obviously despised them totally for their oppor-

19 Marina Sabinina, 'How We Were Re-educated: The End of February 1948', short story commissioned for this book.

tunist lack of principle, for the extraordinary ease with which they could change their opinion, and not least for their lack of talent and pedantic vacuity. The whole spectacle made him recall an amusing story.

'Once when I was a boy, I came for a piano lesson at Leonid Nikolayev's home. As was usual in those years, I was emaciated and hungry, and Nikolayev ordered his nephew Misha to "make an omelette for Mitya". The nephew obediently set about it; as I was eating the omelette Nikolayev started to expound: 'Just think, Misha cooked the omelette, you are eating it, but a third person passes by who neither knows how to prepare an omelette nor wants to eat one, but he comes just in order to talk about the omelette. That person is the musicologist, whose sole aim is to hold a discourse about the essence of an omelette. Who needs him? Do you, the hungry person eating it, or Misha who prepared it? No, absolutely nobody needs him.'

Obviously this tirade was aimed at our Conservatoire frauds, and not at all professors in principle. For instance, Shostakovich had a deep respect for Sollertinsky and had gained an enormous amount from him. But the circumstances of 1948/49 were enough to arouse disgust and revulsion, if not hatred, against the whole race of musicologists who so diligently helped in the persecution of the 'formalists'.[20]

The campaign against cosmopolitanism

Simultaneous to the purges in the arts and sciences, the campaign against 'rootless cosmopolitans' (the euphemism coined for Jews) intensified, culminating in the 'Doctors' Plot' of 1953. The Soviet press accused the implicated doctors (who were dubbed 'assassins in white coats') of belonging to a terrorist group which had confessed to murdering Zhdanov in 1949, and which was now conspiring to assassinate the military and political leaders of the country.

It is believed that Stalin had his own personal reasons for requiring a further witch hunt. In his last paranoid years, the dictator had come to distrust his erstwhile crony, the NKVD chief Lavrenti Beriya. Now he wished to implicate him in the 'Doctors' Plot' and have him liquidated. The fact that Beriya had organized the Jewish Anti-Fascist Committee at the beginning of the war with the purpose of mobilizing Jewish public opinion in the USA against the

20 Marina Sabinina, 'The Man Who Spoke about the Omelette', short story commissioned for this book.

Germans was now to be used against him. However, in the event, Stalin died before this could be carried out. Beriya only outlived Stalin by a few months.

Seven of the nine doctors arrested in connection with the 'Doctors' Plot' were Jews, including Professor Miron Vovsi, a cousin of the actor Solomon Mikhoels, who was a member of the Jewish Anti-Fascist Committee. Both men were also accused of being agents of American Intelligence and of JOINT, the acronym for the Jewish-American Charitable Organization.

Shostakovich, who abhorred all forms of injustice and racism, had to be silent in public, but in his music and in his private actions, he showed his moral fibre. His immediate response was to aid the repressed, irrespective of race or creed. To do so required enormous selflessness and courage.

During the period of the anti-cosmopolitan campaign, Natalya (Tala) Vovsi-Mikhoels suffered the stigma of being a close relation of two prominent figures classed as 'Enemies of the People' – her father and her uncle. Her father, the brilliant actor and founder of the Moscow Jewish Theatre, Solomon Mikhoels, and her uncle, Professor Miron Vovsi, were victims of the last Stalinist purges.

Solomon Mikhoels had left for Minsk on 7 January 1948. By coincidence this was the day of the first meeting of the 'activists of music' convoked by Zhdanov. On the eve of his departure for Moscow, Mikhoels died in mysterious circumstances on 12 January. Later it transpired that Stalin had ordered his murder.

Mikhoels was on friendly terms with Shostakovich and had spoken out in defence of his Eighth Symphony in 1944. In the post-war years NATALYA VOVSI-MIKHOELS enjoyed close contacts with Russian musical circles through her marriage to the composer Moisei (Metak) Weinberg. She describes the loyal support Shostakovich accorded to her and Weinberg in those dark days:

On 13 January 1948, a meeting took place at the Central Committee building under Zhdanov's chairmanship. Its purpose was to discuss the question of 'formalism in music'. The composers Shostakovich, Prokofiev, Myaskovsky and others were censured for being formalists and pessimists, 'for distorting our reality, for not reflecting our glorious victories, and for eating out of the hands of our enemies'. In a word, if they were not actually labelled 'Enemies of the People', they were at any rate at least their accomplices. The meeting lasted from 1 to 6 p.m. As soon as it was over Dmitri Dmitriyevich came straight to see us.

We ourselves had been living on another plane for the last seven hours; the news of Father's death earlier that day had left us completely devastated. The doors of the flat were open and a stream of people came and went in silence – an endless stream of stunned and frightened people. We wandered amongst them, without lingering or talking to any of them. Suddenly I heard my name called out; on seeing Dmitri Dmitriyevich, I went up to him. Silently he embraced me and my husband, the composer Moisei Weinberg, then he went over to the bookcase and, with his back to everybody in the room, pronounced quietly but distinctly and with uncharacteristic deliberation, 'I envy him . . .'. He didn't say another word, but stood rooted to the spot, hugging us both around the shoulders.

It was only later that I learnt the truth about the course of the previous days' events. Although I was told about them, I suppressed my reactions as if I myself had not been present and was not a participant in them. But this single phrase of Dmitri Dmitriyevich's pierced my very consciousness. I never forgot it, although we were never to mention it again.

By that time we had known each other for five years. We met often in our homes, at friends' houses and at concerts and restaurants. What did we talk about? As far as I remember, nothing in particular. Sometimes somebody would tell a flat joke, and Dmitri Dmitriyevich, after downing a large glass of vodka, would proceed to repeat it in his quick patter, thereby transforming it instantly into something comical and absurd. Sometimes the discussion touched on some composition that we had heard recently, and, if the conversation was taking place in somebody's home, then the speaker would demonstrate his point on the piano.

From the viewpoint of today, even I, as one who took part in those friendly gatherings, find it hard to believe that people never talked about what was going on around them. It wasn't that they were trying to hush up things, but, quite simply, they kept silent, and this was the norm. Anyone who broke this silence was immediately suspect; he who talked in the presence of four or five people was bound to be an informer.

The conversation often touched on our children. Dmitri Dmitriyevich's love for his children was boundless, and he was continually anxious about them. If a well-known paediatrician came to see us, Dmitri Dmitriyevich immediately brought his daughter Galya around for a consultation. We used to talk about our friends, or read aloud our favourite bits of Saltykov-Shchedrin. We revelled in those excerpts that evoked 'surrounding reality'. But we never spoke about politics.

Once, after the Decree on Zoshchenko and Akhmatova appeared in the Leningrad magazine *Zvezda* in 1946, Shostakovich told us that he had met Zoshchenko, and that he was in a dreadful state and completely destitute. In his quick patter, so familiar to us, he kept repeating: 'One must help him. It's essential that he gets help.' And Dmitri Dmitriyevich himself did help, in the most discreet and tactful way.

It is difficult to choose the right word to define Shostakovich's gift for helping people discreetly. It was not just his tact, but his deep-seated fear of causing offence that qualified his charity. I remember how my husband once asked Dmitri Dmitriyevich if he could borrow a small sum of money for a short period of time. Dmitri Dmitriyevich's response was immediate: 'Don't worry, I've got lots of money just now . . .' They agreed that Weinberg would collect the sum from him the following afternoon at three. The next morning Dmitri Dmitriyevich rang to tell me that, as it happened, he himself would be in the vicinity of our flat, and to ask if I was going to be in. He arrived shortly, cash in hand. This was typical of his courtesy. He did not wish to humiliate anyone who had asked him for some favour; rather, he tried to save them from such embarrassment. He, similarly, would ask us a favour, and we always did our best to help each other out. After all, those were years when many composers had their works banned from performance and were forced to accept any kind of hack work. What terrible humiliations they had to endure!

In 1948, some months after the Decree on *The Great Friendship*, Shostakovich wrote his cycle of Jewish songs. On 25 September 1949, Dmitri Dmitriyevich's birthday, we were invited to his home. It was on that occasion that I first met Mstislav Rostropovich, a slim youth with an intelligent, sardonic look, and an incredible winning charm. At eight o'clock precisely, Dmitri Dmitriyevich announced that we were to go into his study where we were to hear a new work of his. The impact of the poems of those simple Jewish songs (at Dmitri Dmitriyevich's request the texts had been translated word for word) at that particular time was simply shattering for me and my husband Moisei Weinberg. After all, not a day passed without those 'rootless cosmopolitans' (who all bore Jewish surnames) being slandered and abused in the press. This cycle voiced what we dared not ever express in conversations. It was an open protest by Shostakovich against the hounding of the Jews in this last five-year plan of Stalin's.

The work received its première much later, in the time of the 'Thaw'. As always, whenever a work of Shostakovich's was premièred, the concert hall was full to bursting. In those years, a presenter always came out to announce the works. Despite the fact that the cycle was sung in Russian, the presenter gave an 'explanation' of the text of each song. He declared that in 'Lullaby', where the song contains the words 'Your father is in Siberia, sleep, little one, but I cannot sleep', 'it all took place in Tsarist Russia.' With that he left the stage. There was animation in the hall and people barely restrained themselves from laughing. For a long time after that Dmitri Dmitriyevich loved to repeat, 'It all took place in Tsarist Russia, it all took place in Tsarist Russia.'

On that occasion, and at any concert where his works were being performed, Dmitri Dmitriyevich sat with his family, all tense and tapping his fingers against his lips. People went up to greet him, and he jumped up to thank them, kissing the ladies' hands. Although we all knew that it was tiring and irritating for him, it was impossible not to go up to him.

Concerts of Shostakovich's music were distinguished by an atmosphere of incredible festivity, and Dmitri Dmitriyevich's tension communicated itself to the public. We all had the feeling that we were present at some kind of mystery. At the end, there was a moment of hushed silence, then the hall exploded into ovations. Dmitri Dmitriyevich would bow without ever smiling, and when I looked at him at such moments, my heart would go out to him, as I sensed his inner loneliness. We went backstage, where his admirers expressed their delight, and Dmitri Dmitriyevich convulsively shook everyone by the hand and thanked them, and then in a whisper and with a kindly, if perplexed and somewhat conspiratorial smile, he would say, 'And now, come over to our place, we must drink and have a bite to eat.'

At home, he would quickly down two large tumblers of vodka, and then he would slip off unnoticed to sleep. The guests continued to drink and eat. So it was during Nina Vasilyevna's lifetime, and also after her death. Dmitri Dmitriyevich did not change his habits. As time passed, the company changed. But his friendship with Weinberg was constant to the very end of his days.

Although Weinberg was not a pupil of Shostakovich's, Dmitri Dmitriyevich always showed great interest in his work. From the very beginning of their acquaintance, they established a law whereby each played his new compositions for the other. I remember one day Weinberg telling me of a dream he had had in which Shostakovich invited him to listen to a new work where he heard themes from many of his previous compositions. As he was telling me this story, the telephone rang; it was Shostakovich, who indeed was inviting him to come and listen to a work he had just completed. It turned out to be the Eighth Quartet, which Dmitri Dmitriyevich considered to be his musical autobiography. Weinberg returned home shaken to the very core by the music, and by his prophetic dream.

In February 1953 Weinberg was arrested. Stalin was still alive. To be arrested in those times meant departure for ever. The families of those arrested were ostracized. I rushed between the Moscow prisons, the Lyubyanka and the Butyrka, and didn't know whom to approach.

A few days after his arrest, a great friend of ours rang me and suggested we met. While we paced the dark and narrow Moscow lanes, he told me that Shostakovich was writing a letter to Beriya and needed me to come and help him edit it. It was sheer lunacy to go to Shostakovich in my situation! But I went and read the letter in which he, Shostakovich, vouched that Weinberg was an honest citizen and a most talented young composer, whose chief interest in life was music. I understood how dangerous it was for Shostakovich to vouch for an enemy of the people, a Jew, and furthermore, Mikhoels's son-in-law, that same Mikhoels who had been accused posthumously of collaborating with 'Joint'! I felt stunned, grateful and terrified all at the same time. I expressed these emotions as best I could to Dmitri Dmitriyevich, but he, shy of being thanked, just continued to repeat, 'Don't worry, don't worry, they won't do anything to me.'

Apart from this letter, his wife Nina Vasilyevna suggested that I should write a statement, giving her power of attorney, thereby allowing her to take our things and sell them to support my seven-year-old daughter Vitosha, when they came to get me and my sister. (As our arrest seemed absolutely inevitable, she allowed herself to say 'when' and not 'if'.) In fact, as it transpired later, she had decided that they would look after Vitosha.

But all this was not to be. On 5 March Stalin died. A month later, my father was rehabilitated in the press. Soon after this Shostakovich and his wife went to the south on holiday, making me promise to send a telegram as soon as Weinberg was released.

And shortly we were able to send them this telegram: 'Enjoy your holiday. We embrace you, Tala and Metak.' Two days later the Shostakoviches were back in Moscow. That evening we celebrated. At the table, festively decked out with candles in antique candlesticks, Nina Vasilyevna read out the power of attorney that I had written. Then Dmitri Dmitriyevich got up and solemnly pronounced, 'Now we will consign this document to the flames,' and proposed that I should burn it over the candles. After the destruction of the 'document', we drank vodka and sat down to supper. I rarely saw Dmitri Dmitriyevich as calm, and even merry, as he was that evening. We sat up till the early hours of the morning. Nina Vasilyevna laughingly recounted how I was worried that Vitosha would get a bad upbringing in the orphanage; it was then that I discovered that they had decided to take her into their own home.

On 4 December 1954 Shostakovich rang us from Armenia to inform us of his wife Nina's death. He asked us to go to his home so that the children would not be alone when he telephoned them with the news half an hour later. When we got to the flat we found his son Maxim on the phone. When he put down the receiver he said, 'Now they'll devour him,' and burst into tears. Although Maxim was only sixteen years old then, he understood what a tremendous moral support his mother had been to his father. He realized that Shostakovich was now alone, defenceless before the system that was destroying him, and that, on his own, he would be unable to hold out against it.[21]

Support and discretion in the hour of need

The conductor THOMAS SANDERLING gives his views on Shostakovich's public persona. He believes that the composer consciously used his position to give help in private wherever possible:

Shostakovich didn't try to promote his own career or reputation. He didn't go in for heroic deeds, but nevertheless he knew that his reputation as a great composer could be put to use to help people quietly and practically. This was a necessity to him.

In the same way his music could not but express the suffering and horror he saw around him. Here we see Shostakovich continuing the great Russian tradition, where art, most particularly in literature,

21 Natalya Vovsi-Mikhoels, 'Reminiscences of Shostakovich', article commissioned for this book.

assumes a predominantly moral role. This morality was the salient feature both of Shostakovich's music and of his everyday conduct. One can point to the dual origins of the moral principle, which undoubtedly also reflect the influence of Mahler, one of Shostako-vich's favourite composers. Mahler's music is likewise born of a strong moral stance.

In the West many people cannot comprehend how Shostakovich could give public utterance to certain ideological statements delivered at Composers' Congresses or Peace Conferences. But for Shostakovich this was a calculated choice. The path he trod was not a popular one, but it allowed him to use his authority and position in order to help people. He did so unobtrusively, behind the scenes. Indeed, in those times the only real and practical way of helping people was through personal intervention, as public or open protest got you nowhere. One might say that he consciously bought this right by throwing the odd bone to the dogs. Thus, he gained the necessary breathing space for himself by writing occasional music or making public statements to placate the officials. I think that Shostakovich dismissed these public utterances as worthless, knowing that their effect on people's lives was virtually nil.

Amongst the people that Shostakovich helped was my father, Kurt Sanderling. Shortly before Stalin's death, when my father held the position of conductor of the Leningrad Philharmonic (a position he shared with Mravinsky), he was openly attacked at a meeting of the Obkom[22] by a certain official who was responsible for the Party line on culture in Leningrad. In those times such an attack meant at the very least that a person would lose his job, and probably much worse. There were many such cases in Leningrad in particular, in circles very close to us.

Everybody knew what such an attack meant. Our family was in a state of shock, not knowing what might follow. Mravinsky contacted Shostakovich in Moscow on my father's behalf. Dmitri Dmitriyevich in turn petitioned some very important Party official and pleaded for my father. He was not afraid to use his contacts in high-up places.

The director of the Leningrad Philharmonic treated my father quite decently. He was informed that he was now 'on leave' from the Philharmonic, although officially he was still registered there for work

22 Local Party Committee.

purposes. Effectively my father was not allowed to appear in public and was out of work. Fortunately, Shostakovich succeeded in proving that a 'misunderstanding' had occurred in Leningrad. About six months after the original attack, the director of the Philharmonic called my father to see him and asked him when he would like to schedule his next concert. Before long the concert took place and the Leningrad newspapers printed notices saying that Kurt Sanderling had conducted such and such a concert. This amounted to a signal that the situation had returned to normal, and hence my father was once more *persona grata*. This was the result of Shostakovich's doing.

I know of other such instances where Shostakovich's intervention was vital for the reversal of some injustice. For instance, Dmitri Dmitriyevich helped André Volkonsky's mother to regain permission to live in Moscow, after she had been exiled immediately after their repatriation to the USSR in 1949. This was just one of many cases where he actively helped in the rehabilitation of innocently persecuted victims in the period immediately following 1953.[23]

From Jewish Poetry

Shostakovich's interest in Jewish music preceded the Stalinist anti-semitic campaign of the late 1940s and early 1950s. The Finale of the Second Piano Trio, and the First Violin Concerto had already used Jewish themes, and they were to appear in several of the composer's next works, including the Fourth String Quartet, the Preludes and Fugues for Piano, and the Four Monologues on Pushkin poems.

By 1948 Shostakovich was familiar with a remarkable collection of Jewish folk music in Kiev. This collection had been destroyed by the Germans in the early years of World War II and then painstakingly reconstructed by a certain Moshe Beregovsky, who in 1938 had compiled and published a work entitled *Yiddische Volks-Lieder*. Beregovsky presented his PhD thesis on the theme of Jewish folk music at the Moscow Conservatoire in 1946, and Shostakovich was nominated as his examiner. In 1948, when Beregovsky fell into disgrace in Kiev, Shostakovich invited him to stay in his Moscow flat, where he hid him until he was able to help rescind the arrest order.[24]

In August 1948 Shostakovich bought a recently published book entitled

---

23 Thomas Sanderling: recorded interview with EW.
24 Rafiil Matveivich Khozak (1928–) came from a Jewish community in Latvia which was annihilated by the Germans at the beginning of World War II. Although he lost all his relatives, Khozak, a boy of twelve, made a miraculous escape. Shostakovich showed

Jewish Folk Songs, edited and translated into Russian by Y. M. Sokolov. The words of these songs inspired him to start writing his vocal cycle *From Jewish Poetry* for three solo voices and piano.

The intonations of Jewish folk music appealed to the composer. As Shostakovich explained: 'The distinguishing feature of Jewish music is the ability to build a jolly melody on sad intonations. Why does a man strike up a jolly song? Because he feels sad at heart.[25]

Shostakovich's music speaks of the universal condition of man, the misery of each individual and his helplessness in the face of overwhelming odds. Undoubtedly, Shostakovich also identified with the Jew as the victim of thousands of years of injustice, and now as the victim of Nazi and Stalinist persecution.

Shostakovich fully realized that the song cycle *From Jewish Poetry* would not be allowed a public performance. In fact its composition was tantamount to a challenge to the politics of Stalin. Nowithstanding the public ban on much of the composer's work, *From Jewish Poetry* and other 'unofficial' works, such as the Third and Fourth String Quartets, were widely heard in musical circles in private performances.

The soprano NINA L'VOVNA DORLIAK was the daughter of the famous St Petersburg Wagnerian soprano Xenia Dorliak. Her family was acquainted with the Shostakoviches from their childhood years. In 1948 Shostakovich invited her to perform the soprano part of his newly-created *From Jewish Poetry* Op. 79. Dorliak had recently married Sviatoslav Richter, and both musicians were to become part of the composer's close circle of trusted interpreters:

From my earliest childhood I have never ceased to worship Shostakovich. I remember him as a young boy, as he was portrayed in Kustodiev's famous portrait in the sailor suit. In those days, we knew him as a pianist and student of Alexandra Rozanova, who was also my piano teacher. Whereas I never became a pianist, Dmitri Dmitriyevich continued his piano studies with Professor Nikolayev at the Conservatoire. He was a wonderful pianist.

I never missed a single concert where Shostakovich performed or where his works were played. I also went to see every production of Shostakovich's stage works, apart from *The Nose*. I well remember the performances of his ballets *The Golden Age* and *Bolt*. I have to say that the public was dismayed by them and did not understand them. Even musicians were unable to accept these ballets because the music was

---

the boy great kindness and encouraged him in his early attempts at composition. I am grateful to Mr Khozak for providing me with this information in a private interview.
25 Same source.

unlike anything else they had heard before. On the other hand, *Katerina Izmailova* (or *Lady Macbeth of Mtsensk*, as it was called in the MALEGOT production) immediately captured the public's imagination and enjoyed an enormous success. It was a complete victory both with connoisseurs and with the general public.

Shostakovich had a genuine and outstanding dramatic talent. He knew how to convey the flow of drama through his music. I think that he would undoubtedly have continued writing operas if it were not for all those dreadful decrees and criticisms. Although these events broke something in him, he was still able to say everything he wanted in his symphonies; it is important not to underestimate their dramatic content and almost theatrical impact.

But this is something we never talked about. All my life I felt dwarfed by Shostakovich and could never aspire to his level. Hence I was always shy of engaging in conversation with him. But I had a profound passion for his music, and I felt that I understood the essence of his every work right up to the final Viola Sonata.

Early in the autumn of 1948 Dmitri Dmitriyevich completed the cycle *From Jewish Poetry* and brought the score to me at home, saying that he wished to play it through for me. Sviatoslav Richter was also with me. The cycle touched us to the very core. He suggested that I should sing the soprano part and choose the two other soloists, a mezzo-soprano and a tenor. Immediately I approached Tamara Yanko and Alec Maslennikov. One has to remember that at the time of its composition there could be no possibility of a public performance of the cycle. Although I was not bothered by this, I was worried that my colleagues might balk at the idea of singing 'unacceptable' music. After all it was the year of that terrible, stupid and shameful 'historic Decree'. Fortunately, in this instance, both singers were quick to agree.

We soon performed the cycle for the first time, privately at Dmitri Dmitriyevich's flat. He invited many musicians and his own friends. The new work was striking and profound, and everybody was moved by its intense and simple sincerity. We gave private performances on more than one occasion, and we rehearsed a lot for them – Dmitri Dmitriyevich liked rehearsing. He was very strict and we were not allowed to be so much as a minute late. There was only one occasion in my life when he was angry with me, when, through unavoidable circumstances, I arrived some minutes late. He himself was always terribly exact and punctual to the second, a characteristic he shared, incidentally, with Sergei Sergeyevich Prokofiev.

Several years went by before we were able to give the first public performance of *From Jewish Poetry* in Leningrad.[26] By that time Zara Dolukhanova had taken over the mezzo part, so she, rather than Yanko, had the honour of giving the first official performance. Thereafter we gave several performances in Moscow, Leningrad and in the Baltic Republics. Dmitri Dmitriyevich always played the piano part; while he was able to perform he never let anybody else play it. Richter wanted to accompany us in this cycle, but Dmitri Dmitriyevich insisted on playing all the concerts himself; he obviously enjoyed them!

Shostakovich really loved his own works, and got a real pleasure from listening to them. You only had to see him at a rehearsal or concert; his state of agitation was painfully evident. I remember Dmitri Dmitriyevich saying how much he liked Richter's recording of six of his Preludes and Fugues made in Czechoslovakia: 'I listen to this record over and over again.' Generally, listening to good performances of his work made him very happy. I remember his joy on the occasion of the first performance of the Violin Sonata given by Richter and Oistrakh at the Grand Hall of the Moscow Conservatoire. Despite the fact that by then he was ill and could hardly walk, he insisted on coming out on stage with them to acknowledge the applause and to thank them. He told them, 'Today I am a really happy man.'

In his youth Dmitri Dmitriyevich was very handsome. He was also extremely nervous, and remained so throughout his life. He preserved his wonderful good looks until his last years, when he was beset by ill health and his face assumed a tortured aspect. He had a very infectious laugh, which was irrestistible when he told some funny story – he really appreciated humour. It was a great sadness for us to witness the ordeal of his last years of illness. Yet, being a very buttoned-up person, he never complained. He knew that we felt for him in his cruel and inhuman sufferings, although he would never have wanted us to give voice to our sympathy. He retained his dignity until the last.[27]

26 On 15 January 1955, at the Glinka Hall, Leningrad.
27 Nina Dorliak: recorded interview with EW.

Even before Stalin's death Shostakovich did try and get the cycle *From Jewish Poetry* sanctioned for performance through the Union of Composers' audition procedure. ABRAAM GOZENPUD recalled:

Shostakovich first showed his cycle *From Jewish Poetry* at the Moscow Union of Composers early in 1953, just after the news bulletin in the press had appeared denouncing the Doctors. This provoked an immediate reaction from many well-known and famous persons demanding punishment of 'the murderers in white coats' (who were mostly Jews). Therefore, the performance of this cycle at that time was an act of great civic courage. Shostakovich had to overcome much resistance from the officials responsible for the arts eventually to get permission for a public performance.[28]

Evidently *From Jewish Poetry* was known to enough people before its first public performance in 1955 for it to be a source of danger to the composer.

EDISON DENISOV recorded Shostakovich's reaction to anonymous threats received in connection with this work:

On 3 March (1954) I visited Dmitri Dmitriyevich. He was very upset as he had discovered about a campaign against the Jewish songs. He received two very coarse and vulgar anonymous letters of the 'You've sold yourself to the Yids' type. He told me he never read anonymous letters, but this time he read them because they had been typed and were very short.

He said, 'I try to cultivate a philosophical attitude to such matters, and I didn't think I would be so distressed by these letters.'

He told me that he had always loathed anti-semitism, and he referred to Lenin's forgotten decree. . . . He presumed that all the trouble over the Jewish songs stemmed directly from Alexandrov, the Minister of Culture.'[29]

The 1st World Peace Congress

The 1st World Peace Congress in New York took place between 25 and 28 March 1949. Shostakovich was sent as a Soviet peace delegate at the express wish of Stalin. Apart from having to make a speech in public, the composer

28 Abraam Gozenpud, 'Encounters with Shostakovich', article commissioned for this book.
29 Edison Denisov, unpublished diary.

performed the second movement from his Fifth Symphony on the piano to an audience of 19,000 at Madison Square Garden on 27 March.

The visit of the Soviet delegation was heralded by much publicity in the USA. Prior to its visit, Igor Stravinsky received a telegram from Olin Downes requesting him to add his signature to a telegram of welcome to Shostakovich. Stravinsky's curt reply: 'Regret not to be able to join welcomers of Soviet artists coming this country. But all my ethic and esthetic convictions oppose such gesture,'[30] was published in the international press on 18 March. The Soviet press reacted instantly by calling Stravinsky a 'traitor and enemy of our fatherland'.[31] This exchange created a charged atmosphere between supporters of the two composers, and this was the background that existed when Shostakovich was forced to give public expression to his (or rather official Soviet) sentiments on Western music.

Amongst those present on the American side was the composer NICHOLAS NABOKOV, a cousin of the writer Vladimir Nabokov. It is hardly surprising to learn that Shostakovich could not forgive Nabokov for publicly embarrassing him by making him repeat and stand by these sentiments. On the other hand, it must be remembered that Nabokov, like so many Russian emigrés of the period, nurtured an undying hatred for Soviet communism and the methods it used. Undoubtedly, Shostakovich would have respected and much preferred Stravinsky's response, who, when asked by journalists to enter into a public debate with the Soviet composer, replied: 'How can you talk to them? They are not free. There is no discussion in public with people who are not free.'[32]

By January 1949 Shostakovich was well on the way out of the doghouse. His film scores had won cautious approval by the critics and his name began to be mentioned again as a 'gifted composer' of the Soviet Union, rather than the 'formalist' and 'bourgeois decadent'. In March of the same year, still bruised from the thrashing he had received, he was picked out of the clothes hamper and like dirty laundry he was washed, ironed out and sent to America to meet with the peace-makers, peace addicts and peace dupes of the Waldorf-Astoria conference. He arrived in New York in company with five other gentlemen in blue serge suits and over-sized sleeves à la Stalin, and was exhibited as the biggest publicity and propaganda attraction of that Communist-inspired performance.

I saw him for the first time at a Press conference given by the various delegations (chiefly from behind the Iron Curtain), and so appropri-

30 Igor Stravinsky, *Selected Correspondence*, vol. I, p. 359.
31 *Krasnaya Zvezda*, 19 March 1949.
32 Stravinsky, *Selected Correspondence*, vol. I, p. 358.

ately held in the Perroquet Room of the Waldorf-Astoria. I found myself sitting opposite him, in fact so close that our knees nearly met. Throughout the tumultuous conference, I watched his hands twist the cardboard tips of his cigarettes, his face twitch and his whole posture express intense unease. While his Soviet colleagues on the right and left looked calm and as self-contented as mantelpiece Buddhas, his sensitive face looked disturbed, hurt and terribly shy. I felt, as I lit his cigarette or passed a record to him from an American admirer, that he wanted it over with as quickly as possible, that he was out of place in this crowded room full of rough, angry people, that he was not made for public appearances, for meetings, for 'peace missions'. To me he seemed like a trapped man, whose only wish was to be left alone, to the peace of his own art and to the tragic destiny to which he, like most of his countrymen, has been forced to resign himself.

Two days later I saw him again. This time he spoke at a public meeting of the conference's music panel. He was the centre of attention and the object of adoration of a vast crowd of admirers, so many of whom were not admiring Shostakovich, the composer, but the abortionists of his art and the bosses of his destiny – the Soviet Government. Everybody except me rose when he came into the hall and everybody except me applauded furiously. Escorted by two of his colleagues, he walked to the podium and sat down at the left of the president of the panel, not far from the microphones in the centre of the long green table. Again his face twitched, and he looked uncomfortable and awkward.

When, after several trying and ludicrous speeches, his turn came to speak he began to read his prepared talk in a nervous and shaky voice. After a few sentences he broke off, and the speech was continued in English by a suave radio baritone. In all the equivocation of that conference, Shostakovich's speech was at least direct. Written in the standard style of Agitprop speeches, it was quite obviously prepared by the 'party organs' in charge of the Waldorf-Astoria conference, on the Soviet side of the picture. In it these 'organs', through their mouthpiece, the composer Shostakovich, condemned most Western music as decadent and bourgeois, painted the glories of the rising Soviet music culture, attacked the demon Stravinsky as the corrupter of Western art (with a dig at Prokofiev) and urged upon the 'progressive Americans' of the conference the necessity of fighting against the reactionaries and warmongers of America and . . . and admitted that the 'mouthpiece' (Mr Shostakovich) had itself often erred and sinned against the decrees of the Party.

I sat in my seat petrified by this spectacle of human misery and degradation. It was crystal clear to me that what I had suspected from the day that I heard Shostakovich was going to be among the delegates representing the Soviet Government was true: This speech of his, this whole peace-making mission was part of a punishment, part of a ritual redemption he had to go through before he could be pardoned again. He was to tell, in person, to all the dupes at the Waldorf conference and to the whole decadent bourgeois world that loved him so much that he, Shostakovich, the famous Russian composer, is not a free man, but an obedient tool of his government. He told in effect that every time the Party found flaws in his art, the Party was right, and every time the Party put him on ice, he was grateful to the Party, because it helped him to recognise his flaws and mistakes.

After his speech I felt I had to ask him publicly a few questions. I had to do it, not in order to embarrass a wretched human being who had just given me the most flagrant example of what it is to be a composer in the Soviet Union, but because of the several thousand people that sat in the hall, because of those that perhaps still could not or did not wish to understand the sinister game that was being played before their eyes. I asked him simple factual questions concerning modern music, questions that should be of interest to all musicians. I asked him whether he, personally, the composer Shostakovich, not the delegate of Stalin's Government, subscribed to the wholesale condemnation of Western music as it had been expounded daily by the Soviet Press and as it appeared in the official pronouncements of the Soviet Government. I asked him whether he, personally, agreed with the condemnation of the music of Stravinsky, Schoenberg, and Hindemith. To these questions he acquiesced: 'Yes,' he said, 'I completely subscribe to the views as expressed by . . . etc. . . .' When he finished answering my questions the dupes in the audience gave him a new and prolonged ovation.[33]

Official and non-official works

On his return from his visit to the USA in April 1949 Shostakovich started work on his Fourth Quartet, which he finished on 27 December of that year. It

33 Nicholas Nabokov, *Old Friends and New Music*, pp. 203–5.

was dedicated to the memory of his close friend, the artist Pyotr Villiams. The Finale of the Fourth Quartet uses a theme of unmistakable Jewish intonation.

Shostakovich interrupted work on the quartet to compose *The Song of the Forests*, an oratorio celebrating Stalin as 'the great gardener' for his grandiose plans to transform the steppe into forestland. It was the first of several works where Shostakovich used texts by Evgeny Dolmatovsky, an officially approved poet of limited talent.

In 1948 Shostakovich had written music for three films: *The Young Guard*, *Michurin* and *Meeting on the Elbe*. In a letter dated 12 December 1948, Shostakovich complained to Isaak Glikman how this hack work drained his strength:

> Physically, I feel quite low, and this in turn does not foster my creative powers. I suffer from frequent headaches, and besides that I feel constantly nauseous, or, to put it simply, I feel like throwing up. I must say it's most unpleasant. While shaving I have a chance to examine my face. It's swollen, there are great bags under my eyes, and my cheeks are puffy and lilac-coloured. In this last week or so, I have aged considerably, and this ageing process races ahead at incredible pace. Furthermore this physical ageing is accompanied by a loss of youthful spirit. Maybe it's simply a case of being over-tired. After all, I've written lots of film music this year. It allows me to eat, but it causes me extreme fatigue.[34]

Indeed Shostakovich needed his earnings from this source not only as bread and butter money, but to demonstrate that he was participating in patriotic work.

It is worth pointing out that Shostakovich had been in no great hurry to produce a serious symphonic work that would rehabilitate him in official favour. However, *The Song of the Forests*, first performed by Mravinsky and the Leningrad Philharmonic on 15 December 1949, served the purpose. The oratorio was favourably received and gained Shostakovich the Stalin Prize in December 1950. This was worth 100,000 roubles, a considerable sum. In addition, after his participation at the Peace Congress in New York, the State awarded Shostakovich a dacha (or country house) outside Moscow at Bolshevo. Thus, in the material sense, life had started to improve slightly for the composer.

The Borodin Quartet, formed in 1946, had been closely associated with Shostakovich's music from its first days. The quartet was originally called the Quartet of the Moscow Philharmonic; its founder members were Rostislav Dubinsky, Rudolph and Nina Barshai, and Valentin Berlinsky. In 1953, Dmitri Shebalin, the son of Shostakovich's close friend Vissarion Shebalin became the

34 Isaak Glikman, *Letters to a Friend*, p. 77.

quartet's viola player, and two years later the group assumed the name of the Borodin Quartet, under which guise it has achieved world-wide fame.

While Shostakovich remained constant in his loyalty to the Beethoven Quartet, giving them the exclusive right to première his quartets, he sometimes expressed the wish in private that he could give a first performance to 'the Borodins'. The composer Edison Denisov recorded that:

> Dmitri Dmitriyevich is satisfied with the Beethoven's performance of the Fifth Quartet. But, he says that they don't play the Fourth Quartet well. He wanted to give the première to Dubinsky (the Borodins), but the Beethovens announced that this would lead to a break in their relations (they were offended). Dmitri Dmitriyevich said, 'I don't like relations between people to be too friendly or too hostile. Relationships should be kept simple.' This explains much in his behaviour.[35]

The cellist VALENTIN BERLINSKY recalls his experience of working with Shostakovich:

My close acquaintance with Shostakovich began in 1944, during the war. He was a professor at the Moscow Conservatoire, and I was a student. Our student quartet (to be professionally established two years later) was preparing a programme for a class concert at the Small Hall of the Conservatoire that included Shostakovich's First String Quartet. Teryan organized for Shostakovich to hear our performance prior to the concert, and a time was fixed for this audition at the Conservatoire. I'll remember that meeting as long as I live. It was to take place at nine o'clock in the morning. We arrived two hours earlier to warm up; naturally we were very excited to be meeting the composer. It had been agreed that I would meet Shostakovich in the downstairs cloakroom and take him to the classroom that we had been allocated. I came downstairs at five to nine; Shostakovich arrived a couple of seconds after nine. To my amazement, he started apologizing for being late. That was the first shock I had. He was amazingly punctual, and couldn't bear others to be late.

Just as we were about to start playing for him, he asked us if we had a score. But we only had the parts we were playing off. 'That doesn't matter,' he said. 'Go ahead and play.' We played right through the quartet. When we finished, Dmitri Dmitriyevich said, 'I won't say anything to you now, instead I'll try and play the quartet for you on the piano.'

35 Entry for 1 December 1953 from an unpublished diary.

Now I was in for a second shock. Dmitri Dmitriyevich played through the whole work note-perfect without a score and without even sitting down at the upright piano. Then he repeated certain passages that he wished to draw our attention to. He was such a lump of nerves, and was so agitated that he couldn't even sit down!

From that day on, we played every quartet up to and including the Thirteenth to Shostakovich before performing it in public.

Our first performance with Shostakovich took place on 12 October 1947, when he played his Piano Quintet with us. I remember various details of the preceding rehearsals, which took place at his home. In the Prelude, he asked us not to make a ritenuto, despite it being marked in the score. 'But ritenuto is written here,' we exclaimed. He came up to us very nervously, took out a pen and crossed out the marking in every part. Rudolf Barshai was the viola player in the quartet at the time. In the Finale there is an imitation between the cello and viola. It's in the score now, but it wasn't then. The cello and viola were supposed to play together, but Barshai made a mistake and came in after I did. Shostakovich stopped playing and said, 'Please, mark it the way you played it just now.' In all the editions published after that date, that is how it is printed.

We performed the Quintet with him again on 3 December 1949. Shostakovich performed very little in public at that time. Those years (1949–50) were particularly hard for him, after he was dismissed from the Conservatoire. Altogether, he played the Quintet with us eight times. The last performance was in Gorky on 23 February 1964, at a festival of his music organized by Rostropovich and Guzman. Shostakovich was already ill, and his right arm didn't function well. He could only play the Intermezzo. It was his last performance as a pianist.

Shostakovich was a very anxious performer. Because of that all our tempi tended to be too fast. The amazing thing is that he appeared to be ashamed of his own music. He used to say, 'Let's play it fast, otherwise the audience will get bored.' He particularly rushed the slow movements. For instance, in the Third Quartet, he hurried us on in the great funeral march of the fourth movement. 'No, no,' he would say, 'while you're stretching out that first C sharp, the audience will fall asleep.' In general, his marking of the tempo often contradicted what he really wanted.

We would say, 'But, Dmitri Dmitriyevich, your metronome mark is such and such.'

He replied, 'Well, you see, my metronome at home is out of order, so pay no attention to what I wrote.'

Sometimes he wrote in the metronome markings after the first performances by the Beethoven Quartet. Its leader, Dmitri Tsyganov, was by nature a fast player, and this influenced Shostakovich's tempo markings. We never played in the same tempi that the Beethoven Quartet took.

Many years later, we recorded the first eleven quartets in Japan, and we presented Shostakovich with the records. Shortly afterwards, he wrote us a very detailed letter, which didn't contain a single reference to the tempi. Most of his complaints were in regard to the dynamics (usually he asked for more subtle nuances within the dynamic range), and to some wrong notes. These mostly turned out to be misprints in the score.

Shostakovich hardly ever changed anything in his works. He was very meticulous in his fair copy. Once we prepared the Third Quartet to play for him. The first movement opens with the cello playing a bottom F, written *arco*. For some reason we decided that it sounded better played *pizzicato*, while the second violin and viola continue to play arco. In our youthful folly, we decided to play it like that for Dmitri Dmitriyevich without any prior warning. This again took place at his home. No sooner had we started, when he stopped us and said, 'Excuse me, but you are meant to play *arco* there.'

I said, 'Dmitri Dmitriyevich, you see, we've given it some thought, and maybe you would like to reconsider. It seems to us that *pizzicato* sounds better here.'

'Yes, yes,' he hastily interrupted, '*pizzicato* is much better, but please play arco all the same.'

In the late 1940s and early 1950s, only very few pieces by Shostakovich could be performed in public. Immediately after the publication of the Zhdanov 'Decree', and before punitive action was taken against the disgraced composers on the Conservatoire staff, we rehearsed the Third Quartet in Shebalin's office. Shebalin was still director of the Conservatoire, although he was shortly to be dismissed, along with Shostakovich. I purposely left the doors of the room wide open, and the music of this wonderful quartet resounded all over the Conservatoire. Students came running to hear it.

Shostakovich wrote his Fourth Quartet in 1949, the most difficult year for him. We played this quartet at an audition with the purpose of

having it commissioned by the Ministry of Culture, so that Shostakovich would get paid some money for it. Alexander Kholodilin was the
chief of the Ministry's Directorate of Musical Institutions, and responsible for taking the decision. He came from Leningrad and was a
cultured, intelligent man, with progressive attitudes. He tried to help
Shostakovich. The audition succeeded in its purpose, and the Ministry
bought the quartet and paid Shostakovich a fee. However, it was only
performed in public after Stalin's death. There is a story in circulation
that we had to play the quartet twice on this occasion, once in our
genuine interpretation, and a second time 'optimistically', to convince
the authorities of its 'socialist' content. It's a pretty invention, but it's
not true; you cannot lie in music.[36]

The Eighth Quartet is one of my particular favourites. It is a
landmark, the summing up of a whole period in the composer's life.
The quotations from Shostakovich's previous works give it the
character of autobiography. Naturally, we decided to learn the
quartet. First, after many rehearsals, we played it in an out-of-town
concert in Krasnoyarsk. Only then did we feel prepared to play it for
Shostakovich. We performed it for him at his home; when we finished
playing, he left the room without saying a word, and didn't come
back. We quietly packed up our instruments and left. The next day he
rang me up in a state of great agitation. He said, 'I'm sorry, but I just
couldn't face anybody. I have no corrections to make, just play it the
way you did.'

The Beethoven Quartet were always the first to play Shostakovich's
works. We only received the parts after their performance. When I
was young, I used to get upset by this; I would have loved to give first
performances of Shostakovich's new works! But later, I realized that
Dmitri Dmitriyevich was right. He was a loyal friend, and he was loyal
to his musicians. Sometimes, word reached us that he was impatient
to hear our performance of a newly-written quartet; but he never
broke the rule that the 'Beethovens' had the right of first performance.

After concerts, we often used to sit around the table with Shostakovich. Either we went to his place for a meal or he came to visit us. On
these occasions he was relaxed and full of humour. Once, when we
were in London in 1962, I met Shostakovich in Hyde Park. We were

36 This story is included in Rostislav Dubinsky's *Stormy Applause: Making Music in a
Workers' State*, p. 279.

both staying in the Prince of Wales Hotel nearby. When I saw the composer's familiar figure walking down an alley of trees, I decided it was better not to disturb him, so I walked the other way. But suddenly we found ourselves face to face; there was no escape. I said, 'Dmitri Dmitriyevich, you probably don't feel like company now.'

'No, no,' he said, 'I'm very glad to see you, let's take a stroll together.'

We spent the next hour together. I never saw him so relaxed, he was a different man. I spoke to him of a recent meeting in Venice with Luigi Nono, who had promised to write us a quartet. Usually Shostakovich preferred not to divulge his attitude towards avant-garde music. He never said anything derogatory or negative to anyone's face, but sometimes he expressed his opinion. And a man's entitled to an opinion.

On this occasion, Dmitri Dmitriyevich suddenly went glum. Then he said, 'Tell me, have you played all the Haydn Quartets?'

'No, Dmitri Dmitriyevich, of course not.'

'Well, please play all the Haydn Quartets, then all the Mozart Quartets, then all of Schubert's Quartets. Only then should you play Luigi Nono's music.'[37]

The Preludes and Fugues for Piano Op. 87

Between 1950 and 1953, Shostakovich's compositional activities continued to alternate between 'pure' composition and official music. To the latter category belonged the music for two propaganda films, The Fall of Berlin (1950) and The Unforgettable Year 1919 (1951), 'Ten Poems on Texts by Revolutionary Poets' for mixed chorus and the patriotic cantata The Sun Shines on the Motherland (1952). This work, originally to be entitled Cantata of the Party, used words by Dolmatovsky, who had become Shostakovich's official Party-approved librettist.

Shostakovich's predilection for vocal music prompted the composition of two works written for private consumption: Two Lermontov Romances (1950) and Four Pushkin Monologues (autumn 1952). As in 1936, Shostakovich turned to the great poet Pushkin to seek the assurance that, however isolated, genius will win through. Significantly, he quotes part of the second mono-logue, 'What Is in My Name?' in the first movement of his Tenth Symphony (just as the first Pushkin Romance 'Rebirth' turns up in the Fifth Symphony). Like the Fifth String Quartet (completed on 1 November 1952), these song

37 Valentin Berlinsky: recorded interview with EW.

cycles had to await public performances till after Stalin's death. Furthermore, there is evidence that the Tenth Symphony was conceived during this period, and was likewise withheld for over two years prior to performance in December 1953.

Paradoxically, even if Shostakovich continued to be condemned as a 'formalist' composer, the Soviet authorities exploited the composer's international reputation, demanding his participation in further Peace Congresses. (He travelled to Warsaw in November 1950 and Vienna in December 1952 as an official delegate.) In February 1951 he was elected deputy to the Supreme Soviet of the RSFSR, and as such showed his willingness to be a 'true son of the People and Party'.

In 1950, Shostakovich headed a Soviet delegation to East Germany for celebrations of the bicentenary of J. S. Bach's death. In Berlin his own music was also performed and he played as one of the soloists in Bach's Concerto for Three Harpsichords (Pianos). In Leipzig he heard the pianist Tatyana Nikolayeva play at the International Bach Competition. Nikolayeva's understanding of Bach's music was a direct inspiration to Shostakovich, and on return to Moscow in the autumn he started his cycle of Twenty Four Preludes and Fugues, which he worked on intensively at the Composers' Retreat at Ruza in December and completed in February 1951. Shostakovich showed the work at an audition at the Union of Composers on Miusskaya Street, where he was urged by the Union Secretaries, Zahkarov and Koval', his erstwhile persecutors in 1948, 'not to repeat his old mistakes'.

Shostakovich never played the complete cycle in public although he was to record it. But he soon started performing groups of four to six Preludes and Fugues from Op. 87 at public concerts. It was first performed as a complete cycle by Tatyana Nikolayeva in Leningrad on 23 and 28 December 1952.

The writer LYUBOV' RUDNEVA recalls the audition and ensuing discussion of Shostakovich's Twenty-Four Preludes and Fugues at the Union of Composers. She bases her account on her own detailed notes, made at the time, and also the archival stenographic record of the meeting. Rudneva was not acquainted with Shostakovich at the time, although they had many composer friends in common:

In the middle of May of 1951 an extraordinary happening occurred at the Small Hall of the Union of Composers. What was most amazing is that the participants did not regard it as in any way out of the ordinary.

On two successive evenings Shostakovich played his latest work, the Twenty-Four Preludes and Fugues for piano. He appeared to be oblivious to the tense situation around him. After he had finished playing, the chairman gave him the floor.

When he addressed his colleagues Dmitri Dmitriyevich's face

showed extreme fatigue, as if he had just run a long-distance race. A naive credulity shone through his words, something most unusual for those times. His defencelessness and willingness to state his opinions openly had a shattering effect on me. Dmitri Dmitriyevich spoke as if he assumed that at such a motley gathering it was possible to have a selfless, creative and equal exchange of ideas worthy of the music he had just played.

I had been invited to the audition and the discussion by some young composer friends; for them a new work by Shostakovich was a real event. The audience included the outstandingly talented pianists, Mariya Yudina and Tatyana Nikolayeva. But, occupying prominent places in the front rows were those colleagues of Shostakovich who, as it were, had been invested with the power of prosecution. Besides those colleagues, who were ungifted, envious and all too ready to make judgements and lay down the law, there were also those who could claim a certain professional experience in both an open and covert persecution of Shostakovich and his fellow-composers, Proko-fiev and Myaskovsky.

My friends and I were quite alarmed by how these musical bureaucrats reacted during Shostakovich's performance of his music. All the signs were negative: the shaking of heads as they wrote down their comments, the perfunctory shrugging of shoulders typical of a condescending dignatory, and a significant exchange of jotted-down messages.

Dmitri Dmitriyevich did not think of distancing himself from this herd, when he spoke he did not use weighty words which might have forced them to abandon their self-confident manner during the ensuing discussion. Evidently Dmitri Dmitriyevich expected a genuine professional discourse, a discussion on the birth of something new, a composer's excursion into unknown territories.

Shostakovich spoke with extreme simplicity: 'I wrote this work from October to February of this year. What was my aim? The first circum-stance which stimulated me was my visit to the Bach celebrations in Leipzig. Hearing so much of Bach's music prompted me to create something in this genre. Even before my trip to Leipzig, I had read how Rimsky-Korsakov, when he was already a mature and experienced composer, wrote sixty fugues as a sort of training in polyphony. I had also heard, I can't remember where exactly, that Tchaikovsky wrote such a work to exercise his technique as a composer.

'I have always found it quite hard to compose, and therefore, so as to make it easier for me perhaps, I too have to practise this sort of scribbling. But as I started composing this work, I found that it was transcending the limits of a purely technical exercise. After I had written the first Preludes and Fugues it seemed to me that to write with a merely technical aim would not be very interesting.'

At this moment we heard rustling and whispers from the front rows, where his official detractors were interpreting what Dmitri Dmitriyevich had said as an admission of his 'formalist tendency'. Later that evening, they were to accuse him of this at the open discussion.

But Dmitri Dmitriyevich continued: 'When we listen to Bach's music, it is impossible not to suspect that a whole series of his works, including the Forty-Eight Preludes and Fugues, were written as a way of keeping his polyphonic techniques polished. I too wanted a more serious task than just practising my technique. It is difficult for me to judge the result, as the work is so fresh off the stocks. Although this composition in some way almost seemed to write itself, I worked on it a great deal. Undoubtedly I now have to ask myself whether I have succeeded in my aim of writing preludes and fugues that have a substantially artistic content, and do not constitute a mere technical exercise.'

Then Dmitri Dmitriyevich spoke about the various performing possibilities of the Preludes and Fugues, as a cycle or as separate pieces. He must have already foreseen the inevitable reproaches as to the difficulties of performance, and that they would be impossible to overcome. And this, despite the fact that he already knew the genuine opinions of Yudina and Nikolayeva.

But, alas, these were times of a simplified approach to art, a boorish, 'standardization', and of narrow-minded, utilitarian attitudes. Therefore, in all probability Shostakovich was also issuing a warning to his listeners:

'I wish to say that I do not regard this composition as a cycle. It does not need to be played from the first to the last prelude and fugue. In my opinion this is not essential, in fact it might even harm the work, as it is indeed difficult to comprehend. It would be more correct, therefore, to play a group of six, or maybe even three or four of the pieces. It is not a cycle, where one piece must perforce follow on from another. It is just a collection of piano pieces, and not a work that is connected throughout.'

Dmitri Dmitriyevich then thanked the audience for their attention: 'It would be most interesting and useful for me to hear your comments as to how far I have succeeded in these Twenty-Four Preludes and Fugues, whether I have created a work of artistic value, or whether it seems arid and boring.'

Then, one after another, the Union secretaries, all musical functionaries, voiced their disapproval. Amongst them, alas, was Kabalevsky: 'This work is based on a grave miscalculation. It could not have served you, Dmitri Dmitriyevich, for instance as a preparation for *The Song of the Forests.*'

After some peremptory remarks about the composer's undoubted gifts and professionalism, the officials competed with each other in unmasking him. They had no hesitations in accusing Dmitri Dmitriyevich of sinning against 'surrounding reality' and of failing to reflect the image of his contemporaries. They confidently instructed him, using mind-bogglingly ghastly bureaucratic clichés. A typical instance was the diatribe of a certain S. Skrebkov, then a secretary of the Union of Composers:

'In the instances where I dislike these Preludes and Fugues, I would describe the music as ugly. I can say with certainty that I did not like the D flat major fugue. I absolutely reject such music. I see this as a formalist fugue. And in my view, the A minor fugue sounds distorted and false, erroneous in its modulations and chords. The G major Prelude and Fugue shows tendencies of those sins, those grave sins, committed by Dmitri Dmitriyevich in past years. What sort of images is he presenting us? Are they the images, I ask, of Soviet reality?'

And here followed a mass of reproaches as to the composer's subjectivity; his contrived affectations were heaped on poor Shostakovich: 'Not typical of our life . . . The musical image given in the D flat major is no reflection of our reality, only a caricature of it . . . I refute it with impunity. Dmitri Dmitriyevich has committed an error in allowing himself to write such a Fugue . . .'

And thus the slanderous calumny rolled on.

Next it was the turn of the musicologist T. Livanova to harangue Shostakovich. She had some trouble expressing herself: she spoke 'on the basis of my ears' experience', and of 'material thematics' and how 'the different images antagonize each other'. She accused the creator of the G major Fugue of expressing 'emotions that are morbid, gloomy and unhealthy. Like many other comrades, I would like something different here.' She then made the practical suggestion that 'certain of the pieces do not merit being widely popularized'.

The stenographic report that has survived from this discussion is curious. It has been partially doctored to suit those 'Valued Party Cadres', who subsequently edited their own speeches and also withdrew those parts of other texts which were not to their taste or which they deemed unfit to be seen by their 'bosses'. For instance, two-thirds of my speech is no longer in the archive today. Also, some of the extended and conspicuous heckling in the hall has been deleted. These jeers and baits served as a warning to the defenders of the work, a means to bring them to their senses. Israel Nestyev, a member of the Central Committee (in 'the field of music', as was the expression), was one who took on the role of rabble-rouser, as did Tikhon Khrennikov.

Neither the pianists Yudina and Nikolayeva, nor the composer Sviridov, were able to save the discussion from these absurd demagogical pronouncements. Sviridov tried to use a certain degree of diplomacy to swing the discussion on to a more dignified level. But that evening they were completely ignored.

Yudina produced a striking contrast to the impersonal chorus of self-appointed prosecutors and judges in her outward image, gestures and tone of voice, and her spontaneous manner of speaking her thoughts. Strange as it may seem, it was difficult to distinguish between the ample figure of the lady-instructress Livanova and the heavy-faced musicologist Koval', the dispenser of grim pronouncements, and the fawning Nestyev and others of their ilk. They appeared to feel no shame; it was as if all their statements were covered with a film of dirt. But had a complete outsider walked into the hall and seen the large figure of Yudina in her voluminous dark dress, he would have immediately recognized in her face and manner of speech a great personality and artist.

Yudina first made the point that she was 'speaking on behalf of all pianists'. I felt that she was attempting to raise the level of discussion on to a more spiritual plane, so as to dam the mire that had seeped into the hall. Having spoken of the great necessity of such new compositions, she fixed this band with her fearless gaze and declared, 'Much of what is composed today has no life in it because it lacks inner content, mastery and pathos. But we pianists are eternally grateful to Dmitri Dmitriyevich! It is said truly that you can identify a bird by its flight!

And to argue whether there exists a need for polyphony is sheer child's prattle which is not even worth discussing.'

Her speech was sincere and spontaneous. She spoke a language completely unknown to these pseudo-musicologists, these anonymous zealots. She proceeded to explain that Dmitri Dmitriyevich had created something practical and useful to the Conservatoire students, which would serve as a way to master their instrument. And I was reminded how Shostakovich's elder friend Meyerhold had emphasized the tremendous importance of young talent being in contact with great art, as it led to self-discovery.

Yudina gave her evaluation of the new work as 'a real heroic exploit! And if certain comrades remained unimpressed, then all the worse for them.' And responding to Škrebkov's ironic and insulting description of the D flat major as a 'caricature' she exclaimed, 'And if indeed there are amongst the Preludes and Fugues instances of caricature, tell me what's wrong with that? Maybe some of us deserve to be caricatured. And indeed life is far richer and more varied than the recipe provided by Comrade Skrebkov. He couldn't even write a single prelude and fugue, whereas Dmitri Dmitriyevich has . . .' In conclusion she asked that those who were concerned with the real meaning of Shostakovich's music should allow performers to play it for a wide audience.

Nikolayeva gave a dignified speech. She said that, having listened to this work several times, on each hearing it produced a deeper and deeper impression. The work was striking for its variety and multifaceted qualities, and also for the unusual sense of unity it conveyed. After this Yudina raised her voice again.

Her sensitive antennae had picked up the hostile and hardened attitude of the 'prosecutors' and the hidden anguish of those who were too frightened to oppose them. Athough part of the audience had applauded her and Nikolayeva's words, she sensed that everything they said was being ignored by the self-appointed 'key figures'.

Yudina challenged her listeners: 'Life will overthrow all these condemnations by you armchair theoreticians. It will be left to us, the practical musical 'activists', to overcome your criticism by making the work available to the People. Your quibbling, negative judgements will wither away at their roots. And thank God for that!'

The 'activists' sat there with stony faces, while Shostakovich sat right at the very edge of the front row. His pose was incredible – no artist would take upon himself to depict it! His head hung towards the floor, and at certain moments it slumped so very low that it dangled between his widely spread-out knees. No doubt this explosion of abuse seemed so agonizing and obtusely academic that he was possessed by an irrepressible desire to shake off all this filth from his person.

Now Nestyev was at it again, sending his oaths spiralling into the air with his pointed index finger: 'We very much wish that Shostakovich's outstanding talent should be channelled to the road of advanced socialist art, that he should not waste himself on compositions with so little ideological significance. Despite certain successes, this work does not correspond to the strict criterion of today's Soviet art.'

However comic it may seem, Nestyev's accusations and abuse fell almost exclusively on me, a figure from the literary world; and this despite the fact that his worthiest opponent was undoubtedly Yudina. My speech had aroused his irritation and fury; he called it perfidious. I had been prompted to take the tribune by my friend, the composer Alexander Lokshin. Nestyev and Khrennikov had tried to prevent me from speaking and demanded that I should be thrown out of the hall.

I was not so much distressed by Nestyev's assault on me; he and his ilk were, after all, behaving according to stereotype. But it was inexpressibly bitter to see this petty gang yelping around their victim, Dmitri Dmitriyevich.

Nestyev ignored the sense behind my words. He set himself and his fellow-thinkers up as the composer's saviours from those invidious influences that permeated his latest work. 'This work hardly corresponds to those high pinnacles of achievement that we have come to expect from Dmitri Dmitriyevich.'

From the outset, I made the point that Dmitri Dmitriyevich had no need for champions, and that a whole lot of professionals had spoken amateurish nonsense with such arrogant confidence in the belief that they were justified in their attempts to regulate artistic style and creativity. I asked where such a vulgar scheme of 'sacred commandments' had been laid down. And how did they measure this gamut of illusory values?

Interestingly enough, the essence of my speech is preserved in the stenographic record, despite the fact that my judges destroyed three-quarters of it. Some of the Preludes and Fugues did not pass the censor's eye. Therefore only a part of the absurdities uttered remain in the archives.

My speech was nearly shouted out by the officials in the front rows. I had hardly opened my mouth when I was interrupted: 'I wish to ask you, when we are living through difficult and tragic times' – A roar from the hall – 'when each of us feels the necessity to help the People and the comrade in question' – 'Remove her from the hall.' – 'and if at such a time a composer presents a work of the highest mastery where he has shown bold invention, has depicted the image of thinking man with a rich variety of experience and suffering – surely all this is indeed a reflection of "surrounding reality"?'

The word 'tragic' and my reference to the composer's innovation roused intense fury amongst Dmitri Dmitriyevich's detractors. I continued by asking them what were the 'true values' they kept referring to? And I pointed out that, in a truly musical country like Czechoslovakia, a large festival had opened with performances of Shostakovich's music. What would the Czechs say if they could see what was going on tonight?

And finally, how ignorant and vulgar to say that Bach was creating images of the time he lived in in his Preludes and Fugues, whereas Shostakovich was not: 'Are such narrow scholastic arguments lawful? Why demand that art should be illustrative? I do not see any well-wishers amongst the composer's colleagues that are present. One should help an artist by sensing what was uppermost in his mind in his striving and achievement. And how can you turn Dmitri Dmitriye-vich's words, spoken with real sincerity, against him? He was not counting on making an effect when he spoke of the aims he had set himself, and you reproach him with "formalism and technical tricks".'

From the back of the hall I heard applause; but hardly had I finished speaking than I was approached by a certain 'somebody' who threatened me, speaking of my 'ideological' errors. I heard nothing in my despair; my attention was completely riveted by the image of an anguished Shostakovich, who remained in the same pose, his head bent low between his spread-out legs.[38]

The pianist TATYANA NIKOLAYEVA recalls the creation of Shostakovich's Preludes and Fugues. She also recounts how, during the period of their composition, the composer started writing his Tenth Symphony. Her testimony places the conception and composition of the Symphony well over two years earlier than the normally accepted date (1953):

38 Lyubov' Rudneva, 'How It Happened . . .', article commissioned for this book.

I first met Shostakovich while I was a student of piano and composition at the Moscow Conservatoire. My composition teacher was Shebalin, and Shostakovich and Myaskovsky took our orchestration classes. They were both wonderful, good men, kind teachers and excellent judges.

But I got to know Shostakovich really well in July 1950, when we were in Leipzig for the Bach celebrations. This was the start of a friendship which lasted twenty-five years – until Dmitri Dmitriyevich's death.

It has been said that Shostakovich was inspired to write his Preludes and Fugues after hearing my performance of Bach's Forty-Eight Preludes and Fugues during the Bach competition. It is true that I proposed the complete Forty-eight for the competition programme, but in the event the jury only selected one! – the F sharp minor from the first Book. Hence it was my performance of Bach's music in general, rather than the Preludes and Fugues in particular, that might have impressed Dmitri Dmitriyevich.

Soon after our return to Moscow, Shostakovich started composing his Preludes and Fugues. As he was writing them he would call me up and invite me over to his place, so that 'he could play something for me.' The first time I went he had already written the C major and A minor Preludes and Fugues. By the next day he had written the G major. After he had written the first eight, I said, 'Dmitri Dmitriyevich, would you mind playing them all through now from the beginning?' And he did.

But one day I came to the house (in the early months of 1951), and saw a large score on the piano. He said to me, 'Today I will play you something different.' It was the exposition of the first movement of his Tenth Symphony. He started writing this wonderful work simultaneously with the composition of the Preludes and Fugues. Indeed he played me everything he wrote in that period as it was created – the Fifth Quartet, the Pushkin Monologues.

Shostakovich conceived his works in an enormous span from beginning to end; they are born of an amazingly intense creative process. In this he is comparable to Bach. Shostakovich's symphonic works were composed and written down in full score – the Tenth Symphony was no exception. Soon Dmitri Dmitriyevich went on to play me the other movements of the Tenth Symphony as it was being composed. I can't remember now the exact date when he completed it, but it was during 1951, and not in 1953, the date always given in programme notes and textbooks.

On 16 May 1951, a meeting was convoked at the Union of Composers to discuss Shostakovich's newly completed Preludes and Fugues. Its purpose was to authorize public performance and publication of the work. Dmitri Dmitriyevich himself played from the music, and I turned the pages for him. It was unbearably hot and stuffy in that small crowded hall. He was extremely nervous, and did not play at all well. It is perhaps not so surprising that nobody understood the work on that one hearing – after all, the music is of great polyphonic complexity. For me it was different, as I was totally immersed in the world of the Preludes and Fugues, having lived with them from their birth, so to speak.

But the discussion that followed was utterly shameful, and it left the most dismal impression on me. I have to say that I don't think that the criticisms directed at Shostakovich were in any way motivated in political circles. Unfortunately, first and foremost to lead the attack against him were his colleagues and fellow musicians. They exploited the political situation to give vent to their black envy, and were only too ready to label Dmitri Dmitriyevich a formalist or cosmopolitan. You could say that a new work by Shostakovich hit these envious, petty-minded musicians like an atomic bomb. Any politically damaging effects on Shostakovich were the consequence of a ricochet effect produced by their condemnation and censure.

All this made me the more determined to learn the Preludes and Fugues myself, and to prove to its critics that the work was a masterpiece.

The following summer (of 1952) a second meeting was called in Moscow by the Committee for the Arts. I made sure that it was arranged at a time when Shostakovich was in Leningrad. I wanted to go through this on my own, not wishing Dmitri Dmitriyevich to endure another humiliation. The audience was largely the same as the previous year. However, Skrebkov, Kabalevsky, Livanova and Nestyev – all of whom had previously torn the work to shreds – now praised it to the skies. My aim was achieved as the work was authorized for publication – incidentally, this meant that Shostakovich could get paid for it. He was extremely happy at this outcome, and sent me telegrams of gratitude. Indeed, he dedicated the Preludes and

Fugues to me, but this was a secret between us; the dedication was not printed in the published editions.

Soon I myself played eight of the Preludes and Fugues at the Grand Hall of the Moscow Conservatoire. Then, at Dmitri Dmitriyevich's request, I gave the first performance of the whole cycle in December 1952 in Leningrad. We weren't sure then whether they would allow the complete cycle to be performed in Moscow.

I must emphasize that Shostakovich intended this work to be played in its entirety, as a cycle. When played separately, the pieces acquire a 'divertimento' character. I have always insisted that Dmitri Dmitriyevich's wish be respected. Therefore, although I played the cycle many times in the Soviet Union, during his lifetime I only once played it abroad – in Poland at a concert in Krakow arranged by two ardent admirers of Shostakovich's music – Cserny Stefanska and Krzsystof Meyer. And it is only in recent years that I have performed the complete cycle in the West – I preferred to wait than give in to impresarios' demands for 'easy' programmes.

However, Dmitri Dmitriyevich never played the work in public as a complete cycle. He did play groups of the Preludes and Fugues; and in concerts dedicated to his music so did I. A typical programme of Shostakovich's music was made up of an 'old' Quartet, a group of Preludes and Fugues, followed by the première of a new Quartet. Every time Dmitri Dmitriyevich asked me to participate in such a concert, I would drop everything to do it. I always asked him, 'Which Preludes and Fugues would you like me to play?' And he invariably answered, 'Choose whichever you please, but, come to think of it, play this one, that one and that one . . .' This was his answer to me for twenty-five years, and it always made me laugh.

The last time he addressed me with this request was only a week before his death. He phoned to tell me that he had completed a viola sonata, and asked me to play a group of Preludes and Fugues in the concert with its première on his birthday. Alas, the concert took place without him.[39]

39 Tatyana Nikolayeva: recorded interview with EW.

CHAPTER SIX

The Thaw

The political background of the Thaw years

In the first months after Stalin's death, the collective leadership formed from the dictator's closest political associates acted with the appearance of apparent unanimity. But under the surface there started a jostling for power within the Party hierarchy. Nikita Khrushchev, the Party First Secretary, emerged as a political force to be reckoned with, initially in an alliance with Nikolai Bulganin. It took him until 1958 to remove all opposition to his leadership.

The open power struggle commenced with the removal of Lavrenti Beriya, the chief of the dreaded NKVD and a member of the initial triumvirate. With his arrest in July 1953 and subsequent execution the arbitary power of the Secret Police was somewhat curtailed, signifying a gradual process of 'de-Stalinization' and the easing of political repression.

Khrushchev speeded up this process when he exposed the atrocities of Stalin's regime in a secret speech to the delegates of the 20th Party Congress in 1956. It took five years before he was ready to denounce Stalin publicly, which he did at the 22nd Party Congress.

The revelations of Khrushchev's secret speech (which soon were leaked in the Western press and spread faster than fire at home) turned the Soviet people's way of thinking upside down; moreover they unleashed a series of strikes and revolutions in the Eastern European satellite countries. The Soviet authorities were prepared to resort to rude force to restore the damaged prestige of the Party and impose order both at home and in Eastern Europe. The invasion of Hungary by Soviet troops in October 1956 was the culmination of a series of events triggered off by the 20th Party Congress unmasking of Stalin.

Another important consequence of the speech was the release and rehabilitation of large numbers of people from the camps and prisons (true, the process had been initiated after Stalin's death.) Inevitably a profound disenchantment with the Party and its methods took root among the populace at large, and slowly people found the courage to voice their protests. The 'Thaw',[1]

1 Ilya Ehrenburg's novel *The Thaw* was published in 1954, and this title became synonymous with the 'liberal' politics of the 1950s.

as this post-Stalin decade became known, oscillated between liberalization and repression. Ultimately it was a divisive period, confusing for both hard-line supporters of Stalinist communism and reformers and liberals alike.

In the meantime, as the Soviet Union emerged from years of isolation, contacts were cautiously established with the outside world, including the Western powers (albeit the country's 'ideological enemies'). While Soviet citizens had their horizons widened, their society was also subject to external scrutiny. The Soviets upheld their international prestige by pouring money into the space and arms race, and also by exporting culture. A brilliant generation of Soviet musicians (Oistrakh, Richter, Rostropovich and Mravinsky, to name but a few) started to travel, taking the West by storm and proving the undiminished supremacy of the Soviet performing tradition. These artists championed new Soviet music, with Shostakovich's music at the forefront of their repertoire. At home the ban on art, literature and music that had been previously labelled as 'decadent and formalist' was lifted (although by no means indiscriminately), allowing people to rediscover their own cultural heritage and giving them a glimpse of modernist developments in the West.

As Shostakovich was restored to grace after his years of disfavour, he soon realized that the rewards of official recognition were not always comfortable to live with. Khrushchev, with his policy of 'peaceful co-existence' and a sharp eye to Western reaction wanted to be seen to have the support of the intellectual community. Having disastrously mismanaged the 'Dr Zhivago' affair, with the shameful ousting of Boris Pasternak from the Writers' Union and the ensuing brouhaha over his Nobel Prize award in 1958, Khrushchev stepped up the pressure on prominent intellectuals to voice their support of the Party line. Shostakovich's inability to resist this mounting coercion undoubtedly was a factor in his choice of theme for his two 'revolutionary' symphonies, and in his application for Party membership in 1960.

The last years of the Khrushchev era gave birth to two new concepts – at home the phenomenon of dissidence, and on the international front the policy of detente. The long-term consequences of the repercussions of the 'Thaw' years were far-reaching indeed. Despite the intervening years of Brezhnevian 'stagnation' they reached their ultimate conclusion with the disbanding of the whole communist system itself.

FLORA LITVINOVA describes Shostakovich's immediate reaction to the death of Stalin:

With Stalin's death in March 1953, I noticed Dmitri Dmitriyevich's sense of relief. Although the enormous pressure that weighed on him throughout life was somewhat eased, he felt no sense of euphoria. We were left with the feeling that the regime was indestructible under the ruling triumvirate of Molotov, Malenkov and Beriya. The latter still cast a heavy shadow on the country, although rumours started to gain ground that it was actually Beriya who would bring order into the KGB, establish justice and release the prisoners from the camps. We had this information from the wife of Maisky, the ex-ambassador to London, who had been arrested and sent to the camps. I came to see the Shostakoviches to tell them this news. Suddenly Dmitri Dmitriyevich pounced on me:

'How can you believe such deliberate lies, lies that have been put into circulation by *that* department! *Beriya*, who personally cut up corpses and flushed them down the toilet, now wants people to believe that he has grown wings. And you are inclined to believe it!²

The Tenth Symphony

Immediately following Stalin's death, Shostakovich's main preoccupation was to release the works that he had been forced to hold back from performance. In the last two months of 1953, three substantial works were given their premieres: the Fourth Quartet (13 November), the Fifth Quartet (3 December) and the Tenth Symphony (17 December).

In 1955, another two important works, the Violin Concerto and the song cycle *From Jewish Poetry* received their long overdue public premiere. That same year Shostakovich's thoughts returned to his cherished opera *Lady Macbeth of Mtsensk*, and as a first step to rehabilitating the work he asked Isaak Glikman to modify the libretto.

Hitherto it has always been accepted that the Tenth Symphony, a work widely regarded as Shostakovich's central masterpiece, was largely created in the summer months of 1953 at the Komarovo dacha outside Leningrad. The date of completion is given as 25 October, by which time the composer was back in Moscow.

But according to Tatyana Nikolayeva, one of Shostakovich's closest musical friends of the period, the Symphony was composed, at least in part, during 1951, parallel to the creation of the Preludes and Fugues. Whereas Nikolayeva was emphatic about the dating of the first movement – early in 1951 – she indicated that the other movements were finished within that year, without being precise about the dating.

It is possible that having started the Symphony in 1951, Shostakovich either completed it or substantially rewrote it in the summer of 1953. In his letters written between June and October 1953 to various correspondents the composer refers unequivocally to the creation of his Tenth Symphony,

2 Flora Litvinova: article commissioned for this book.

movement by movement. It would seem far-fetched for him consciously to wish to create the fiction of writing a work two years after its actual completion. Yet there is other evidence which supports Nikolayeva's claim. Manashyr Yakubov, the curator of the Shostakovich archive, has pointed to the existence of sketches of a movement of an unfinished violin sonata dating from 1946, where the first theme bears a marked resemblance to that of the Tenth Symphony's first movement, and the second subject themes are identical. This implies that Shostakovich had been mulling over this musical material for many years before it eventually got written down in finished form as the Tenth Symphony.

Certainly, if Shostakovich did deliberately withhold and 'mis-date' the Symphony, then one must assume that he was motivated by the fear that it would be subjected to the same kind of attacks inflicted on its two pre-decessors. The recent debates at the Union of Composers on the Preludes and Fugues and *From Jewish Poetry* will have done little to alleviate such apprehensions. It took an event as momentous as Stalin's death to shift the prevailing wind of cultural repression.

In the stifling atmosphere of the post-1948 climate, Shostakovich had dedicated most of his serious effort to writing chamber works. The Tenth Symphony without doubt represented an urgent need to return to large symphonic form. In this sense it picks up a link with the Violin Concerto of 1947/48, rather than with the previous Ninth Symphony.

It was in late October 1953 that Shostakovich (together with Moisei Weinberg) played a two-piano version of the score to Mravinsky in Leningrad, and afterwards to a gathering of Moscow musicians and composers. Mra-vinsky, sufficiently impressed, set aside all other tasks to learn the work and presented it in public only six weeks afterwards.

The Tenth Symphony enjoyed a huge public success, and was highly praised in reviews by such authorities as Aram Khachaturian and David Oistrakh. The music must have seemed like the summing up of a tragic epoch to the contemporary listener, with its raging Scherzo depicting the forces of evil (if not indeed an actual portrait of Stalin[3]), while the life-affirming force of the artist is celebrated as the DSCH motif resounds triumphantly at the end of the Finale.

A few months after its first performance Shostakovich wrote an apology for the work which verges on the ridiculous; indeed its absurdity is so patent that on this occasion the composer must have penned it himself, dispensing with the services of a ghost-writer. Shostakovich explains that he had written the symphony in too much of a hurry; then, the first movement isn't a proper sonata allegro, the second movement is a bit too short in relation to the other

3 Solomon Volkov, *Testimony: The Memoirs of Dmitri Shostakovich*, p. 107.

movements which are too long, and the third movement suffers from being drawn out in places and cut down too much in others. As for the Finale, the introduction is long-winded, although it fulfills its compositional function.

This extraordinary exercise in 'healthy self-criticism' served to deflect anyone pursuing the trail of interpretative explanation. Having thus denied the existence of any programme, the composer signs off with a passing comment: 'in this work I wished to portray human feelings and passions.'[4] But this seemingly innocent remark reveals more than one might think.

In the third movement Shostakovich dwells insistently on his 'autobiographical' musical signature – the four notes DSCH (D, E flat, C, B). This motif was already used in his Second Piano Sonata and his First Violin Concerto and was to become a recurrent feature of his works. A passing reference to his setting of Pushkin's poem (the second of the Op. 91 Four Monologues), 'What Is In my name for you?', acquires a poignant significance in the light of a recent revelation that the five-note horn motif in the third movement is also a musical signature – that of a woman's name, Elmira.[5] The horn call is heard no less than twelve times during the movement, and in addition it bears a striking and self-conscious resemblance to the horn motif in Mahler's first song from *Das Lied von der Erde*.

The person behind the inspiration was the Azerbaijani pianist and composer Elmira Nazirova, who had studied with Shostakovich in the year prior to his dismissal from the Moscow Conservatoire. During the summer months of 1953 Shostakovich carried on an intense (and probably largely one-sided) correspondence with her. Although Nazirova undoubtedly served as his muse during the period of composition, it seems that it was a temporary obsession with her image that sustained Shostakovich's inspiration, rather than a need to fuel a concrete physical relationship.[6]

The Symphony's reception amongst Party and Union officials was hardly enthusiastic. At a conference called by the Union of Composers in spring of 1954 to discuss the work, the music was condemned for not meeting with the

---

4 *Sovietskaya Muzyka*, no. 6, 1954.
5 Tenth Symphony, third movement, figure 114:

The notes, written of course at transposed pitch a fifth higher, of the signature *E L(a) Mi R(e) A*, derived from using both the French and German systems of notation.
6 Nelly Kravets, 'A New Insight into the Tenth Symphony of Dmitri Shostakovich', a paper delivered at the conference 'Shostakovich: The Man and His Age', University of Michigan, 28 January 1994. Publication forthcoming.

requirements of current Soviet ideology, with its emphasis on the 'optimistic, bright future of Soviet Man'. Pavel Apostolov accused Shostakovich of the sin of 'modernism' and 'a gloomy, introverted psychological outlook'. Another of Shostakovich's erstwhile detractors, Boris Yarustovsky objected to the lack of 'an active struggle for the good', and questioned, 'Where are the positive ideas in this symphony?'

The head of the Composers' Union, Khrennikov, played it safe by pointing to Shostakovich's own *Song of the Forests* as a suitable model for composition.[7]

These carping criticisms by petty bureaucrats and Union officials were issued along the same 'ideological' lines as those levelled at Shostakovich during the Union's assessment of the Preludes and Fugues in 1951. But the political climate had defrosted sufficiently to protect Shostakovich and his new work from repressive measures.

The Symphony was immediately taken up and widely performed within the Soviet Union and abroad. After five years of disgrace in the aftermath of the 1948 Decree, Shostakovich emerged with his reputation enhanced, the quality of his composition attesting to his moral and artistic integrity.

The Festive Overture

This work was written for the thirty-seventh anniversary of the October Revolution, and received its première on 6 November 1954, with Melik-Pashayev conducting the Bolshoi Theatre orchestra. LEV NIKOLAYEVICH LEBEDINSKY recalls how the piece came into being:

Shostakovich composed the Festive Overture before my very eyes. It was commissioned by Vasili Nebol'sin, a conductor at the Bolshoi Theatre, who was a master of producing works for every conceivable public holiday or ceremonial occasion. Beforehand there would be a lot of commotion. Meetings were called at the Bolshoi and at the Ministry of Culture, where, in heated discussions and pompous arguments it was decided what particular work Stalin (or his successors) should listen to and which composer should be commissioned to write the necessary piece. These commissions incidentally were much sought after as they were very well paid, and composers fell over themselves to get one. Shostakovich was the only one never to get one. The other composers wrote terrible shit.

On this occasion for some reason nothing suitable was ready for the celebration of the October Revolution. Nebol'sin was in trouble. Very

7 Sofiya Khentova, *Shostakovich: Life and Work*, vol. II.

little time remained, rehearsals had been called, there were no parts ready, and what's more there wasn't even a piece written! In desperation Nebol'sin came to see Shostakovich at his flat. I happened to be there at the time.

'You see, Dmitri Dmitriyevich, we are in a tight spot. We've got nothing to open the concert with.'

'All right,' said Shostakovich.

Nebol'sin said that he would send a courier round to collect the score as soon as it was ready and get the copyists lined up, and with that he left.

Dmitri Dmitriyevich, with his strange, unpredictable, almost schizophrenic character, had the notion that I brought him good fortune, although to my knowledge I never brought him any particular luck. He said, 'Lev Nikolayevich, sit down here beside me and I'll write the overture in no time at all.'

Then he started composing. The speed with which he wrote was truly astounding. Moreover, when he wrote light music he was able to talk, make jokes and compose simultaneously, like the legendary Mozart. He laughed and chuckled, and in the meanwhile work was under way and the music was being written down. About an hour or so later Nebol'sin started telephoning:

'Have you got anything ready for the copyist? Should we send a courier?'

A short pause and then Dmitri Dmitriyevich answered, 'Send him.'

What happened next was like the scene with the hundred thousand couriers out of Gogol's *Government Inspector* Dmitri Dmitriyevich sat there scribbling away and the couriers came in turn to take away the pages while the ink was still wet – first one, then a second, a third, and so on. Nebol'sin was waiting at the Bolshoi Theatre and kept the copyists supplied.

Two days later the dress rehearsal took place. I hurried down to the Theatre and I heard this brilliant effervescent work, with its vivacious energy spilling over like uncorked champagne.[8]

8 Lev Lebedinsky: recorded interview with EW.

Nina's death – and a second marriage

Shostakovich's personal happiness was shattered when his wife Nina Vasilyevna Varzar died suddenly in Armenia on 4 December 1954. Despite its open
nature, their marriage had been harmonious, and family life had been its
mainstay. Moreover, Nina had always protected her husband from the
outside world and seen to the smooth running of the household. Nina's close
working and emotional relationship with the physicist Artem Alikhanyan, as
well as Shostakovich's involvement with his Leningrad pupil Galina Ustvolskaya were open secrets.

Now, without Nina, Shostakovich found he had to deal with mundane
practicalities himself, and to steer his children through the difficult period of
adolescence. His daughter Galina soon was to enrol at the Biology faculty of
Moscow University, while his son Maxim was studying at the Central Music
School, and at the time wished to become a pianist. Shostakovich wrote two
works to encourage him: the Concertino for Two Pianos (1954) and the Second
Piano Concerto (1957).

Shostakovich complained to Edison Denisov shortly after Nina's death: 'If
only you knew how hard my life is now.'[9]

And in the summer of 1955 he wrote to Denisov from Komarovo: 'Everything here reminds me of Nina Vasilyevna. She loved this place and put much
energy into making our home here. The summer is passing by sadly without
my producing anything. Mama is ill. Nina's father can hardly move. It's very
hard to witness all this continually.'[10]

Soon Shostakovich suffered a second blow with the death of his mother on 9
November of that year. In her he lost the person who had done most to
develop and fulfil his genius.

Hoping to ease his loneliness, Shostakovich sought for companionship in
marriage, but finding a suitable companion to help him run his household was
not such an easy matter.

Shostakovich's feelings for Galina Ustvolskaya were strengthened by his
admiration of her original talent as a composer. As a token of his esteem he
gave her many of his manuscript scores (including the unfinished *Gamblers*
and the Preludes and Fugues Op. 87), and furthermore quoted themes from
her composition in his own work (as in his Fifth Quartet, where he uses a
theme from Ustvolskaya's Clarinet Trio).

When Shostakovich married in July 1956, his friends were bewildered by his
unexpected decision; he not only acted in haste, but his choice seemed
eminently unsuitable.

9 Edison Denisov, unpublished diary.
10 Letter dated 31 July 1955.

He had met his new bride, Margarita Kainova, the previous month at a composers' competition at the World Festival of Youth in Moscow, where Shostakovich headed the jury. Kainova worked for the Communist Youth Organization (Komsomol) and had no love or understanding of music. Khentova claims that the poet Evgeny Dalmatovsky effected the introduction.[11] Galina Vishnevskaya assumed that Kainova's main attraction was a certain physical resemblance to Nina.[12] The composer's friends' fears were vindicated, as the marriage proved a disaster from which Shostakovich disentangled himself three years later.

After Nina's death Shostakovich underwent a rare compositional crisis. On 11 March 1956 he wrote to his former pupil, Kara Karayev:

> I have very little news. And even less good news. The saddest thing is that after the Tenth Symphony I have hardly composed anything. If this continues I'll soon be like Rossini, who, as is well known, wrote his last work at the age of forty. He then went on to live till seventy without writing another note. This is small comfort to me.[13]

Interestingly enough, Shostakovich had been able to compose throughout the years of his disgrace. But now, despite the more relaxed political climate, he felt that he had written himself out, measuring himself by the previous standards of his own extraordinary 'tempo' of serious composition. Nevertheless, by August 1956 he had composed his Sixth String Quartet, while the massive Eleventh Symphony, written the following year, showed that his grasp of large symphonic form was as secure as ever.

FLORA LITVINOVA describes the effect of Nina's unexpected death on Shostakovich's life:

> After a long interval without working, Nina returned to her scientific research. She worked in the laboratory of their friend, the Academician Alikhanyan, who was head of an Institute of Physics in Armenia. Every summer Nina went to a station high up in the mountains of Armenia, almost on the summit of Alagez, where research was carried out into cosmic radiation.
>
> Once, shortly before she left for an expedition, I suddenly noticed that Nina was wearing glasses.
>
> 'Are you sad?' she asked. 'Soon we'll be old and playing blind man's buff.'
>
> We were walking down the street and a cold wind was blowing. I

11 Sofiya Khentova, 'Women in Shostakovich's Life', p. 264.
12 *Galina: A Russian Story*, p. 227.
13 L.-V. Karagieva (ed.), *Kara Karayev: Articles, Letters and Opinions*, p. 54.

realized that Nina didn't look as well or as youthful as usual. Her face was pale and her complexion grey. 'Well,' I thought to myself, 'she's not so young after all.' That was in the summer of 1954. Nina was only forty-three years old.

On 3 December of that year I was at home, having stayed away from work to look after my little girl, Nina. The telephone rang. It was Dmitri Dmitriyevich. 'Flora, Nina has a blockage of the intestine. She has been taken down to Yerevan from the mountains, and they are going to operate. I am taking the next plane to Yerevan. Can you come with me? I think that it will be psychologically easier for Nina to have a woman friend with her at such a time.'

I was at a loss: 'You see, Dmitri Dimtriyevich, my little girl is ill, and Mama is unwell, so there is no one for me to leave her with. I am sure that the operation will be successful; after all Nina is so healthy and positive.'

The next day Nina died. Her intestine was infested by a cancerous tumour. Her body was brought back to Moscow. I remember little of the funeral. I only remember that when I walked into the flat, I saw Nina lying in the open coffin on the table; she looked tranquil, beautiful, and appeared to be only asleep. Dmitri Dmitriyevich stood next to her. We kissed and both burst into tears. I could not forgive myself that despite everything I had not flown down to be with her. I was incapable of imagining such a terrible outcome, as Nina was the personification of life itself. Next to Dmitri Dmitriyevich stood Galya, a young woman now, and the adolescent Maxim. How Nina watched over them, and solicitously looked after their upbringing.

After Nina's death, we spent less time at the Shostakoviches. Once, when I came over on Nina's name day, 27 January, Dmitri Dmitriyevich, who had had a bit to drink, suddenly announced that he found it difficult to live on his own. And it was hard dealing with the children.

'You know, by nature, I am incapable of frivolous liaisons with a woman. I need a wife, a woman to live with me and be at my side.'

Some time later I received a letter from Dmitri Dmitriyevich, where he informed me, as Nina's friend, that he intended to marry Margarita Kainova: 'She is a kind woman, and I hope that she will be a good wife to me, and a good mother to my children. I hope that you will remain, as before, a dear friend of our household.'

Anusya Villiams passed on to me some frightening rumours about Dmitri Dmitriyevich's intended: that she worked for the Central

Committee of the Komsomol, was a Party member, that she was unattractive and uncharming, and knew nothing about art. Misha and I were invited to meet her. We felt ill at ease, and I remember little about that visit. But I wrote down in detail everything about our following visit to Dmitri Dmitriyevich.

On 24 October 1956 we went to hear a concert of new compositions. Dmitri Dmitryevich's Sixth Quartet was premièred, a Trio by Boris Tchaikovsky and a String Quartet by Revol Bunin were also performed. We were breathtaken by Shostakovich's music. Dmitri Dmitriyevich himself had aged a lot, and looked grey. He bowed nervously in acknowledgement of the applause, flapping his hands absurdly at the performers. It was agreed that we would go to see him the coming Saturday. Here is my diary entry for 27 October 1956:

'Yesterday we went to see Shostakovich. Since Nina's death, we had only been around a few times. There is always an unpleasant feeling, a loss for words, a sense of awkwardness. Besides the absence of Nina and my own sadness at the loss of a genuine friend, I also miss that simplicity in my relations with Dmitri Dmitriyevich. When she was alive, he used just to come into the room and be with us as long as he felt like it, and talked only if he felt like it. He would then go off to work in his study. Then he would appear and say, 'Shall we have a cup of tea? I do love having breaks. And do you know, it's a rule with me that I never work on holidays or days off, only on weekdays." If we lunched or dined together, he liked to have a glass of cognac, and then he would get animated and recount something interesting. Often it would be a malicious, sarcastic or funny story about some mutual friend.

But on this occasion, Misha and I were just paying a visit. And there was no Nina, but an alien and unattractive woman, who, thank God, left the room after greeting us. We sat in Dmitri Dmitriyevich's study. He quickly put some questions to Misha: "Have you heard any news on the BBC? What's happening in Budapest? And Poland? The empire is falling apart at the seams. It always happens – the fist must be tightly clenched – it's enough for it to relax just a little for the empire to crack. And only Stalin was capable of that."

'We talked of his songs written to texts of Dolmatovsky.[14] I said that

---

14 Litvinova is probably referring to *Five Romances on Verses of Dolmatovsky* Op. 98 (1955) which were published early in 1956 and had received several performances by the bass, Boris Gmyrya. In 1951 Shostakovich had also composed *Four Songs to Words by*

I didn't like them much (in reality I didn't like them one little bit), and the words were terrible. "Why did you write music to those texts?" I asked.

'Shostakovich replied, "Yes, the songs are bad, very bad. They are simply extremely bad."

'And I piped up again, "But why did you write them?"

'He answered, "One day I will write my autobiography, and there I will explain everything, and why I had to compose all this." He spoke with some discomfiture, and a feeling of awkwardness arose between us.

' "But did you like the quartet?" he said, wishing to change the subject.

'But I kept on, "But why do you allow these songs to be performed if you don't like them?"

' "But this is an opus of mine. It has been published. Anyone who wants to has the right to include this work in their programme; I cannot refuse them."

'His embarrassment was painfully obvious. I know what it was that drove me on. Knowing his views, I could not bear to hear that he intended to join the Party. I was sure that, had Nina been alive, none of this would have occurred. We had been told how pressure had been exerted on him from certain quarters, but we did not know if this was so for sure, and we hardly dared to ask him outright.

'Misha, seeing that I was behaving tactlessly, changed the subject by saying how much he had enjoyed Boris Tchaikovsky's Trio.

'Dmitri Dmitriyevich's face lit up: "Yes, his Trio is wonderful, excellent. Boris is very talented, and works hard. And that's important, because in music professionalism means so much. Many things can be studied and learned, so it should be possible for anybody to compose music. But professionalism combined with talent, as in Boris's case, gives rise to wonderful music. And that is true of Bunin as well."

'I then asked about his other pupils and friends. "Is Weinberg composing, and Levitin?"

'Dmitri Dmitriyevich answered disapprovingly, "Only theatre and film music."

Dolmatovsky Op. 81; the first of these, 'Rodina Slyshit', acquired a special fame when the first man in space, Yuri Gagarin, sang it while in orbit in 1961.

' "And Sviridov, is he still drinking?"

' "No, Sviridov has stopped drinking, and is composing. His songs on Esenin poems are very good. And, d'you know, I've also stopped drinking? I don't drink at all. Today I wanted to drink something, but discovered that Maxim and his friends had drunk a whole bottle of cognac."

'We were most surprised; I still thought of Maxim as a young boy. Dmitri Dmitriyevich said that they had had a serious talk, and he thought that Maxim would stop. Maxim appeared at dinner time. A real popinjay, a handsome and twitchy youth. He was preparing to go hunting. We heard him boorishly abuse the chauffeur on the phone for not providing him with a tyre.

'Dmitri Dmitriyevich spoke of the brief period of "Thaw", saying that it should be enjoyed while the going was good. "The novel is bad, but Ehrenburg found the right word – the Thaw. We must relish it while it lasts, as experience shows that frosts will follow, and hard ones at that."

'Misha and I spoke of a film, where Picasso was shown painting a picture before our very eyes. Shostakovich said that he understood nothing about visual art. We were full of our impressions of the Picasso exhibition in Moscow. People had reacted excitedly to it, both young and old, and it provoked much argument and waving of hands. The majority of people were seeing such art for the first time.

'Suddenly Dmitri Dmitriyevich burst out, "Don't speak to me of him, he's a bastard."

'We were stunned.

' " Yes, Picasso, that bastard, hails Soviet power and our communist system at a time when his followers here are persecuted, hounded, and not allowed to work."

'I interjected, "But your followers are also hounded and persecuted."

' "Well, yes, I too am a bastard, coward and so on, but I'm living in a prison. You can understand that I'm living in a prison, and that I am frightened for my children and for myself. But he's living in freedom, he doesn't have to tell lies. I am now being invited by all countries of the world to travel, but I'm not accepting, and I don't intend to travel anywhere until I can speak the truth, until I can answer the question as to what I really think about the Central Committee's 'historic' Decree. And Picasso, who's forced him to speak out? All those Hewlett

Johnsons, Picassos, and Joliet-Curie, they're all vermin. They live in a world which no doubt has its problems, but they are free to speak the truth and to work, and they can do what their conscience dictates. And Picasso's revolting dove of peace! How I hate it! I despise the slavery of ideas as much as I despise physical slavery."

'Misha and I tried to explain that Picasso probably didn't know what was going on in our country, and that he and others like him no doubt thought that our artists enjoyed being "socialist-realists", painting like Gerasimov. We pointed out that Picasso probably backed the idea of communism in general, as indeed did we. "And you, too, Dmitri Dmitriyevich, are for the ideas of communism."

'He answered, "No, communism is impossible. But let Picasso be, I don't want to talk about him anymore."

'At supper time, Madame came to sit at table. She is terribly uninteresting, and there is something horse-like about her. She tries terribly hard to please everybody, from the guests to the children, and to adopt the right tone. But, goodness, how vapid and unpleasant she is – particularly after Nina, and altogether. . . !'[15]

LEV LEBEDINSKY describes Nina's open nature and sense of humour, and how later he helped effect the introduction of Margarita Kainova to Shostakovich:

I knew all of Shostakovich's wives. Nina Vasilyevna (or Nita) was an energetic, vivacious woman, who, for all the complexities of their marriage, provided Shostakovich with a family and protected him somewhat from the outside world. She had a great sense of humour. I remember Nita's infectious and unconstrained laughter when she told me the details of the famous telephone conversation with Stalin, which she had listened in to on the other receiver.

A few weeks after this conversation with Stalin, the Party Organization decided it was time to do something about Shostakovich. So they appointed a 'sociologist' from the Conservatoire to instruct him. This man was an incredible fool, thick-headed to a degree. He was invested with the responsibility for guiding Shostakovich's thoughts, for 'powdering his brains', and explaining the meaning of 'political economy' in terms of Marxist terminology. The instruction took place at Dmitri Dmitriyevich's flat. Poor Shostakovich simply had to grin

15 Flora Litvinova, article commissioned for this book.

and bear it, and somehow disguise his boredom. Even so, he managed to find some humour in the situation.

One day the instructor said to Shostakovich, 'Is it true, Dmitri Dmitriyevich, that Joseph Vissarionovich rang you up in person?'

'Yes it is true.'

'What a truly great man Stalin is! With all the cares of state, with all he has to deal with, he knows about some Shostakovich. He rules half the world and he has time for you.'

Dmitri Dmitriyevich was happy to play him along, and said, 'Yes, yes, it is truly amazing.'

'I know you are a well-known composer,' continued the instructor, 'but who are you in comparison with our great Leader?'

Dmitri Dmitriyevich was not lost for a reply. Thinking of Dargomyzhsky's famous romance with its text, 'I am a worm in comparison to His Excellency,' he immediately interjected, 'I am a worm.'

'Yes, that's just it, you are indeed a worm,' this idiot said, 'and it's a good thing that you possess a healthy sense of self-criticism.'

Dmitri Dmitriyevich knew how to act a role; he hung his head and repeated, 'Yes, I'm a worm, a mere worm.'

Nita, who had been present during this 'instruction' laughed until the tears streamed down her cheeks.

Nita's early death in 1954 was a tragic blow to Shostakovich, and he was never able to fill the void she left in his life.

Once a few years later, Dmitri Dmitriyevich approached me with a strange request: to help him make the acquaintance of a young lady who had caught his attention.

'So who is this lady?' I asked.

'She works for the VLKSM, the Komsomol.'

'Well, where on earth did you see her?'

'At a competition run by the Komsomol for the "Best Massed Song". I was there and she was constantly hovering around me.'

'So, what do you know about her?'

'Nothing much, only I know that she's called Margarita Kainova.'

'Why didn't you get yourself introduced while you were there?'

'Well, you know what those meetings are like. How could I approach her and introduce myself in those surroundings?'

'So, what's your plan?' I asked.

'It's very simple, very simple. I've worked it all out. Tomorrow we'll go to the opera. I have already got two tickets. I want to ask you as a favour to deliver one of them to her.'

I agreed to help. I experienced certain difficulties in my mission, as I didn't know her address, but eventually I discovered where she lived and delivered the ticket. Dmitri Dmitriyevich was as happy as a child and clapped his hands with joy.

I met him the day after. 'How did it go?' I asked.

He looked a bit confused. It turned out that when Dmitri Dmitriyevich got to the theatre, sitting on the seat next to him – the one destined for Kainova – was a young man. He bore a certain resemblance to her.

'Probably her brother!' I said.

'Yes, no doubt, the scoundrel.'

'And then what happened?'

It transpired that he and the young man sat through the whole opera without exchanging so much as a word.

Not long afterwards I was urgently called to his home. I was to meet and 'inspect' Margarita Kainova. She made no impression on me. We sat down to drink tea, and it was a fairly tedious occasion. After she had left, Dmitri Dmitriyevich told me, although it was the first time that she had come to his house, he had proposed to her.

'Why on earth did you do that?'

'Well, that's what has happened and I can't get out of it now.'

'Excuse me, but have you got to "know" her in the biblical sense? Are you in love with her?'

Of course the answer was a mumbled 'No'. He was so shy, that he didn't know how else to find a contact with her. 'And now I've promised her.'

'The devil take it,' I remonstrated, 'what if she's totally unsuited to you?'

Two or three days later he told me that he was off to Leningrad, to Komarovo, and that he was taking Margarita with him as his wife. My hair stood on end. Then a few days later I got a postcard from him saying that their marriage had been formalized. I phoned him and voiced the necessary polite phrases; but I knew from his tone of voice that Dmitri Dmitriyevich was embarrassed and felt far from happy. He brushed me off, 'Yes, yes, thank you, thank you.'

One day in the summer of 1959, Maxim informed me that Dmitri Dmitriyevich asked me to go up to Komarovo as soon as possible. I found him with his sister Mariya Dmitriyevna. She came out to meet me with these words: 'Lev Nikolayevich, Dmitri Dmitriyevich and Margarita are separating; please don't make any objections or exert any pressure on Dmitri Dmitriyevich.' I found this very strange.

'Mariya Dmitrievna, surely you don't think that I want to keep them together? I was always against such a hasty match.'

When we were all in the house and started talking, Dmitri Dmitriyevich started giving me somewhat guilty, sidelong glances. It then dawned on me that he had decided to cast the blame on me, and had accused me of being the instigator of this unsuccessful match. His children had always been against the marriage, and Margarita had been continuously critical of the children. Dmitri Dmitriyevich had told me previously that they weren't getting on too well, and that their disagreements centred around Margarita's inability to understand the children. One day, when she was complaining, he said to her with a completely straight face, 'Why don't we kill the children, then we can live happily ever after.' She didn't understand that this remark was typical of his quirky, paradoxical sense of humour.

Dmitri Dmitriyevich stayed in Komarovo until divorce proceedings were under way, leaving Maxim to get Margarita out of their Moscow flat.[16]

The première of the First Violin Concerto

MARINA SABININA describes the long awaited première of Shostakovich's First Violin Concerto:

In the autumn of 1955, the première of the First Violin Concerto was to take place in Leningrad. Its author had witheld this work from the world for many years. In addition all his preceding substantial works (the Preludes and Fugues, the Tenth Symphony) had aroused malicious attacks from the champions of 'Socialist Realism' and had caused Shostakovich no small amount of injury and bitterness.

The conductor, Mravinsky, had called as many orchestral rehearsals for the new concerto as for a monumental symphony. The soloist, David Oistrakh, was extremely concerned for the fate of this concerto and how it would be received by the press and the public; he had been

16 Lev Lebedinsky: recorded interview with EW.

working at the piece for a very long time, getting 'right inside' the music, until he was incurably enamoured of this brilliant concerto. In a word, the composer, conductor and soloist were all in a state of extreme agitation. A whole group of their friends and admirers were set to go to Leningrad for the première, and they were themselves no less nervous.

The magazine *Sovietskaya Muzyka* had commissioned me to attend the première to review it. Before that I had studied the score, and had listened to a rehearsal at Shostakovich's flat, when Oistrakh, accompanied by Victor Yampolsky, first played the Concerto through to the composer. On that occasion, Oistrakh advised Dmitri Dmitriyevich to give the main theme in the opening of the Finale to a resonant brass instrument, and to save the timbre of the violin for later. Dmitri Dmitriyevich immediately agreed.

On the evening of 29 October, the Grand Hall of the Leningrad Philharmonic was overflowing, and there was an atmosphere of jubilation and exhilaration. After the performance ended there was a storm of delirious applause, ovations, expressions of delight, and the composer, soloist and conductor were called out an endless number of times. Returning to the 'European' Hotel I bumped into a group of four people by the lift, the Glikmans, Galina Ustvolskaya and Dmitri Dmitriyevich, who cordially invited me to come up to his room 'to celebrate, you understand, to celebrate this event'.

'Thank you, of course I'd be delighted to come, thank you.'

In fact I then had to sort out an awkward situation as previously Oistrakh had invited me to supper with him; I ran up to his room and left a message explaining the matter. Of course it would make sense to drop a delicate hint to Dmitri Dmitriyevich that it would be a good idea to combine this improvised festivity. And when Dmitri Dmitriyevich started to talk of 'how brilliantly, extraordinarily, and marvellously' the soloist had played that evening, I made a tentative suggestion to that effect which was greeted very enthusiastically. Shostakovich rang Oistrakh's room, but alas, he had not returned – no doubt he had been delayed changing his soaked-through concert clothes in the artists' room.

In the meantime Dmitri Dmitriyevich had prepared a 'feast' in his room: he produced out of some paper bags some stale pies, which he had bought on the street and were as hard as stones, and some equally rock-like and inedible green apples. This was the accompaniment to the vodka. However there were no receptacles to pour it in, so we made use of a glass decanter stopper turned upside down, and some plastic cups found in the bathroom. Dmitri Dmitriyevich, with his 'glass' in hand paced up and down the room with quick steps, muttering, 'I am so glad, so glad, I'm so happy. I'm utterly, utterly happy.' We clinked glasses and drank, and our host touchingly thanked 'everybody, everybody, absolutely everybody', toasted the ladies, resumed his pacing up and down, occasionally tripping up on the carpet. He took a bite from the rock-like pie, but was defeated by it and let it drop on the table. Then suddenly he fell silent and collapsed on the bed in the alcove. In a childishly helpless, plaintive voice he said, 'And now all of you please go away, I am terribly tired, I want to sleep, to sleep . . .' We naturally hurried to bid our farewells, to which he did not respond.

When I told Oistrakh about this curious 'feast', he was most alarmed. 'But, my goodness, Dmitri Dmitriyevich must be absolutely ravenous, he didn't eat anything all day long, I must drag him up to my room, look at all these marvellous dishes here!' He rang, and to my surprise Dmitri Dmitriyevich picked up the receiver, but declined the invitation. 'I'm already in bed, I'm completely drained of strength, completely without strength.' The nervous tension that he had endured that day had been too much for him.[17]

The Shostakovich households

The Shostakovich family moved to their Moscow flat on Mozhaiskoye Highway (later renamed Kutuzovsky Prospect) in 1947. In 1949, after participating in the peace delegation to the USA, Shostakovich was awarded a country house (or dacha) outside Moscow in Bolshevo. Later, in 1961, he bought a dacha in Zhukovka and, to the bewilderment of all and sundry, gave back the Bolshevo dacha to the state. (After all, he could have sold it at a profit!)

The Shostakoviches also enjoyed visiting their dacha in Komarovo in the Gulf of Finland (known by its Finnish name, Kellomiaki, before the Revolution). It was here that Shostakovich did most of his composition during the summer months. The house belonged to the Varzar family, and was originally shared with various of its members; it was later bequeathed to Maxim and Galina. From 1961, Shostakovich himself stopped using this house, and

17 Marina Sabinina, 'I Am Utterly Utterly Happy', short story written for this book.

instead went to rest and compose in the Union of Composers' House of Creativity in nearby Repino. There he was allocated on a permanent basis a small house, 'cottage number 20'.

After Nina's death, Shostakovich ran his household with the help of various servants, who were treated like members of an extended family. He continued to support them after their retirement. The children's nurse, P. Demidova (who had also looked after Nina when she was a child), was allocated a room in their old flat on Kirov Street. Fedosya Kozhunova (Fenya) retired to look after the dacha in Bolshevo, while her niece Mariya looked after the family in the town flat. Additionally, Shostakovich employed a personal secretary, Zinaida Gayamova (also known by her maiden name, Merzhanova), and a chauffeur, Alexander Limonadov.

The soprano GALINA VISHNEVSKAYA got to know Shostakovich after her marriage to the cellist Mstislav Rostropovich in 1954. She writes of her impressions of the Shostakovich family's somewhat chaotic household and modest and unpretentious way of life:

In those years Dmitri Dmitriyevich was living on Kutuzovsky Prospekt. When I first entered the apartment I was amazed by the disorder that reigned within – the lack of comfort, despite the fact that two women lived there: the maid, Mariya Dmitriyevna, and the old nanny, Fenya. Everything bore the stamp of neglect. Dmitri Dmitriyevich was only forty-eight when, on 4 December 1954 his wife, Nina Vasilyevna suddenly died, leaving him to raise the two children: a daughter, Galina, seventeen years old, and a son, Maxim, who was fourteen.[18] Dmitri Dmitriyevich transferred all his love for his wife to his children, and was a dedicated family man. I never heard him raise his voice to either of them, although their upbringing had been turned over to the maid, and they were growing up spoiled and undisciplined. He loved them with a kind of abnormal, morbid love, and lived in constant fear that some misfortune would befall them.

. . .

Dmitri Dmitriyevich liked to invite his close friends to his place and seat them at his table. Russians drink vodka rather than wine with their meals, and he was no exception. He didn't use small vodka glasses, and preferred to do the pouring. He would start by pouring himself half a tumbler and drinking it off right away. Then he would pour himself another half, and begin to eat – that was his 'quota'. He

18 In fact Galina was eighteen years old and Maxim sixteen.

got tipsy rather quickly, especially in his last years; and when he did he would quietly disappear into his room for the night.

In those days he was hard-pressed for money, and there would be only sausage, cheese, bread and a bottle of vodka on the table. But he never seemed to notice what he was eating. He had few friends (life itself had made the selection for him), and his guests were usually the same people – those whose loyalty had been proven by time. But even then he rarely visited unless it was to celebrate birthdays. (He always remembered those birthdays, and never failed to send a telegram of congratulations.)

Most often he would sit at these affairs in silence, not taking part in the general conversation. He never sat long. After drinking his 'quota' he would stand up suddenly and say (using almost always the same words): 'Well, we've drunk and we've eaten. It's time to go home. Time to go home.' And he would leave.[19]

Shostakovich's son-in-law, EVGENY CHUKOVSKY, comes from a well-known literary family – he is the grandson of Kornei Chukovsky. His uncle Nikolai was a well-known novelist and his aunt Lydia was a close friend of Akhmatova and a supporter of fringe and dissident writers. His own father, Boris, a biologist, died in active service during World War II, and consequently he was brought up partially in his grandparents' home, thereby acquiring an awareness of the pre-Stalinist Russian cultural background, something that had been lost by many of the young generation growing up in the 1950s.

Here Chukovsky writes of his first impressions of the Shostakovich family. He had met Maxim Shostakovich, a student like himself at the time, at a rowdy Moscow party to see in the New Year of 1957. In the early hours of the morning, well fortified by their hostess's lethal punch, the merry-makers decided that it was time to listen to some music:

Maxim announced that if we wanted to hear music then we were to come to his home without a moment's delay. We rushed into the street in a crowd and bundled ourselves into a large taxi and set off for the Mozhaiskoye Highway. But on the way most people realized that they had had enough and it was time to go home. Soon, only Maxim and I were left in the car, and as I lived out of town and had nowhere to go at that hour it didn't matter to me where I went.

At the Moscow end of the Mozhaiskoye Highway, only 800 metres

19 Vishnevskaya, *A Russian Story*, pp. 223, 224.

from the large road sign 'Moscow', indicating the boundary of the big city, stood block number 37/45 where Shostakovich lived. It was situated between two neon signs: 'Cinema – Prizyv – Cinema' and 'Cinema – Pioneer – Cinema'. The block belonged to the Foreign Ministry and it was inhabited by ambassadors extraordinary and plenipotentiary, counsellors and other staff. But some flats had been delegated by the Powers Above to 'workers in the arts': actors, artists and composers. Shostakovich occupied two flats, numbers 86 and 87, which had been converted into one. The door of number 86 had been nailed up, and it was evident that it was never used. Maxim rung the bell of number 87 and we were let in.

What an extraordinary phenomenon the events of that New Year's night were. Normally I would be flabbergasted at the idea of arriving at somebody's home after three in the morning, but on that night it didn't seem odd at all.

Maxim had an excellent 'professional' tape recorder in a corner of his room. Soon the tape was running and the saccharine voice of some American singer was being reproduced so purely that you could hear her breathing. But I didn't listen. I was transfixed by the sight of a large festive cake on the piano, and thought to myself, 'My goodness, he's only a boy, and he has his own cake!'

The door opened and Dmitri Dmitriyevich entered. I was a bit scared, it was after all very late, but he only greeted us politely and asked Maxim if he had had a good time. Having received an affirmative answer, he made off to his own room.

I got friendly with Maxim and spent a lot of time in their apartment. I liked the Shostakovich home and involuntarily compared it to ours. It seemed that despite the differences there were many similarities. For instance, instead of having the postbox on the outside of the door as was common, there was a slit in the door covered on the outside by a metal flap, inscribed with the word 'Post'. On the inside of the door there was no box, and the letters, newspapers and magazines fell higgledy-piggledy on to the floor.

And, as in our home, it was the custom to address one's elders only by their names, without using the customary 'Auntie' or 'Uncle' which I found incredibly irritating.

And again, as we did at home, they called the Fathers of Communism 'Karlo–Marlo'. I also heard repeated a rhyme dating from 1914 that Grandfather was fond of:

'Hail Russia, my fatherland.
And Hail her plucky Allies!'

Although I spent a lot of time in Maxim's company, I didn't enter the other rooms in the flat, as there was never any reason to do so. But one day Maxim said, 'My father wants to meet you. He's in the dining room.'

I felt very diffident, but I had no choice but to go. I opened the door and stood on the threshold. Dmitri Dmitriyevich sat facing me at the table with his back to the window. He was eating meat with potatoes. The two-tiered redwood sideboard was the same as one we had in our dining room, and the table too looked very much like ours. The walls were cream coloured with crudely painted golden flowers and leaves. Golden? Painted in a revolting bronze paint!

'It can't be true,' I thought.

Such a thing was impossible in the home of Shostakovich. But there it was, and my attention was so caught up by this that I hardly heard the question my host was asking. It was simple enough: who was I? I replied as best I could, and was given permission to withdraw. As I was going out, I noticed the telephone by the door. A piece of paper was stuck behind the wire to it. The following list was typed on it:

All newspapers
All magazines
Radio
Television
TASS
Dolgopolov

I was quite familiar with such lists. It indicated the organizations to which Shostakovich was not at home should they wish to speak to him on the phone. To this day I wonder what were the possible sins of Mr Dolgopolov, the only private individual on the list.

When the whole country was busy eradicating the faults of Soviet music highlighted in the 'historic' Decree of 1948, Stalin decided to phone Shostakovich personally in order to see what effect the measures taken were having on the culprit.

Therefore the traditional, 'Hello, Dmitri Dmitriyevich,' was followed by, 'How are you?'

Shostakovich replied, 'Very poorly.'

I'm convinced this is true.

Stalin, feigning ignorance, expressed his concern and said in conclusion, 'We'll take care of your health!'

And they did just that.

Shostakovich received a pass to the Kremlin Hospital and an official document stamped with seals stating that the composer was to be provided with a summer house outside Moscow equipped with every modern convenience. The document was signed by Stalin himself.

The people charged with carrying out the doddering General-issimo's wishes managed to find a house which had no modern conveniences. Yet fearing the Generalissimo's wrath, they urged Shostakovich to accept money for the renovation of the house and sign a receipt for a new and properly equipped dacha.

Furniture was brought to the house, and the Shostakoviches made an attempt to settle there, but they were balked by the absence of conveniences. A well was dug but it soon filled with sand. They sunk an artesian well, but the steel pipes burst somewhere deep in the bowels of the earth. They laid a pipeline, but the pipes burst with the first frost. Besides, the place was very difficult to get to and the family didn't have much time at their disposal. Nina Vasilyevna, Dmitri Dmitriyevich's wife, was busy with work, the children were at school, and they spent the summers near Leningrad. They only paid occasional short visits to the house.

It's no joke to live without water. A number of experts were called in to solve the problem. The experts floated around in shoals like herring, and each one had some project which proved to be impractical or highly dubious. One of them, a mad inventor known locally as 'the Kettle', came up with the idea of converting sewage into pure drinking water. He was willing to do this at his own expense.

'Doesn't it smell somewhat?' enquired Shostakovich squeamishly.

'Not at all,' the 'Kettle' assured him. 'Well, maybe in the spring thaws you get the odd whiff. Otherwise there's no smell at all.'

In the meantime the solution was to use the old methods prevalent in Central Asia. Kuzma, the water carrier from the village, a quiet, subdued man, and somewhat of an invalid, took a bucket and walked the half kilometre to the spring. Every day, come rain, come snow, he filled up a large barrel with bucket-loads of water.

Maxim used to complain because his father insisted on him going to their dacha in Bolshevo. He found it unbearably boring there, there was absolutely nothing to do, and it was incomparably nicer to stay in town. So one day he suggested that I should go with him to keep him company and cheer him up. Limonadov was to take us there.

Limonadov, or simply Lemonade, was the chauffeur's name. However his family acquired this strange surname is a mystery. It certainly produced a startling effect on people, as when a traffic inspector, scrutinizing his driving licence and unable to believe his eyes, told him, 'Giddy up then, Lemonade – syrup!'

Alexander L'vovich Lemonade was a nice fellow, and everybody called him just Sasha; that is everybody except Dmitri Dmitriyevich, who always addressed people, irrespective of who they were, with the formal name and patronymic. Dmitri Dmitriyevich didn't like familiarity, and was constantly bewildered at how, in the cinema studio, for instance, harassed and grey-haired employees who had worked there all their lives continued to call each other by the diminutives 'Petya' and 'Kolya'. He told us that even when he had had occasion to teach at a children's music school he had imposingly addressed all the children by their name and patronymic, preparing them for their future adult life. In the same way he never used the familiar 'thou', except with his most intimate friends. Only once towards the end of his life did he forget himself so far as to use the 'thou' form when speaking to me, something I can only be proud of.

Lemonade appeared and we set off, first to the garage where he deposited his master's car and got out his own. For Lemonade lived in Bolshevo and was travelling home.

It was a rarity in those days for a chauffeur to own a car. And it turned out that the car had been Shostakovich's, who, when he had bought a new car, sold off his old one for peanuts. He was completely disinterested in the fact that on the black market you could sell a second-hand car for double the price of a new one in the shops. Limonadov, of course, took advantage of this circumstance, quite rightly supposing that it wouldn't be easy to find a second such idiot. (Incidentally I knew of another one; his name was Kornei Chukovsky, not that I would tell Limonadov.)

And here we were in Bolshevo. Along the roadside factory buildings loomed, with piles of trash lying scattered around nearby, the usual accompaniment to such buildings in Russia. The highway was intersected by untidy railway crossings; out of some turning came a string of six carts loaded with wooden barrels, each dragged by a tired old

jade slithering on the snow. The unsavoury smell explained everything – sewage disposal in progress. My goodness, what a place! What
kind of dacha could there be here?

The house stood somewhat apart from the highway, and in winter it
was impossible to drive up to its gates because the snow was never
cleared. Limonadov deposited us on the road and drove off in haste.
We walked down a path made where the deep snow had been trodden
down and found ourselves in front of a gate, part of a continuous
wooden board fence. A knot in one of these boards fell out to reveal a
hole. Maxim pushed his finger in the hole and we heard a bell ring
somewhere.

'It's disguised so the local boys don't fool about with it!' Maxim
explained.

We heard footsteps and a squeaky woman's voice from behind the
fence asked, 'Who's there?'

'It's friends, Fenya,' said Maxim, and the gate opened.

The old babka Fenya lived permanently at the dacha as its guardian.
She was monstrously ugly. Her nose looked like a large potato on
which new little potatoes had sprouted. Her thin legs carried a
triangular body which lacked shoulders, so that her long jointy arms
appeared to grow right from the neck. In addition, she was constantly
muttering in a squeaky voice. In this muttering there was no real
malice; indeed her eyes shone with such love for people that her old
wrinkled face beamed. It was enough to see her to trust her immediately; respect for her followed soon after.

She had started her service in the Shostakovich household in
Leningrad before the war. She considered herself downgraded in this
position, as in the old times she had been the servant of a rich
merchant. In the interval between the merchant and Shostakovich she
had seen some pretty difficult times, and had barely survived the
famine on the Volga. Since then she had developed a nearly religious
respect for bread and never threw out a crumb. She converted stale
bread into rusks which she stored in a cardboard box. Once the box
was full, she filled up another, then another, and many more. Fenya's
room was stacked with these boxes, and mice abounded. They made
plenty of noise, eating their way through the rusks from inside the
cartons, and they roamed freely around the house. Life became
unbearable. An attempt was made to persuade Fenya to part with her
treasure; it was proposed to take her to the shops so that she could see

with her own eyes that there was plenty of bread to be had, as well as other good food. But nothing helped. So they resorted to more drastic measures. When Fenya was out of the house the boxes were removed. She returned to discover the theft, and sat down and cried quietly. Then she started all over again.

But during the war, through her frugal foresightedness, Fenya survived and saved her relatives. And now that the war was over who was to forbid Fenya her rusks? She lived all year round at the Shostakovich dacha, and, although nothing was asked of her, from habit she continued to work. She cultivated a vegetable garden and grew carrots, parsley, onions and tomatoes; she made jam, salted cucumbers, marinated cabbages and looked after the hens. All this produce was then sent with Limonadov to the family in town, and Limonadov brought back tea, coffee, soap, sausage and, to use Chekhov's words, other 'colonial produce'. For herself the old babka Fenya kept only the rusks with which she barricaded her room.[20]

EVGENY CHUKOVSKY goes on to describe the Shostakovich household at Komarovo:

At the end of May 1959 Maxim suddenly announced that the whole family were shortly to depart for Komarovo. In a characteristically peremptory manner he dismissed as fools anyone who spent the summer elsewhere.

I knew of no 'Komarovo', so I asked him what was so special about it. In reply came the single word 'dacha', and Maxim's eyes lit up, as in a burst of fiery oratory he described the charms of the place and the heroic exploits that he and his buddies got up to (which, in retrospect, I now see as nothing short of malicious hooliganism). I set my heart on going to that remarkable place, Komarovo.

Maxim quickly left the room but returned immediately – 'Papa's calling you.'

Shostakovich was sitting in the dining room under a lampshade made from paraffin waxed paper. Such lampshades had just become all the rage; they were produced by bereft widows with no other means of support.

'Hello, Dmitri Dmitriyevich,' I said.

'Hello,' he replied. 'Do come and stay with us at our dacha in Komarovo.'

20 Evgeny Chukovsky, novella commissioned for this book.

I wanted to say something, but Maxim literally pushed me out of the room as an indication that the audience was over.

The invitation had been pronounced very drily. Its intonation – or rather complete lack of intonation – made me think of a recalcitrant child whose mother makes him repeat over and over again, 'Forgive me please, I won't do it again.'

Now it's clear to me that a very awkward thing had happened. I hardly knew Dmitri Dmitriyevich then, and his manner of expression was not familiar to me. Therefore in my naivety it never occurred to me that it was Maxim that had forced him to issue this invitation to their dacha.

Komarovo. I climbed down on to the platform and at once caught the air of the mysterious gulf, the touch of iodine of its breath giving it a heightened vigour not quite like that of normal fresh air. The electric train thundered past me and turned into a green caterpillar creeping along the railway tracks, whose lines stretching into the distance refuted the axiom that parallel lines never meet. Beyond the platform the satanic golden eye of a signal light glowed; the soil around us was sandy, grass didn't grow under the pine trees, only moss, and along the line on my left there stretched a low granite platform, a remnant from the old times when the station used to be called Kellomiaki.

I remembered that I was to turn right at the second crossroads into the Academicians' Village and then to ask for Korablestroitelei Street. Here was the crossroads where the main village street, Kellomyaks-kaya, now called Akademshosse, began. I thought that I must be nearly there, but strangely enough nobody knew where this Korab-lestroitelei Street was. All was lost! I'd never find this mysterious place. Just then I noticed a clump of young pine trees beneath which the yellowish white sandy soil barely showed for the thick carpet of pine needles. From there Shostakovich emerged.

It turned out that this clump of pine trees was none other than Korablestroitelei Street. It boasted only five or six houses, and one of these – number 20 – was Shostakovich's.

Before my eyes was a strange edifice, surrounded by a paling which looked as if it had come from the set of Little-Russian opera. In the distance, screened by this paling stood something between a house, a log cabin and a dacha. It resembled more than anything else a Spanish galleon with broken masts which had been dragged out of the sea for repairs after a terrible gale. It didn't seem much like a dacha to me. And to add to my astonishment a dirty green electric train thundered past just above the level of the roof. The property was situated in a ravine just under the high railway embankment.

Dmitri Dmitriyevich informed me that Maxim and Galya had gone to Tallinn and were expected back any time now. He handed me over to the care of some old women, who had suddenly appeared in a throng from goodness knows where. I found myself in a room with an old upright piano. It was decorated with cheap wallpaper, and the flimsy window frame held three pieces of glass instead of one. There was a round stove in the corner, clad with corrugated iron. It all seemed very rickety and shoddy, with only an inadequate lick of white paint on the doors and windows. In such a house one could only expect the food to be bad; but the 'cultivated poverty' actually stopped short here and the old women fed me very well.

I went out on to the road to wait for Galya and Maxim. I sat on the warm sand by the roadside, dumped there for the purpose of repairs. After some time a 'Pobeda' car with a Moscow number-plate appeared in the distance. Maxim and Galya were sitting inside and at the wheel was the chauffeur Limonadov with his teeth bared in a poisonous smile.

We then all supped together on the veranda, eating fish caught that evening by the local fisherman and drinking extraordinarily delicious milk. Then, in the outlandish dusk of the White Nights, I was dragged off to the gulf, which they called the sea, even though it hardly had enough water to merit the name.

Shostakovich wrote on the veranda of the first floor, which he called with a noticeably wry smile his 'creative laboratory' or his 'tvorilka'. Tracery window casements took up three of its four walls, and against one of these stood a heavy oak desk. On it stood a set of coloured glass inkwells, white, yellow and red, which had as an appendage a glass beacon crowned by a sharply pointed lightning conductor. Every time I approached that desk I shuddered as I imagined that it might pierce the eyes of the composer as he bent down to write.

Dmitri Dmitriyevich used these inkwells as he liked to work with an ordinary dip-pen. It was easy to write notes with it: you pressed and it left a blob, then you steered it up – it left a line. A Parker or other fountain-pen would have been much worse for this purpose, and it took Shostakovich a long time to get used to writing with a ball-point pen. He preferred to dip the old-fashioned steel-nibbed pen in the violet ink of the inkwell.

He composed in his mind. I suspected that he went on doing so round the clock. In any case I failed to establish any specific time when he composed, because he never approached the old upright piano on the ground floor. Once he said, although in jest, that all instruments should be taken away from composers, as they should have no need for them.

To observe him writing down what he heard was like a miracle. Placing a large sheet of manuscript paper in front of him, with hardly an interruption and practically no corrections or rough copies, Shostakovich created his new scores. They were created in entirety and instantaneously. It looked as though he wasn't composing, but just copying down sounds heard in his innermost self. And then, when the score was ready, he wrote out the orchestral parts himself.

Maxim once asked him, 'Papa, why are you writing out the parts when the score is there? Anyone who knows how to read and write music could do it for you.'

Dmitri Dmitriyevich replied, 'Everyone should do his own work from beginning to end.'[21]

The Rehabilitation of Lady Macbeth

As Shostakovich released the last of his suppressed works from the 1948–53 period, he cherished high hopes that his opera, Lady Macbeth of Mtsensk, would be revived after nearly twenty years of ignominious silence. (True, the opera had occasional performances outside the Soviet Union, as at the Venice Biennale Contemporary Music Festival in 1947.) In March 1955 the composer played the opera, with certain revisions, for the Leningrad Maly Opera Theatre (MALEGOT), who wished to stage the work in the forthcoming season. According to Isaak Glikman, the composer had already composed the two entr'actes that constitute one of the significant changes in the 1961 version of the opera, re-named Katerina Izmailova.

The following month Shostakovich asked Glikman to review the libretto, and gave him permission to make changes to the text (to fit the existing music) at his discretion. Shostakovich's chief concern was to eradicate some of the cruder vulgarities of the original.

21 Evgeny Chukovsky, novella commissioned for this book.

Before being able to programme the opera, MALEGOT needed to have the go-ahead from the authorities. Here Glikman describes how, in the spring of 1956, despite the musical and textual changes, *Lady Macbeth* was rejected by the State-appointed commission. This bitter humiliation must have reinforced Shostakovich's fears that fundamentally the Party had no intention of changing its policies towards the arts. Over the next few years Shostakovich nevertheless made several tentative efforts to have the new version of the opera re-staged. But it was only in 1961 that it received approbation by the Union of Composers, thereby allowing it to be staged in Moscow at the Nemirovich-Danchenko Theatre the following year.

The published score of Op. 114 (as the composer catalogued the new version of *Katerina Izmailova*) does not credit Glikman (or anybody else) with the textual changes to the libretto. Certain voices have claimed that Irina Antonovna Shostakovich, the composer's third wife, was responsible for the rewritings, in her capacity as literary editor of the published score.[22] As yet there is no concrete evidence to cast doubts upon Glikman's claim to their authorship.

ISAAK GLIKMAN recalls the humiliating experience for Shostakovich of having *Lady Macbeth* re-auditioned – and rejected:

I return to the unhappy fate of the opera *Lady Macbeth*. I remember that in March 1955 Shostakovich asked me to look at the whole libretto of the opera with a critical eye, and to make any corrections and changes that I thought fitting. Within a month I had put words to many pages of the piano score, attempting always to preserve the spirit of each phrase, but investing them with different verbal forms.

On 19 April 1955 I showed this version of my vocal text to Dmitri Dmitriyevich, and it was approved by him. Soon I received a letter from Dmitri Dmitriyevich sent from Moscow dated 21 April 1955, which included the following lines: 'Dear Isaak Davydovich, Many thanks for your hard work. I am now adjusting it in my piano score; my only regret is that you have only completed this task now and not twenty-two years ago.'

In the winter of the following year I received another letter from Shostakovich: 'I fulfilled Zagursky's request and had a talk with Molotov, who repeated his instructions about an audition of *Lady Macbeth* by a competent Committee.

'Yesterday I saw Comrades Mikhailov, Kaftanov, Kemenov, and

22 These include Lev Lebedinsky, who wrote the introduction to the 1963 edition of the piano score of Op. 114, Mstislav Rostropovich and Maxim Shostakovich (in each case, in conversation with EW).

other leading functionaries of the Ministry of Culture, and while engaging in pleasant chat, they made no reference to the matter of *Lady Macbeth*. I feel it's awkward for me to raise the matter myself. Kabalevsky is unwell at the moment, and evidently they are waiting for his recovery, before appointing the relevant Committee. I think that it would be better if Zagursky, rather than I, pressed the urgency of the matter. I am not going to apply for an audition of *Lady Macbeth*. It seems to me that as it is I have done more than enough.

'If the Committee is called to audition *Lady Macbeth*, then I earnestly ask you to be present. Not to defend the opera, but simply as a friendly face and moral support.'

This letter requires some clarification. The director of the Leningrad Maly Opera Theatre, Zagursky, was trying to get the necessary permission to stage *Lady Macbeth* (*Katerina Izmailova*) – without this the disgraced opera could not be put on. With this aim in mind, he had urged Shostakovich to apply in person to the First Deputy Chairman of the Council of Ministers of the USSR, Vyacheslav Molotov.

Gritting his teeth, Dmitri Dmitriyevich carried out this request – he absolutely hated promoting his own interests and petitioning on his own behalf, and in particular having any dealings with high-up officials. As a result of his meeting with Molotov a Committee was set up to review the second version of *Lady Macbeth*. Kabalevsky, a member of the Collegium of the USSR Ministry of Culture, was appointed to preside over it, and the other members elected were the composer Chulaki, the musicologist Khubov, and the conductor Tselikovsky, head of the Department of Music Theatres attached to the USSR Ministry of Culture. Zagursky, Doniyakh, the chief conductor of the MALEGOT, and myself (as author of the corrected texts) were invited from Leningrad to attend the Committee's sessions.

It would be untrue to say that Shostakovich did nothing about the forthcoming audition of the opera. In early February 1956 he asked me to come down to Moscow to talk about procedure, and at the same time to listen to the Moscow première of the Violin Concerto (performed with enormous success by Oistrakh and Mravinsky).

The audition of *Lady Macbeth* eventually took place on 11 and 12 March 1956. It took the Ministry of Culture roughly three months to organize it; their lack of haste was evidently no accident. It seemed to me that they had already decided on a negative outcome.

Probably it was Kabalevsky's suggestion that the Committee should meet at Shostakovich's flat on the Mozhaiskoye Highway rather than at either the Ministry of Culture or the Union of Composers. It would be seen as a gesture of respect to the famous composer.

At the appointed hour the Committee members had appeared in Dmitri Dmitriyevich's study. They greeted the master of the house cheerfully. Nothing seemed to augur the collapse of the whole enterprise. Shostakovich, immensely agitated, distributed the typed-out copies of the new edition of the libretto. Dmitri Dmitriyevich was most concerned that this second version of both the music and the text of the opera would be regarded as definitive, and that there would be no going back to the first edition. Subsequently, as a caution to conductors and directors, the title page of the score of *Katerina Izmailova* states this categorically. Then he sat down at the piano and performed the opera marvellously.

There followed a short interval, during which time the members of the Committee became aloof and severe; then the discussion started. The opera was subjected to the harshest criticism in the spirit of the notorious article 'Muddle Instead of Music'.

Zagursky and Doniyakh, shaken by this turn of events, maintained the silence of the grave. Shostakovich sat alone on a large sofa listening to the speakers. He leant against its wide back as if seeking support. His eyes were closed; he probably couldn't bear to see his colleagues outshining themselves in abuse. From time to time a sickly grimace distorted his face.

To the great displeasure of the Committee I spoke out twice, talking with agitation about the urgent necessity to produce this great opera, whose music had been declared to be a 'muddle' twenty years ago. Khubov kept rudely interrupting me, shrieking and shouting. His attempts to distract me were unsuccessful. Ultimately my words were no more than a single voice crying out in the wilderness. The Committee were unanimous in their recommendation that *Lady Macbeth* should not be staged in consideration of its enormous ideological and artistic defects.

I returned home from Moscow on 14 March, still reeling from this second execution of *Lady Macbeth*, this time carried out by enlightened musicians. While these memorable events were still fresh in my mind I wrote down a short account of them, which I will now quote:

'The discussion of *Lady Macbeth* can only be described as a disgrace. Khubov, Kabalevsky and Chulaki all kept referring to 'Muddle Instead of Music'. In particular Khubov and Kabalevsky surpassed them-selves. They compared certain parts of the music with the worst invective from the article. They pointedly repeated that the article had not been 'withdrawn' and that it still retained its force and relevance. (After all it states that 'the music creaks, groans, and pants . . .')

'Kabalevsky complemented certain things in the opera, and this was doubly unpleasant to hear. In his capacity as chairman of the Committee he concluded that the opera would be impossible to stage as it made an apology for a murderess and seductress – his sense of morals was highly offended . . . I spoke with plenty of conviction, but all my arguments were demolished by the article, which Kabalevsky and Khubov waved about in the air like a truncheon.

'Finally Kabalevsky asked Shostakovich to put forth his point of view, addressing him with friendly familiarity as "Mitya", but Dmitri Dmitriyevich refused to speak, and with remarkable self-possession thanked him "for the criticisms".'[23]

'On the Correction of Errors'

After Khrushchev's unmasking of Stalin at the 20th Party Congress, it was logical that all the policies of Stalin's last paranoid years (including the infamous 'Zhdanov' Decrees) should be reviewed. Discussions about the implications of these reassessments took place behind closed ministerial doors. Undoubtedly there was conflict within Party circles as to how much and how quickly changes in cultural policy should be implemented. Accord-ing to Marina Sabinina, almost immediately after the Congress, proposals were put forward to re-evaluate the 1948 Decree on 'Formalism in Music'. Another two years passed before the Party Central Committee issued a new Decree to supersede it (on 28 May 1958).

Clumsily titled 'On the Correction of Errors in the Evaluation of *The Great Friendship, Bogdan Khmelnitsky* and *From All My Heart*', this document signalled full official rehabilitation of all leading composers who had suffered criticism, although it did not actually rescind the notorious Decree on formalism. Nevertheless, it served to lift the official ban on art that had been labelled decadent (whether Western or 'formalist' Soviet) and acted as a green light for composers to follow new and experimental paths.

In the opinion of Galina Vishnevskaya,[24] the Decree was passed as a concession to international opinion, since Shostakovich had been much in the

23 Isaak Glikman, *Letters to a Friend*, pp. 119–21.
24 *A Russian Story*, pp. 242–4.

public eye in his capacity as chairman of the Tchaikovsky International Competition, which had taken place in April of that year. To maintain Soviet cultural prestige, the Party decided to remove the slur on Shostakovich's name. Vishnevskaya recalls a private celebration at the composer's home, where Shostakovich proposed a toast to 'the great historical Decree "On Abrogating the Great Historical Decree" ', while singing Zhdanov's instructions, 'There must be refined music. There must be beautiful music' to the tune of Stalin's favourite Lezginka (a national Georgian folk dance). Significantly this was no less than a quote from his lampoon *Rayok*.

MARINA SABININA gives an account of Shostakovich's frustration and anger at the inadequate measures proposed to clear the names of the composers criticized in 1948:

One day during February or March of 1956 I had to go and see Shostakovich about some matter concerning the magazine *Sovietskaya Muzyka*. He was a member of its editing committee. And so I found myself in his flat on Kutuzovsky Prospect in his spacious study with two grand pianos. On the wall hung a painting by Pyotr Villiams: a blindingly pink, virtually nude figure of 'Nana'. On his desk a game of patience was laid out, which I had interrupted with my arrival. Patience was one of his favourite occupations, his way of overcoming stress.

I found Dmitri Dmitriyevich in poor spirits and more agitated than usual. He was hurtling round the room from one corner to the other with his short, hurried footsteps. He greeted me curtly, asked me to sit down, and started speaking, first in broken phrases, abrupt exclamations, then, as he became more heated, in whole, feverishly blustering paragraphs. It would appear that he was conversing with himself, as he only occasionally stopped to address me and obviously expected no response from me.

'I was called up to see a certain "high-up official". They, you see, are now interested, as to how they can somehow "correct" the Central Committee's famous Decree of 1948. *Correct it*!! Correct the very thing that carried off Myaskovsky to his grave, broke Prokofiev, and poisoned the lives of many young, talented musicians, and opened up careers for all kinds of filthy trash . . . Do you know that I visited Nikolai Yakovlevich Myaskovsky literally on the eve of his death, about two days before he died. He lay in bed, terribly emaciated, pale and weak, and suddenly he gasped in a barely audible whisper: "As I lie here, I keep thinking, could it possibly be that everything I did and taught was 'against the People'? Perhaps there is some bitter truth in it after all, and we were indeed on the wrong path." You understand, this most noble, modest of men lay there dying, tortured by these thoughts, torn apart by doubts, seriously looking for a grain of truth in that illiterate, revolting document!

'I answered this high-up official, saying, "No, nothing should be corrected, the only thing is to revoke the Decree, *revoke* it." And to revoke it categorically, like that inhuman, shameful law which forbids abortion, which has cost the lives of thousands, if not hundreds of thousands of women. They have been reduced to poking knitting needles up themselves, they have maimed themselves and died, because in these hard and hungry times they didn't want to bring into the world children who would be neglected and starving.'

For a while Dmitri Dmitriyevich broke off his monologue.

'Then in 1948, we "*formalists*" were ordered to make speeches of self-criticism at the Union of Composers' Congress. I shouldn't have gone. Prokofiev was more intelligent than me, he sent a letter excusing himself – a rather dry, cold letter in which he, as it were, agreed that he was guilty of certain errors; the authorities, of course, were not satisfied by his letter. Myaskovsky had already taken to his bed and didn't appear at this meeting. And I went along. My name was called, and I got up without any idea as to what I was going to say, only knowing that I had to repent. I thought, "Well, I'll muddle through somehow." As I walked towards the speakers' tribune from the hall – you know there are those steps and railings on the right – a certain person[25] caught me by the sleeve and shoved this bit of paper in front of me. "Take this please," he said. At first I didn't understand what he wanted, then he whispered in a sort of condescending and cloying voice, "It's all written down here Dmitri Dmitriyevich, just read it out."[26]

'And I got up on the tribune, and started to read out aloud this idiotic, disgusting nonsense concocted by some nobody. Yes, I humiliated myself, I read out what was taken to be "my own" speech.

25 The 'certain person' was Vasili Kukharsky, a Party official who in those years was making a rapid career for himself. He became Minister of Culture in the 1960s. Reputedly Shostakovich was frightened of him, yet found it difficult to remember his name.
26 According to some other accounts, Leo Arnshtam wrote Shostakovich's speech.

I read like the most paltry wretch, a parasite, a puppet, a cut-out paper doll on a string!!'

This last phrase he shrieked out like a frenzied maniac, and then kept repeating it. I sat there completely dazed. Involuntarily a scene from this meeting which I too had attended came to mind, a small episode during Shostakovich's speech which had cut like a knife at my heart.

Reading this humiliating self-accusation, after the words 'music against the people' Dmitri Dmitriyevich suddenly tore himself away from the text for a minute, lifted his head and said in a sad and helpless voice, with his short-sighted eyes fixed on the auditorium, 'It always seems to me that when I write sincerely and as I truly feel, then my music cannot be "against" the People, that after all, I myself am a representative . . . in some small way . . . of the People.'

I recalled everything that he recounted that day very clearly, when, in the mid 1960s, I was trying to get to the bottom of the idea of the second subject of the theme of the Allegretto in the Tenth Symphony, with its DSCH motif. This motif sounds strange and mechanical, lifeless but persistent, just as if the composer had, with terror and revulsion, seen himself as a puppet, a 'doll on a string', which is being arbitrarily manipulated in the merciless hands of the Puppeteer . . . And here the analogy with Stravinsky's *Petrushka* automatically springs to mind.

I happened on the antecedent to this image in a work by a certain I. Ermakov, *Sketches for an Analysis of Gogol's work*, a work published in the 1920s and soon to be condemned as Freudian. There Ermakov refers to Gogol's pathological tendencies, and in particular to his habit of long and continuous self-contemplation in front of a mirror, when, completely self-absorbed, he would repeatedly call out his own name with a sense of alienation and revulsion. I introduced a quotation from this book into my chapter on the Tenth Symphony,[27] but it was ruthlessly cut out by the editors; our famous helmsman of 'socialist realism', Boris Yarustovsky refuted my 'subversive idea', explaining that 'a great Soviet composer is unable to experience such absurd and morbid emotions'![28]

27 Marina Sabinina is referring to her book *The Symphonism of Shostakovich: The Path Towards Maturity* (Sovietsky Kompozitor, Moscow, 1965).
28 Marina Sabinina, 'During the Days of "the Thaw" ', short story written for this book.

Rayok

Rumours that Shostakovich had written a work 'in secret' satirizing the 'Zhdanov' Decree had been in circulation for some time after the composer's death. The existence of the satirical cantata *Rayok* (variously translated as *The Peep-Show, The Gods*, and *A Learner's Manual*) was finally confirmed when it received a first public performance in Washington in January 1989 by Mstislav Rostropovich. He used a copy made available to him by the musicologist Lev Lebedinsky.

Rayok has its antecedent in Mussorgsky's work of the same name; here Shostakovich lampoons the cultural activists who launched the 'struggle with formalism'.

Shortly after the Washington performance, Shostakovich's widow produced from the family archive the original manuscript(s) together with some preliminary sketches. They are written in the characteristic purple ink Shostakovich used until the early 1960s, and none of them are dated. The work was performed in the Soviet Union a few months after the Washington première in a slightly different version. A few months after that an additional excerpt was found, constituting an extended 'finished' ending (which Venyamin Basner remembers Shostakovich playing to him around 1967).

Lebedinsky claims the authorship of the sung libretto of *Rayok*, where much of the material is derived from the speeches of Zhdanov, Stalin, Zakharov, Dmitri Shepilov and others. He credits the satirical pseudo-literary 'publisher's foreword' to the composer. The Shostakovich Archive, however, attributes the whole work, including the libretto, to Shostakovich alone.

There is also disagreement about the time of *Rayok*'s creation. The Shostakovich Archive alleges that the work was conceived and partly written already in 1948, and that it was completed in two further stages, in 1957, then the late 1960s. This version of events is supported by Isaak Glikman. He alone of Shostakovich's surviving friends claims that the composer played *Rayok* for him in the summer of 1948. Vissarion Shebalin's widow remembers Shostakovich playing *Rayok* at their Moscow flat 'sometime in the 1950s', in any case after Shebalin fell ill. Shebalin's advice to Shostakovich was to destroy all trace of the work as 'you could be shot for such things'.[29]

Lebedinsky dates *Rayok* to the time of the 2nd Union of Composers' Congress, which took place between 28 March and 5 April 1957. Dmitri Shepilov, a secretary of the Central Committee responsible for the arts, in a speech worthy of Zhdanov, exhorted composers to write in the style of their classical forebears. Evidently a 'howler' in this speech was the stimulus for the creation of the lampoon, which deserves interest less for its musical quality

29 Alisa Shebalina: recorded interview with EW.

than as a social document. *Rayok* (and particularly Shostakovich's parodying 'pseudo-literary' introduction) reflects Shostakovich's intolerance of the ignorance and pomposity of the petty functionaries and political big-shots who ruled his life for so many years.

Lebedinsky's dating is supported by others of Shostakovich's friends (including Mikhail Druskin) and the composer's daughter Galina, who remembers the fun and games that accompanied the 'creation' of *Rayok*. Indeed, Maxim and Evgeny Chukovsky were inspired to start writing a libretto along similar lines, which Shostakovich promised to set to music the moment it was finished. Like so many ideas born of the heat of the moment, this one came to nothing.

Shostakovich's satirical frame of mind is confirmed by his letters of 1957. On 31 March of that year he wrote to Isaak Glikman of his attendance at the Composers' Conference: 'I particularly like Comrade Lukin's speech. He reminded us of Zhdanov's inspired directives that music should be melodic and graceful.'[30] In a letter to Edison Denisov dated 22 July, written while he was busy composing his Eleventh Symphony, Shostakovich refers scathingly to the musicologist Pavel Apostolov, one of the 'heroes' of *Rayok*: 'From the village of Stepanichkov Foma Fomich Opiskin[31] has come to settle in Moscow under the pseudonym of P.A. . . . He makes statements in the press. Particularly effective is his latest newspaper article, where he throws himself into the struggle for music to be melodic and graceful.'[32]

In the opinion of many friends and family, Shostakovich would never have dared write such blatant satire in 1948, when he feared for the lives of himself and his family. *Rayok* belongs to a genre that is usually created in the privacy of the home in the company of friends to the accompaniment of a few glasses. Therefore the view that Shostakovich gave vent to his rancour by composing a satire on the top political leaders in strict secrecy does not necessarily hold water. Perhaps the writer Abraam Gozenpud sums up the argument best:

I find the current view that *Rayok* was created as a spontaneous reaction to the Decree very difficult to accept. It could hardly have been so; a satire on your executioners is not created under the shadow of the guillotine. I do not think that Shostakovich's civic courage is in any way diminished if we move the date of *Rayok*'s composition forward by a few years. We should remember that Anna Akhmatova did not entrust her Requiem to paper in those times. The important fact is that Shostakovich created a scathing lampoon on the ignorant

30 Glikman, *Letters to a Friend*, p. 125.
31 This name could mean either 'Scribbler' or 'Pisser'.
32 D. D. Shostakovich, 'Letters to Edison Denisov'.

assassins of culture headed by Zhdanov. By being able to laugh at them, he claimed victory over them.'[33]

Lev Lebedinsky gives his verson of the creation of *Rayok*.

Rayok was conceived during the 2nd Congress of Composers of the USSR, which was as insignificant and boring as all such occasions. In the name of the Central Committee of the CPSU, we were instructed by the Party Secretary, Shepilov, on questions of ideology. Wishing to flaunt his 'scholarship', his speech groaned with a mountain of weighty names. In one phrase he pointed to our great Russian classics – Glinka, Tchaikovsky and Rimsky-Kor*sa*kov. Shepilov's illiterate howler, misplacing the accent on the *a* of the middle syllable of the composer of *Scheherezade* galvanized Shostakovich to life. He had been languishing from boredom, but he suddenly perked up and started to laugh out loud at this example of 'scholarship'. He came over to sit next to me and whispered to me that as soon as the session was over, we were to go out to his dacha at Bolshevo. During the journey there, he spoke of nothing but Shepilov's speech: 'No doubt, the text of this speech was written by some Ya*sru*stovsky, S*ryu*lin or Opo*sty*lov,'[34] Shostakovich chuckled. 'And why didn't he pronounce Bo*ro*din, or *Se*rov, or *Ta*nyeev, instead of Tan*yee*v?'[35] He simply couldn't forget Kor*sa*kov, and kept returning to Shepilov's linguistic discovery. Thus in an almost arbitrary manner, he formulated a poetic strophe in the dactylic metre:

Glinka, Tchai-/kovsky,
Rimsky-Kor-/*sa*kov.

We arrived at his dacha and had supper.
'You're going to write the text of *Rayok* this very day,' Shostakovich told me in complete seriousness.
'But I don't know how to write poetry.'
My refusal was not heeded.

33 Abraam Gozenpud, 'Encounters with Shostakovich', article commissioned for this book.
34 These are distortions of the names of Yarustovsky, Ryumin and Apostolov, all Party functionaries, who had over the years hounded Shostakovich, and had been active in the campaign against 'formalism'. These changes immediately give the names vulgar connotations, i.e. Yasrustovsky could be conveyed as 'I-shit-ovsky'.
35 The change of accents in these composer's names render them ridiculous. The etymology of Bo*ro*din now is based on beard, etc.

'We don't need poems,' Dmitri Dmitriyevich retorted. 'All we need is a good laugh. Here's a pencil and paper. Write.'

'But it's night-time already,' I protested in an attempt to evade the authorship of the libretto.

'I'll drop by every now and then to make sure you haven't fallen asleep.' And with these words Dmitri Dmitriyevich went to his own room.

An hour later he came in with some strong tea, and gave me a severe look. At this stage I could only outline my plan; I called the libretto *A Free Discussion*. I also read out the list of dramatis personae. I assumed that the poverty of my suggestion would make him drop the idea. But the opposite happened: he accepted my plan, waxed the merrier, and suggested that we should camouflage the names of the characters. Stalin became Edinitsyn, Zhdanov Dvoikin, Shepilov Troikin.[36]

We met a couple more times in Moscow to finish *Rayok*. The following day at my flat on Lesnaya Street, I gave Dmitri Dmitriyevich my final version of Stalin/Edinitsyn's speech. Dmitri Dmitriyevich was extremely satisfied and chuckled away. The next day we gave *Rayok* the final polish, and had lots of fun. Dmitri Dmitriyevich played it only for his family and chosen friends. He then gave me the manuscript for safekeeping. After his marriage, his wife Irina Antonovna asked me for it back. I returned it to Dmitri Dmitriyevich, but naturally I kept my own copy. Before he left the Soviet Union, Solomon Volkov came to see me to try and get hold of my copy.[37]

Shostakovich perceived by the younger generation

In the post-Stalinist years, a new generation of composers formed their perceptions on life and music as the cultural barriers of Soviet isolationist policies broke down. Many of these young composers started looking westwards for information and influences. Composers such as Sofiya Gubaidulina, Edison Denisov, Alfred Schnittke and Nikolai Karetnikov started to compose in the 'Shostakovich' tradition, which was seen by the more enlightened Conservatoire teachers as the 'positive' side of socialist realism.

36 Edinitsyn, Dvoikin and Troikin have more than one connotation. On the one hand, they imply Number One, Number Two, and Number Three; on the other hand, these numbers are associated with school grades. A Three is the lowest pass mark, Two is already failure to pass, whereas One means abysmal failure.
37 Lev Lebedinsky, compiled from recorded interviews with EW and unpublished articles.

By the late 1950s, they were experimenting in compositional techniques that Shostakovich had himself rejected. Although Shostakovich's presence remained the greatest single influence in Soviet music, the composer gradually appeared to lose his relevance and, up to a point, his moral authority for these composers.

EDISON DENISOV comes from Tomsk, Siberia, where he studied mathematics at university, while simultaneously attending musical high school. He decided to approach Shostakovich – as the highest authority – to seek advice as to whether he should devote himself to composition. The Master responded with firm support and encouragement, and opened the way for Denisov to become a composer:

In 1949 I sent all my compositions to Shostakovich in Moscow without even knowing his address. He replied with a very kind, long letter giving a detailed analysis of my naive student works. Although these works had no real musical quality, he confirmed that, in his opinion, I should definitely become a composer. I was eventually accepted as a student at the Moscow Conservatoire in 1951, and it was during my student years that I became very friendly with Shostakovich.

Despite his complex personality, Dmitri Dmitriyevich was fundamentally a good and warm-hearted man. Certainly, he showed great kindness to me. I always took my compositions to show him and greatly valued his opinion. At the same time I adored my own professor, Shebalin, to whom I owe so much in life. But Shostakovich was of all importance to me.

Shostakovich and Shebalin had a deep love for each other. Shostakovich always enquired after 'Ronya' after I had been for a lesson. We studied many of Shostakovich's works in class, and Shebalin always gave us judicious advice. He didn't point to Shostakovich's melodic language, as he felt that this was one of the weaker aspect of 'Mitya's' composition, and indeed, he told us that writing melodies was an agonizing effort for him. Nor did he approve of the mechanical rhythmic features, or the Hindemith-like polyphony in Shostakovich's works. He taught us to admire Shostakovich's wonderful ability to construct large forms, and his unique skills of orchestration, and urged us to learn from these particular qualities. I am very grateful that Shebalin encouraged us to be discerning, and stopped us from idolizing a composer blindly, whoever it might be. He considered it important to identify a composer's less successful features as well as his best qualities.

Each visit to Shostakovich's home was a celebration for me. I hardly ever saw Nina Vasilyevna, Dmitri Dmitriyevich's beloved wife, because she was mostly away on working trips. Therefore I spent most of the time alone with Dmitri Dmitriyevich. I would ask him lots of questions and our conversation ranged over many topics. I kept a record of those meetings.

While I was a student, I used to coach Dmitri Dmitriyevich's son Maxim in maths at home. He was then a pupil at the Central Music School and had trouble with his school subjects. Later, when he entered the Conservatoire, Maxim studied score-reading with me, and was a very poor student. But, rather than fail him at his exams, the compositional faculty decided to give him the best marks. We did this only for Dmitri Dmitriyevich's sake. I always had the feeling that Maxim didn't really want to study at the Conservatoire. Dmitri Dmitriyevich knew this and once said to me that it had been a mistake to send him to music school, and that his real talent was for engineering.

I never missed a première of Shostakovich's works. For instance, I travelled to Leningrad for the première of the Tenth Symphony.

After graduating from the Conservatoire I continued to see Dmitri Dmitriyevich frequently. I not only visited him at his town flat, but also at his dacha at Bolshevo. I remember when I arrived there he would bury a bottle of vodka in a snowdrift. When it was chilled we would drink it together, and talk long into the night. Often I would stay over at his place.

I see Shostakovich's importance on many levels, and this includes all the oblique contradictions which in fact make up the true essence of his nature and evolution. Shostakovich was full of paradox. He was very nervous by nature; he never sat still, and while speaking he usually paced up and down. When he was silent, he might sit in a comfortable chair, but then he was always fiddling with something – his hands were always in motion.

Once I came to see him and found him sitting at a table writing furiously. He asked me to wait till he had finished. Soon he completed the score he was writing. Then he took it and tore it up into tiny shreds and threw them into the waste-paper basket.

I was dumbfounded: 'But Dmitri Dmitriyevich, that was your score . . .'

He answered, 'Well, I'm finding it hard to compose, it just won't come to me, and I'm not used to sit about without working, so I've decided to orchestrate all Rimsky-Korsakov's Romances. I've got the complete volume of his songs and I orchestrate them one by one. As soon as I've finished doing one, I tear it up and throw it into the waste-bin.'

Dmitri Dmitriyevich manifested an inner nervous agitation, whereby the work process always functioned whether or not he was able to compose music. This was a feature of his highly strung personality.

Shostakovich was very attached to his pupils and suffered when they behaved tactlessly towards a colleague, or betrayed the principles in which he believed. Georgi Sviridov was a particularly sore point for him. He found it hard to take Sviridov's aggressive attitude towards him, and his obsession to prove himself a greater composer than his teacher. Shostakovich, knowing his own worth, never felt threatened by Sviridov's wish to surpass him. But this betrayal by his favourite pupil distressed him. Shostakovich had had great faith in Sviridov's talent, and he could not bear to see him work for the licensed officials. He repeated to me several times one and the same phrase: 'Yura has passed through the trials of fire and water, but the brass trumpets have destroyed him.' And he added that Sviridov was a real person and a real composer in those days when he had nothing to eat or to sober up on, when he used to run from door to door to beg a rouble. Now he was unrecognizable both as a human being and as a composer. Shostakovich used to say, 'I don't understand Yura. If I wrote *The Song of the Forests* and *The Song of the Torch* that was because I was forced to. But who has forced him to write *The Pathétique Oratorio*? Why did he do it?'

Of course Sviridov wasn't alone in this. But Shostakovich didn't take people like Karen Khachaturian or Yuri Levitin seriously, regarding them as composers of limited talent. In general, he was very attached to all his pupils, even to those who were not particularly good composers, like Venyamin Basner. He treated them with understanding and took a lot of trouble for them. In his last years he was devoted to Boris Tishchenko. He would write letters to the Ministry asking for material support on their behalf and also requesting publication and performances of their works. On the other hand, he usually didn't help composers who had not been his pupils.

Shostakovich suffered personally for what went on around him. He felt for the people, and was distressed by many things that went on in our country. When I first arrived in Moscow fresh from Siberia, I was a naive and foolish young man. Although I never wrote a cantata about Stalin, like most of my generation I very much idealized our politicians. Once I said something nice about Voroshilov; for some reason I felt particular sympathy for him. Dmitri Dmitriyevich said to me, 'Edik, if Budyonny is up to his knees in blood, then Voroshilov is up to his balls in blood.'

'And Kaganovich?'

'Kaganovich is up to his neck in blood.'

I remember his exact words. Such things upset him greatly. When Gagarin went up into space, he reacted by saying, 'Why throw away money like that? Think of the villages where old woman have to walk a kilometre to fetch water from freezing wells and lug it all the way home. The State wastes money on its space programme, on propaganda and political contest with the Americans – none of us need it.'

Another of Shostakovich's bugbears was Boris Asafiev.[38] When I was a student I read Asafiev's books, and every time I mentioned Asafiev's name Dmitri Dmitriyevich bristled. He would repeat: 'I have met many good people and many bad people in my life, but never anybody more rotten than Asafiev.' He would refer to him as 'the Great-Russian chauvinist'. Shostakovich crossed out his original dedication to Asafiev in *Lady Macbeth*. He told me that Asafiev had written him a letter which, if it were ever to be published, would demolish his good name for ever. However, Asafiev's wife, who was a kind-hearted soul, came round to see Shostakovich and begged him to give her the letter

'She got down on her knees in front of me, weeping, and implored me to return it. I didn't have the heart to refuse her, so, against my better judgement I let her have the letter. Then in front of my very eyes she set a match to it and burnt it.'

---

38 In an autobiographical article published in *Sovietskaya Muzyka* in September 1956, DDS stated that 'Under Asafiev's influence I wrote the opera *The Nose* and the piano pieces *Aphorisms*. Later our ways parted. I have frequently been made aware of the untenability of his views on art – but I have always respected him as a music scholar.' This is a good example of Shostakovich's ability to be subtly subversive. The two works he claims to have composed under Asafiev's influence were still labelled as 'decadent' in 1956, and had not been performed for over twenty-five years. His friends would have known what a back-handed compliment Shostakovich dealt when referring to his 'respect' for Asafiev as a 'music scholar'.

I never found out what the letter contained.

Asafiev was an unprincipled bastard and caused extensive harm to Soviet music. Even in the late 1920s he manifested his complete lack of principles, declaring that Tchaikovsky's *Eugene Onegin* was unfit to be staged in the Soviet Union. And in 1948 he denounced the music of Britten and Messiaen from the tribune, saying it was 'a mixture of formalism, obscurantism and depravity; comrades – this is the bottom of the pit.' And all the comrades clapped and applauded, thinking what a clever man Asafiev was to have come up with these extraordinary observations. It was not for nothing that Asafiev was made an academician, like Lysenko. I would say that he is the musical equivalent of Lysenko and his intellect as a musician is comparable to that of Lysenko's as a scientist. Up till now there has been no reevaluation in our musical thinking, and Asafiev is still considered an authority, and his books are still read today.

I once talked to Shostakovich about Solzhenitsyn's *One Day in the Life of Ivan Denisovich*.[39] I had just read the book and it had a shattering effect on me, and not only psychologically, but for its artistic merit as well. Shostakovich said, 'Edik, it's reality varnished over, it's reality varnished over. The truth was ten times worse than that.'

Once we were at the Composers' Plenary session in Sverdlovsk.[40] It was one of the few times that I attended such an occasion. One evening Shostakovich wasn't feeling well, and therefore didn't go to the concert. He asked me to come to his room, and we stayed up talking till midnight. He recalled his past and kept returning to the same phrase: 'When I think about my life, I realize that I have been a coward. Unfortunately I have been a coward.' He then added that if I had seen the things that he had, then I too would have become a coward. For instance, he told how during the period of the purges he would go to visit a friend, only to discover that this friend had disappeared without trace, and nobody knew what had happened to him. His possessions had been bundled up and thrown out on to the street, and strangers were occupying his flat.

Another reason for his cowardice was his profound and obsessive love for his children. Many of the bad things he did in life were done

39 Solzhenitsyn's novel, published in 1962 in *Novy Mir* literary journal, describes one day in the life of an inmate of the Stalinist camps.
40 Shostakovich attended the plenary session of the Urals Branch of the Union of Composers in October 1957.

–304–

on behalf of his children. His position and authority, all his honours and medals and his excellent material position allowed him to make comfortable provision for them during his lifetime, accommodating them in large flats and giving them cars. He devoted a lot of effort in helping Maxim, despite his limited talents as a musician. Eventually, Maxim became a successful conductor, but he had his father to thank for his position as chief conductor of the Moscow Radio Orchestra.[41]

The composer SOFIYA GUBAIDULINA was, like Denisov, brought up far away from the metropolis, Moscow. She came to Moscow in 1952 to study composition at the Conservatoire. At her graduation Shostakovich sat on the examination committee and, duly impressed by her talent, saw to it that she was awarded the highest grade. Having rejected 'socialist realism' and developed her own highly individual compositional style, Gubaidulina's career was effectively blocked by the Union of Composers, and she encountered enormous difficulties in getting her music performed and published:

Shostakovich is of utmost importance to people of my generation, not only because of the influence he exerted as a composer, but also as a person. We grew up at a time when everything around us became one unending question. We were obsessed with asking questions, because at the time there was a complete absence of information about everything from politics to art. The crude attacks on literature and music that appeared in our press were utterly bewildering. One day you're in love with a story by Zoshchenko or a poem by Akhmatova; then suddenly they're proclaimed 'bad' and 'terrible', and their works are aggressively attacked in all the major newspapers.

It's now difficult for people to imagine what a young person felt in such a situation. Suppose that you are fourteen or fifteen years old, you discover with delight a particular work by Shostakovich, and suddenly it turns out that this work is suspect, even dangerous. You are left with an urgent question, and there is no answer to be had anywhere.

The questions arose when our fathers were being arrested. We knew for certain that they were remarkable and honest men, yet they were being arrested. Maybe the man who was the first to be picked up by the Black Maria was the most respected, the purest person we knew. We had no doubts whatsoever as to his honesty; but also there

41 Edison Denisov: recorded interview with EW.

was no doubt that he had been arrested. We all knew that what was going on was horrible, but nobody could understand why it was going on. What was the purpose of all this?

It's only now, possessing such a huge amount of information, that we know the whys and wherefores. At the time our life was a nightmare, and many people went mad. I also went mad at the time – clinically mad. So did the composers Roman Ledenyov and Hermann Galynin. Russia underwent a kind of psychological catastrophe, which particularly affected the young.

My personal acquaintance with Dmitri Dmitriyevich could never be close because of our age difference. My own teacher, Nikolai Peiko, had been Shostakovich's assistant at the Moscow Conservatoire, and they retained a close friendship after Shostakovich was dismissed from his professorship. Peiko introduced me to the circles in which he moved. I used to visit Shebalin, and we played four-hand music on the piano. I met Dmitri Dmitriyevich on several occasions and I hung on to his every word. When I was in my fifth year at the Conservatoire, Peiko took me to see Shostakovich so that I could show him a youthful symphony that I was working on. He listened to it, and made some remarks, generally praising the music. But what struck me most was his parting phrase: 'Be yourself. Don't be afraid of being yourself. My wish for you is that you should continue on your own, *incorrect* way.'

One phrase said to a young person at the right moment can affect the rest of his or her life. I am infinitely grateful to Shostakovich for those words. I needed them at that moment, and felt fortified by them to such an extent that I feared nothing, any failure or criticism just ran off my back, and I was indeed able to pursue my own path.

Shostakovich's sensitivity to a musical phenomenon which lay outside his own sphere stemmed from his own vulnerability and experience. In this instance it allowed him to sense my pain. Despite his outward irony, and his manner of expressing himself in paradoxes, he felt and understood the suffering that Russians are doomed to endure, and the manner in which it defines their behaviour and relationships. In this way Shostakovich belongs to the Russian humanitarian tradition.

Shostakovich, with his youthful vulnerability, experienced things in the same way as we did. His influence was all-important to us, and it formulated our attitude to life. He was the person from whom young people hoped to receive the answers. When he failed to provide them, we felt tremendously let down, and again a terrible question raised its ugly head.

When Shostakovich joined the Party in 1960, our disappointment knew no bounds. That such a man could be broken, that our system was capable of crushing a genius was something I could not get over. We were left wondering why, just at the time when the political situation had relaxed somewhat, when at last it seemed possible to preserve one's integrity, Shostakovich fell victim to official flattery. What forced him into this action? It made me realize that a man may be able to endure hunger and withstand political crushing, yet be unable to overcome the temptation of a 'carrot'. Shostakovich was defeated by a 'carrot'!

I now realize that the circumstances he lived under were unbearably cruel, more than anyone should have to endure. He had overcome the most important trials, but when he allowed himself to relax, he succumbed to weakness. But I accept him, for I see him as pain personified, the epitomy of the tragedy and terror of our times.

Indeed, I believe that Shostakovich's music reaches such a wide audience because he was able to transform the pain that he so keenly experienced into something exalted and full of light, which transcends all worldly suffering. He was able to transfigure the material into a spiritual entity, whereas Prokofiev's music lacks the contrast between terrible darkness and an ever-expanding light. We listened to Shostakovich's new works in a kind of exaltation. His concerts were events not only of musical but of political significance.

However, the next generation of musicians had a different attitude to Shostakovich's music and personality. They had different landmarks, and found their own answers. What was pain to us was history to them.[42]

FLORA LITVINOVA's perceptions changed in the years of the Thaw, and her attitude to Shostakovich became more critical. Like many of the Russian intelligentsia, she found it hard to accept Shostakovich's apparent cynicism in outwardly conforming to the demands of the establishment. Perhaps it is hardly surprising that increasingly she and her husband felt less at ease with Shostakovich. Whereas the Shostakovich children grew up spoilt and protected, the Litvinov's son Pavel questioned the regime, and soon fell out with it, becoming a leader of the dissidents. In 1968 Pavel staged a protest against

42 Sofiya Gubaidulina: recorded interview with EW.

the Soviet invasion of Czechoslovakia in Red Square. He was imprisoned and deported to Siberia, and eventually forcibly exiled from the Soviet Union:

I want to try and explain why Shostakovich entered the Party, made so many ill-fated 'correct Party-line' speeches, and why eventually he signed the letter against Sakharov.

Shostakovich was quite simply afraid. He feared for his children, his family, himself and his neighbour. Where this fear sprung from originally I don't know. Once he spoke about the despair he experienced after his father's death, when he suddenly found himself alone in a hostile world. A frail boy, he had to shoulder the responsibility of caring for his mother and sisters. Then perhaps it was the terror of seeing so many people disappear, the mass of people who were arrested and perished in the camps. Besides, Dmitri Dmitriyevich was incapable of resisting any form of force and boorishness. When pressure was exerted on him, he was ready to compromise himself, read out or sign anything, so long as he would be left alone.

But at the same time, he showed courage and nobility. Despite his fear, I know how many people he helped, and how often he interceded for people.[43]

NIKOLAI KARETNIKOV was one of the 'alternative' Soviet composers who started their careers in the mid 1950s. In this short passage he describes a dialogue with Shostakovich, showing his keen preoccupation with moral issues even in life's most mundane moments:

After a conversation about music, Dmitri Dmitriyevich suddenly turned to me and asked:

'And now tell me, Nikolai Nikolayevich, have you, so to speak, seen that film, that film, so to speak, that everyone is talking about?'

'What film, Dmitri Dmitriyevich?'

'So to speak, *Your Contemporary*, you know, *Your Contemporary*.'

'Yes, I've seen it, Dmitri Dmitriyevich.'

'I'm most interested, what do you say about it, what do you say, most interesting . . .'

'Well, I don't know, Dmitri Dmitriyevich; I think you would be bored by it . . .'

'And why, so to speak, and why?'

'Well, you see, the principle hero of the film is a certain gas called

43 Flora Litvinova: article commissioned for this book.

"Kaetan", and the moral truths propounded in the film do not transcend the boundaries of what our mothers taught us in childhood: Don't steal, don't lie, respect your elders . . .'

'But that's wonderful! That's wonderful! Indeed now, so to speak, now has come the time, the time when, so to speak, such things are so necessary, these things should be constantly repeated. It must be a wonderful, so to speak, wonderful film. I'll definitely go, so to speak, I'll definitely go to see it.'[44]

Honouring Prokofiev

OLEG PROKOFIEV explains the background to Plate 22.

This photograph was taken on 11 February 1958. I am not particularly proud of it. Yet it is an extraordinary document. It was taken at the unveiling of the commemorative plaque to my father on the house where he lived in Moscow between 1936 and 1941. Khrennikov is making the main solemn speech. I am standing between Shostakovich and my mother, who had returned from concentration camp a year and a half before, and looks sad and beautiful. I am caught at a rather embarrassing moment, as I am trying to make some ironic or witty remark to Shostakovich; perhaps something about what Khrennikov had said.

I do not remember what I was saying, but obviously it was ill-timed. Shostakovich hardly pays me any attention and does not seem to be particularly excited either by me or Khrennikov. Possibly he did not even hear me. Was he thinking of the past, because it was almost ten years to the day since the Zhdanov Decree was published? Or about the future, imagining the same speaker spouting the same clichés and ideological platitudes at his funeral?

Seventeen years later Khrennikov certainly did just that.[45]

MARINA SABININA describes Shostakovich's participation at the ceremony to unveil the second of two memorial plaques to Prokofiev:

On 5 March 1958, on the occasion of the fifth anniversary of Prokofiev's death there was to be the ceremonious unveiling of memorial plaques on the walls of the houses where he had lived in Moscow. At

44 Nikolai Karetnikov, 'Your Contemporary', unpublished article.
45 Oleg Prokofiev, 'On My Few Contacts with Shostakovich', article commissioned for this book.

14/16 Chkalov Street (which Prokofiev had left in the early spring of 1941 to go and live with Mira Alexandrovna Mendelssohn, who became his second wife) the gathering was headed by Tikhon Khrennikov, a personal friend of his first wife Lina Ivanovna. And at the other house at MKhAT[46] Passage Shostakovich was in charge. This was the house where Mira's parents had their flat and where Prokofiev died.

It was a bright and sunny day, about minus 12–15°C, with an icy wind blowing. I arrived exactly on time at three o'clock in the afternoon, naturally to the second venue. Alas, Dmitri Dmitriyevich, for some reason much too lightly dressed, and with his overdeveloped sense of punctuality, had arrived well in advance, and no doubt had already been striding up and down for some time in the frost. He looked miserable and chilled to the bone, his face was a greyish-blue colour. There weren't many people at the gathering; Dmitri Dmitriyevich hurriedly whispered to me, 'Mariya Dmitriyevna, as soon as I've done with the speech, let's slip off upstairs to Mira's flat. She's prepared some eats and drinks. And I'm frozen to the marrow, cold as a dog.'

And that is what happened. As soon as he had made his short introductory speech, Dmitri Dmitriyevich withdrew to the side and gave me a discreet nod. We rushed upstairs. The door of the flat was open in hospitable expectation, the tables were laid with delicious food. Dmitri Dmitriyevich immediately sat down and poured himself a vodka, mumbling, 'Come on, come on, we absolutely must warm ourselves up.'

He downed his glass and seemed somewhat revived; nevertheless his expression was still gloomy, and he appeared to be out of sorts. Trying to cheer him up, I asked, 'Are you upset?'

'Yes, yes, that's exactly it, I'm most upset. You know, it's horrible, it's disgusting – I've just been called up by some high officials.' (His tone of voice was venomously sarcastic, he gestured with his hand to the ceiling.) 'They wanted advice over a declaration made by Prokofiev's first wife, Lina Ivanovna. She's for ever writing to them and to all the bigwigs. She states that, as it were, Mira's relationship with Prokofiev was only an illicit connection, and that she, Lina, was the only lawful and rightful wife and heir; and here she is fussing to prove all this with wonderful, new, convincing and shattering arguments.

46 Moscow Arts Theatre.

First of all she can apparently prove that from 1935/36 Sergei Sergeye-vich was completely impotent and therefore his marriage with Mira cannot have been consummated. "Go and ask the doctor whom Prokofiev went and consulted," she says. "He'll confirm it."

'And secondly, when they re-emigrated to the USSR, certain formalities, some legal niceties, were not observed, so now she says that Prokofiev was not a legal Soviet citizen and therefore any marriage made here must be invalid. There you are – the famous *Soviet composer* Prokofiev! In general women are disgusting, most terribly disgusting!'

Hoping to calm him down, I remonstrated, 'But Dmitri Dmitriye-vich, after all, I'm also a woman . . .'

He apologized: 'Excuse me, I didn't have you in mind,' and then gulped down another glass.

After a short silence he pronounced, at first somewhat grumpily, then waxing more and more indignant, 'Well, if it comes to it, I suppose I too am an impotent, or something of the kind. Then when I die all my former wives will come and desecrate my grave and pour filth on my name. No, no an artist should never marry, definitely should never marry!'[47]

The Leningrad Philharmonic

When composing Shostakovich usually had in mind the qualities of a particular performer, or, in his symphonic works, the hard brilliance and precision of the Leningrad Philharmonic. This orchestra's association with Shostakovich went back to the First Symphony: effectively they were given the right to premiere all his symphonies, which, from the Fifth Symphony onwards, were conducted by Evgeny Mravinsky. This held true except under special circumstances, as during the period of evacuation from Leningrad, when the Seventh Symphony was first performed by the Bolshoi Theatre orchestra and Samosud.

This special relationship later went sour when Mravinsky pulled out of the first performance of the Thirteenth Symphony.

The violinist YAKOV MILKIS joined the Leningrad Philharmonic in 1957, where he worked until he emigrated in 1974. Here he describes the working atmosphere in the orchestra, as well as his personal impressions of Shostako-vich:

47 Marina Sabinina, 'An Artist Should Never Marry', short story written for this book.

During my eighteen years at the Leningrad Philharmonic Shostakovich's symphonies were a part of the staple repertoire. The only symphonies which were not performed in that period were the Second and Third. I participated in the premières of the Eleventh and Twelfth Symphonies, and also of the First Cello Concerto with Rostropovich and the Second Violin Concerto with Oistrakh. Mravinsky always conducted.

These premières were great events, particularly for us musicians, who were the first to have contact with the new score. Usually we had a week's rehearsal on a new work, which meant five full rehearsals and then the dress rehearsal. Dmitri Dmitriyevich sat in on all of them with a score and pencil. During the breaks he would come up to Mravinsky to make his comments about balance and sound. Sometimes they discussed some possible minor corrections or retouchings. Basically Shostakovich never changed anything in his scores, which he always prepared meticulously.

I do remember one exception, when we were rehearsing the Eighth Symphony for a forthcoming performance in the concert season. Dmitri Dmitriyevich had come up to Leningrad as usual for the rehearsal. In the break Mravinsky turned round to us and said, 'Do you know, I have the impression that here in this place Dmitri Dmitriyevich has omitted something; there's a discrepancy between the harmonies of these chords as they appear here and where they occur elsewhere. I've always wanted to ask Dmitri Dmitriyevich about this point, but somehow I have never got round to it.'

Just at this moment, Dmitri Dmitriyevich himself came up to Mravinsky, who put the question to him without further ado. Dmitri Dmitriyevich glanced at the score: 'Oh dear, what a terrible omission, what an error I have committed. But you know what, let's leave it as it is, just let things stay as they are.' We then understood that this 'error' was deliberate.

In fact, Shostakovich never made errors in his scores. During rehearsals, he might make a correction in terms of orchestral balance – one group may have been playing too loudly, or an instrument that should have come to the fore was smothered. But these mistakes did not emanate from his score; they were acoustical misjudgements which were set right during the process of rehearsal.

Dmitri Dmitriyevich used metronome markings to indicate tempi in his scores. He had many preliminary meetings with Mravinsky where

every point, including the tempi, was agreed before orchestral rehearsals began. However, as a general rule the metronome markings in the
scores were always faster than the tempi taken during performance.

The inconsistency in these markings can be found in Shostakovich's
chamber works as well as in the symphonies. For instance, take the
case of the Second Piano Trio. There the metronome marking of the
Scherzo is so fast as to render it virtually unperformable. Once, while I
was studying this Trio, I happened to be in Komarovo when Dmitri
Dmitriyevich was also staying there. I plucked up courage to ask him
about the markings, not only the fast speed of the Scherzo, but the
very slow speed indicated for the third movement.

He answered, 'You know, take no notice. I use this rickety old
metronome, and I know I should have thrown it out years ago, as it's
completely unreliable, but I have got so attached to it that I keep it. But
you, as a musician, should just play as you feel the music and take no
notice of those markings, take no notice.'

Once I spent the summer in Komarovo. I used to practise in my
cottage after breakfast out on the terrace. I was studying Prokofiev's F
minor Violin Sonata for a recital in the coming season. It was Dmitri
Dmitriyevich's habit to take a morning walk down the avenue of trees
which led past our rented cottage. As he passed, he would stop dead
in his tracks and stand there listening. It made me feel very awkward
seeing him standing there. The next time I met him I asked if I
disturbed him with my practice.

'I could easily start playing half an hour or an hour later, after you
have finished your walk.'

But he answered, 'On no account do that, pay no attention to me. I
enjoy listening to the violin, and in any case what wonderful music
Sergei Sergeyevich wrote, wonderful music. Just play and take no
notice of me.'

This goes to show that his supposed dislike of Prokofiev's music is a
myth.

When I first saw Dmitri Dmitriyevich, in the late 1940s and early
1950s, he was in his prime. I often heard him perform his own works,
and I particularly remember his concerts with the Beethoven Quartet.
He was a wonderful pianist, and when performing he was completely
absorbed in his own world. His playing conveyed an ideal sense of
form and structure, but more than that it was an expression of his
innermost world, one that cost him sweat, blood and tears. He played

with a special touch and colour, and often quite intentionally treated the piano as a percussion instrument. It is rare that a composer uses the upper register of the piano like a xylophone, making a sharp, percussive sound. This is how he played the Scherzo from the Piano Quintet, for instance. I still have the particular sound of his sarcastic, dry staccato in my ears today. It completely suited the style of the music.

I don't remember a time when Dmitri Dmitriyevich failed to come up to Leningrad for a performance of his own music and at least some of the preceding rehearsals, irrespective of whether it was a première or not. He always sat alone at rehearsals, preferring some inconspicuous spot in the stalls. He avoided any kind of demonstrativeness, and seemed to retire into himself, melting into his surroundings, so as to be left undisturbed while listening and working. This incredible modesty was apparent also when he was in a gathering of people. Here too he appeared to fade into the background, doing his best not to attract attention to himself.

Certain chosen friends would come along to the final rehearsals: Nikolai Semyonovich Rabinovich, the conductor – a wonderful musician; the composers Venyamin Basner and Boris Tishchenko. Isaak Glikman always attended the premières, and sometimes also came to the dress rehearsals, as did his brother the sculptor, Gavriil Glikman.

Shostakovich's music was very close to us musicians of the Leningrad Philharmonic. We sensed its message as something of particular and great importance. I know of no other instance where a composer consistently takes a patriotic moral stand in his music. This feature of his work was evident right from the start, in the youthful First Symphony, where you already sense profound tragedy and a personal foreboding. I regard the First Symphony as the first chapter of a book where you know that a great drama will unfold. Your interest has been captured, and you remain in suspense awaiting the terror that lies ahead. Shostakovich's whole musical output is logical and consistent in its expression. Through it Dmitri Dmitriyevich found a way of registering a protest and of mocking the Soviet regime. However, the irony and sarcasm in the music are outweighed by a sense of profound tragedy.

There were of course the occasional weak works in his output, such as *The Song of the Forests* and the operetta *Moscow-Cheryomushki*. But those works were written under particular circumstances as occasional pieces and they can be discounted. Dmitri Dmitriyevich didn't care to talk about them.

The Soviet authorities committed a great crime in killing the opera composer in Shostakovich. After 1936, he was frightened of using texts, because of the danger of being tied by the concrete nature of words. However, I hear in all his instrumental music a hidden text and even specific words – and I hear a particular conflict, rather than a general drama. Of course Shostakovich used texts in his romances, but these works were often written as private works. But later his need to express himself through drama and words forced its way through in the great scores of the Thirteenth and Fourteenth Symphonies, where he was unable to restrain this impulse. The texts he used, however, were important for their philosophical content rather than for their poetic expression, and through them he conveyed his particular vision of the world. But who knows what he might not have written if only he had not had to repress his rare gift for music drama?

Although we were all aware of the message in his works, Mravinsky never spoke in associative images during rehearsals when Dmitri Dmitriyevich was present. But if he wasn't there, Mravinsky did allow himself certain remarks that made it clear what he saw in the music. For instance, during a rehearsal of the Fifth Symphony, in the third movement, in the episode where the oboe has a long solo over the tremolos of the 1st and then the 2nd violins, Mravinsky turned round to the violin sections and said, 'You're playing this tremolo with the wrong colour, you haven't got the necessary intensity. Have you forgotten what this music is about and when it was born? Your tremolo sounds too self-satisfied.' I remember another occasion when he was rehearsing the Finale of the Ninth Symphony. He objected to the character of the sound in the celli and double basses when they play in unison with the trombones. 'You have the wrong sound. I need the sound of the trampling of steel-shod boots.' (We knew that he wasn't referring to ordinary soldiers, but to the KGB forces.)

I rarely had occasion to speak to Dmitri Dmitriyevich myself on such themes. But there was a small episode which gave me a glimpse of what he himself experienced in his music. In 1960 the orchestra had a big European tour, and we gave the British première of the Eighth Symphony under Mravinsky at the Royal Festival Hall. Dmitri Dmitriyevich was there of course, and amongst those who attended were Benjamin Britten, Yehudi Menuhin and Nathan Milstein. The Symphony made a shattering impression on the London audience, and was also received very enthusiastically by the critics.

The next day we went to France, and when making the channel crossing by ferry, I found myself standing on deck next to Dmitri Dmitriyevich. I told him what a great impression yesterday's concert had made on me. I explained that for me one of the most remarkable things in the work is the transition to the Finale: two clarinets play a long modulating passage, as if fumbling in the dark, and then at long last, before the bassoon solo, the music resolves into C major like a ray of sunlight. I said to Dmitri Dmitriyevich, 'You know, I always wait for this C major resolution, and even though I know that it will happen, yet every time I greet it as a long-awaited event.' Dmitri Dmitriyevich looked at me, and I will never forget the expression of his eyes. 'My dear friend, if you only knew how much blood that C major cost me.' He then fell silent, and I was left with the feeling that I had touched on something very sacred and private. However many times I have played that transition passage, I am always shaken by it.[48]

The Eleventh Symphony

Shostakovich started work on this symphony immediately after completing his Second Piano Concerto in February 1957 (the composer complained to Denisov the latter work had 'no artistic value').[49] As was his habit, the composer did most of his writing during the summer months in the peace of his Komarovo home. On 25 June he wrote in caustic mood to Edison Denisov:

> In Komarovo it's very hot . . . Every day there are heavy thunderstorms, lightning flashes, severing the sky. Thunder rumbles, and I sit in my 'creative laboratory' composing my Symphony. I'll soon finish, whereupon will ensue what the modernist and formalist (see *Sovietskaya Kultura*) Alexander Skryabin described in the Finale of his First Symphony, where he (in the Finale) takes up a realistic position, writing:
>
> > 'Why does this sweet moment reek of poison?
> > 'Tis the gaining of that far horizon.'
>
> But at the moment I sit at my desk all day long composing.[50]

48 Yakov Milkis: recorded interview with EW.
49 Letter dated 12 February 1957 (D. D. Shostakovich, 'Letters to Edison Denisov').
50 *ibid*.

The massive Symphony was a departure from Shostakovich's other symphonic and instrumental works in so far as it has a programme dedicated to the events of the '1905' Revolution. (The four movements are entitled 'Palace Square', 'The Ninth of January', 'Eternal Memory', 'Nabat' ['The Alarm Bell'].) The musical material is drawn from revolutionary and prison songs of that period.

The composer had first stated his intention of writing on the theme of the first Russian Revolution during the fiftieth anniversary celebrations in 1955. Two years later Shostakovich announced that he was composing the '1905' Symphony to commemorate the fortieth anniversary of the October Revolution. Ostensibly the Symphony's programme was absolutely orthodox, but ironically the very use of popular revolutionary songs (even in a purely instrumental form) imbued it with an ambiguous meaning. It is enough to recall some of the unvoiced texts, for instance, the first prison song 'Listen', used throughout the first movement, whose words pronounce, 'The autumn night is as black as treason, black as the tyrant's conscience. Blacker than that night a terrible vision rises from the fog – prison.' And similarly, the words of the famous revolutionary song used in the last movement of the Symphony: 'Rage, you tyrants –/ Mock at us,/ Threaten us with prison and chains./ We are strong in spirit, if weak in body!/ Shame, shame on you tyrants!'

The Symphony was given its première in Moscow on 30 October 1957 under Nathan Rakhlin, and a few days later Evgeny Mravinsky gave the first Leningrad performance. Public reaction was divided between those who felt disillusioned by Shostakovich's apparent defection to the ranks of officialdom, and those who heard once more rage and despair in a biting exposure of violence and evil. At face value, the music was accepted as an important statement of Shostakovich's allegiance to communism and the precepts of socialist realism.

LEV LEBEDINSKY explains the significance of the 'sub-text' in the Eleventh Symphony:

The Eleventh Symphony was upheld as an example of how music can reflect ideology. True, Shostakovich gave it the title '1905', but it was composed in the aftermath of the Soviet invasion of Hungary. What we heard in this music was not the police firing on the crowd in front of the Winter Palace in 1905, but the Soviet tanks roaring in the streets of Budapest. This was so clear to those 'who had ears to listen', that his son, with whom he wasn't in the habit of sharing his deepest thoughts, whispered to Dmitri Dmitriyevich during the dress rehearsal, 'Papa, what if they hang you for this?'

The officials wrote articles about the triumph of socialist realism, whereas the symphony in reality once again demonstrates Shostakovich's use of Aesopean language. The texts of the revolutionary songs quoted refer unequivocally to the tyrant's black conscience and the horrors of prison.

In *The Gulag Archipelago* Alexander Solzhenitsyn recounts how, while in prison, he heard the Zek[51] Drozdov singing the song 'Listen' used by Shostakovich in the Symphony. He goes on to remark that Shostakovich badly needed to hear a rendering of this song here before writing his Eleventh Symphony. In that case he would never have touched it or else would have given it a contemporary, rather than a dead meaning.

No doubt the writer was implying that Shostakovich had not seen with his own eyes Stalin's death camps, nor witnessed the Zeks' yearning for freedom, nor heard their songs.

But a genius does not need to experience a phenomenon or be a participant in a particular drama for him to understand its essence. Just as Dostoevsky didn't have to kill an old woman to be able to describe in minutest detail not only the external facts of the murder, but Raskolnikov's spiritual condition both during and after the crime.[52] True, Shostakovich didn't go to prison or to the camps, but he was able to transmit the atmosphere of reigning terror truthfully and with enormous force. And in addition all his conscious life Shostakovich lived in expectation of arrest, imprisonment and punishment. With his heightened sensitivity and keen artistic intuition he was constantly imagining and recreating the atmosphere of these prison camps, commiserating with the condition of their inmates, and fueling his undying hatred for the executioners of our age.

The Eleventh Symphony is a truly contemporary work, camouflaged by necessity with a historic programme. Many did not hear what Solzhenitsyn calls its 'contemporary meaning'. But Shostakovich knew that time would prove him right, and that he had been able to expose in his music what Solzhenitsyn was to describe eighteen years later in his *Gulag Archipelago*.[53]

---

51 Russian term for a labour camp detainee.
52 Fyodor Dostoevsky, *Crime and Punishment*.
53 Lev Lebedinsky, 'Shostakovich's Handling of Folk/Popular Song in His Own Works and Those of Other Composers', unpublished article.

Music
by Anna Akhmatova
(Dedicated to Dmitri Dmitriyevich Shostakovich)

It shines with a miraculous light
Revealing to the eye the cutting of facets.
It alone speaks to me
When others are too scared to come near.
When the last friend turned his back
It was with me in my grave
As if a thunderstorm sang
Or all the flowers spoke.[54]

ZOYA TOMASHEVSKAYA comes from a literary Leningrad family. Her father, the distinguished Pushkin scholar Boris Tomashevsky, enjoyed a close friendship with many of the country's most distinguished writers, notably with Anna Akhmatova. Here Tomashevskaya recalls Akhmatova's and Zoshchenko's relationships with Shostakovich:

On returning to Leningrad after the war, we went to almost all the concerts of Shostakovich's music. I think we never missed a première. And almost all the premières took place in Leningrad, with the exception of the Thirteenth Symphony, which Mravinsky did not conduct. Dmitri Dmitriyevich unfailingly attended them all. His chamber works were performed in the Maly Hall, in the house which formerly belonged to Engelhardt, the symphonies in the Philharmonic, the former Nobleman's Assembly.

These premières were always events. Anna Andreyevna Akhmatova almost always came with us to those concerts. My parents and she were linked by a lifelong friendship. At the première of the Eleventh Symphony there was a lot of discontented muttering. The music-loving connoisseurs alleged that the Symphony was devoid of interest. All around one overheard such remarks as, 'He has sold himself down the river. Nothing but quotations and revolutionary songs.'

Anna Andreyevna kept her silence. For some reason my father couldn't attend the concert. When we came home afterwards he asked us, 'Well, how was it?' And Anna Andreyevna answered, 'Those songs were like white birds flying against a terrible black sky.'

That was in 1957. The Hungarian Uprising was still very much in

54 Translated by Grigori Gerenstein.

our minds. And here in this symphony one kept hearing 'Freedom' sing out. Later I was told by the choreographer, Igor Belsky, who produced a wonderful ballet on the music of the Eleventh Symphony, that, when he consulted Shostakovich, the composer said to him, as if in passing: 'Don't forget that I wrote that symphony in the aftermath of the Hungarian Uprising.'

In the postwar years I often had occasion to meet the writer Mikhail Zoshchenko. We lived in the same building, in the same staircase entrance. Our flat was on the fifth floor, his on the one below. On our landing there lived Marina Didorovna Bogratian-Mukhlavskaya. This wonderful woman was the person closest to him during those years that were so terrible for Zoshchenko. Her friendship literally kept him alive for twelve years. In the late evening, when he came home, we would meet on the staircase and hold long conversations on the window-sill.

Whenever I returned from a concert of Shostakovich's music, Mikhail Milhailovich invariably told me some story connected with their friendship. Zoshchenko loved Shostakovich dearly, although he denied that theirs was a true friendship, as their lives took them down such different paths. I found two of these stories particularly remarkable. When Mikhail Mikhailovich was called up to the Soviet Army, he was relegated to the militia, since he had suffered from gas poisoning during the First World War. Dmitri Dmitriyevich found this very amusing, as Mikhail Milhailovich was the quietest and most refined person in the world. So he then composed for him the stridently bellicose 'Militiaman's March'.

And the second story: Dmitri Dmitriyevich would sometimes phone him up, and in his tragic, quick-voiced patter asked him to come immediately to see him: 'I need to talk.' Mikhail Mikhailovich would go. Dmitri Dmitriyevich would sit him down in an armchair, and then start to pace up and down the room in a frenzy. Gradually he would calm down, and finally, soothed and radiant, would say to Zoshchenko in a tired voice, 'Thank you, thank you dear friend, I so much needed that talk with you.'[55]

This reminds me of another occasion, when, many years later, Anna

---

[55] Mstislav Rostropovich also recounts how on several occasions he was urgently called to Shostakovich's house. On arrival he would sit in silence with the composer for half an hour or so before being sent home. (In conversation with EW.)

Andreyevna Akhmatova told me about her visit to Shostakovich. Dmitri Dmitriyevich had invited her to go and see him at Repino. Anna Andreyevna went. She said of that visit, 'We sat in silence for twenty minutes. It was wonderful.' It was remarkable how the fate of these two people, so different and yet so similar, was interlinked.

It is also in keeping to recall the no less striking inscription to Shostakovich made by Boris Pasternak in 1948: 'February 1948. In these days I consider it my duty to press your hand, and to say that we must be true to ourselves. May your great future be of help to you.'[56]

Pasternak could not have liked Shostakovich's music. He was a disciple of Skryabin, a romantic, and he himself wrote music. But what a true understanding of each other these people had, and of all that was happening around them.[57]

The First Cello Concerto

As the window to the West opened, Soviet artists started to travel. Amongst them was MSTISLAV ROSTROPOVICH, who in the second half of the 1950s laid the foundations of his uniquely brilliant international career. At home, he dedicated much effort to the promotion of contemporary music, and was particularly proud of his association with Shostakovich, with whom he gave frequent concerts.

Shostakovich continued performing throughout the 1950s, and finally stopped playing in public only when illness restricted the use of his hands. He most enjoyed playing his chamber works in the company of his friends. However, he found public performances stressful, as he complained to his friend and pupil Kara Karayev: 'I have been giving a lot of concerts, but with no pleasure. I still to this day can't get used to the stage. The strain is of high cost to my nerves. As soon as I reach fifty (God willing), then I will immediately cease my concertizing.'[58]

It was Rostropovich's superb artistry, as well as his musical partnership with his wife, the soprana Galina Vishnevskaya, that inspired Shostakovich to write a series of important works for this couple. The first of them was the

---

56 Olga Ivinskaya noted in her *A Captive of Time*, p. 130–1, that Pasternak wrote that inscription before Shostakovich recanted publicly at the 1st Congress of Composers, which was convened two months later. Pasternak's response was resigned: 'Oh Lord, if they only knew how to maintain their silence!'

57 Zoya Tomashevskaya, 'Reminiscences of Shostakovich', article commissioned for this book.

58 Letter from Bolshevo dated 4 October 1955 (L.-V. Karagieva [ed.], *Kara Karayev: Articles, Letters and Opinions*, p. 53).

Cello Concerto Op. 107, composed in July 1959. Here the cellist recalls his delight at the appearance of this work and how he learnt it in record time:

I often used to play Shostakovich's Cello Sonata with the composer. We played it many times in concerts in Moscow and also toured the Baltic Republics with a programme devoted to his music in 1955. In these concerts, Dmitri Dmitriyevich usually played a couple of his Preludes and Fugues, then some songs from the cycle *From Jewish Poetry*, and we finished with the Cello Sonata. Once we participated in a 'collective' concert somewhere outside Moscow on the Istra River. I normally never played at such occasions, but Shostakovich, in his capacity as Deputy-Candidate to the Supreme Soviet, had been invited to attend some manifestation. In the course of the proceedings, Dmitri Dmitriyevich played some of his music and then, together, we performed a couple of movements from the Cello Sonata.

We also recorded the Cello Sonata.[59] After making this recording with Shostakovich, I don't intend ever to make another one. It took us a long time to complete it, as Dmitri Dmitriyevich was quite nervous – partly because he was in a hurry to get off to lunch with his sister, who lived out of town. In the Finale he kept missing the chords in the two bars before the triplet section in the cello part. The more agitated he got, the more he kept splashing them. I then made a tentative suggestion: 'Dmitri Dmitriyevich, let me help you out here.' So I sat down at the piano and played the left-hand chords with two hands, while he played the right-hand chords with two hands. That's how we recorded them.

The First Cello Concerto was the first work that Shostakovich wrote specially for me. Interestingly enough, I never asked him to write anything. Once, when talking with Nina Vasilyevna, Dmitri Dmitriyevich's late wife, I raised the question of a commission: 'Nina Vasilyevna, what should I do to make Dmitri Dmitriyevich write me a cello concerto?'

She answered, 'Slava, if you want Dmitri Dmitriyevich to write something for you, the only recipe I can give you is this – never ask him or talk to him about it.'

So, with the greatest difficulty I managed to restrain myself. But although I never spoke about it, Dmitri Dmitriyevich knew that I constantly dreamt of his writing a piece for me.

59 This recording was originally issued by Melodiya in 1957.

I think that Shostakovich was speaking the truth when he remarked in an interview for *Sovietskoye Iskusstvo* that he had been inspired by Prokofiev's Symphony-Concertante for cello and orchestra when composing his First Cello Concerto. He loved this work passionately. He told me that he had played the record of Symphony-Concertante so many times that it was completely worn down and only emitted a kind of hiss when played on his gramophone.

There are a host of connections between Prokofiev's work and Shostakovich's Cello Concerto. Not only are many details of the Symphony-Concertante reflected in the First Concerto, but indeed, whole sections of the piece (admittedly much transformed) found their way into Shostakovich's work.

When I played the Symphony Concertante with the Moscow Philharmonic Orchestra, the timpani player in the orchestra was a war veteran with only one leg. At the end of the Finale, the cello ascends the heights as if spiralling up to the very summit of a domed roof; on reaching the highest note it is silenced by one bang of the timpani which puts an end to this frenzied madness. This remarkable player stood on his one leg (he had no artificial limb to support him) and struck that note. After the concert, Dmitri Dmitriyevich joined us to celebrate. 'Slavka, how that one-legged guy thumped his drum! He called a halt to everything with that final blow!' At the end of his own Cello Concerto there are seven rhetorical bangs on the timpani; undoubtedly Shostakovich borrowed this idea from Prokofiev's Symphony-Concertante. And there are other examples.

In his First Cello Concerto, Shostakovich alludes to Stalin's favourite song, 'Suliko'. These allusions are undoubtedly not accidental, but they are camouflaged so craftily that even I didn't notice them to begin with. The first time Dmitri Dmitriyevich hummed this passage through to me, he laughed and said, 'Slava, have you noticed?'

I hadn't noticed anything.

' "Where is my dear Suliko, Suliko? And where is my dear Suliko, Suliko?" '

I doubt if I would have detected this quote if Dmitri Dmitriyevich hadn't pointed it out to me.[60]

When I learned that Shostakovich had finished the Cello Concerto, I

---

60 'Suliko' is quoted in *Rayok* and sung to a ridiculous text. The melody appears in the appendix on pp. 477–9, together with the passage Rostropovich referred to in the Cello Concerto.

immediately went up to Leningrad with the pianist Alexander Dedyukhin. I received the score on the evening of 2 August 1959, and I learnt the work in four days exactly. I practised for ten hours the first day, and had the score memorized within three days. It was the most wonderful pleasure for me.

Then on 6 August, Dedyukhin and I went to Shostakovich's dacha in Komarovo outside Leningrad to play the Concerto through to him. Dmitri Dmitriyevich said, 'Now just hang on a minute while I find a music stand for you . . .'

I had been waiting for this, and said, 'Dmitri Dmitriyevich, but I don't need a stand.'

He said, 'What do you mean, you don't need a stand, you don't need one?'

'You know, I'll play from memory.'

'Impossible, impossible . . .'

Shortly after my return to Moscow I received three letters from Shostakovich, which became my most treasured possessions. They were like love-letters, and became a kind of talisman for me. I kept them by my bedside table and read them constantly. The first letter started with these words, 'Slava, I am completely intoxicated by what you have done to me, by the sheer delight you have given to me.' I don't wish to continue to quote Dmitri Dmitriyevich's words, as they would sound completely implausible. Then one fine day I couldn't find the letters. I asked our maid Rimma where they were. She had seen me hunting for them high and low for three days, but she was too frightened to tell me straight away that she had thrown these treasured letters into the rubbish bin.

I played the first performance of the Concerto in Leningrad with Mravinsky conducting. I cannot say that I ever loved Mravinsky as a musician. I knew him very well, and recognized him to be a great conductor, and more than that, a great psychological instructor. Undoubtedly, he understood music and was meticulous in everything he did. But it seems to me that too much aristocratic breeding deprives one of the possibility to enter fully into the music. In Mravinsky's case, he was so full of his noble origins that he was never able to let go of a certain in-bred reserve. Despite this I played with him frequently until 1962, when we quarrelled – over Shostakovich, what is more.[61]

61 Mstislav Rostropovich: recorded interview with EW.

EVGENY CHUKOVSKY describes how Rostropovich first played the Cello Concerto for Shostakovich at his Komarovo dacha:

Shostakovich had completed his cello concerto. Rostropovich dashed up from Moscow in his car and came to pick up the music. For four days the residents of the Evropeiskaya Hotel would have been suffering intolerably had it not been for the fact that luckily the hotel dated from the time when they knew how to build thick walls. Rostropovich was learning the concerto!

I went into the 'tvorilka', and while contemplating anew the horrifyingly spiked beacon, Shostakovich asked me to get hold of a tape-recorder somewhere in the village so he could record the first performance of the concerto here in his home at Komarovo.

Whatever next! Tape recorders were a rarity in those days, and Leningraders who owned them didn't take them to their holiday homes. Maxim and I sped around the settlement in the Pobeda car, but our search was in vain.

At midday the next day Rostropovich drove up in his Opel, and he entered the house carrying the womanly form of his cello. Behind him appeared a man of small stature wearing a brown suit. This was Alexander Alexandrovich who reproduced the orchestra on the piano.

And then, in this small room on the ground floor of the Komarovo 'galleon', Alexander Alexandrovich opened out the score on the piano desk, and Mariya Dmitriyevna, Shostakovich's sister, took her place standing at his side to turn the pages.

The pianist glanced over at Rostropovich and they started. It is a thankless task to try to describe music through words. The people gathered in this small room yielded to a state of superficial numbness, although passions smouldered within each one of them. They were captives to the will of the composer, who sat there tensely listening to the music which previously he alone had heard.

And when the last sounds died away, before the silence had been broken and while everybody was still recovering from what they had just heard, I thought to myself, 'Who, if not God, has given the author such power over people?'

As for the author, he said of this work, 'I took a simple little theme and tried to develop it.'

The first performance was celebrated with a good dinner on the downstairs veranda. There was much joking, people got slightly tipsy, but Dmitri Dmitriyevich asked me not to drink so that I could drive him into Leningrad. The fearless Rostropovich didn't worry about the police and was prepared to drive even when tipsy, but Shostakovich needed a car for the return journey.

In Leningrad our first stop was at the Eliseyev store where vodka and various snacks were bought, and then we moved on to Mariya Dmitriyevna's place on Sofia Perovskaya Street. Her flat had been severed off from a large apartment that had once been luxurious. Before the Revolution it belonged to a barrister. We climbed up the steep dark stairwell to the fifth floor, where a reinforced padded door protected the flat from would-be burglars. Inside there were two decent-sized rooms: a sitting-cum-dining room and a bedroom. There was no room for the bathtub so it stood in the kitchen. All the windows faced east, and the sun blazed on to them directly, turning the room into a furnace.

As Dmitri Dmitriyevich suffered from heat, the first thing he did was to draw the curtains. The room was plunged into gloom, cut by bright shafts of light which entered through the cracks. It looked like a set for a film about Mexico.

In the meantime, Shostakovich took some beautiful crystal glasses out of the cupboard and lit the candles in a bronze candleholder, and everyone sat down at the table. Everyone except for me, that is, as indeed I obviously could not contribute to the conversation. Incidentally, Alexander Alexandrovich also did not participate in the table-talk, but that didn't stop him from throwing back one glass after another.

The talk was predominantly about the concerto; Dmitri Dmitriyevich remembered that he hadn't written the dedication into the score. The music was immediately produced and, dipping his pen into the inkwell which for some reason stood on the piano, Shostakovich inscribed it: 'Dedicated to Mstislav Leopoldovich Rostropovich.' The dedicatee stood behind him watching him write. Then they leafed their way through the score, and one could tell from the expression on their faces that every page of it sounded for them. I heard Rostropovich suggest an improvement in some passage.

'You're a clever one,' Dmitri Dmitriyevich said. 'If I do it you'll be the only one who can play it; but I write for everybody, you know!'

He closed the score and hurried to sit down at table. Everybody was tired by this time, and the tone of the conversation lightened. They started gossiping about matters at the Composers' Union. At a certain point the name of Kholodilin cropped up.

And what, you might think, is so special about Kholodilin? But the name had a devastating effect on Alexander Alexandrovich. His eyes lit up and he started fidgeting on his seat, and poked his neck out of his collar like a goose. Obviously, for the first time all evening, he too had the desire to say something.

'Nimi Nimich,' (this was how Dmitri Dmitriyevich's name came out when uttered by Alexander Alexandrovich) 'do you know the etymology of the name Kholodilin?' he asked.

Dmitri Dmitriyevich looked bewildered, thought it over then said, 'It must come from the word "kholodits" (to make cold).'

'Goodness me no, Nimi Nimich,' chirped Alexander Alexandrovich. 'It comes from the word "kholodilo", not "kholodits".' He paused, expecting a reaction, but none followed.

'So what?' Shostakovich said.

'Don't you know what "kholodilo" means?'

'No, I don't.'

'It means prick.'

'But why?' Shostakovich demanded in amazement.

Alexander Alexandrovich hurried to explain, 'Because it makes ladies break out into a cold sweat.'

'I don't know about that, I don't know. I should have thought rather a hot sweat, a hot sweat,' Dmitri Dmitriyevich gabbled in reply. He felt embarrassed and was in a hurry to leave for home.

We drove back to Komarovo. Shostakovich sat in the front seat and as was his wont kept silent throughout the journey; he didn't like talking to chauffeurs. At each bend of the road the setting sun shone straight into our eyes. Then Dmitri Dmitriyevich pulled down the sunshield. When the road turned back towards the east, he pushed it up again. Down and up, down and up, until the sun plunged into the gulf.[62]

Official duties

The composer was not allowed to neglect his public duties, and was increasingly used by the Soviet regime as a figure-head to represent the 'free' intelligentsia. This accounts not only for his participation in peace confer-

62 Evgeny Chukovsky, 'Komarovo', novella commissioned for this book.

ences, plenary sessions and congresses of the Union of Composers, but also for the steady flow of public statements and articles on an increasingly wide variety of topics that appeared under his name in the press. Undoubtedly the majority of these publications were written by 'ghost' authors.

Shostakovich was re-elected as a Deputy to the Supreme Soviet in 1955. As his involvement with the administrative affairs of the Composers' Union increased, he was appointed a secretary to the governing body of the All-Soviet Union in 1957, and in April 1960 was elected First Secretary of the RSFSR (Russian) Union of Composers, a post specially created for him.

DANIIL ZHITOMIRSKY describes an occasion when he acted as speech-writer to Shostakovich:

There are dozens of speeches and articles catalogued in *D. D. Shostakovich: Musicological and Bibliographical Guide* (Moscow, 1965) as having been published under his name, including a large number that were political and propagandist, such as 'Moscow – the Hope of Humanity' (1950), 'On the Path Indicated by the Party' (1957), 'Let Us Be Worthy of the Glory of the Great Motherland' (1959) and 'The Party Inspired Us' (1962). It was a secret to no one that these and such-like articles were written by professional journalists, and only signed by the supposed author. This was a regular, everyday technique employed for 'speeches by famous people'. Even in the preparation of his articles about music, the participation of the author was a mere formality, and sometimes it was altogether lacking. I can judge this from my own experience as one of Shostakovich's literary 'collaborators'.

I remember, for instance, how his speech about Beethoven (to be delivered in Berlin on the occasion of the Beethoven celebrations in 1952) came to be composed. I went to see Shostakovich with a prepared typescript. Immediately after my arrival various extremely important functionaries from the Committee for the Arts appeared. I read out 'Shostakovich's speech' distinctly and loudly. Then the Ministry officials expressed their profound thoughts. They gave one to understand that they were better and more thoroughly informed on all matters concerning Beethoven than 'Shostakovich' was in his written speech. They were particularly well-informed about 'Beethoven and Revolution' and 'The Love for Beethoven in the USSR'. They issued dozens of invaluable 'directives', which I diligently wrote down, while Dmitri Dmitriyevich sat in the darkest, furthest corner of the room in complete silence. What did he know about Beethoven!

This all happened in the late evening before his departure to East Germany early next morning.

I stayed on, correcting the speech in Shostakovich's study until the early hours. At dawn he awoke me. For the sake of appearances he leafed through my finished text. 'Thank you, thank you, it is excellent, many thanks!' With a quick gesture he scratched the crown of his head and disappeared.

As I recall this incident I can't help pondering on how I too was a participant in this falsification. And after all, several times I had occasion to observe that Dmitri Dmitriyevich had his own ideas on these subjects, which were far more original and profound than any contained in the texts prepared for him by others. I can gain little comfort from the fact that I tried to write as I imagined he would himself. And on more than one occasion I had reason to believe, as I still do today, that Dmitri Dmitriyevich was reconciled to these falsifications not through indolence, and obviously not through moral indifference. Rather I think that he abdicated any real responsibility for these publications for serious reasons. He regarded the official press (and indeed, there was no alternative press) with scepticism as a dismal establishment. His attitude seemed to be, 'Let them write whatever they want. After all, I know its worth. Nobody cares in essence what I am and what I think. Moreover, it would be stupid and highly undesirable to let them see *what* I really am . . .'

I also remember Dmitri Dmitriyevich's wonderful expressive manner of speech when conversing in private. He had his particular style, using short, almost aphoristic phrases, always direct and to the point. He couldn't bear stereotyped phrases and superfluous words. He was impeccably considerate, but in uttering the standard words of greeting, thanks or good wishes he was extremely succinct, thereby sometimes appearing to emphasize the superficiality of such ritual phrases and gestures.

The idiosyncrasy of Shostakovich's speech consisted in the fact that humour and sarcasm loomed through an unperturbed serious-ness of manner. One was always aware of his natural artistic gift in his use of pointed but restrained hints, allegory, imitation, in the way he acted out a whole theatrical scene or told the most vacuous anecdote (which he was not above telling). I remember him telling a joke in a small circle of friends with so much success that he immediately had to repeat it, of course with extra embellishments –

he didn't like literal repetitions in his speech any more than in his music.

However, Shostakovich was quite different when speaking from the tribune in an official capacity. I reproduce an entry from my diary from the 1950s:

'I listened to Dmitri Dmitriyevich's speech with growing irritation, but also with compassion and sympathy. How alien and artificial seemed the text he was pronouncing. Banal, journalistic phrases, textbook quotations, cumbersome and wordy statements. And the way he read this all out! In a quick patter, omitting all punctuation marks, and with an intonation that seemed intentionally lacking in sense. It was as if he was poking fun at himself in the role of official orator.'[63]

Shostakovich attended the 4th Plenum of the Executive of the Siberian Composers' Organization in Novosibirsk in April 1961. On that occasion MARINA SABININA travelled as his official escort. Here she describes the experience:

Usually when Dmitri Dmitriyevich made his frequent trips around the country in his capacity of Chairman of the Union of Composers of the RSFSR he was accompanied by Ivan Ivanovich Martynov, who helped him to prepare the necessary texts of speeches, resolutions and reports. On this occasion Martynov was ill and therefore was unable to accompany Dmitri Dmitriyevich to Novosibirsk. I was told that it was Dmitri Dmitriyevich's personal wish that I should take this role upon myself.

On the flight, sitting next to Dmitri Dmitriyevich, I asked him, 'Dmitri Dmitriyevich, how are your children these days?'

'Children, children! Small children don't allow you to sleep, and older children don't allow you to live! Maxim is now crazy about pop and jazz, and turns on the most rubbishy cheap music in his room at full volume. That makes it very hard for me to work, even to breathe, to exist . . .'

'But Maxim intends to become a pianist?'

'Yes, he intends to be a pianist, but I don't know what will become of it all. He doesn't like real, good music, he simply can't stand it.'

In Novosibirsk times were cold and hungry. I didn't have much success in my attempts to buy something for breakfast and supper –

63 Daniil Zhitomirsky, 'Dmitri Shostakovich: Reminiscences and Reflections', unpublished article.

just some kefir and stale rolls. But we were often invited to people's homes where we were given a very warm reception and fed with true Siberian hospitality in the merchant style of old – 'pelmenye' (Siberian dumplings), various kinds of pies, caviar and salmon.

We expressed our appreciation of the luxurious fare, and I could not contain my curiosity and asked where our hosts had managed to find it. The wife of a local composer proudly let us in on the secret: she had gone to the local Party Committee. 'I told them, "You see, we have to entertain the great Shostakovich, winner of so many prizes and awards." And they answered, "Right, we understand," and gave us a pass just for this occasion to use the provision store of the local Party Committee, saying, "Take whatever you fancy." The prices were cheap into the bargain!'

Dmitri Dmitriyevich ate with relish, praised the dumplings and our clever hostess. He obviously enjoyed these festivities. Somebody struck up a folk song, and he joined in with obligatos and decorations. He even inveigled me into singing along. And for a long time we sang one song after another, improvising God only knows how. Our singing was out of tune, with bags of wrong notes, and I thought, 'surely this must be agony for his refined hearing.' But no, Dmitri Dmitriyevich was thoroughly entertained, and exuded an air of boyish mischief at all this sport.

Generally he was in a very cheerful frame of mind those days. In particular, he came to life at the rehearsals of the Siberian Folk Choir, which presented a very dull, ordinary repertoire and mediocre voices. But they made every effort to please their eminent guest. Shostakovich fidgeted and smiled and kept asking, 'Don't you think that blonde girl, third from the left, is awfully pretty? Do you think I should marry her, eh?' And on the way back to Moscow he remembered that fresh young beauty: 'What a lovely girl, and I am all on my own, all on my own, there's nobody to sew on a button for me. . . !' (In fact one of the buttons on his coat had fallen off, and I sewed it back on for him one free evening.)

We also visited the grave of Ivan Ivanovich Sollertinsky at the Novosibirsk cemetery. The grave was well tended, although it looked somewhat unloved and official. I wondered if it had been specially tidied up for his visit, or if it was always so well cared for. Dmitri Dmitriyevich stood motionless, locked in silence. It seemed to me that he was inhibited by the presence of so many strangers, and that this semblance of an official ceremony jarred. No doubt this enforced remoteness clashed with the loving images and intimate memories of that most brilliant man, the bosom friend of his youthful years.[64]

Victim of oppression or faithful Party member?

Universally recognized at home and abroad, recipient of a host of awards from within the Soviet Union and abroad, by the late 1950s Shostakovich found himself to all intents and purposes regarded as an establishment figure.

Nevertheless, his sudden application in September 1960 to join the Communist Party came as a surprise to his colleagues and a bitter disappointment to his friends.

It was evident that Shostakovich was uninterested in any privilege or gain to be had as a Party member, having resisted membership throughout the Stalinist decades. However, in the wake of the 20th Party Congress, the Party's position had changed. Stalin's old faithfuls, Lazar Kaganovich, Vyacheslav Molotov, and Georgi Malenkov were removed from high office, although saved from public disgrace. With an eye to public opinion (particularly in the West), Khrushchev felt the need to raise the credit of the Party and introduce fresh blood into its ranks. Therefore he now looked for support from the leading lights of the intelligentsia. Like many in his situation, Shostakovich must have found it increasingly difficult to resist mounting pressure to join a party which had disassociated itself from some of the worst atrocities of the regime, laying the blame firmly at Stalin's door.

Furthermore, to fill the void left by Stalin's dethronement, the cult of Lenin was intensified. This meant that by 1961 Shostakovich, now a Party member, was forced to stand by his long-standing declarations to write a large-scale work dedicated to Lenin. Hence his decision to tackle the sacred cow of Soviet ideology and to dedicate the programme of the Twelfth Symphony to Lenin.

But the element of paradox that was always present in the sequence of Shostakovich's compositions provides an insight into the composer's inner conflict and continuing 'double life' of this period. The Eleventh Symphony was written shortly after *Rayok*, and the light-weight operetta *Moscow-Cheryomushki* (whose 'topical' subject deals with the new housing co-operatives being raised in the cities at this time) before the First Cello Concerto with its parodying references to Stalin's favourite song. In 1960, the year of his application to join the Party, Shostakovich created two of his most highly personal works, the Seventh Quartet (dedicated to his late wife, and written to commemorate her fiftieth birthday), and his tragic autobiographical master-

64 Marina Sabinina, 'About Children and Other Things', short story written for this book.

piece, the Eighth Quartet. Wedged between these two works was the vocal cycle *Satires* on words by Sasha Chyorny, a parody on the evils of society (disguised with the apt subtitle 'Pictures from the Past').

Perhaps most surprising for fans and critics alike was the delayed première of the Fourth Symphony, following hard on the heels of the Twelfth Symphony in December 1961. The overwhelming vitality of this work, dating from 1936, testified to Shostakovich's amazing creative resilience, and served as a reminder of the quality of his early music, which had been largely neglected and unperformed over the last two decades.

ABRAAM GOZENPUD describes Shostakovich's attitude towards worldly fame:

It is true that Shostakovich was not indifferent to worldly recognition, to honours and awards; but he regarded them with a certain scepticism and irony. Once, when awarded yet another Honorary Diploma from a Foreign Music Society, he said, 'I am frightened that I will choke in an ocean of awards.' And another time, after attending *Eugene Onegin* at the Bolshoi Theatre, he remarked that all the performers wore their prestigious award medals, leaving only two people in the company without decorations denoting rank and position: Pushkin and Tchaikovsky![65]

Lev Lebedinsky probably attracted Shostakovich's friendship because he was so different from him – warm, earthy and forthright. He shared with Shostakovich a sense of humour and a hatred of Stalinism and communism. Shostakovich was able to accept Lebedinsky's political background and his former allegiance to proletarian ideology, no doubt because Lebedinsky, disillusioned with the communist system early on, was the first to admit that these ideas had been erroneous.

Undoubtedly, Lebedinsky was a controversial figure, and his role as a founder and ideological spokesman of RAPM rankled with many. However, by the 1950s his status in the Composers' Union had declined to that of 'the oldest Bolshevik' member. On the other hand, Lebedinsky's work in musical folklore was highly regarded.

Evidently there was an element of casual informality and a natural simplicity in the relationship between the two men – something that Shostakovich rarely encountered. Even his close friends felt inhibited by Shostakovich's genius, as testified by the soprano Galina Vishnevskaya: 'All those of his circle were especially deferential towards him, and would be transformed by his presence. We all tried not to talk too much, to be more

65 Gozenpud, 'Encounters with Shostakovich'.

reserved – and often we ended up acting entirely unlike ourselves.'[66] Lebedinsky lived within walking distance of Shostakovich's Moscow flat, and Shostakovich often asked him to drop by on the spur of the moment.

Here Lebedinsky's wife, MARIYA KONNISKAYA, describes the background from which her husband came:

Lev Lebedinsky was born in 1905, the son of an enlightened doctor and socialist revolutionary from Chelyabinsk. From the age of twelve he was active in politics, defending Bolshevism (alas!). At the age of fourteen he ran away from home to fight at the Front. Within a year he had been appointed political commissar to a Cavalry Reconnaissance Division of the 23rd Kazan Regiment attached to Tukhachevsky's Fifth Army. He joined the Bolshevik Party. He travelled from one end of Siberia to the other, suffered from frostbite and was demobilized. He was sent to Moscow to work under Dzerzhinsky as a reward for his outstanding ability. Here he saw things in a different light, and asked to be transferred to work 'with the People' as a simple worker in a steel factory.

Soon he decided to make music his profession. On the basis of the thorough musical education he had received as a child, he was able to enter the Moscow Conservatoire. He became a musicologist whose speciality was polemics, always fighting for or against something. He was one of the initiators of RAPM in 1925, remaining an active member until its dissolution in 1932. Their credo was for music of the 'People', proletarian music; for social problems and the heroic (for Beethoven, for Mussorgsky); against the sentimental and 'personal' (against Tchaikovsky, Rachmaninov). But this was the fervour of youth. He even fought for his views with Marshal Voroshilov over the Aviators' March ('Always Higher') with its melody more suited to a cheap chansonette.

After 1932 he fell into disgrace. In the Second World War he served in the Army at the Home Front. During the following period of 'cosmopolitanism', to avoid punitive measures, he removed himself for long periods from Moscow, spending much time in Bashkiriya studying and collecting folklore.

In 1955 he was allowed to work in Moscow again. He became the chief editor of the Folklore Department of the Musgiz Publishing House, and was shortly appointed president of the folklore commis-

66 Vishnevskaya, *A Russian Story*, p. 225.

sion. Lebedinsky was the editor of the published score of Shostako-vich's *Katerina Izmailova* in its second version. Although he met Shostakovich many years before, his close friendship with the composer dates from the years after the war, and was particularly intense during the 1950s and first years of the 1960s.[67]

LEV LEBEDINSKY recalls the events surrounding Shostakovich's application for Party membership:

Shostakovich not only was a great composer but a remarkable person. His extraordinarily heightened sensitivity forced him to live with exposed nerves. Already traumatized by life from early childhood, in his adult years his painful perception of reality was aggravated by persecution from a totalitarian regime. As a true democrat, he deeply detested the communist system, which continuously threatened his very life. In his first major work, his First Symphony, he already challenges the forces of evil. I was the first to note that the timpani in the last movement sound like a depiction of an execution on a scaffold. When I remarked to Dmitri Dmitriyevich, 'You were the first to declare war against Stalin,' he did not deny it. Already, from his early years, Shostakovich understood what was going on in our country and what was to come.

Shostakovich's parents educated their children in the great human-itarian traditions of Russia. Before the Revolution, they used to hide refugees in their house without discriminating between people of varying political views. According to family legend, once when Shostakovich's uncle, Maxim Kostrykin, was hidden in their apart-ment along with some Kadets or Oktyabristy,[68] tremendous quarrels broke out between them. 'We'll kill you first when we get into power,' they shouted at each other.

This uncle was a fervent bolshevik, and reputedly took the young Shostakovich to the Finland Station to see Lenin's arrival.

'What did you go to the Finland Station for?' I asked Shostakovich.

'I wanted to hear Lenin's speech,' he said. 'I knew a dictator was arriving.'

---

67 Mariya Konniskaya: extract from unpublished letter.
68 The Constitutional Democrats, known as the Kadet Party, promulgated the idea of a constitutional monarchy on British lines. The Oktyabristi took their name from the October Manifesto of 1905, where Tsar Nicholas granted an elected body, the Duma, and guaranteed civil rights of citizens.

Shostakovich was the only Soviet composer who expressed his hatred of the totalitarian regime in his music. Despite the fear that he might be physically destroyed for his views, as many of his colleagues were, he continued his struggle, following the footsteps of the great humanists of the past. Often he was compelled for the purpose of self-defence to disguise his music and his views. As a result he was often misunderstood even by those who shared his attitudes. Their lack of understanding and unjust accusations caused him considerable pain.

His autobiographical Eighth Quartet contains quotations from his most important works, and ends with the popular dirge 'Tormented by Grievous Bondage'.[69] It was hard to misunderstand, but the critics did misunderstand it and wrote, 'In the Finale the composer quotes Lenin's favourite song.'

Time-serving was alien to Shostakovich's nature. But, over the years, he assumed a mask, and played the role of an obedient Party member. Nevertheless, he often lost his orientation in the complex labyrinths of political behaviour. His writings often contradicted what he said, and, even worse, his actions contradicted what he had written.[70]

The most tragic example of his neurotic behaviour was his joining the Communist Party in 1960, which he hated and despised. It's hard to tell what made him join, although he had been under much official pressure for some time. He didn't tell his friends and family that he had made the application for membership; we only found out when we received the official Party circular in the post.

It was only then that it dawned on me what had happened. Shostakovich had never heeded my warnings that certain invitations issued by certain friends brought him into the society of licensed officials, and were nothing short of a trap. On one such occasion some bureaucratic trickster put a prepared text in front of him. No doubt Dmitri Dmitriyevich had been plied with drink, and was under its influence when he signed the 'request' to be admitted to the Party.

As the date of the meeting where Shostakovich was to be 'admitted

---

69 Variously translated as 'He Died in Hard Slavery' or 'Tormented by Lack of Freedom'.

70 It is also worth remembering that Shostakovich was amongst the signatories of a letter to the Central Committee demanding that Solzhenitsyn be allowed a normal way of life and proper working conditions. (The other signatories included the writers Kornei Chukovsky, Konstantin Paustovsky and the physicist Pyotr Kapitsa).

to the Party ranks' drew near, Dmitri Dmitriyevich's life became a torment. He went up to Leningrad, where he hid in his sister's flat, as if escaping from his own conscience. I followed him there. The meeting was to take place the next morning in Moscow. Shostakovich was a tangle of nerves; he was so conditioned by fear that no logical argument or reasoning could reach him. In the end I literally physically restrained him from going to the station to take the night train, and forced him to send a telegram saying that he was ill.

Hence the widely publicized Party meeting was a flop because of the absence of . . . Shostakovich himself! The authorities had to resort to a deception, announcing that Shostakovich had been taken ill so suddenly that there was no time to notify all the invited Party members. Since an unprecedented number of people had gathered to witness Shostakovich's ultimate humiliation, in their eyes the cancellation of the Party meeting acquired the proportions of a major public scandal. They all formed the impression that Shostakovich was being pushed into the Party by force.

I will never forget some of the things he said that night, sobbing hysterically: 'I am scared to death of them.' 'You don't know the whole truth.' 'From childhood I have been doing things that I wanted *not* to do.' 'I'm a wretched alcoholic.' 'I've been a whore, I am and always will be a whore.' (He often lashed at himself in strong words.)

The tragi-comedy of admitting Shostakovich to the Party was played out a few months later. He became an exemplary and obedient Party member. Without fail he attended every possible ridiculous meeting of the Supreme Soviet, every plenary session, every political gathering, and even took part in the agitprop song rally. In other words, he eagerly took part in events which he himself described as 'torture by boredom'. He sat there like a puppet, his thoughts wandering far away, applauding when the others applauded. Once I remember him clapping eagerly after Khrennikov had made a speech in which he had made some offensive remarks about Shostakovich. 'Why did you clap when you were being criticized,' I asked. He hadn't even noticed!

What moved him was not lack of principles, but a deep-rooted contradiction of character. Take his attack on Solzhenitsyn and Sakharov. It is well known that Shostakovich sympathized with both of them. He kept re-reading Solzhenitsyn's short stories and intended to write an opera called *Matryona's House* right after the story had been published in *Novy Mir* magazine in the January 1963 issue. Unfortunately, he could not find a writer to whom he could entrust the writing of a libretto for the opera; once he even turned to me, although I hardly took his proposal seriously.

God only knows what possessed him to put his signature to that filthy official slander of Sakharov and Solzhenitsyn. Nobody forced him to do it. He was ill at the time, and it would have been very easy for him not to admit the petty official of the secretariat of the Composers' Union who had come with a 'request' to sign the letter. However, he did sign the shameful calumny. Afterwards he cursed himself, saying that he'd never forgive himself for having done it.[71]

ISAAK GLIKMAN gives a harrowing account of Shostakovich's condition in June 1960, brought on by his enforced recruitment into the detested Communist Party:

In the last ten days of June 1960, Shostakovich came to Leningrad and, instead of booking into the Evropeiskaya Hotel as was his wont, went to stay with his sister.

On 28 June I paid Dmitri Dmitriyevich a short visit. He informed me that he had recently written *Five Satires on Verses by Sasha Chyorny*, and he hoped to familiarize me with this opus. But early on the following morning, Dmitri Dmitriyevich rang and asked me to come and see him immediately.

When I glanced at him, I was struck by his suffering aspect, his troubled and confused expression. He hurriedly led me into the small room where he slept and limply sank on to his bed and started crying, weeping out loud. In horror, I wondered if something dreadful had happened to a member of his family. In response to my questions, he mumbled indistinctly through his tears: 'They have been hounding me, they have been pursuing me.'

I had never seen Dmitri Dmitriyevich in such a state. He was quite hysterical. I gave him a glass of cold water, which he drank with his teeth chattering, and he gradually calmed down. About an hour later, he took hold of himself sufficiently to tell me what had happened to him a short while ago in Moscow.

On Khrushchev's initiative, it had been decided to make him Chairman of the RSFSR Composers' Union, and Party membership was a required criterion for this position. P. N. Pospelov, a member of

71 Lev Lebedinsky: compiled from recorded interviews with EW and unpublished articles.

the Central Committee bureau of the RSFSR had been entrusted with the mission of enlisting Shostakovich.

These are Dmitri Dmitriyevich's actual words to me that June morning, at the height of 'the Thaw':

'Pospelov tried to persuade me by every means to join the Party, where one breathes so easily and freely under Nikita Sergeyevich's leadership. Pospelov greatly admired Khrushchev, his youthful vigour, his grandiose plans, and said it was essential that I should enroll in the ranks of a Party headed not by Stalin, but by Khrushchev.

'Completely dumbfounded, I did my best to refuse this honour. I clutched at any straw, saying that I had never managed to master Marxism, that they should wait until I did. Then I pleaded my religion. Then I said that it would be possible to be Chairman without Party membership, citing as examples Konstantin Fedin and Leonid Sobelyov, who both occupied leading positions in the Writers' Union without being Party members. Pospelov rejected all my arguments, and several times alluded to Khrushchev, who was anxious for the fate of musical matters, saying that I must respond to his calls for help. I was utterly exhausted by this conversation. At a second meeting, Pospelov once again cornered me. My nerves cracked up, I gave in to him.

. . . 'In the Composers' Union, they shortly discovered the outcome of my negotiations with Pospelov, and soon somebody had concocted a statement which I was to parrot at a meeting. I want you to know I have decided not to appear at the meeting. I've come to Leningrad in secret to stay with my sister, and to hide from my tormentors. It still seemed to me that they would come to their senses and leave me in peace. And then, if all else fails, I'd lock myself in up here. But yesterday evening telegrams arrived demanding my immediate arrival. But I'm not going. They can only take me to Moscow by force, only by force.'[72]

The Circumstances behind the creation of the Eighth Quartet

Shostakovich wrote his Eighth Quartet during a visit to East Germany in July 1960. Ostensibly it was conceived under the impression of the horrific scale of

---

72 Glikman, *Letters to a Friend*, pp. 160, 161.

destruction wrought on Dresden, the subject of Arnshtam's film *Five Days and Five Nights*, for which Shostakovich was to write the music. However, this theme served, at most, as a superficial stimulus.

While in Germany the composer stayed at the beautiful resort of Gorlits in Saxony. It was there that, instead of working on the film, he composed his five-movement Eighth Quartet, which he ironically described in a letter to his friend Isaak Glikman as 'ideologically flawed and of no use to anybody'.

Shostakovich went on to explain to Glikman that:

> When I die, it's hardly likely that someone will write a quartet dedicated to my memory. So I decided to write it myself. One could write on the frontispiece, 'Dedicated to the author of this quartet.' The main theme is the monogram D, Es, C, H, that is – my initials. The quartet makes use of themes from my works and the revolutionary song 'Tormented by Grievous Bondage'. My own themes are the following: from the First Symphony, the Eighth Symphony, the Piano Trio, the [First] Cello Concerto and *Lady Macbeth*. Wagner's Funeral March from *Götterdämmerung* and the second theme from the first movement of Tchaikovsky's Sixth Symphony are also hinted at. And I forgot – there's also a theme from my Tenth Symphony. Quite something – this little miscellany!
>
> The pseudo-tragedy of the quartet is so great that, while composing it, my tears flowed as abundantly as urine after downing half a dozen beers. On arrival home, I have tried playing it twice, and have shed tears again. This time not because of the pseudo-tragedy, but because of my own wonder at the marvellous unity of form . . . that's all that happened while I was in 'Saxon Switzerland'.[73]

LEV LEBEDINSKY recalls how Shostakovich played him the Eighth Quartet on his return from Dresden:

The failure of his first attempt to join the Party throws light on the Eighth Quartet written during that period. The quartet begins with the composer's monogram, DSCH, followed by quotations from his earlier works, and ending with the folk dirge, 'Tormented by Grievous Bondage'. The composer dedicated the Quartet to the victims of fascism to disguise his intentions, although, as he considered himself a victim of a fascist regime, the dedication was apt. In fact he intended it as a summation of everything he had written before. It was his farewell to life. He associated joining the Party with a moral, as well as physical death. On the day of his return from a trip to Dresden, where he had completed the Quartet and purchased a large number of

73 Letter dated 19 July 1960 (*ibid.*, p. 159).

sleeping pills, he played the Quartet to me on the piano and told me with tears in his eyes that it was his last work. He hinted at his intention to commit suicide. Perhaps subconsciously he hoped that I would save him. I managed to remove the pills from his jacket pocket and gave them to his son Maxim, explaining to him the true meaning of the Quartet. I pleaded with him never to let his father out of his sight. During the next few days I spent as much time as possible with Shostakovich until I felt that the danger of suicide had passed.[74]

The *Satires*

By 1960 the soprano Galina Vishnevskaya, the Bolshoi Theatre's leading soprano, enjoyed an enormous reputation as an opera singer both at home and abroad. She was also renowned for her sensitive performances of Russian romances with her husband Mstislav Rostropovich.

The vocal cycle *Satires* was the first of three works that Shostakovich dedicated to her (they were followed by his orchestration of Mussorgsky's *Songs and Dances of Death* in 1962 and the Seven Romances on Poems by Alexander Blok in 1967). In addition the composer had her voice in mind when writing his Fourteenth Symphony.

In 1960 Shostakovich received as a gift a recently published book of Sasha Chyorny's verse from his son-in-law, Evgeny Chukovsky, which no doubt served as a stimulus to write the song cycle. But Shostakovich evidently knew Chyorny's work from much earlier, as Flora Litvinova can testify: 'Way back in Kuibyshev, I remember Dmitri Dmitriyevich reading the *Satires* to us, especially,

> Our forebears crawled into cells,
> And often reminded themselves in an evil hour:
> 'It's tough, friends, but probably
> Our kids will be freer than us.'[75]

Here GALINA VISHNEVSKAYA recalls how the cycle came into being, and how composer and performers overcame the problem of making 'dubious' texts acceptable to the authorities:

In the summer of 1960, during the time I was working on the Mussorgsky [*Songs and Dances of Death*], Shostakovich called us to his place and asked us to listen to his new work, a song cycle called *Satires*,

74 Lev Lebedinsky: compiled from recorded interviews with EW and unpublished articles.
75 Flora Litvinova, article commissioned for this book.

based on the verse of Sasha Chyorny, for soprano with piano accompaniment. Dmitri Dmitriyevich himself played and sang, while Slava and I remained rooted to our chairs, overwhelmed by the unimpeded flow of sarcasm and black humour.

'Do you like it, Galya?'

I could only whisper, 'Dmitri Dmitriyevich, it's phenomenal!'

'I wrote it for you in the hope that you wouldn't decline to sing it.'

'Decline?' I was hoarse with excitement.

Dmitri Dmitriyevich got up from the piano, took the music, and before handing it to me, said, 'If you don't object, I'd like to dedicate this work to you.' He wrote in the manuscript: 'Dedicated to Galina Pavlovna Vishnevskaya,' and made me a gift of it.

Slava and I hurried home toting the precious gift – we were crazy with happiness. How had Dmitri Dmitriyevich, who knew me only as an opera singer, surmised my past career as a music-hall singer? His cycle had been written for none other than a music-hall singer with an operatic voice!

A few days later we performed the new work for Dmitri Dmitriyevich.

'Remarkable! Simply remarkable! There's just one thing: I'm afraid that they won't let it be performed.'

And he was right. One of the poems was 'Our Posterity'. Though written in 1910, it had recently been published in the Soviet Union. Yet with the music of Shostakovich it took on an entirely different meaning – it became an indictment of the current Soviet regime and its insane ideology.

> Our forebears crawled into cells,
> And often whispered there:
> 'It's tough, friends, but probably
> Our kids will be freer than us.'
> The kids grew up, and they too
> Crawled into cells in time of danger,
> And whispered: 'Our kids
> Will greet the Sun after us.'
> And now, as for all time,
> There is but one consolation:
> 'Our kids will be in Mecca
> If we are not fated to be.'

They have even predicted the times:
Some say two centuries, others say five.
Meanwhile, lie in sadness
And babble like an idiot.
Obscene gestures are in disguise,
The world is scrubbed, combed, nice.
In two centuries! To hell with that!
Am I Methuselah?
And I'm like an eagle-owl among the ruins
Of broken gods.
I have neither friends or enemies
Among descendants not yet born.
I want a little light
For myself, while I'm still alive.
Everyone from the tailor to the poet
Understands my call.
And our posterity? Let our posterity
Fulfilling their fate
And cursing *their* posterity
Beat their heads against a wall!

It was clear that the authorities would not allow such verse to be sung on stage. The words refer to today, and could not be said better. I had an idea. 'Dmitri Dmitriyevich, instead of calling the cycle *Satires* call it *Pictures of the Past*. Throw them that bone and they might sanction it. Yesterday is part of the past, too; the public will see it that way.'

He was satisfied, and snickered at the irony of it. 'Beautifully thought out, Galya! Beautifully thought out. Under *Satires* we'll put 'Pictures of the Past' in parentheses, like a kind of fig leaf. We'll cover up the embarrassing parts for them.'

In that way the cycle got its name. But we were never sure, right up until the time of the concert, that they wouldn't take it off the programme. The authorization came only at the last minute.

On the evening of 22 February 1961, the concert hall was jammed with people. All of Moscow waited impatiently for Shostakovich's new work with the seditious verses. Slava accompanied me. For the first part of the programme, I sang Mussorgsky's *Songs and Dances of Death*. For the second part, I sang a number of works by Shostakovich, including 'Pictures of the Past'. As I began 'Our Posterity', I could see that the audience was taut with the tension. Stalin's and Beriya's crimes were being exposed, the verses were hitting the bull's-eye:

> And I'm like an eagle-owl among the ruins
> Of broken gods.

Some of Russia's gods had been overthrown, but others had arrived in their place.

When I finished, the audience did not so much shout as roar. They demanded an encore, and we repeated the whole cycle for them, but they still refused to let us go; we performed the entire work yet another time.[76]

Despite the fact that a concert performance of the *Satires* had been sanctioned, Vishnevskaya and Rostropovich were unable to record the work for television because 'Our Posterity' was deemed ideologically unsuitable. Naturally the artists refused to perform the cycle without this song, as was suggested by the television producers.

Two symphonic premières

As far back as 1924, Shostakovich had announced that he wished to dedicate a symphonic work to the memory of Lenin. His most recent statement to this effect had been published in *Sovietskaya Kultura* in June 1959. The following year he was at work on a programme symphony in four movements. The first was to be a musical narrative of Lenin's arrival in Russia in April 1917; the second was dedicated to the events of October 1917; the third to the civil war; and the Finale was to depict the triumph of the Great October Revolution. Sofiya Khentova[77] speaks of the existence of the 1960 sketches of the symphony in the family archive. Surprisingly, amongst them appears a substantial chunk with a parodying waltz based on material from the fourth song, 'Misunderstanding', of the vocal cycle *Satires*. The waltz motif coincides with the song's text, 'he did not understand the new poetry'. It is an intriguing thought that Shostakovich might have intended to include this material as hidden satire in the symphony.

By the autumn of 1960, Shostakovich had changed his original conception of the work, and reduced the programme to represent the events of 1917, rather than a portrayal of Lenin. In Soviet musicological circles, it is believed that he substantially changed the musical material as well. Certainly it was unusual

76 Vishnevskaya, *A Russian Story*, pp. 267–70.
77 Khentova, *Shostakovich*, vol. II, p. 363.

for Shostakovich to make full sketches or write more than one variant of any major work, the exception being his controversial Ninth Symphony, where he changed his initial concept of the piece as time progressed.

The Twelfth Symphony, subtitled 'The Year 1917', was finally completed on 12 August 1961 as an offering for the forthcoming 22nd Party Congress, and just before Shostakovich's second application to join the Communist Party on 29 August. He was confirmed as a full member at a special meeting convoked at the Union of Composers on 14 September.

After its first performances[78] the Symphony met with a cool response from musicians and the general public. Many felt that the quality of the music did not match his preceding symphonic works. The enlightened Soviet listener, always with a sharp ear for the 'sub-text', could identify with the sombre music of the Eleventh Symphony, hearing in it not only the crushing of the recent Hungarian Revolt, but all the atrocities committed in the name of Revolution in their own country. The Twelfth Symphony seemed to speak at face value, without lending itself to a secondary level of meaning.

In Volkov's *Testimony* the following statement is attributed to Shostakovich: 'I began with one creative goal and ended with a completely different scheme I wasn't able to realize my ideas – the material put up resistance. You see how hard it is to draw the image of leaders and teachers with music.'[79]

Maxim Shostakovich[80] has spoken of the universal rather than the specific nature of the music's message, where the violence, the struggling crowds and chaos of revolution can be seen as a constant feature of world history. The composer's widow, Irina Shostakovich[81] puts forward the view that the composer wished to describe a vision of the ideal ruler inspired by Pushkin's verses addressed to Nicholas I ('In Hope of All the Good and Glory' [1826]). In this case, the triumphant major apotheosis of the Finale can perhaps be interpreted as the victory of a much hoped for utopia.

With complete disregard for any of these arguments, the officials pronounced the Symphony a triumph for socialist realism.

Lev Lebedinsky has asserted that Shostakovich had originally wished to compose a symphony parodying, rather than glorifying Lenin. For this reason, then, the composer had to re-write the work at short notice, as he feared that the subversive nature of the music was dangerously transparent. As of today there exists little evidence to support this claim, but there are also no grounds to refute it. Here is Lev Lebedinsky's account of the matter:

78 The première was given in Leningrad on 1 October 1961 under Mravinsky, and three performances were given on 14, 15 and 16 October in Moscow under Konstantin Ivanov.
79 Volkov, *Testimony*, p. 107.
80 In private interview with EW.
81 In private interview with EW.

In 1961 Shostakovich made another attempt to express his true attitude to what was going on in his country. He decided that his Twelfth Symphony was to be a satire of Lenin. When he told me this I tried to talk him out of it. It was too dangerous and nobody would understand anyway. He brushed off my advice with, 'He who has ears will hear' (a favourite Shostakovich expression). Then he went to Leningrad to attend the first performance. One evening he rang me up in a panic. 'Lev Nikolayevich, tomorrow my symphony will be played for the first time. Can you come up to Leningrad?'

'What, right now?' I asked.

'Yes, please come.'

I immediately went to the station, and tipped the guard so as to get on the night train. I arrived early in the morning. He was waiting for me at his hotel. He was as pale as death. He looked awful. In the lobby he said to me, 'I've written a terrible symphony. It's a failure. But I managed to change it.'

'Change what?'

'The whole symphony. But we can't talk any more. My room is full of journalists and all sorts of strange people.'

When we entered his room, I had a feeling that we had stumbled into a lunatic asylum. There were representatives of hundreds of organizations there. They put some questions to him and he answered somehow. The conversation was being recorded, and the cameras were whirring, filming this historic occasion for the cinema news. After all, Shostakovich had written a symphony about Lenin! Finally, the ordeal was over and everybody left.

Shostakovich then explained: 'I wrote the symphony, and then I realized that you had been right. They'd crucify me for it because my conception was an obvious caricature of Lenin. Therefore I sat down and wrote another one in three or four days. And it's terrible!' With his insane technique he could do anything. He could have written an opera in three days.

We went to the rehearsal. He pleaded, 'Sit next to me, don't leave me on my own now.' They started playing. The music was frightening in its helplessness. I experienced some terrible moments, and I thought I was about to go mad. Shostakovich was holding my hand, and he kept asking, 'Is it really awful?'

I knew that if I said it was awful he would go mad too. I restrained myself and said, 'No, it's perfectly all right.'

'What do you mean, all right? It's terrible.'

'Stop it,' I said, 'don't be so nervous. It's perfectly passable.'

My only thought was to prevent him from losing his reason.

'No one must know what I told you about this symphony's history,' he said.

'God forbid!' I reassured him.

Afterwards people like Isaak Glikman and others accused me of having forced Shostakovich to write about Lenin. They also implied that I made him join the Party – as if my suggesting a symphony about Lenin wasn't enough! I never condemned the Symphony because I could not betray a friend, even when he was wrong. I invented various phrases in praise of the Symphony, and Glikman looked at me with disgust. I understood how he felt. I believe that part of the original manuscript was destroyed, while Shostakovich kept the rest, intending to re-use the material in the future. His widow, Irina Antonovna, must have what remains of the original score.[82]

Only a few months after the Twelfth Symphony was first performed Muscovites were able to hear the long-delayed première of the Fourth Symphony, given under Kondrashin on 30 December 1961. Many of the composer's friends assumed that Shostakovich had bargained the right to resuscitate his favourite 'lost child' by producing the Twelfth Symphony as a placatory offering to the authorities. Here KIRILL KONDRASHIN recounts how he came to conduct the first performance of Shostakovich's Fourth Symphony:

In 1961 the artistic director of the Moscow Philharmonic, M. Grinberg, a very intelligent man, advised me to have a look at Shostakovich's Fourth Symphony, which was written in 1936 and had still never been performed.

The performance of the Fourth Symphony had been cancelled in the wake of the attacks on Shostakovich's opera, Lady Macbeth. During the war, the score had been lost. In Leningrad just about everything got burnt for heating during the gruelling winters of the siege. It was only later that one of Shostakovich's close friends, Levon Atovmyan, found the surviving orchestral parts of the Symphony in Leningrad. Using them as his basis, he was able to reconstruct the score. He also made a reduction of the Symphony for two pianos, and it was this version that I first saw. It was very carelessly done, with few dynamic markings

82 Lev Lebedinsky: recorded interview with EW.

and tempo instructions. Nevertheless, it was immediately clear to me that this was an outstanding work.

I told Grinberg that I would be delighted to perform the Symphony. Shostakovich didn't know about our plan at the time, as Grinberg had decided to tell him only when he was certain that I would agree to the performance.

I went to see Shostakovich. He said, 'Here on the piano is the version of the score that you have seen. As the full score was lost I've forgotten much of it. I need to look at it again to see whether the Symphony is worth performing, and whether it requires any changes.'

The next day he rang me. 'Kirill Petrovich, I'd be very happy for you to perform the Symphony. No changes need to be made. The piece is very dear to me as it is.'

Soon after that, the Fourth Symphony received its first performance.[83]

The following is an extract from FLORA LITVINOVA's diary:

31 December 1961. Yesterday we went to hear the Fourth Symphony, we had been invited by Dmitri Dmitriyevich. It was the first time we heard it, and it made a shattering impression on us. Why do Dmitri Dmitriyevich's later works lack those qualities of impetuosity, dynamic drive, contrasts of rhythm and colour, tenderness and spikiness? One involuntarily thinks what a different path he would have taken, how different his life would have been, if it were not for the 'historic' Decree which warped the living spirit in him.

Now the Symphony enjoyed an enormous success. Dmitri Dmitriyevich said that he had not corrected one note in it. Its exceptional maturity and finished perfection shone through from the first to the last note. *Lady Macbeth* and the Fourth Symphony surely marked the apogee of Shostakovich's creative career.'[84]

83 Kirill Kondrashin: recorded reminiscences.
84 Article commissioned for this book.

CHAPTER SEVEN

Regeneration

Revival and renewal

The year 1962 was a year of particular importance in Shostakovich's life, bringing him private happiness and creative success. Early in the year he met Irina Supinskaya, a young literary editor, whom he married in November. She brought to his life the freshness and energy of youth, and stability and order to his home. As his health deteriorated, she was to look after him with tactful care and devotion.

In the spring, Shostakovich completed a cantata on Evtushenko's poem 'Babi Yar'. He shortly went on to extend it into a five-movement symphony, his Thirteenth, scored for bass soloist, bass chorus and full symphony orchestra. Shostakovich's departure from the purely instrumental symphonic form (albeit his last two symphonies were tied to programmes) fulfilled a need for dramatic expression that had been stifled in the wake of the criticisms of *Lady Macbeth* in 1936. For Shostakovich, the choice of Evtushenko's poems seemed most auspicious. The poet belonged to a generation young enough to be unintimidated by the years of terror. Shostakovich saw these poems as an expression of 'the problems of civic responsibility'. Hence, in this symphony he was able to openly demonstrate his concern for the horrors and injustices of recent Soviet history.

Soon Shostakovich found himself embroiled in a political controversy on account of the texts. For him this was a further corroboration of the fact that the explicit nature of words always spelt trouble. The Party aired its 'opinion' on the ideological faults of 'Babi Yar'. This had the desired effect of frightening off performers of the Thirteenth Symphony, and indeed of making Evtushenko revise the poem. However, even if the 'Thaw' was drawing to a close, the freedom tasted in the last few years had also given artists a new courage. In the conductor Kirill Kondrashin Shostakovich found an artist absolutely committed to his work. The authorities were unable to stop the première of the Thirteenth Symphony, which went ahead to wild public acclaim on 18 December 1962.

Only days after this concert, the première of *Katerina Izmailova* (the revised version of the opera *Lady Macbeth*) took place at the Stanislavsky and

Nemirovich–Danchenko Theatre in Moscow. The rehabilitation of this work was of great symbolic importance to Shostakovich.

Although the Stanislavsky Theatre's production of *Katerina Izmailova* had been sanctioned by the Minister of Culture, Ekaterina Furtseva, she had not reckoned with Khrushchev's recent outbursts against the intellectual community and the furore surrounding the Thirteenth Symphony. It was decided to test the reactions of the officials responsible for culture at a closed performance of the opera on 26 December. For the sake of caution it was camouflaged by being billed as *The Barber of Seville*!

Two weeks later, under its own title, *Katerina Izmailova* opened officially to a triumphant reception. The opera regained its former status and popularity, and was soon staged in new productions in Western and Eastern Europe, as well as in other Soviet cities. Shostakovich, anxious for the opera's smooth rebirth, decided to devote much of his time and attention to supervising the forthcoming productions. Not only did he attend all the rehearsals at the Stanislavsky Theatre from October 1962, but in 1963 he took an active part in the rehearsals for two new productions in London and Riga. In November he spent the best part of a month at Covent Garden, interrupting his visit there to attend the dress rehearsal in Riga, and returning for the London première on 2 December. Similarly he attended rehearsals and performances in Zagreb (January 1964), Vienna (February 1965), Kazan (February 1965), Kiev (March and April 1965) and Leningrad (April 1965).

The composer felt that his presence was essential to the opera's new life; for instance, he stated that he had in some measure been able to tone down exaggerations in the London and Zagreb productions, where undue emphasis had been given to the erotic element. In Vienna he insisted that some proposed cuts be restored, while he categorically forbade La Scala to use the first variant of *Lady Macbeth*. He singled out the Kiev production both for the excellence of the musical side and for its superb production. Therefore the conductor Konstantin Simeonov and the Kiev cast were entrusted with the sound recording of Mikhail Shapiro's 1966 film of the opera, where the 'outsider', Galina Vishnevskaya both sang and acted the title role.

Shostakovich was now accepted unquestionably in his own country as the leading voice in music, and his fame was celebrated no less abroad. The first large retrospective of Shostakovich's works was programmed at the Edinburgh Festival in August 1962, and in February 1964, the city of Gorky devoted its festival exclusively to his music. This was followed by other 'Shostakovich' festivals in Volgograd and Leningrad in 1966.

Shostakovich also continued to be busy with his civic duties, both at the Union of Composers, and as a deputy to the Supreme Soviet, in which capacity he was elected to represent his native city of Leningrad in 1962. Also in that year Shostakovich returned to teaching at the Leningrad Conservatoire, when he agreed to take on a select class of post-graduate composition students, amongst whom was his favourite pupil, Boris Tishchenko.

Marriage to Irina Supinskaya

In 1961 the Union of Composers were allocated a new multi-storey block on Nezhdanova Street in the heart of old Moscow. The Union moved its offices from Miusskaya Street there, and allocated the flats in the building to its members and musicians from the Conservatoire. Thanks to the efforts of his secretary, Zinaida Gamayova, Shostakovich was given a five-room flat in the building. With both his children married (and still living at home) and grandchildren appearing, the composer had felt restricted in his old flat on Kutuzovsky Prospect.

In the same year he bought a dacha in Zhukovka, an exclusive settlement to the south-west of Moscow given over principally for the use of academicians. Here, in contrast to the Bolshevo dacha, the facilities included running water and central heating, so that the house could be inhabited in winter as well as summer.

Early in 1962, Shostakovich met Irina Supinskaya. They were introduced by Lev Lebedinsky. Supinskaya worked as a literary editor in the publishing house Sovietsky Kompozitor, where, amongst other things, she helped prepare the published scores of *Moscow-Cheryomushki* and *Katerina Izmailova*. Irina hailed from Leningrad. She lost her parents at a very early age. Her father was a victim of the Stalinist purges, and her grandparents perished during the siege of Leningrad. As a seven-year-old child she was evacuated across Lake Lagoda to Kuibyshev. Brought up by an aunt, she studied at the Moscow Pedagogical Institute.

Shostakovich wrote to his old friend Shebalin: 'An event of great importance has happened in my life. My wife is called Irina Antonovna. She has one small defect: she's only twenty-seven years old. In every other respect she is sweet, clever, gay, simple and loveable. She wears glasses and can't pronounce her l's and r's.'[1]

In writing to Isaak Glikman, Shostakovich noted in his dry, sardonic manner that Irina's father had suffered from the 'Personality Cult and infringement of revolutionary law'. He went on to add that she had spent time in a 'dyet-dom' – a euphemism for the orphanages which housed children of the enemies of the people. 'A girl with a past,' he summed up.[2]

The couple spent part of the summer staying in the country at Solotcha near

---

1 Sofiya Khentova, *Shostakovich: Life and Work*, vol. II, p. 416.
2 Isaak Glikman, *Letters to a Friend*, p. 176.

Ryazan with Irina's aunt. It was here that Shostakovich orchestrated Mussorgsky's *Songs and Dances of Death*.

In the second half of August Shostakovich attended the Edinburgh Festival with his son Maxim; he was unable to take Irina because the Soviet authorities had not provided her with the necessary travel documents. In November that year, when Supinskaya's divorce from her first husband was granted, their marriage was formalized, and in future Shostakovich never travelled or appeared in public without his young wife.

Lebedinsky's relationship with Shostakovich deteriorated in the years after his marriage to Irina Supinskaya. Feeling that Shostakovich was now cut off from his old friends and increasingly surrounded by officials and sycophants, Lebedinsky stopped frequenting the household. The final impulse to terminate their relationship was ostensibly provoked by Lebedinsky's unwillingness to accept the bleak message of the Finale of the Fourteenth Symphony – 'Death is all-powerful.' Lebedinsky wrote Shostakovich an uncompromising letter, assuring him of his love, but declaring their friendship over. According to Irina Shostakovich, this letter provoked a laconic reaction from Shostakovich: 'Unfortunately Lebedinsky has grown old and stupid.'[3]

Here LEV LEBEDINSKY recalls how Shostakovich came to meet Irina Supinskaya:

Shostakovich's third marriage was no more considered than his second, although ultimately it worked out well for him. It was I who introduced Dmitri Dmitriyevich to Irina Supinskaya.

Our close friendship allowed us to speak to each other as man to man. Shostakovich used to complain: 'I've got no women. I'm afraid to approach them.' He didn't have much luck with women, or you could say more accurately that he had had a number of failures.

Once he said to me, 'You know that girl in glasses, I've taken a shine to her. I'd like to get to know her better, but I haven't been introduced.'

The girl in question worked as a literary editor under my charge at the publishing house. I promised to introduce her, but deliberately put off doing so. However, one night we were coming up the stairs at the Small Hall of the Conservatoire, and there she was talking to some other lady. As I greeted her, Shostakovich hovered at my side, whispering in my ear, 'Do introduce me.' How could I avoid it? Then he said, 'I'll give her my telephone number straight away.'

'Go ahead', I said, pleased that he was consulting me.

3 In private conversation with EW.

Soon afterwards they started meeting. I was very happy for him, although I assumed that this new relationship would only be short-lived. After all Irina was already married to an older man. But one day Shostakovich told me that he had proposed to her. He was lonely and needed a woman to help him in his life.

Their marriage served as a fragile shield behind which Shostakovich hoped to hide from the cruel world. Irina took it upon herself to establish a new order in the Shostakovich household. As their life became more bourgeois, their home became open to a different class of guest, which didn't exclude officials. For this reason our meetings became rarer, and eventually I decided to terminate our friendship, rather than give in to compromise.

However, when all is said and done, it was Irina who provided Shostakovich with stability and comfort, and who nursed him with devotion through his grave illness.[4]

GALINA VISHNEVSKAYA writes of the beneficial influence that Irina Supinskaya had on Shostakovich's life:

Shortly after his grandson was born, Dmitri Dmitriyevich came to our place looking very out of sorts. At dinner, everything became clear.

'Imagine, Galya!' Slava said to me. 'Dmitri Dmitriyevich tells me that he intends to get married.'

'But that's wonderful!'

'That's what I think. Dmitri Dmitriyevich is worried that she's too young.'

'Yes, Galya, it's an awkward situation. She's younger than my daughter,[5] and I'm embarrassed to tell the children. There's more than thirty years' difference between us. I suppose I'm too old for her.'

'Old? But look what a stallion you are! If I hadn't been married to Slava, I'd have grabbed you for a husband long ago. Old? But you're only fifty-six!'

He was delighted and showed it. 'Do you mean that – that I'm not old?'

'I swear it!'

'Let me bring her by and introduce her to you, then. Her name is Irina.'

---

4 Lev Lebedinsky: recorded interview with EW.
5 In fact she was born in 1934, and was two years older than Galina, DDS's daughter.

The very next day, Dmitri Dmitriyevich and Irina paid us a visit. It was the first time that they had appeared anywhere together. She was very young, modest, and sat all evening without raising her eyes. Seeing that we liked her and approved of his choice, Dmitri Dmitriyevich grew more and more relaxed and lighthearted. All at once, like a little boy, he shyly took her hand. Never had I known Shostakovich to act out of an inner impulse like that, and touch another person – man or woman. At most he would pat his grandsons on the head.

That petite woman with the quiet voice proved to be a vigorous mistress of the household, and quickly organized the life of that huge family. It was with her that Dmitri Dmitriyevich finally came to know domestic peace. He had just moved from Kutuzovsky Prospekt into our building, to the apartment next to ours – his bedroom shared a wall with our living room. His young wife got the new apartment into shape and rearranged things at the dacha in Zhukovka so that Dmitri Dmitriyevich would be spared the noisy goings-on of the young people and their growing families. Now he had his own bedroom and study on the second floor of the house. A devoted wife, she assumed all household concerns and created the ideal atmosphere for his work. Surely, she prolonged his life by several years.[6]

The Thirteenth Symphony

Two of the high points of the 'Thaw' had been the publication of Evtushenko's poem 'Babi Yar' in *Literaturnaya Gazeta* in September 1961, and that of Solzhenitsyn's novel *One Day in the Life of Ivan Denisovich* in *Novy Mir* in December 1962. The latter was only published after persistent pressure from the journal's editor, Alexander Tvardovsky, who persuaded Khrushchev himself to read the story. Khrushchev's approval secured the necessary authorization to publish from the Presidium of the Party. This was in itself an unprecedented step, but it did not betoken a new or consistent policy on literary freedom. Only a few months earlier, the KGB had confiscated all the manuscript copies of Vasili Grossman's great novel *Life and Fate*, which the author never saw again and assumed were lost for ever.

Khrushchev perhaps failed to foresee the enormous reaction provoked by the publication of such literature. When, in the wake of *Ivan Denisovich*, publishers were flooded with novels, short stories and memoirs dealing with the painful Stalinist years, the authorities took fright. In the backlash of

6 Galina Vishnevskaya, *Galina: A Russian Story*, pp. 273, 274.

pressure from the right wing of the Party, Khrushchev and his ideologues implemented measures to bring artists and writers into line with Party thinking, to correct his 'over-hasty' liberalization. Whereas Khruschev himself may have been initially sympathetic to the abolition of literary censorship, by early 1963 he had abandoned this position.

On 27 March 1962 Shostakovich completed his setting of Evtushenko's poem 'Babi Yar' to music; initially his concept was to write a one-movement cantata. By this time Evtushenko was already being subjected to a campaign of criticism. The poet was accused of belittling the role of the Russian people, who had taken the brunt of suffering during the war years, by writing of the exclusively Jewish victims of the 1941 Nazi massacre at Babi Yar, a ravine in the town of Kiev.

By the end of May Shostakovich had decided to extend 'Babi Yar' into a symphony, using other poems by Evtushenko. On 20 July he put the finishing touches to the score of his five movement Thirteenth Symphony while staying in hospital. That very day, on being discharged, he and Irina Supinskaya took the night train to Kiev to show the score to the bass, Boris Gmyirya, an artist whom Shostakovich particularly admired. From there he went to Leningrad to give the score to Mravinsky. By mid-August, Gmyirya, under pressure from the local Party Committee, wrote to Shostakovich to say that, in view of the dubious text, he refused to perform the work.[7] This rejection was followed by an even more galling humiliation: Mravinsky, the performer most closely connected with Shostakovich's works, declined to perform the Thirteenth Symphony. Undoubtedly he too was unnerved by the 'risky' nature of the poems, although ostensibly he excused himself for other reasons.

It was at this point that Shostakovich turned to Kirill Kondrashin, who readily agreed to perform the Symphony.

On 1 December 1962 the Party leader, Nikita Khrushchev, attended an exhibition entitled Thirty Years of Moscow Art at the Manège. When confronted with works by such avant-garde artists as Ernst Neizvestny and Boris Zhutovsky, Khrushchev, a complete philistine in matters of art, who was advised by philistines, broke into a spontaneous tirade against these 'abstractionists and pederasts'. Although people wondered whether he understood the meaning of either term, there could be no doubt that the leader's attention was now focused on the unruly intellectual community.

On 17 December writers and artists were called to a Kremlin reception. Here

---

7 Gmyirya had lived in occupied territory during the Second World War, and had been forced to collaborate with the Germans. This fact made him vulnerable to pressure from the authorities, and therefore he gave in quickly to their demand that he should refuse to participate in the performance of the Thirteenth Symphony. As Gmyrya was quite open with Shostakovich on this account, the composer was able to accept his withdrawal, whereas he regarded Mravinsky's refusal as tantamount to betrayal.

Khrushchev and his spokesman on ideological matters, Leonid Ilyichyov, issued severe warnings against 'contamination' by Western bourgeois influences. Artists were urged to adhere strictly to the precepts of socialist realism and to leave the task of exposing the 'cult of personality' to the Party.

On that evening artists and sculptors were at the forefront of the attack. Pointing at a sculpture by Ernst Neizvestny, Khrushchev ranted:

> Is this sculpture? I already asked them if they weren't pederasts? But one is a pederast at ten years of age, and how old are you? [The leader had evidently muddled pederasts with masturbators.] . . . And Shostakovich – his music's nothing but jazz – it gives you belly ache. And I'm to clap my hands. But with jazz – you get colic. Maybe I'm a man of the old regime, but I like Oistrakh. We stand for old times so we don't give in to decadence. What are we to do with Neizvestny and Zhutovsky? If they don't understand, let them leave the country.[8]

Ilyichyov gave Evtushenko a similar dressing-down for writing 'Babi Yar' – it was the Party who should fight anti-semitism: 'Is this a time to raise such a theme? What's the matter with you? And then it gets set to music. Babi Yar wasn't just Jews but Slavs.'

At this point the poet defended an artist's right to speak the truth: 'It cannot be that the government should decide for us. And abstractionism, like realism, can be good or bad art. Who would deny that there are examples of great art amongst the abstractionists . . . Can we exclude Picasso. . . ?'

Khrushchev expressed his reaction to these arguments by quoting a Russian proverb: 'The grave cures the hunchback.'

Evtushenko had the courage to retort, 'I think that nowadays it's no longer the grave, but life.'[9]

These arguments may have seemed primitive and banal, but they had a direct relevance to the première of the Thirteenth Symphony the very next day. Despite eleventh-hour attempts to prevent the concert, the performance went ahead and the Symphony was acclaimed by an ecstatic audience. Mariya Yudina represented the view of the liberal intelligentsia when she wrote to Pierre Souvchinsky that 'Shostakovich has become "one of us" again with his Thirteenth.'

On the other hand the symphony was publicly met by complete critical silence, and further performances were actively discouraged.

KIRILL KONDRASHIN recounts the difficulties in getting the Thirteenth Symphony its first public performance:

8 Boris Zhutovsky, 'Returning to My Notes of 1962/63', *Literaturnaya Gazeta*, 5 July 1989.
9 *Ibid.*

In the autumn of 1962 Shostakovich rang me and said, 'Kirill Petrovich, I've written a new symphony. I'm going to play it through for a few people; you'd be welcome to come too.'

Naturally, I went along. Khachaturian was there, Weinberg and Yuri Levitin, all composers and Shostakovich's friends. Shostakovich told us that the symphony was not composed in traditional form; it used a bass soloist and chorus as well as orchestra. It was a setting of five poems by Evtushenko published over the years. Before he started playing, Shostakovich read us the poems. As he played and sang through the symphony, we followed the score.

The first movement, 'Babi Yar', is a requiem for the Jews shot in Kiev in the autumn of 1941 at the very beginning of the war. Then comes 'Humour', followed by 'In the Shop', which tells of Russian women, heroines in their own way, who waste their lives queuing for food. The next poem, 'Fears', evokes the Stalinist era when everybody lived in terror of the NKVD and possible arrest. The last poem, 'Career', affirms that careers are made not by those who keep silent, but by those who raise their voices and sacrifice themselves, thereby becoming immortal.

The poem that provoked most conflict was, of course, the poem about the Jews. Although officially unacknowledged, anti-semitism had existed in Russia since the war. Shostakovich was much preoccupied by this problem. He was not a Jew, but he sympathized with the Jewish people, as is testified firstly by the many Jewish themes to be found in his music, and secondly, by the fact that he twice raised the Jewish theme specifically in his works. I am referring firstly to *From Jewish Poetry*, the song cycle written in 1948, during a period of great anti-semitism. And secondly to 'Babi Yar', the first movement of the Thirteenth Symphony. Evtushenko's poem had recently been published in the *Literaturnaya Gazeta* and at once acquired great popularity.

The Symphony had a very disturbing effect on me. On that occasion there was no mention of performance. But, two days later, Shostakovich rang me and said, 'Kirill Petrovich, if you liked my Symphony and are agreeable, I would like you to conduct the first performance.'

Of course I was greatly honoured by this request, and immediately agreed. Usually all of Shostakovich's symphonic works were first performed by his friend, the conductor Evgeny Mravinsky, and the Leningrad Philharmonic Orchestra. I was surprised that things were different this time.

Later I discovered that Shostakovich had indeed showed the score to Mravinsky, who had refused to play it under some ludicrous pretext. The real reason was that at the time the press was full of criticism for Evtushenko's poem. They said that Evtushenko had distorted the historical truth, ascribing to the Jews alone the right to be victims of the war, whereas in fact at Babi Yar people of all races had been slaughtered, including Ukrainians and Russians. This was a lie; according to survivers, there were only Jews. There was a lot of heated discussion among the intellectuals. But it was clear that this was just an extension of an anti-semitic campaign. The official line proclaimed that it was incorrect to give such emphasis to the Jewish question.

Evidently, Mravinsky had been advised from above not to perform the symphony, and he withdrew like a coward. Shostakovich was very hurt.

Shostakovich invited me to discuss the details of the performance, including the choice of soloist.[10] I suggested a young singer from the Bolshoi Theatre, Victor Nechipailo. Dmitri Dmitriyevich said that he didn't know him, but if I recommended him, he had nothing against my choice. Grinberg advised me to get another singer to learn the part, 'just in case'. He suggested a young singer, Vitali Gromadsky, who was employed as a soloist of the Philharmonia. In two or three weeks' time, after I had started working with the singers, Shostakovich said he wanted to hear them. The three of us and a pianist went to see Dmitri Dmitriyevich. He was quite satisfied with their interpretations and had no complaints. He was usually very tactful and sparing with his criticism. This was because he was always so grateful to people for playing his music, and he trusted a good musician's intuition.

A little incident occurred on that occasion. Gromadsky, who was a kind but not over-intelligent young man, must have been reading all the criticism of 'Babi Yar' in the press. He suddenly piped up, 'Dmitri Dmitriyevich, why did you choose this poem when there is no anti-semitism in the Soviet Union? Why write about it in your symphony?'

Shostakovich was terribly upset. Gromadsky had touched a sore spot. He was almost shouting when he replied, 'No, there is, there is

---

10 Galina Vishnevskaya recounts how at Shostakovich's request she approached the Bolshoi Theatre bass, Alexander Vedernikov. Initially delighted to be asked, he quickly withdrew on realizing the risky nature of the texts. Only after this episode was Nechipailo invited to sing the solo part (*A Russian Story*, pp. 275–77).

anti-semitism in the Soviet Union. It is an outrageous thing, and we must fight it. We must shout about it from the roof-tops.' His words stuck in my memory and they explain a lot in his work.

We started work on the Symphony. As usual we started with orchestral rehearsals, without the choir and soloist. Shostakovich was always in attendance. It is unnecessary to make any corrections to Shostakovich's scores. Only minor dynamic alterations are sometimes needed, and they happen of their own accord. Dmitri Dmitriyevich never interfered with my work. He always held in his hands a box of Russian cigarettes ('papirosi'),[11] on which he noted down whatever he wanted to tell me afterwards. With great pride I remember him saying to me, 'Kirill Petrovich, you're a hard man to work with. Just as I write down some point, you're already making it to the musicians!'

Occasionally I would stop the orchestra and address Shostakovich from the stage, 'Dmitri Dmitriyevich, have you got anything to say?'

He usually replied, 'Nothing, nothing, everything's fine.'

Only once did he make a remark, 'Kirill Petrovich, in the last movement the second violins have an A flat to B flat modulation. It's very beautiful. Could you bring it out a bit more please?' It was the only correction he ever made.

Meanwhile news reached me that, in high Party circles and in the Ministry of Culture, various functionaries were alarmed by the rumour that Shostakovich had written a symphony about Jews. They were all waiting for the first performance, scheduled for 18 December 1962. I made sure that both singers rehearsed with the orchestra so that we would be ready for every eventuality.

On the previous day, Khrushchev had given a reception for the Moscow intellectuals, where, in his unbridled way, he applied ideological pressure on the artistic community. The reception signified the end of the 'Thaw'. Shostakovich, with his bad luck, was always the first victim of such changes, as happened in 1936, in 1948 and now again in 1962.

Shortly before writing this symphony, which provoked so much talk about 'ideological errors', Shostakovich had joined the Communist Party. I know that the district Party secretary was heard to complain later on, 'This is outrageous, we let Shostakovich join the Party, and then he goes and presents us with a symphony about Jews.'

11 Russian cigarettes with a hollow cardboard filter.

Since the theme of the Thirteenth Symphony was fraught with conflict, an order had been issued from the top to prevent the performance on the very eve of the première. But the authorities were afraid actually to ban the Symphony. The following day, at ten o'clock in the morning, we were supposed to start the dress rehearsal. The atmosphere was very tense and Shostakovich was extremely nervous. In the last few days some strange faces had appeared in the hall, but nobody paid too much attention, because many musicians and interested people liked attending these rehearsals.

The singer at the concert was to be Nechipailo. At about quarter to ten he rang up to say that he was ill and could not sing. I believe that this was the result of pressure put on him.[12] We started looking for Gromadsky, who lived quite far from the city centre and had no telephone. As he was not scheduled to sing that night, there was no knowing whether he even intended to come to the concert, let alone the dress rehearsal.

But after about twenty minutes Gromadsky appeared. Fortunately, he had decided to come and listen to the final rehearsal. We told him that he was now to rehearse immediately and to perform that night. In former years, he had been a sailor and was a brave man. So he came out on stage and we started to rehearse. He made some mistakes, because, naturally, he was not as well prepared as our main soloist. After we had played through the first movement, the orchestral manager appeared on the stage, saying, 'Kirill Petrovich, you are wanted on the telephone.'

I interrupted the rehearsal and proceeded to the artists' room where the telephone was. It was Georgi Popov, the Minister of Culture of the Russian Republic.

'Kirill Petrovich, how is your health?'

This apparent polite concern for my health was nothing more than the usual trick of our bureaucrats. First they enquire about something totally irrelevant – your health or the weather.

'Very well,' I said.

Then a menacing note was introduced.

'Is there anything that might prevent you conducting tonight?'

12 In her account of the same events, Galina Vishnevskaya absolves Nechipailo from blame. He had been ordered at the last minute to sing that night at the Bolshoi Theatre to replace the scheduled singer, who had been 'taken ill', no doubt following Party instructions (*A Russian Story*, p. 278).

20   DDS with Isaak Glikman

21   From a performance of *From Jewish Folk Poetry* in mid-1950s. Nina Dorliak, soprano, in the white dress; Alec Maslennikov, tenor; mezzo soprano unidentified

22 With Oleg Prokofiev at the unveiling of the plaque in memory of his father, 11 February 1958. See Oleg's own commentary to this picture in main text

24 Lev Lebedinsky, 1950s.

23 DDS with Evgeny Mravinsky, 1961

25   DDS with Marina Sabinina, assembled musicologists and army members,
early 1960s

26   At a Kremlin reception given by Khrushchev in honour of the Composers
Union Congress, 1962. Khrushchev is talking to Tikhon Khrennikov, between
them, Yuri Shaporin. Kabalevsky stands middle right, tall, in glasses; to his right,
Vasili Solovyov-Sedoy. To the right of DDS, Mikhail Chulaki.

27 Première of Thirteenth Symphony with Evgeny Evtushenko and Kirill Kondrashin, 1962

28 DDS with Sviatoslav Richter and Mstislav Rostropovich, mid-1960s

29   Première of Fourteenth Symphony, DDS with Galina Vishnevskaya, Mark
Reshetin, Rudolph Barshai and members of the Moscow Chamber Orchestra,
1968

30   With David Oistrakh, before the première of the Fifteenth Symphony

31   *Left*, DDS speaking at Composers' Union Congress, Tikhon. Khrennikov
seated, late 1960s.   32   Mstislav Rostropovich, Kurgan, 1970

33   DDS with Mikhail Waiman, Irina Shostakovich and Venyamin Basner,
early 1970s

34   *Left*, DDS at a rehearsal of the Fifteenth Quartet, with Irina Shostakovich and Vladimir Ovcharek, 1974.   35   With Benjamin Britten, April 1971

36   With his son Maxim, *c.* 1974

37 With Evgeny Shenderovich and Evgeny
Nesterenko, December 1974

38 Vissarion Shebalin

39 Isaak Schwartz

40 Fyodor Druzhinin

'No, I'm in splendid form.'

Although I realized at once what he was driving at, I carried on as if I hadn't a clue about anything. A silence followed.

Then he said, 'Do you have any political doubts in relation to "Babi Yar"?'

I answered, 'No, I don't have any. I think that it's very timely and very relevant.'

Silence again. Then he said, 'Tell me your expert opinion, can the Symphony be performed without the first movement?'

I said, 'That is completely out of the question. First of all it would distort the form of the Symphony; and secondly everyone knows already that the first movement is a setting of 'Babi Yar'. If we miss it out, it will cause a most undesirable reaction.'

Silence again.

Then he said, 'Well, do as you see fit.'

After this telephone call I resumed the rehearsal without mentioning the conversation to Shostakovich. The evening's performance was a triumph, and almost caused a political demonstration. At the end of the first movement the audience started to applaud and shout hysterically. The atmosphere was tense enough as it was, and I waved at them to calm down. We started playing the second movement at once, so as not to put Shostakovich into an awkward position.

We gave two performances. Then it was announced that a third performance was to take place on 15 January 1963. Until now, Evtushenko had been all over Shostakovich and me. But around the New Year, Evtushenko, as keen on publicity as ever, decided to publish a second version of 'Babi Yar' in the *Literaturnaya Gazeta*. You could hardly call this second version poetry — just a combination of rhymes. The poem was now nearly twice as long because he had inserted lines about the role of the Russian people and the Party. He made sure that it was seen that he had taken the authorities' criticism to heart.

Shostakovich then asked me to come and see him. He was very confused. He said something along these lines: 'That wasn't a nice thing to do on Evtushenko's part. The poem now belongs to us both, I've become a kind of co-author. He could at least have notified me that he was going to make these changes. What am I to do about it? If I set the new version to music, I will have to change the whole Symphony. Obviously, I can't do that. But, they have let it be known that performances of the Symphony in its present state will not be permitted. Evtushenko has responded to criticism, while I haven't.'

After some soul-searching, Shostakovich decided not to change the music; he just changed a few lines of the text. But the Symphony then suffered an organized campaign of silence – a positively deafening silence. After the initial two performances it was suppressed for five years.[13] Of course, no official ban was published; they simply said, 'We don't recommend that this work should be performed.'

They left the final decisions with you, but God help you if you decided against their recommendations. You were then dealt with like a naughty Party member.[14]

The Siberian poet, Evgeny Evtushenko, made his name with the publication of his lyric poems in the mid 1950s. He went on to tackle controversial social themes in his verse, and to win enormous popularity through his rhetorical poetry recitations (indeed, in the Soviet Union he has performed in packed-out football stadiums).

Initially much admired for his courageous outspokenness, Evtushenko came to be identified more and more with the official line. He was accused of compromising his integrity, when, after creating a remarkable poem, such as 'Babi Yar', he would curry official favour by writing on strictly 'authorized' topics.

His association with Shostakovich continued after the Thirteenth Symphony when the composer set his poem 'The Execution of Stepan Razin' to music in 1965.

Here EVGENY EVTUSHENKO recalls his meetings with Shostakovich in connection with the Thirteenth Symphony:

From childhood the name of Dmitri Dmitriyevich Shostakovich meant something eternal to me, and I never thought that I would meet him in the flesh. However we did meet. In 1962 I had been in Kiev. A university friend of mine took me to see a place called Babi Yar. I had read something about it – there was a poem by Ilya Ehrenburg and another one by Lev Ozerov with the following memorable lines:

13 Kondrashin slightly exaggerates. In fact there were two performances of the Thirteenth Symphony with the revised text in Moscow in February 1963. Vitali Katayev performed the Symphony in Minsk with the old text shortly afterwards. Further performances took place outside Moscow in Gorky in December 1965, and in Novosibirsk and Leningrad during 1966.
14 Kirill Kondrashin, Reminiscences of DDS.

> I have come to you, Babi Yar,
> Sorrow's age can't be told.
> I must be unthinkably old –
> You'd lose count, even if counting by the century.

But the true story of what had happened at Babi Yar was not widely known. My friend led me up and down those ravines, hills and gullies, where at the time you could still come across a human bone. He told me the terrible story of how the Nazis had brought here tens of thousands of Jews, Ukrainians and Russians, and murdered them without pity.[15] At once I had a feeling of historical injustice. There was no monument. The next day, at my hotel, on odd scraps of paper, I wrote a poem, 'Babi Yar'. The first line reflected my refusal to accept the injustice of history, the absence of a monument to so many innocent slaughtered people.

> There are no monuments over Babi Yar,
> The steep precipice, like a rough-hewn tomb,

The publication of 'Babi Yar' provoked extremely stormy reactions, much greater than I had expected. I received an avalanche of telegrams and letters from all over the country. People came to see me to express their feelings, and they sent me flowers. On the other hand the newspaper *Literaturnaya Rossiya* published an immediate reply to me by the poet Alexei Markov.

> What kind of a true Russian are you
> When you forget your own people?
> Your soul is as narrow as your trousers,
> As empty as a flight of stairs.

Literaturnaya Rossiya also published articles attacking me, among other things for having forgotten the heroic struggle of the Russian people in the Great Patriotic War, obscuring it with the depiction of the mass execution of innocent but passive victims of 'Babi Yar'. To tell the truth, these articles had a certain nationalistic and even chauvinistic flavour to them. What hurt most was that my opponents, in criticizing me, claimed the support of people like Sholokhov and Ehrenburg.

15 Here, as in the revised version of 'Babi Yar', Evtushenko talks of the massacre of three national groups, and not exclusively of the Jews, as in his first version of the poem.

When I came back to Moscow, one day the telephone rang in my mother's apartment where I was staying at the time. Neither the neighbours nor my mother ever used my patronymic when addressing me; they always called me Zhenya. The voice on the phone asked for Evgeny Alexandrovich. My mother replied that it must be the wrong number, because there was no Evgeny Alexandrovich here. She didn't realize that I was being called.

The telephone rang again.

'I would like to speak to Evgeny Alexandrovich Yevtushenko. This is Shostakovich speaking.'

At last my mother realized that Evgeny Alexandrovich was her son Zhenya. I heard his amazing, inimitable voice. It was slightly hoarse, stuttering, vibrating and jerky.

'Evgeny Alexandrovich. Shostakovich here. I've read your poem, 'Babi Yar' in the *Literaturnaya Gazeta*. It's a remarkable poem. Will you allow me to set it to music?'

I was in seventh heaven. Not only because such a request from Shostakovich was the most remarkable token of support at a difficult moment when I was being attacked from every side; I would still have been delighted if somebody just praised the poem. But Shostakovich himself was asking my permission to set my poem to music!

I replied hurriedly, fearing that he might change his mind. 'Of course, please do.'

He said briskly and matter-of-factly: 'Splendid. Thank God, you don't mind. The music is ready. Can you come here right away?'

I went to his apartment where for the first time I heard his setting of my poem 'Babi Yar'. It was not a symphony yet. What a shame that his performance then was not recorded. It was quite extraordinary. He sang in his hoarse voice. When he came to the line, 'It seems to me that I am Anna Frank,' he wept. The music there changed from an epic requiem to a spring-like lyricism. I was overwhelmed. I'm no expert in music. Some of my poems had been set before, but the music hardly ever coincided with the melody I had heard in my inner ear when writing the poetry. I hope it doesn't sound like conceit, but if I were able to write music I would have written exactly the way Shostakovich did. By some magic telepathic insight he seems to have pulled the melody out of me and recorded it in musical notation. That was my feeling. He amazed me with his profound rendering of the poem. His music made the poem greater, more meaningful and powerful. In a word, it became a much better poem.

I gave Shostakovich my book *The Wave of a Hand*, which had just come out. We talked for a long time, not about literature or music, but about history, those past times which had caused him so much suffering. They had also affected my childish soul, because I had lost both my grandfathers, and witnessed how unjustly people were treated, and how sometimes they disappeared.

We discussed all this. I don't remember him asking me to write something specific, but as a result of our conversation, I wrote the poem 'Fears'. I gave it to him.

After a while he phoned me. 'Evgeny Alexandrovich, you know I've concocted something really big here. Would you like to come and hear it?'

Then I heard the whole of the Thirteenth Symphony uniquely performed by the composer. I was stunned, and first and foremost by his choice of such apparently disparate poems. It had never occurred to me that they could be united like that. In my book I didn't put them next to each other. But here the jolly, youthful, anti-bureaucratic 'Career' and the poem 'Humour', full of jaunty lines, were linked with the melancholy and graphic poem about tired Russian women queue-ing in a shop. Then came 'Fears Are Dying in Russia'. Shostakovich interpreted it in his own way, giving it a depth and insight that the poem lacked before. I still regret that in the text he used some of the lines aren't very good, a result of my haste. In that sense I let Shostakovich down. I hope one day to fulfil my duty to his memory and to revise the poem.

In connecting all these poems like that, Shostakovich completely changed me as a poet. I would never have written 'Bratskaya GESS', my most important long poem, with all its varied composition, unexpected changes of rhythm, bold transitions from, say, Stepan Razin to girl Nyushka, from a rhythm of slaves to my purely personal story. I would not have had the nerve to attempt such a composition had not Shostakovich united my disparate poems in the Thirteenth Symphony.

In a sense, it is a unique symphony, making the audience cry in 'Babi Yar' and laugh in 'Career' when the soloist sings:

> The Artist, a contemporary of Galileo
> Was no more stupid than the latter –

> He knew the Earth revolved,
> But he had a family –

It was to me a great school of composition because Shostakovich proved that there are no elements in art that cannot be put together. One must be brave and try to unite what seems to be incompatible.

We became friends and I came to see him often. He was the first to hear many of my poems. We argued sometimes about history and about himself. He took me to the first performance after all those years of *Katerina Izmailova*. After that I wrote a poem which had the following lines:

> The music was not to blame,
> Hiding as in a jungle inside the copies of the score
> Because once it had been haughtily hounded as Muddle.
> For nearly thirty years the score gathered dust
> And the music of sadness and love,
> Crucified on the staves,
> Strained against them during the nights,
> Craving to be heard.
> But to return to the opera, – on the stage
> A thin bespectacled man, not a God,
> Awkwardness in his clawing fingers
> And his tie sticking out awry,
> Looks in confusion, his breath uneven
> Like a boy, his eyes downcast.
> And he bows so awkwardly,
> He hasn't learnt how, that's why he's triumphant now.[16]

I would like to mention the profound impression made by the Fourteenth Symphony. During the première I sat next to Shostakovich, and from time to time he nervously clutched my hand. At the end come Rilke's words:

> Death is all powerful – it is on guard.
> At the hour of happiness, at the highest moment of life
> It comes upon us, alive and thirsty, – it cries within us.

16 From the poem 'A Second Birth' written in late December 1962. Shostakovich commented to Isaak Glikman in a letter dated 7 January 1963: 'I don't like the title "A Second Birth". My music never died, and therefore it doesn't need to be born a second time' (Glikman, *Letters to a Friend*, p. 184).

I think the Symphony was inspired by his foreboding of an imminent departure from life and music. For all Rilke's greatness, I disagree with his line 'Death is all powerful'. Over people like Shostakovich death has no power. His music will sound as long as humankind exists. Great art succeeds where medicine fails – victory over death. When I wrote 'Babi Yar' there was no monument there. Now there is a monument, and I am happy that Fate gave me an amazing chance to work with Shostakovich.[17]

Mravinsky's defection

ISAAK SCHWARTZ recalls the events surrounding Mravinsky's disassociation from Shostakovich's Thirteenth Symphony:

From the Tenth Symphony onwards, I sat in on all the rehearsals and concerts of Shostakovich's new works, including the Eleventh and Twelfth Symphonies. Mravinsky didn't like outsiders to be present at these rehearsals, but at Shostakovich's insistence, he allowed me to come and arranged for the necessary pass. As I lived close to the Philharmonic Hall, I never missed a rehearsal.

The painful history of the Thirteenth Symphony unfolded before my very eyes. To the astonishment of all and sundry, Mravinsky did not perform it.

During the early 1960s, I spent the summers in Repino at the Union of Composers' Retreat, where Mravinsky and his second wife, Inna Serikova, whom he passionately adored, also spent their holidays. His love for Inna was so absolute that he preferred to surround himself with friends and acquaintances from her circle, rather than his own. Inna and I had been students together, so his good-will extended towards me as well. He treated me kindly, although, of course, with his inherent detachment and arrogance.

Once, when the Mravinskys were in my cottage, the conversation touched on the impending performance of Shostakovich's new symphony – the Thirteenth. It became clear from the conversation that Mravinsky had received the score, and was now experiencing certain doubts – something was inhibiting him. To start with, the nature of these doubts was unclear to me. But as Mravinsky voiced them out loud, seeking Inna's advice, she put forward an irrefutable argument

17 Evgeny Evtushenko, Reminiscences of Shostakovich and his Thirteenth Symphony.

for a refusal to perform the work: Mravinsky never conducted choral works, and this symphony called for a bass soloist and a male choir.

'You must only conduct pure music.'

I found it amusing how, in this situation, the expression 'pure music' acquired ambiguous overtones. This, indeed, was the explanation given to Shostakovich for Mravinsky's refusal to conduct the Thirteenth.

At the time, and to this very day I cannot accept such a lamentable excuse for Mravinsky's refusal. I saw clearly that there was another reason that influenced him: despite his influential and high position in life, Mravinsky, alas, was a man of his time. He was wary of Shostakovich's choice of Evtushenko's verse. Inna played a decisive role here. As someone groomed in the school of Party thought (she had for a time worked in the Party District Committee [OBKOM]), she felt that Evtushenko's verses and their settings by Shostakovich could have a pernicious effect on the career of her beloved husband. Mravinsky's rejection of the Symphony horrified his friends and admirers, and it marked the end of my contacts with him.[18]

MSTISLAV ROSTROPOVICH talks of Shostakovich's loyalty towards performers, and his views on Mravinsky's betrayal of Shostakovich. He himself severed his connection with the Leningrad Philharmonic – both the orchestra and the institution – after quarrelling with Mravinsky:

There were two causes for my falling out with Mravinsky: the first was over the Thirteenth Symphony, the second over the Second Cello Concerto. Although Shostakovich later made his peace with Mravinsky, I nevertheless believe that he despised him as a human being for his cowardice in the whole affair of the Thirteenth Symphony. There was no excuse for such behaviour. Mravinsky must have understood what a brilliant work the Thirteenth Symphony was, as well as its importance to Shostakovich.

As for the Second Cello Concerto, Mravinsky announced to me literally only two weeks before I was due to play the première in Leningrad that he refused to conduct the concert. The excuse he gave was inadmissible: he said that he hadn't had time to learn the Concerto for the opening concert of the season, which was to be in honour of

18 Isaak Schwartz, 'Reminiscences of Shostakovich', article commissioned for this book.

Dmitri Dmitriyevich's sixtieth birthday. I think that, after the affair of the Thirteenth Symphony, Mravinsky was left with a feeling of extreme awkwardness towards Shostakovich, and he virtually stopped performing his new works. He never conducted the Thirteenth or Fourteenth Symphonies, and only much later conducted the Fifteenth on one or two occasions. So the première of the Second Cello Concerto took place in Moscow with Evgeny Svetlanov conducting.[19]

Shostakovich later tried to reconcile me with Mravinsky, during one of my visits to Komarovo. I only remember that we all drank an awful lot, as it seemed the only way to find a common language.

This brings me to the interesting question of Shostakovich's attitude to first performances. Dmitri Dmitriyevich had an incredible loyalty to all the first performers of his music. When he was writing his last quartets, he dedicated one to each of the members of the Beethoven Quartet, who had given the first performances of nearly all the quartets. I attended the rehearsals of these late quartets right from the start when the musicians were literally sight-reading. Dmitri Dmitriyevich would tell me, 'You know, the "Beethovens" no longer play so well. But when I see that they are still together, it gives me a feeling of security – I know that everything in the world is still all right, because they continue to exist.'

For instance, the Borodin Quartet played a lot better than the 'Beethovens' in their last years, but Shostakovich was absolutely loyal to them. I knew that if he were to write something for cello, he would automatically turn to me, even if I had forgotten how to play. As far as Mravinsky was concerned, Dmitri Dmitriyevich would have trusted him with all his works till the end of his days if Mravinsky had not proved himself to be an unprincipled turncoat.[20]

A philosophical outlook

The film and theatre director, Grigori Kozintsev, worked with Shostakovich over a period of forty years. In the last years of his life, Shostakovich was finally able to dispense with writing film music, which he had come to regard as an annoying distraction from his main life's work. But in the last fifteen years of his life he made exceptions for his friends, writing music for five films,

19 On 25 September 1966.
20 Mstislav Rostropovich: recorded interview with EW.

two each for the directors Leo Arnshtam and Kozintsev, and as a long-standing promise for the writer Galina Serebryakova.[21]

Shostakovich's last contact with Kozintsev in the cinema had been in 1950, when he wrote the music for the biographical film about the noted nineteenth-century literary critic Vissarion Belinsky (1811–48). The sad fate of that film left both men with a sour taste.

But with better times Kozintsev turned to Shakespeare's great tragedies, *Hamlet* (1964) and *King Lear* (1971). Shostakovich's music was to be an integral part of both films. For *Hamlet*, the composer produced thirty-four incidental pieces, refusing, as a matter of principle, to use any music that he had written previously for two stage productions of the play.[22]

GRIGORI KOZINTSEV was one of Russia's most respected intellectuals, and his artistic sensibility lent him a unique insight into the working process of the composer's mind:

Belinsky

The film *Belinsky* was maimed by insistent demands for never-ending, absurd remakes; it was released on hire only several years after its completion. I didn't have the strength of heart to sit through it. I left the hall and roamed the streets for a long time. After this experience, I stopped working in the cinema and transferred my efforts to the theatre.

'I saw *Belinsky*,' Dmitri Dmitriyevich said to me when we met – a similar hatchet job had been done on his music, incidentally. 'All this, of course, doesn't go to enhance the picture, to enhance the picture, of course.'

Our conversation took place at his dacha. Dmitri Dmitriyevich finished smoking his cigarette in silence, and then slowly and doggedly ground the butt into the ground.[23]

Shostakovich's professionalism. His score of Hamlet

An old hack will harp about his 'creativity' and his 'unique personal themes'. Shostakovich, on the other hand, is never offended when asked to write exactly one minute thirteen seconds of music, and when told that he must fade the orchestra to make way for dialogue at the twenty-fourth second, and bring it up again at the fifty-second to

---

21 Arnshtam's films were *Five Days and Five Nights* (1960), *Sofiya Perovskaya* (1967/8). Galina Serebryakova wrote the scenario (based on her trilogy of the life of Marx) for the film *A Year as Long as a Lifetime* (1965).

22 Akimov's production of 1932, and Kozintsev's 1954 production, where the director used Shostakovich's music written for his earlier production of *King Lear* (1941).

23 Grigori Kozintsev, *The Complete Works*, vol. II, p. 436.

synchronize with a cannon shot. Art that is specially commissioned and functional does not necessarily have to be bad art!

It was in vain that I tried to get some critical response to our film *Hamlet* from Shostakovich. I see so many faults in it, that I wanted to test my sensations and have them reinforced by the opinions of a man whose artistic sensibility I can trust. But, alas, after seeing all the material for the fourth time, all one succeeds in eliciting from Dmitri Dmitriyevich are kind words.

Is the film faultless? Of course not. The problem lies elsewhere: what is commonly called 'critical analysis' is a foreign concept to Shostakovich. If he likes the essential drift of the film, then, like an ideal spectator, he is so engrossed by the life of the screen that he cannot be distracted to formulate judgements in cold blood.

Besides which, he abhors our Soviet critical terminology of 'achievements and errors'; easy familiarity is alien to his nature. Shostakovich thereby instructs us not only in great art, but in modesty, purity and respect for other people's work.[24]

Shostakovich's music serves as a great example to me. I could not direct my Shakespearean films without it. What is its main feature? A feeling for tragedy? Indeed, an important quality. . . . Philosophy, an intrinsic concept of the world. . . ? Of course, how can one speak of *Lear* without Philosophy. . . . But it's a different feature that is important, and one that's hard to describe in words. Goodness . . . virtue compassion. But a particular goodness. In Russian we have a wonderful word – virulent. No good exists in Russian art without a virulent hatred of all that degrades man. In Shostakovich's music I hear a virulent hatred of cruelty, of the cult of power, of the persecution of truth . . .[25]

Shostakovich's personality
Dmitri Dmitriyevich's modesty and utter truthfulness are amazing. He is completely unable to pay compliments, and this despite his position as chairman of various unions, meetings, delegations, conferences, presidiums. He maintains his silence, then says, 'You know, it's marvellous.' That's all.

24 *Ibid.*, vol. II, pp. 423, 430.
25 *Ibid.*, vol. III, pp. 155, 156.

When listening to compliments, his face distorts into a grimace, and he's unable to find an apt or polite reply. Apart from his natural modesty, he has an extreme dislike of anything smacking of superficial pomposity, exaggerated exultation or lofty words.

There are artists who, in their appearance, their manner of speech and their behaviour, resemble their own art. Such were Mayakovsky and Alexander Dovzhenko. But is there anything in Dmitri Dmitriyevich's exterior that for a moment suggests the tragic power of his symphonies? At first glance, not so much as a hair. Nevertheless, on closer acquaintance, one particular feature, perhaps the most pertinent, manifests itself. I would call it the hypersensitivity of his skin. The power of his artistic response is revealed in his instantaneous vulnerability, the palpitating contact of his nervous structure with the outer world, and the extraordinary receptivity of his spiritual organism.

He leads two lives: the exterior life of everyday conversation and behaviour, where he notes down football results in a large accounting book, and lays out endless games of patience. Before making a speech, he indulges in cards as a way of resting and of distracting his attention from the outside world.

But simultaneously, his inner life runs like an incessantly working motor, an ever-open wound. It is impossible to define this part of his life in words. His working day is as long as a lifetime. He can be extremely weak, be morbidly vulnerable, and he finds it impossible to resist pressure. Then suddenly he produces the Scherzo from the Thirteenth Symphony.

Shostakovich has been accused of neuroticism, and much has been written about his nervous disposition. But his detractors would like our age to be portrayed in stereotyped images of the plump, red cheeks and the cute and innocent gaze of a child staring out from a soap ad.

Dmitri Dmitriyevich's face goes into contortions when reminded of a recording of the Thirteenth Symphony sent from abroad: 'If only you knew what torture it is to listen to a bad performance of one's work.'[26]

Reflections on the Thirteenth Symphony
The essence of Shostakovich's music lies in the conflict between the

26 *Ibid.*, vol. II, pp. 427, 430, 431, 435.

spirituality of man and the inhuman forces that are hostile to this spirituality.

Such a man can withstand oppression of unprecedented power. In the Thirteenth Symphony, this force, from the first appearance of the image 'Babi Yar', grows and acquires an ever more mechanical character, totally devoid of spirit. But the 'reed' does not bend. If you like, this is how Shostakovich's optimism is expressed. In Shostakovich's music the 'thinking' reed is empowered with exceptional spiritual qualities. First and foremost with a conscience, an obsessive need to react in an almost physiological way to the suffering of others (what Dostoevsky calls 'the compulsive response'), with a refinement and nobility of feeling. It reflects his own pure and unsullied response to life.

Then comes [the Scherzo] 'Humour'. This, probably, is the one quality that allows Shostakovich to live. [In this movement] the merry wind of the 1920s blows in from all sides. Is this music? No, it is everything that we suffered and experienced seizing you by the throat.

I re-read Evtushenko's poem 'Humour' after listening to the Thirteenth Symphony. It's worth comparing to Shostakovich's setting, not only in form, but in the power of the associative connections. Shostakovich produces images of 'Humour', and Evtushenko juggles with easy rhymes and rhythms. Evtushenko's poem is a facile composition, graced with witty invention. Shostakovich's setting is the fruit of suffering. His prison *is* a prison, his humour is fearless and joyful, a victorious, life-affirming force. Evtushenko flirts amusingly with the antithesis. In Shostakovich, each conflicting source acquires the momentous sweep of history. On the one hand, you have a talented facility, a superficial play, and on the other, a Scherzo harnessed to historical tragedy.

Shostakovich was able to enrich Evtushenko's images with strength and passion. The superficial poems, which play with words, acquire tragic depths and express veritable suffering. Shostakovich, in his exposition of all the poems, has homed in on the associations of suffering to such an extent that, on hearing the Symphony, one is totally gripped.

There is a line in Evtushenko's poem 'Career' [the fifth movement of the Symphony]: 'I am making my career by *not* making it.'

Many people have made careers for themselves. And there are also those who made their careers through *not* making them. Anything was possible. Nevertheless, none of this sordid world applies in Shostakovich's case. And it is unpleasant to hear any such implications in reference to Dmitri Dmitriyevich. He has worked unflinchingly, because, like all great Russian artists, 'he could not be silent.'

Music is not a profession for Shostakovich, it is the necessity to speak out and to convey what lies behind the lives of people, to depict our age and our country. Nature has endowed him with a particular sensibility of hearing; he hears people weep, he hears their low murmur of anger, the tearing of hearts, the trembling groans of despair. He has hearkened to the rumbling of the earth, the crowds marching for justice, the strikers' whistles, the angry songs erupting in the city outskirts, a penny-harmonium screeching out trite melodies, and the wind that carries them to every corner of the earth. He introduced revolutionary songs into the severe world of the symphony. Then, when the sirens of war whined over Europe, he heard the hoarse cries and the moans, the grating and jangling of steel on the bloodied battlefields.

And in these times Idea and Thought were muzzled and yoked. Whips were cracked and Art was made to dance, to beg favours in front of petty despots; it had to guard over the Good and stamp on the Seditious.

Dmitri Dmitriyevich laboured throughout his life. Then times changed. He had to listen to laudations long overdue, was garbed in the mantle of Honorary Doctor of Oxford University; he read out speeches and reports from scraps of paper. World-wide fame had arrived.

The childish features of his face changed; the corners of his lips drooped, his eyebrows rose upwards; a mask showed through his face, the ancient mask of tragedy. His great destiny, albeit uneasy, was now defined. What kind of career could one talk of?[27]

Stravinsky's return visit to Russia

Igor Stravinsky returned to his native country on 21 September 1962 after nearly fifty years of exile and unrelenting hostility by the Communist regime. Not only was Stravinsky a living legend, but a symbol of a lost culture. His

27 *Ibid.*, vol. II, pp. 431, 432, 433, 444.

visit had an enormous impact on musical life in Moscow and Leningrad, signalling the right to perform his works and those by other 'modernist' Western composers which had been banned to silence over so many years.

Stravinsky was received as a guest of the Union of Composers. The composer KAREN KHACHATURIAN, a secretary of the Union, was appointed by Khrennikov as his escort during the visit:

When Stravinsky made his return visit to Russia in 1962, I was at his side from the first day of his visit to the last, remaining with him from morning to night each day. From the moment he arrived Stravinsky kept asking, 'Where is Shostakovich?'

It so happened that while we were in Moscow, Shostakovich was in Leningrad, and Dmitri Dmitriyevich returned to Moscow just as we were going up to Leningrad; so we kept missing each other. Stravinsky was most intrigued and kept saying, 'What's up with this Shostakovich? Why does he keep running away from me?'

Eventually, just before Stravinsky's departure, Ekaterina Furtseva, the Minister of Culture, whom Dmitri Dmitriyevich used to call 'Ekaterina the Third', gave a banquet at the Metropole Hotel. There were a lot of people there, and finally the two composers came face to face. It was a very tense meeting. They were placed next to each other and sat in complete silence. I sat opposite them. Finally Shostakovich plucked up courage and opened the conversation:

'What do you think of Puccini?'

'I can't stand him,' Stravinsky replied.

'Oh, and neither can I, neither can I,' said Shostakovich.

So Puccini, who was completely alien to both these composers, gave them the impetus for a conversation and some kind of initial contact. But a sort of confusion set in, and these two great and complex individuals couldn't find any real ground for contact. This was their only meeting.

Shostakovich was a great admirer of Stravinsky and loved and knew all his works inside out, starting with the Russian and neo-classical period. He particularly loved the *Symphony of Psalms*. Perhaps he knew the later works less well.

Stravinsky regarded Shostakovich as a composer with a brilliant gift who had started well, but who had been broken by the 'Zhdanovsh-china'. He was right from one point of view. Notwithstanding Shostakovich's enormous resources and powers of resistance, the events of 1936 and 1948 had a profound influence on his personality and on his composition. Certainly those crass criticisms inhibited his urge to write operas – and stage works were the major preoccupation of his younger years.

Shostakovich hated being asked questions about his music and whether this or that theme represented something or had any particular meaning. When asked, 'What did you want to say in this work?' he would answer, 'I've said what I've said.' Either you had it in you to understand, or, if not, then it would be fruitless to try and explain anyway.[28]

Stravinsky was accompanied on this visit to the USSR by ROBERT CRAFT. Contrary to Karen Khachaturian's evidence, Stravinsky met Shostakovich twice, both times at government receptions given at the Metropole Hotel. The first took place on 1 October 1962, the second on the eve of Stravinsky's departure on 10 October. Craft recorded the two meetings in his diary:

October 1st
This is the most extraordinary event of the trip, a kind of 'last supper' (for non-disciples) during which I.S. reveals his Russianness more completely than at any time in the fifteen years I have known him. Mme Furtseva presides at the centre of the table with I.S. to her right, and Shostakovich to her left; seeing the two St Petersburg-born composers so close together, one is struck by the fact that their complexions and sandy hair are exactly the same. . . .

Shostakovich's is the most sensitive and intellectual face we have so far seen in the USSR. He is thinner, taller, younger – more boyish-looking – than expected, but he is also the shyest and most nervous human being I have ever seen. He chews not merely his nails but his fingers, twitches his pouty mouth and chin, chain smokes, wiggles his nose in constant adjustment of his spectacles, looks querulous one moment and ready to cry the next. His hands tremble, he stutters, his whole frame wobbles when he shakes hands – which reminds us of Auden – and his knees knock when he speaks, at which time others look anxious for him, as indeed they might. He has a habit of staring, too, then of turning guiltily away when caught, and all evening long he peeks illicitly at I.S. around the nicely rounded corners of Mme Furtseva. There is no betrayal of the thoughts behind those fright-ened, very intelligent eyes. His new wife is beside him. An adoring

28 Karen Khachaturian: recorded interview with EW.

pupil, perhaps, but by age, looks, and her equally shy, serious, distant manner, a daughter . . .

October 10th
Farewell banquet at the Metropole, a happy occasion and no formality. . . .

Shostakovich, this time at I.S.'s side, looks even more frightened and tortured than at the first conclave, probably because he thinks a speech is expected of him. He converses neutrally at first, then like a bashful schoolboy blurts out that he had been overwhelmed by the *Symphony of Psalms* when he first heard it, and that he had made his own piano score of it which he would like to present to I.S. Seeking to return the compliment, I.S. tells Shostakovich that he shares some of his high regard for Mahler.

Poor Shostakovich starts to melt, then quickly freezes again as I.S. rather cruelly continues: 'But you should go beyond Mahler. The Viennese troika adored him also, you know, and Schoenberg and Webern conducted his music.' Toward the end of the evening, and after drinking several *zubrovkas*, Shostakovich pathetically confesses that he would like to follow I.S.'s example and conduct his own music. 'But I don't know how not to be afraid.'[29]

Shostakovich's own judgement of his elder colleague was very clear-cut: 'Stravinsky the composer, I worship. Stravinsky the thinker, I despise.'[30]

The creation of the Gorky Festival

MSTISLAV ROSTROPOVICH recalls Shostakovich's conducting debut

I was responsible for the organization of the first music festival in the Soviet Union, which took place in Gorky in June 1962. I organized it as a bet. Of course nowadays music festivals have sprouted up all over the place, but at that time there wasn't a single festival in the Soviet Union. I had written a somewhat visionary article for the magazine *Sovietskaya Muzyka*, recounting how many wonderful festivals are organized abroad by musicians, and wouldn't it be marvellous if we too had a music festival in our country. Then once, when in conversation with the director of the Gorky Philharmonic Orchestra, Nikitin,

---

29 I. Stravinsky and R. Craft, *Dialogues and a Diary*, pp. 291–2, 306–9.
30 Letter dated 9 September 1971 (Glikman, *Letters to a Friend*, p. 279).

and its conductor, Guzman, I told them, 'You know I'm thinking about setting up a music festival.'

They replied, 'Thinking's not much good, a bit of action is what's needed.'

So I said, 'Fine, let's take action, let's have the festival here in Gorky.'

'All words, no action' was their reply, and I fell for this bait of 'No Action'. We laid bets as to whether it would ever happen. Effectively we agreed to organize this first festival together. When it opened, and I was driving through the main street of Gorky, which was bedecked with banners and flags, I remember thinking to myself, 'I'll probably finish up in jail for setting this up. They'll say, "Just think, for some piece of nonsense we went and decorated the town with flags." '

Shortly after the first Gorky Festival,[31] we organized a concert in Gorky devoted to Shostakovich's music. It took place on 12 November of that same year and was a special event, as Shostakovich conducted the first half of the concert himself. This was the first (and last) time he ever conducted an orchestra, apart from one occasion in his student days.

Earlier that summer Galina and I had received a rather soiled-looking packet from Shostakovich containing his orchestration of Mussorgsky's *Songs and Dances of Death*. He had recently met Irina Antonovna Supinskaya, his third wife, and they had gone to visit her relatives in the country at Solotcha, outside Ryazan, for a holiday. And it was from there that he sent us this masterpiece wrapped up in old brown paper as an unexpected gift. Like everything he did, it was absolutely brilliant. We decided to give the first performance in Gorky.

The programme was the Festival Overture and the First Cello Concerto, which Shostakovich conducted. Then, in the second half, I conducted the *Songs and Dances of Death* in Shostakovich's orchestration, with Galina as soloist.

Shostakovich and I arrived together for the concert on the night train from Moscow at about five or six o'clock in the morning. Dmitri Dmitriyevich was very nervous. Before the first rehearsal that morn-

31 At this Festival one concert was dedicated to Shostakovich's works, where Rostropovich played the First Cello Concerto, participated in a performance of the Eighth Quartet, and accompanied Vishnevskaya in the *Satires*. Shostakovich was present on this occasion.

ing, he was particularly anxious. He turned to me and said, 'Slava, I'm not going, I'm not going to the rehearsal.'

'What do you mean, you're not going. We have to go!'

'But I can't, I can't.'

I said to him, 'No, we have to go.'

'All right, then, but let's have a little drink together – then perhaps I'll go.'

So an hour before the rehearsal was due to start, we polished off half a litre of vodka. Afterwards I think I had a harder time playing the cello than he had conducting.

Dmitri Dmitriyevich conducted very well, very precisely and clearly. It's true that beforehand both Guzman and I had rehearsed the orchestra so much that the musicians could have played the notes with their eyes shut.

After the success of this concert, it was decided to dedicate the second Festival[32] in Gorky totally to Shostakovich's music.[33]

Non-official culture

On 14 October 1964 Nikita Khrushchev was removed from office by a vote of the Party Plenum. His successors, Leonid Brezhnev (who assumed the position of First Secretary of the Party) and Alexander Kosygin (appointed Chairman of the Council of Ministers), seemed faceless bureaucrats by comparison to the impetuous and earthy Khrushchev, and it took some time before the new regime showed its true colours.

To begin with, the leadership established as a priority the need to reform the backward economy and to solve the inherited problem of an agricultural policy in disarray. For this purpose it sought increased contacts and investment from the West. Secondly, under the conservative influence of such ideologues as Mikhail Suslov and Alexander Shelepin, it wished to reverse the recent trend towards liberalism. Aiming to drive home the message that it was not going to tolerate either literary freedom or political dissidence, the Party decided to make scapegoats out of the writers, Yuli Daniel and Andrei Sinyavsky. In February 1966, at a closed and flagrantly unfair trial, exceptionally harsh sentences were meted out to the two men.

But again the authorities had miscalculated, not reckoning with the angry reaction of the intellectual community. Over sixty members of the Writers' Union remonstrated to the Supreme Soviet against the form of the closed trial,

32 The Festival took place in February 1964.
33 Mstislav Rostropovich: recorded interview with EW.

and the poet Alexander Ginzburg succeeded in compiling a record of the court proceedings which were published in 'samizdat'. The authorities' policy of intimidation was beginning to backfire.

But it was events in a satellite country that finally dashed any hopes for liberalization at home. The Soviet authorities, frightened by the repercussions of the freedoms granted under Alexander Dubček's government during the brief 'Prague Spring' of 1968, decided to send troops into Czechoslavakia in August that year. This wilful use of force was deeply shocking to the Soviet liberal community, who increasingly felt the need to express open protest. A small group of people (including Pavel Litvinov) staged a demonstration in Red Square against the invasion, and were promptly arrested for their pains.

The appearance of 'samizdat' (meaning 'self-publication'), a sort of underground press which circulated its publications in typescript, assumed an enormous importance. Through attention in the Western press, and Russian broadcasts by Western radio stations, writers had an opportunity to reach readers, and dissidents lived in the knowledge that their cases would receive publicity, and the hope that eventually the regime would be called to task.

This period in Soviet history is characterized by the authorities' defensive attitude to cultural policy. In a void created by the conflicting desires to show a semblance of normality to the outside world, and rigidly to control the arts, there grew up a phenomenon of a 'non-official' culture. Art that was officially not tolerated – exhibitions, poetry readings, theatre and concert performances – was permitted in small halls and spaces, with word of mouth and hand-painted posters the only means of publicity. At the same time, officially tolerated fringe theatres, notably Lyubimov's TAGANKA Theatre, succeeded in staging thought-provoking performances, using sub-text and subversive interpretation as a means of outwitting the censorship. Progressively, the real Soviet culture of the 1960s and 1970s functioned in this semi-underground way.

In the musical world, the official policy saw the extension of power to the conservative faction of the Union of Composers under the leadership of Tikhon Khrennikov, who continued the long-standing 'struggle against modernism'. But a younger generation of 'unofficial' composers, including Schnittke, Denisov, Valentin Silvestrov and Gubaidulina, was gradually making a name for itself in the musical community, supported by performers who in the future would play their music abroad. Shostakovich's position was outwardly unaffected by this situation. He continued to take an active part in the administrative duties of the Union of Composers, and to voice his loyalty to the Party in public. Ostensibly a figure of the 'official' establishment, Shostakovich didn't fit into this scheme of things naturally. It was blatantly obvious that he disassociated himself inwardly from the official statements he was expected to sign and parrot in public. Yet nobody questioned the inherent morality of a work like the Thirteenth Symphony. But there was a growing mood of dissatisfaction with the position he assumed amongst the younger generation of composers. As they fought the constraints of the conservative forces at the Union, they expected – and didn't necessarily receive – support from a figure whom they could not but admire, and in whose liberal sympathies they could not but believe.

Politics at the Composers' Union

The Leningrad composer SERGEI SLONIMSKY recalls Shostakovich in his capacity as First Secretary of the RSFSR Composers' Union in various situations:

It was an autumn day in 1964. In the morning it was broadcast on the radio that Nikita Sergeyevich Khrushchev had been dismissed from all his posts and duties. Later on that day I met Shostakovich on Sofiya Perovskaya Street, where his sister lived, almost next door to my home. His lips were pursed in a barely discernible ironic smile.

'Well, Sergei Mikhailovich, now we will most certainly enjoy an even better life?'

I chuckled out loud, and Dmitri Dmitriyevich's smile broke into a broad grin, virtually baring his teeth.

Just a few years previously, after yet another Composers' Congress,[34] Khrushchev had given a splendid banquet at the Kremlin. It was attended by a throng of people, and all the musicians pushed their way forward to be nearer to the great leader. Grouped around him were Yuri Shaporin, Vano Muradeli and Konstantin Dankeyevich. Shostakovich stood somewhat to the side, listening quietly and with apparent indifference to the interminable speeches of 'Nikita the Corncob'.

The Leader was instructing his People: 'Well, if the music is half decent, you know, then I can just about listen to the radio. Something like the Ensemble of Violinists of the Bolshoi Theatre, or a good tune like "You Little Stream" or some other Ukrainian folksong.'

Here he added something in Ukrainian, and, pointing at Dankeye-

---

34 The occasion referred to is probably the RSFSR Congress of Composers held in April 1960, when DDS was elected First Secretary.

vich, said jovially, 'Now, Konstantin is also a "Khokhol"[35] – he understands me,' and at this the tears streamed down Dankeyevich's wide cheeks. Muradeli froze like the Town Governor in the dumb scene of Gogol's *Government Inspector*. Shaporin cleared his throat, coughed and stepped aside, and Kabalevsky immediately appeared in his place.

Khrushchev continued: 'But, on the other hand, if they transmit the kind of music, well, how shall I put it, music that resembles the croaking of crows . . .'

'Ha-ha, ha-ha!' a Leningrad composer and democrat standing beside me whooped right into my ear, and an awkwardly suppressed chorus of chuckles echoed around the hall. Khrushchev, lost in thought, gazed around at those standing around him. Suddenly his eyes rested on Shostakovich standing in the distance.

'Now, Dmitri Dmitriyevich saw the light at the very beginning of the war with his . . . what d'you call it, ah, his Symphony.' There was a stir of commotion amongst the elite. Khrushchev approached Shostakovich and shook his hand. Dmitri Dmitriyevich smiled politely but rather drily. Applause broke out. Suddenly, from across the table, the composer of popular songs, Lyudmila Lyadova, whisked over and threw herself at Shostakovich and kissed him.

'Oh, Dmitri Dmitriyevich, how we all love you.' And she was followed by others, and a flood of congratulations ensued which Dmitri Dmitriyevich received with the usual polite restraint.

That same year he had become First Secretary of the Union of Composers of the RSFSR. Khrushchev persuaded him to join the Party. And only shortly afterwards the same Khrushchev was angered by Shostakovich's 'Babi Yar' from the Thirteenth Symphony. At the Leningrad Party HQ at Smolny a functionary of the OBKOM informed us with a smirk, 'I saw next to Dmitri Dmitriyevich, and I saw how his hands trembled.' I don't doubt but that this man's legs would have been shaking if the all-powerful leader had bestowed on him his attention and given him a similar dressing-down.

In the spring of 1964 Shostakovich decided to change the leadership of the Leningrad Union of Composers, and proposed that it should be headed by some younger musicians. He rang me and asked me to

35 This term originates from the Ukrainian word for crest or topknot. In Russian the word denotes a Ukrainian, in reference to the Ukrainians' habit of shaving their heads, leaving only a topknot.

come to his room at the Evropeiskaya Hotel, where he was with his deputies Alexander Kholodilin and Sergei Balasanyan.

'Sergei Mikhailovich, we want to put forward Andrei Petrov as the chairman of the Leningrad Union, and you as his deputy.'

My argument seemed perfectly rational: 'Dmitri Dmitriyevich, I would rather you didn't; besides which, my candidature will not be accepted by the OBKOM. After all I'm a formalist!'

At this last word a slight grimace distorted the Master's serious face.

'We want the best composers at the head of our Union. We wish to recommend you.'

I thanked him, but soon discovered that the OBKOM had indeed rejected my nomination, although they agreed to the candidature of Andrei Petrov as Chairman of the Union to replace Vasili Solovyov Sedoy.[36]

From the mid 1960s EDISON DENISOV started to make his reputation in the West as the leading voice of a new generation of Soviet avant-garde composers. One of his first works to be played outside the Soviet Union was 'Le Soleil des Incas' for soprano and small ensemble, written in 1964.

Undoubtedly Shostakovich found Denisov's music increasingly alien, although outwardly he continued to encourage him. Here Denisov describes how sometimes Shostakovich would lose his nerve and, instead of supporting the younger composers, take sides with the Union officials:

'The Sun of the Incas' was the first of my works to be performed widely abroad. It was an important work for me, as it was here that I started to speak my own musical language. Before that I had not found myself, and expressed myself in the musical language of others. It was in connection with this work that I had reason to be offended by Shostakovich's behaviour for the first time in my life.

It was at his initiative that I presented this piece at the Secretariat of the Union of Composers. To my surprise, when the piece was examined and played, Shostakovich sharply criticized it, instead of lending his support as he had led me to expect. Afterwards I asked him why he did this.

'Well, you see, Edik, when I walked into the hall, the first person I saw was Vasily Kukharsky, and, you know, I was frightened.' I suppose it was an honest answer.

36 Sergei Slonimsky, 'Brush Strokes for a Portrait of a Great Musician', article commissioned for this book.

I remember another occasion at the Union of Composers, when Dmitri Dmitriyevich lent his prestige and name to a piece of business that he could not have approved. At this meeting, the composer Roman Ledenyov proposed that certain names (all of the old-guard type of official composer, including Kirill Molchanov) should be removed from the membership council. After his proposal, Shostakovich read out the list that had been put forward with the Party names – the opposition's proposal. He did this quite often. He urged that we vote with Khrennikov against Ledenyov's proposal.

Then Khrennikov stood up and announced rhetorically, his voice rising in a frenzied crescendo: 'There are two proposals, that of Roman Semyonovich Ledenyov, and that of the Winner of the Lenin Prize, the State Prize, People's Artist of the USSR, Hero of Socialist Labour, Professor, our universally beloved and respected Dmitri Dmitriyevich Shostakovich . . .' After this bombastic performance, thunderous applause broke out in the auditorium in the packed-out Hall of Columns. Of course Ledenyov's proposal only received fifteen votes, and the rest of the Hall voted for Shostakovich.

I remember going to see Shebalin just after this happened, and he said, 'I can't understand Mitya. After all he could have simply not showed up, saying that he was ill. Why does he sully his name with such things?'[37]

A commission from the Bolshoi Theatre

Over the years, spasmodic reports circulated to the effect that Shostakovich was writing an opera on the Soviet 'classic' *Quiet Flows the Don*, rather in the same way as he was forever embarking on a 'Lenin' symphony. But from January 1964 these press reports appeared with regular persistence, stating that Shostakovich was composing an opera based on the second part of Sholokhov's epic novel, whereas Feliks Dzerzhinsky's earlier opera of that name dealt with events from the first part of the book.

Between 1964 and 1966 Shostakovich himself made frequent statements on this subject, saying that he was about to or was already composing the music. Indeed, a contract for the opera was drawn up between the composer and the Bolshoi Theatre which announced plans to stage it in the 1966/7 season. Y. Lukin, a Sholokhov expert, produced a libretto which Shostakovich accepted in October 1964. The composer met Sholokhov a few months earlier

37 Edison Denisov: recorded interview with EW.

and announced his intention of going to visit the writer at his home 'to breathe the air of the Don steppes, to meet the fellow-countrymen of the novel's characters, to hear Cossack songs in their native surroundings and to glean advice from Sholokhov himself, the author of the immortal epic'.[38]

While Shostakovich continued to make public assurances that this most important work 'would take up all of 1966, if not 1967', by May 1966 he had confided in his friend and pupil, Boris Tishchenko, that 'his enthusiasm for the project had evaporated'.[39] By the summer of that year he had decided definitely not to continue (or start) work on the opera. It appears that no sketches or music for *Quiet Flows the Don* have survived.

Although during the 1950s Shostakovich had been employed by the Bolshoi Theatre as a consultant, his work was never staged there in his lifetime, with the exception of the short-lived production of *Lady Macbeth* (December 1935–January 1936), which incurred the wrath of Stalin. Even in the 1960s the Theatre preferred the idea of commissioning a work that was 'ideologically' safe than of reviving his previous operas. Here the director, BORIS POKROVSKY expresses his indignation at the Bolshoi Theatre's blinkered attitude to Shostakovich's operas:

I got to know Shostakovich in 1943, when I came to Moscow to work with the Bolshoi Theatre. I soon got in with a group of artistic people, including the conductor Samosud and the artists Vladimir Dmitriev and Pyotr Villiams. They introduced me to Dmitri Dmitriyevich. To start with our relationship was quite formal; Dmitri Dmitriyevich was very kind to me, and being a self-confident young man, I assumed this was normal. Only later did I realize how fortunate I was.

Before long, I felt that Dmitri Dmitriyevich had somewhat cooled in his attitude towards me. Then suddenly, one evening at a party, he came up to me, embraced me and seemed to be almost apologizing. Later I asked Dmitriev what all this was about. It turned out that Shostakovich had made enquiries about me: Dmitriev had vouched for me, saying, 'Pokrovsky's a very decent person.'

Dmitri Dmitriyevich exclaimed, 'A decent person! How simply wonderful.'

Shostakovich's greatest mistake – indeed it was a crime – was to leave his opera *The Gamblers* unfinished. I have staged the marvellous fragment that exists at the Moscow Chamber Theatre – it constitutes about a third of Gogol's play.

38 M. Yakovlyev (ed.), *D. Shostakovich on Himself and His Times*, p. 275.
39 Khentova, *Shostakovich*, vol. II, p. 454.

Dmitri Dmitriyevich gave me the most primitive reason for his not having completed the work. He thought it would be too long. In fact, when he was writing the work in Kuibyshev, he kept ringing the Bolshoi Theatre to check the length of such operas as *The Queen of Spades*. He himself reckoned that if he continued *The Gamblers* on the principle of setting all of Gogol's text the opera would last between four and six hours. But what business of his was its length? That's a producer's problem, not a composer's. There are plenty of long operas. It's true many people consider Prokofiev's *War and Peace* a bad opera for the sole reason that it's very long. And yet it is we directors who are to blame – Prokofiev originally wrote a shorter work, and added two long scenes at my request. In fact I decided to produce it in two parts; there exists a reduced version, which is the one usually performed now.

Shostakovich wrote *The Gamblers* because he felt like it – it wasn't commissioned and there was no project to stage it. However, in the Bolshoi Theatre there were persistent rumours, even firm assurances that Shostakovich was writing an opera, *Quiet Flows the Don*, to celebrate some anniversary – or as a gift for the October Revolution. In fact the newspapers also carried these reports. One of the Bolshoi's senior directors, Iosif Tumanov, told me many times that he was to direct it, and that Shostakovich was already composing it. Then Vishnevskaya would appear and say, no, Shostakovich was writing a quartet! I don't think he ever wrote a note of this opera – but he did write forty minutes of music to *The Gamblers*!

Today (1992) you will find that the Bolshoi Theatre doesn't have a single Shostakovich or Prokofiev opera in its repertoire, despite the fact that over the last ten years or so no restraints have been implemented in the choice of repertoire. Nobody has forbidden these operas, but neither does anybody want to stage them: the singers don't want to sing them, the audience doesn't want to listen to them and the management doesn't want the bother. I know this to my cost.

After Shostakovich's death I put on *Katerina Izmailova* at the Bolshoi Theatre, and I consider it the best work I ever did. It enjoyed considerable success with the public. But the reviews were damning. What's more they were written by the so-called friends and heirs of Shostakovich – composers and musicologists who took upon themselves the right to judge. These included people I know myself, like Isaak Glikman and Yuri Levitin. The latter wrote an article accusing me of 'destroying Shostakovich's concept.' And there was a general outcry from these self-appointed heirs because I 'demolished the Shostakovich tradition' by staging the orchestral entr'actes in the same way as I staged the entr'actes and intermezzo in *The Nose*. Shostakovich approved these *mise en scènes*, saying that it gave a marvellous impetus and a unity of movement throughout the opera. He gave me his support, and I think, had he been alive, he would have allowed me to apply the same principle in *Katerina Izmailova*.

All these criticisms put ammunition into the hands of those who wished to see my production removed from the stage of the Bolshoi. I had the greatest difficulty in getting the Theatre to agree to a production of *Katerina Izmailova* in the first place. Instead of supporting me, the composer's 'friends', in their anxiety to defend Shostakovich, have deprived the public of a production which could have had a long life. We have them to thank that his operas are not in repertoire at the Bolshoi.

Those people who surrounded Shostakovich in his later years, who visited him in his home and today publish memoirs claiming the closeness of their relationship, these are the enemies of Shostakovich, not Stalin and Zhdanov. When it comes to understanding Shostakovich's music, a sixteen-year-old boy with talent understands it more than any of the 'friends'. You need a gift to understand Shostakovich, just as you do to understand Mozart, Bach or Beethoven.[40]

'The Beethovens'

In the aftermath of the Thirteenth Symphony, Shostakovich's pace of composition slackened somewhat, not least due to his busy schedule of travel, teaching, attending Plenums of the Composers' Union, as well as rehearsals and performances of his own music. In 1963, Shostakovich limited his musical output to writing an Overture on Russian and Kirghizian Themes, and orchestrating the Schumann Cello Concerto for Rostropovich.,

Shostakovich finished the first version of his Ninth Quartet in the autumn of 1961. In a fit of depression, or, to quote his own words, 'in an attack of healthy self-criticism, I burnt it in the stove. This is the second such case in my creative practice. I once did a similar trick of burning my manuscripts, in 1926.'[41]

It took Shostakovich nearly three years to settle down and write another

40 Boris Pokrovsky: recorded interview with EW.
41 Letter dated 18 November 1961 (Glikman, *Letters to a Friend*, p. 168).

quartet. His 'second' Ninth Quartet was completed on 28 May 1964. Dmitri Tsyganov, the leader of the Beethoven Quartet, recalled that Shostakovich told him that the quartet he had consigned to the flames was based on themes 'from childhood'; the new quartet was 'completely different':[42]

The Ninth Quartet was shortly followed by the Tenth, written between 11 and 20 July while on holiday at the Composers' Retreat in Dilizhan, Armenia. The first was dedicated to Irina Shostakovich, his wife, and the latter to his friend, the composer Moisei Weinberg.

Shostakovich's muse was making up for the fallow year of 1963. Early in 1964 he had composed a score for Kozintsev's film of *Hamlet*, and by September of that year he had completed a cantata for bass, chorus and orchestra, *The Execution of Stepan Razin*.

As far back as May 1963, the composer had stated his intention of writing a work using Evtushenko's texts dedicated to the theme of man's conscience.[43] His choice of text settled on excerpts of Evtushenko's epic narrative poem *The Bratsk Hydro-Electric Station*, which dealt with Stepan Razin's revolt and execution.

Shostakovich did not accept Evtushenko's poem uncritically. He wrote to Isaak Glikman: 'Its interesting that when I composed my Thirteenth Symphony, I was in absolute agreement with the poet's every word. In the *Execution of Stepan Razin* there are lots of verses which stir up protest in me; it is as if I enter into polemics with this poetry.'[44] Although Shostakovich discarded some lines, Evtushenko did not agree to his suggestions for actual changes in his verses.

The Execution of Stepan Razin was first performed under Kondrashin's baton, in Moscow on 28 December 1964. History repeated itself on that occasion, when the bass soloist, Ivan Petrov, without any prior warning, failed to turn up at the morning dress rehearsal. Again it was Vitali Gromadsky who stepped in and sang that night. Although the cantata did not produce the furore of the Thirteenth Symphony, its official reception was cool, and its performance was met by total silence in the Soviet press.

Shostakovich's new quartets fared better. The Beethoven Quartet gave the première of both the Ninth and Tenth Quartets in Moscow on 20 November, and in Leningrad the day after. The 'Beethovens' had come into Shostakovich's life long before he himself started writing string quartets. It was a natural choice for the composer to give them the premières of all his quartets; the two exceptions were the First, which they played six days after the Glazunov Quartet premièred it, and the Fifteenth.

42 Khentova, *Life and Work*, vol. II, p. 465.
43 Glikman, *Letters to a Friend*, p. 190.
44 Letter dated 15 September 1964 (*ibid.*, p. 196).

Tsyganov recalled that in 1960, when rehearsing the Seventh Quartet, he informed Shostakovich that the recording company Melodiya

'wishes us to record your last quartet.'

'Last quartet?' exclaimed Shostakovich. 'When I've written all my quartets, then we'll talk about my last quartet!'

'And how many do you intend to write?' enquired Tsyganov.

'Twenty-four,' he answered. 'Haven't you noticed that I never repeat a key? I'll write twenty-four quartets, so as to have a complete cycle.'[45]

After more than thirty years together, changes started to take place in the 'Beethovens'' original formation. In 1964 the viola player, Vadim Borisovsky, retired. The following year the second violinist, Vasily Shirinsky died. They were replaced by Fyodor Druzhinin and Nikolai Zabavnikov.

After Vasili Shirinsky's death Shostakovich emphatically insisted that the Beethoven Quartet should carry on its existence at all costs, as it had acquired the status of a national institution. He himself responded to the loss of his friend and colleague by writing the Eleventh Quartet (completed on 30 January 1966) in Shirinsky's memory. After that each member of the original ensemble received 'his own' quartet. Shostakovich dedicated the Twelfth Quartet to Dmitri Tsyganov, the Thirteenth to Vadim Borisovsky and the Fourteenth to the cellist, Sergei Shirinsky. With the latter's death in 1974, during a rehearsal of the Fifteenth Quartet, the 'Beethovens' were unable to tackle the première, and it was given by the Tanyeev Quartet of Leningrad.

FYODOR DRUZHININ joined the Beethoven Quartet in 1964. Here he recalls his working relationship with Shostakovich:

I first heard Shostakovich's music when I was a boy in Moscow during the war years. In the freezing Grand Hall of the Moscow Conservatoire he played his Piano Quintet with the Beethoven Quartet. The audience were wearing fur coats. The hall was fairly empty, and I sat in the first balcony with my father, who had just returned from the Front after being wounded. Brought up on Mussorgsky, Glinka and Tchaikovsky, I listened to this new music as if under hypnosis, and my only wish was for it to go on for ever. From then on I tried never to miss a concert with a new work by Shostakovich, particularly his quartets and symphonies.

While still a schoolboy, I was present at the famous meeting at the Grand Hall of the Conservatoire in 1948, the most shameful moment of our cultural history. The civic punishment of such artists as Shostakovich, Shebalin, Prokofiev, Akhmatova and Zoshchenko,

45 Khentova, *Shostakovich*, vol. II, p. 508, 509.

with ignorant nonentities cast as their executioners, had been prophesied in Shostakovich's music. It's our good fortune that, thanks to the abstract nature of music, they were unable to put the composer before a firing squad.

People who lived in Shostakovich's epoch have no need to dig in the archives or to marvel at the evidence of repressions and executions and murders. It is all there in his music. Following the best traditions of Russian art, the murky and ugly side of terror, repression and suffering lead us finally to the tragic apotheosis of the Finale of the Fifth Symphony, and to the mysterious transformation into eternal light and conciliation in the Third Quartet and the Viola Sonata.

During the 1930s, fear became the uppermost emotion for Shostakovich and for our intelligentsia. It was a fear not only for their personal existence, although that was real enough, but a fear for their families, their work and their whole country.

When, after Stalin's death, the lid was slightly lifted off our hellish cauldron, Dmitri Dmitriyevich went through an ordeal that was even more terrible for an artist: temptation by official fame and flattery, and identification with the prevailing ideology, which was alien to him.

Then the heavy hammer of official honours, belated glorification, dealt Shostakovich a much more terrible blow than all the criticism of the 1930s and 1940s. Taken under the aegis of the watchful Party eye of the Union of Composers, Shostakovich underwent the most anguished period of his life and art. He was painfully torn between a sincere desire to repay all the unsolicited honours through his work, and his real artist's view of what was going on in the country.

It seemed to me that Shostakovich's already battered and morbid psyche would buckle and shatter under this collective onslaught of 'progressive forces'. And he was also beset by illness and old age, thoughts of death and the pointless waste of time entailed by his official duties. But fortunately, in the early 1960s, he met and married a charming and intelligent woman, Irina Supinskaya, who played a purifying and resurrective role for him throughout the rest of his life. It was at this time that I became a member of the Beethoven Quartet.

When my teacher, Vadim Borisovsky, became so ill that he could no longer play, I was asked by Dmitri Tsyganov to help them out by reading through with them Shostakovich's two new quartets, the Ninth and the Tenth. Tsyganov told me that Shostakovich was impatient to hear what he had written. He gave me the copied parts at the Conservatoire at around lunchtime, and I was to come that evening at seven o'clock to the flat of Sergei Shirinsky for a play-through.

I arrived at quarter to seven, worried that I might be too early. However, when I entered the room, to my horror I saw not only all the other musicians in their places, but Shostakovich in an armchair right next to my empty place. This modest 'sight-reading session' turned out to be a three-hour endurance test. Not only was I replacing my teacher in the Beethoven Quartet, but I was having to sight-read sensing the presence of the composer beside me – and I mean sensing, as I didn't dare look at Dmitri Dmitriyevich.

When we had played the last chord of the Ninth Quartet, Dmitri Dmitriyevich said in a satisfied voice, 'Masters are playing.' Thus my place in the Quartet was assured for the forthcoming premières of these two quartets. From then on, most of our meetings with Dmitri Dmitriyevich took place during our lengthy rehearsals either in Sergei Shirinsky's flat, or in Shostakovich's study – his flat was in the same building.

The relaxed atmosphere of these rehearsals had a very beneficial effect on Shostakovich. He reacted painfully to the point of anguish to any external or alien presence. When he was amongst strangers, especially if there were present people ill-disposed towards him, his critics, other composers, or simply someone he didn't know, his nervous tension never slackened. His body kept twitching, his mouth drooped dolefully, his lips trembled and his eyes exuded such oppressive tragic energy that he was frightening to look at. When we were alone he was a different person. (I myself was only involved at a later stage of rehearsal, when the work was almost prepared.) He was calm but concentrated, ready to smile and joke.

When we were preparing the Eleventh Quartet, dedicated to the memory of Vasili Shirinsky, we played it through to Dmitri Dmitriyevich in his study and then stayed on for a meal. This was early in 1966 and Shostakovich could still drink. At the table we drank to the memory of Vasily Petrovich.

A few days previously the funeral of Anna Akhmatova had taken place, and Shostakovich spoke warmly of her poetry. We all stood up to honour her memory. Then Dmitri Dmitriyevich suddenly changed the subject. Greatly agitated, he burst out, 'What I want to say is that everyone writes music as well as he can, but why play dirty tricks on other people? They say we should never speak ill of the dead. But what I want to say is that certain people should be dug out of the grave so I could spit in their face, spit in their face!' Then he thumped the table with his hand as if to indicate that this conversation was closed.[46]

Illness

Throughout his life Shostakovich suffered from bad health. His fragile constitution had been undermined in childhood and adolescence by cold and hunger, and by a bout of tuberculosis. With his sensitive, almost neurotic disposition, he tended to react physically to the outward circumstances of his life. Even before the first symptoms of a debilitating illness manifested itself in 1958, the composer spent much time in hospitals and sanatoria for cures and check-ups.

In early 1958 Shostakovich was admitted to hospital in Moscow in the hope that his condition could be diagnosed. He wrote to Isaak Glikman about his symptoms:

> My right hand has become very weak. I often have pins and needles. I cannot lift heavy things. My fingers can grip hold of any suitcase, but I cannot hang a coat up on a hook. I find it difficult to brush my teeth. When I write, my hand gets tired. I can only play [the piano] slowly and pianissimo. I noticed this condition in Paris, where I was barely able to play my concerts. I just took no notice. The high priests of medicine are unable to answer my question as to what name to give this illness; they have condemned me to a stay in hospital.[47]

In his letters and conversation, Shostakovich was to become increasingly sceptical about the healing powers of the medical profession.

In 1960, at his son Maxim's wedding, his legs suddenly gave way, resulting in the fracture of his left leg. Seven years later he broke his right leg, and remained visibly lame for the rest of his life. With stoic humour he reported from hospital to Glikman: 'We're 75 per cent there: my right leg is broken, my left leg is broken, my right hand is damaged. All it needs is for me to hurt my left hand, and then 100 per cent of my extremities will be out of order.'[48]

It was only towards the end of 1965 that his condition was successfully diagnosed by the Leningrad doctor D. K. Bogorodinsky as a form of poliomyelitis which affected the nerve endings and the bones. Shostakovich

---

46 Fyodor Druzhinin, article commissioned for this book.
47 Letter dated 6 September 1958 (Glikman, *Letters to a Friend*, p. 141).
48 Letter dated 30 September 1967 (*ibid.*, p. 234).

jokingly referred to his having contracted a 'children's disease', but came to resent more and more the humiliations of a debility which made it difficult to walk and use his hands.

Progressively, Shostakovich was forced to spend more time in clinics and hospitals for observation and treatment. In addition to the pains and weakness in his bones and muscles, a bad heart condition necessitated a month's stay in a cardiological clinic in January 1965.

In view of the deteriorating condition of his right hand, Shostakovich had virtually stopped playing the piano in public. Exceptionally, he decided to accompany the singers Galina Vishnevskaya and Evgeny Nesterenko at a concert in Leningrad on 28 May 1966 devoted to his own works, which included the first performances of 'Five Romances on Texts from *Krokodil*', and the 'Preface to My Collected Works and a Short Reflection upon This Preface', as well as the Leningrad première of the Eleventh Quartet. Vishnevskaya remembers that on the night of the concert, Dmitri Dmitriyevich 'was not only nervous, he was afraid – terrified that his hands would fail him.'[49] Isaak Glikman remembers that the weather was unseasonably hot and humid, and that the hall was stifling hot. In addition, Nesterenko, himself suffering from nerves, twice failed to come in at the right place during the performance, causing the composer visible distress.[50]

The nervous strain had been too much for Shostakovich. The following night he suffered a serious heart attack. He spent the following two months in hospital, and on being discharged he was sent for further treatment and observation to a sanatorium outside Leningrad in Melnichny Ruchei for the month of August. By sheer coincidence Shostakovich was allocated the rooms that were once occupied by Andrei Zhdanov. On return home, he was forced to observe an invalid regime, and there were further hospital visits. Describing such a visit to Glikman, Shostakovich displays a mixture of stoicism and black humour worthy of Zoshchenko:

> During my stay in hospital I was examined by Professors Michelson (a surgeon) and Schmidt (a neurologist). They are both extremely satisfied with the condition of my hands and legs. After all, the fact that I cannot play the piano and that I can walk up steps only with the greatest of difficulty has no importance. One need not play the piano, and one can avoid going up steps and stairs. One can just sit at home, there's no need to traipse about slippery pavements and steps. Quite right: yesterday I went for a walk, fell over and banged my knee. Had I stayed at home this wouldn't have happened. And as for everything else, things are also going

49 Vishnevskaya, *A Russian Story*, p. 362–3.
50 Glikman, *Letters to a Friend*, p. 216.

excellently. As before, I can't smoke or drink. There have been temptations. But my foolish terror is stronger than any such temptations.[51]

The composing process was so much part of his nature that Shostakovich was able to adapt to any surroundings, and continued writing in hospital. If the doctors forbade him to compose, then he read avidly, regarding reading as an active process of mental exercise, and not just a pleasant pastime. Many texts for his works were chosen while in hospital, including the verse that was set in the Seven Romances on Poems of Alexander Blok, and the poems set in the Fourteenth Symphony.

Sixtieth birthday

Shostakovich enjoyed celebrating birthdays and anniversaries. For his own sixtieth birthday he wrote two works – the Second Cello Concerto, and the 'Preface to My Collected Works and a Short Reflection upon This Preface', both written in the spring of 1966. In the 'Preface' Shostakovich takes Pushkin's 'Story of a Rhymer' as a starting point, and in a mood of subversive caricature goes on to cite a long list of his own titles and duties, delighting in self-parody. A foretaste of this work can be found in the 'Five Romances on Texts' from *Krokodil's* written in one day on 2 or 3 September 1965. These settings of aphoristic communications from the satirical journal *Krokodil* are full of skittish humour, having their antecedent in such works of the 1920s as Alexander Mosolov's 'Newspaper Announcements'.

Shostakovich saw the New Year of 1966 in at Zhukovka together with a close circle of friends, including Rostropovich and Vishnevskaya. While indulging in a game of 'my favourite tune', Shostakovich played a street song originating from Odessa: 'Bubliki, Kupitye Bubliki'.[52] This innocent little tune unexpectedly made its appearance as the theme of the second movement of the Second Cello Concerto. In that context it soon loses its innocuous quality, going on to acquire virulently menacing overtones.

After finishing his Eleventh Quartet in early March, Shostakovich immediately turned his thoughts to writing another work for Rostropovich. From 20 April Shostakovich spent three weeks in the Crimea, resting at the Sanatorium of Oreanda. By the end of the first week, he had completed the Second Cello Concerto. The work was conceived more as a symphony for cello and orchestra; in contrast to the First Concerto, which seemed the perfect vehicle for Rostropovich's extrovert virtuosity, the Second Concerto is darker and more introspective.

51 Letter dated 10 November 1966 (*ibid.*, p. 221).
52 'Bread rolls – buy our bread rolls.' Bubliki have a hole in the middle, and are somewhat like Jewish bagels.

The Concerto was given its first performance on Shostakovich's sixtieth birthday at the Grand Hall of the Moscow Conservatoire, with Svetlanov conducting and the dedicatee as soloist.

While officially convalescing at home, Shostakovich wrote the Seven Romances on Verses by Alexander Blok for soprano and piano trio, his first composition after suffering a heart attack in May 1966. It was completed on 2 February 1967, and intended for Vishnevskaya, Oistrakh and Rostropovich. Shostakovich hoped to be able to tackle the piano part himself, and he wrote it bearing in mind the restrictions of his illness.

The work occupies a special place in his vocal output for its quality of personal confession, ranging from the intimacy of 'Ophelia's Song', an invocation of Shostakovich's native city of St Petersburg, stormy premonitions of destruction and concluding with a hymn to the therapeutic power of music.

MSTISLAV ROSTROPOVICH recalls the genesis of these two important works by Shostakovich:

The Second Cello Concerto was, like the First, written without a commission, and came as a surprise for me. But for the first time in years, Shostakovich showed me the piece before it was completed. As a rule Dmitri Dmitriyevich never even mentioned a work until it was finished, whereas Prokofiev showed me what he wrote virtually bar by bar, delighting in each new note! In Shostakovich's case, I don't know who else can boast of such an honour, except maybe Mravinsky or Isaak Glikman. On this occasion I was even able to give Dmitri Dmitriyevich one piece of clever advice, which he made use of.

In general I never dared to offer any advice to Shostakovich, as I knew that I hadn't achieved sufficient stature myself. Once Prokofiev said to Myaskovsky, 'Nikolai Yakovlevich, you need to be watered.' Afterwards I asked Prokofiev what he had meant by this. He answered, 'He's like a flower; if he's watered, perhaps he might grow.' In this sense, I knew that I needed watering if I were ever to be able to enter into discussion with a genius.

All the works that Shostakovich wrote for me and for Galina appeared spontaneously. Possibly you could say that the exception were the Seven Romances on Poems by Blok. I had asked Dmitri Dmitriyevich to write some vocalises which Galina and I could perform together. When I made this request, he made no response. When he had finished the cycle, he said to me, 'Slava, you understand, you see, I wanted to satisfy your request – I found some suitable texts to set. And I wrote the first song as you wanted, "Ophelia's

Song'', for voice and cello. But then I started the second song with a whacking great pizzicato on the cello, and I realized that I didn't have sufficient instruments to continue, so I added the violin and piano.'

Shostakovich in general never made any sketches for his compositions. He held the whole preparatory process in his head. Then he sat down at his desk, and without ever touching the piano, he simply wrote down the complete work from beginning to end. He wrote so fast that the urgency of the compositional process is tangibly evident in his uneven and jerky handwriting.[53]

VENYAMIN BASNER describes how Shostakovich wrote the Blok songs after recovering from illness and a creative block:

Dmitri Dmitriyevich often asked advice from performers and composers, although he knew what he was doing better than any of us. It never ceased to surprise me. In his later years, we were very close friends indeed, and he used to telephone me and consult me too.

'Venya, I hope it's not too late, you're not asleep are you? What do you think, can the cor anglais manage those high notes?'

It was ridiculous for him to be consulting me, but I realized that he, too, liked reassurance in regard to his ideas. On that occasion he was writing the Eleventh Symphony, where there is a long solo for cor anglais.

'Do you think it's worth a go, will it work?'

'Of course, Dmitri Dmitriyevich, it'll sound wonderful.'

He knew it without me telling him. I remember him similarly seeking my advice when he was orchestrating Mussorgsky's *Songs and Dances of Death*.

Dmitri Dmitriyevich also valued advice at rehearsals. He liked a friend to come to the rehearsal and sit and follow the score beside him. I myself must have attended all the rehearsals of his new works from the Tenth Symphony onwards. He would make a lot of notes, usually on the back of a packet of 'papirosi'. His comments concerned the dynamics and balance – something might sound too intense or, on the contrary, might get lost in the texture. Dmitri Dmitriyevich always prepared his scores meticulously, to the extent of marking in all the bowings in the string parts. Although he was a pianist himself, he nevertheless demanded that these bowings should be observed.

53 Mstislav Rostropovich: recorded interview with EW.

Shostakovich never addressed his comments directly to the orchestral musicians. With his unfailing politeness, he passed on his requests through the conductor, Evgeny Mravinsky. Dmitri Dmitriyevich was hardly ever known to make any corrections once a composition was in the process of rehearsal. Only in very rare cases would he change anything. Usually he said, 'I'll change it in my next work.'

But I also heard many of Shostakovich's works for the first time before they reached rehearsal stage, when he played them through on the piano, sometimes for the very first time ever. I remember the particular instance of the Seven Romances on Poems by Blok. They were written a few months after Dmitri Dmitriyevich had suffered a heart attack, while playing a concert in Leningrad. He had to spend a long time in hospital, before being allowed home to Moscow. Furthermore, his doctors forbade him to appear in public for several more months.

It was the time of his sixtieth birthday celebrations, when the Second Cello Concerto was given its first performance by Rostropovich. Despite the doctors' instructions to the contrary, he insisted on attending that concert.

I was in regular contact with him during this period. I know that he was very depressed, because, as he told me at the time, he was suffering from a 'composer's block', and for several months he felt 'outside' music. The doctors had also forbidden him to smoke or drink. His morale was at rock bottom, because there was nothing he hated more than not being able to write. All his attempts to compose were futile.

One day I came to Moscow, and, as was my habit I rang him first thing at his dacha in Zhukovka, He said, 'Vova, how wonderful that you're in Moscow. Can you come out here at once, this very moment, without delay?'

I said that I'd be down as soon as I could. I arrived to find him in excellent spirits, walking up and down. He was on his own, as Irina Antonovna had gone away for a few days. He greeted me with these words: 'I've just finished a new work.'

Shostakovich was always tremendously happy after completing a new composition. He told me that the idea of this work came to him when he was still in hospital, recovering from his heart attack. Although he carried the idea with him, since then he had been unable to compose. He had started to doubt himself, suspecting that perhaps his talent had dried up.

But that day, as soon as I walked through the door he said, 'Listen, you're not too tired, are you? Let me play this new work through for you.'

And he sat down at the piano and sung through those wonderful Blok songs. I was thrilled and amazed by the music, and he was delighted to see my genuine pleasure.

He then told me, 'Three days ago, Irina Antonovna left the house. I was alone. I opened a cupboard, and, lo and behold, there on the bottom shelf was half a bottle of brandy. She had hidden all the drink in the house, but by chance I discovered this bottle. And, you know, I had this sudden urge to drink, which I couldn't resist, so I had a glass. And you know, it was so good that I sat down and everything came to me at once, and I finished the work in three days.'

Certainly, I rarely saw him as happy as on that day. He said that from now on he was going to ignore the doctors' advice. One thing is certain though, he never took up smoking again, although he allowed himself the odd glass of spirits.[54]

The composer's association with his peers

Shostakovich had endless curiosity about music, and listened avidly to new works by composers good and bad alike. Although he lent his support and encouragement to his colleagues, there were few composers of his stature with whom he enjoyed a close rapport. Whereas his long-standing friendship with Vissarion Shebalin will have provided Shostakovich with opportunities for professional discourse and creative stimulus, his links with Sergei Prokofiev and Benjamin Britten merit special attention.

Encounters with Prokofiev

Prokofiev and Shostakovich first met in 1927, when the former, on a return visit to Leningrad, heard the 21-year-old composer play his own Piano Sonata. After Prokofiev returned permanently to the USSR in 1936, the composers established a somewhat formal relationship based on mutual respect. Their attitude towards each other's music was coloured by no little ambiguity. Shostakovich regarded Prokofiev as an uneven composer, although he held certain of his works in the highest regard. For instance, he passionately loved Prokofiev's opera *Duenna*, and he valued *War and Peace* highly enough to agree

54 Venyamin Basner: recorded interview with EW.

to orchestrate a fragment of the last act (at Rostropovich's request) for the 1969 Bolshoi Theatre production (which Rostropovich conducted).

OLEG PROKOFIEV, the composer's son was born in France, but returned with his parents to Russia aged nine. In 1941 his parents separated, and Sergei Prokofiev married Mira Mendelssohn-Prokofieva, the librettist of his opera *War and Peace*. Oleg and his brother lived with their mother.

Oleg Prokofiev remembers falling under the spell of Shostakovich's music during the war years, when his mother took him to rehearsals of the Seventh Symphony. He attended the Moscow premières of both the Seventh and Eighth Symphonies, and understood their acute relevance to the situation in the Soviet Union:

I never spoke to my father about my fascination with Shostakovich's music. I think that this happened because when I spoke to him about music and composers, which was rarely, I was older, and already interested in different music. I also might have felt instinctively that in a way my father and Shostakovich were 'in different camps' and I shouldn't mention it. And yet the camps were not so different when, in 1949, they were all labelled a bunch of 'composers writing formalistic, decadent music, which is against the people', and so on.

It is difficult to imagine how the general public tacitly accepted this opinion. In any case, I just remember how two months later, during the May Day Demonstration Parade, I stumbled upon the oldest son of the composer Shebalin in the crowd, and we shared our grievances, lamenting the ugliness and absurdity of all the slanders and accusations addressed at our fathers and other composers. We were surrounded by a crowd from which it was impossible to get away, so we did not drop too many names, and used a kind of Aesopian language. It was a beautifully warm, sunny day, and an atmosphere of festivity prevailed. This somehow made our conversation even more poignant.

Despite the fact that my father and Shostakovich found themselves 'in the same boat' – and a rather sinking one at that – their relationship was not an easy one. There was neither friendship nor natural communication between them. When one reads the few letters that they exchanged, one is struck by a mixture of polite respect and indifference (each of them ignore all the 'friendly remarks' about their music).

The only actual meeting which I witnessed between my father and Shostakovich happened in 1950. It was the first performance of the

Cello Sonata in the Small Hall of the Conservatoire. As it happens, it was probably the only time when just the two of us went to a concert together. My father was not feeling very strong after another bout of illness. The Sonata was played in the first half of the concert, so after congratulating the performers, Rostropovich and Richter, we decided to leave. In the empty foyer Shostakovich approached my father and started speaking to him.

'I would like to congratulate you, Sergei Sergeyevich, on the wonderful Sonata that you have written.'

'Thank you, Dmitri Dmitriyevich, but really it's nothing special. It was an old idea. I have just put together a few bits and pieces.'

Shostakovich, suddenly embarrassed, pattered on, 'Oh no, Sergei Sergeyevich, you shouldn't diminish its value, it's a real masterpiece, I assure you.'

My father was embarrassed too, but also pleased. 'Thank you . . . but . . . no, it's just a trifle.'

And so they went on for some time along these lines, both trying to maintain this extremely courteous and self-deprecating, humble line of conversation. What struck me most was the extraordinary contrast of their physiques and complexions. Two totally different characters united in their respectful uneasiness!

My next close encounter with Shostakovich took place three or four years later, after my father had died. Stalin had also died, and this was the reason for the meeting, as things were beginning to change in a dramatic way. My mother, who had been arrested in 1948, a week after the Zhdanov Decree on Formalism in Music, was languishing in a concentration camp in the North Urals and needed help. The first rumours were circulating that it might now be possible to plead for her release (something unthinkable before). In fact there was talk of people already having been freed on grounds of 'unjustified accusations'. My brother and I thought that Shostakovich, as the most prominent Soviet composer, could help us in this task.

We went to see him in his flat on Kutuzovsky Prospect. He received us without ceremony, dressed casually and wearing slippers in what seemed an enormous sitting room by Moscow standards. In fact our conversation took place right in the middle of the room, which made us feel a bit uneasy.

Without any preamble, we went straight to the point. Shostakovich listened to us with great attention and characteristic intensity. Yet at the same time he never seemed to stop moving. He would continually change his position on the chair, as if he never felt comfortable, crossing one leg over the other, then swapping legs; then a slipper would fall off, and he would try and pick it up from the floor and put it back on; then he would drop it again. Occasionally he would try to light a cigarette, but matches kept breaking, and the cigarette would refuse to light, and so he would take a new one, but couldn't find the packet immediately. This went on throughout our interview.

Surveying the large room, with its two grand pianos covered with dark material, I could not help thinking of a story about Shostakovich which circulated in Moscow at that time. Apparently, one evening a friend dropped by, and on entering this room he found it in darkness, except for the corner where Shostakovich was sitting at a table illuminated by a single lamp. He was reading a book, which he rather awkwardly tried to conceal on seeing his friend.

'What are you reading?' his friend asked.

'Oh, nothing interesting,' was the answer.

When later Shostakovich had to leave the room for a minute, his friend rushed over to the corner and found behind the table the book he had been reading. It was the official – and only existing – biography of Stalin.

I have to say that Shostakovich was very willing to help us. He promised to do whatever was in his power, and we left the house with more hope. In fact, he tried to help so many people that eventually, because he had written such a lot of letters to the government, less and less attention was paid to his pleas, which were considered by and large to be an expression of his 'artistic eccentricity'.[55]

Friendship with Benjamin Britten

The only Western composer with whom Shostakovich entered into a relationship of genuine friendship was Benjamin Britten. Shostakovich claimed that had it not been for the language barrier, they would have become close friends. He intensely admired Britten's *War Requiem*, placing it on a level with Mahler's *Song of the Earth*.[56] The two composers met in London in 1959, when seated together in a box at the Royal Festival Hall to hear Rostropovich perform Shostakovich's First Cello Concerto.

55 Oleg Prokofiev, 'On My Few Contacts with Shostakovich', article commissioned for this book.
56 Letter dated 1 August 1963 (Glikman, *Letters to a Friend*, p. 190).

From then on Rostropovich was instrumental in nurturing the friendship between the two composers. Exchange visits were arranged between Aldeburgh and Moscow. Britten first visited Moscow to conduct the première of his Cello Symphony (written for Rostropovich) in February 1962. Shostakovich visited Aldeburgh in the summer of 1962. Thereafter, Britten and Peter Pears visited Moscow on concert tours on several more occasions.

Britten and Pears also came on two private visits to the Soviet Union as a result of personal invitations from Rostropovich and Vishnevskaya. Thus they spent the summer of 1965 in Armenia, and ten days in Moscow during December 1966 and January 1967 as guests of these Russian musicians. On the latter occasion Britten and Pears gave an inspired performance of Schumann's *Dichterliebe* and Britten's *Michelangelo Sonnets* at the Grand Hall of the Moscow Conservatoire, which Shostakovich attended.

Peter Pears kept a diary record of his visit. Here he describes how he and Britten celebrated Christmas as Rostropovich's Moscow flat, and saw in the New Year of 1967 at his dacha in Zhukovka outside Moscow:

Christmas dinner at Slava's . . . The Russian Orthodox Christmas remains in the middle of January (hence no church bells audible in these days), but the Orthodox Soviet Atheists are only interested in the New Year. All Russians love Christmas trees however, and Father Christmas (if not Santa Claus) is in evidence everywhere. At Slava's there was no tree, but the dinner table was brilliant with candles, and the chandelier over the table (a very beautiful old one bought 'from a very old woman in Leningrad') sparkled. Dmitri and Irena Shostakovich were there, punctual as always, and we exchanged presents . . . We sat down to a splendid spread, with an excellent goose, and talked of many things. Shostakovich in good form, talkative, nervous, Irena gentle, quiet, a marvellous foil for him. After dinner, we produced a specially brought pack of Happy Families (not the old original illustrations alas!) Slava had been champion at Aldeburgh, Christmas 1965, but this time in Moscow it was Dmitri who triumphed. We all enjoyed it, a great success, much laughter, every breach of 'Thank you ver' much' pounced on and punished.

Talk about Stravinsky and the drivelling muck written about Dmitri by Nabokov,[57] etc. Ben tells of his recent dream of Stravinsky as a monumental hunchback pointing with quivering finger at a passage in Ben's Cello Symphony – 'How dare you write that bar?' Dmitri quickly excited and depressed. We drank healths and break up not too late,

57 Reference to Nicholas Nabokov, the composer.

and back to our orange suite and the too short bed and the pillows stuffed with woollen pebbles, and a deep, deep sleep.

Sunday January 1st

Last night, was, as expected, a great occasion and many preparations were made. The idea was that we had the first course (hors d'oeuvres etc.) chez Dmitri, the next, hot, at Slava's, and the sweets at Dmitri's opposite neighbour's, Professor D.[58] whose speciality 'ist mit Kochende Wasser zu tun' (Slava's description of an atomic scientist). The Prof. has a friendly capable wife, a pretty French-speaking daughter and perhaps a sister, anonymous.

We were summoned for 10.00 pm at Dmitri's, we were of course late. The surprise was a special showing of an ancient copy of 'The Gold Rush' upstairs in someone's bedroom. (It is the most wonderful film and full of superb sophisticated photography – don't forget the Chaplin-into-Hen sequence). We had a quick nip of vodka before, and the film lasted exactly the right length of time (until 11.50) when with champagne bottles in hand we went out to the brightly lit Christmas Tree and toasted the New Year to the Soviet National Anthem, and went around kissing one another, the Shostakoviches, the Professor and his family, Dmitri's daughter, Galya, and her very odd beatnik husband, and us. Next came a meal around a long table groaning with drink and eats, and presents (indoors needless to say). We each got some cognac or vodka, a false nose (not expected to be worn for more than a minute or two) and, later, a score of Dmitri's recent 'Stepan Razin'[59] (Yevtushenko) for Ben, and a record of the same for me.

At this point Dmitri, tired, and with a recent heart attack in mind, was packed off to bed, and we came back to 'ours', where Galya, Ben and Slava made a little music while our meal was being prepared. Boiled Soodak (fish) with an egg-sauce, simple and suitable. And then (2 am) we went over to the Prof.'s for tea and sweet things – jolly good, too.

There was a rather amusing contrast between the houses and their owners: (i) Dmitri and the sweet, very gifted, tactful Irene, with a

---

58 Professor Nikolai Antonovich Dolezhal, an eminent nuclear physician and academician. Shostakovich enjoyed his company, and often visited him for a game of cards (usually partnered by his daughter Galina).

59 The recording of *The Execution of Stepan Razin* Op. 119 was made with Kondrashin conducting the Moscow Philharmonic, the RSFSR Academic Choir and Vitali Gromadsky, bass soloist in 1965.

house varying from too much clutter to apparent discomfort. She is in her 20's, he just 60, twice a widower: his children are older than she, I fancy.

(ii) Slava and Galya with tremendously expensive gadgets, chandeliers from Venice, four or five American fridges, which don't work, cupboards full of hair-dryers and electric toasters.

(iii) The Prof. who is obviously a V.I.P. living like an Edwardian bourgeois with nice Persian rugs, discreet and well-arranged lampshades, small dark pictures, a small grand piano. Madam Prof. is Ukrainian and specializes in rich Ukrainian cakes.

At about 3.30 we called it a day and went back through the crisp night snow-white to bed. Not a sound before 9.30 am, then creaks, whispers, and slow emergences towards the bathroom, followed by tea, or breakfast (untouched) upstairs at 11 or so.

News came that Dmitri expected us for lunch at 2. We insisted on a walk, sunny, but very cold, among other reasons for the sake of the endearing dog Jove JOFF, pronounced Dgoff, a young highly intelligent Alsatian, who is tied up outside even in this snow (he has a cosy little Datchya) because indoors he is too big and too incontinent. He adores these walks and loves everyone except Dmitri Shostakovich's beatnik son-in-law who, by the way, is not so cretinous as he looks, speaks reasonable slow English and loves 'drizzle'. D.S. loves the winter and hates the summer – too many mosquitoes. (Remember this!)

For lunch chez D.S. we had (as on our previous post-Armenian visit) exactly the same menu as the night before, and in due course tramped home to sleep, summoned to meet again at 7 pm at the Prof.'s for 'some tea and a little eat'. We couldn't reach the Prof.'s before 8.15, to find D.S. and daughter Galya + Prof. + Frau Prof. playing the card-game called KEENK (?King), a rather dull subversion, with variants of whist. In the other half of the parlour, television was intruding senselessly, for the sole benefit of a non-speaking Chekhov character, (an aunt of Mrs. Prof.'s cousin?) who stared non-stop at it and to whom we were never introduced. After two hours (?) of KEENK, watched with growing impatience by Ben (he was horrified to see D.S. part with 12 roubles to the Prof.) the hint was taken and we sat down to tea, cognac, wine, brawn, ham, and Ukrainian cakes. D.S. rather soon disappeared; we sat on and finally got away at 10, and in furious despair Ben called for 'Winterreise'. I saw what he meant, and it was a very good cleanser for the palate and the mind . . . we sang the first half straight through to our dear Galya, Aza,[60] and Slava. This was as much as I could manage, without practice and with a furious tummy-ache, and in spite of Ben's sulks, refused the second half.

Monday January 2nd [Moscow]
Off up the icy snow – safe to the flat. Before this, we had looked in, at Slava's (and Irene Sh.'s) suggestion, at the final rehearsal of Dmitri's Thirteenth Symphony, the one to texts by Yevtushenko (including 'Babi Yar' – the passionate anti-semitic poem). The performance is tonight, Kondrashin and the Moscow Philharmonic. Owing to our late start, we could only hear some of the last movement, to a text (Baritone Solo and Bass Chorus – 60 of them) which contrasts Galileo with a colleague who also knew that the earth revolves round the sun but, on account of his large family, did not allow himself to say so. 'Give me a career like Pasteur, Galileo or Tolstoi (Chorus: which Tolstoi? Solo: Leo!)' (There was a ghastly career-Soviet-novelist Alexei Tolstoi). It ended very simply, very beautifully, strings, solo string, a bell – really the work of a master – how we wish we could have heard it all.

We leave the Hall for Slava's, Dmitri and Irena to come later at 4 pm to say Goodbye before we go. Lunch is to be at 1 pm and we are to shop again later. Our lunch guests are to be (at Slava's special urgent suggestion) Z. and wife. This man has to our certain knowledge been the arch-enemy of liberal artistic musical thought, for 20 years, and when we get home we must read again Alexander Werth's 'Musical Uproar in Moscow' to see just how foul the things were which he said about Dmitri Sh. and Prokofiev (not to mention Ben). We have met him several times. This Gruyère-faced man is immensely dislikeable.
    . . .
All goes affably and serenely enough until after coffee and/or tea at 3.30 the arrival of Dmitri and Irena. We have always understood that Z. was loathed by Dmitri (why not?) and we felt very guilty and awkward to have these two in the same room. All Ben could do, in the few minutes that Dmitri allowed himself to stay, was to express his great admiration for the piece we had heard this morning (which at its first performance a year or two ago was slaughtered by the political critics). Then the light went out with D. and Irena, and we just passed

60 The pianist Aza Amintayeva, who worked as accompanist in Rostropovich's class at the Conservatoire.

the time until at 4 we were due to start to go, and the Z's with much pleasantry (she is I think, agreeable) took themselves off.

Britten and Pears visited Moscow and Leningrad once more for the Days of British Music in April 1971. In Moscow they were the guests of the British Ambassador, Sir Duncan Wilson. Here his daughter, ELIZABETH WILSON, recalls various encounters with Shostakovich during those days:

In Moscow Britten conducted the London Symphony Orchestra in a concert at the Conservatoire Hall where his Piano Concerto and his Cello Symphony were programmes with Sviatoslav Richter and Rostropovich as the respective soloists. Shostakovich came to that concert, and he also attended a private concert that Britten and Pears gave at the Embassy Residence, where the artists performed a group of Schubert lieder and Britten's *Winter Words*. (I am sure that the white Daneman piano in the grand ballroom of the Embassy has never before or since produced such a subtle and beautiful range of sound!)

But the two composers met twice again in less formal circumstances. A 'rehearsal' performance of Shostakovich's recent Thirteenth Quartet was arranged at Dmitri Dmitriyevich's flat on Nezhdanova Street for Britten and Pears' benefit. I accompanied them as chauffeur and interpreter, mainly so that they could rid themselves of the official Soviet interpreter who had been allotted to them. Ben had taken against her, after noticing the paralyzing effect she had on sensitive Soviet citizens.

We were welcomed at the door by Shostakovich, and sat down in the adjoining study where the 'Beethovens' were already assembled. To our dismay, the official interpreter arrived unbidden – proof that the Embassy walls had ears of their own, as nobody had told her the time and place of this meeting. Still, she was unable to mar this occasion – an exclusively musical experience. We listened in tense silence to the Beethoven Quartet perform this extraordinary music – its effect was all the more powerful because of the intimacy of the occasion – indeed, we were seated almost on top of the performers.

A few days later there was a small gathering at Rostropovich's flat in the next-door building. Britten had just completed his Third Suite for Cello Solo, and had brought it to Moscow as a present for the cellist. That day he was to play the Suite through for him on the piano.

Shostakovich and his wife, Peter Pears, Susan Phipps and myself made up the rest of the audience.

The effect of the Suite was all the more profound for its having been written with a keen awareness of the harassment Rostropovich was recently suffering on account of his open support of Solzhenitsyn. The work, based as it is on Russian themes, was a manifest tribute to a Russian patriot.

When Britten had finished playing, he got up from the piano amidst acclamations of 'Bravo'. He appeared to disclaim all credit for what we had just heard, shrugging his shoulders in embarrassment. With a perplexed expression, he apologized for his inadequate performance and for having played the music too fast. At this Shostakovich chipped in and said, 'Yes, yes, Ben, we composers always tend to play our music too fast . . .'

Dmitri Dmitriyevich went on to make a point about the Kontakion ('Rest with All the Saints') from the Orthodox Liturgy which Britten uses as one of the Suite's themes, all the themes are stated in their pure form at the end of the work, after a set of variations.

Shostakovich knew another version of the melody, using a B flat rather than a B natural, and questioned the source of the variant that Britten had used. Ben was very upset: 'Of course, Dmitri must be right – and now what am I going to do?' (here he addressed Peter Pears) 'I can change the theme, but what about the preceding variations. . . ? I'll have to rewrite the whole thing.'

Seeing his agitation, Dmitri Dmitriyevich tried to calm Ben down, and started apologizing profusely, saying it didn't matter, no doubt there were at least two versions in existence, only he was familiar with the other one. Throughout these exchanges Rostropovich was as excited and affectionate as an overgrown schoolboy. He was intent on driving home to Shostakovich that Britten had written a series of marvellous solo works for cello, whereas Dmitri Dmitriyevich didn't seem to be writing any new chamber work for cello yet. The implication was clear enough, but, alas, these hints went unheeded.

When Britten returned to England, he confirmed with authorities from the Russian Orthodox Church that his version of the Kontakion was generally accepted. However, in deference to Shostakovich, Britten gives the two versions of the Kontakion in the published edition of the Suite, thereby leaving the choice to the performer.

Like Shostakovich, he didn't believe in changing what he had written.[61]

More sixtieth birthdays

In his later years Shostakovich was increasingly drawn to the intimate world of chamber music. Not only do his later works (starting with his Ninth Quartet) have what Alfred Schnittke calls the quality of 'philosophical lyricism',[62] but they were designed as a vehicle for self-discovery and private confession. In this Shostakovich seemed to be relinquishing the public world of the large symphonic canvases, where he spoke from a moral stand as the voice of civic conscience.

Moreover, as if to refute his increasing physical infirmities, Shostakovich was to show an infinite capacity for renewal in the sphere of chamber music, together with a youthful flexibility in his ability to absorb and rework new influences.

This predilection for intimate musical forms went hand in hand with a need to surround himself with an intimate circle of performers. After the bitter lessons of the Thirteenth Symphony, Shostakovich preferred to write for trusted friends. Having composed his two most recent works for Rostropovich and Vishnevskaya, Shostakovich went on to dedicate his next work, the Second Violin Concerto, to his old friend David Oistrakh.

Whereas the First Cello Concerto closely followed the scheme of the First Violin Concerto, this time it was the Second Cello Concerto that served as a model for the Second Violin Concerto. Written in May 1967 it was intended as a sixtieth birthday present for the great violinist, but the composer had anticipated the celebration by one year. However, it is unlikely that Shostakovich, with his extremely accurate memory, actually muddled the date of Oistrakh's birth. In probability he had already conceived the piece and did not want to delay writing it.

Oistrakh remarked on some of the peculiar features of the work: the extreme awkwardness of the C sharp minor key for a string player, and other technical instrumental problems, such as the double stopping, which at first sight appeared insurmountable. But Oistrakh realized that Shostakovich knew exactly what he was after, and had a precise understanding of the violin's possibilities.[63]

---

61 Elizabeth Wilson, 'Reminiscences of Benjamin Britten's Visit to Moscow, April 1971', article written for this book.
62 Alfred Schnittke, 'Circles of Influence', in G. Shneyerson (ed.), *D. Shostakovich: Articles and Material*, p. 225.
63 David Oistrakh, 'A Great Artist of Our Time', in G. Shneyerson (ed.), *D. Shostakovich: Articles and Material*, p. 28.

The Violin Concerto was first performed in Moscow on 26 September 1967 (Shostakovich's birthday), just a month before the première of the Blok cycle, in which Oistrakh also participated.

And there was a pleasant surprise in store for Oistrakh:

> Evidently Dmitri Dmitriyevich considered that, having mistaken the date of my anniversary, he should correct the error. This is how the Sonata for Violin and Piano appeared, written 'in honour of David Oistrakh's sixtieth birthday'. I hadn't in any way expected it, although I had long dreamt that Shostakovich would write a violin sonata.[64]

This splendid three-movement work was completed on 23 October 1968, and was given its official première on 2 May 1969 with Sviatoslav Richter partnering Oistrakh.

In the meantime, Shostakovich had not forgotten another violinist friend. On 11 March 1968 he wrote to Dmitri Tsyganov from Repino: 'Dear Mitya! Tomorrow is your sixtieth birthday. I have just completed a quartet and ask you not to refuse the honour of accepting my dedication to you.'[65] The work in question, the two-movement Twelfth Quartet, represented a new departure for Shostakovich. Here he made use of elements of serialism within the framework of tonality, using the twelve note rows thematically (as indeed he had already done partially in the Blok cycle and the Second Violin Concerto) rather than serially. In view of the official Soviet stand against the Western avant-garde and the New Viennese School, Shostakovich felt the need to justify trespassing on dodecaphonic territory: 'If a composer sets himself the aim of writing purely dodecaphonic music at all costs, then he is artificially limiting himself. But using elements of this system can be fully justified when dictated by the actual compositional concept.'[66] When Tsyganov anxiously brought up the subject of serialism, Shostakovich retorted, 'But one finds examples of it in Mozart's music.'[67]

In any case the composer had rarely been so satisfied with a new work of his own. He informed Tsyganov that the Twelfth Quartet had worked out 'splendidly'; it was more a 'Symphony' than a chamber work. The music emphasizes the importance of the first violin; Tsyganov remarked:

> It was as if he reached the very core of my musical nature. Shostakovich praised my playing in the funereal episode of the second movement, in the lengthy violin pizzicato section, where one seems to hear the tread of death itself. And another peculiar feature of this quartet: only three instruments play for quite some time at the beginning. The Eleventh Quartet was

64 Oistrakh, 'A Great Artist of Our Time', p. 29.
65 Khentova, *Shostakovich*, vol. II, p. 509.
66 *Ibid.*, vol. II, p. 511.
67 *Ibid.*, vol. II, p. 512.

designed for Vasili Shirinsky, but he was no longer with us by the Twelfth Quartet, as the music shows – three instruments remain, only afterwards does the fourth enter.[68]

68 *Ibid.*, vol. II, p. 521.

CHAPTER EIGHT

The Last Years

The Fourteenth Symphony

While orchestrating Mussorgsky's *Songs and Dances of Death* in 1962, Shostakovich became fascinated by the idea of writing a similar cycle and extending it into a vocal symphony. The composer identified not only with the musical idiom of Mussorgsky's overwhelmingly original work but with its angry protest against man's mere temporal existence. Its theme, as well as its music, therefore provided the initial inspiration for his Fourteenth Symphony.

First mention of the composition of a new symphony is made in a letter from Shostakovich to Isaak Glikman dated 11 February 1966.[1] No further reference is made to a new symphonic work in that correspondence until 1 February 1969, when the composer told Glikman that he was writing an oratorio for soprano and bass soloists and chamber orchestra.[2] A fortnight later he reported:

> Yesterday I finished the piano score of my new work. I am not going to call it an oratorio – one can't, as an oratorio calls for a choir. My work doesn't include a choir; just two solo singers – soprano and bass. . . . One probably shouldn't call it a symphony either. For the first time in my life, I remain perplexed as to what name to give a composition of mine.[3]

In this work, as in its predecessor, Shostakovich abandoned the traditional form of the symphony. Scored for strings, percussion and two solo singers, the Fourteenth Symphony is a setting of eleven short poems, which are nevertheless musically linked and form a unified structure. Confrontation with death is at the heart of this work, undoubtedly reflecting Shostakovich's ever-growing preoccupation with mortality. However, through careful ordering of the texts, the composer conveys a specific message of protest at the arbitrary power exercised by dictators in sending the innocent to their deaths. This idea was little commented on during his lifetime, since Shostakovich

---

1 Isaak Glikman, *Letters to a Friend: Dmitri Shostakovich to Isaak Glikman*, p. 209.
2 *Ibid.*, p. 249.
3 Letter dated 17 February 1969 (*ibid.*, p. 250).

himself helped perpetuate the concept of a work primarily concerned with man's personal fears in the face of death.

Shostakovich wrote the Symphony during a month-long stay at the Moscow Kremlin Hospital, when he was gravely ill. During his stay, as a result of an outbreak of influenza, the hospital imposed quarantine, and no visitors (even close family) were allowed in. Forced to observe a strict invalid regime, the composer gave himself over to reading. Thus literature provided an additional stimulus for the new work, which he started to sketch on 21 January 1969. Shostakovich chose his texts from a disparate selection of poetry in translation (Federico Lorca, Guillaume Apollinaire and Rainer Maria Rilke), adding only one original Russian poem by Pushkin's lycée companion, the Decembrist Wilhelm Küchelbecker, addressed to their common friend Anton Delvig. In consultation with his wife, Irina, Shostakovich worked on the poems, adapting and shortening them to his needs.

Writing again to Glikman, Shostakovich summed up what lay behind the choice of texts:

> It occurred to me that there exist eternal themes and eternal problems, amongst which are those of love and death. I had already turned my attention to themes of love, at least in the 'Kreutzer Sonata' on Sasha Chyorny's verses. I had not touched upon the theme of death. Just before entering hospital, I listened to Mussorgsky's 'Songs and Dances of Death', and the idea of tackling death came to fruition.
>
> I would not say that I am reconciled to the phenomenon. I started selecting the verse. My choice of poems is probably quite random. But it seems to me that they are given unity through the music. I composed very fast; I was continually afraid that while writing the Fourteenth Symphony, something would happen to me – that my right hand would cease to function, that I would suddenly go blind, etc. These thoughts gave me no peace.[4]

Later in the letter Shostakovich confessed that he regarded the symphony as a landmark in his output: 'Everything that I have written until now over these long years has merely served as a preparation for this work.'[5]

Indeed, it was the inclusion of texts that once again raised the suspicions and fears of the authorities. It was decided to vet the work at a closed concert on 21 June 1969. During this performance, one of Shostakovich's former persecutors, Pavel Apostolov, had a heart attack and died. Many Russians held the superstitious belief that his death represented a vindication of the sufferings inflicted on the composer over the years; indeed Apostolov's funeral was virtually boycotted by his colleagues.

4 Letter dated 19 March 1969 (Glikman, *Letters to a Friend*, p. 252).
5 Letter dated 19 March 1969 (*ibid.*, p. 252).

The official premières of the Symphony took place in Leningrad on 29 September and 1 October.

RUDOLF BARSHAI had first come into contact with Shostakovich in the 1940s in his viola playing days, when, as a member of first the Quartet of the Moscow Philharmonic (later known as the Borodin Quartet), and then, from 1953, the Tchaikovsky Quartet, he performed Shostakovich's Piano Quintet with the composer.

In 1958 Barshai founded the Moscow Chamber Orchestra together with Andrei Volkonsky, and was its chief conductor until he left the Soviet Union.

Here Barshai recalls how Shostakovich's Fourteenth Symphony came into being:

It all started early in the year of 1969, when Shostakovich sent me a telegram asking me to phone him at home. At the time I had no telephone, although I had made many requests for one to be installed These requests were ignored initially, but eventually an answer was sent to the Moscow Philharmonic, where I was registered as 'an employee', saying: 'The District Union of the Workers of Such and Such a District has established that Comrade Barshai has no need of a telephone.'

I went out to a call box and rang Shostakovich at once. He put various questions to me. The first question regarded the exact formation and numbers of the Moscow Chamber Orchestra. We only used one double bass.

Dmitri Dmitriyevich asked, 'Would it be possible to have two players?'

'Of course.'

'And how many percussionists?'

'As many as you need.'

'Thank you very much, thank you very much. That was important for me. Goodbye and thanks.'

And not another word. It did make me suspect something was brewing, of course.

Two weeks later I got a second telegram from Shostakovich asking me to phone him urgently.

Again I rang him immediately.

'Rudolf Borisovich, what are you doing at this very moment?'

'I'm free now.'

'Then come around at once to see me.'

I rushed over to his place. Dmitri Dmitriyevich then played through his Fourteenth Symphony on the piano – he had only just completed it. He showed me the score and asked me various questions in regard to orchestration, concerning the divisi and similar details. We spoke for two hours. He then said, 'If you don't have any objection, let's invite Vishnevskaya to sing the soprano part.'

'Of course I have no objection. What about the bass?'

'Well, let's wait a little and think about it. And when will you start rehearsals?' he added.

I said I was willing to start as soon as the soloists were ready and knew their parts.

After this we met frequently; Dmitri Dmitriyevich made some minor corrections to details in the score. Each time he made a change he showed it to me. It is interesting how jealously he regarded even the smallest change. In general he never wanted to correct anything, and considered that corrections were an unnecessary evil. He would advise his pupils, 'Don't change anything. Make your corrections in your next composition.' And should somebody be so bold as to make some suggestion to him, he would say, 'Thank you very much for your advice, thank you very much . . . I'll make that correction in my next work.'

But in this case, things were a little different. For instance I had a small point to make (I would never have gone so far as to offer Shostakovich advice). There is the moment in the last bars of the Symphony when the whole orchestra is not required to play, although the music finishes loudly. I know of course that in some of Mahler's symphonies the music finishes softly and the number of players in the orchestra decreases accordingly. But in this case the Symphony finishes loudly and not all the players participate – only strings, no percussion. I suggested utilizing some percussion. Shostakovich said that this was a valid point and he tried to write additional percussion parts for the ending.

After the first 'unofficial' performance in Moscow in June 1969, he wrote to me while I was on holiday with some suggestions for the additional percussion parts. He pencilled in the staves on the letter and notated these parts. But in the end he decided against using them.

One day Dmitri Dmitriyevich informed me that Vishnevskaya was having to delay learning her part as she had a busy schedule and was touring abroad. Therefore she could not make any promises as to when she would be ready.

I said, 'Never mind, we'll wait for her.'

But Dmitri Dmitriyevich answered, 'No, no, I don't want to wait, I'm afraid I'll die soon, and I want to hear my work. I was afraid that I wouldn't live to finish the Symphony, but I managed in time, I managed in time. If you have no objections, I'd like to propose another singer, Margarita Miroshnikova, who sings my music. Let's go and hear her.'

So we went to the Bolshoi Theatre to hear her sing, and I liked her voice. He said, 'Let's ask her to learn the part.'

We then chose Evgeny Vladimirov as the bass. The two singers started to learn their parts, and as they were getting on very well we started the orchestral rehearsals. I rehearsed separately with the singers. What was really remarkable was that Shostakovich came to every single rehearsal from the very first orchestral read-through to the individual piano rehearsals with the singers. He didn't miss a single one. He sat and listened, completely absorbed in his own music, excited and thrilled by its sound.

Once we were rehearsing in the large rehearsal room of the Piatnitsky Choir at the Philharmonia. As usual he was sitting behind me with Irina Antonovna. We were playing the second movement, Malaguena – that passionate smouldering Spanish music – when suddenly I felt a painful blow on my shoulder. It quite frightened me! I turned around to see Shostakovich at my side. He whispered in my ear, 'Keep going, keep going. The devil take it, I never thought it would sound so good.'

We scheduled a great number of rehearsals, so as to try out the corrections. Shostakovich actively participated in this process of work. He usually didn't make outright suggestions. For instance, when it came to the question of tempi, he tended to be rather sly. He would say, 'Yes, the tempo that you are playing now is exactly right.' But if I suggested, 'Should it be a bit faster or slower?' he would only answer, 'No, just go on like that.'

One could sense Shostakovich's real agitation during these rehearsals. I attribute this to the fact that he particularly valued this Symphony. I had known Shostakovich over thirty years, but I never saw him in such a state of excitement. He was like a small boy completely carried away by his passions.

We experienced many difficulties with the first performance. Initially we were not allowed to perform the Symphony. As often happened in the Soviet Union, nobody actually *forbade* the performance, but, by withholding a performance space, the officials succeeded in temporarily implementing a ban. Then some big-wig decided that it would be better if the first performance were not given in public. We were allocated the Small Hall of the Conservatoire for a 'closed' concert. Special invitation tickets were issued to a select audience.

This performance took place on 21 June. The orchestra and I were on stage, ready to start, when Shostakovich got up to address the audience. He talked about the nature of the Symphony. He stood below in the stalls; he didn't want to come on stage at that point. Miroshnikova and Vladimirov sang the solo parts, and Galya Vishnevskaya sat in the front row of the audience.

It was during the performance that Pavel Apostolov died. While we were playing, I heard a noise. Well, I thought to myself, some noise in the hall, it's something that happens during concerts. We went on playing. Afterwards I was told that somebody felt unwell and had been carried out. Apostolov died almost at once. Afterwards, Shostakovich appeared backstage chewing his fingernails (he had the habit of biting his nails when he was nervous).

'I didn't want *that* to happen, I didn't want that.'

He of course knew exactly who it was that had died. There was a terrible symbolic coincidence in the death of the man who, in effect, had been Shostakovich's persecutor for years on end.

Solzhenitsyn was at that first 'closed' performance in Moscow. I was told afterwards that he had said that the Finale lacked 'light'. But I don't think that this was an issue between him and Shostakovich, as has been claimed. It is more a question of one's own religious and aesthetic outlook. It is true that in Mahler's symphonies, for instance, there is a lot of light in the Finales. But Mahler was deeply religious, whereas Shostakovich was not. Shostakovich portrayed reality in his work.

The official premières of the Fourteenth Symphony took place a few months later, at the end of September, first in Leningrad and then in Moscow. During the summer vacation Shostakovich wrote to me saying that there was a wonderful opportunity to perform the Symphony at the Hall of the Leningrad Capella.

At the end of August, when we were all back in Moscow after our holidays, Dmitri Dmitriyevich rang me up and asked if I would go to see him at once.

'Rudolf Borisovich, I'm terribly agitated.'

'What's happened?'

'Come at once – I'll explain everything.'

I hurried to his home to find him in a ghastly state. He was a bundle of nerves. He implored me, 'Rudolf Borisovich, release me from these terrible intrigues between the soprano soloists. They're torturing me. They came to see me, one of them shrieking, the other weeping. They both want to perform the official première. Miroshnikova claims that she was the first to learn the part and has already given a performance. Well, that's true of course. And as for Vishnevskaya, well, you understand the situation, you understand the situation.'

'Why don't we have two casts of singers, like in opera houses, so if one were to fall ill, the other would stand in,' I suggested.

'What a wonderful idea, a wonderful idea, that's what we'll do.'

So it was that both in Leningrad and in Moscow there were two premières, one concert immediately following the other, with two sets of singers. Vishnevskaya and Mark Reshetin were the soloists in the first of the two concerts, Miroshnikova and Vladimirov in the second.

But the first recording was made with Miroshnikova singing, rather than Vishnevskaya. This happened because Shostakovich wanted a recording made as soon as possible. He was convinced that he did not have long to live, and he wanted to have the Symphony on record immediately. He himself rang the Melodiya record company to make the arrangements. Unfortunately, Vishnevskaya was busy for the next six months and had no time to make the record. Who was I to insist, if Shostakovich was in such a rush and so adamant that he wanted to listen to his Symphony before he died? So the record was made with Miroshnikova as soprano soloist.[6]

The violinist MARK LUBOTSKY first met Shostakovich in 1955, but he never had more than a passing acquaintance with the composer. Like the majority of Soviet musicians, Lubotsky regarded every new work by Shostakovich as an event, and attended as many performances of his works as possible. Here he describes the 'closed' première of the Fourteenth Symphony:

'Death is terrifying, there is nothing beyond it. I don't believe in life beyond the grave.'

That's what Shostakovich said before the first closed performance of

6 Rudolf Barshai: recorded interview with EW.

his Fourteenth Symphony in the Small Hall of the Moscow Conservatoire in June 1969. Rudolf Barshai conducted the Moscow Chamber Orchestra. The audience was made up largely of Moscow composers, and students and professors of the Conservatoire.

On my right sat a nice-looking middle-aged lady, an administrator at the Composers' House, and next to her a shortish somewhat elderly gentleman.

Concluding his brief commentary on the new symphony, Shostakovich quoted from Nikolai Ostrovsky's novel, *How the Steel Was Tempered*. The essence of the passage was that one should die with a clear conscience, 'so that one need not be ashamed of oneself'.

And lastly, before the start of the performance, he asked the audience to remain as quiet as possible as the concert was being recorded. A hush fell on the hall. The sinister symphony of death was played in dead silence. During a passage of intensely quiet music in the fifth movement, 'On Your Guard', suddenly a chair seat closed abruptly with a loud bang. The elderly man sitting next to the lady at my side jumped to his feet and hurriedly rushed out of the hall, not so much as glancing round. She whispered to me, 'What a bastard. He tried to destroy Shostakovich in 1948, but he failed. He still hasn't given up, and he's gone and wrecked the recording on purpose.'

'Who is he?' I enquired.

'Apostolov,' she whispered in reply. In 1948 Apostolov was a member of the music department of the Central Committee; he was a notorious persecutor of Shostakovich.

When the Symphony was over, the first people to come out of the audience saw ambulance men carrying a body out of the building on a stretcher. Apostolov had had a heart attack while the music was still being played. 'Death is on his guard, think of your conscience,' the Symphony had been warning us.

The next day I ran into Shostakovich near the entrance of the Union of Composers. I started to tell him what an enormous impression the Fourteenth Symphony had made on me, and I thanked him for it. But he kept repeating, 'No, it is I who should thank you.'[7]

The Fourteenth Symphony became something of an issue amongst the Russian intelligentsia. Shostakovich was much criticized for his bleak and

7 Mark Lubotsky, extract from unpublished memoirs.

pessimistic attitude to death, his rejection of religious consolation. In particular Rilke's words in the Symphony's Finale, 'Death is all-powerful', caused great offence, and Shostakovich was accused of betraying the Russian's mystic belief in eternal life in this Symphony forlorn of light and hope.

Amongst those who allegedly disagreed with Shostakovich's position was the writer Alexander Solzhenitsyn. Irina Shostakovich remembers the writer expressing his outrage in a letter to Shostakovich over the composer's inclusion of Apollinaire's poem 'In Prison – at the Santé Jail', where he pointed out that Apollinaire had spent only a few days in prison, and his sufferings were as nothing when compared to those of the millions who had languished in Soviet prisons and camps.[8]

Another point of view is postulated by Grigori Kozintsev, who believed that life-affirming forces shine through the most tragic and grotesque elements of Shostakovich's music: 'Even in the face of extreme horror, what one hears is not the victory of darkness and death, but the victory of creativity.'[9]

The first performances of the Thirteenth and Fourteenth Symphonies in Germany

The conductor THOMAS SANDERLING was born in Leningrad, but returned with his family to East Germany in 1960 aged eighteen. There he completed his studies and started his career. In 1969 he was invited to conduct the Moscow Philharmonic Orchestra in the Soviet Union. Shostakovich attended Sanderling's concert in Moscow, and invited him to his home:

The first thing that struck me about Dmitri Dmitriyevich was the immense power which emanated from him. I remembered this quality from my childhood, and it is something I have never encountered before or since. Anyone who came into contact with Shostakovich, whoever he might be, could not but be intensely aware of being in the presence of a person of great spiritual purity and moral fibre. Shostakovich had an almost hypnotic effect on people. I myself felt virtually paralyzed during the first hour of that visit. There was nothing imposing about his exterior, and no affectation in the way he was dressed. But a sort of magical stillness surrounded him.

What Shostakovich actually said during my visit had less importance than my awareness of his presence, which I experienced as a unique phenomenon. By then, he was already suffering from illness

8 In private conversation with EW.
9 Grigori Kozintsev, *The Complete Works*, vol. II, p. 441.

and spoke very little, and mainly about music. At the end of the visit he gave me the scores of his Thirteenth and Fourteenth Symphonies, both inscribed to me. At this point, Dmitri Dmitriyevich remained silent, and I felt some reaction was expected from me. I asked him tentatively if he would permit me to perform these works. He agreed, and, by giving his approval, he granted me the right to the first German language performances of these two vocal symphonies.

Shostakovich always insisted that vocal texts should be performed in the language of the audience. He used to say, 'You understand, it is absolutely awful when you hear everybody at the concert turning their programme pages simultaneously.' This detail was an additional reason for him to ensure that comprehension of words was direct and did not necessitate printed translations.

And so our working contact started. For instance, as one of the poems in the Fourteenth Symphony by Rilke was a Russian translation of the original German poem, Dmitri Dmitriyevich was very curious to know if the music would fit the original text. Because Russian, unlike German has no articles, we found that we needed more notes for the amount of syllables. Shostakovich agreed to add the necessary extra notes for this original German text.

I approached the East German poetess, Waltraut Levine, who specialized in translating opera librettos. I started by providing her with a literal word for word working translation of the Russian verse, which she then polished. In the original Russian Shostakovich often added an accent to create a special effect, so as to emphasize a particular word or syllable. The musical effect, whether it is made through an accent, a tremolo, or orchestral colouring, loses its meaning if it is not retained in translation. So certain words had to remain on certain notes. We took a lot of trouble to get this right.

After my performance of the Fourteenth Symphony in East Berlin, I sent a tape from the concert to Dmitri Dmitriyevich. Shortly afterwards Shostakovich came to Berlin and rang me.[10]

'Thomas, this is Shostakovich. Are you free now? It would be wonderful if you would come and visit us, or better still, we'll come to visit you.'

And literally within the space of an hour he and his wife, Irina Antonovna, had arrived at our doorstep. He first of all asked my

10 Shostakovich visited East Berlin in May 1972.

mother to show him around the flat. He was curious to know where the kitchen was.

'Where's the kitchen, where's the kitchen? The kitchen must be comfortable, that's important.'

There was something very touching about his attention to such details, a sign of his caring attitude towards people. I can therefore believe what is said about his answering every letter ever sent to him, however trivial. This punctiliousness was no mannerism, but the essence of his nature.

At the end of this visit to Berlin, it was arranged that I would give the first performance of the Thirteenth Symphony in East Germany. It must be remembered that, as East Germany completely depended on Moscow for 'guidance', it had not yet been possible to perform this symphony there. And indeed, the Thirteenth Symphony, after the Moscow première, was virtually banned from performance within the Soviet Union, and hence in all East European countries as well. Even Kurt Mazur, with his dynamic energy, had been unable to procure permission to play the Thirteenth Symphony with the Gewandhaus.

However, I knew a wonderful woman, Ruth Brennecke, from the East Berlin Radio, who was able to organize the performance. Knowing that Shostakovich was to return to Berlin for the opening night of the production of *Katerina Izmailova* at the Staatsoper,[11] she planned the performance of the Thirteenth Symphony to take place immediately afterwards. The officials were delighted, as they had forgotten to check the status of the Symphony with Moscow, and assumed that this would be a great honour. In other words, they were bluffed into permitting an event of great musical importance, which could have carried 'dangerous' political overtones.

In the event there was no uproar or scandal at the East Berlin performance, despite the fact that the Thirteenth Symphony had never been performed in Germany (either East or West). Not that anything was done to promote the event; there was no advance publicity and the Symphony's performance was not so much as mentioned in the Press.[12]

11 The Berlin première took place on 24 February 1973.
12 Thomas Sanderling: recorded interview with EW.

Treatment at Dr Ilizarov's clinic in Kurgan

Shostakovich's last years were plagued by health problems. Despite this he spent as much time travelling as his health permitted to attend performances of his music abroad and within the Soviet Union. He preferred to compose in the peaceful surroundings of the Composers' Retreats, notably at Dilizhan in Armenia and at Repino outside Leningrad, or at his own dacha in Zhukovka outside Moscow. But even when hospitalized Shostakovich never lost his determination to compose. His courage in the face of illness was indomitable, and to the end of his life, despite the bad condition of his right hand, he always wrote down his music himself.

Shostakovich had read about the remarkable story of Valery Brumel, a high jumper and member of the Soviet Olympic team, who had broken both legs in an accident. Surgeons in Moscow performed fourteen operations, but were unable to help him. A form of treatment developed by the orthopaedic surgeon Gavriil Ilizarov, known as osteo-synthesis, produced amazing results, saving limbs, lengthening bones and straightening out deformations. In Ilizarov's orthopaedic clinic in Kurgan, a small town east of the Urals, Brumel recovered fully and was able to return to sport.

Shostakovich now placed all his hopes on the magical powers of Dr Ilizarov. He informed Isaak Glikman in early January 1969 that he hoped that Ilizarov would return the 'working use of my right hand'.[13] In a further letter dated 1 February 1969, he states that, unlike Brumel, he has no desire to jump: 'But I want to be able to climb on to a bus or a tram. I want not to cringe with terror as I step on to an escalator in the metro (Underground). I want to be able to walk up and down stairs easily. My wishes are quite modest.'[14]

When his illness was finally diagnosed at the end of that year as poliomyelitis, Shostakovich wrote pessimistically to Glikman from his hospital bed that Ilizarov's course of therapy could not be expected to help this condition.[15] However, Dr Ilizarov decided that, on the contrary, the composer would profit from intensive treatment at his Kurgan orthopaedic clinic. Hence Shostakovich spent two long periods in 1970 in Kurgan under Ilizarov's care, from 27 February to 9 June, and from 27 August to 27 October. He went back on a third, shorter visit for further treatment in June 1971.

The strenuous regime in the Kurgan orthopaedic clinic included massage and physiotherapy, gymnastic exercises and medication.

By mid-April Shostakovich was already feeling the benefits of the cure. On 11 May 1970 he reported to Glikman, 'My achievements are manifold: I can

13 Letter dated 2 January 1969 (Glikman, *Letters to a Friend*, p. 248).
14 *Ibid.*, p. 249.
15 Letter dated 23 November 1969 (*ibid.*, p. 265).

play the piano, walk up and down stairs, climb on to a bus (true, with difficulty). . . . I can use my right hand to shave, do up my buttons. I don't miss my mouth with my spoon.'[16] Ilizarov had given him back not only physical strength in his limbs, but hopes for the recovery of his well-being.

During this period, despite great fatigue from the treatment, Shostakovich started work on the music for Kozintsev's film *King Lear* and wrote *Loyalty*, settings of Dolmatovsky's patriotic ballads for unaccompanied male choir. In between his two courses of treatment Shostakovich completed the music for *King Lear* and his Thirteenth Quartet.

Encouraged by the good results, the composer spoke about his renewed capacity for work, and even of the possibility of resuming his pianistic activity. However, this respite was relatively short-lived. Two months after completing his Fifteenth Symphony in July 1971, the composer suffered a second heart attack. It seemed that all that had been achieved under Ilizarov's regime was wasted, and Shostakovich's weak condition excluded resuming any of the physical exercises that made up an essential part of the treatment. From then onwards, it became increasingly difficult for Shostakovich to walk and write, and more and more he suffered the humiliation of his debilitating condition.

MSTISLAV ROSTROPOVICH introduced Shostakovich to Ilizarov, and lent his support to the creation of the special orthopaedic clinic in Kurgan:

As Dmitri Dmitriyevich's illness advanced he expressed a desire to have treatment from Doctor Ilizarov in his clinic in the Urals, in the town of Kurgan. Dr Ilizarov had achieved incredible things with patients suffering from a variety of bone complaints, and Dmitri Dmitriyevich said that in his belief this was the only doctor who could help him.

I was able to organize this contact for him, and then I helped gather money for the clinic. As a volunteer unpaid day worker (a 'Leninist subbotnik' or Saturday worker), I also helped to build the second storey of the new hospital that Ilizarov was building then. During the months that Dmitri Dmitriyevich was having treatment, I came to Kurgan to give some concerts with the Sverdlovsk Philharmonic. I made an appeal to the orchestra to join me in this enterprise, and so with this volunteer force we virtually finished building the second storey of the clinic in a day. I personally built the toilet on the second floor. I insisted that we were given 200 pairs of gloves with our bricks and cement, saying that if any harm was done to the musicians' hands, the local party organization would be held responsible. We had

16 Letter dated 11 May 1970 (*ibid.*, p. 271).

an instructor with us, of course, otherwise the whole building would have collapsed. But we all worked hard, and for two days afterwards my back was completely rigid.

My purpose in organizing these concerts in Kurgan with the Sverdlovsk Orchestra was to perform Shostakovich's music, so that people there would know who this Shostakovich was. In the end, I played so many concerts in Kurgan that I bored everybody to tears. When people saw me carrying my cello on the street, they quickly crossed to the other side. But Dmitri Dmitriyevich knew what I was doing and appreciated my efforts on his behalf.[17]

GRIGORI KOZINTSEV started work on his film *King Lear* in the autumn of 1969. He invited Shostakovich to write the music, and met him early in the New Year of 1970 to discuss the project:

We were speaking in the study of Cottage number 20 in Repino, where in the past we had slaved over *Hamlet*. How much better the cottage looks now – new carpets and furniture, a sideboard with a tea set and crystal glasses edged in gold.

And how much worse Shostakovich looks. He limps, and can no longer play his music. He has been ill for a long time. His hand has shrivelled up, his bones are brittle . . . The surgeon from Kurgan has cured Brumel's leg. Dmitri Dmitriyevich wants to go to him.

'Do you know,' said one of the world's most famous people, 'all over this country people are trying to get into his clinic. But, you know, fortunately I've found a sponsor: Dolmatovsky has arranged for me to go to him.'

We decided on the first musical piece. The theme is grief, misfortune. That's how we'll start our work on *King Lear*.[18]

[Repino, July 1970]
Dmitri Dmitriyevich walks, or rather advances slowly from his cottage to the car, as if all those months of treatment in Kurgan had never happened.

But at the recording of the music [for *King Lear*], he takes off his jacket, and, full of energy, in a different rhythm, runs up to the conductor with ease, as if he had forgotten about his illness. There's

17 Mstislav Rostropovich: recorded interview with EW.
18 Kozintsev, *Complete Works*, vol. II, pp. 437, 438.

no canteen, so from nine in the morning till six in the evening he doesn't eat anything. What kind of strict regime is this?

Next morning he greets me with an exalted quotation, completely untypical of Shostakovich's normal speech: 'Music is my soul, as Glinka said, you know. Yesterday I forgot about everything, and, you know, I felt really well. One must be absorbed in one's work.'

His work, naturally, he performs excellently. I was particularly struck by the introduction to the storm, Lear addressing the sky. The sounds grow, intensify, then recede, and it all starts again. One note, F, remains.

'There may be few notes,' says a satisfied Shostakovich, 'but there's lots of music.'

We both immediately rejected any form of illustration for the storm. The forces of evil break out into liberty, celebrating and exulting in victory.'[19]

FLORA LITVINOVA recalls her last meeting with Shostakovich:

My last conversation with Dmitri Dmitriyevich took place at the House of Creativity at Ruza in 1970. Dmitri Dmitriyevich had returned from having treatment at Dr Ilizarov's clinic with the use of his right hand partially restored. He even tried to play the piano, but he would tire very easily. On that occasion Irina Antonovna had gone to the cinema. Although Dmitri Dmitriyevich did not like to complain, the conversation took a sombre turn. First Dmitri Dmitriyevich spoke of Maxim's success as a conductor with great pride, how well he performed his symphonies, and what successes he had scored on his tours to the West. 'But, of course, he doesn't want to live there. And think how proud Nina would have been of him.'

Then we spoke of the Fourteenth Symphony, and how each of the authors of the texts had undergone personal tragedy.

'But I myself am not ready to die. I still have a lot of music to write. I don't like living here at Ruza, I prefer working at home, at the dacha at Zhukovka. But Irina Antonovna gets tired looking after me, and she too needs a rest. Here we are taken care of, and there is nothing to worry about. It's true that I have to endure those interminable meetings with my colleagues where there is a lot too much talk.'

We remembered how we had seen in the New Year of 1948 here at Ruza.

19 *Ibid.*, vol. II, pp. 438, 439.

'Yes, those were desperate times. Things are a bit easier now; but, goodness, how they managed to contort us, to warp our lives! . . . You ask if I would have been different without 'Party guidance'? Yes, almost certainly. No doubt the line that I was pursuing when I wrote the Fourth Symphony would have been stronger and sharper in my work. I would have displayed more brilliance, used more sarcasm, I could have revealed my ideas openly instead of having to resort to camouflage; I would have written more pure music.

'But I am not ashamed of what I have written, I like all my compositions. "A child may be crippled and lame, but he's dear to his parents all the same." And besides that, think how much music I have written for the cinema. It's not bad either. And it gave me and my family a chance of a reasonable living. But it used up so much of my energy and time . . . I wrote music to more than thirty films, some of it perfectly decent music. That was possible with directors like Kozintsev and Arnshtam, who understood that the function of music in films is not just accompaniment, but the means of revealing the essence and idea of the film.'[20]

The rise of the dissident movement

The 1968 Soviet invasion of Czechoslovakia not only marked a turning point in the thinking of the liberal intelligentsia, but a low point in relations with the outside world. Western governments and press were united in condemning the Soviet use of force and interference in the affairs of another state.

In addition the Soviet leadership now had to contend with the combative spirit of the growing dissident movement, which was learning to fight back in the face of repression. The dissidents' demands that the regime should at least observe the legitimacy of laws embodied in the Soviet constitution provided them with a powerful weapon. Infringements by the Soviet authorities of their own laws were now documented and publicized through such means as 'The Chronicle of Current Events' in samizdat, and later by the Helsinki Watch Groups.

As the Soviet human rights movement grew inexorably, its aim widened to include demands for religious and national freedom, as well as an end to political repression. Soon voices from the scientific community, notably those of Andrei Sakharov and Zhores Medvedyev, joined ranks with the dissenters in order to protest against continuing restraints on freedom of information and damaging authoritarian policies imposed from above.

20 Flora Litvinova, article commissioned for this book.

The Soviet authorities used two basic methods to deal with dissidence. On the one hand they stepped up their campaigns against protestors, using harassment and intimidation, and arresting those who annoyed them on such pretexts as violation of public order or discrediting the Soviet system. In particular an intensified campaign was started against the writer Alexander Solzhenitsyn, who was awarded the Nobel Prize in 1970.

The authorities also sought to weaken the dissident movement by removing its most active members from the scene. Such significant figures as Pavel Litvinov, Iosif Brodsky, and Vladimir Bukovsky were compelled to leave the country. When Alexander Solzhenitsyn was bundled on to a plane and forced into exile in February 1974, this had far-reaching repercussions. Only a few months later Rostropovich and Vishnevskaya, whose professional activity had been stifled in the wake of their support for the writer, applied for (and were granted) permission to leave the country for a two-year period. Before this time was out, they were stripped of Soviet citizenship, thereby being forced into exile. Shostakovich surely had Solzhenitsyn, if not his musician friends, in mind when he set Michelangelo's sonnet on Dante, 'To the Exile' in his great vocal cycle Op. 145, composed later that year.

A new policy permitting the emigration of Jews to Israel (a loophole through which Russians married to Jews could also leave the country) was implemented simultaneously to these events. Not that the right to emigrate was automatically granted – the authorities could choose to withhold an exit visa, thereby subjecting the would-be emigrants (soon dubbed 'refusniks') to harassment and deprivation of civic rights. Pressure groups at home and in the West fought against the unjust persecution of protesters and refusniks who languished in Soviet jails or psychiatric wards.

Musicians were amongst those who chose to emigrate (ostensibly to Israel) and seek a better life in the West. They included such diverse figures as the composer André Volkonsky, the conductor Rudolf Barshai and the violinists Mark Lubotsky and Rotislav Dubinsky.

The repressive policies implemented by the Soviet authorities were ultimately counter-productive. Samizdat may have had a limited numerical readership nationwide, but its impact was enormous. On the other hand a large part of the population owned short-wave radio and had access to information through broadcasts of Russian language radio stations (notably the BBC Russian Service) from the West. Hence, with every year that passed a mood of disenchantment and cynicism became increasingly prevalent at many levels of society.

The Brezhnev era, now dubbed as the period of 'stagnation', was marked by a growth of corruption and a consolidation of the Nomenklatura, the enormous class of Party apparatchiks who ruled the bureaucracy. For artists, scientists and all professional people who wished to avoid confrontation and yet to live an 'honest' life, these were difficult years. Their problems received less attention from the outside world, but were the cause of constant aggravation at home and at work. With so many of the country's most eminent figures either forced to emigrate or deprived of the possibility of practising their professions, the rule of mediocrity, if not down-right incompetence, became the order of the day.

'Yurodivy' or cynic?

By his later years Shostakovich had achieved a position of undisputed fame, and the authorities did not dare touch him. But in his composition and his personal conduct he seemed to retreat more and more into his own inner world.

The argument first mooted in the West by Solomon Volkov[21] that Shostakovich consciously took on the role of 'Yurodivy', or holy fool, has gained general acceptance. The 'holy fool', who protests 'in the name of humanity, and not in the name of political changes',[22] was long recognized in Russia as having the historical right to expose evil. His use of arcane symbols or simplistic parables to express the truth was later adapted to the conditions of Soviet Russia, where every statement could have more than one message. However, instead of aiming to create a meaningful paradox, the modern yurodivy revealed the truth at the level of the 'sub-text', making this apparent by deliberately communicating banalities on the surface level. This concept shaped Russian cultural consciousness during the years of totalitarian rule.

However, as times changed, it was important to make challenges that were direct and explicit. If the Russian intelligentsia was to confront the political system, it had to shoulder its civic responsibilities in a manner that was not open to misinterpretation.

As Volkov puts it, 'Shostakovich was a moralist . . . but he never had a political programme.'[23] And it was here, in his failure to lend open support to the human rights movement, that the composer laid himself open to criticism. In his late years, as a public figure, he allowed himself to be manipulated unscrupulously, adding his signature to official letters and making speeches expressing the Party line. Although he participated in these events with growing disgust and cynicism, his reputation as a 'signer' became an issue with the liberal community.

Whether Shostakovich actually went as far as physically adding his signature to letters and articles released under his name in the Soviet press is

21 Solomon Volkov, *Testimony: The Memoirs of Dmitri Shostakovich*, p. xxi.
22 *Ibid.*, p. xxxiii.
23 *Ibid.*, p. xxxiii.

beside the point; but he certainly didn't bother to disown his signature or disassociate himself from published statements if they did indeed appear without his knowledge or permission. The controversy reached its height in 1973, when his name appeared as a signatory in a letter in *Pravda*[24] denouncing André Sakharov. That he regretted this act, there can be no doubt. He was called to task by Lydia Chukovskaya and given the cold shoulder by many colleagues.

One should remember that in the past Shostakovich had intervened privately on behalf of many, many people. As late as 1966 he was a signatory (with the writers Kornei Chukovsky, Konstantin Paustovsky, and the academician Pyotr Kapitsa, amongst others) of a letter to the Central Committee demanding that Solzhenitsyn should be given proper living conditions so that he could continue his literary activity.

On the other hand, two years later, when Solzhenitsyn wished to round up signatories for a condemnation of the Soviet invasion of Czechoslovakia, he initially thought of calling on various eminent personalities, including Shostakovich and Kapitsa. But he soon changed his mind, realizing that, despite the fact that these men sought social contact with him, they would never bring themselves to sign such an uncompromising denunciation. Their outlook on life had been formed under different circumstances: 'The shackled genius Shostakovich would thrash about like a wounded thing, clasp himself with tightly folded arms so that his fingers could not hold a pen.'[25]

Shostakovich had an uneasy relationship with those who had chosen the road of open protest, thereby risking if not imprisonment at least harassment at work for themselves and their families. When Solzhenitsyn moved into Rostropovich's little guest house at Zhukovka, the two great men became neighbours, but did not form a friendship. Irina Shostakovich remembers how Solzhenitsyn paid a visit to their home to express his anger over a statement demanding the release from prison of the Greek composer Mikis Theodorakis that had appeared in the press with Shostakovich's signature. Allegedly the writer felt outraged that the composer had never remonstrated in public against the illegal detention of thousands of prisoners within his own country – by comparison Theodorakis's case hardly merited attention. Apparently in this instance Shostakovich was not guilty: he was in hospital, and therefore would have been unable to add his signature to this published statement.[26]

Irina Shostakovich also recalls how, in order to escape the imminent arrival of a pestering official, she and Dmitri Dmitriyevich spent the whole day away

24 3 September 1973. The other signatories included those of Kabalevsky, Shchedrin, Khrennikov, Aram Khachaturian and Sviridov.
25 Alexander Solzhenitsyn, *The Oak and the Calf: Sketches of Literary Life in the Soviet Union*, p. 221.
26 In private conversation with EW.

from home, visiting the cinema, seeing one old film after another. But their efforts were in vain; shortly after their return home late at night, the door-bell rang and the unwelcome official appeared with the document ready for signature.[27] Shostakovich was not one to argue, and in such cases conceded quickly to the request.

GALINA VISHNEVSKAYA gives her view on the political position adopted by Shostakovich:

Although Shostakovich knew he was considered a leader among musicians, he could not fail to see that he was being reproached by those who felt he had declined the political struggle. He saw that people expected him to speak out openly, to fight for his soul and creative freedom as Solzhenitsyn had done.

. . .

He often told us when we erupted over yet another injustice, 'Don't waste your efforts. Work, play. You're living here, in this country, and you must see everything as it really is. Don't create illusions. There's no other life. There can't be any. Just be thankful that you're still allowed to breathe!' He felt that we were all participants in the farce. And having agreed to be a clown, one might as well play that role to the final curtain.

Once he had made his decision, Shostakovich unabashedly followed the rules of the game. He made statements in the press and at meetings; he signed 'letters of protest' that, as he himself said, he never read. He didn't worry about what people would say of him, because he knew the time would come when the verbiage would fade away, when only his music would remain. And his music would speak more vividly than any words. His only real life was his art, and into it he admitted no one. It was his temple: when he entered it, he threw off his mask and was what he was.[28]

SERGEI SLONIMSKY recalls an embarrassing blunder in a press article signed by Shostakovich:

Shostakovich hardly ever wrote the texts of his articles and speeches.[29] Once, in the middle of the 1960s, one of his 'editors' carelessly made

27 In private conversation with EW.
28 Galina Vishnevskaya, *Galina: A Russian Story*, p. 398, 399.
29 This is amply confirmed by Isaak Glikman. In his correspondence with Glikman, Shostakovich many times asks his friend to write an article on his behalf, on subjects ranging from the poet Mayakovsky, the centenary of the Leningrad Conservatoire, to

an ass of him with a real howler. An article signed by Shostakovich appeared in *Pravda*. It was directed against the musical avant-garde, and came out with the memorable statement: 'I am unable to distinguish Boulez's music from that of Stuckenschmidt, they sound so similar.' But Stuckenschmidt was a musicologist. The anonymous ghost-writer had evidently muddled him with Stockhausen.

At a meeting of the Composers' Union, V. Ferré started quoting this article in exalted tones. Shostakovich's face darkened, and he got up and left the Presidium for the wings of the stage. Stuckenschmidt himself reacted with astonishment in the West German press: 'I did indeed write music in my youth, but never showed it to anybody. How did Mr Shostakovich discover it?' This provoked a rare occurrence – *Pravda* admitted its mistake. In one of the next issues the error was corrected with this clumsy phrase: 'the music promoted by the musicologist Stuckenschmidt in his articles . . .'

Another, even more preposterous mistake appeared in *Pravda* in 1971 through my fault. Reviewing Shostakovich's Thirteenth Quartet, I wrote saying that it was dedicated 'to the memory of the viola player, V. Borisovsky'. But Vadim Borisovsky was alive and in good health; simply, he had retired and no longer played in the Beethoven Quartet. I was at the time in a state of great depression; I had just discovered that my father had cancer and was near to death. I was also influenced by Isaak Glikman's emotional exclamations on the gloomy nature of the music: 'It's a requiem!'

When I recovered my presence of mind, I rushed about sending telegrams and letters of apology to the newspaper, to Shostakovich and to Borisovsky in person. I swore never to write another review, a promise I have kept to this day. In reply I received from Dmitri Dmitriyevich a wonderfully kind and tactful letter, in which he advised me not to pay too much attention 'to the slip of the pen', and reminded me with characteristic humour of Mark Twain and his announcement that 'the rumours of my death are exaggerated . . .' He was able to reassure me in respect of Borisovsky's feelings.

In the next issue of *Pravda*, as a sort of 'refutation' of this error, a short communication signed by Borisovsky himself was published which stated that he vigorously objected to the machinations of the

---

the pianists Emil Gilels and Sviatoslav Richter. Shostakovich was always fastidious about passing on the fee that he received for such articles to the actual writer.

Zionists in Palestine. This ridiculous statement was the newspaper's way of informing its readers that Borisovsky was indeed alive.[30]

EDISON DENISOV claims that Shostakovich's cynicism allowed him to sign press articles and Party statements, even while disassociating himself from these actions. He also saw how the composer was subjected to humiliating public censure as a result:

Shostakovich signed many letters mostly without so much as reading them through. There were certain things in life that he regarded very cynically. In particular, he never so much as glanced at the articles that were published in *Pravda* and *Sovietskaya Muzyka* under his name. I once asked him how he could have signed a certain article that appeared in *Pravda*. I knew the person who had written it and it stated: 'I cannot distinguish between the music of Boulez, Henze and Stuckenschmidt.'

Shostakovich replied, 'Edik, at twelve thirty at night the door bell rang. I had already gone to bed and was asleep. They had brought this article from *Pravda* which was to be printed in the morning edition. I was meant to read it and sign it there and then. All I wanted was to sleep. I had had enough of all this ages ago, so I just signed the thing there and then and went back to sleep.'

All these articles that people attribute to him of course were not written by him. I once asked him why he did not write his memoirs, and he said, 'Edik, I am not a writer, I am not a writer.' He didn't like writing. True, in his youth he did write some articles, but I don't believe he ever wrote anything after 1936.

The worst instance was his letter against Sakharov. I felt that he had every right to refuse to write or sign such a letter, in fact he was duty bound *not* to do so. Why he did so is incomprehensible to me.

This gave rise to certain scenes which I found very painful to witness. For instance, when my *La Vie en Rouge*[31] was performed at the Composers' Union, Dmitri Dmitriyevich came and sat at the end of a row in the middle of the hall. Everybody had to pass by him to get to their seats. When Yuri Lyubimov went by, Dmitri Dmitriyevich got up to greet him. It was difficult for him to get up; he could hardly walk

---

30 Sergei Slonimsky, 'Brush Strokes for a Portrait of a Great Musician', article commissioned for this book.
31 Premièred in Zagreb in May 1973.

and then only with the aid of a stick. Struggling to his feet he approached Lyubimov with hand outstretched. But Lyubimov looked him in the eye and, turning away, demonstratively sat down on his own. Shostakovich went white.

I asked Lyubimov, 'Why did you do such a thing?'

He answered: 'After Shostakovich signed that letter against Sakharov and Solzhenitsyn I can't shake his hand.'

There were many others who felt the same way.

Incidentally, this was the last time that Shostakovich attended a performance of a work of mine. I was very touched when he rang me the next morning: 'Edik, I congratulate you on a remarkable work born in your house.'

I remember the last time we met at the Composers' House in Ruza about five years before his death. Dmitri Dmitriyevich always returned to one and the same theme: 'In my youth we were brought up on the Ten Commandments: "Don't kill; Don't steal; Don't commit adultery." But nowadays there exists only one commandment: "Don't sully the purity of Marxist–Leninist teaching." '

In general, during the last years I found the people who flocked around Shostakovich extremely unpleasant. They took advantage of his kindness. It resembled the situation during the last years of Lev Tolstoy's life, when a pack of jackals panted around the great man, waiting to divide up the remains after his death. This was one of the reasons I didn't see much of Dmitri Dmitriyevich in those last years.

However, in 1974 he rang me up to invite me to the première of *The Nose* at the Moscow Chamber Opera. He said, 'Edik, I very much want you to attend the première. But don't judge me harshly – these are the sins of my youth, the sins of my youth!' I said that I would gladly go and pick up the tickets, but he interrupted me, 'Don't worry about that. Irina Antonovna has already left to deliver them to you. She'll be at your place in five minutes.' And indeed five minutes later the doorbell rang and Irina Antonovna was there with two tickets. In this respect, Dmitri Dmitriyevich was impeccably attentive towards people; his punctiliousness was remarkable.

When all is said and done, I value Shostakovich first and foremost as an outstanding musical personality. He of course was more than just a remarkable composer; he possessed a unique and deeply impressive personality. He never struck poses and was always himself. It is true that our ways drifted apart and I became increasingly indifferent to his music. But Shostakovich is very dear to me, and I continue to love the man and admire his music, despite the passage of time.[32]

Yuri Lyubimov founded the TAGANKA Theatre in 1963. With its small intimate space, the theatre soon became a focus for artistic experiment and lively intellectual argument. Lyubimov's provocative productions were barely tolerated by the officials. But the public responded to his direct theatrical style, urgently communicated by a school of powerful actors, and the Taganka immediately acquired enormous popularity. Its principal actor, poet and song-writer, Vladimir Vysotsky, acquired a cult status amongst Soviet youth and later became the Theatre's chief attraction. Here YURI LYUBIMOV recalls Shostakovich's connection with his theatre.

Shostakovich used to come to my Taganka Theatre. I asked him to write music for my production of *The Fallen and the Alive*, which was based on poetry by Pasternak and Tvardovsky and also on that of poets who had lost their lives during the War – Kogan, Kulchitsky. He didn't have time to write a special score, but very generously he said, 'Use any music of mine you like.' He must have trusted me because he never objected to the way I used his music.

When I put on Bertolt Brecht's *Galileo* I asked Dmitri Dmitriyevich for permission to use the music he had written for the Vakhtangov Theatre production of *Hamlet*. I wanted to use the theme of the Royal Hunt in a different context. It seemed to me to express very well Galileo's hope for change. He made no objections. I don't think it was mere politeness on his part, he could see that the music worked well in the new context. I always urged him to tell me if he disagreed with my use of his music. But he never complained, which never ceased to amaze me.

Shostakovich often came to see my productions with his wife Irina. He was always very nervous, and in later years he was too ill to climb the stairs to my office. He would wait downstairs and ask me to take him to his seat before the audience arrived. He couldn't stand the crush and didn't like talking to strangers. He always thanked me after the show: 'Very good, very good. Very interesting.'

He came to see my production of *Tartuffe*, where I used music from his Thirteenth Symphony (from the second movement, 'Humour') played considerably speeded-up. I was afraid it would make him angry. But he said, 'Splendid, splendid. Very original.'

32 Edison Denisov: recorded interview with EW.

Once the Minister of Culture, Ekaterina Furtseva, commissioned me and Shostakovich to organize a gala concert at the Kremlin Palace of Congresses for an anniversary of Lenin's birthday. I suggested that we start with Wagner's 'Twilight of the Gods'. Dmitri Dmitriyevich got very excited. I went to see him at his dacha and we went for a walk in the woods. He said: 'It's a fantastic idea to start with 'The Twilight of the Gods'. . . . You go ahead and do it, but I'll have to excuse myself. I just can't take part in all of this.' He simply couldn't overcome his disgust on such occasions. He said to me, 'You must do it, otherwise they'll take your theatre away from you.' It all goes to show how painful all this activity was to him and what scars and traumas it left on him.

Once he signed a letter against Sakharov and Solzhenitsyn. I was very upset. One night at the theatre, just after this letter appeared in the press, they told me that Shostakovich was waiting downstairs. I refused to go down and see him as usual. However, later I felt guilty and decided to show him to his seat. I thought he must be miserable enough without my censorious demonstrations. But he sensed my disapproval.[33]

The Fifteenth Symphony

In his last symphony (1971) Shostakovich returned to a purely instrumental work and a four-movement traditional form. Although the composer refuted any open programme, the Fifteenth Symphony nevertheless represents a summing-up, a sort of retrospective glance over a musical lifetime, extending into the realm of memory through the numerous quotations (not to mention self-quotation) from composers as diverse as Rossini and Wagner. Although it conveys an introspective loneliness in the face of approaching death, the music also reflects a sense of serenity and resignation – a contrast to the protest and anger of the Fourteenth Symphony.

Shostakovich started sketching the Fifteenth Symphony in April 1971. According to Isaak Glikman, the first movement was written in Kurgan during June of that year.[34] Shostakovich spent the whole of July in Repino, where he completed the symphony on 29 July 1971.

VENYAMIN BASNER talks about Shostakovich's composition process with particular reference to the Fifteenth Symphony:

33 Yuri Lyubimov: recorded interview with EW.
34 Glikman, *Letters to a Friend*, p. 277.

Very often, just before reaching the end of a work Shostakovich would get stuck. But suddenly, the right solution would come to him, and he would then complete the work very quickly. On these occasions, he was as happy as a child. I think the moments just after completing a composition were the best of his life.

A case in question is the Fifteenth Symphony. Dmitri Dmitriyevich had already written three movements when he came to stay at the Composers' Union Retreat in Repino. I also have a dacha at Repino and so we were neighbours. While we lived in Repino we religiously observed a little ritual. We both spent the mornings working. Then I would go to his cottage at one o'clock, and we went for a short walk before lunching together. We would buy a measure of vodka, and enjoyed a small drink with our lunch. We also used to listen to the BBC Russian Service. These programmes were transmitted on the radio at 1.45 p.m. Dmitri Dmitriyevich only let it be known to his most intimate circle of friends that he listened to the BBC. I was always struck by a detail, typical of his punctiliousness: after listening, he was always careful to tune the radio back to the bandwave of Radio Moscow – just in case anybody bothered to check!

When he was writing the Finale of the Fifteenth Symphony, he complained that his work was moving very slowly and nothing came to him. Then one day he said, 'I think, if you don't mind, we won't meet today.' And again the next day he asked me not to come.

I once asked Dmitri Dmitriyevich what time of day he worked best. He answered, 'When things are going well, then I am driven by the music, as if it were some outside force, and I write all day, at any time of day, morning, noon or night.' During those days when our meetings were suspended he finished the Finale of the Symphony, locked inside the house, writing day and night. I nevertheless phoned him daily to see if all was well. One morning he answered, 'Yes, Venya, I think we can go for our walk today.'

I arrived at one o'clock as usual. But Dmitri Dmitriyevich hadn't quite assessed his time properly. He asked if I wouldn't mind waiting a few moments. I sat down quietly and watched Dmitri Dmitriyevich write the last few bars of the score and date it.

I must say that it was most instructive to watch Shostakovich compose. Most composers write their scores horizontally, having ruled the bar lines on the manuscript paper. But Dmitri Dmitriyevich never ruled any lines beforehand. He just wrote down a bar at a time, but in vertical order, starting with the piccolo and flute, followed by the oboe and working his way down to the strings at the bottom of the score. Then he got his ruler out and drew in the bar line. I said to him once, 'Dmitri Dmitriyevich, that's not a very convenient way of writing, surely it's easier to write out the parts horizontally with the bar lines ruled in?'

He replied, 'You know, I also used to do it that way. But once I had written a cadenza passage full of black notes in the clarinet part, and it didn't fit in to the bar, so I had to rub out everything and write out the whole page again. Since then, I decided to write my scores this way.'

As it was no problem for him to hold the whole of a symphony in his head, he just wrote out his music directly in full score. He never bothered with a piano score and usually didn't make any preliminary sketches. As far as he made a skeleton outline of a work, it would fit on to one or two lines of manuscript paper. This would be the plan of a whole composition.[35]

The late string quartets

The string quartets form the most remarkable output of Shostakovich's last years, where the composer left a legacy comparable in originality and depth of expression to that of Beethoven's late period. Shostakovich did not live to write twenty-four quartets, one in every key, as he had planned. But it was in this medium, more than any other that he put his stylistic and philosophical ideas to the test.

The last three quartets are arguably the summit of his achievement, ranging from the dark, deathridden intensity of the one-movement span of the Thirteenth, the swings between tender passion and wistful serenity in the Fourteenth, to the distilled utterances of the six awesome elegiac Adagio movements of the Fifteenth.

The Thirteenth Quartet was written for Vadim Borisovsky, the original viola player of the Beethoven Quartet. Although conceived in August 1969, it was finished a year later, after a period of intensive treatment in the Kurgan orthopaedic clinic.

After completing the Fifteenth Symphony, Shostakovich underwent an extremely difficult period. His health was shattered by a second heart attack, and as a composer he felt 'dried up'. Writing to Glikman with a light-hearted irony that barely disguises his real despair, Shostakovich warned:

35 Venyamin Basner: recorded interview with EW.

Look after your health. It's terrible to lose it. Heart attacks and the like creep up on you unawares. Should you feel that your first measures of vodka afford you no pleasure, that spells trouble. I noticed while in Repino that I got no pleasure from drinking vodka. And that meant a heart attack was on the approach.[36]

After eighteenth months of creative silence he got down to writing his Fourteenth Quartet, which he completed at Repino in April 1973. The work was dedicated to Sergei Shirinsky, the cellist of the Quartet, whom Shostakovich had known since 1926. Whereas in the Thirteenth Quartet the viola is pre-eminent, here the dominant role is given to the cello.

Like the Sixth Quartet, the Fifteenth bears no dedication. It was completed on 17 May 1974. When Sergei Shirinsky died after a rehearsal of the Quartet on 18 October, it was decided to give the score to the Tanyeev Quartet who gave the Leningrad première on 15 November. Nevertheless, the Beethoven Quartet, with Tsyganov the only remaining founder member, played the Moscow première on 11 January 1975.

Here FYODOR DRUZHININ gives his memories of the Thirteenth, Fourteenth and Fifteenth Quartets:

For me the Thirteenth Quartet, dedicated to my teacher Borisovsky, occupies a special place in the cycle. Starting with the Ninth Quartet I played all the premières of the quartets that followed. But the Thirteenth Quartet is a hymn to the viola, giving the viola-player a special responsibility.

I wish to recount a small incident which preceded the writing of this quartet. We were recording the Twelfth Quartet (dedicated to Tsyganov) in the church where 'Melodiya' had its studio. I had arrived a little early to warm up. At the time I was learning Kodály's transcription of Bach's Chromatic Fantasy, which has an enormous number of arpeggios of every kind in it. I was playing with some panache a diminished seventh chord that went up to a high B flat in the third octave, playing *ff* as marked with loads of vibrato.

Suddenly I heard the familiar grating voice behind me. 'Fedya, that's a B flat, a B flat,' said Dmitri Dmitriyevich who had unobtrusively crept up behind me.

I affirmed that it was indeed.

'Well, try it once more if you don't mind,' Dmitri Dmitriyevich asked.

I whirled up the arpeggio again.

36 Letter dated 28 November 1971 (Glikman, *Letters to a Friend*, p. 280).

'Yes, now sustain it with vibrato; it's not a harmonic, is it? . . . Well, well, yes, yes, so that's how,' Dmitri Dmitriyevich murmured in response to some private thought. Then he asked if I could land straight on that note, without the preceding passage. I answered that it was possible, and indeed that it was more difficult to come down from it than to go up.

Sometime later we received the new score of the Thirteenth Quartet; we had had no inkling of its existence. I saw that the Quartet ends with a long viola solo in the high register (known jokingly as the heights of eternal resin), and that the last note is that same B flat which is then passed on to the first and second violins to give the effect of a snowballing crescendo. I would say that the performance of the Thirteenth Quartet brought me much closer to Shostakovich.

I felt his goodwill towards me many times. On one particular occasion we were playing through the Thirteenth Quartet at Dmitri Dmitriyevich's home for some British guests: Benjamin Britten and Peter Pears, who were accompanied by two charming ladies, Susan Phipps and the cellist Elizabeth Wilson. We played the Quartet through twice. We were showered with compliments, and Britten gave me a copy of his Lacrimae. Not knowing how to write my name in his inscription, he turned to Shostakovich. Dmitri Dmitriyevich first gave my full official name and patronymic, then he suddenly said with incredible tenderness, 'Fedya Druzhinin, just Fedya.' This was in 1971, after the première of the Fourteenth Symphony, which Shostakovich had dedicated to Britten. Britten, moved and shaken after hearing the Thirteenth Quartet, kissed Shostakovich's hand. This proved to be their last meeting.

After every performance of this quartet, Dmitri Dmitriyevich shook hands with all the members, but he would give me a kiss. This was in recognition of the special difficulty of the viola part.

Despite his great tact and delicacy, if Dmitri Dmitriyevich was displeased by a performance, it was frightening even to look at him, let alone approach him. I remember his state when we gave the first performance of his Twelfth Quartet in Leningrad. In the first half of the concert the Blok cycle was performed, and we were to play in the second half. When we went into the artists' room in the interval, we saw Shostakovich sitting on his own; there was nobody near him, and he was striking the ground with his stick and muttering words to the effect: 'Unforgivable, disgraceful, inexcusable.' Seeing us, he got up and said, 'Well, my friends, it's up to you; I am behind you like a stone wall.'

If one can consider artistic satisfaction as happiness, then there were occasions when Shostakovich was happy. He admitted as much to us, when one day we arrived at his home to acquaint ourselves with the newly-written Fourteenth Quartet without our second violinist, Nikolai Zabavnikov, who was ill. Dmitri Dmitriyevich opened up the score at the piano and said that he would play the second violin part himself. So in this unusual formation we read through the whole quartet. When the rehearsal was over, Dmitri Dmitriyevich was visibly excited. He got up and addressed us with these words: 'My dear friends, this has been for me one of the happiest moments of my life: first of all, because I think that the Quartet has turned out well, Sergei,' (the Quartet was dedicated to the cellist, Sergei Shirinsky) 'and secondly I have had the good fortune to play in the Beethoven Quartet, even if I only played with one finger! And how did you like my Italian bit?' We immediately knew what he meant by this last remark, as in the second movement and in the Finale's coda there is a short but wonderfully beautiful and sensual melody. It evokes a nagging but unquenchable ache of the heart, perhaps because this vocal phrase verges on banality.

Shostakovich not only trusted the musicians he loved, but he also heard their way of playing when he composed. Tsyganov once said while working on the Second Quartet that it seemed that the recitative in the 'Romance' had been specially written for him.

'Yes, indeed it was, Mitya. I wrote it for you,' replied Shostakovich.

He was extremely precise in the indications written in his scores, but the final tempo markings and some other directions were only added after several rehearsals with the Quartet.

All the more reason for me to feel proud that after we read through the Fourteenth Quartet, he suddenly came up to me and said, 'I'll now take my pen and write down exactly what you did when you played the "Chaconne".' This is how he called the solo episode for viola in the first movement.

I protested, 'But Dmitri Dmitriyevich, I'm not played into this music yet, perhaps it's too early – I'll play it better later on.'

'No, no it should be played just like that,' and he wrote in the nuances of the recitative as I played it then.

When the performance of a quartet had 'ripened', Dmitri Dmitriyevich started to invite some guests to the rehearsals. To start with it would be his closest friends and members of our families, but this circle widened, and on the eve of the premières he would gather together at his home the cream of Moscow and Leningrad musicians. Looking back now to these home 'concert-rehearsals', I think that they were our very best performances. We played with great élan, freely and uninhibitedly, and our daily meetings with the composer gave us confidence and inspiration.

According to Tsyganov, the Beethoven Quartet had two equal musical patrons – Beethoven and Shostakovich. After the death of Vasili Shirinsky, Nikolai Zabavnikov, a pupil of Tsyganov's, became the second violinist. In order for me and Zabavnikov to become full and equal members of the Quartet, it was decided to play the two cycles at the Moscow Conservatoire – all the Beethoven and all the Shostakovich quartets. Dmitri Dmitriyevich expressed his wish to work on his quartets with us. This active contact with Dmitri Dmitriyevich was the most serious and wonderful schooling in the art of performance that can be imagined.

Shostakovich's quartet writing is in direct continuation of the traditions of Haydn, Mozart and Beethoven; however, Shostakovich uses the individual qualities and timbre of each instrument, extending their range, especially that of the cello and viola, to unheard-of possibilities. It can also be said that the quartets are Shostakovich's most profound and intimate works.

Dmitri Dmitriyevich as it were relived his life in the process of working with us. He tirelessly sat through almost all our rehearsals. He was interested in everything from the technical aspects of bowings and fingerings to the more refined details of interpretation.

For instance, he liked a full-sounding rich pizzicato. He warned us, 'Don't let it sound as if you're playing on some threadbare piece of string!'

This brings to mind an episode concerning the Twelfth Quartet.

Dmitri Dmitriyevich addressed the cellist, Sergei Shirinsky: 'You know there is something I have wanted to say to you for ages about the way you play a certain passage, only I am afraid that if I do you will then spoil it.'

Shirinsky smiled in confusion but promised Dmitri Dmitriyevich that he would do his best not to spoil it.

'Well, when you play the pizzicato motif (quaver quaver crotchet

crotchet, repeated twice) while the twelve-tone theme is played on the viola, your notes don't quite coincide vertically with the viola's quavers; that in all probability is the real essence of musical luxury!'

Dmitri Dmitriyevich never allowed us to wallow in our emotions while playing, however much we liked the music. His attitude was akin to Beethoven's in that respect. 'You don't need to listen to the music!' he exhorted us. 'You must work, work. Let the audience listen.'

Only once did we see Shostakovich visibly moved by his own music. We were rehearsing his Third Quartet. He'd promised to stop us when he had any remarks to make. Dmitri Dmitriyevich sat in an armchair with the score opened out. But after each movement ended he just waved us on, saying, 'Keep playing!' So we performed the whole Quartet. When we finished playing he sat quite still in silence like a wounded bird, tears streaming down his face. This was the only time that I saw Shostakovich so open and defenceless.

Despite this inner vulnerability, his exterior manner was always strict and objective; he never failed to point out any errors in the performance, especially if they referred to the musical form.

When a new quartet was to receive its première, Dmitri Dmitriyevich always wanted us to play an earlier quartet in the first half of the concert, maybe together with a group of the Preludes and Fugues for piano, so as to fix the audience's attention on the new work in the second half. We often played his First Quartet or a work from the classics, in particular Mozart. But we never programmed the Third or the Fifth Quartets in the first half of such a concert, bearing in mind their amazingly forceful effect.

Shostakovich invited Dmitri Kabalevsky to one of the later rehearsals of the Fifteenth Quartet, an orthodox ideologue with a rather dubious aesthetic outlook, who had repeatedly criticized Shostakovich in the past. I was afraid of Kabalevsky, well remembering his reactions and critical remarks after the first performance of the Fifth Quartet in the Union of Composers in 1952. This quartet had a shattering effect on all those who heard it (including Kabalevsky). It was decided that after a brief interval it should be played a second time. During this brief pause Kabalevsky had been talking behind the scenes, and after the second performance all his enthusiasm for the piece suddenly evaporated. I could never forgive him this hypocrisy.

When we had finished playing the Fifteenth Quartet, the first thing that Kabalevsky said was that, in his opinion, Shostakovich should change the titles of the movements and he would be well advised to borrow them from Romain Rolland, for instance, 'Meditations over the Plateau of Life'. With innocent amazement Shostakovich demanded, 'But why the *plateau*?'[37]

VLADIMIR OVCHAREK, the leader of the Tanyeev Quartet, recalls playing the Fifteenth Quartet to the composer prior to the première in Leningrad:

Starting with his Fourth Quartet, Shostakovich used to send us the scores of his quartets regularly, giving us permission to perform them immediately after the Beethoven Quartet had played the première in the Small Hall of the Leningrad Philharmonic.

Dmitri Dmitriyevich always found the time to listen to us and to offer his comments on our interpretation. His remarks were made in a correct and laconic manner, as he was always careful not to hurt the self-esteem of the performers.

In October 1974 Dmitri Dmitriyevich approached us with the suggestion that we should be the first performers of the Fifteenth Quartet. What immense joy we felt! We set aside all our other commitments and started to tackle the piece. We were shaken to the core by the scale and tragedy of this quartet, and tried to give it every ounce of our soul.

We were shortly to go on a concert tour of Sweden, where we had programmed Shostakovich's Fourteenth Quartet. As we were to leave from Moscow, we made an arrangement to meet Shostakovich in his Moscow home. Dmitri Dmitriyevich had said that he could hardly bear to wait for the moment when he would finally hear his new work.

Our appointment was for five o'clock, but as usual our documents had not been prepared in time by Gosconcert, and we only received our passports from the Ministry of Culture at eight o'clock in the evening. Therefore we only managed to reach Shostakovich's flat at nine-thirty that evening.

We found him in a state of tremendous anxiety; he had thought that we would never arrive, and he was impatient to hear the new quartet played 'in the flesh'. His wife, Irina Antonovna, and the musicologist G. Khubov were also present. I can never forget Dmitri Dmitriyevich's state of nervous tension as he waited for us to begin the performance.

37 Fyodor Druzhinin: article commissioned for this book.

Finally after Irina Antonovna had switched on the microphone, we were ready to begin.

After our performance, Dmitri Dmitriyevich remained in a state of agitation for quite some time. He then thanked us for 'having penetrated so deeply the essence of this philosophical work, which I hold most dear'.

We wanted to profit from this meeting, and asked Shostakovich also to listen to us play the Fourteenth Quartet, as we were about to perform it on tour. Initially Dmitri Dmitriyevich refused outright, saying that he did not want to spoil the enormous impression left by the Fifteenth Quartet. But when we insisted he eventually agreed. He was satisfied with our performance, and wrote a flattering inscription into our score.

Having heard both quartets, Dmitri Dmitriyevich calmed down somewhat. He was in magnificent spirits, told lots of jokes, and even sang the Songs of Captain Lebyadkin to us; at the time they had still not been performed in public.[38] The simple, relaxed atmosphere of that evening left an indelible impression. For us, it was an inspiration to be with Shostakovich the great artist, who nevertheless remained simple and unaffected in his human relationships.[39]

The Nose

In 1971 Boris Pokrovsky staged the first production of *The Nose* in Russia (after the original 1930 Leningrad production) with student forces from GITIS, the State Institute of Theatre and Art, conducted by Vladimir Delman. The performances were not publicized, and in Moscow only a restricted circle of listeners went to this revival. However the GITIS production was taken on tour in the south of Russia.

At this point Pokrovsky proposed to the Bolshoi Theatre that they should stage *The Nose*. The artistic management procrastinated, claiming they could not make a decision as they did not know the score, and no recordings existed. Pokrovsky arranged a special performance of his student production which would serve the Bolshoi Management as an opportunity to 'audition' the piece. To his amazement, only twenty minutes into the performance, all

38 Shostakovich informed Isaak Glikman in a letter dated 23 August 1974 that he had completed two new 'opuses': the Michelangelo Suite and the Four Verses of Captain Lebyadkin (*Letters to a Friend*, p. 302). The usual date given for the composition of the Lebyadkin songs is spring 1975.

39 Vladimir Ovcharek, article commissioned for this book.

representatives of the Bolshoi had left the hall, with the exception of the conductor Boris Khaikin.

In the wake of the Bolshoi's cynical lack of interest in *The Nose*, Pokrovsky decided to put on the opera at his newly founded Moscow Chamber Theatre. When he told Shostakovich of his plan, the composer was sceptical about its realization for several reasons. He was not sure that Pokrovsky could find singers able to cope with the music, and pointed out that the orchestral forces of the Theatre were inadequate, in view of the unusual scoring which calls for balalaika, domra and percussion. But chiefly Shostakovich did not believe that Pokrovsky would have the persistence to push for the necessary permissions from the authorities to stage his opera.

Pokrovsky, however, proved Shostakovich wrong on all counts. Rehearsals for *The Nose* started even before the Moscow Chamber Theatre had a space of its own; they were held in hired clubs, theatres and studios. At an early stage of the proceedings, Pokrovsky got into conflict with his original conductor, Delman, who soon left the production team, and shortly afterwards emigrated from the Soviet Union.

Left without a musical director, Pokrovsky now turned to Gennadi Rozhdestvensky. Initially Rozhdestvensky expressed doubts about the feasibility of staging *The Nose* for much the same reasons as Shostakovich. But after seeing rehearsals in progress, he immediately agreed to participate. As it happened, he held no position at that time, having recently terminated his association with the Bolshoi Theatre, so he was able to join the Moscow Chamber Theatre as chief conductor and musical director.

On learning of Rozhdestvensky's involvement, Shostakovich became more confident of the project's success. He lent his active support to Pokrovsky in the acquisition of a suitable venue for the Theatre by interceding with Tikhon Khrennikov, who himself supported Pokrovsky, and using his authority at the level of the Central Committee. Soon the Theatre was given the venue that it occupies today, in the basement of an old cinema near the Sokol Metro station.

Here is Boris Pokrovsky's account of the staging of *The Nose*.

Before I staged *The Nose* myself, I saw some very good productions of the opera in Dresden and East Berlin, put on by most talented directors, solid, daring and well studied in the German manner – but not what Shostakovich had in mind. I was asked by these directors to contact Dmitri Dmitriyevich on their behalf and to ask him for a concrete description of the concept behind the work.

When I was back in Moscow I saw Shostakovich, and while we were chatting I mentioned the query of the German directors. Dmitri Dmitriyevich just laughed and said, 'There's *no* concept there.' It is one thing to understand a work, another to feel it. Even today I can honestly say that I don't understand *The Nose*, any more than you can understand Gogol or Shostakovich.

Maybe Shostakovich was joking when he denied that there was a concept behind *The Nose*, but I don't think so. As far as he was concerned he had done his job and written the piece. Either the piece has an effect on you, and you feel it and relate to it, or it doesn't.

I remember what an enormous impression Shostakovich's words made on me when I suggested that he might like to correct the balalaika part in the score. In the original production two players had to play the part as it was impossible for one player to play the notes as written. Dmitri Dmitriyevich exclaimed, 'On no account should you correct it! Don't change anything, even though there may be some bad things there.'

When we started to rehearse in our own theatre, Shostakovich was anxious to attend. But he was very ill at the time and could hardly walk. He sent his wife, Irina Antonovna to see what we were up to and whether it was worth taking seriously. She came and was evidently sufficiently impressed to encourage him to come. For Dmitri Dmitriyevich walking was so painful that it was virtually impossible for him to cope with the staircase that led from the foyer at street level down to the hall. He didn't wish people to see his infirmity, he was very touchy and fastidious in his sensibilities, and hated any form of pity. Our actors were quite ready to carry him down the stairs, but he refused their offer. Instead he used a back entrance in the courtyard where there were less stairs and he was not exposed to public view.

At the rehearsals Shostakovich was completely immersed in the music. He had no interest whatsoever in the staging and never interfered with it. In this respect, he was like Prokofiev – he would watch, listen, sometimes show surprise or delight when things happened which he hadn't expected. He was very tactful, but very business-like in his dealings.

As it was he only intervened twice. The first time was when he asked the baritone singing the part of Kovalyov to try a phrase an octave higher. He told us that in Scene 8, when Kovalyov tries unsuccessfully to put his nose back in place, the singer Zhuravlenko in the original Leningrad production had sung the words, 'Nu, nu, polezai, durak,'[40] up an octave. Dmitri Dmitriyevich was almost

---

40 'Go on, you fool, back in your place.'

-446-

apologizing when he asked our singer if he wouldn't mind trying it. It didn't matter if he couldn't manage it, it wasn't essential, but perhaps he'd have a go all the same? Of course the baritone (and all subsequent ones who have sung the role of Kovalyov in my production) had time to learn it and always performed it as Dmitri Dmitriyevich requested.

The second case was quite comic. During a break in rehearsals, Dmitri Dmitriyevich called me over to make the following suggestion: 'Please forgive me for making a suggestion. It's just spilled out of me, maybe it's a stupid idea, if you don't like it, you know, forget it, forgive me . . .' and so on.

In fact his suggestion was radically daring, and my only regret is that we cannot continue to implement it without him being there. It concerned a piece of original Gogol text that I had added at the end of the opera. Here the crowd enter into a discussion of the story and of how they had experienced these bizarre happenings. 'How can a nose disappear, what can have happened, how could it be cut off, let alone stuck back on again, what a stupid idea! An altogether ridiculous story, quite outrageous – in the first place it brings no benefit to the Fatherland, and in the second place it brings no benefit for the Fatherland,' and so on – a truly Gogolian dialogue. It finished with these lines: 'It is most surprising that authors should address themselves to such subjects. We've never heard the likes before.'

Shostakovich suggested to me that the actor who spoke these lines should come up to him in the hall, and, pointing a finger accusingly at him, recite the words.

Of course I loved the idea. I would say that Shostakovich revelled in high-spirited pranks and daring ideas. But the musicologist Yarustovsky was incensed at my taking such liberties: 'How dare Pokrovsky meddle with Shostakovich's opera!' Shostakovich had reacted with an open mind, and was delighted: 'Why didn't I think of it myself in the first production?'

Shostakovich came to all the rehearsals, which at some point were filmed for a small documentary. Although it wasn't that well put together, there is one amazing moment, when the cameraman filmed Shostakovich's face simultaneously with the chorus in the Summer Gardens – one of the most difficult scenes in the opera, written with a youthful daring bordering on malice. Here one can see the spontaneity of Shostakovich's reactions, his surprise, his delight, his humour – you sometimes see him mouthing the words as the music is sung. It is a remarkable study of how a composer responds to what he sees (as opposed to what he hears) in his own work.

Overall, this production of *The Nose* was a happy experience for Dmitri Dmitriyevich. He saw a favourite child re-born, performed by young and enthusiastic performers, led by artists he trusted, in this small 'underground' theatre.[41]

The conductor GENNADI ROZHDESTVENSKY recalls finding the long-lost score of *The Nose* in the basement of the Bolshoi Theatre:

At the end of the 1950s I was working at the Bolshoi Theatre in Moscow. One Saturday, a communist 'subbotnik'[42] was announced; our 'voluntary' task was to clean up a bomb shelter deep in the cellars of the theatre. It was reached by a side entrance, no. 15. During the war, people had hidden there from the enemy bombs. This bomb shelter was chock-a-block with planks, boards and old buckets, and our mission was to tidy it up. The first thing I noticed on entering was a large book under a plank. I retrieved it, brushed off the dust and gave it a wipe. On opening the book, what did I see written on the title page but the words *The Nose*. I froze in my tracks. It was a copyist's score (not the original manuscript) of Shostakovich's opera. The composer had entered his comments and markings on almost every page, including his corrections to the copyist's errors in both music and text.

I had no intention of throwing this volume into one of the old buckets with the boards and planks. I grabbed it and rushed off home. However, as the score had the stamp of the Bolshoi Theatre Library in it, it was clear that I had effectively stolen it. Since it is taught in the Bible that theft is a sin, I thought to myself I had better make amends by formalizing some sort of exchange with the Bolshoi Theatre.

Here chance was on my side. Shortly afterwards, I happened to go to the music shop on Neglinnaya Street, which formerly housed Jurgenson Publisher's showrooms. They have a second-hand section, which usually has a rather slow turnover. But that day the salesgirl addressed me: 'Here's something of interest for you. We've just acquired a copy of Anton Rubenstein's opera *The Demon*.'

It was in two volumes with a wonderful binding, published by

41 Boris Pokrovsky, recorded interview with EW.
42 An unpaid voluntary day's work, usually organized on Saturdays ('subbota', Saturday, hence subbotnik).

Roders of Leipzig during the composer's lifetime. In fact it was a lithograph copy, with a number on the flyleaf; only about a hundred copies of the score had been printed for hire purposes. I immediately bought the score, not yet foreseeing its final destiny.

When the question arose of a swap with the Bolshoi, I recalled that *The Demon* was in their repertoire, performed in the nearby Bolshoi studio theatre, where the Moscow Operetta now has its home. It struck me as a brilliant idea to offer the score of *The Demon* in exchange for *The Nose*. The Bolshoi Theatre's copy of *The Demon* was in a terrible state. Their production had been in existence for an interminable age. The corners of the score were dog-eared, or had disintegrated altogether. Over the years, lots of different versions had been produced, each involving different cuts which had been scribbled in, then rubbed out, then marked in again.

I realized that this could be my trump card. I said to the librarians: 'Just look at the condition of your *Demon*, no self-respecting conductor is going to conduct from a score in that state. I'll give you a completely new one. Take a look at it, what a beautiful binding it has, what a stroke of fortune for you, a completely unused copy, you'll never find the likes again.'

They answered, 'Yes, it is exactly what we need. Let's draw up a document legalizing this exchange.'

I have preserved this document and have glued it into my score of *The Nose*. It confirms that the exchange of these two scores has been approved between the administration of the Bolshoi Theatre and the conductor Rozhdestvensky. It was effectively an admission that the Bolshoi Theatre did not see any need to own a score of Shostakovich's *Nose*, whereas another copy of Anton Rubenstein's opera *The Demon* was essential to their existence.

I was very happy and I rang up Dmitri Dmitriyevich to tell him of my acquisition. Before the war he had sold the rights of *The Nose* to Universal Edition in Vienna, and they now owned all the material, including the manuscript. Then with the advent of the war and other events, all communications were lost between Shostakovich and Universal. He was left with nothing, not even a copy of the score. I remember when I spoke to him, he asked if I could temporarily lend him this copyist's score – just for a few days.

I said, 'Of course, I will have a photocopy made for you.' I suppose it was mean-spirited of me not to give him this copy as a present. As it was I had decided to keep it as my working score, and indeed it was the copy I used to conduct the 1974 revival of *The Nose* at the Moscow Chamber Theatre.

This production of *The Nose* was the first to take place in Russia since the original Leningrad staging in 1930. Dmitri Dmitriyevich attended almost all the rehearsals at the underground theatre at Sokol, where the Moscow Chamber Theatre has its home. He was by then very ill, and his arms and hands hardly functioned. He would sit in the stalls, completely absorbed in following the singers, mouthing their every note and word. I remember how during the Epilogue, when Kovalyov reappears with his nose in place and everything, so it seems, is once again in order, the singer sang the words, 'Dushechka, Raskrasotochka.' Dmitri Dmitriyevich shouted out from the stalls, 'Not "dushechka", but "dushenka", that's how it is in Gogol.'[43]

Some extraordinary things happened during this rehearsal period. For instance, once Dmitri Dmitriyevich stopped me after the orchestral entr'acte and asked, 'Why did the harpist play a stopped note instead of the natural harmonic that was written?'

I couldn't believe my ears – this was in the middle of a loud full tutti section, where it was hard to distinguish any detail. I approached the harpist and asked her what she had played.

She replied, 'Excuse me, I played a stopped note at ordinary pitch instead of the harmonic marked in my part.'

I recall another occasion which astounded me no less. After we had recorded *The Nose*, Dmitri Dmitriyevich came to the studio on Kachalov Street to listen to the result of our recent work, prior to the final editing. He had been unable to attend the actual recording sessions because of ill health.

I then committed a terrible blunder. I had come to this playback session with this self-same score, rescued from the cellar. I offered it to Shostakovich, but he turned round to me and said, 'It's all right, fortunately I can still remember the whole work.'

He proceeded to listen to the opera right the way through with his eyes closed. He never even glanced at the score. Afterwards he made a series of comments of a very concrete nature, saying exactly where there were errors to be corrected or adjustments to be made.

43 The final words of the opera: 'My darling, my beauty.' The diminutive 'dushechka' is virtually interchangeable with 'dushenka'.

A few years before I conducted the Moscow Chamber Theatre production, I was invited to Prague to perform the 'Suite' from *The Nose* in the composer's version, which includes Ivan's song to the accompaniment of balalaika. The Czechs said that they couldn't find a balalaika player and asked me to bring one from Moscow, where they should be easy to come by. I was also confident that I would find a balalaika player in Moscow, and approached a certain Aksentyev, a wonderful player and winner of a mass of international competitions, and no fewer national ones – the genius of the balalaika. He agreed with pleasure to come and play this single number with the singer.

A bit later I rang him and said, 'Let's meet in Moscow and rehearse the song.' He sounded somewhat reluctant. Each time I phoned him, he appeared to sink further into gloom. He announced that it would be better to rehearse in Prague. We travelled by train, and it so happened that my compartment was next to his. No sooner had the train pulled out of the station, than he started practising his balalaika. It became immediately apparent to me that this paragon, this prize-winner of hundreds of international competitions couldn't even play two bars in a row.

I thought to myself, 'What's going to happen?'

Aksentyev kept going out into the corridor to have a smoke.

I said, 'Please, may I listen to your solo?'

He answered, 'No, I'm not ready yet.'

'How do you mean, not ready? We have a rehearsal in Prague tomorrow.'

'No, I'm not ready.'

Then he told me, 'Do you know, this piece is completely unperformable.'

Aksentyev couldn't stretch the intervals, or play the chords. He was very upset. 'I play all the Paganini caprices on my balalaika, and here I can't manage a simple accompaniment.'

It turned out that the problem was caused by an error on Dmitri Dmitriyevich's part. He had assumed that the balalaika was tuned in fifths like a violin, whereas it is actually tuned in fourths. The piece as written really is unperformable.

When I told Shostakovich about the problems we had, he said, 'Yes, it's true that I wrote thinking of a violin. It's my fault. Please either retune the balalaika, or have the solo played on two balalaikas.'

Such a thing was a very rare occurrence for Dmitri Dmitriyevich. He was terribly embarrassed: 'Yes, yes, I committed a terrible error, a terrible error, it's inadmissable, quite unforgivable. I completely forgot that the balalaika is tuned in fourths. And now I am suffering for my mistake.'

In the Chamber Opera we re-tuned the balalaika in fifths and it was played by a violinist on stage wearing a red shirt. He had no difficulties playing this accompaniment.[44]

The last vocal cycles

With the Fifteenth Symphony, Shostakovich bade farewell to symphonic music, although he created orchestral versions of his last two superlative vocal cycles. The Six Poems of Marina Tsvetayeva for contralto and piano were completed in the summer of 1973 and are dedicated to Irina Bogachova. In this sensitive portrayal of the highly personal world of this tragic Russian poetess, Shostakovich aptly renders not only Tsvetayeva's lyrical tenderness, but her stoic fortitude in the face of affliction. Significantly, the last song is a dedication to his Leningrad contemporary, the poetess Anna Akhmatova.

The greatest of all Shostakovich's song cycles, the Suite on Verses of Michelangelo Op. 145 (completed on 30 July 1974) was written with the voice of the bass Evgeny Nesterenko in mind, and was dedicated to his wife, Irina Shostakovich. Originally conceived as a commemoration of the fifth centenary of Michelangelo's birth, Shostakovich consciously links himself with this great artist in a celebration of the immortality of Art. Like the Fourteenth Symphony, the work is in eleven movements; however, here the composer transcends mortal fears and suffering, and, refuting the idea of protest in the face of death, offers the serenity of acceptance as the final resolution to life itself.

In complete contrast to the grandeur of this conception is his penultimate work, the Four Verses of Captain Lebyadkin Op. 146 (completed immediately after the Michelangelo Suite), a portrait of Dostoevsky's grotesque buffoon. Here the composer mocks the boorishness of petty officialdom, which he himself had suffered in silence over the years.

The mezzo-soprano Irina Bogachova, and the pianist SOFIYA VAKMAN were invited by Shostakovich to give the first performance of Six Poems by Marina Tsvetayeva, which took place on 27 December 1973 at the Small Hall of the Moscow Conservatoire. The composer had been discharged from hospital that very day, but, with his usual determination, would not have dreamed of missing the concert which also featured the Moscow première of the Four-

44 Gennadi Rozhdestvensky, recorded interview with EW.

teenth Quartet. Here Vakman describes their rehearsals with the composer in his Moscow home:

Irina Bogachova and I went to see Shostakovich twice. We were astonished by many things. First that in his study Shostakovich tried to sit as far away from us as possible, so as to be outside the acoustic 'performance zone'. But the main thing that struck us was his own curiosity in regard to what he had himself composed. He sat absolutely motionless, only his hands fidgeted nervously, maintaining a complete silence, as he listened to us perform the cycle right through.

Then he got up and asked, 'And would you mind doing it again?' And the second time through he listened in the same manner without uttering a word, as if trying to penetrate the very sound that issued from us. He was intent on listening in order to assess his own achievement, as a continual re-examination of himself. Thus on these occasions we performed the cycle three or four times before he started making comments. And these were made almost as if in apology.

In some of the music, Irina felt that the range was uncomfortable for her voice. She asked if Dmitri Dmitriyevich would be willing to transpose the cycle up a semi-tone. 'No, please, leave it as written. I'd rather not change it.' The idea behind his words was that although he was willing to transpose the music, he did not wish to change the key.

Shostakovich respected and trusted his performers. If one should question him, 'Dmitri Dmitriyevich, you wrote allegro, and the metronome marking is . . .' he would interrupt and say, 'Take no notice – I never know if I mark the metronome correctly.' He granted the performers the right to their interpretation, and never exerted pressure on them. His remarks were made shyly, with great tact, almost as if they carried little significance.[45]

In the early 1970s the celebrated Soviet bass Evgeny Nesterenko formed a duo with the pianist EVGENY SHENDEROVICH. They were the first performers of the Suite on Verses of Michelangelo and the Four Verses of Captain Lebyadkin. Shostakovich wrote of their interpretation of the Michelangelo Suite (recorded for Melodiya in late March 1975): 'This performance surpasses all words of praise.' Here Shenderovich recalls his close working contact with Shostakovich in the last twelve months of his life:

We were to play through the Michelangelo Suite for Shostakovich in mid-October 1974 for the first time. But when Nesterenko suddenly

45 Sofiya Vakman, article commissioned for this book.

fell ill this plan had to be changed. We asked Dmitri Dmitriyevich if I might come on my own to play some fragments of the Suite for him to check on our proposed tempi and to seek answers to some of our queries in relation to the text. Dmitri Dmitriyevich agreed and within fifty minutes of the call I was at his flat.

I sat at the piano with Dmitri Dmitriyevich beside me. I was very nervous, but I felt that Dmitri Dmitriyevich was even more anxious than I was – it meant so much to him to hear his new work played and given life. He himself was unable to play the piano any more due to the illness that incapacitated the use of his hands.

Shostakovich asked me to repeat several episodes over and over again. It was as if he could never have his fill of the music, and wanted to re-live the whole process of its creation.

Dmitri Dmitriyevich possessed a rare and remarkable quality – he showed a special trust to the performers of his music, allowing their fantasy free play. I found this fact extremely helpful when performing, all the more so when playing in his presence. I was amazed how readily he accepted our interpretation, including my somewhat risky 'imaginative' pedal techniques.

When I asked him why a work with so perfect a form, constructed on monothematic principles, should be called a Suite, Shostakovich explained that he disliked the term 'cycle' but that he would give some further thought to the title.

Nesterenko and I were amazed at the philosophical power of the cyclic links between the movements, for instance, in the introduction to the first movement, 'Truth', and the tenth movement, 'Death'. In both cases the music is absolutely equal to its theme. I asked Dmitri Dmitriyevich only one question: whether these two introductions should be performed in the same way? He answered, 'Absolutely identically.'

This introduction should be performed with a harsh trumpet-like sound reminiscent of the fanfares signalling the start of an ancient Greek tragedy. It seems to me that Shostakovich's work is indeed on a par with a tragedy by Sophocles in the profundity of its philosophical concept, its universal, all-embracing force. The music is written as a dialogue for piano and voice, as a duet of equal partners, and in this it is new and original.

Dmitri Dmitriyevich never made declarations about his musical principles and overall intentions. At best, one could hope to hear some specific comment concerning a certain phrase or change of tempo. Here all I had to do was to hint at something, say, the clarinet-like timbre of the piano's refrain in the third movement, 'Love', and Dmitri Dmitriyevich would quickly respond, 'Yes, yes, very good, that's the right timbre.'

Before starting the eighth movement, 'Creation', I timidly suggested, 'Dmitri Dmitriyevich, I cannot rid myself of the association of the first chord in this movement with your music for . . .'

'My music for *Hamlet*?' Dmitri Dmitriyevich finished my sentence for me. He did not deny it, but he informed me that this movement contained another association: he had read that Michelangelo possessed such power and precision that with his very first blow he could hew out of a boulder all the superfluous marble. He very rarely ever needed to correct his work.

And indeed this image is almost visually present in Shostakovich's music, with the abrasive chords, the syncopated rhythms and the short passages spiralling upwards like a whirlwind. You can vividly hear the great sculptor's hammer blows and the scraping of his chisel on the marble.

For the introduction to the ninth movement, 'Night', I wanted to create a sense of tense and hushed silence, a sort of numb detachment resulting from long reflection on grief. I decided to allow myself a trick to achieve this mysterious colour, whereby I pressed down both the sustaining and the muting pedals, getting a smudy, smoky effect. Instinctively I wished to recreate the impression made on me by Michelangelo's unfinished sculptures, where a large part of his conception remains imprisoned in the original marble block, and yet the sculpted contours of the figure fuse with the unworked marble.

Shostakovich's reaction was totally unexpected. He put his hands on mine and said quietly, 'Don't change it. Leave that sonority exactly as it is.'

Dmitri Dmitriyevich also accepted a similar pedal technique in the analogous postlude of number ten, 'Death', where the bell-like sound of the bass resounds for a long time, sustained by the pedal, while the introductory theme rings like a distant reminiscence in the high register of the piano.

When Nesterenko was well again, we performed several movements from the Suite for Shostakovich. Then, in the presence of Dmitri Dmitriyevich's friends and colleagues, we played the work right through. We were more nervous than at a concert, which can be attributed not only to the highly select audience, but to the fact that Shostakovich insistently requested that we should perform with the piano lid fully open.

Shostakovich believed that the piano lid should always be open, even when the piano served as an accompanying instrument. Dmitri Dmitriyevich said that the construction of a piano was calculated to make it sound at its best with the lid fully open. 'After all, the natural position of a level-crossing is open! It is shut in case of necessity,' he quipped. He told us that his teacher, Nikolayev, had created a whole theory about the harm caused to the piano soundboard by keeping the lid closed, because it subjected the soundboard to an unforeseen phenomenon, an enormous amount of vibrations reflected by the lid.

For instance, Dmitri Dmitriyevich told us that he always played the cello sonata with the lid fully open. In regard to any doubts about the balance, Shostakovich defended his point: 'A soloist doesn't shut the lid when he is required to play softly – it would be like a violinist playing his instrument without taking it out of its case.' He regarded the pianist in ensemble as an equal partner.

The première of the Michelangelo Suite took place on 23 December 1974, at the Small Hall of the Leningrad Philharmonic. The dress rehearsal, which Dmitri Dmitriyevich attended in the company of various friends and pupils, was filmed, and some fragments were included in a TV documentary about Shostakovich.

The programme was chosen in accordance with Dmitri Dmitriyevich's wishes: in the first half, a selection of Glinka Romances and Mussorgsky's *Songs and Dances of Death*; the Michelangelo Suite occupied the second half.

Late at night, after the concert, Dmitri Dmitriyevich, as thoughtful and attentive as ever, rang us to thank us for the performance.

On 8 January 1975 we played the Suite at Shostakovich's Moscow home for his colleagues, composers and Union Secretaries. The guests, including Aram Khachaturian, Khrennikov, Kabalevsky and Maxim Shostakovich, all arrived together. Maxim sat next to me to turn the pages.

The work left an overwhelming impression. Aram Khachaturian asked if Dmitri Dmitriyevich intended to orchestrate the Suite. Shostakovich answered that no, for the moment he didn't intend to. Khrennikov wanted to know of the origins of the first melody in

'Eternity'. Dmitri Dmitriyevich told him he had composed his theme in his youth, but it was the first time he had used it in a finished work. With its sound of angelic bells in the piano's upper register, its effect in this mature masterly work is loaded with profound meaning.

Dinner followed, the usual postlude to such an evening. Dmitri Dmitriyevich was in lively spirits, and recounted all kinds of curious incidents from his life as a concert artist. He told us about the origin of the Spanish Songs. The soprano, Zara Dolukhanova had brought these simple folk melodies with their original texts to him, asking him to harmonize them. However, when the texts were translated into Russian, it turned out that they were intended for a male performer. One can but imagine Dolukhanova's disappointment. Nevertheless, Shostakovich created one of his best works at her instigation.

At the end of the evening, the poet Andrei Voznesensky dropped by, bearing his new translations of Michelangelo's poems. Shostakovich had used translations by A. M. Efros, but these did not satisfy him. He had told Nesterenko to wait before learning the initial text from memory, as he expected to correct it. In the meanwhile, Dmitri Dmitriyevich had asked Voznesensky to 'polish' these translations with his expert ear.

However, Voznesensky wrote completely new versions of the poems, using a different metre. Despite the fact that in themselves they were wonderful translations, there was no hope of them coinciding with the melodic line of the vocal part. Shostakovich was most upset that he had troubled Voznesensky for nothing. Efros's translations became the established text.

But that evening Voznesensky read us his translations. In the future Dmitri Dmitriyevich used his influence to help their publication.

In the early months of 1975 Nesterenko and I received from Shostakovich the music of a new, highly original composition, the Four Verses of Captain Lebyadkin, with the texts from Dostoevsky's The Possessed.

Again Nesterenko and I had to learn the work apart, as I had to return to Leningrad. Shostakovich in the meantime came up to Leningrad. He worked at Repino, where he also underwent treatment for his illness. During that time I visited him several times. His right hand was in appalling condition, and I saw what heroic effort it required for him to write down the music. He leant his hand on a specially constructed sloping stand which lay next to the manuscript paper on his desk. Overcoming severe physical pain, he succeeded in writing down his music.

I spoke to Dmitri Dmitriyevich about various points in the Lebyadkin songs. He agreed to some of my suggestions about the fingerings in the piano part. Then, after a moment's pause, he said: 'You know, Lebyadkin is of course a buffoon and laughing stock. But there is something frighteningly creepy about him. Tell this to Nesterenko, maybe it will give him an indication of the image I had in mind.'

Soon Nesterenko and I went to Kiev for concerts, and we rehearsed intensively for three days. I have to say, despite the fact that we had performed Shostakovich's humorous cycle 'Five Romances on Texts from *Krokodil*', we found the Lebyadkin cycle very hard; it required much more technical mastery, a more incisive satire, and much more subtle innuendos and variation of intonation than in the *Krokodil* cycle.[46]

Links with Dostoevsky

Shostakovich had a remarkable knowledge of Russian classical literature, and throughout his life followed developments in contemporary Russian (and Soviet) literature with interest. His own bent for satire was reflected in his love of Gogol, Saltykov-Shchedrin and Zoshchenko – the latter, in particular, appealed to him for his merciless exposure of the petty realities of the 'new Soviet man' and his restricted vision of the world.

The film director Grigori Kozintsev remarked on Shostakovich's ability to adopt as his own Gogol's axiom that the Russian language has the potential to transform itself within a single sentence from the elevated to the everyday, from the frivolous to the tragic. 'This feature permeates the atoms and cells of Shostakovich's musical themes.'[47] Furthermore, he pointed out that in the composer's everyday behaviour and mannerisms of speech there was much that could be traced back to his favourite writers. For instance, the way Shostakovich peppered his everyday speech with such interjections as 'you know', 'one might say', 'so to speak' and 'as it were' was typical of the language of Dostoevsky's and Gogol's heroes.[48]

Gogol's grotesque fantasy world had enormous appeal for Shostakovich, and it was a natural choice for him to turn to Gogol for his opera libretti. But he

46 Evgeny Shenderovich, article commissioned for this book.
47 Kozintsev, *Complete Works*, vol. II, p. 432.
48 *Ibid.*, vol. II, p. 426.

evaded setting texts by his favourite authors, Chekhov and Dostoevsky, until the very end of his life. One of his last projects was to write an opera on Chekhov's story 'The Black Monk'; unfortunately it was not to be realized. His penultimate work, Four Verses of Captain Lebyadkin, was a setting of poems from Dostoevsky's novel *The Possessed*, sung by the grotesque, clown-like figure of Captain Lebyadkin.

The distinguished Leningrad literary critic and musicologist, ABRAAM GOZENPUD, writes about his contacts with Shostakovich at the time that he was preparing for publication a book on Dostoevsky and music. Gozenpud had been introduced to Shostakovich by their mutual friend Sollertinsky in 1934. Their relations thereafter were formal and never close. However, Gozenpud must have won Shostakovich's respect through his unpretentiousness and his refined sensitivity of perception:

A compassion for the wretched and unfortunate, a desire to help them and to defend them from abuse, injustice and the power of the forces of darkness – these are characteristic features of Shostakovich's work. And in this he is close to Dostoevsky. There is much that links the composer to this author: identification with the humiliated and distressed, hatred of man's violence against man, an amazing capacity to penetrate the secret recesses of the soul, a merciless accuracy in depicting the terrors of this world, irony, sarcasm, a combination of the tragic and the comic.

Shostakovich, like Dostoevsky, shows how evil is born, and how what appears to be harmless in origin can turn into something dangerous and destructive. In *The Possessed*, Lyamshin improvises on the piano and combines 'The Marseillaise' with the sentimental song 'Ach, mein lieber Augustine'. Gradually this harmless little song changes its character and acquires a threatening note; it starts to rage and rampage monstrously and terrifyingly.

In the first movement of Shostakovich's Seventh Symphony the harmless marching song gradually acquires the force of a hurricane which blows everything from its path. There is of course a radical difference between Lyamshin's improvisation, which was derived from France's defeat in the 1870 war with Prussia, and the Seventh Symphony created during the Second World War, which depicts not only the theme of the enemy's attack, but a faith in a Soviet victory. But it seemed to me that the idea behind the conception of the central episode in the Symphony's first movement shares a certain similarity with Lyamshin's improvisation.

Although Shostakovich turned to Gogol and Leskov in his operas, I think that it was Dostoevsky who was particularly close to him. And this closeness is not just deduced from the fact that Kovalyov's lackey in *The Nose* sings Smerdyakov's song 'With Unconquerable Strength', borrowed from *The Brothers Karamazov*.

In his opera *Lady Macbeth* the composer touched on Dostoevsky very closely (and not just in the last act). Leskov condemns the heroine of his story, whereas Shostakovich attempts to justify her in depicting the unbearably cruel conditions of the Izmailov household, and elevating her love for Sergei. . . .

In writing *Lady Macbeth* Shostakovich wished to create both a satire and a tragedy. Dostoevsky wrote in his workbook: 'Why should satire exclude tragedy? Tragedy and satire are two sisters and belong to each other; thus jointly, their name is – the truth.' These words could serve as an epithet to this opera.

I wanted Shostakovich to confirm my conjecture on these points, so I wrote to him in Kurgan, where he was undergoing treatment at Dr Ilizarov's clinic.

Despite the illness which made writing for him very difficult, he answered my letter. He wrote that 'it is very hard for me to convey to you what Dostoevsky's work stirs up in me. He has too powerful an effect on me, so powerful that it is difficult for me to organize my impressions.' Dmitri Dmitriyevich went on to write about the contradictions of the great writer's personality, which are reflected in his work, particularly in *A Writer's Diary*. Shostakovich was more than anything offended and outraged by those 'creators' of lampoon and parody in literature who claim in Dostoevsky a like-minded thinker. . . .

In a subsequent conversation with me, he said that writers of genius are motivated by love, whereas creators of lampoons and parody are indulging in the religion of hatred. 'And hatred is the soil which gives life only to poisonous plants.'

In the same letter Shostakovich wrote of his attitude to Dostoevsky: 'I love him and admire him as a great artist, I admire his love for people, for the humiliated and wretched.'

In the summer of 1971 Dmitri Dmitriyevich came to the Composers' House of Creativity at Repino, and I gave him a typescript of my book *Dostoevsky and Music*. A week later he wrote inviting me to visit him. He mentioned in his letter that he had been re-reading *The Possessed* and was more firmly convinced than ever that this was a prophetic book, a warning about the dangers that threaten mankind if political murderers, demagogues and executioners seize power.

He informed me that when he was composing *Lady Macbeth* he never parted with Dostoevsky's *From the House of the Dead*. In regard to the similarity of Lyamshin's improvisation to the central episode of the Seventh Symphony, he could not answer. Maybe somewhere in his subconscious the memory of 'Ach, mein lieber Augustine' had flashed by. 'But here we need the help of a Freud.' He added, 'I have many times thought of writing on themes from Dostoevsky, but cannot bring myself to do so. It is too frightening. I thought of *The Meek and Oppressed*, and that most Dostoevskyan of all his works, *Bobky*, and also the scene from *Crime and Punishment* with the crazed Marmeladov and his children. But I always retreat from these ideas. Do you know that it is easier to have dealings with Shakespeare than with Dostoevsky? I envy the courage of those composers who dare to handle Dostoevsky. In truth I am frightened to do so – like Herman in *The Queen of Spades*.'

Dmitri Dmitriyevich responded to my book with praise. However, he voiced a request: 'Dostoevsky did not like Offenbach, perhaps because he was put off by the frivolity of his performers (particularly the female ones) and their abandoned behaviour on stage. But Offenbach cannot be dismissed because of this. Your own attitude is not clear to me. I cannot believe that you do not love this great composer. Therefore, if you don't object, please define your own position clearly. Offenbach is dear to me for his ability to combine irony and lyricism, sarcasm and poetry.'

Naturally I did not hesitate to carry out Dmitri Dmitriyevich's wish.

A few months later I approached Shostakovich again in writing. And despite the deterioration of his health, he immediately hastened to answer my letter from hospital, attaching to it a short note, recommending my book for publication. This recommendation played a decisive role, and my book was brought out in the Jubilee year of Dostoevsky.

A few years later Dmitri Dmitriyevich turned to Dostoevsky, creating the cycle Four Verses of Captain Lebyadkin. The doggerel composed by this character from *The Possessed* fulfils a function of parody verging on absurdity which debases the 'exalted' genre of poetry.

In the novel fragments of poems by Afanasy Fet and Kukolnik float into Lebyadkin's memory. And into that of his musical double drift intonations of Count Monterrone from Verdi's *Rigoletto*, then Tchaikovsky's Romance 'In the Silence of the Mysterious Night', but of course in a debased rendering. In 'The Cockroach' the melodic basis is derived from a version of the children's song 'Chizhik'[49] in the minor key. And 'The Ball in Aid of the Governesses', with ringing of bells, has features of a triumphal cantata. However, this show of grand festivity is but a parody. Shostakovich succeeded brilliantly in creating an image of a drunkard aspiring to the role of romantic hero 'with a grenade in his breast'.

In the Lebyadkin cycle the composer continues the satirical exposure of bourgeois petty-mindedness and trivial vulgarity. And in this his ally is no less than his favourite Dostoevsky.[50]

Fortitude in the face of affliction

The Polish composer KRZYSZTOF MEYER enjoyed a close rapport with Shostakovich, whom he met in 1961. His authoritative biography, *Dmitri Shostakovich*, was published in Poland during the composer's lifetime, and appeared in 1980 in German translation. Meyer, himself a prolific composer, completed Shostakovich's opera *The Gamblers* in 1980. It was first staged in Wuppertal in 1984.

Shostakovich was a closed person. He spoke in laconic, simple sentences; this same characteristic was evident in his journalistic articles, written throughout his life. But his face always expressed the depth of his feelings. He was hypersensitive, especially in regard to anything connected with music. In 1962, when Jan Krenz conducted the Eighth Symphony in his presence at the Edinburgh Festival, the composer, overcome, burst into tears like a child.

He always appeared extremely nervous. His face was a bag of tics and grimaces: he would either twitch his lower lip, or unexpectedly blink, or keep correcting his glasses and stroke his hair, which, as a result, was in a state of permanent chaos. While talking, he would

49 Chizhik-Pyzhik is the name of the most familiar of all children's songs, which nearly every Russian child can play with one finger on the piano. Literally, 'chizhik' means siskin, which is a bird, a yellow and black Eurasian finch.
50 Abraam Gozenpud, 'Encounters with Shostakovich', article commissioned for this book.

insert a lot of asides, 'so to say', 'a kind of', 'you understand', which often had no connection at all with the sentence he was uttering at that given moment. I have at home a tape of a rehearsal of the Fifteenth Quartet held at the composer's home. After the rehearsal, Shostakovich thanked the performers, saying, 'Thank you all, you know, for this kind of concert, you understand.' When he sat at his desk or at a table, he would always nervously drum at it with his fingers, or, pressing his left palm to his cheek, he would tap various rhythms with his fourth and fifth fingers.

He was absentminded. When engaged in conversation, his eyes always wandered past his interlocutor, and he continually jumped from subject to subject. Often he couldn't remember which opus he had just completed, and to find out he would have to ask his elder sister who lived in Leningrad. For that reason his works often lacked opus numbers, or had double numbers. When I look at the letters he sent me I am amazed that not one of them has been correctly addressed, each time there is a different mistake, and he found my name so complicated that he never managed to write it without an error.

He had an idiosyncratic sense of humour and a love of acting. I remember visiting him once at his home and finding a militiaman there who had come from Gorky to Moscow on business relating to Shostakovich's duties as Deputy to the Supreme Soviet.[51] When eventually the man left, Shostakovich spent nearly half an hour laughing and imitating his salutes, bows and mannerisms. Another time he enacted for me the scene of a misunderstanding with an optician who had prescribed spectacles which were too strong for him. He enjoyed all this like a child, and maintained this sense of humour until the end of his days.

He used to say to me, 'I don't know if you are aware that there was a composer called Hindemith, who . . .' or, 'Here in this score a trumpet is used – you no doubt have heard of such an instrument.'

Once he wrote to me, 'I am now on Lake Baikal,' which was followed by an asterisk; at the bottom of the page he added: 'It's a long way from Moscow.' Another time he introduced the composer Eshpai to me, 'He is a very talented composer, he even knows how to orchestrate all by himself.'

51 Shostakovich had been elected a deputy to the Supreme Soviet of the town of Gorky in June 1966.

I could quote many examples like that. I also remember with what glee he would boast his knowledge of Leningrad tram numbers. This sense of humour would appear unexpectedly; then equally unexpectedly he would revert to his serious manner.

His politeness to other people was at times disarming. I was told that, when he was lying in hospital after his heart attack, the doctors categorically forbade him any movement, but he would still greet his visitors, lifting himself on to the pillows and almost sitting up. Despite the fact that towards the end of his life he walked with the greatest difficulty, he would accompany all his guests not just to the door, but to the lift on the landing outside. He would greet anybody he knew with, 'Well, well, so tell me how is your health?' He finished most of his letters with a similar phrase: 'You must look after your health.'

His last years were plagued with health problems. Apart from his developing illness, he started to undergo difficulties in writing music. Despite his having composed such unquestionable masterpieces as the Fourteenth Symphony, and the Twelfth and Thirteenth Quartets, he seemed to lose faith in his own possibilities. 'Nothing goes right,' he once told me. 'I've dried up, why should I continue with all this . . .' In one of his letters to me he complained that he could not complete the music for the film of *King Lear*.

In 1971 I received a very depressed letter:

'Dear Krystof, Thank you for your Third Quartet . . . It's a great joy and honour for me that you have dedicated your new work to me for my sixty-fifth birthday. Thank you. As for myself, I've recently been ill for a long time. I'm not well now either. But I still hope to recover my strength. I am very weak. Last summer, I completed one more symphony, the Fifteenth. Probably I shouldn't be composing any more. But I cannot live without it. . . . I would love to show you the score.'

These words were written on the eve of his second heart attack. This letter is the best illustration of his modesty. It is rather unusual in that Shostakovich hardly ever mentioned his own music, and he hated questions that were in any way connected with his work.

But we often talked about the music of others. In the earlier years of our friendship we used to play through works on the piano. Shostakovich had a phenomenal ear and a phenomenal memory. I remember one day he suggested, 'Let's play Beethoven's Grosse

Fugue,' and handed me the score. In his study there were two pianos which were always out of tune.

'You play the first violin and viola parts on that piano, and I'll play the second violin and cello parts on the other one.'

As we only had one copy of the score, I asked, 'How are we going to divide the music?'

Shostakovich waved his hand. 'It's all right, I'll play it from memory,' and then proceeded to play the whole quartet with me without a single mistake.

He always raved about Mahler. When I asked him which of his symphonies he rated highest, he hesitated and answered: 'The First, to be sure, also the Second . . . and the Third . . . and also the Fourth, Fifth, Sixth and Seventh . . . and the Eighth is marvellous . . . and the Ninth! And also the Tenth! But if someone told me that I had only one more hour to live, I would want to listen to the last movement of The Song of the Earth.'[52]

For years I had been trying to persuade him to write a clarinet quintet. Shostakovich hesitated. 'Who knows? Maybe it is even an interesting idea, although I don't particularly like the Brahms Quintet . . . the Mozart is excellent, but Brahms? . . . Brahms is probably first and foremost a symphonic composer . . .' Suddenly he got agitated. 'Oh, how I love the Fourth Symphony, most of all of course, and then the Second, and the First, and, without doubt, least of all the Third.'

He once violently burst out: 'Debussy and La Mer? It's just a piece of candy in the mouth, nothing more.'

When we had such discussions, most often in his huge and spacious study, Shostakovich would often interrupt the conversation, jump up from his chair and either go to the piano or leave the room. I had the impression of someone so highly stimulated that he lived in a state of constant excitement. I never knew the cause of these interruptions. They might happen several times within an hour, but did not last longer than one minute.

His study was an enormous room. Just next to the door stood a very old and dilapidated sofa and a small bookcase whose shelves were

---

52 Boris Tishchenko recalls that, while a post-graduate student of Shostakovich's, the composer told him, 'I used to consider The Song of the Earth the best work ever written, but now it seems to me that Bach's music is even more forceful.' And also that he loved 'all of Mahler, except perhaps for the Eighth Symphony' ('Study for a Portrait', in G. Shneyerson, D. D. Shostakovich, p. 100).

strewn with books in fantastic disorder. Over the sofa hung a portrait of the thirteen-year-old Mitya Shostakovich by a family friend of his childhood, the painter Kustodiev. On the opposite side of the room were two pianos, and over them hung all manner of things: posters of the composer's concerts (always the most recent), diplomas of honorary doctorates, photos of the composer, and also of Mahler, Mussorgsky and the Soviet composer of children's songs, Blanter.

Between the two windows stood an enormous desk, the composer's work place during his healthy years. Placed on the desk was a huge antique lamp with a shade, and two very large silver candlesticks. Shostakovich kept two photographs under glass on his desk top; one of himself surrounded by the members of the Beethoven Quartet, and a large portrait of Stravinsky, for whom Shostakovich never publicly expressed any sympathy. But after the death of the composer of *The Rite of Spring*, he placed his portrait under the glass.

Additionally, there was always a clutter of things scattered about: a box with traditional nib-holders and an old ink blotter, which he used to the very end when writing his music; a number of ballpens; scissors for cutting papirosi; boxes of various kinds; a calendar; two huge inkholders; the telephone; and many other objects.

There was also a large antique clock, which ticked loudly and chimed on the half hour. I always wondered if this loud ticking didn't interfere with his work. Not far from the desk stood a small table with a tape recorder, which he never learned to use.

Thinking back to the last years of Shostakovich's life, I try to guess the man's thoughts and feelings, living in the knowledge that he was terminally ill. He mentioned death only once, when I saw him after his second heart attack. 'I knew someone,' he said suddenly, 'who had eight heart attacks . . . he is no longer alive . . . but I know that soon . . . over there . . .' (here he made a vague gesture with his hand) 'we will meet.'

He devoted his penultimate symphony, the Fourteenth, to the theme of death. Fatalistic touches of a specifically personal nature appear in some of his last pieces: in the 'Michelangelo Suite' and in the tragic Fifteenth String Quartet.

For the last few years, death (before it claimed Shostakovich) was making the rounds of his close friends and colleagues from his younger days. One of the first to go was Vasili Shirinsky, the second violinist of the Beethoven Quartet, to whose memory Shostakovich dedicated his

Eleventh Quartet. Then it was the turn of his elder sister Mariya; a friend from his student days, Valerian Bogdanov-Berezovsky; the film director Grigori Kozintsev. Then Vadim Borisovsky, the viola player of the Beethoven Quartet died, and after him Lev Oborin, Shostakovich's friend from his youth, with whom he took part in the first Chopin competition. His secretary of many years, Zinaida Merzhanova, also died; and eventually, in the last year of his life, he lost almost simultaneously two friends, David Oistrakh and the cellist Sergei Shirinsky. Broken, Shostakovich didn't have enough strength to stay to the end of Oistrakh's funeral.

Shostakovich maintained close relations with Polish composers. He always spoke with the highest respect of Lutoslawski, whom he called 'master'. He also had a high opinion of Penderecki. I have in front of me a letter addressed to the author of the St Luke's Passion, which he wrote in January 1975: 'Thank you very much for the record of your excellent music. [It included among other things Penderecki's First Symphony.] I've listened to this record several times already. Your music has made a great impression on me. I wish you from the bottom of my heart all further success. I would love to come to Cracow. However at the moment my health does not allow me to undertake such a journey. Maybe in the future I will feel better, and then I will most certainly come.'

Unfortunately, he didn't live to see that moment. He had enough strength to go to Leningrad for a whole month from 20 February until 20 March. It coincided with the première of Moisei Weinberg's opera *The Madonna and the Soldier*. He always loved and valued Weinberg's music, and had dedicated his Tenth Quartet to him.

Throughout this month's stay in his native city Shostakovich felt unexpectedly well. He went to the theatre every evening and attended all the rehearsals of Weinberg's opera. On 20 March he returned to Moscow and left for his dacha, where he stayed till the end of the month. All of April was spent at the Barvikha Sanatorium near Moscow. The condition of his hands and legs suddenly improved; he partially regained the use of his right hand, and he also put on weight.

In the first part of May he stayed in his Moscow flat, where he made a draft of his new opera, *The Black Monk*, based on Chekhov's story, for which Alexander Medvedyev was to write the libretto. He planned to work on this new piece in August, when he was to stay in the small village of Yadrino (not far from Cheboksar). The previous year he had been made one of the village's deputies to the Supreme Soviet. He wanted, as he told one of his friends, 'to meet – dead or alive – the people who have elected me'. From 5 to 25 May he stayed in Repino near Leningrad. There he met with a few of his former students, who brought him their compositions. For the first time he noticed that his eyes were failing, and the tiny notes of the score started to become invisible. All his life he had been short-sighted, but recently his myopia exceeded 15 diopters. He understood that he was beginning to go blind.

For the last five days of June he stayed again at his dacha outside Moscow. On 1 July, he suffered from a severe malfunction of the heart. He stayed in hospital throughout July, and came home on 1 August, very weakened. On 3 August, while eating a peach, he choked, and as a result of a prolonged attack of coughing which lasted several minutes, the malfunction of the heart got worse again. He was taken to hospital for a few days. Nothing however indicated that the end was near. On 9 August at six fifty he unexpectedly started to suffocate. This time it was not caused by the heart. For the past two and a half years Shostakovich had suffered from one more fatal illness, about which he and his wife had known for a long time – lung cancer. Double treatments with cobalt had not produced any results. In the past few months new growths were found in the kidneys and the liver. This evening the cancer attacked the artery between the heart and the lungs. The agony lasted for forty minutes, and for the last fifteen the composer was unconscious. At half past seven in the evening, he passed away. His death coincided with the anniversary of the first performance of the Seventh Symphony in besieged Leningrad, and with the eleventh birthday of his grandson Dmitri, Maxim's son.

A few days before, I received the last letter from Shostakovich written in hospital. In it he wrote:

'Dear Krzysztof, thank you for remembering me, thank you for the letter. I am again in hospital, due to lung and heart problems. I manage to write with my right hand only with the greatest difficulty. Please excuse my scribbles. Best wishes to Zosia. A warm handshake. D. Shostakovich.

'P.S. Although it was very difficult for me, I wrote a sonata for viola and piano.'[53]

53 Krzysztof Meyer, extracts from an article written as an extended obituary of DDS.

The Viola Sonata

The Viola Sonata, completed a month before his death on 9 August 1975, was Shostakovich's swansong. Here, as in the Michelangelo Suite, Shostakovich overcomes worldly trivialities and suffering in a mood of exalted philosophical resignation. The Viola Sonata can be regarded as a fitting requiem for a man who had lived through and chronicled the scourges of a cruel age.

Throughout his difficult life, Shostakovich succeeded in keeping his personal integrity intact. Even when plagued by health problems he never diminished his working pace. Undoubtedly, as the debates and arguments recede into the mists of time, the single greatest testament to Shostakovich's indomitable spirit and powers of mental discipline will remain the body of music.

Fyodor Druzhinin and Mikhail Muntyan gave the first performance of the Viola Sonata at Shostakovich's home in Nezhdanova Street on 26 September, which would have been his sixty-ninth birthday, in front of a select audience of musicians, squeezed to overflowing into his study. The official première was given on 1 October 1975 in Leningrad in the Glinka Hall.

FYODOR DRUZHININ recalls the process of Shostakovich's last urgent creative act:

The Sonata Op. 147 for viola and piano was destined to be Dmitri Dmitriyevich's last work. (Incidentally, Dmitri Dmitriyevich hated being asked, 'And what was the last work you wrote?'

'What d'you mean, last work? Why, you know, maybe I'll still manage to write something else . . .')

It was also to be the last bridge in our long-standing relationship. It was all the more dramatic as Dmitri Dmitriyevich knew that he was dying, and that his days were literally numbered when he wrote this work.

The theme of death dominated all his late works, starting with the Fourteenth Symphony: the Fifteenth Symphony, the Fifteenth Quartet, the Michelangelo Songs, and finally the Viola Sonata.

On 1 July 1975 the phone rang at nine o'clock in the morning. I heard the familiar, slightly rasping voice, 'Fedya, this is Dmitri Dmitriyevich Shostakovich speaking.' He always presented himself thus, using his full name, although I immediately recognized his voice. 'Fedya, you know I have the idea of writing a viola sonata.'

My heart was pounding, because I knew that when Dmitri Dmitriyevich spoke of having 'an idea' of writing something, it meant that the concept had ripened and the work was probably complete. He would never speak of something that was only a projected work.

'I would like to consult you, to ask your advice on some technical points.' There followed some questions about my family, my health and so on. 'Where are you going to spend the summer?' I assured Dmitri Dmitriyevich that I was entirely at his disposal, and if he wanted I was ready there and then to come and see him with my viola.

'That would be wonderful, but I am not allowed to see anyone. I am at my dacha, but I am going into hospital very soon; as soon as I am discharged, then we will meet. I will ring you to inform you of the progress of the work; and I will write to you from the hospital.'

In two hours' time, Dmitri Dmitriyevich rang me again: 'I wanted to ask you this: can you play parallel fourths on the viola? I know that double stopping is traditionally in thirds, sixths and octaves. But here I want fourths, and at quite a quick speed.' Here he sang me what he had in mind. I encouraged Dmitri Dmitriyevich to write whatever he liked – viola players would stretch their technique and learn to play scales in fourths. For several days we had conversations like this on the phone. Dmitri Dmitriyevich was touching in his punctiliousness, and kept me informed of the progress of his work. He complained about his hand: 'You know it's very difficult for me to write, or rather to write down the notes. I spend an awful lot of time at it as my hand shakes, and won't obey me.'

His phenomenal creative energy was in no way impaired. He finished his magnificent work in a few days.

On 5 July Dmitri Dmitriyevich rang me and said, 'Fedya, you would probably like to know at least in outline the programme of the sonata?' He had never before talked, at least to me, of the inner content of his works. Sometimes he would drop a hint such as, 'This passage should sound divine. . . ,' 'Here the walls are collapsing around you. . . ,' or of the first movement of the Fifteenth Quartet, 'Play it so that flies drop dead in mid-air, and the audience start leaving the hall from sheer boredom.'

'The first movement is a novella, the second a scherzo, and the Finale is an adagio in memory of Beethoven; but don't let that inhibit you. The music is bright, bright and clear.' Evidently, Dmitri Dmitriyevich wanted to emphasize that the music was not morbid and should not be regarded as a funeral march. 'The Sonata lasts about half an hour, and should take up one half of a concert. With whom do you propose to play?'

It was only then that I had understood that I had been chosen to give the first performance. I told him that I was playing these days with Mikhail Muntyan. Shostakovich interrupted me and said, 'Yes, that's wonderful, I know him, he's a superb musician.'

That same day in the evening Irina Antonovna rang to say that Dmitri Dmitriyevich wished to speak to me.

'Fedya, I have buckled down to it, and managed to complete the Finale. I am having the score sent to the Union of Composers to be copied, as no one could possibly read from my manuscript. As soon as the copying has been done, I'll let you have the music. I have to go into hospital now, but I'll have a telephone there by my bed, so we can talk. Are you intending to go away at all?'

I said that if my presence was not necessary, I would as usual go to Tarus for the summer.

'God be with you, you must go, of course. Leave me your address so I can write to you there. Then in about two weeks' time I think I'll be out of hospital and we'll meet.'

I left for Tarus to practise like mad, so as to be in top form for the new sonata.

And indeed in a few days time I received a letter from Dmitri Dmitriyevich in hospital, which calmed my fears. He gave me his telephone number in hospital. But when I tried to ring, there was no answer. I tried ringing his wife, Irina Antonovna, but discovered that she was with him in the hospital. Eventually I discovered that Dmitri Dmitriyevich's condition had deteriorated, and he had been transferred to a special ward where there was no telephone. I immediately rushed up to Moscow so as to be in touch with him.

The preparation of the score was dragging on, and this upset and irritated Shostakovich, although he was used to these kinds of delay. But he regarded them as a discourtesy. Eventually I got through to Irina Antonovna, and I calmed down a little, as she said that Dmitri Dmitriyevich felt somewhat better, and the music was now ready, so I would receive the score probably on 6 August. It was arranged that I would pick it up from their flat on Nezhdanova Street. When I arrived I was handed the score. On opening it I stood rooted to the spot as I read the inscription on the title-page: 'Dedicated to Fyodor Serafimovich Druzhinin.'

I rushed home and immediately rang Misha Muntyan. He came flying over to my place and we thereupon started playing the sonata and continued playing it till late at night. Immediately afterwards I sat down to write a long letter to Dmitri Dmitriyevich to express my profound gratitude to him and my immense admiration for the sonata, which sounded marvellous, and to reassure him that there wasn't a note in it that could not be played. I promised to be ready as soon as possible to perform it to him, and at latest, if he approved of our interpretation, to schedule it for a concert on his birthday, 25 September.

This letter was written during the night of 6 and 7 August. On 9 August Dmitri Dmitriyevich died in hospital.[54]

Mortal Decay Does Not Touch Me . . .

> Here fate has sent me eternal sleep
> But I am not dead.
> Though buried in the earth,
> I live in you,
> Whose lamentations I listen to,
> Since friend is reflected in friend
> . . . Is reflected in friend.
>
> I am as though dead
> But as a comfort to the world
> With thousands of souls, I live on
> In the hearts of all loving people.
> That means I am not dust,
> Mortal decay does not touch me
> . . . Does not touch me.

From the setting of Michelangelo's verse in the final song, 'Immortality' of Shostakovich's Suite on the Poems of Michelangelo Op. 145.

MARK LUBOTSKY describes the ultimate farce of Shostakovich's civic funeral at the Grand Hall of the Moscow Conservatoire, followed by the burial at the Novodevichi Cemetery on 14 August 1975 (this is an extract from his diary):

August 14th
9.30 a.m. Police in Hertzen Street and in the side streets standing around in groups, ready to cordon off the area. The Grand Hall of the Conservatoire has already been blocked off. Backstage, various

54 Fyodor Druzhinin, article commissioned for this book.

officials from the Ministry of Culture run about with black bands on their arms. I came across Maxim Shostakovich and the composer Yuri Levitin, a one-time pupil of Dmitri Dmitriyevich. They say that during the ceremony Shostakovich's music will be played only in recordings. None of the Moscow orchestras are in town in mid-August. Nobody has even tried to put together an orchestra of some kind. They refer to the will, which it appears forbade the funeral to be accompanied by orchestra. It all seems somewhat strange.

10.15 a.m. The coffin is in the hall. A black pedestal with three steps at right angles to the platform. Shostakovich. Too much pinkish-red make-up. Unrecognizable. Except for his arms. Unnaturally small from shoulders to wrists, and the hands dead and waxy, but his own, in some terrible way his own. A crowd of organizers in black suits with armbands and people who had obviously never been in this hall before. Although they were wearing different clothes, they were all alike in some way, as if the mark of Cain distinguished all those plain clothes 'music scholars'. They were in constant action – forever sniffing around.

A detachment of soldiers marched in and took positions facing each other down the central aisle, each one cutting off a passage between two rows. The family, Shostakovich's wife, Irina Antonovna, his daughter Galya and son Maxim, the grandchildren and other relatives, sat on special benches on the right. There were four or five rows of similarly reserved benches on the left, but as yet they were empty.

I found a place forward on the right side of the first amphitheatre with a good view of what was going on down in the stalls.

Tapes of Shostakovich's music were being played: the Piano Quintet, slow movements from the quartets and the Fifth Symphony.

The stalls began to fill up. Two 'music scholars' stood in the aisle asking questions and issuing directions. The reporters bustled about – their manner was obnoxious. One of them, he must have been from the television, kept running about with an exposure metre, shoving it now at Shostakovich's face, now at the huge wreath at his head, whose ribbon he smoothed out to expose the words 'From the Central Committee of the Communist Party, Presidium of the Supreme Soviet, and Council of Ministers of the USSR', and now under the noses of the dead man's relatives.

Aram Khachaturian and his wife appeared. They put flowers on the pedestal and then approached Irina Antonovna, the widow, and

Maxim. Khachaturian kissed them in his idiosyncratic way; from above one can see it all too evidently – at the last minute he turned his face away, so that he got kissed, thereby avoiding having to give a kiss himself.

An elderly woman carrying a bag approached the coffin. 'Who's that, who's that?' one of the nearby 'musicologists' cried out. He was wearing a soiled black suit and outmoded black boots and a short red tie; he had on a pair of glasses in a narrow metal frame *à la* Beriya. He was ready to dive into the stalls from the balcony – who knows what that lady was carrying in her bag! But she approached the family and kissed Irina Antonovna, and he calmed down.

The head of the queue which had formed out in the street was let in through the central door. People were openly grieving. They started playing the Eighth Quartet, and immediately there formed a 'triangle' of true things: the music, the coffin, these people. They walked slowly, many of them wanted to remain a little, but they were not allowed to; when they lingered they were hurried on. Those who had flowers asked timidly whether they could put them on the coffin. Permission was given but they were told not to tarry. A plump, middle-aged man looking vaguely Chinese detached himself from the procession, threw flowers at Shostakovich's feet in the coffin and fell to his knees.

Various composers walked past the coffin. Yuri Butsko stopped to take a long last look at Shostakovich's face. The soldiers hurried him on too.

Gradually the hall filled up. There were very few familiar faces, mostly functionaries and people who had nothing to do with music. Yurlov's chorus arrived and delegations from the Moscow orchestras. They were playing the slow movement of Shostakovich's Piano Trio. It didn't sound like a recording. The playing was excellent; it transpired that Oleg Kagan, Natalya Gutman and Vladimir Skanavi were the performers. Then the chorus sang one of the revolutionary poems. Next a female singer, followed by a male one. Something excessively loud in Italian – probably Verdi. Why? Then for some reason Bach, the first movements from the B minor and C minor sonatas for violin and harpsichord. It was out of tune and not together, the musicians were probably sight-reading. How could they do that? True he was dead, but he was still Shostakovich.

There was a constantly changing guard of honour. At one point it consisted of the music scholar L. Danilevich, the cellist L. Evgrafov, the composers D. Kabalevsky and R. Shchedrin, the pianist D. Bashkirov and the violinist L. Kogan. Mravinsky appeared and sat on the bench next to the relatives. The pianist Nikolai Petrov, followed by the Glinka Quartet playing Tchaikovsky,[55] then the pianist Tatyana Nikolayeva played Shostakovich's C major Prelude and Fugue. Among the people processing past the coffin a portly young man stopped and gave a deep bow.

1.00 p.m. The memorial service was about to begin. The benches for the guests of honour to the right of the coffin were occupied by the guests of honour: Tikhon Khrennikov, Pyotr Demichev, Vasili Kukharsky and other deputy ministers; a plumber (or carpenter) – hero of labour from Leningrad; a dozen other characterless faces unknown to anybody; Kabalevsky, Kondrashin and Kogan.

So many people were missing; it was mid-August and they were on holiday. An unfortunate time to die.

Suddenly all the 'musicologists' in mufti disappeared. They must have been waiting for someone important who hadn't turned up. At 1.30 Khrennikov started the civic memorial service.

'We have lost . . .' etc. 'When Shostakovich and I were in California he proudly declared to the journalists that "first and foremost he was a communist" . . . etc.'

Kukharsky spoke from the Ministry of Culture, followed by the plumber/carpenter from the workers of Leningrad, and then by Shchedrin as Shostakovich's successor as First Secretary of the Russian Composers' Union (RSFSR). In Shchedrin's speech every word was in its proper place. One only wished for a bit less self-assertion and a bit more of the grief felt by the people outside the Hall.

All the speakers declared that they considered Shostakovich a genius (the plumber spoke of 'the Seventh Symphony' and 'The Song of the Counterplan' beloved by all the working class in Leningrad). These were approved statements – the official obituary had stated as much after all, and it had been signed by all the heads and even 'Himself'.

But – 'first and foremost he was a communist', and so on.

55 I was told by one of the Quartet's members that they were 'instructed' to play the second movement of Tchaikovsky's Second Quartet. They had protested, on the grounds that they had it from Shostakovich's widow that Dmitri Dmitriyevich particularly disliked this movement. But the authorities were adamant in their choice.

At the end a couple of foreign representatives spoke, some president of a creative union from East Germany and the vice-president of the Austria-Russia society. Poor Khrennikov must have found it difficult to provide foreigners representing 'the correct trend' at such notice. They spoke in German, in a sentence or two at a time, followed immediately by an interpreter reading out two whole pages of text.

A notice on the gate of the Novodevichi Cemetry said, 'It is forbidden to visit the cemetery on Thursdays.' It was cold. A military band was butchering its way through Chopin's Funeral March. We stood around a platform listening to more speeches. The composer Otar Taktakishvili, the Georgian Minister of Culture, made a monotonous, lengthy speech. He was followed by Andrei Petrov, the Leningrad composer, who at least spoke more concisely and with a certain sincerity. To my side stood Rudolf Barshai who had just applied for permission to emigrate. In front of me the professor of the Central Music School, Anaida Sumburyan who had been Vladimir Ashkenazy's teacher. She said, 'This is the end of the road – a full stop.'

Fyodor Druzhinin, the viola player in the Beethoven Quartet, came up to me. He told me of Shostakovich's viola sonata, his last work. Dmitri Dmitriyevich had put the finishing touches to it just before his death.

Hammers banged. They were nailing down the lid of the coffin. Then they moved. Then they stopped. The Soviet anthem was played. It was cold and it started to drizzle.[56]

56 Mark Lubotsky, extract from unpublished memoirs.

The First Cello Concerto

Here is 'Suliko' as quoted in *Rayok*:

(Boosey & Hawkes, London, 1990)

The first time the theme appears in the First Cello Concerto is in the Finale:

Rostropovich was referring to the last appearance of the theme:

(left and right: Musikverlag Hans Sikorsky, Hamburg, © 1960)

Biographical Notes

Unless otherwise stated, it can be assumed that all persons included in this appendix were born and lived in Russia (or after 1917 in the Soviet Union). I decided not to use the term 'Soviet', as in 'Soviet composer', 'Soviet film-maker' or 'Soviet writer', because it has acquired a secondary meaning: by implication a 'Soviet composer', for example, is one who is connected with the regime and writes in the socialist-realist style.

Note: A starred name indicates a contributor.

Afinogenov, Alexander (1904–41), playwright. Influenced by Proletkult philosophy, one of the leaders of RAPP. DDS wrote the music for his play *Salute to Spain* (1936). Killed during Nazi bombing of Moscow.

Akimov, Nikolai (1901–68), theatre director and artist. In 1932 produced his first play at Vakhtangov Theatre, a highly eccentric *Hamlet*, for which DDS wrote the music.

Alekhine, Alexander (1892–1946), chess player. World champion 1927–35, 1937–46. Emigrated to France in 1921. Died in Portugal.

Alexandrov, Alexander (1883–1946), composer and choral conductor. Founder of Red Army Ensemble of Song and Dance. Composed Soviet national anthem; well known for his popular and patriotic songs.

Alikhanov, Abraam (1904–70), physicist. Graduated from Leningrad Polytechnic in 1929. Made important discoveries with his brother Artyom Alikhanyan in 1930s.

Alikhanyan, Artyom (1908–78), physicist. Born Tbilisi. Studied Leningrad University, graduating in 1931. Discovered (with his brother Abraam Alikhanov) phenomenon of emission of electron-positron, and in 1939 stream of fast protons in cosmic rays. Founded Erevan Physics Institute in 1943. In 1945 created high-altitude station on Mount Aragats for research into cosmic radiation.

Apostolov, Pavel (1905–68), musicologist, specialist in military music, composed for military bands. Cultural activist who hounded DDS, especially during the campaign against formalism.

Arapov, Boris (1905–92), composer. Student of V. Shcherbachov at Leningrad

Conservatoire, where he himself taught composition from 1930. Like DDS, he was dismissed from his position in the wake of the 'anti-formalist' campaign in 1948.

*Arnshtam, Leo (1905–80), cinema director. Lifelong close friend of DDS. Studied piano at Petrograd Conservatoire. From 1925–28 worked as pianist at Meyerhold's Theatre in Moscow. Under Meyerhold's influence, abandoned music in favour of cinema. Shostakovich wrote the music for five of his films, starting with *The Girlfriends* (1935).

Asafiev, Boris (1884–1949) (literary pseudonym: Igor Glebov), composer, writer, founder of Soviet school of musical criticism. Had a radical influence on many composers (including DDS) during the 1920s. Withdrew his support for *Lady Macbeth* in 1936. Was responsible for organizing the backstage proceedings of the 1948 'Zhdanov' campaign. In recognition for his services, Stalin had him elected to the Academy of Sciences, a unique honour for a musician.

Babel, Isaac (1894–1939), prose writer. Arrested and shot in 1939.

*Balanchivadze, André (1906–92), Georgian composer. Studied at Leningrad Conservatoire, where his brother, the choreographer George Balanchine, had studied piano. He developed a lasting friendship with DDS in his student years.

Balasanyan, Sergei (1902–82), composer and founder of Tadzhik professional school of music.

*Barshai, Rudolf (1925–), viola player and conductor. Founder member of Borodin Quartet. In 1953 joined Tchaikovsky Quartet, led by brilliant violinist Julian Sitkovetsky. In 1958 B. and André Volkonsky founded Moscow Chamber Orchestra; B. was its chief conductor until 1976, when he emigrated to Israel. First performer of DDS's Fourteenth Symphony.

*Basner, Venyamin (1925–), composer. Studied violin at Leningrad Conservatoire, graduating in 1949. Attended Shostakovich's composition classes as an observer, playing new works on violin at request. Developed and maintained close friendship with DDS, seeking advice on composition from him.

Belinsky, Vissarion (1811–48), influential literary critic.

Berg, Alban (1885–1935), Austrian composer. His expressionist opera, *Wozzeck*, premièred in 1925, was performed two years later in Leningrad, where DDS saw it, and remained much impressed.

Beriya, Lavrenti (1899–1953), head of NKVD 1938–53. Renowned for his atrocious cruelty. Formed part of triumvirate that succeeded to power on Stalin's death. Arrested in July 1953 and executed later that year.

*Berlinsky, Valentin (1925–), cellist. Founder member of Borodin Quartet with which he still plays (original names: 1943–6, Quartet of Students of Moscow Conservatoire; from 1946–55, Quartet of Moscow Philharmonic). Performed Piano Quintet frequently with DDS.

Bezymensky, Alexander (1898–1973), 'proletarian' poet. Participated on Bolshevik side in October Revolution. Active in Komsomol movement and prominent member of RAPP. DDS set his verse in the Second Symphony, and wrote music to his play *The Shot*.

Bogachova, Irina (1939–) mezzo-soprano, soloist of Kirov Theatre, Leningrad. First performer of DDS's Six Tsvetayeva Songs Op. 143.

Bogdanov, Alexander (1873–1923), philosopher. Developed ideas under influence of German idealist philosopher Mach's theory of economy of life's forces. Founded PROLETKULT in 1917 as a non-party organization of intellectuals wishing to develop new proletarian culture on principle of collectivism. Non-proletarian classes were to be refused admission to the laboratory studios where the new culture would be created. Proletkult was taken over by the Ministry of Education, but disbanded on Lenin's orders in 1920.

***Bogdanov-Berezovsky, Valerian** (1903–71), composer and musicologist. Studied at Petrograd Conservatoire, close friend of composer in early 1920s.

Brodsky, Iosif (1940–), most respected poet of post-war generation. Arrested in 1964 on charges of parasitism, sentenced to five years exile, although later allowed to return to Leningrad. Emigrated to USA in 1972. Awarded Nobel prize for literature in 1987.

Budyonny, Semyon (1883–1973), Marshal of Soviet Cavalry Army, which he led during civil war. Despite being a crony of Stalin, he lost his command during World War II due to his incompetence and inability to understand new technology.

Bukovsky, Vladimir (1942–), scientist and dissident. In 1976 allowed to leave the Soviet Union in exchange for Luis Corvalan (head of Chilean Communist Party).

Bunin, Revol (1924–76), composer, whose mildly experimental work of the 1950s was valued by DDS.

Chernyshevsky, Nikolai (1828–89), radical publicist and critic, who had a profound influence on Russian revolutionary movements of nineteenth and early twentieth centuries.

***Chukovsky, Evgeny** (1938–), cameraman. His grandfather, Kornei Chukovsky (1882–1969), was an eminent man of letters and children's writer. His uncle, Nikolai Chukovsky (1905–66), was a successful novelist. His aunt, Lydia Chukovskaya, well known for her memoirs of Anna Akhmatova, was an active supporter of many dissident writers. His father, a biologist, died in active service during World War II. As a boy, he was brought up partially in his grandparents' home, acquiring an awareness of the pre-Stalinist Russian cultural background, which had been lost by most of the young generation growing up in the 1950s. Met Maxim and Galina Shostakovich while a student at GITIS. (Institute of Theatre and Cinema). In 1959 he married

Galina Shostakovich, by whom he had two sons. Divorced in 1991.

*Chulaki, Mikhail (1908–89), composer. Before World War II he was artistic director of the Leningrad Philharmonic. From 1963–70 he worked as artistic director of the Bolshoi Theatre, Moscow. Also taught composition at the Moscow Conservatoire. Took an active part in the affairs of the Union of Composers.

Chyorny, Sasha (real name Alexander Glikberg) (1880–1932), poet and satirical writer who emigrated from the Soviet Union in early 1920s.

Dankeevich, Konstantin (1905–84), Ukrainian composer and teacher. His best-known work, the opera *The Great Friendship* (1951), considered a classic of Ukrainian socialist realist music, was attacked for a wrong interpretation of nationalist issues. In 1958 it was restored to favour in the Decree 'On Re-evaluating the Errors of *The Great Friendship*.

Dargomyzhsky, Alexander (1813–69), composer. His opera *The Stone Guest*, a setting of one of Pushkin's 'Little Tragedies', had a formative influence on Mussorgsky and thus on Russian opera in general.

Davidenko, Alexander (1899–1934), composer, leader of RAPM. Was dubbed 'The Red Beethoven'. His choruses and mass songs achieved great popularity.

*Denisov, Edison (1929–), composer. Studied mathematics at Tomsk University, simultaneously attending musical high school. Encouraged by Shostakovich, came to study composition with Shebalin at Moscow Conservatoire. One of the first Soviet composers to embrace 'avant-garde' techniques and to make contacts with the leading figures of Western modernism. Has played an important role as teacher and leader of all Soviet 'progressive' musicians from the 1960s to this day. His compositions were the first of Soviet 'avant-garde' to be performed in the West.

Deshevov, Vladimir (1889–1955), composer and teacher. In 1920s wrote in 'constructivist', urbanistic style, under influence of Honegger et al, with an additional political edge to his work. His opera *Ice and Steel* was one of the first Soviet operas to be staged, and was compared to *The Nose*.

Dmitriev, Vladimir (1900–48), artistic, stage designer. Studied with Petrov-Vodkin. Worked at Vakhtangov, Moscow Arts and Bolshoi Theatres.

Dobuzhinsky, Mstislav (1875–1957), painter, illustrator, theatre designer, member of Mir Isskustva (World of Art). Emigrated from Soviet Union in 1925.

Dolmatovsky, Evgeny (1915–), patriotic poet, best known for his popular songs. Despite his being an 'official' writer, DDS consistently set his poems during the 1950s. Wrote text of DDS's oratorio *Songs of the Forests*.

Dolukhanova, Zara (1918–), mezzo-soprano. First performer of DDS's *From Jewish Poetry*.

*Dorliak, Nina (1908–), soprano. Her mother was the operatic singer Xenia

Dorliak, renowned for her Wagnerian roles. Nina studied singing at the Petrograd Conservatoire, and had a successful career as a lieder singer. First performer of Shostakovich's cycle *From Jewish Poetry*. Amongst her recordings are the above cycle (with the composer at the piano), and Prokofiev's *Ugly Duckling* with Sviatoslav Richter, to whom she is married. Professor of singing at the Moscow Conservatoire for over forty years.

Dovzhenko, Alexander (1894–1956). One of the most important Soviet filmmakers and cinema theorists.

*Druskin, Mikhail (1905–91). Studied piano at the Leningrad Conservatoire, and from 1930 to 1932 in Germany. Based in Leningrad, he pursued a successful career as pianist and teacher. Has also published books and articles on a large range of subjects, from J. S. Bach to the New Viennese School. His authoritative book on Stravinsky was translated into English by Martin Cooper. Had a great influence in musical circles as a thinker and a man of impeccable integrity.

*Druzhinin, Fyodor (1934–), viola player and composer. After completing his studies at the Moscow Conservatoire, he embarked on a soloist's career. Joined the Beethoven Quartet in 1964. DDS dedicated his last work to him, the Viola Sonata Op. 147.

Dubinsky, Rostislav (1923–), violinist. Founder member of Borodin Quartet. Emigrated in 1970s, first to Holland then to the USA.

Dulova, Vera (1909–), harpist. She and her husband, the baritone Alexander Baturin, were friendly with DDS during evacuation in Kuibyshev. Baturin gave first performances of DDS's Pushkin Romances Op. 46.

Dunayevsky, Isaac (1900–55), composer of operettas and songs; achieved great popularity for his optimistic marches ('March of the Enthusiasts', 'The Jolly Kids', etc.). Influential figure in Leningrad Union of Composers.

Dzerzhinsky, Feliks (1887–1926), founder of CHEKA (Commission for the struggle with Counter-revolution) in 1917. Renamed the GPU in 1923, this organization effectively acted as a secret police force and was the antecedent of the KGB.

Dzerzhinsky, Ivan (1909–71), composer. Of mediocre talents. Studied with Gnessin, Gavriil Popov and Ryazanov. Shostakovich helped him in the orchestration of his opera *Quiet Flows the Don* (1932–4), which achieved considerable success and was upheld as a model of socialist-realist opera after the *Lady Macbeth* scandal of 1936.

Dzhabayev, Djambul (1846–1945), Kazakh bard. His songs in praise of Stalin (many of which were fabricated by Russian translators) brought him fame, and he was awarded the Order of Lenin. DDS set some of his texts, but was adamant that such creative frauds should be exposed.

Ehrenburg, Ilya (1891–1967), writer and journalist. Worked as a foreign correspondent in Paris (1908–17), Berlin (1921–4), in Spain during the civil war and with the Soviet Army during World War II. His memoirs *People, Years and Life* (1961–5) had a great impact on the younger generation of Russians, to whom Ehrenburg represented a lost culture.

Eisenstein, Sergei (1898–1948), theatre and film director. Joined Moscow Proletkult Theatre in 1920. Developed theory of 'montage of attractions'. Early silent films include *Strike* and *Battleship Potemkin*. His two later films, *Alexander Nevsky* and *Ivan the Terrible*, with scores written by Prokofiev, are acknowledged classics. DDS regarded the latter film with hostility, regarding it as an apology for Stalinism.

Eliasberg, Karl (1907–78), chief conductor of Leningrad Radio Orchestra during 1940s, with whom he gave performance of DDS's Seventh Symphony in besieged Leningrad.

Ermler, Friedrich (1898–1967), film director. Directed *Counterplan* with Yutkevich for which DDS wrote music.

*Evtushenko, Evgeny (1933–). One of the most talented poets of the post-war generation. While much admired for such outspoken poems as 'Babi Yar' and his epic 'Bratskaya GESS', he was accused of compromising his integrity and poetic talent by writing on 'authorized' topics and currying official favour. Shostakovich set his poems in the Thirteenth Symphony and in the cantata *The Execution of Stepan Razin*.

Ezhov, Nikolai (1895–1940), People's Commissar of NKVD from 1936 to 1938. In 1938 was arrested and subsequently shot. Succeeded by Lavrenti Beriya.

*Ferkelman, Arnold (1914–). Studied cello in Tbilisi with the distinguished teacher Konstantin Miniard-Byeloruchev. Lived in Leningrad from 1930. Won second prize in All-Union competition for performing musicians in 1933. Soloist of Leningrad Philharmonic. Worked in Moscow Orchestra of Cinematography after World War II.

Ferré, Vladimir (1902–71), composer. Studied with Myaskovsky. Member of 'Prokoll' (1925–6), the Moscow group of proletarian composers. Director of the Kirghiz Philharmonic in Frunze 1936–45. Taught composition at the Moscow Conservatoire from 1945.

Filonov, Pavel (1883–1941), avant-garde painter. He associated with the Futurists before the Revolution and developed a theory of analytical art. He created his own school (the Leningrad Collective of Masters of Analytical Art), which was dissolved in 1932.

Frederiks, Vsevolod (1885–1943), physicist. Of Danish extraction. Met Nadezhda Kokaoulina while studying at university and befriended Shostakovich family. Professor at Leningrad Polytechnical Institute. Husband of DDS's sister Mariya. He was arrested in 1937 and died in the labour camps.

*Fried, Grigori (1915–), composer. He studied at the Moscow Conservatoire with Shebalin and Litinsky, and founded the youth club at the Moscow Union of Composers in 1965 with the aim of promoting contemporary music, and initiating discussions between composers, performers and an educated 'general' public. He thereby created a platform for enterprising performers to present new works by Western and Soviet composers long before they reached the general Soviet public.

Furtseva, Ekaterina (1910–74), Minister of Culture 1960–74.

*****Galli-Shohat, Nadezhda (Nadejda)** (*née* **Kokaoulina**) (dates not known). Maternal aunt of DDS. Educated in native Siberia and studied physics at the Bestuzhev Courses at St Petersburg. Was involved in revolutionary politics, joining the Social Democrat Bolshevik Party after the 1905 Revolution. Was close to Sofiya, her elder sister and mother of DDS, and for some time lived with the Shostakovich family. In 1923 she left Russia with her second husband and settled in the USA. Collaborated with Victor Seroff in writing the first English-language biography of DDS, which was printed in the USA in 1943.

Galynin, Hermann (1922–66), composer. Studied at Moscow Conservatoire with DDS, who acknowledged his original and striking talent. He suffered from schizophrenia.

Gamov, Georgi (1904–68), physicist. Studied in Leningrad and worked in Denmark and Cambridge (UK) before emigrating to the USA. Worked with E. Teller on theory of Beta decay.

*****Gauk, Alexander** (1893–1963), conductor. Studied with Nikolai Cherepnin at Petrograd Conservatoire. Started his career as opera and ballet conductor in Leningrad at GATOB and MALEGOT. Chief conductor of the Leningrad Philharmonic 1930–3. Appointed chief conductor of Moscow Radio Orchestra in 1933, and soon afterwards of the newly founded Moscow State Orchestra. Taught at Leningrad and Moscow Conservatoires.

Glazunov, Alexander (1865–1936), composer. Followed traditions of the Mighty Five and Rimsky-Korsakov, whom he succeeded as head of St Petersburg/Leningrad Conservatoire from 1906 to 1928. Emigrated to Paris in 1928. Glazunov's music forms part of the Russian classical repertoire. Remembered for his devotion to the Conservatoire, and for his generous encouragement of many musicians, notably the young Shostakovich.

Glière, Rheingold (1875–1956), composer. Studied with Tanyeev at Moscow Conservatoire, where he himself taught for many years. Chairman of organizational committee of Union of Composers 1938–48.

Glikman, Isaak (1911–), literary and drama critic. Professor of Leningrad Conservatoire. Lifelong friend of DDS. During 1930s he worked unofficially as a secretary for DDS.

*****Glivenko, Tatyana** (1906–). Daughter of well-known Moscow philologist. Met DDS in 1923; their on and off romantic attachment lasted for nine years. She married A. Berlin, a professor of chemistry, in 1929.

Glyasser, Ignati (1850–1925), pianist. Of Polish extraction. Studied with K. Klindwort and J. Kullak, possibly also with Hans Bülow, whom he idolized. Founded courses in St Petersburg. Worked out an intensive technical system for his piano school. Wrote and published two textbooks: *Drills as the Basis of Piano Technique* and *Rhythmic Repetition*.

Gnessin, Mikhail (1883–1957), composer. Pupil of Rimsky-Korsakov. Professor at the Leningrad and Moscow Conservatoires, and also at the Gnessin Institute, Moscow. Created a national Jewish 'school' of music in Russia, which was actively discouraged in the Stalinist years. Had a great influence as a teacher, being respected not only as an excellent professional, but for his dignified and supportive behaviour to his colleagues during the Zhdanov campaign etc.

Golodny, Mikhail (1903–49), poet. Member of 'Young Guard'. Party member from 1933. Well-known for his patriotic ballad songs.

***Gozenpud, Abraam** (1908–), literary critic and musicologist. Met Shostakovich through Ivan Sollertinsky (a close friend) in 1934. Was friend of Vissarion Shebalin. Wrote the libretto of Shebalin's opera *The Taming of the Shrew*. Amongst his many publications are a biography of the tenor Ershov, a monograph on Dostoevsky, etc.

***Gubaidulina, Sofiya** (1931–), composer. Studied with Nikolai Peiko at the Moscow Conservatoire. After graduating, she encountered enormous difficulties in getting her music performed and published. In the late 1960s and 1970s, she experimented with electronic music and formed an improvisation group called 'Astrea'. From the 1980s her music has received worldwide recognition.

***Ikonnikov, Alexei** (1905–), musicologist. Studied at Leningrad Conservatoire.

Ilizarov, Gavriil (1921–92), orthopaedic surgeon. Developed procedure to correct and lengthen deformed bones. Formed Research Institute of Experimental and Clinical Orthopaedics and Traumatology in Kurgan, Siberia. DDS underwent two periods of treatment with him in 1970.

Ilyichyov, Leonid (1906–), one time chief editor of *Izvestia*. Head of Department of Propaganda and Agitprop of Central Committee of Communist Party 1958–61. Secretary of Central Committee 1961–5.

Ivanovsky, Alexander (1881–1968), theatre and cinema director.

Johnson, Hewlit (1874–1966), English cleric. Head of Anglo-Soviet Friendship Society, member of peace movement. Awarded Lenin prize.

Joliot-Curie, Frederick (1900–58), French nuclear physicist of 'progressive' views. President of France–USSR Society from 1947. From 1950 head of World Committee of Peace. Awarded Lenin prize.

Kabalevsky, Dmitri (1904–87), composer associated with the regime. Won popularity for his concertos dedicated to 'Youth'.

Kaganovich, Lazar (1893–1992), Bolshevik, one of Stalin's right-hand men, associated with some of the worst excesses of the Stalinist period (including the deportation of the Kulaks). Removed from Presidium by Khrushchev in 1957.

Kamenev, L. B. (real name Rosenfeld) (1883–1936), Bolshevik, member of Lenin's Central Committee and Politburo. Married Trotsky's sister. Together with Zinoviev, formed opposition of the left after Lenin's death. Expelled from Party in 1927, 1932 and 1934. Arrested in 1935 for membership of 'terrorist counter-revolutionary Trotskyist–Zinoviest bloc'. Charged at the notorious show trial of 1936 with treason, the assassination of Kirov and planning that of Stalin. Sentenced to death and shot.

Kapitsa, Pyotr (1894–1984), physicist, member of Academy of Sciences. Worked with Rutherford at Cambridge 1924–34. Refused to develop atomic bomb for Stalin, who held him under house arrest.

Karayev, Kara (1918–77), Azerbaijani composer. Studied at Moscow Conservatoire with Alexandrov and DDS. In his writing used a colourful national idiom together with modern compositional techniques (neo-classicism, twelve-tone series, etc.).

*Karetnikov, Nikolai (1930–), composer. Belongs to the alternative stream of Soviet composers. From the 1960s he developed his compositional style on serialism, under the influence of Webern's music.

Keldysh, Yuri (1907–), musicologist allied to official line. Taught at Moscow Conservatoire.

Kerensky, Alexander (1881–1970), politician. Occupied positions of Minister of Justice, Minister of War, then Prime Minister in the provisional government of Russia between February and October 1917. Emigrated in 1918.

*Khachaturian, Aram (1903–78), Armenian composer. Studied at Moscow Conservatoire with Myaskovsky. Gained recognition with Piano Concerto in 1936. His striking use of nationalistic music was particularly suited to his ballet scores, such as *Gayane* (1942) and *Spartacus* (1954). Active in the affairs of the Union of Composers.

*Khachaturian, Karen (1920–), composer. Studied with Shostakovich and Shebalin in the Moscow Conservatoire, graduating in 1949. His subsequent career was much supported by the Union of Composers and Khrennikov. In 1962 he was entrusted by Tikhon Khrennikov to accompany Stravinsky during his return trip to Russia. One of the Principal Secretaries of the Union of Composers.

*Khaikin, Boris (1904–78), conductor. Worked mainly in the field of opera. Started his career at the Leningrad Kirov Theatre; worked at the Bolshoi Theatre in Moscow 1954–78.

Kharms, Daniil (real name Yuvachyov) (1906–42), writer and poet. Member and founder of the short-lived Leningrad absurdist school, Oberiu. Was arrested in early 1930s, released, then arrested again and perished in the Gulag camps.

Khlebnikov, Velimir (1885–1922), Russian experimental poet, one of the founders of the futurist movement. Developed theories on the renovation of language which were tied into his mystic philosophy. Although a cult figure amongst the intelligentsia of the time, his poems were not published during the Soviet era.

Kholodilin, Alexander (1908–71), musicologist. Head of the music department of the Ministry of Culture. On friendly terms with DDS. Responsible for commission of complete edition of DDS's works published in the Soviet Union.

Khrapchenko, Mikhail (1904–86), literary critic. President of Committee of Arts of the USSR during the war years.

Khrennikov, Tikhon (1913–), composer. Studied with Shebalin 1932–6. His realistic opera *Into the Storm* (1939) brought him success, and was upheld as an example to Prokofiev, when his opera *Semyon Kotko* was subject to attack. In 1948 was elected First Secretary of the Union of Composers, a position he still holds. In 1948 he led the attacks on the 'formalist' composers, Shostakovich, Prokofiev, Khachaturian *et al*. His defenders point out that in the Stalinist years no composer was arrested; also that he always looked after the welfare of composers. While he moderated his views, 'moving with the times', his name was anathema to the younger generation of composers.

Khubov, Georgi (1902–74), musicologist, editor of *Sovietskaya Muzyka*.

Kirov, Sergei (real name Kostrikov) (1886–1934), Bolshevik leader. From 1926 worked in Leningrad, succeeding Zinoviev. During 17th Party Congress he won more votes for Party leadership than Stalin, who falsified the results to show himself victor. Stalin resented his popularity and independence from central Party control in Leningrad. His assassination in December 1934, almost certainly on Stalin's orders, signalled the start of the Terror.

Klemperer, Otto (1885–1973), German conductor. Music director at Cologne (1917–24) and Wiesbaden (1924–7). Head of Berlin Kroll opera (1927–31), which was set up to stage new works. Performed frequently in the Soviet Union in late 1920s. Last visit to USSR in 1936, when he declined the post of chief conductor of Moscow Philharmonic.

Knipper-Chekhov, Olga (1868–1959), actress, wife of Anton Chekhov. Created heroines of Chekhov's plays at first Moscow Arts Theatre productions.

Kokoshkin, Fyodor (1871–1918), founder of KADET Party. Member of Provisional Government of 1917. Both he and fellow Kadet Shingaryov were arrested by Bolsheviks in November 1917, and assassinated by sailors in January 1918.

*Kondrashin, Kirill (1914–81), conductor. Studied at Moscow Conservatoire with Zhilyaev and Khaikin. Worked at MALEGOT 1936–43. From 1943 conductor at Bolshoi Theatre. Artistic Director of Moscow Philharmonic

1960–75. Applied for political asylum in Holland in 1978, where he was appointed to the Concertgebouw Orchestra. First met DDS in 1937 in Leningrad. Gave first performances of Fourth Symphony (1961) and Thirteenth Symphony.

Konniskaya, Mariya (1905–), artist. During World War II she lost most of her family during the siege of Leningrad, but escaped across Lake Lagoda with her two small children. Was taken prisoner by Nazis and transported with her children to Germany. After the war she was 'repatriated', and hence was regarded as 'a potential enemy of the people' and deprived of all citizen's rights. For ten years she led a precarious existence, earning her living as a charwoman, manicurist, nanny, etc. Married Lev Lebedinsky in 1955.

Konstantinovskaya, Elena (1914–75), translator. DDS met her in Leningrad in 1934 while she was acting as interpreter during official meetings with foreign musicians. DDS took English lessons with her, which led to romance during 1934–5. She was arrested in 1935 as a result of an anonymous denunciation, but released the following year. Went to Spain during civil war, where she met and married Roman Carmen. Later remarried and taught foreign languages at Leningrad Conservatoire.

Kornilov, Boris (1907–38), poet. Married to Olga Bergolts. Author of 'Song of the Counterplan'. Perished in Stalinist purges.

Kostrykin, Maxim (d. 1937), revolutionary. The brother-in-law of D. B. Shostakovich. Married (1903) to DDS's paternal aunt, Mariya Boleslavovna Shostakovich. An ardent revolutionary and member of the Bolshevik Party, he was exiled to Siberia in the early years of this century. The Shostakovich family was very friendly with the Kostrykins, and during the 1920s DDS often stayed with them in Moscow. Maxim Kostrykin perished in the purges of 1937.

Koussevitsky, Sergei (1874–1951), American conductor of Russian birth. In 1909 founded his own publishing house and his own orchestra. Champion of new music; in 1910 premièred Skryabin's *Prometheus*. Left Russia after 1917 revolution. From 1924 chief conductor of Boston Symphony Orchestra.

Koval', Marian (Kovalyov) (1907–71), composer and musicologist. Studied with M. Gnessin at the Moscow Conservatoire. Member of Prokoll in 1920s/ 1930s. In late 1940s/early 1950s was chief editor of *Sovietskaya Muzyka*. A follower of Asafiev. During the Stalinist period he outdid himself in his active persecution of 'formalists', and hence was one of Shostakovich's most dangerous critics.

***Kozintsev, Grigori** (1905–73). One of the most distinguished of Russia's film and theatre directors and a theatrical/cinema theorist. Founder (with Trauberg and Yutkevich) of the 'FEKS' experimental group – the Factory of the Eccentric Actor. Worked as a film director with L. Trauberg until the

1940s. DDS consistently wrote music for Kozintsev's films through the years from 1928 (*New Babylon*) till 1970 (*King Lear*).

Kozolupov, Semyon (1884–1961), cellist and teacher. Professor at Moscow Conservatoire.

Kubatsky, Viktor (1891–1971), cellist. Founder of Stradivarius Quartet. Later worked in Bolshoi Theatre Orchestra, where he was active in organizing concerts. Dedicatee of DDS's cello sonata.

Kustodiev, Boris (1878–1927), artist, illustrator. Famous for his portraits, and his colourful 'primitive' scenes of Russian life. Continued to paint even when confined to a wheelchair through illness. Painted DDS when a boy. DDS reputedly influenced by his illustrations to Leskov's 'Lady Macbeth of the Mtsensk District'.

Landau, Lev (1908–68), physicist. Studied at Leningrad, and in Denmark at the Niels Bohr's Institute. Founded school in Kharkov which became leading centre of study of theoretical physics. Known for his work in atomic and low-temperature physics.

*****Lebedinsky, Lev** (1904–92), musicologist and expert in musical folklore. One of the founders and chief ideologues of RAPP. Close friend of DDS during the 1950s. In his capacity as editor at the Sovietsky Kompozitor publishing house, he edited the piano score of the second version of *Katerina Izmailova*.

Ledenyov, Roman (1930–), composer. Student of Shebalin. One of the post-World War II generation of Soviet composers who was criticized for his tentative experiments in 'Western' styles. Teaches composition at the Moscow Conservatoire.

Leskov, Nikolai (1831–95), realist writer, whose story, 'Lady Macbeth of the Mtsensk District' was the basis of Shostakovich's second opera.

*****Levitin, Yuri** (1912–), composer. Studied with DDS at Leningrad Conservatoire 1937–40. His symphonies and oratorios are written in the conventional 'socialist-realist' style. Composed much light music, popular songs, etc.

Litvinov, Maxim (1876–1951), Bolshevik revolutionary. Arrested and escaped to Britain in 1902, where he met his English wife, Ivy Low. Arrested by British Government in 1917, who allowed him and his family to return to Soviet Union the next year in exchange for James Lockhart. Commissar for Foreign Affairs 1930–9. Ambassador to Washington 1941–3. Deputy Commissar for Foreign Affairs 1943–5. Retired in 1946.

*****Litvinova, Flora** (*née* **Yasinovskaya**) (1920–), biologist. Brought up by mother, who worked as a seamstress in a Moscow factory. Married Mikhail Litvinov (1917–) in 1940. Spent years of evacuation in Kuibyshev where she got to know DDS and family. Her son Pavel (1940–) trained as a physicist, became prominent member of the dissident movement, suffered arrest and exile to the USA. In recent years she has been actively involved in the Moscow organization MEMORIAL (created in the years of Glasnost') which rehabilitates all survivors of Gulag, obtains evidence from newly opened-up archives and arranges pensions for the needy.

*Litvinova, Tatyana (1918–), artist, translator. Married sculptor Ilya Slonim in 1941 while in evacuation in Kuibyshev. After the war she studied art and the classics, but was expelled from college as a 'formalist' before she was able to graduate. Returned to England in early 1970s with her mother Ivy Low-Litvinova.

Lopukhov, Fyodor (1886–1973), choreographer 1933–6. Director of ballet group at MALEGOT. Produced DDS's ballets *Bolt* and *Limpid Stream*.

*Lossky, Boris (1905–), art historian. Son of Nikolai Lossky, Russian idealist philosopher (1870–1965). Left Russia with family in 1922. Studied at Sorbonne; from 1947 curator of the Tours Art Gallery; and from 1967 until his retirement curator of Palace of Fontainebleau.

Lourié, Arthur (1892–1966), avant-garde composer linked to futurists. Under the influence of Scriabin, he was one of the first Russians to experiment with elements of dodecaphony, graphic notation, etc. From 1917 acted as Commissar of the Music Division of the Ministry of Education under Lunacharsky. In 1922 emigrated to Paris.

*Lubotsky, Mark (1931–), violinist. Studied in Moscow with Yampolsky and Oistrakh. Currently resides in Hamburg.

Lukashevich, Klavdia (1859–1937), children's writer. Godmother of DDS.

Lunacharsky, Anatoly (1875–1933), Bolshevik Commissar for Enlightenment 1917–29. A literary critic and playwright, and unlike all his successors in Soviet times a man of considerable culture.

Lysenko, Trofim (1898–1976), biologist, member of Soviet Academy of Sciences. Lysenko denounced the theory of intraspecific competition as bourgeois formalist deviation. Instead he promoted the theory of 'class' biology, stating that acquired characteristics can be inherited, enabling the creation of new species and the transformation of old ones. His ideas appealed to Stalin, who readily supported him in his attempts to destroy all his opponents among Soviet geneticists.

*Lyubimov, Yuri (1917–), actor, theatre director. Founder of Taganka Theatre in 1964, which was noted for its controversial productions. In 1983 remained in London while on tour; in 1984 was stripped of Soviet citizenship. In 1988 invited to return to work in Russia.

Lyubimsky, Zahkar (1887–1983), Director of Leningrad state theatres.

Maazel, Lev (1907–), music theorist whose work, unlike so many of his Party-minded colleagues, was highly regarded. Professor at Moscow Conservatoire.

Malenkov, Georgi (1902–88), Bolshevik leader. Chairman of Council of Ministers after Stalin's death. Removed from office in 1957 by Khrushchev as member of 'anti-Party' group.

Malevich, Kazimir (1873–1935), painter. Founder of suprematist school, which evolved from abstract cubism. His Leningrad studio was influential in the 1920s. Died in obscurity and poverty.

*****Malko, Nikolai** (1883–1961), conductor. Director of Leningrad Philharmonic 1925–9. Left the Soviet Union in 1929. Worked frequently in London and Denmark before World War II. Settled in Chicago in 1940. Conductor of Yorkshire Symphony Orchestra (1954–5) and from 1957 till his death conductor of Sydney Symphony Orchestra.

Marshak, Samuiil (1887–1964), poet and translator. Well-known as children's writer and for his translations of Shakespeare.

Martynov, Ivan (1908–), musicologist. Wrote book on DDS's music. Worked as DDS's assistant in running the RSFSR Union of Composers.

Mayakovsky, Vladimir (1893–1930), poet, playwright, artist and actor. Together with Burlyuk brothers, founder of Russian futurism. After 1917 he allied himself and futurism with the Bolshevik regime. In 1920s editor of LEF.

Melik-Pashayev, Alexander (1905–64), conductor. Worked at Bolshoi Theatre 1931–64.

Mendeleyev, Dmitri (1834–1907), chemical scientist. Discoverer of Periodic Law of Chemical Elements. His daughter Lyubov' was married to the poet Alexander Blok.

Mendelssohn-Prokofieva, Mira (1915–62), translator and writer. Second wife of Sergei Prokofiev, for whom she wrote libretto of *War and Peace*.

Messerer, Asaf (1903–92), choreographer and dancer, famous for his performance in the role of Petrushka. Worked at Bolshoi Theatre.

*****Meyer, Krzysztof** (1943–), Polish composer. Author of *Dmitri Shostakovich* (PWM, Krakow, 1973), which was also published in Germany (Reclam, Leipzig, 1980). He is a prolific composer, whose works have been widely performed. Completed Shostakovich's opera *The Gamblers* (1980–1), which was staged in Wuppertal in 1984. Since 1987 teaches composition at the Hochschule für Musik in Cologne.

*****Meyerovich, Mikhail** (1920–), composer and pianist. Studied at Moscow Conservatoire. Played Shostakovich's Eleventh Symphony with DDS in four-hand versions at audition at the Union of Composers.

Mikhailkov, Sergei (1913–), writer, children's poet. Held influential position as Secretary of Writers' Union.

Mikhailov, Nikolai (1906–82), Minister of Culture 1955–60.

Mikhoels, Solomon (1890–1948), actor. Founder of the Jewish Theatre in Moscow.

Milhaud, Darius (1892–1974), French composer. Member of 'Le Six'. Visited Leningrad and Moscow in 1926 with Jean Weiner, when he met DDS.

*****Milkis, Yakov** (1931–), violinist. Studied at Odessa and Moscow Conservatoires (with Lev Zeitlin). He became leader of the Maly Opera theatre orchestra in Leningrad in 1955, and played in the Leningrad Philharmonic 1957–74. Currently holds position of associate leader of the Toronto Symphony Orchestra.

Molchanov, Kirill (1922–), composer who made career in official circles; author of Friendship Cantata, patriotic songs, etc.

Molotov, Vyacheslav (real name Skryabin) (1890–1986), Bolshevik statesman. As Commissar for Foreign Affairs he negotiated the Soviet-German non-aggression pact in 1939. Belonged to 'anti-Party group' who tried to depose Khrushchev in 1957, after which was demoted to position of Soviet ambassador to Mongolia. Expelled from Communist Party in 1964.

Mosolov, Alexander (1900–73), composer who achieved renown for his constructivist, mechanistic music in the 1920s (i.e. the 'Iron Foundry'). Unable to adapt his considerable talents to the demands of socialist realism, Mosolov became a marginal figure in Soviet musical life.

*Mravinsky, Evgeny (1903–88), conductor, whose reputation was established after giving the premiere of DDS's Fifth Symphony. This marked the beginning of a long and close working contact with DDS. Chief conductor of the Leningrad Philharmonic from 1938 till his death.

Muradeli, Vano (1908–70), Georgian composer and musical activist. Now remembered for his opera *The Great Friendship*, which provoked Stalin's wrath and was the subject of and gave the title to Zhdanov's 1948 'Decree' against formalism. He was quick to recant and rehabilitate himself in the eyes of the officials.

Myaskovsky, Nikolai (1881–1950), composer. Taught at Moscow Conservatoire. His earlier works demonstrate experimental ideas, with expressionist and constructivist influences. Was able to adapt successfully to the demands of Soviet 'socialist realism' without compromising his integrity. Many of his twenty-seven symphonies remain in repertoire today.

*Nabokov, Nicholas (1903–78), emigré composer. Cousin of writer Vladimir Nabokov.

Neizvestny, Ernst (1926–), sculptor and dissident. Was subject of Khrushchev's tirade against 'abstractionism' in 1962. Later he and Zhutovsky designed memorial stone on Khrushchev's grave. Emigrated to USA.

Nesterenko, Evgeny (1938–), bass, soloist of Bolshoi Theatre. First performer of DDS song cycles 'Five Romances on Texts from *Krokodil*', Michelangelo Suite, Lebyadkin Songs, etc.

Nestyev, Israel (1911–93), musicologist. One of leading 'Party line' critics during the campaign against formalism. Author of books on Prokofiev.

Nikolayev, Leonid (1878–1942), pianist and composer. Remembered as remarkable piano teacher. Amongst his pupils were Vladimir Sofronitsky, Mariya Yudina and DDS.

*Nikolayeva-Tarasevich, Tatyana (1924–93), pianist and composer. Studied at Moscow Conservatoire. In 1950 won first prize at Leipzig competition held for bi-centennial commemoration of Bach's death. During this festival DDS, replacing Mariya Yudina, performed in concert with her and Serebryakov Bach's Concerto for three pianos. DDS wrote his Preludes and Fugues as a result of his profound impression of her playing.

Oborin, Lev (1907–74), pianist and composer. Member of Moscow group of 'Six' ('Shestyorka'). Winner of Chopin competition in 1927. Close friend of DDS in student years. Member of duo and trio with violinist David Oistrakh and cellist Sviatoslav Knushevitsky.

*Oistrakh, David (1908–74), violinist and conductor. Studied with Stolyarsky in his native Odessa. Professor at Moscow Conservatoire. Dedicatee of DDS's two violin concertos and violin sonata.

*Ovcharek, Vladimir (1927–), violinist. Studied at Leningrad Conservatoire. While still a student, formed quartet which in 1963 became known under its present name of 'Tanyeev' Quartet. Their Melodiya recording of DDS's fifteen string quartets won a Grand Prix in 1978.

Pasternak, Boris (1890–1960), one of Russia's greatest twentieth-century poets. Unable to publish his poetry during Stalinist era, he earned his living as a translator (notably of Shakespeare's plays). His only novel, *Dr Zhivago*, was published outside the Soviet Union in 1957, caused a furore at home and his expulsion from the Writers' Union. Awarded Nobel Prize for literature in 1958, but refused it under pressure from the authorities.

Paustovsky, Konstantin (1892–1968), novelist. Appreciated for his fine prose writing.

Pavlov, Ivan (1849–1936), scientist, specialist in animal physiology and psychology. Discovered the 'Pavlovian reflexes' in chimpanzees and dogs. In USSR Pavlov was championed, as his theories confirmed the materialistic view of man. Privately he remained an Orthodox believer.

*Pears, Peter (1910–86), English tenor, whose professional career was closely associated with Benjamin Britten's music. Met DDS with Britten both in England and on various visits to Russia.

Peiko, Nikolai (1916–), composer. Acted as Shostakovich's assistant at the Moscow Conservatoire 1943–8.

*Perelman, Nathan (1906–), pianist and teacher. Studied with Nikolayev. Professor of piano at the Leningrad Conservatoire. When Maxim Shostakovich enrolled at Leningrad Conservatoire to study conducting, Perelman accepted him in his class at DDS's request.

Piotrovsky, Adrian (1898–1938), theatre and literary critic. Organized revolutionary mass spectacles in early 1920s. Worked as dramaturge at MALEGOT and TRAM. Perished in the purges.

Polyakin, Miron (1895–1941), violinist, pupil of Auer.

*Pokrovsky, Boris (1912–), opera and theatre director. Studied piano. Has worked at Bolshoi Theatre on and off for fifty years, from 1943. Amongst innumerable new productions at Bolshoi was Vano Muradeli's *The Great Friendship* (1947). In reaction to the frustrations of working with the large, unwieldy administration of Bolshoi Theatre, he and Gennadi Rozhdestvensky founded the Moscow Chamber Theatre in 1972. Under his directorship, the theatre has acquired an enormous reputation for its intimate and imaginative productions and its adventurous repertoire.

Popov, Gavriil (1904–72), pianist and composer. Studied with Shcherbachov at Leningrad Conservatoire. Earned a reputation as a 'modernist' in the 1920s.

Popova, Lyubov' (1889–1924), avant-garde artist. Worked in cubist style and evolved a theory of dynamics of movement and colour. From 1918 onwards was involved with new system of practical artistic instruction.

Preis, Alexander (1906–42), writer. Librettist, with DDS and Ionin, of operas *The Nose* and *Lady Macbeth of Mtsensk*.

*Prokofiev, Oleg (1928–), art historian, painter and sculptor. Son of the composer Sergei Prokofiev (1891–1953) and the singer Lina Prokofieva (1897–1989). Since 1971 has been living and working in England.

Rabinovich, David (1900–78), musicologist. Author of first Soviet biography of DDS. Arrested in 1949.

Rabinovich, Nikolai (1908–72), conductor. Worked principally in Leningrad. Esteemed as outstanding musician and personality. Conducted much of Shostakovich's film music (the Maxim trilogy, *Hamlet*, etc).

Radlov, Nikolai (1889–1942), painter. Son of prominent Russian philosopher. With his brother Sergei, the theatre director, was active in Leningrad's avant-garde circles in 1920s.

Raikh, Zinaida (1894–1939), actress. Wife of Meyerhold. Brutally murdered after her husband's arrest and the closing of his theatre.

Rakhlin, Nathan (1906–79), conductor. Gave world premiere of DDS's Eleventh Symphony and Leningrad premiere of Second Cello Concerto.

Richter, Sviatoslav (1914–), pianist. Student of Heinrich Neuhaus. First performer of many of Prokofiev's works (the Ninth Piano Sonata is dedicated to him). Acquired a legendary reputation before he was allowed to travel and perform in the West. First performer, with Oistrakh, of DDS's Violin Sonata.

Rodchenko, Alexander (1891–1956), avant-garde artist. Gave up painting in 1921 to work on poster, book and textile designs, photography, etc. In 1920s active as instructor in the Commissariat of Education's Applied Arts section, promulgating the incorporation of art into everyday life. Stage designer for production of Mayakovsky's *The Bedbug*, for which DDS wrote the music.

Roslavets, Nikolai (1881–1944), avant-garde composer. Developed a system of tone organization which contained elements of serialism. A Marxist by conviction, he worked for the Bolshevik regime in education and agitprop. Supporter of ASM, rather than RAPM, with whom he came into conflict in 1927. Died in Moscow in total obscurity.

*Rostropovich, Mstislav (1927–), cellist, conductor and pianist. Studied cello initially with his father, then at Moscow Conservatoire with Semyon Kozolupov. Also student of composition with Shebalin and DDS. During the 1950s established a uniquely brilliant career. Has commissioned innumerable new works from the world's leading composers, enriching the cello repertoire and extending the instrument's possibilities. DDS dedicated his two cello concertos and his orchestration of Schumann's cello concerto to him. In consequence of his protection of the disgraced writer Solzhenitsyn, his activities were severely restricted by the Soviet authorities. Hence his request to leave the Soviet Union with his family in 1974. First returned to Russia in 1990, conducting the Washington National Symphony Orchestra, and was hailed as a national hero.

Rozanova, Alexandra (1876–1902), pianist. Taught at St Petersburg Conservatoire as assistant of Malazemova, a disciple of Anton Rubenstein. Teacher of DDS and, a generation earlier, his mother Sofiya Vasilyevna Shostakovich.

*Rozhdestvensky, Gennadi (1931–), conductor. During the lifetime of DDS he held positions of chief conductor at the Bolshoi Theatre, the Moscow Radio Orchestra and the Moscow Chamber Theatre. Reputed for his championship of contemporary composers, and many neglected scores from the past. His research has brought to light some of DDS's previously forgotten scores, including the music to the film *New Babylon*, and other theatre, ballet and cinema music. Currently chief conductor of the Stockholm Symphony Orchestra.

*'Rudneva, Lyubov' (Fegelman) (1915–), writer. Author of numerous novels and short stories, and also of critical studies of Mayakovsky and Meyerhold

Ryazanov, Pyotr (1899–1942), Leningrad composer and teacher. Follower of V. Shcherbachov.

Ryumin, Pavel (dates not known), Secretary of Central Committee of Party, where he worked in the Cultural Department. Ridiculed by DDS as 'Sryulin' in introduction to *Rayok*.

*Sabinina, Marina (1917–), musicologist, writer and teacher at Moscow Conservatoire. Author of several books on DDS's music, including an authoritative survey of his symphonies.

Sakharov, Andrei (1918–89), nuclear physicist. Dissident and founder of Russian human rights movement. Like DDS, owned a dacha in Zhukovka outside Moscow.

Saltykov-Shchedrin, Mikhail (1822–89), greatest satirical writer of the nineteenth century.

Samosud, Samuel (1884–1964), conductor. Opera conductor at MALEGOT (1918–36), at Bolshoi Theatre (1936–43) and at Stanislavsky and Nemirovich–Danchenko Theatre (1943–56). First performer of DDS's *The Nose, Lady Macbeth of Mtsensk* and Seventh Symphony.

*Sanderling, Thomas (1942–), German conductor. Born in Novosibirsk, but grew up in Leningrad. His father, Kurt Sanderling, fled from Nazi Germany to USSR in the late 1930s, and shared the position of director of the Leningrad Philharmonic with Evgeny Mravinsky 1941–60, during which time he was closely associated with DDS and his music. The family returned to East Germany in 1960, where he studied and started his professional career. Gave first German performances of DDS's Thirteenth and Fourteenth Symphonies.

Schnittke, Alfred (1934–), composer. Studied with Golubiev at Moscow Conservatoire. Came to prominence in late 1960s as one of the most interesting of Russia's avant-garde composers. Experimented with serialism, polystylism, etc. Today is regarded as the most important composer to emerge from Russia. Currently lives in Hamburg.

Schnittke, Benedict (1905–66), teacher of music theory at Leningrad Conservatoire, where his wife Ala Schnittke (1908–87) taught musical analysis and form.

*Schwartz, Isaak (1923–), composer. Studied at Leningrad Conservatoire with Arapov and Evlakhov. Composer of many lyrical songs and chamber works. Best known for his stage and film music.

Serebryakov, Pavel (1909–79), pianist. Pupil of L. Nikolayev. Director of Leningrad Conservatoire 1938–52, 1962–79.

*Serebryakova, Galina (1905–), writer and specialist on Karl Marx. Her husband, the diplomat Sokolnikov, was shot in 1937, while she languished for twenty years in the Gulag prisons. DDS renewed contacts with her after her release. In 1965 DDS wrote music for the film *A Year as Long as a Lifetime* based on her book on the life of Karl Marx.

Serov, Alexander (1820–71), opera composer, whose music and ideas influenced Dargomyzhsky and Mussorgsky.

Shaporin, Yuri (1887–1966), composer, teacher and activist. His most famous work is the opera *The Decembrists* (1953).

Shcherbachov, Vladimir (1889–1952), composer. Had considerable influence in the 1920s. Led a school of reformist 'modernist' composers in Leningrad, where he taught 1923–31. In 1931 was 'demoted' to a professorship at the Tbilisi Conservatoire. His music (including his monumental Symphony no. 2 on words by Alexander Blok, and his 'Izhorsk' Symphony no. 4) has been unjustly neglected over the last fifty years or so.

Shebalin, Vissarion (1902–63), composer and teacher. Studied with Myaskovsky. Member of Moscow group called The Six. Close friend of DDS from

1925 until his death. Director of Moscow Conservatoire 1943–8. Criticized by Zhdanov in 1948, together with DDS, Prokofiev, etc. Had an important influence as a teacher; his pupils included such diverse figures as Edison Denisov, Nikolai Karetnikov and Tikhon Khrennikov. DDS not only valued Shebalin as one of his few loyal friends, but admired him as a composer. Much of their life-long correspondence was dedicated to musical discussion.

*Shebalina, Alisa (*née* Gubé) (1901–), paediatrician. Trained in Moscow and Germany. Met the composer Vissarion (Ronya) Shebalin in 1924. As was the fashion in the 1920s, the couple despised the 'bourgeois' trappings of matrimony, and only officially registered their marriage in the late 1930s, after the birth of their two children. To this day she dedicates her energies to honouring her husband's memory, and has published several books of reminiscences, documents, etc.

*Shenderovich, Evgeny (1918–), pianist. Studied at Leningrad Conservatoire, specializing in accompaniment. Met DDS during his student years. Duo partner of bass Evgeny Nesterenko, with whom he gave first performances of DDS's two last vocal cycles. Taught at Leningrad and Moscow Conservatoires. Since 1991 lives in Israel.

Shepilov, Dmitri (1905–), Secretary of Central Committee of Communist Party. One of the ideological spokesmen who led the attack against 'formalism' in 1948. Ridiculed by DDS in *Rayok*.

Shillinger, Iosif (1895–1943), composer and music theorist. Was influential in Leningrad musical life during the 1920s.

Shneyerson, Grigori (1911–), musicologist allied to the official establishment. Editor of book of reminiscences and articles on DDS published in 1976.

Sholokhov, Mikhail (1905–84), writer. Established his reputation with epic novel *Quiet Flows the Don*. Quickly became an establishment figure, who was accorded the highest honours and lived in unheard-of luxury, even though he virtually stopped writing. Often acted as Party spokesman on literary matters.

Shostakovich, Irina Antonovna see Supinskaya

Shostakovich, Mariya Dmitriyevna (1903–73), pianist. Composer's elder sister.

Shostakovich, Sofiya Vasilyevna (1878–1955), pianist. Composer's mother.

*Shostakovich, Zoya Dmitriyevna (1908–90), veterinary scientist. Younger sister of DDS. Married Grigori Khrushchev in 1920, a histologist by profession who later became director of the USSR Academy of Sciences.

Simonov, Ruben (1899–1968), actor and theatre director. Worked at Vakhtangov Theatre from 1926, becoming its director in 1939.

Sitkovetsky, Julian (1925–58), violinist. Winner of Queen Elizabeth Competition. Leader of Tchaikovsky Quartet.

*Slonim, Ilya (1906–73), sculptor. Best known for his bust portraits. After being accused of 'formalist' tendencies, he experienced great difficulties in exhibiting his work. Married T. Litvinova in 1941.

*Slonimsky, Sergei (1932–), composer. Son of the writer Mikhail Slonimsky. Graduated from the Leningrad Conservatoire in composition under Professor Evlakhov, a former DDS pupil. Published a book on Prokofiev symphonies in 1958. Much of his work in 1960s and 1970s was written in experimental, radical style; hence he experienced difficulties in getting his music performed. In recent years he has also achieved a reputation outside Russia for his symphonies, operas and chamber works.

Smolich, Nikolai (1888–1968), opera and theatre director. Artistic director at MALEGOT 1924–30. Later he worked at the Bolshoi in Moscow, where he also taught at the Conservatoire.

*Sokolov, Nikolai (1903–), artist. In 1924 formed the 'Kukryniksy' group with two other artists, M. Kupriyanov and P. Krylov (the 'Ku' and 'Kry' of the group). The 'Kukryniksy' (an anagram of the three artists' names) had a wide range of team activity, working in the theatre and illustration. They achieved nation-wide fame for their satirical cartoons, created for the magazine *Krokodil*.

Sokolovsky, Mikhail (1901–41), theatre director. Created TRAM, the avant-garde experimental youth theatre, based on collective principles and influenced by Brecht, which was closed down in 1935. At the beginning of World War II he enlisted with the People's Volunteer Brigade and died in the defence of Leningrad.

Sollertinsky, Ivan (1902–44). A man of incredible erudition and wit, equally at home in the many professions of which he was master: theatre and art specialist, linguist, specialist in Romance and Hispanic languages. Eventually chose to follow career in music as a professor at Leningrad Conservatoire, artistic director of the Leningrad Philharmonic and brilliant lecturer in music. From 1927 was DDS's closest friend and confidant.

Solovyov-Sedoy, Vasili (1907–79), composer of popular songs. Best known as the composer of the song 'Moscow Nights'. Chairman of the Leningrad Composers' Union 1945–64.

Solzhenitsyn, Alexander (1918–), writer. Served in Soviet Army in World War II; arrested on trumped-up charges, languished in the Gulag camps until rehabilitation in 1958. Although tentatively published in Russia during the Thaw years, from 1968 he was subjected to ferocious campaign of criticism and forced to emigrate from Russia in 1974. Won Nobel Prize in 1970.

Souvchinsky, Pierre (1892–1985), writer and musicologist. Emigrated to France, where he became a leading figure of the Russian emigré community. Was on close terms with Stravinsky. After World War II he helped

Boulez form the Domaine Musicale etc. Corresponded with Pasternak until the poet's death.

Spassky, Boris (1937–), chess player. World champion 1969–72.

Stakhanov, Alexei (1905–). Miner who achieved fame by breaking the record for mining coal on the night 30/31 August 1935, when he produced in one shift fourteen times the expected norm. A few weeks later he doubled his own record. Gave his name to the Stakhanovite movement of shock workers, whose aim was to boost morale and increase industrial productivity. Later he was an administrator in the Ministry of Coal and Industry and a deputy to the Supreme Soviet.

Stanislavsky, Konstantin (1863–1938), theatre and opera director. Co-founder of Moscow Arts Theatre in 1898. First director of Chekhov's late plays. In 1918 organized Bolshoi Theatre Opera studio, renamed Stanislavsky Opera Theatre.

Steinberg, Maximilian (1883–1946), composer. Taught composition at the Petrograd/Leningrad Conservatoire for over forty years. Son-in-law of Rimsky-Korsakov.

Stiedri, Fritz (1883–1968), Austrian conductor. Director of Leningrad Philharmonic 1932–6. Promoted much new music, notably Schoenberg's.

Stuckenschmidt, Hans Heinz (1901–88), German musicologist. Schoenberg's last pupil. Has written books on Busoni, Schoenberg, *et al.*

Supinskaya, Irina (1934–), literary scholar. DDS's third wife from 1962.

Sveshnikov, Alexander (1890–1980), chorus master. Director of Moscow Conservatoire from 1948. Director of State Academic Choir.

Sviridov, Georgi (1915–), composer. One of DDS's most talented pupils. Best works are settings of Russian lyrical poetry (Esenin, Pasternak) for chorus or solo voice. Became an establishment figure, a yes-man in the Union of Composers.

Tarkhanov, Mikhail (real name Moskvin) (1877–1948), actor and theatre director. Worked at Moscow Arts Theatre. Head of GITIS (Theatre Institute) 1942–8.

Tatlin, Vladimir (1885–1953), avant-garde painter. Influenced by Picasso's cubist paintings. From 1917 worked in Lunacharsky's Commissariat for Enlightenment as head of Moscow Department of Painting. In 1920s worked in design and three-dimensional art, his most famous construction being the 20 ft spiral tower dedicated to the Third International. From the 1930s his work was no longer tolerated.

Theodorakis, Mikis (1925–), Greek composer of revolutionary outlook and communist sympathies. Arrested in 1967 by right-wing Colonel's regime. His music was banned in Greece. Released in 1970.

Tishchenko, Boris (1939–), composer and pianist. Studied at Leningrad Conservatoire with Evlakhov and as post-graduate with DDS. One of most outstanding talents of his generation. DDS rated him highly, and particularly admired his setting of Akhmatova's Requiem.

Tolstoy, Dmitri (1923–), composer. Son of the writer Alexei Tolstoy (1883–1945). Studied with Shebalin in Moscow, and Arapov and DDS (1947–8) in Leningrad.

*Tomashevskaya, Zoya (1926–), architect. Comes from well-known St Petersburg/Leningrad intellectual family. Her father, the distinguished Pushkin scholar Boris Tomashevsky, enjoyed close friendships with some of Russia's most distinguished writers, notably Anna Akhmatova. The Tomashevskys always kept open house for musicians and writers in their flat on the Griboyedev Canal at the heart of old St Petersburg.

Toscanini, Arturo (1867–1957), Italian conductor. As an anti-fascist, he refused to conduct in Italy and Germany. Spent the war years in the USA as head of the NBC orchestra 1938–45. One of the first conductors to promote DDS's music outside the USSR, giving first Western performance of the Seventh Symphony in New York in 1943.

Trauberg, Leonid (1902–), film director. Founder of FEKS with Kozintsev and Yutkevich. All his films 1924–46 co-directed with Kozintsev.

Trifonov, Yuri (1925–81), writer.

Trotsky, Lev (real name Bronstein) (1879–1940), revolutionary. Originally a Menshevik before joining forces with Lenin early in 1917. Founded Red Army and was responsible for its political training and tough discipline. From 1924 he was in opposition to Stalin, who ousted him from power, had him exiled from Russia in 1928 and assassinated in Mexico.

Tsekhanovsky, Mikhail (1895–1965), film director and animator. DDS wrote the music for two of his cartoon 'opera' films, *The Tale of the Priest and His Servant Balda* and *The Silly Mouse*.

Tsyganov, Mikhail (1905–93), violinist. Leader and founder of Beethoven Quartet, which gave the first performance of DDS's quartets (with the exception of No. 1 and No. 15).

Tukhachevsky, Mikhail (1893–1937), Marshal of the Soviet Army. One of the most brilliant Soviet military strategists. Eliminated by Stalin, along with the elite of the Red Army, in the 'generals' purge.

Tuskiya, Iona (1901–63), Georgian composer. Studied with Shcherbachov.

Tvardovsky, Alexander (1910–71), poet and writer. Editor of progressive literary journal *Novy Mir*; responsible for publishing Solzhenitsyn's *One Day in the Life of Ivan Denisovich*.

*Tyulin, Yuri (1893–1978), composer and music theorist. Follower of Shcherbachov's reformist school in the 1920s. Taught at Leningrad Conservatoire for fifty years. Together with Asafiev and Yavorsky he deeply influenced musical thinking in Soviet Russia during the first half of this century.

Tyutchev, Fyodor (1803–73). Russian metaphysical poet.

Ulanova, Galina (1910–), ballerina. Outstanding soloist of Kirov Theatre.

Ustvolskaya, Galina (1919–), composer. Studied with DDS 1938–47 at Leningrad Conservatoire. DDS regarded her compositional talent most highly, quoting themes from her music in his work and giving her many of his own manuscripts. Her uncompromising radical music, together with a retiring, impractical personality, has meant that her music suffered neglect until a recent revival of interest.

*****Vakman, Sofiya** (1911–), pianist and accompanist. Studied at Kiev and Leningrad Conservatoires. Gave first performance of Tsvetayeva Songs Op. 143, accompanying I. Bogachyova.

Varzar, Nina (1910–54), physicist. Studied at Bestuzhev Courses and Leningrad University. Married DDS in 1932. Mother of his children, Galina (1936–) and Maxim (1938–).

*****Vecheslava, Tatyana** (1910–), ballerina. Soloist of Leningrad Kirov Theatre. Participated in the production of *Bolt* in 1931.

Villiams, Pyotr (1902–47), painter and theatre designer. Worked with VKHUTEMAS in early 1920s. Best work done at Bolshoi Theatre 1941–7.

*****Vishnevskaya, Galina** (1926–), soprano. Soloist of Bolshoi Theatre 1952–74. Married M. L. Rostropovich in 1956. Dedicatee of three vocal works by DDS. Britten wrote 'The Poet's Echo' and the soprano part of the War Requiem for her voice.

Volkonsky, André (1933–), composer and harpsichordist. Born in Geneva of old aristocratic Russian family. They returned to USSR in 1947. Expelled from Moscow Conservatoire in 1954. One of the most talented musicians of his generation, profoundly influencing composers' avant-garde circles, as well as stimulating interest in early music. Founder of Moscow Chamber Orchestra and Madrigal Group.

Voroshilov, Kliment (1881–1969), Bolshevik and close associate of Stalin. Full member of Politburo from 1926. In 1941 was stripped of his command for failing to prevent the German blockade of Leningrad. Chairman of the Presidium of Supreme Soviet 1953–7. Lost his Party and government posts after unsuccessfully trying to depose Khrushchev in 1957.

Vovsi, Miron (1897–1960), therapist and paediatric surgeon. Arrested in 1953 as part of 'Doctors' Plot'.

*****Vovsi-Mikhoels, Natalya** (1921–), linguist. Daughter of the famous Jewish actor Solomon Mikhoels, and the niece of Professor Miron Vovsi. First marriage was to composer Moisei Weinberg. After her divorce in 1972 she emigrated to Israel. Author of *My Father, Solomon Mikhoels*.

Vvedensky, Alexander (1904–41), poet. Member of Oberiu, the Leningrad group of absurdist writers.

Vysotsky, Vladimir (1938–80), actor at Taganka Theatre. Achieved incredible popularity for his songs, which were written in the style of 'street' or 'camp' ballads to guitar accompaniment.

Weinberg, Moisei (1919–), composer and pianist. Graduated from Warsaw Conservatoire. In 1939 escaped to USSR. Became close friend of DDS from 1943. Arrested in 1953, released after several months. DDS never taught him, but had high opinion of his gifts.

Weisberg, Julia (1880–1942), composer and critic. Pupil of Rimsky-Korsakov and Glazunov. Married A. N. Rimsky-Korsakov, son of the composer. In 1920s edited the music journal *Muzikalny Sovremmenik*.

Welter, Nadezhda (1899–), mezzo-soprano. Worked with GATOB (Kirov Theatre) in Leningrad as soloist of the company 1930–3 and 1945–53. Also worked at MALEGOT 1933–45, where her roles included a remarkable portrayal of Carmen and the Countess in Tchaikovsky's *Queen of Spades*.

Yarustovsky, Boris (1911–78), musicologist and teacher. Responsible for ideological matters at the Union of Composers. Was one of Shostakovich's persecutors even before 1948. However, he moved with the times, as is evidenced by his two books on Stravinsky, the first being a crude attack on the renowned master, while the second gave a more favourable appraisal. DDS ridiculed him in the preface of *Rayok* as 'Yasrustovsky'.

Yavorsky, Boleslav (1877–1942), composer and music theorist. Pupil of Tanyeev. Developed theory of 'modal rhythm' and created a symmetrical system based on tritone and its resolution, which he applied to all music. Had an enormous influence as a teacher at the Kiev and Moscow Conservatoires. His personality and theories had a profound influence on DDS, as testified by the intensive correspondence between them during DDS's student years.

*Yelagin, Yuri (1910–87), violinist, writer. Played in orchestra of Vakhtangov Theatre. Emigrated after World War II to Houston, USA, where he became leader of the Houston Symphony Orchestra. Published a biography of Meyerhold, *The Black Genius*.

*Yudin, Gavriil (1905–91), conductor. Cousin of Mariya Yudina. Studied at Petrograd/Leningrad Conservatoire. Had a modest career as a conductor within the Soviet Union.

Yudina, Mariya (1899–1970), pianist. Pupil of Leonid Nikolayev. A person of enormous erudition and great enthusiasms for new causes. Hence she studied philosophy, architecture, poetry, etc. Had an enormous following in Russia, but never performed outside the country. Her unpredictable behaviour (e.g. reciting poetry during concerts) and espousal of religion were anathema to Soviet 'officialdom'. Her performances were characterized by highly individualist and sometimes eccentric interpretation, which could inspire, but could also irritate. From mid 1950s devoted her energy to the cause of new music, corresponding with Stravinsky and Stockhausen.

Yutkevich, Sergei (1904–85), film and theatre director, designer and artist. Pupil of Meyerhold. Director of Agitgroup 'Sinyaya Bluza'. Worked with Eisenstein in his theatre productions. Co-founded FEKS with Kozintsev and Trauberg. DDS wrote the music for three of his films, including *Counterplan*.

Zakharov, Vladimir (1901–56), member of RAPM in 1920s. From 1932 director of Piatnitsky Choir. In 1948 he was appointed one of the Union of Composers' Principal Secretaries, and in this capacity was one of the most ferocious persecutors of 'formalist' composers.

Zamyatin, Evgeny (1884–1937), writer. Acquired fame in the 1920s with his utopian novel *We*. In 1931 he wrote to Stalin asking permission to leave the Soviet Union, rather than suffer the ignominious moral death of silence by censorship. His request was granted. Zamyatin died in Paris. Collaborated briefly with DDS and Preis on the libretto of *The Nose*.

Zaslavsky, David (1890–1961), political publicist. Close to Lenin pre-1917. During 1930s to 1950s he worked on the editorial board of *Pravda*. Confessed author of the article 'Muddle Instead of Music' that appeared anonymously in *Pravda* on 28 January 1936.

Zhdanov, Andrei (1896–1948), party activist. From 1944 he worked as Central Committee secretary in charge of ideological matters. Was responsible for post World War II decrees attacking writers, film-makers and composers.

Zhilyaev, Nikolai (1881–1942), composer and music theorist. Teacher at Moscow Conservatoire. DDS regarded him as one of his musical mentors. His loyalty to his friend Marshal Tukhachevsky led to his own arrest in 1937 and death in prison.

*Zhitomirsky, Daniil (1906–92), writer and musicologist. Studied at Moscow Conservatoire during late 1920s. Member of RAPM and of its splinter group PROKOLL. Started a journalistic career in the late 1920s. In 1929 he wrote a polemic article in *Proletarsky Muzikant* condemning DDS's *The Nose*, noting that DDS 'had strayed from the main road of Soviet Art'. After dissolution of RAPM in 1932, Zhitomirsky changed his radical ideological position, and suffered a period of disgrace.

*Zhukova, Lydia (dates not known), pianist. Studied at the Petrograd Conservatoire. Emigrated to USA.

Zhutovsky, Boris (1934–), artist of 'unofficial' trend. Attacked by Khrushchev in 1962 for his 'abstract' painting. Later he befriended Khrushchev and was briefly married to his daughter. Recently he has acquired a reputation outside Russia.

Zinoviev, Grigori (real name Radomyslsky) (1883–1936), Bolshevik revolutionary close to Lenin. Controlled Leningrad Party Organization 1921–6. Formed 'left' opposition with Kamenev. Expelled from Party three times from 1927. Arrested in 1935. Tried and condemned at the notorious show trial of 1936.

Zoshchenko, Mikhail (1895–1958), humorous writer. Acquired great popularity in the 1920s for his short sketches about the 'new way of life' in Soviet Russia. Was also loved for his deadpan manner when publicly reciting these sketches. Attacked (together with Akhmatova) in the Leningrad newspaper *Star* in 1946 as part of Zhdanov's campaign against 'formalists'. DDS much admired his work, and was on friendly terms with him.

Annotated List of Sources

Note: All translations from Russian to English have been done by
Elizabeth Wilson, unless otherwise stated

Arnshtam, Leo Oskarovich, 'Immortality' ('Bessmertiye'), in G. M. Shneyerson (ed.), *D. D. Shostakovich: Articles and Materials (Shostakovich: Stat'i i
materialy)* (Sovietsky Kompozitor, Moscow, 1976).

Asafiev, Boris Vladimirovich, *Selected Works in Five Volumes (Izbranniye trudi v
pyati tomakh)* (Izdatel'stvo Akademii Nauk SSSR, Moscow, 1952).

Balanchivadze, André Melitonovich, 'Contemporaries Write on D. D. Shostakovich' ('Sovremmoniki o D. D. Shostakovichc'), in L. V. Danllevich (eu.),
Dmitri Shostakovich (Sovietsky Kompozitor, Moscow, 1967).

Barshai, Rudolf Borisovich. A recorded interview with EW, London, October
1988.

Basner, Venyamin Efimovich. A recorded interview with EW, Leningrad,
December 1988.

Berlinsky, Valentin Alexandrovich. A recorded interview with EW, London,
December 1990.

Bogdanov-Berezovsky, Valerian Mikhailovich, 'Adolescence and Youth'
('Otrochestvo i yunost''), in G. M. Shneyerson (ed.), *D. D. Shostakovich:
Articles and Material (D. D. Shostakovich: Stat'i i materialy)* (Sovietsky
Kompozitor, Moscow, 1976).

– *The Roads of Art (Dorogi iskusstva)* (Muzyku, Leningrad, 1971)

Chukovsky, Evgeny Borisovich. Two novellas commissioned for this book.
The first is untitled and gives a description of the Shostakovich household in
Moscow. The second is entitled 'Komarovo' and describes their summer
residence. Both novellas have been somewhat cut. I have tried to retain all
the material that is directly relevant to a description of Shostakovich and his
everyday surroundings.

Chulaki, Mikhail Ivanovich, 'Today I Will Talk about Shostakovich' ('Segod-
nya ya rasskazhu o Shostakoviche'), *Zvezda*, no. 7, 1987. These memoirs
were written towards the end of his life in the Glasnost era, and Chulaki
presents himself as a liberal, which is hardly how others saw him. But his
first-hand account of the reception of the Fifth Symphony gives an insight
into the mechanism of the Soviet bureaucrats' way of thinking, where
ideology reigned supreme over art. I have taken the liberty of correcting a
few errors in the dates.

Danilevich, Lev Vasiliyevich (ed.), *Dmitri Shostakovich* (Sovietsky Kompozitor, Moscow, 1967).

Dansker, O. L. (ed.), *S. A. Samosud: Articles, Reminiscences, Letters* (S. A. Samosud: Stat'i, vospominaniya, pis'ma) (Sovietsky Kompozitor, Moscow, 1984). Contains reminiscences of Nadezhda L'vovna Welter.

Denisov, Edison Vasiliyevich. A recorded interview with EW, Moscow, December 1988.

– 'A Diary Record of My Meetings with Dmitri Shostakovich'. An unpublished typescript made available by courtesy of the author.
See also Dmitri Shostakovich, 'Letters to Edison Denisov'.

Dorliak, Nina L'vovna. A recorded interview with EW, Moscow, January 1990.

Druskin, Mikhail Semyonovich, 'Shostakovich in the 1920s ('Shostakovich v 20-e gody'), in *Sketches, Articles, Notes* (*Ocherki, stat'i, zametki*) (Sovietsky Kompozitor, Leningrad, 1987). I am grateful to Mr Druskin for giving me permission to use this article selectively. My choice was influenced by the three-hour interview (unrecorded at his request) I had with him in his Leningrad home in January 1990.

Druzhinin, Fyodor Serafimovich. An article of reminiscences commissioned for this book.

Dubinsky, Rostislav, *Stormy Applause: Making Music in a Workers' State* (London, Hutchinson, 1989).

Evtushenko, Evgeny Alexandrovich. Reminiscences of Shostakovich and His Thirteenth Symphony. Melodiya stereo A10 00285000, side 4 of album of 2 records. This is a spoken introduction to the Thirteenth Symphony, conducted by Gennadi Rozhdestvensky and played by the Orchestra of the Ministry of Culture. The interview with Evtushenko was recorded in 1987. Translated by Grigori Gerenstein.

Ferkelman, Arnold. A recorded interview with EW, Moscow, September 1989.

Fried, Grigori Samuilovich, *Music, Contacts and Destinies* (*Muzyka, obshcheniye – sud'by*) (Sovietsky Kompozitor, Moscow, 1987).

Galli-Shohat, Nadejda Vasiliyevna *see* Seroff, Victor.

Gauk, Alexander, 'Creative Encounters' ('Tvorcheskiye vstrechi'), in L. Gauk, R. Glezer and Y. Milstein (eds), *Alexander Vasiliyevich Gauk: Memoirs, Selected Articles, Reminiscences of His Contemporaries* (*Alexander Vasiliyevich Gauk: Memuary, izbranniye stat'i, vospominaniya sovremmenikov*) (Sovietsky Kompozitor, Moscow, 1975). An article in a book of collected articles and reminiscences. Gauk's article, which is largely about Shostakovich, was written in 1961. It reflects contemporary perception of the composer, and in certain instances his silences are revealing.

Gauk, L., Glezer, R. and Milstein, Y. (eds), *Alexander Vasiliyevich Gauk:*

Memoirs, Selected Articles, Reminiscences of His Contemporaries (Alexander Vasiliyevich Gauk: Memuary, izbranniye stat'i, vospominaniya sovremmenikov) (Sovietsky Kompozitor, Moscow, 1975).

Glikman, Isaak Davydovich, *Letters to a Friend: Dmitri Shostakovich to Isaak Glikman (Pis'ma k drugu: Dmitri Shostakovich Isaaku Glikmanu* (Sovietsky Kompozitor, St Petersburg; 'DSCH' Publishers, Moscow, 1993).

Glivenko, Tatyana Ivanovna. A recorded interview with EW, Moscow, March 1989. I met Tatyana Glivenko through Zoya Dmitriyevna Shostakovich. The interview took place in her homely kitchen at her flat on Ulitsa 261 Bakiinskikh Kommissarov. Tatyana Ivanovna was a woman of great charm, and despite her years she retained a youthful spirit. Although on the one hand she was reluctant to speak about her early life and emotions, she also spoke with spontaneous warmth about her relationship with DDS, which still meant much to her, despite her having lived a full life centred on a loving family. On that occasion Tatyana Ivanovna also made available to me an edited typescript of excerpts of DDS's letters to her. These excerpts referred exclusively to musical matters, and all parts referring to their personal and intimate relationship had been cut out.

In January 1990 I visited again, bringing with me the transcript of her interview, which I asked her to check through with me.

In December 1991 Shostakovich's letters to Glivenko came up for auction at Sotheby's in London. They were acquired by Shostakovich's son Maxim, who was thus able to fulfil his father's wishes in stopping prying eyes from reading a personal correspondence. Maxim Shostakovich specifically asked me to refrain from quoting from these letters, with the exception of the small quotations that were printed in the Sotheby's catalogue (see Dmitri Shostakovich, Letters to Tatyana Glivenko).

Gnessin, Mikhail Fabianovich, *Thoughts and Reminiscences about N. A. Rimsky Korsakov (Mysli i vospominaniya o N. A. Rimskom-Korsakove)* (Muzgiz, Moscow, 1956).

Gozenpud, Abraam Akimovich, 'Encounters with Shostakovich' ('Vstrechi s Shostakovichem'). An article commissioned for this book.

Gubaidulina, Sofiya. A recorded interview with EW, Huddersfield/London, December 1990.

Ikonnikov, Alexei Alexandrovich, 'Some Strokes for a Portrait of Shostakovich' ('Shtrikhi k portretu Shostakovicha'), *Nashe Naslediye*, no. 4, 1989.

Ivinskaya, Olga, *A Captive of Time* (Collins, London, 1976).

Kapralov, V. A. (ed.), *Boris Mikhailovich Kustodiev* (Khudozhnik RSFSR, Leningrad, 1967).

Karagieva, L.-V. (ed.), *Kara Karayev: Articles, Letters and Opinions (Kara Karayev: Stat'i, pis'ma i vyskazivaniya)* (Sovietsky Kompozitor, Moscow, 1978).

Karetnikov, Nikolai Nikolayevich, 'Your Contemporary' ('Vash sovremmenik') (1975). Over the years Karetnikov has written a series of reminiscences in the form of novellas, some of which have now been published in Russia in the wake of Glasnost. They include several short sketches relating to Shostakovich. 'Your Contemporary' was made available by the author from an unpublished typescript.

Khachaturian, Aram Ilyich, *see* Khentova, Sofiya.

Khachaturian, Karen Surenovich. A recorded interview with EW, Moscow, December 1988.

Khaikin, Boris Emilovich, *Discourses on Conducting* (*Besedy o Dirizhirovanii*) (Sovietsky Kompozitor, Moscow, 1984).

Khentova, Sofiya Mikhailovna, 'Dmitri Shostakovich: We Live in a Time of Stormy Passions and Actions' ('Dmitri Shostakovich: Miy zhivyem vo vremya silnykh strastei i burnykh postupkov'), *Niva*, no. 2, January 1991.

– *Shostakovich: Life and Work* (*D. Shostakovich: Zhisn' i tvorchestvo*), 2 vols (Sovietsky Kompozitor, Leningrad, 1985).

– 'Shostakovich and Khachaturian: They Were Drawn Together by 1948' ('Shostakovich i Khachaturiyan: Ikh sblizil 1948-i god'), *Muzikalnaya Zhisn*, no. 24, 1988.

– 'Women in Shostakovich's Life' ('Zhenshchiny v zhisni Shostakovicha'), *Vremya i My*, no. 112, 1991.

Kisilev, V. (ed.), 'Letters from the 1930s' ('Iz pisem 1930^{kh} godov'), *Sovietskaya Muzyka*, no. 9, September 1987, pp. 85–91. Contains letters of DDS to Zakhar Lyubinsky and various correspondents.

Komarovskaya, N. L., 'My Meetings with B. M. Kustodiev' ('Moyi vstrechi s B. M. Kustodievyem'), in V. A. Kapralov (ed.), *Boris Mikhailovich Kustodiev* (Khudozhnik RSFSR, Leningrad, 1967).

Kondrashin, Kirill Petrovich. Reminiscences of DDS. Transcribed from a recorded conversation with Nolda Broekstra-Kondrashin in Holland in 1979 and used with her kind permission.

Konniskaya, Mariya Yuryevna. Extract from an unpublished letter made available by the author.

Koritsky, N. I., Melnik-Tukhachevskaya, S. M. and Chistov B. N. (eds), *Marshal Tukhachevsky: Memoirs of His Friends and Comrades in Arms* (*Marshal Tukhachevsky: Vospominaniya druzyei i soratnikov*) (Voennoye Izdatel'stvo Ministerstva Oborony SSSR, Moscow, 1965). In this collection of memoirs there is an article by DDS which is quoted in the text.

Kozintsev, Grigori Mikhailovich, *The Complete Works* (*Sobraniye sochinenii v 5^i tomakh*), 5 vols (Isskustvo, Leningrad, 1982). Particular reference is made to 'Notes about Art and Artists' ('Zametki ob iskusstve i lyudyakh iskusstva') from vol. II, where there is a section devoted to DDS. There Kozintsev comments on many aspects of the composer's personality, sometimes in aphoristic jottings, sometimes in extended paragraphs.

Kozlova, G. M. (ed,), [*Letters of Lev Oborin*] ' "I'm Eighteen Years Old": Letters of D. D. Shostakovich to L. N. Oborin' (' "Mnye ispolnilos' vosemnadtsat' lyet": Pis'ma D. D. Shostakovicha L. N. Oborinu'), in *Encounters with the Past (Vystrechi s proshlym)* (Sovietskaya Rossiya, Moscow, 1984).

Kustodieva, Irina, 'Dear Memories' ('Dorigiye vospominaniya'), in V. A. Kapralov (ed.), *Boris Mikhailovich Kustodiev* (Khudozhnik RSFSR, Leningrad, 1967).

Kuznetsov, A. (ed.), 'D. D. Shostakovich: Reminiscences of Friends and Relatives' ('Vospominaniya rodnykh i druzyei'), in *Mariya Venyaminovna Yudina: Articles, Reminiscences and Materials (M. V. Yudina: Stat'i, vospominaniya i materialy)* (Sovietsky Kompozitor, Moscow, 1978).

Lamm, Olga Pavlovna, 'Vissarion Yaklovlevich Shebalin', in A. Shebalina, *In Memory of V. Y. Shebalin: Reminiscences, Materials (Pamyati V. Y. Shebalinu: vospominaniya, materialy)* (Sovietsky Kompozitor, Moscow, 1984.

Lebedinsky, Lev Nikolayevich. Recorded interviews with EW, Geneva, August 1900, Moscow, December 1900 and March 1909. Material also collated from Lebedinsky's unpublished articles, with the author's approval.

– 'Shostakovich's Handling of Folk/Popular Song in His Own Works and Those of Other Composers' ('Obrashcheniye D. D. Shostakovicha k narodno-pesennomu materialu, k proizvedeniyem drugikh kompozitorov i svoim sobstvennym'). Unpublished article. Checked and additional information added in a consultation interview with EW, Moscow, March 1989.

Levitin, Yuri Abramovich, 'The Year 1948' ('1948 god'). One of various unpublished articles of reminiscences written in the late 1980s that were kindly made available to me by the author.

Litvinova, Flora Pavlovna. A commissioned article. Flora Litvinova, prompted by my request for reminiscence material, wrote a long and fascinating memoir of 67 pages, dealing with the years of her friendship with the Shostakovich family, additionally giving much background and autobio graphical material for the sake of context. She also used extensive quotations from her diaries of those years. I have used as much of her article as possible, spread through five chapters of this book. However, for reasons of space, I was forced to cut many pages of her memoirs. I was guided in my selection of what to omit by two rules: not to repeat material I already had from another contributor, and to leave out material that did not relate directly to DDS or his family.

Litvinova, Tatyana, 'Shostakovich in Kuibyshev' ('Shostakovich v Kuibysheve'). An article commissioned for this book and translated by Grigori Gerenstein. Litvinova wrote in Russian, despite her complete fluency in English. I therefore asked her to check the translation, which she most kindly did.

Lossky, Boris Nikolayevich, 'New Facts about Shostakovich' ('Novoye o Shostakoviche'), *Russkaya Mysl'*, no. 3771, 24 April 1989, Paris. I quote from this article and from his extensive unpublished notes, 'Reactions of a Schoolmate of Mitya Shostakovich to Sofiya Khentova's "Shostakovich's Young Years" ' ('Reaktsii shkolnogo tovarischa "Mityi" na tyext tsenogo truda S. Khentovoi "Molodiye gody Shostakovicha' otnosyashchiyeska k 1915–1922 godam'). I am most grateful to Boris Lossky for reading and checking this version and translation of his text, and for his most useful suggestions. I also thank him and the editors of *Russkaya Mysl'* for waiving the copyright for this publication.

Lubotsky, Mark Davidovich. Extracts from his unpublished memoirs, made available by kind permission of the author, translated by Grigori Gerenstein and EW.

Lyubimov, Yuri Petrovich. A recorded interview with EW, London, November 1988. Translated by Grigori Gerenstein and EW.

Malko, Nikolai, *A Certain Art* (Morrow, New York, 1966). Nikolai Malko emigrated from the Soviet Union in 1929. The long chapter on Shostakovich in his book was written in 1944. It testifies to the importance of his relationship with Shostakovich as the first champion of his music. However, because it was written nearly two decades after the events it describes, and without recourse to Soviet documentation, it is hardly surprising that Malko's memory was not always totally reliable in regard to dates and facts.

– Philharmonic Diary, Archive of the Leningrad Institute of Theatre, Music and Cinema.

Maranchik, Pavel, *The Birth of Komsomol Theatre* (*Rozhdeniye Komsomolskogo Teatra*) (Iskusstvo, Moscow and Leningrad, 1963).

Meyer, Krzysztof, extracts from an article written as an extended obituary of Shostakovich, *Ruch Muzyczny*, no. 19, 1975, Poland. Translated by Jagna Wright. My thanks to K. Meyer for waiving the copyright.

Meyerovich, Mikhail Alexandrovich. A recorded interview with EW, Moscow December 1988. Translated by Grigori Gerenstein.

Mikheeva, Lyudmila Vikentyevna, *In Memory of I. I. Sollertinsky: Reminiscences, Material and Research* (*Pamyati I. I. Sollertinskogo: Vospominaniya, materiali i issledovaniya*) (Sovietsky Kompozitor, Leningrad/Moscow, 1974).

– 'The Story of a Friendship' ('Istoriya odnoy druzhby'), *Sovietskaya Muzyka*, Part 1, no. 9, September 1986; Part 2, no. 9, September 1987. A literary editor, Mikheeva is married to Ivan Sollertinsky's son Dmitri. This article chronicles Ivan Sollertinsky's friendship with DDS, backed up by letters selected from the family's private archive.

Milhaud, Darius, *Notes without Music* (Da Capo Press, New York, 1970).

Milkis, Yakov. A recorded interview with EW, Camerino, Italy, August 1989.

Mravinsky, Evgeny Alexandrovich, 'Thirty Years of Shostakovich's Music'

('Tridtsat' lyet s muzykoi Shostakovicha'), in L. V. Danilevich (ed.), *Dmitri Shostakovich* (Sovietsky Kompozitor, Moscow, 1967). This book was prepared for the composer's sixtieth birthday.

Nabokov, Nicholas, *Old Friends and New Music* (Little, Brown, London, 1951).

Nikolayev, Alexei (ed.), ['Letters to Shebalin'] 'He Was a Wonderful Friend' ('Eto byl zamechatel'ny drug'), *Sovietskaya Muzyku*, no. 7, 1982. Letters of DDS to V. Y. Shebalin.

Nikolayeva, Tatyana. A recorded telephone interview with EW, Italy, February 1993.

Oistrakh, David Fyodorovich, 'A Great Artist of Our Time' ('Velikii khudozhnik nashego vremeni'), in G. M. Shneyerson (ed.), *D. D. Shostakovich: Articles and Materials* (*D. D. Shostakovich: Stat'i i materialy*) (Sovietsky Kompozitor, Moscow, 1976).

Orlov, Georgi, *Shostakovich's Symphonies* (*Symphonii Shostakovicha*) (Gosudarstvennoye Muzykalnoye Izdatel'stvo, Leningrad, 1961).

Ovcharek, Vladimir Yurevich. An article commissioned for this book.

Pears, Peter, *Moscow Christmas. A Diary* (private publication). The extracts are © The Executors of Sir Peter Pears and are not to be further reproduced without written permission. I express my gratitude to the Britten-Pears Library for permission to use extracts from this book.

Perelman, Nathan Yefimovich. A recorded interview with EW, Leningrad, December 1988.

Pokrovsky, Boris Alexandrovich. A recorded interview with EW, Amsterdam, April 1992.

Prokofiev, Oleg Sergeyevich, 'On My Few Contacts with Shostakovich'. An article commissioned for this book and written in English.

Rabinovich, David Abramovich, *Dmitri Shostakovich, Composer* (Foreign Language Publishing House, Moscow, 1959).

Ruzhkov, Mark, *Reminiscences of an Old Musician* (*Vospominaniya starogo muzikanta*) (Overseas Publication Interchange, West Germany, 1984).

Rostropovich, Mstislav Leopoldovich. A recorded interview with EW, London, November 1989.

Rozhdestvensky, Gennadi Nikolayevich. A recorded interview with EW, London, October 1989.

Rudneva, Lyubov' Savvishna, 'How It Happened . . .' ('Kak eto sluchilos''). An article commissioned for this book.

Sabinina, Marina Dmitriyevna. She wrote the following series of short stories specially for this book:

'About Children and Other Things' ('O detyakh i prochem')
'An Artist Should Never Marry' ('Khudozhnik ne dolzhen zhenitsya')
'During the Days of "The Thaw" ' ('V dni "ottepeli" ')
'How We Were Re-educated' ('Kak nas perevospityvali')

' "I Am Utterly, Utterly Happy" ' ('Ya sovershenno, sovershenno schastliv')

'The Man Who Spoke about the Omelette' ('Chelovek, kotory govorit o yaichnitse').

Sanderling, Thomas. A recorded interview with EW, London, December 1989.

Schnittke, Alfred Garrich, 'Circles of Influence' ('Krugi vliyaniya'), in G. M. Shneyerson (ed.), *D. D. Shostakovich: Articles and Materials* (*D. D. Shostakovich: Stat'i i materialy*) (Sovietsky Kompozitor, Moscow, 1976). A collection of articles on DDS.

Schwartz, Isaak Iosifovich, 'Reminiscences of Shostakovich' ('Vospominaniya o Shostakoviche'). The extracts are from an article commissioned for this book. I met Isaak Schwartz in March 1989 and recorded an interview with him. When I sent him the transcript (in translation), he was not altogether happy with it, but fortunately agreed to write down his reminiscences. I am most grateful to Lyudmila Kovnatskaya for her help in preparing this article.

Serebryakova, Galina, *About Myself and Others* (*O drugikh i o sebye*) (Sovietsky Pisatel', Moscow, 1971).

Seroff, Victor, in collaboration with Nadejda Galli-Shohat (aunt of DDS), *Dmitri Shostakovich: The Life and Background of a Soviet Composer* (Alfred A. Knopf, New York, 1943). This book was published during the Second World War, when relations between the USA and the Soviet Union had suddenly improved due to the two countries having become allies. Shostakovich was 'all the rage' throughout the Western World after the widely publicized performances of his Seventh Symphony in the Soviet Union, the USA and Great Britain.

In writing the chapters concerning the composer's childhood, Victor Seroff must have relied almost entirely on the memory of his collaborator Nadejda Galli-Shohat and documents (including family letters) provided by her. In his foreword, he writes, 'I have checked every statement; every fact in this story is backed up by documents and material either in my possession or at the New York Public Library. I have even checked up on my collaborator, and it is my pleasure to compliment her on the accuracy of her memory' (p. x).

Shostakovich himself must have been embarrassed and upset by the appearance of the book. Immediately after its publication, he made a statement calling it a bad book with many inaccuracies. However, we cannot be sure if this reflects a genuine opinion, or was an expedient disassociation from the Western press.

Shebalina, Alisa Maximovna. A recorded interview with EW, Moscow, March 1989. Alisa Maximovna received me in her Moscow flat. At 89, she was a woman of undiminished spirit, with a memory as sharp as ever. She had prepared for my visit by getting ready various documents and letters to show me to use as evidence in her story. This is a tribute to her as a highly skilled and professional editor of six books of reminiscences and letters on her husband Vissarion Shebalin.

– *In Memory of V. Y. Shebalin: Reminiscences, Materials (Pamyati V. Y. Shebalinu: Vospominaniya, materialy)* (Sovietsky Kompozitor, Moscow, 1984.

Shenderovich, Evgeny Mikhailovich. An article commissioned for this book.

Shneyerson, Grigori Mikhailovich (ed.), *D. D. Shostakovich: Articles and Materials (D. D. Shostakovich: Stat'i i materialy)* (Sovietsky Kompozitor, Moscow, 1976). A collection of articles on DDS.

Shostakovich, Dmitri Dmitriyevich, untitled article, *Muzikalnaya Zhisn*, no. 21, 1960.

– 'Autobiography' ('Avtobiografiya'), *Sovietskaya Muzyka*, no. 9, 1966.

– 'Description of Life' ('Zhisneopisaniye'), written in June 1926 for his curriculum vitae, TsGALI Archive, Moscow, F.2048, op. 1, ed Khr. 66.

– Letters to Boleslav Leopoldovich Yavorsky, TsGALI Archive, Moscow, F.2049, op. 3, ed. Khr. 96.

– 'Letters to Edison Denisov'. From an unpublished typescript kindly provided by E. Denisov.

– 'Letters to Mother' ('Pis'ma k materi'), ed. R. S. Sadykhova and D. V. Frederiks, *Neva*, no. 9, 1986. These letters form part of the Shostakovich archive in the possession of Dmitri Vsevolodovich Frederiks, who is the son of Mariya Shostakovich and hence the nephew of DDS.

– Letters to Tatyana Glivenko, Sotheby's Catalogue, December 1991.

See also:

Glikman, *Letters to a Friend*.

Hulluv, 'Letters from the 1930s' TsGA letters to Zakhar Tyulinsky and various correspondents.

Kozlova, *Letters to Lev Oborin*.

Mikheeva, 'In Memory of Sollertinsky'.

Nikolayev, Alexei, 'Letters to Shebalin'.

Yudin, 'Letters to Smolich'.

Shostakovich, Zoya Dmitriyevna. I recorded my interview with Zoya Dmitriyevna in the kitchen of her Moscow flat on Ulitsa Gubkina. Initially she was somewhat reluctant to recount the story of her famous brother's childhood (told many many times before, no doubt), but, fortified by large cups of strong tea, she soon warmed to her task. Her style of speaking was blunt and direct and she gave a picture of a happy and secure childhood. In certain instances, she found it difficult to be precise in her memories of events from so far back in time. A year later I went back to Moscow with her interview transcribed and translated. Unfortunately she was too ill to receive me, and I was only able to check the text through with her niece Galina, the composer's daughter.

Slonim, Ilya L'vovich, 'Shostakovich as a Model for a Portrait' ('Shostakovich – v kachestve modeli dlya portreta'), *Sovietskaya Muzyka*, no. 8, 1980.

Slonimsky, Sergei Mikhailovich, 'Brush Strokes for a Portrait of a Great Musician' ("Neskol'ko shtrikhov k portretu velikogo muzykanta'). An article commissioned for this book.

Sokolov, Nikolai Alexandrovich, 'On My Meetings with D. D. Shostakovich' ('O moyikh vstrechakh s D. D. Shostakovichem'), in *Sketches from Memory* (*Nabroski po pamyati*) (Iskusstvo, Moscow, 1987).

Solzhenitsyn, Alexander Isayevich, *The Oak and the calf: Sketches of a Literary Life in the Soviet Union* (Collins/Harvill, London, 1980).

Stravinsky, Igor Fyodorovich, *Selected Correspondence*, ed. Robert Craft, 2 vols (Faber & Faber, London 1982).

– and Craft, Robert, *Dialogues and Diary* (Faber & Faber, London, 1968).

Tishchenko, Boris Ivanovich, 'Study for a Portrait' ('Etyd k portretu'), in G. M. Shneyerson (ed.), *D. D. Shostakovich: Articles and Materials* (*D. D. Shostakovich: Stat'i i materialy*) (Sovietsky Kompozitor, Moscow, 1976). A collection of articles on DDS.

Tomashevskaya, Zoya Borisovna, 'Reminiscences of Shostakovich' ('Vospominaniya o Shostakoviche'). An article commissioned for this book.

Tsurtsumiya, R. (ed.), *André Melitonovich Balanchivadze: Collection of Articles and Material* (*André Melitonovich Balanchivadze: Sbornik statei i materialov*) (Sovietsky Kompozitor, Tbilisi, 1979).

Tyulin, Yuri Nikolayevich, 'The Youthful Years of D. D. Shostakovich' ('Yuniye gody D. D. Shostakovicha'), in L. V. Danilevich (ed.), Dmitri Shostakovich (Sovietsky Kompozitor, Moscow, 1967).

Vakman, Sofiya Borisovna. An article commissioned for this book.

Vecheslava, Tatyana Mikhailovna, *About All That Is Dear* (*O tom, chto dorogo*) (Sovietsky Kompozitor, Leningrad, 1989).

Vishnevskaya, Galina Pavlovna, *Galina: A Russian Story* (Hodder & Stoughton, London, 1984). In her book, Vishnevskaya gives a perceptive portrait of Shostakovich that is touching for its warmth and humour. This book, more than any other to date, gives an accurate picture of the atmosphere of Moscow musical life in the post-war years.

Volkov, Solomon, *Testimony: The Memoirs of Dmitri Shostakovich as Related to and Edited by Solomon Volkov* (Hamish Hamilton, London, 1979).

Vovsi-Mikhoels, Natalya, 'Reminiscences of Shostakovich' ('Vospominaniya o Shostakoviche'). An article commissioned for this book.

Welter, Nadezhda L'vovna, *About Opera and Myself: Pages of Reminiscences* (*Ob opernom teatre i o sebye: Stranitsy vospominaniya*) (Sovietsky Kompozitor,

Leningrad, 1984). See also her reminiscences in Dansker, *S. A. Samosud: Articles, Reminiscences, Letters.*

Wilson, Elizabeth, 'Reminiscences of Benjamin Britten's Visit to Moscow, April 1971'. An article written for this book.

Yakovlyev, M. (ed.), *D. Shostakovich on Himself and His Times* (*D. Shostakovich o vremeni i o sebye*) (Sovietsky Kompozitor, Moscow, 1980).

Yelagin, Yuri, *The Taming of the Arts* (*Ukroshcheniye iskusstv*) (Chekhov Publishing House, New York, 1952).

Yudin, Gavriil Yakovlevich, *Beyond the Frontiers of Past Years* (*Za gran'yu proshlykh lyet*) (Muzykal'noye Nasledstvo-Muzyka, Moscow, 1966).

– ['Letters to Smolich'] 'Your Work Will Remain an Event for Me All My Life' ('Vasha rabota dlya menya sobytiye na vsyu zhisn'), *Sovietskaya Muzyka*, no. 6, 1983. Contains DDS letters to Nikolai Smolich.

Yusefovich, V. A. (ed.), *D. F. Oistrakh* (Sovietsky Kompozitor, Moscow, 1985).

Zelov, N. S., 'Scholarships of the Commissariat of Enlightenment', *Yunost'*, no. 10, 1967.

Zhitomirsky, Daniil Vladimirovich, 'Dmitri Shostakovich: Reminiscences and Reflections' ('Dmitri Shostakovich: Vospominaniya i razmyshleniya') (unpublished). This extended article was given to me by Zhitomirsky when I was in Moscow in early January 1990 as material unpublished to date. Subsequently, a substantial part of this material, although in a slightly different form, formed the basis of an extended article entitled 'Reminiscences, Materials, Comments' ('Vospominaniya, materialy, vyskazyvaniya') in *Daugava*, no. 4, 1990.

Zhukova, Lydia, *Epilogues: First Book* (*Epilogi: Kniga pervaya*) (Chalidze, New York, 1983).

Zhutovsky, Boris Iosifovich, 'Returning to My Notes of 1962/63' (Vozvrashch-cheniye k zapisyam 1962–1963 g.g.'). *Literaturnaya Gazeta*, 5 July 1989.

Index

Figures in bold refer to people quoted

Babel, Isaac 169, 190
Babi Yar (site of massacre) 355, 356, 358, 362, 363
Bach, Johann Sebastian 211, 465n; DDS heads delegation to East Germany for bicentenary celebrations 248, 249; Nikolayeva compares DDS with 256
WORKS: Chromatic Fantasy (Kodaly transcription) 438–9; Concerto for Three Harpsichords (Pianos) 248; Preludes and Fugues 11, 250, 255, 256; Sonata in B minor for Violin and Harpsichord 474; Sonata in C minor for Violin and Harpsichord 474
Balanchivadze, André **79–80**, 113
Balasanyan, Sergei 383
'Ballet Falsehood' (*Pravda* article 6 Feb 36) 90, 109, 112, 114, 124, 132, 133
Barinova, Mariya 20–1
Barshai, Nina 242
Barshai, Rudolf 242, 244, **413–17**, 418, 427, 476
Bartók, Béla 36
Barvikha Sanatorium, Moscow 467
Bashkirov, Dmitri 475
Basner, Venyamin **123–5**, 190, **206–7**, 296, 302, 314, **396–8**, 435, **436–7**
Batumi (Black Sea resort) 94
Baturin, Alexander 158n, 160
BBC (British Broadcasting Corporation) 269, 427, 436
Bedbug, The (Mayakovsky) 44, 68, 74, 77, 78
Beethoven, Ludwig van 106, 187, 334, 442, 470; DDS's speech in Berlin on 328–9; Klemperer conducts 116, 118; legacy of late period 437
WORKS: Grosse Fugue 460–1; Piano Sonata No. 5 in C minor 13–14; Piano Sonata No. 14 in C# minor (Moonlight) 36; Piano Sonata No. 23 in F minor (Appassionata) 16, 36; Piano Sonata No. 29 in B^b major (Hammerclavier) 36, 56; quartets 441; symphonies 22, 23; Symphony No. 3 116; Symphony No. 5 116; Symphony No. 8 14; Symphony No. 9 14, 22, 178n; violin sonatas 199
Beethoven Quartet 131, 160n, 199, 243, 245, 246, 313, 369, 388–91, 406, 431, 437–43, 466, 467, 476

Begiashvili, Soso 160
Belinsky, Vissarion 370
Belsky, Igor 320
Beregovsky, Moshe 234
Berg, Alban 56
Beriya, Lavrenti 181, 226–7, 231, 259, 260–1, 344
Berlin: DDS's music played and plays Bach in 248; Beethoven celebrations (1952) 328; DDS attends first performance of Thirteenth Symphony in Germany 420–1; production of *Katerina Izmailova* at Staatsoper 421
Berlinsky, Valentin 242, **243–7**
Bestuzhev Courses for Women, St Petersburg 3, 161
Beyond the Frontiers of Past Years (Yudin) 37
Bezmensky, Alexander 61, 62, 78
Birth of Komsomol Theatre, The (Maranchik) 78–9
Bizet, Georges: *Carmen* 98
'Black Monk, The' (Chekhov) 459, 467
Blanter, Matvei (composer) 466
Blaramberg, Pavel 108
Blok, Alexander 43, 341
Bloody Sunday (St Petersburg massacre, 1905) 1
Blue Blouses 95
Bobky (Dostoevsky) 461
Bodaibo, Eastern Siberia 3, 5
Bogachova, Irina 452, 453
Bogdanov, Alexander 70
Bogdanov-Berezovsky, Valerian 7, **24–7**, **36**, 63, 467
Bogorodinsky, D. K. 392
Bogratian-Mukhlavskaya, Marina 320
Bolshevism/Bolsheviks xiv, 3, 4, 17, 19
Bolshevo 321n, 351; DDS awarded dacha at 242, 277; Kozhunova looks after 278, 284–5; Maxim bored at 282–3; lack of water at 282; Chukovsky describes 283–4; Lebedinsky at 298–9; Denisov at 301
Bolshoi Theatre, Moscow 182, 216, 333; and *The Nose* 73, 444–5, 448, 449; stages new production of *Lady Macbeth* (1935) 108, 385; and DDS's orchestration of *Boris Godunov* 141; and *Khovanshchina* 143; evacuated to